# VICTORIAN
# THINGS

# VICTORIAN THINGS

_____

## ASA BRIGGS

B. T. Batsford Ltd *London*

TYPESET BY KEYSPOOLS LTD
GOLBORNE, LANCASHIRE
AND PRINTED IN GREAT BRITAIN BY
BATH PRESS, BATH

PUBLISHED BY B. T. BATSFORD LTD
4 FITZHARDINGE STREET, LONDON W1H 0AH


BRITISH LIBRARY CATALOGUING IN PUBLICATION DATA


Briggs, Asa, *1921–*
    Victorian things.
    1. English civilization, 1837–1901
    I. Title
    942.081

    ISBN 0-7134-4519-X
    ISBN 0-7134-4520-3 Pbk

Signs and the signs of things are used only when we are lacking things.

UMBERTO ECO, *The Name of the Rose*, 1983

The other [project] was a Scheme for entirely abolishing all Words whatsoever ... Many of the most Learned and Wise adhere to the new Scheme of expressing themselves by *Things*; which hath only this Inconvenience attending to it; that if a Man's Business be very great, and of various kinds, he must be obliged in Proportion to carry a greater Bundle of *Things* upon his Back, unless he can afford one or two strong servants to attend him.

JONATHAN SWIFT, *Gulliver's Travels*, 1726

Most of the marks that man has left on the face of the earth during his two-million year career as a litter-bugging, meddlesome and occasionally artistic animal have one aspect in common: they are things, they are not deeds, ideas or words.

GLYNN ISAAC, *Whither Archaeology?* 1971

•

# CONTENTS

# PREFACE

I am grateful to many people for their help in writing this book, particularly to Susan Hard and Janet Lovegrove, who have dug out, usually the right term, some of the detailed evidence, and to Carol Freeland and Yvonne Collins, who have typed my manuscript. The research has been mine, however, and it has been exceptionally interesting – and I bear sole responsibility for the text which has gone through many versions.

Many people have helped me at different times with particular points of interest, among them my wife, to whom I owe much, and my son Daniel Briggs. I would also like to thank Richard Adams, Mordaunt Crook, Monique Charlot, Marcus Cunliffe, Leo de Freitas, Antony Hobson, Susan Lasdun, Richard Latner, Carolyn Marvin, Ileen Montijn, Maurice Rickards, Lesley St. Clair, Pauline Sergent, Frank Swartz, Clive Wainwright, Phillip Waller, Alexander Welch and John Raybould.

Librarians have been, as always, helpful and considerate. I owe a particular debt to the staffs of the London Library, of the British Library, and of The British College of Opthalmic Opticians.

I am deeply grateful to Anthony Seward, my publisher, for his unfailing understanding, courtesy, patience and help, and to Caroline Taverne at Batsford and to my friend Dr B. Mellor for carefully reading the proofs.

*Worcester College,*                                                             Asa Briggs
*Oxford*
November 1987

# ACKNOWLEDGEMENTS

The publishers gratefully acknowledge the following sources of illustrations: *Photographs* IIa The Bridgeman Art Library; III William Heinemann Ltd and John and Jennifer May; IV Barrie and Jenkins Ltd and Charles and Dorrie Shinn; V Mary Evans Picture Library; VIII *Illustrated London News*; IX Courtauld Institute of Art; X, XI National Postal Museum; XII, XIII Christopher Wood Gallery. *Line illustrations* pp. 65 and 184 *Illustrated London News* pp. 412 and 413 Mary Evans Picture Library.

# I

This book, long in the making, completes a trilogy. When I wrote *Victorian People* a generation ago, I had already decided that I wanted in due time to turn from the people, then so often misunderstood, even caricatured, first into the cities in which they lived, and then into their homes. I wanted to consider the *things* which they designed, named, made, advertised, bought and sold, listed, counted, collected, gave to others, threw away or bequeathed. Sometimes, Victorian people enjoyed these things: just as often, they displayed them. Frequently, for the majority were poor, they had no access to them. Sometimes, when they were rich, the things possessed them rather than they the things. Sometimes, of course, the things – even the most modest things – had to be pawned; sometimes they were stolen; increasingly, with encouragement, they were insured. My research has led me not only from library to library, but from museum to museum and from shop to shop.

I have set out in this book, as I did in *Victorian Cities*, not only to deal with the kinds of questions professional historians ask about the nineteenth century, but to place in historical perspective shelves of specialized books, in this case on such subjects as pottery, furniture, textiles and photography, which are not usually studied by professional historians. I have also had in mind readers of books like Dorothy H. Jenkins's *A Fortune in the Junk Pile* (1978), readers who may still have interesting Victorian things hidden away in a cupboard or an attic or even 'sitting unrecognized in the living room'. Of course, the lead – or even the zinc – out of which the objects were made may now be worth more than some of the things in their finished state.

It was not by chance that my book *Victorian People* appeared in 1953, for it was during the 1950s, the decade when the Victorian Society was founded, that attitudes to the Victorians were beginning to change significantly. Indeed, the word 'Victoriana' began to be used generally only around 1951, the time of the Festival of Britain which, in retrospect, was more of a landmark in relation to the appreciation of the nineteenth century than it was in relation to the making of the twentieth. The change, however, was not confined to Britain. In 1950 the American author Carl W. Drepperd had called Victoriana, a term used on both sides of the Atlantic, 'the Cinderella of Antiques'. By 1963, however, another American author, George Grotz, in his *The New Antiques: Knowing and Buying Victorian Furniture* remarked that Victorian antiques were 'the only ones that the great majority of us can turn to with any honesty'; and in a later edition in 1970 he noted how the prices of all the things he had mentioned then had risen by at least one hundred per cent in seven years.

Attitudes to the appearance of Victorian things changed too during the same period. One of the best known British scholar dealers, G. A. Godden, third-generation authority on porcelain and Stevengraphs, has written that until the 1950s, Victorian objects 'excited little sympathy and often suffered ridicule'. By 1963, however, both collectors and scholars had learnt how to discriminate not only between categories of things, but within each category between a thing thought 'good' and a thing judged 'bad'.

In this book, unlike the specialist collectors and scholars, I have tried to deal not only with specific Victorian things but with the relationships between the various categories of Victorian things. There were often surprising links between them, not only common themes but transfers of technology. These are often omitted in the specialist studies, although they figure in histories of design, which themselves have multiplied in very recent years. There were links, too, in the guidance that was given about taste. 'There is a direct analogy', we read in a book of the 1870s on furniture, 'between the spirit which induces a vulgar woman to dress beyond her station in life at a sacrifice of more necessary requirements, and the silly demand of small householders that the fittings of their dwellings should ape those of a much higher rent.'

Inevitably this book is selective, as *Victorian People* and *Victorian Cities* were. It leaves much out. I have begun, however, with the kinds of lists of things which the Victorians liked to draw up. Nor were they the last people to do so. The novelist, Brian Moore, produced one of the most evocative of them in his dream sequence novel *The Great Victorian Collection*, which was published in 1975, when the Victorian revival was complete. In it he described 'the most astonishing collection of Victorian artefacts' appearing mysteriously in twentieth-century California – from *objets d'art* to bric-à-brac and curios, among them furniture, household appliances, scientific instruments, toys, silverware, books, furs, looms, small arms and a railway locomotive.

In the same year, in Japan, a country which for good Victorian reasons figures at many points in my book, the author of *A Hundred Things Japanese* began by explaining that his title had 'a nicely nineteenth-century sound about it. One remembers Victorian books with titles like this'. In fact, one book called *Things Japanese*, covering far more than objects, had been published in 1888, to be followed by Dyer Ball's *Things Chinese* in 1892.

The literary critic Humphry House, who noted with some apprehension in 1948, before the revival really started, how everything produced in the Victorian age was now beginning to be thought 'worthy of affectionate study as well as of critical analysis', was more sensitive to words than to objects. He knew then that the convenient but slippery word 'thing', which has long puzzled philosophers, had acquired a peculiarly Victorian sound in the nineteenth century along with 'thingummy' and 'thingummybob', older words surviving from a once bigger range. 'All things bright and beautiful' was the opening line of a favourite Victorian hymn by Mrs C. F. Alexander, and in Robert Louis Stevenson's poem written later in the century two of the most famous lines ran:

The world is so full of a number of things
I'm sure we should all be as happy as kings.

Lewis Carroll, mathematician as well as story teller, was almost as interested in things as in numbers, recognizing just how important things – and their names – were for the secure scaffolding of Victorian life. 'Things flow about so here', Alice complained 'in a plaintive tone' when that scaffolding was absent: she had just spent 'a minute or so vainly pursuing a large bright thing that looked sometimes like a doll and sometimes like a workbox'.

'Reality' required things, as one prominent Victorian put it, but there was more to things than reality. A very different novelist from Brian Moore, Robertson Davies, has referred to the 'exaltation of the World of Things' in the nineteenth century, and Peter Conrad, who has noted how 'the Dickensian city is made up of interiors, not of public places', has observed memorably in his book *The Victorian Treasure House* how Victorian lists of things could become 'idylls'. This was as true of Henry Mayhew, he points out, as it was of Dickens, and Mayhew's miscellanies included blacking, corn salves, grease-removers, and rat and beetle poisons as well as prints and porcelain ornaments. He knew, too, how people who owned very few things of permanence could hold them especially dear.

I am more interested in nineteenth-century things as they were used and appreciated within their own context than in the things or parts of things which have survived into the twentieth century and in how we now regard them. John Ruskin and William Morris, who had more to say about things than any of their contemporaries, and who figure prominently in this book, thought that there were too many unbeautiful things around. They added that however much they changed with technology or with fashion, they remained unbeautiful, even got worse. They knew, too, how many people were deprived.

Meanwhile, one of Morris's mentors, Karl Marx, who believed that 'to discover the various uses of things is the work of history' and that in his own age 'the first category in which bourgeois wealth presents itself is that of the commodity', had found the countless commodities that surrounded him 'full of metaphysical cunning' and the machines which helped to make them worthy of a mythology. 'Nature builds no machines', he noted with excitement, 'no railways, electric telegraphs, self-acting mules'. The whole earth was being explored 'in all locations to discover new things of use as well as new qualities in the old'. The American sage Ralph Waldo Emerson had noted more than a decade earlier how the English loved 'the lever, the screw and the pulley'. While they had depended for their materials on 'indispensable staples' like coal, iron, pottery, brick and glass, it was by their 'steady combinations' that they had succeeded.

Marx's excitement, not in this case shared by Morris or for that matter by Emerson, was as apparent as his searching criticism, which centred on the relationship between people and things and the way in which people could be treated not only as 'hands' but as things. While his views were little known in England – the first volume of *Capital* (1867) was not translated into

English until 1886, three years after his death – Marx collected most of his evidence from England, where he included among the social consequences of capital accumulation and the spread of commodities 'a mania for possessions', a 'fetishism' which 'clung to the products of work once they became wares', and a worship of money which made it possible, if not always tempting, to acquire 'non-necessities'. Nor was Marx alone in drawing such conclusions. 'It is a folly to suppose when a man amasses a quantity of furniture', we read in a completely non-Marxist article of 1854, 'that it belongs to him. On the contrary, it is he who belongs to his furniture.'

The 'market place' has become far more sophisticated, of course, in the late twentieth century than it was when Marx was writing, and it has acquired new 'mass' dimensions. So, too, has the advertising which signposts things; and it is interesting to observe that the sophistication increased during the 1950s, around the time when interest in Victorian things was growing. The sophistication has grown still more since then throughout what has come to be thought of as a continuing 'communications revolution', and it has influenced the historiography of things as well as publicity surrounding them.

The Victorians, caught up though they were in their own preoccupations and terminology, had hints of such a 'shape of things to come', including a mass market. 'Persons and things do turn up so vexatiously in this life and will . . . insist on being noticed', wrote the old servant Gabriel Betteredge in Wilkie Collins's novel *The Moonstone*, which appeared in 1868, one year after the first volume of Marx's *Capital*, and thereafter things never ceased to turn up. It is only recently, however, that the idea of a 'consumer culture' has been traced back in time by Sir John Plumb, Neil McKendrick, Roy Porter and others to the eighteenth century, to the age of Josiah Wedgwood and Matthew Boulton, and by John Thirsk even further back to the seventeenth century.

The nineteenth century, attracted by the concept of 'plenitude', widened the range of things much further, eventually reshaping all earlier versions of economics to explain 'demand' more fully than supply. Thus, for example, in Philip Wicksteed's marginalist economics, very different from the economics of Ricardo, Mill or Marx, 'a vast number of things which I desire' entered into a 'circle of exchange' based on choice. For Wicksteed, however, 'the ultimately desired objects of choice' were not commodities but subjective experiences of some kind. Contemporary advertisers would agree. So, too, would have agreed the brilliant nineteenth-century showman Phineas Taylor Barnum, much admired by Queen Victoria. No account of Victorian things could be complete without him. Yet it was less spectacular advertisers who were usually at the centre of the scene, like those advertising 'washing, wringing and mangling machines combined' in the small advertisement column of the *Illustrated London News* in 1855: 'this important invention is calculated to effect a saving [in time as well as money:] of more than fifty per cent.'

# II

While it is tempting in considering Victorian things to treat them entirely archaeologically, as if they were the only evidence available to the historian, and to approach the 'material culture' of Victorian England like the study of ancient or medieval pottery, solely through a study of materials, design of products and their spatial distribution, such an approach would have been too restrictive. *Pace* the great French historian Marc Bloch, who suggested misleadingly that with objects 'there is no need to appeal to any other human mind as an interpreter', an examination of the contemporary publicity surrounding things – much of it rhetorical – is a necessary and enriching part of my subject. It puts the psychology as well as the economics into the archaeology. So, too, do surviving ephemera like undertakers' bills which must be considered along with lavish cemetery art. So, too, do solidly bound volumes of sermons, designed, like gravestones but unlike bills, to last.

Advertisements, bills and sermons provide evidence throughout the whole reign. 'Professor' Thomas Holloway, the pills and ointment maker, started his business in 1838: four years later he was spending £5,000 a year on advertising, twelve years later £20,000. 'Millions who have never heard of Napoleon ... have heard of Holloway', an American advertising agent claimed in 1870. By the end of Queen Victoria's reign Beecham, who also reached a mass market, was better known than Holloway had been; and advertising was employed to sell many other articles beside pills, ointments – and, most often in the news, soap. An *Illustrated London News* advertisement of 1901, the year Queen Victoria died, described, for example, Peter Robinson's 'Mourning Warehouse' in Regent Street where there were 'garments in stock for every degree'.

'Puffery' can be just as misleading for the historian of things as the boosting of cities, discussed in *Victorian Cities*, can be for the critical historian of the environment. Yet it is fascinating confirmation of a point already made by the *Edinburgh Review* in 1843 that 'the grand principle of modern existence is notoriety'; and it influenced even the cooperative societies which dealt in working people's necessities.

There is supplementary verbal evidence about things in popular literature, particularly that substantial segment including articles, novels and verse, which was immediate in its response (including the illustrations) to current tastes and trends. Within the context of my book there is a special place, therefore, for authors like the energetic Mrs Haweis and the prolific George Augustus Sala, a star of the *Daily Telegraph* – during the 1860s, in its own phrase, 'the paper with the largest circulation in the world'. From his Brighton base Sala always liked to be in touch with the latest fashions: favourite shops were 'the Everything shops' which he was at pains to explain had existed long before the great new department stores, which liked to call themselves *emporia*.

*'Cleans All Places': Monkey Brand wartime advertisement, 1901*

*Mourning for a Jubilee Year, 1887*

Books with a longer life than those of Mrs Haweis or Sala can have great value, too, for many of them are rich in what David Masson in his *British Novelists* (1858) called 'descriptions of the ordinary places of social resort, and of all their objects and circumstantials'. Writers who have appealed to more than one generation – Dickens and Thackeray, for example, or Trollope and Eliot – had significantly different ways of referring to objects, while of a later novelist, Thomas Hardy, John Bayley has written perceptively that 'things matter to him more than the words that describe them, the latter being treated absentmindedly'. Hardy himself was well aware of what he conceived of as the poetry of simple things. After a friend in the course of a conversation on comparative culture had suggested that Dorset peasants held to 'the barbaric idea that confuses persons and things', Hardy wrote in his diary that 'this barbaric idea ... is, by the way, also common to the highest imaginative genius – that of the poet'. If people could be treated as things, things could sometimes behave like people.

Novels and poems do not simply illustrate or decorate: they compel attention through their insights, and they frequently point to explanations. Many of them are thick with things, although Trollope, who cared for things, usually did not list them or dwell on them at length. 'The baker lives here, and that respectable woman, Mrs Frommage', he wrote succinctly in *The Small House at Allington* (1882): she sold 'ribbons and toys, and soap and straw bonnets, with many other things too long to mention'. By contrast, Thackeray loved to linger on things, particularly those which carried a heavy 'freight of associations'; and Barbara Hardy and others have focused their attention on his propensity to visualize, not to conceptualize. George Eliot, a very different novelist from both, dwelt more than once on the relationship between honest 'common things', as they later came to be called, and 'showy, vulgar things', common or not: she noted at Munich, for example, in 1858, how there had been 'an immense expenditure on wax and china ornaments and the least possible outlay in basins'.

The name of the Veneerings in Dickens's *Our Mutual Friend* (1864-5) speaks for itself, and the paragraph which introduces them and their expressions of new wealth is unforgettable. They were 'bran'-new people in a bran'-new house in a bran'-new quarter of London' and everything about them was 'spick and span new'. 'Their carriage was new, their harness was new, their horses were new, their pictures were new, they themselves were new ... If they had set up a great-grandfather he would have come home in matting from the Pantechnicon without a scratch upon him, French polished to the crown of his head.'

Dickens's novels are necessary reading for the historian of things, which are often brilliantly – and poetically – described. General points are raised also. *Dombey and Son* (1846-8) introduced the young Paul's innocent question 'What is money?' which received a totally inadequate reply from his father: *Our Mutual Friend* found money in rubbish. *The Old Curiosity Shop*, published early in the reign, 1841, provided me with a lead in to favourite Victorian things which belonged to the dusty past. It is necessary to note also that Dickens had much in common not only with Trollope or Thackeray but with Sala. His journals – *Household Words*, launched in 1850, 'Cherishing that light of Fancy which is inherent in the human breast', and *All the Year Round*, launched nine years later – are laced with illuminating articles on specific things from needles to wine bottles. 'The mightier inventions of the age', Dickens stated, 'are not to our thinking, all material, but have a kind of soul in their stupendous bodies', and his magazines set out to explain his feeling as much as his thinking.

Although Trollope, who died in 1882 twelve years after Dickens, could be sparing in his listing of things, he could occasionally introduce things very specifically and go on explicitly to draw general conclusions. 'Why doesn't What's-his-name have real silver forks?' old Mrs Van Siever asks Mr Musselboro, a guest at a terrible dinner party given by a *nouveau riche* in *The Last Chronicle of Barset* (1867). 'What's the use?' responds Musselboro.

'Everybody has these plated things now. What's the use of a lot of capital lying dead?' 'Everybody doesn't', Mrs Van Siever replies. 'I don't. You know as well as I do, Musselboro, that the appearance of the thing goes for a great deal. Capital isn't lying dead as long as people know that you've got it.' Arnold Bennett might have said the same. He was well aware of what it meant *not* to have things or to have silver plate rather than silver.

Given such varied evidence, much of it detailed and dated, the historian of the archaeology of Victorian Britain, including the industrial archaeology, itself rediscovered during the 1950s, is more fortunate than those archaeologists who are concerned with periods where there are no written materials or than those anthropologists who are concerned with cultures without a preserved historical record. He is able to turn also to explicit contemporary accounts of crafts and techniques – some in blue books like the Report of the Select Committee on Arts and Manufactures, which ended its sittings in 1836 just before Queen Victoria came to the throne, some in monographs, like George Dodd's *Days of the Factories* (1843), some in textbooks, some in dictionaries and encyclopaedias like G. Phillips Bevan's *British Manufacturing Industries*, one volume of which covered paper, printing, bookbinding, engraving, photography and toys, and some in periodicals like *The English Mechanic*, which first appeared in 1865, or *The Illustrated Carpenter and Builder*, which first appeared in 1867.

# III

The 'connection' between 'art' and 'manufactures', stressed in 1836 and above all in 1851, by influential Victorians like Henry ('King') Cole and Lyon Playfair, demanded constant re-examination as the reign went by, not least during the 1880s and 1890s, in the light of advances in technology and in the chemistry that often lay behind them. Electroplating was only one obvious – and early – example of early change, discovered in Birmingham in the 1830s and commercialized after 1840. The 'vulcanizing' of rubber was another discovery of the 1840s – in several places, more or less in parallel.

*Gum-Elastic*, the title of Charles Goodyear's book (1853), had little that was romantic about it, but the substitution of the word 'vulcanized' for 'heated' or 'fire-proofed' brought in the right hint of mythological mystery: Marx, too, had brought Vulcan into his range of reference. Even earlier, Charles MacIntosh, who died in 1843, had introduced into the language a new word as well as a new product – waterproofed coats, misspelled thereafter as 'mackintoshes'. The wide range of possible uses of rubber took time to establish often through the evolution of other things (pneumatic tyres followed after bicycles in 1887), and already in 1862 there may have been glimpses of a more distant technical frontier when Alexander Parkes, an English metallurgist, produced the first fully artificial polymer to which the name 'celluloid' was to be given.

The role of chemistry, a key subject for the Victorians, had been clearly recognized in relation to agriculture throughout the reign. While Edwin Chadwick, sanitary reformer and administrator, was extolling the benefits of well distributed natural sewage, chemists were producing in their laboratories smells unknown to nature. Chadwick had read the great von Liebig's *Chemistry of Agriculture* (1840), but he had little sense of the wide range of 'useful' things that can be transformed (including 'extract of beef') as a result of Liebig's work. 'There is no problem more important to mankind than the presentation of the objects which organic chemistry contemplates', Liebig had told a Liverpool audience in the year Queen Victoria came to the throne; and nearly forty years later *The Chemical News* wrote that 'the application of chemistry to agriculture and to many of the wants of daily life received so powerful an impulse from Liebig that the popular mind has taken him for the representative of the science in its application to practical purposes'.

By then, in the industrial sector, the by-products of coal, which seemed innumerable, were as interesting to chemists as the coal seams were to geologists. The economic and social implications of by now forgotten chemical discoveries could generate great excitement. Thus, when Walter Weldon, who had never entered a chemical laboratory before 1865, discovered a new process for producing soda in 1869/70, contemporaries recognized immediately that it revolutionized much else: 'by his invention', a French chemist declared, 'every sheet of paper and every yard of calico has been cheapened throughout the world'. Not surprisingly then, it was from the great cotton capital, Manchester, that the loudest nineteenth-century cry came that chemistry was 'the creator of wealth'.

'If England still continues to advance', wrote one of Liebig's pupils, Lyon Playfair, born in India and educated in Scotland but drawn to Manchester, 'it will not be from the abundance of her coal and her iron, but because, uniting science with practice she enables her discoveries in philosophy to keep pace with her aptitude in applying them'.

Playfair himself advanced with the age. Before 1851 he had been a pioneer of public health reform and he had served as 'Special Commissioner to Communicate with Local Communities' preparing for the Great Exhibition: in 1868 he entered Parliament as a supporter of Gladstone and made his first speech in favour of the abolition of religious tests. He went on to press for civil service and educational reform. He was knighted in 1883 and made a baron in 1892.

There were recognized problems in Victorian Britain in achieving the kind of effective applications of chemistry that Playfair demanded. Some of them figured in their environmental context in *Victorian Cities*, and more of them figure in this book. Playfair feared – he was not the last to do so – that his fellow-countrymen would not respond as he wished, and when he served as a juror at the Paris Exhibition of 1867, he reported a consensus that 'our country had shown little inventiveness and made little progress in the peaceful arts of industry since 1862'. The causes, he affirmed, were a lack of 'industrial education for the masters and managers of factories', a cry still heard in the late-twentieth century, and 'a want of cordiality between the employers of labour and workmen', a cry still heard even more often. The *Edinburgh Review* in 1868 noted with a touch of melancholy that we can no longer hope to 'fill half the markets of the world with products of our looms and factories unless we can advance beyond our former selves'. 'Not to be the first is soon, in this age of activity, to be the last.'

It was obvious that the resources on which Britain's industrial revolution had been based were not unlimited. Other countries were richer in iron, and there were even fears about coal. Resources as well as artefacts figure, therefore, in my account of Victorian things, and with them geology figures as well as chemistry. Indeed, geology was a key subject for both amateurs and professionals, and while it could provoke controversy, challenging the authority of the Scriptures by encouraging speculation, it was generally recognized as being both 'instructive' and severely practical. Ruskin's father described his son as 'a geologist from infancy' and later in his life Ruskin himself stated with more than a touch of irony that it was the summit of his earthly ambition to become President of the Geological Society.

Some basic resources, notably cotton and paper, always depended on imports, although it was frequently pointed out that cotton, the 'magic shrub' imported from foreign fields, was related botanically to the English hollyhock. Paper, the making of which was transformed during Victoria's reign, was so important that the Victorians themselves described their age not only as an age of coal and of iron but as 'an age of paper'.

Within the world of things transformed by chemistry, dyeing has been studied at length by economic historians largely because W. H. Perkin, who patented his first aniline dye when he was only 18 years old, found that his discoveries, like the Gilchrist-Thomas steel discoveries, were exploited more quickly and effectively in Germany than in Britain. Significantly, too, the French were the first to honour him – with a gold medal in 1859. Such comparative economic history is basic – in the age of Cobden and after. Nonetheless, the history of such a technology as dyeing is interesting for social and cultural reasons too. Perkin's 'Tyrian purple', popular in France before it became popular in Britain, was called 'mauve' in 1856: it was a sufficiently fashionable colour to pass quickly into Victorian funeral cultures, recently much studied, doubtless on account of its purple pedigree. *Punch* could write of 'mauve measles', noting that 'one of its first symptoms ... consists in the eruption of a measly rash of ribbons above the head and neck'.

Another aniline dye, Verguin's 'fuchsine' of 1859, had quite a different history when it was happily renamed 'magenta': 'a very soluble substance of magnificent crimson colour', it soon proved even more popular than mauve.

And there were many other artificial dyes to follow. Perkin introduced Britannia violet; Caro and Martius the less propitiously named 'Manchester yellow' and 'Manchester brown'. Other Victorian dyes included 'London Dust' and 'Dust of Ruins'. Morris was horrified by the new aniline dyes and the uses to which they were put – at parties or at funerals. Fortunately W. R. Lethaby, twenty-three years younger than Morris and a prophet in line with him, could write of Morris's own funeral that it was the only one which he had attended that did not make him feel ashamed to have been buried.

Many Victorians gave their name to a product. Others gave their name to processes, many of which were at least as controversial as the new products. The controversy started, indeed, with motive power. For Dionysius Lardner and most of the many historians of steam, the steam engine was 'a moving power of unparalleled inportance and efficiency in all the industrial arts'. There were others, however, who saw it as a source and symbol of exploitation. Given the impetus of steam power – and it affected the industrial arts unequally and within different chronological sequences, sometimes surprisingly late – the most significant development was the growth of the machine tool industry, by now as well charted a historical development as dyeing.

With the greater opportunities for standardization, the difference between 'the workmanship of chance' and the 'workmanship of precision', elaborated by David Pye in his *The Nature and Art of Workmanship* (1968), was fully appreciated by the Victorians. Most of them were happy about the consequences, however, and irritated only that foreigners, in this case the Americans, were leading the way. The range of new skills was extolled. So, too, were examples of 'ingenuity' in the use of materials and the widening of markets through replication. Consumer goods were offered not only in batches but in ranges. For example, during the 1890s you could purchase at a distance cast iron umbrella stands by catalogue at prices ranging between 17s 4d and 61s 10d subject to 25 per cent discount. You could also buy a very wide range of umbrellas, some of them 'fashionable' and expensive. Not surprisingly, luggage was widely advertised – and never standardized.

Even in relation to materials, art and technology were never completely separate at any point in Victoria's reign. At the Great Exhibition, for example, you could see a zinc table and an extraordinary and much admired statue in zinc, Professor Kiss's *Amazon*, which had first been cast in bronze in 1839. It was hoped that, like much of the furniture, it would last for ever. Zinc was extolled too as a metal that made possible both 'cheap baths' and 'handsome cornices within the means of all'. Meanwhile, tin, like 'portable iron', was being used with equal confidence in the fashioning of cans for food ('tinned food' mainly for the working classes) and 'impermanent building structures', some of which, it was claimed, were attractive as well as useful: in prefabricated form they too could be exported round the world.

The beauties of cast iron, used for many everyday objects in the kitchen and the cellar, were noted by people who had nothing to say about utility. Exported throughout the world and turned into balconies and railings, cast iron was and has been acclaimed in Melbourne, Cape Town, and Georgetown – despite Ruskin's fierce ideological objection to it – as well as in British cities. Thus, E. Graeme Robertson has called his book on 'ornamental cast iron in architecture' *Victorian Heritage*.

Corrugated iron, scarcely an art material, was so much in demand in prefabricated building that by the end of the century William Cooper of London could offer among other items in his catalogue 'hospitals despatched within twenty-four hours of the receipt of order and erected complete for occupation within fourteen days'. As a 'modern product' corrugated iron seemed to go with linoleum, invented in 1860 by Frederick Walton: linseed oil was mixed with resin and cork dust on to a cotton or flax backing. 'Many a man has doubtless put to himself the question "What is linoleum, and how is it made?"' wrote a Dr McGowan in *Knowledge* in 1896, and he gave a full answer which went back to the seventeenth century, described another Victorian product called 'kamptulicon' which preceded linoleum, and maintained the right note of drama to keep his readers' interest. Walton had told McGowan that after experience of both materials he would rather handle 'dynamite in bulk than cork in a loose state'.

In the great growth of international trade, which involved huge exports of new nineteenth-century manufactured products, from tea services to bicycles, some 'raw' materials lost in the process. For example, British imports of madder, a natural dye known to the ancient Egyptians, fell by nine-tenths in the ten years from 1868 to 1878 and the price per ton by five times from £50 to £10. Nonetheless, despite the triumphs of chemistry, Nature still figured prominently in the provision of things – and their ecology – at the end of the century – cotton; horn and shell; guano; nitrates; oil (see below p. 291). Paper was made from rags until the middle of the century: by the end of the century most of it came, like rubber, from the trees of the forest. Much was still made, therefore, of the 'bounty' of the natural world, for even artificial products like soap and margarine depended on imports of natural ingredients from West Africa.

# IV

In *Victorian Things*, as in *Victorian Cities*, I have chosen to cover the whole time span of Queen Victoria's reign. This is because the experience of the early, middle or late Victorian years taken by themselves would have been incomplete. I have had to look backwards and forwards also, for the reign was not self-contained. There was Victorianism before Victoria, and many characteristically Victorian things continued to be produced in Edward VII's reign. In the beginning there were so many pre-Victorian survivals that recent historians have tended to direct more attention to what had survived than to what had changed; and at the end, through such business concerns as Liberty's, founded in 1875, or an equally famous old firm, Gillow's, with its origins not in London but in Manchester, there were obvious, if often complex, continuities.

Within Victoria's reign itself changes do not follow a simple chronological sequence. In silverware, for example, which has been described as 'the chief status symbol of the Victorian era', Gilbert Marks was still insisting on doing everything by hand in his workshop at the end of the reign, while C. R. Ashbee, who steadfastly objected to 'unregulated machine competition' and created a Guild and School of Handicraft in 1887, was prepared notwithstanding to use machines for rolling plate. Eighteenth-century silver was still being copied at that time, although there were more hybrids than imitations. Ralph Wornum had criticized over-elaborate ornament during the 1850s, and during the 1860s Christopher Dresser had produced simplified designs and his own versions of Japanese styles at a time when the fashion for the elaborate and the ornate was overpowering. Yet even during the 1880s and 1890s – after Dresser had urged explicitly that 'silver objects ... should perfectly sense the end for which they have been formed' and after there had been both a Japanese boom and an Adam revival – there were many buyers who paid little attention to such expressions of change. Elkington and Company who introduced electroplating during the 1840s could re-issue in 1884/5, when re-silvering was much in demand, a jug displayed a whole generation earlier in 1853.

For W. J. Loftie, writing in 1876 in his *A Plea for Art in the House*, the 'revival in painting, architecture and many other arts' had not reached the silversmith: 'there are few more distressing sights to the sensitive eye than a sideboard set out with yachting or racing prizes. A "cup" consists of a block of silver on which is a cast metal representation of a cutter in full scale or a stag after Landseer ... The most ambitious efforts of our designers resemble the Prince Consort memorial, or a wedding cake indifferently'.

In furniture and furnishings, as F. Gordon Roe wrote in 1952, when interest in the Victorians was quickening, 'to talk of a Victorian period is incorrect: there were a number of Victorian periods, overlapping and contending with one another'. Colours had their ups-and-downs also. Mid-Victorian crimsons and golds gave way to 'aesthetic' 'greenery-yallery' (there were many shades of green from verdigris to *vert d'eau*) and to *fade* tints, and they in their turn gave way to much 'fuller-bodied' shades.

Roe set out to identify changing 'moods', describable in terms of colours, while at the same time demonstrating, like historians of other categories of things, that 'a quantity of things regarded as characteristically Victorian had in fact a pre-Victorian past'. He never generalized about curves or corners, knowing well that a writer like Loftie could be just as sceptical about the merits of much of the ornamental furniture of 1876 as he was about silverware. 'It must be remembered', Loftie pointed out, 'that ornament is not necessarily beautiful. Too often a handsome, strong, well arranged bookcase is ruined in appearance by useless and meaningless ornament. Books are the best ornament of the bookcase.'

For Mrs Haweis, writing four years later in her *Art of Beauty*, 'cultivated persons' were reacting naturally against the 'vulgarity' of all the forms of furniture 'to which they have been too long accustomed'. Criticism went further during the 1890s. For example, an article in *The Studio* in October 1893 complained that 'the production of ornament instead of growing out of organic necessity has become a marketable affair controlled by the salesman and the advertiser and at the mercy of every passing fashion'.

*Police Constable (to Boy).* "Now then, off with that Hoop! or I'll precious soon Help you!"
*Lady (who imagines the observation is addressed to her).* "What a Monster!"  [*Lifts up the Crinoline, and hurries off.*

*The crinoline and the hoop:* Punch, *1856*

In women's dress the 'age of the crinoline', described by James Laver as 'the first great triumph of the machine age' – 'the application to feminine costume of all those principles of steel construction employed in the Menai Bridge and the Crystal Palace' – fits neatly – though briefly – within the mid-Victorian years. Yet taking the Victorian years as a whole, there were many quick twists and turns of fashion associated both with 'manias' and 'revivals'. Was it coincidental that during the early 1890s there was a return to the fashion for wide sleeves which had dominated the 1830s? The Royal Scottish Museum organized in 1983 an exhibition on 'the rise and fall of the sleeve, 1825–1840'. Yet the silhouettes of 1830 and 1895 have been described as almost identical.

Every thing has its history as every person has his own biography. Nonetheless, it is helpful, as it was in *Victorian People* and *Victorian Cities*, to begin by dividing Queen Victoria's reign into three parts. The Great Exhibition of 1851 demands at least as important a place in it, therefore, as it did then, even if other Exhibitions, sometimes of very different kinds, inside and outside Britain, like the Paris Exhibition of 1867, have to figure more prominently in this book than they did there. It ushered in a new period.

The beginning of Victoria's reign had seen the end of 'the Rule of Taste' and a clash of styles; there was a reaction against uniformity. As John Steegman put it in his fascinating *Consort of Taste*, published in 1950 on the eve of the Festival of Britain, the change was not merely one of direction. 'It lay rather in abandoning the signposts of authority for the fancies of the individual.' New wealth had much to do with this, but also romantic aesthetics.

During the polychromatic middle years styles could run riot, but there was no shortage of compromises. Nor was there ever a shortage of 'taste-makers'. One of the most famous of them was Charles Lock Eastlake, nephew of Sir Charles Eastlake, President of the Royal Academy. His *Hints on Household Taste* (1868) sharply criticized 'productions of conventional taste which result from the caprice of fashion or the whims of manufacturers'. There were, in fact, many 'hints' in Victorian Britain about what to do with things – including how to make them last longer in order to keep them and how to adapt them for new purposes. 'It should be a rule in every house', wrote Mrs C. E. Humphrey ('Madge' of the periodical *Truth*) in 1895, 'that nothing is to go into the dustbin except dust, ashes and paper'.

By then in the third part of Queen Victoria's reign there had been a self-conscious element of revolt in the 'aesthetic' movement, a revolt against the conventions of the earlier period, and many intimations, also often through revolt, of twentieth-century preferences and tastes both in the Arts and Crafts movement and in *art nouveau*. What had once seemed solid could now seem monstrously absurd. Yet there were carry-overs even then from the mid-Victorian years just as there had been (particularly through 'Gothic') from the early-Victorian years into the mid-Victorian years; and while it has been claimed, with more than a touch of exaggeration by Nikolaus Pevsner, that 'the Modern Movement in design owes more to [William] Morris than to any one artist of the nineteenth century', some of the most cumbrous and unattractive Victorian things were produced in greater quantities than ever before during the 1880s. The late-Victorians were reacting against their contemporaries as well as their parents.

There was another feature of the late-Victorian years. A cluster of 'new things' (described in Chapter 10) was brought into existence. They figure prominently both in social histories and in histories of design, and it is notable that Lethaby was to write in his *Form in Civilization* (1922) that 'aeroplanes and motors and even bicycles [were all] in their way perfect. We need to bring this ambition for perfect solutions into housing of all sorts and scales'.

Already it could be claimed in 1889 that 'we are living in the age of electricity' just as former ages have been called 'the ages of stone, bronze and iron'. The remark was exaggerated as far as Britain was concerned, for Britain was still in the age of steam and for the most part content to stay there. Nevertheless, from the late 1870s and 1880s onwards, as Stephen Kern has written in his book *The Culture of Time and Space* (1983), 'a series of sweeping changes in technology and culture created distinctive new modes of thinking about and experiencing time and space'.

The re-orientation was to separate twentieth-century experience from nineteenth-century experience, in the home as much as in the workshop. There were many continuities here too, however. Before the telephone and 'wireless' was the telegraph: before the cinema photography; before the automobile the bicycle.

## V

In turning from the description of things to their analysis, French historians long pointed the way – at least, in their precepts. 'The variety of historical evidence', Marc Bloch wrote in his *Craft of the Historian*, 'is nearly infinite. Everything that a man writes or says, everything that he makes, everything he touches can and ought to teach us about him'. In the same tradition as Bloch, Fernand Braudel went on after 1950 (he was specific about the date) to study in detail the dynamics of 'capitalism and material life from 1400 to 1800' and in a set of 'afterthoughts' pointed explicitly to 'the boom that constituted the world's first mass production' in the nineteenth century and to the specific role of Britain in the story. He well knew what was round the corner after 1800.

There is as much meditation as explanation in Braudel, however, and it is a different writer from a different society whose work provides what is perhaps the most appropriate introduction to *Victorian Things*. Sigfried Giedion, Norton Lecturer at Harvard in 1939, published his *Mechanization Takes Command* in 1948. 'The true critique of any age', Giedion believed, 'can only be taken from the testimony of that age', and the most revealing testimony can be found in 'the furniture of daily life . . . all things we look at hourly without seeing'. 'To turn backwards to a past age' was not 'just to inspect it'. 'The backward look', he insisted, 'transforms its object. Absolute points of reference are no more open to the historian than the physicist.'

Giedion collected abundant detailed testimony from the past – and as a good historian (and historiographer) he loved the detail – in order to demonstrate how mass production, 'the dominant principle of the twentieth century', had in all its essentials been put into practice in the United States – and elsewhere – 'more than sixty-five years before this century began'. When I wrote *Victorian Cities*, I was reacting against the stimulating simplification of Lewis Mumford, who, in my view, overemphasized the uniformity of nineteenth-century industrial and urban life. In *Victorian Things* I am often able to build on the work of Giedion, sensitive student both of objects and of processes, although, as Adrian Forty, like others before him, has recently shown in his *Objects of Desire* (1986), he should never be treated uncritically.

Giedion first approached the history of things through the discipline not of history but of architecture: in 1941 he had written *Space, Time and Architecture*. There are many other disciplinary approaches to the study, besides archaeology and architecture, just as there are in the study of cities. It was not in a historical journal, therefore, but in the *Geographical Review* that Yi-Fu Tuan examined 'the significance of the artefact', and it was the distinguished Swedish geographer Torsten Hägerstrand who in seeking to survey the whole field of 'time geography' complained that 'we have no sociology or ecology of men and things seen together'.

In fact, while interdisciplinary studies of 'man-made things' may be in short supply, two other converging disciplines besides geography – both with Victorian origins – have put men and things together in revealing fashion – anthropology and semiology. Again France led the way. After Bloch and Braudel came Barthes and Baudrillard, setting out systematically to uncover 'signs and meanings in everyday life'. It was in England, however, that the story began. By a coincidence it was in the year of the Great Exhibition, 1851, that Captain Harry Lane-Fox, later to take the name of Pitt-Rivers, began collecting fire arms before going on to collect almost everything else from all parts of the world, including utensils, machines, ornaments, dress and 'any other ponderable object produced or used at home'. His purpose was not to select 'unique specimens', but to assemble examples of what was 'ordinary and typical', and he went on to trace in an elaborate evolutionary system of classification of things 'the succession of ideas by which the minds of men ... have progressed from the simple to the complex, and from the homogenous to the heterogeneous'.

Pitt-Rivers emphasized how agricultural tools, furniture and utensils 'revealed the lineaments of past ordinary lives'. He wanted men and women who saw his collection to be able 'to hold in their hands an idea expressed by hands'. For him, 'material' and 'spiritual' (or 'magical') went together – armour and charms, compasses and horoscopes, waistcoats and ornamental aprons. A case marked 'religious emblems and ritual objects' in the Pitt-Rivers collection included a medieval crucifix, a Chinese geometric compass and a set of Nigerian divining bones.

Pitt-Rivers was influenced by evolutionary ideas in science as was Herbert Spencer, who referred to the Pitt-Rivers collection in his *Principles of Sociology* (1876). 'Primitive men', Spencer believed, were not to be credited even with such inventiveness as their simple appliances seemed to indicate. 'These have arisen by small modifications ... without any distinct devising of them.' It had been left to nineteenth-century men to invent new things like photography, which the Pitt-Rivers Museum put to good use.

The first museum display of Pitt-Rivers's 'universal collection' of things was in the unlikely setting of Bethnal Green in London's deprived East End – and not far from where C. R. Ashbee was to live in Toynbee Hall – but in 1883 it was transferred to a specially built museum in the then almost equally unlikely setting of Oxford behind Ruskin's Museum. It seemed like an 'Aladdin's cave' to most of the people who visited it. Indeed, the new museum was as characteristic of its period as the Tradescants' collection of 'rareities', 'a world of wonders', had been in the late-seventeenth century when it was moved from Lambeth to form the nucleus of Oxford's Ashmolean Museum.

Pitt-Rivers wanted visitors, but he also wanted researchers; and it was a sign of the still imperfect academic specialization of the late-Victorian period that once moved to Oxford his collection of artefacts was placed under the control of the Professor of Zoology and Comparative Anatomy on the simplest of all grounds that man was a mammal. Even the Tradescants had distinguished more sharply between 'natural' objects and 'artificills', and during the eighteenth century a new generation of antiquarians, fascinated by the ancient world and seeking in spirit to return to it, had already turned from literary texts to coins, statues and vases.

The first lecturer on the Pitt-Rivers collection, E. B. Tyler, later to be knighted, was one of the founding fathers of anthropology – his *Primitive Culture* appeared in 1871 – and parallel to his lectures on ethnology and archaeology other related Oxford lectures were soon arranged with what was still the most Victorian of titles – 'arts and industries'. This was a proof in itself that Victorian anthropology could be no more completely separated from economics than economics from aesthetics.

It was through nineteenth-century anthropology that the concept of 'material culture' was explicitly introduced into the study of things, from the start bringing into the reckoning materials as well as artefacts, while at the same time relating man-made things to 'minerals, flora and fauna, which compose the environment in which people live'. Such a concept of 'material culture' has been described as 'wondrous and gargantuan', 'with everything thrown in except the kitchen sink'; and more recently the kitchen sink has been thrown in too, along with the grate and the hearth. The concept has been extended further, indeed, not least by geographers, in studies of 'eco-systems' and of the things associated specifically with them. As a concept, it clearly needs refinement, if not narrowing of scope: and twentieth-century 'economic anthropology', as developed by Mary Douglas and others, a very rewarding subject in the context of this book, has focused, like the work of the French semiologists, more on the hidden meanings of things than on the range of things available, noting the 'refusal to transact' as well as the 'impulse to circulate'.

'Goods can be cherished or judged inappropriate, discarded and re-placed', Mary Douglas and Baron Isherwood have written in their stimulating and important book *The World of Goods, Towards an Anthropology of Consumption* (1978). 'Unless we appreciate how they are used to constitute an intelligible universe, we will never know how to resolve the contradictions of our economic life.' *The World of Goods* sets out to dissolve as Wicksteed had dissolved long before them, the Cartesian dichotomy between physical and psychical experience. 'Goods that minister to physical needs – food or drink', they insist, 'are no less carriers of meaning than ballet or poetry.'

My object in *Victorian Things* is to try to reconstruct 'the intelligible universe' – or, more properly, universes, for there was more than one – of the Victorians; and I have never ignored the fact, though it is easy for collectors to do so, that the economic inability to transact was even more significant in Victorian Britain than the refusal to do so. In 1900/1901 only 17 per cent of the population left enough property for it to be recorded in the probate records. I have concentrated, however, as French semiologists have done, on the things that were transacted as witnesses, in my case dealing with them not through abstraction or through generalization about categories of objects and their typology – for example, clothes or milk or wine or toys – but rather through the detailed study of particular things. My approach is different from French semiologists in one other respect. While I have noted how, in the words of Barthes, 'newspapers, art and common sense (not to speak of advertising) commonly dress up reality', so that 'Nature and History become confused', I have been concerned with far more than what he calls 'ideological abuse'. There is always a danger that semiologists get caught within the limits of their own expository frames, and there is a further danger that when they try to relate everything to everything else in a culture, they are imposing rules on disorderly 'intelligible universes' rather than discovering them.

Historians have to be very careful to avoid this danger, particularly when they claim to be cultural rather than economic or social historians. As Ernst Gombrich has written, 'it is one thing to see the interconnectedness of things, another to postulate that all aspects of a culture can be traced back to one key cause of which they are the manifestations'. In considering a 'material culture', they know that things are related to each other in many different ways – economically, spatially, functionally, symbolically. Pots are related not only to pans or to vases or to food or to drink, but through their labels and covers – and their advertising – to quite different things falling within their price range, so many, indeed, that the historian can become as confused as Alice was.

31

Transfers of technology are particularly fascinating. For example, hair clippers, patented in the United States in 1879, were anticipated by two handed clippers used for trimming horses, and during the 1870s American youths are said to have used them on their own hair in what was called – with another transfer, this time of ideas – 'a pineapple style'. Such permutations of things fascinated the Victorians as much as the things themselves on offer in a perpetual 'exchange and mart', the title of a new journal published in 1868.

The Victorians' own consciousness of things, late or early in the reign – and it was not lacking in semiological awareness – was expressed in different ways, reflecting not only different degrees of understanding and appreciation, but different, sometimes ambivalent or contradictory, reactions. There was, indeed, just as much ambivalence or contradiction in attitudes to 'things' – from wonder to alarm – as there was in the Victorian responses to cities discussed in the second book of my trilogy. Nor was there any consensus about the design of things, about education in taste, about the evolution of styles or about the values which were associated with consumption or possession.

Local or national, and, above all, international exhibitions, when things were on public display, were always occasions, therefore, for argument as well as for celebration. 'The results of the Exhibition', we read in the official catalogue of 1851, 'are pregnant with incalculable benefits to all classes of humanity'. For Ruskin, however, while the 'quantity of bodily industry' which the Crystal Palace expressed as 'very great', only to that extent was it good. It had only one thought behind it – 'that it might be possible to build a greenhouse larger than ever greenhouse was built before'. At the very end of the century, when the Paris Exhibition of 1900 was news everywhere, there was fierce argument about many of its features, including the symbolic statue 'La Parisienne' which critics described as 'the triumph of prostitution'.

There could be ample argument about 'things' between exhibitions also. Food, for example, was considered not just as a subject for cookery books or for treatises on household management, the most famous of them Mrs Beeton's *Book of Household Management* (1861). It was the theme also of a large volume by George Dodd, of Dr Edward Smith's pioneering collection of diets gathered together in 1863 in 'communities of want', and of a multitude of pamphlets on adulteration, paralleled by similar pamphlets on beer, wine – and water. Dorothy Hartley's *Water in England* (1964), a follow-up to her *Food in England*, is packed with detail about 'water running', 'water caught and conducted and compelled' and 'water domesticated', although there is no chapter as such on water polluted and 'purified'. Water was seldom a free good.

The continuing argument about things always extended to transport. Trouble went with benefits. Railways were symbols of improvement, but they also brought with them disasters, as did steam boilers, and even bicycles. When photography was called a 'foe-to-graphic' art by Landseer's brother, Lord Salisbury, keen on every new invention in every field, complained in the *Quarterly Review* in 1864 that 'bad artists have lavished upon photography a good deal of the contempt which some thirty years ago coach proprietors used to expend upon the dangerous and inconvenient system of travelling by railway'.

Above all, the role of money was almost always treated ambivalently. Early and mid-Victorian books on household economy extolled the advantage of 'principles of economy' – and abstinence – even when their back pages were full of advertisements; and *The Economist*, like Walter Bagehot, its editor, could extol the extension of credit, but condemn in years of financial crisis, like 1857, 'the extent to which credit was misapplied to enable the most worthless part of the community to waste in gigantic follies and disgraceful frauds millions of capital gradually amassed by years of industry and self-denial'. Obviously, in the language of the period money could be 'abused' as well as used. During the 1870s, when there was some pre-Edwardian open praise of 'gorgeous plutocracy', there was a growing sense also, apparent in Trollope, ever-present in Gladstone, of the moral perils that went with it. For Marx, living through good and bad years in Victorian London, greed itself, like 'comfort', the quest for which was never confined to the plutocracy, was 'the product of a definite social development, not natural as opposed to historical', and he related it to a particular capitalist economy at a particular point in its development. In his view, as in Dickens's, money, the 'permanent commodity', 'wealth incarnate', had itself taken the form of a thing.

Meanwhile, great Victorian preachers, turning to older texts than *Capital*, denounced in the name of God against Mammon, 'the demon of greed' and the materialism of an acquisitive society, and looked back, not always convincingly, to a simpler age when there were fewer things (including carpets, among the most obvious symbols of comfort) to tempt the poor and the rich alike. Children were taught not to pray for material things, adults that what the Lord gave he also took away. There were many sermons on St Paul's text in the seventh chapter of the *Epistle to the Corinthians* that 'the fashion of this world passeth', and one well-known hymn by J. G. Whittier began 'All things are thine; no gift have we, Lord of all gifts, to offer thee'.

Even then, that was only one reaction. The novelist Henry Ward Beecher in 1873 claimed just as comprehensively that 'all the things we see are types of things we do not see – visible signs of the things and thoughts of God', while other writers dwelt on the homeliness of 'habit' and the closeness of habit to affection – 'I love it, I love it, that old armchair'. Dickens could even write a story in *Household Words* about a talking hat-stand, 'my mahogany friend', which consoled the narrator when he was crossed in love.

'Sweet are the ties that bind' or, in the different words of the twentieth-century writer, Samuel Beckett, discussing Marcel Proust, habit serves as 'a generic term for the countless treaties' concluded between individuals and their 'countless correlative objects'. A far less well-known French novelist writing long after Proust, Georges Perec, was to portray human life mainly in terms of his characters' acquisition, use and disposal of objects, and his novel *Les Choses* (1965) was to inspire a new twentieth-century *ism*, 'chosism': 'To be is to have.'

# VI

I was tempted in writing my book to eschew all *isms* and focus on single things as I did on single Victorian people and single Victorian cities. I thought among all possible chairs of one particular chair, not a rocking chair, but the Day-Dreamer papier-mâché chair in the Great Exhibition, 'decorated at the top with winged thoughts' and described more fully in Chapter 2; among all possible blocks of coal of one particular block of coal, weighing 24 tons, which was displayed outside the Crystal Palace building in 1851 alongside a statue of Richard Coeur de Lion; and among all possible clocks of a 'century clock' exhibited by J. W. Hile at the 1876 American Centennial Exhibition. It was so arranged, its exhibitor declared, as 'to run a hundred years without re-winding'. From late in the nineteenth century I would have chosen the papier-mâché mechanical dragon exported from London to Bayreuth for Wagner's first festival in 1875.

I might also have included in my list particular imaginary things, like Mr Pickwick's pair of spectacles, which I have referred to in Chapter 3, Edward Lear's 'Washtubbia Circularis', one of a remarkable number of imaginary Victorian inventions, Carron's 'machine for sensational emotions', and, with an intimation more of fact than of fiction, *Punch*'s list of 'curiosities of London' in 1855 which included 'a fresh-laid egg that was less than a month old', 'an omnibus that was not going to start directly' and 'a statue that was not an ornament to the metropolis'.

Yet to have yielded to the temptation to take single things, even in categories, as the subjects of different chapters of this book, would have been just as restrictive as it would have been to consider objects by themselves without considering also the verbal records which place them within their culture. While I have referred, therefore, wherever possible to particular things, I have tried also to consider crucial aspects of categorization. What were the things that Victorians listed, and what constituted a laundry list or a shopping list or the kind of list drawn up by Brian Moore? Which things were signs of status? Which were signs of 'class'?

Differences in the Victorian 'universes of things' began there, but category questions multiply. Which things expressed or set out to express individuality? Which were specifically women's things? Which men's? Which children's? What were the taboos? What were the effects of the Married Women's Property Act of 1870? Which things, including 'images of fame',

*Sacred things: decoration for the Church, 1862*

the theme of Chapter 4, and other 'public things', attempted to integrate or succeeded in integrating the society as well as serving the individual or the family? Which were deemed 'national treasures'? How were habits related to rituals? Which things were treated as 'holy'? Why did Peter Anson call his 1960 study '*Fashions* in Church Furnishings, 1840–1940'? (The *Ecclesiologist* had a thirty page article on church furnishings and decorations at the Paris Exhibition of 1855). Which things were 'imperial' and how many of them came from 'the provinces of empire' rather than from the centre?

In the twentieth century a number of such questions have occasionally been asked in questionnaires, as they were by N. N. Foote, in *Household Decision Making* (1969) or by Mihaly Csikszentmihalyi and Eugene Rochberg-Halton in their American study *The Meaning of Things: Domestic Symbols and the Self* (1981); the latter has one chapter title which would have appealed in particular to the Victorians – 'characteristics of happy homes'. Direct Victorian evidence is fragmentary, however, and scattered, and it raises as many questions as it answers. We know more about kitchens – though not always without research about the functions of the objects inside them – than we do about bedrooms. Who chose iron or brass beds? How much can we deduce from furniture advertisements as to whether it was newly-wed women or men who chose sideboards or chairs? Did husbands or wives in working-class families handle the problems of household management differently from those in middle-class families? The question has been raised in relation to miners by John Benson in his thoughtful study *British Coal Miners in the Nineteenth Century, A Social History* (1980).

In lieu of questionnaires, we are forced to turn to statistics, but while they are there in abundance, most of them were collected not to illuminate individual choices but to chart national 'progress'. Some, too, were just intended to be funny, though they can now seem as unfunny as Victorian puns. *Punch* led the way. 'Professor Persoff', we are told in 1843, 'calculated details of the total number of walking sticks crossing London Bridge during the previous six months – 1,490,720.' More than a third, he concluded, were oak saplings, over a fifth were 'veritable bamboo'. Many of Mayhew's statistics – and he loved to introduce them – have this flavour, as did his lists.

Two generations after G. R. Porter's frequently revised book *The Progress of the Nation*, which first appeared in 1837, Michael G. Mulhall, author of *The Progress of the World*, produced his *Dictionary of Statistics* in 1884, which claimed to be 'the first statistical Dictionary published in any language'. It covered a wide range of items in the form of comparative tables, although the statistics were fragmentary, unsupported by adequate information about sources, and often idiosyncratic. Thus, he pointed out with equal attention that there were 9,800 bicycles in London, more than one in ten of those in England and Wales as a whole, 96,000, and that an offer of £500 for a Persian cat at the Sydenham Cat Show in 1869 had been refused.

Mulhall was just as interested in 'psychic states' as the economist

*The Drawing Room: Maple advertisement, 1887. The suite cost 24 guineas.*

Wickstead and included as one of the items in his dictionary the word 'apoplexy', stating that 'this disease is becoming more prevalent in England'. Ways of life were indicated in many of his items, like the fact that blacking consumption – for 'cleaning' purposes – amounted in value terms in 1880 to no less than £560,000. It would have been interesting to have had the comment of Dickens on this figure, for in 'an evil hour, he had been forced as a child to work in a blackening factory', but he had been dead for fourteen years in 1884. He would doubtless have taken it along with some of Mulhall's other figures, however, as a sign of progress, like the statistics of receipts at bath-houses designed for the working-classes in London. These had risen from £9,800 in 1850 to £25,000 in 1860 and £41,000 in 1880.

Mulhall's generalizations were almost all concerned with evidence of 'progress', and although he chose a French motto for his *Dictionary* 'je n'impose rien, je ne propose même rien, j'expose' – 'I impose nothing, I propose nothing, I expose' – little, if any, of his exposition was to Britain's disadvantage. One of his most interesting generalizations, which had been anticipated in Walter Bagehot's *Lombard Street*, was that between 1840 and 1880 the banking of the world had 'increased eleven-fold, three time as fast as commerce, twenty times faster than population'.

For Mulhall, as for Marx, who died in the year the *Dictionary* appeared, this had been the 'age of capital'. The difference was that where Mulhall saw only plenty, Marx, like Mayhew, saw poverty in the midst of plenty, long before Mulhall wrote. By the 1880s there were many others who did too, including statisticians who pointed out that there were large numbers of people who not only lacked things but did not expect ever to have them: 'poverty in the midst of plenty' could go with 'poverty of desire'. The universe of things was perceived of, as in the distant past, in radically different ways. This is one, although only one, of the reasons why I have included a chapter on spectacles and cameras, the former a very neglected subject, in my book. Perception of things was not just a matter of eyesight. Nor was the camera the 'impartial eye' that some of its first sponsors claimed. Almost at once it was recognized that it could distort reality rather than reflect or record it.

There were certainly differing perceptions among the better-off of the things made in the places which I described in *Victorian Cities*. A. W. Pugin, for example, could bracket together as 'inexhaustible mines of bad taste' Birmingham, which had earned the title of the 'toy shop of Europe' in the eighteenth century, and Sheffield, known for its silver before it was known for its steel and now the home of a superb Ruskin gallery. Meanwhile, the cheap machine-made goods of Manchester, exported to India and the Middle East, could often be compared unfavourably with the fine indigenous textiles of quality which had been made in India for centuries. Nonetheless, the famous Art Treasures Exhibition in Manchester in 1857, which attracted over a million and a quarter visitors, (see below, p. 83 ff), was one of the most impressive Victorian attempts to 'elevate taste'; and although it was not mentioned in *Victorian Cities* in my chapter on 'Manchester, Symbol of a new Age', it has to be mentioned more than once in *Victorian Things*. My chapter on Leeds in *Victorian Cities* was sub-titled 'A Study in Civic Pride'. It is the Leeds clothing industry, however, and not the Town Hall, which must figure in *Victorian Cities*; it was transformed after 1855 as a result of the introduction of sewing machines and band-knives and ready-made clothes.

Victoriana were explicitly referred to in my chapter on Melbourne in *Victorian Cities*. John Betjeman, who wrote the foreword to an edition of Robin Boyd's *The Australian Ugliness* (1960) and who claimed that 'Marvellous' Melbourne, a term coined by Sala, played Edinburgh to Sydney's Glasgow, had more to say, however, about Australian buildings than the objects within them. Perhaps he was right. The Report of the Executive Commissioner for the Centennial International Exhibition in Melbourne in 1888/9 noted in the section on manufactures that 'notwithstanding all the efforts put forth, which were diligent and repeated, the Commission had failed to elicit exhibitors from the manufacturers of Melbourne or Victoria'. It had become 'necessary in certain classes, therefore, to purchase exhibits of clothing, boots and shoes, hats, basket-work etc manufactured within the Colony, so that it might be evident that these industries were carried on, and that the quality of the goods produced was of a superior description'. This might have been thought to be cheating, and it was reassuring to know that by contrast, several Sydney firms entered exhibits of stained glass and engraved glassware.

For the way in which the individuals described in *Victorian People* perceived things, I have turned to their wills. They were significantly different. Bagehot was reticent in describing his possessions, but he liked comfort, and under his wife's influence he could look for more than comfort too. He decorated his house in Queen's Gate Place with Morris papers and de Morgan tiles and described the curtains there as 'a new toy': 'William Morris is composing the drawing room', he wrote, 'as he would an ode'. Bagehot bequeathed all his real and personal property to his wife, his sole executor. So also did Trollope, whom I discussed in the same chapter of *Victorian People*; after his wife's death, it was to be divided equally between his two sons.

Trollope had a greater fear of poverty than Bagehot, if only because at the age of 19 he heard of his father's death in penury, and already in a miserable childhood he had soon learned the difference between wax candles and cheaper tallow candles and had discovered at first hand who bailiffs were. Trollope deliberately sought for himself 'a comfortable home', therefore, and for a time enjoyed its many amenities. Nature, he felt, had intended him for an American rather than an Englishman. His books, he claimed – as did John Bright – were especially precious to him, more so even than his horses. Yet he would never have said of books what Bright said – very pompously – that there was no blessing that could be given 'to our artisans of greater benefit ... The home influence of such a possession is one which will guard them from many temptations and many evils'.

Samuel Smiles, spokesman of self help, recently 're-discovered' afresh long after my own 'discovery' of him, had told his readers that 'riches and ease are not necessary to man's highest culture'. He chose his two sons along with his wife as executors and specified that certain objects – and manuscripts – should go to them: his plate, furniture, china, linen, glass, books, pictures, wines and spirits and other household effects were bequeathed to his wife only if she remained a widow. In the event of remarriage they were to revert to the two sons. Thomas Hughes, a fourth character discussed in *Victorian People*, left only £8,412, most of it to his wife. In his will it was stated that particular articles, to be given to his friends, were specified on a piece of paper on his bureau. Yet a codicil to the will added that the piece of paper had been lost and that he left it to his wife to give away as memorials to his friends such things as she chose. Smiles would certainly never have been so careless.

I have compared such evidence relating to the persons named in *Victorian People* with evidence from other sources dealing with wills, inventories, heirlooms, insurance, and the role of the pawnshop and the bankruptcy court. The disposition of wines and spirits seems to have figures in wills more frequently than books, although when books did figure they were often given very special attention: thus, Lord Macaulay allowed his executor to choose from his collection a hundred favourite volumes. Furniture was often singled out too. The widow of a Northampton pork butcher, Mrs Ann Vials, was more specific in all her bequests even than Hughes. In 1868, two years before the passing of the Married Women's Property Act, she left the portrait of her late husband, 'the mahogany table and cover in the front parlour of my dwelling house', her writing desk, six silver spoons, and 'one pair of sugar tongs marked with the letters GV' to a neighbouring farmer. 'I hold, as the wise legislators of the Married Women's Property Act must have wished', wrote Mrs Craik in her book *About Money* (1886), 'that every woman who has any money to dispose of, either earned or inherited, ought to keep it in her own hands, and learn to manage it herself, exactly as a man does'.

Insurance, like banking, changed the security boundaries of the world of things so that a writer in *Belgravia* in 1868 could already observe that 'the community have a general and indistinct notion that all kinds of things can be insured and all kinds of contingencies provided for by paying a certain sum of money yearly or half-yearly into an office'. The yearly or half-yearly payments were by then far more demanding than church rates, which were disappearing, though not as inexorable as hire purchase payments, already common for furniture in the late-nineteenth century, were to be in later times, or the mounting pressure (*pace* Dickens) to give Christmas presents.

Charity, a main expression of giving away, went back long before the age of insurance, and charitable dispositions figured more prominently in a sample of wills which I have examined than in the wills of persons in *Victorian People* – or in Macaulay's. Other evidence suggests that during the 1890s one in ten published wills included benefactions to charities. Many of these were devoted to 'public things', including hospitals, chapels and churches. The late Professor David Owen has written in detail of Victorian philanthropy before and after death: it was far-reaching, and it was often expressed not through the creation of new things to last but to the giving away of old things, notably food and clothes, as well as of money. 'There is reason to think', wrote the Charity Commissioners in 1895, 'that the latter half of the nineteenth century will stand favourably in respect of the greatness and variety of the Charities created within its duration to no other half-century since the Reformation.' We are still living on a Victorian infrastructure.

'Bring and buy sales' were favourite means of disposing both of new and of second-hand things in the philanthropist's lifetime. Another was to advertise them at ten words for a penny in *Exchange and Mart*, a 'journal', in its own words, 'through which to buy, sell, or exchange anything.' On its opening page the first category of items in the exchange lists was headed 'bric-à-brac' and the second 'country houses'. 'I have a very handsome curly, liver-coloured retriever', one of the first advertisers explained, 'which I should like to exchange for any good ornament for the drawing room. I am open to offers.'

It was not only because of that advertisement, one of many like it, that animals (and birds) figure in my book: like plants and flowers they were an important element in the 'intelligible universes' of the Victorians, cats and dogs as well as horses, although they often had to be treated anthropomorphically in order to become intelligible: they figure prominently in Lewis Carroll also, even if, as Harry Levin has noted, Alice's relations with them were 'far from idyllic'. 'What are you?' the pigeon asks Alice, who replies 'I'm a little girl'. 'A likely story', says the pigeon. The animals in *Tommy Smith's Animals* by Edmund Sallous (1899) were of a different disposition, and in this case it is Tommy who is cruel. 'He would throw stones at the birds . . . and if he did not hit them, . . . he always *meant* to hit them.'

Animals (and birds) usually played no part, however, in pawnshops, another place to dispose of things. Pawnbrokers could only carry on their ancient trade if they could attract customers with suitable possessions to pledge, and it was fortunate for them that by the mid-nineteenth century there were far more such possessions than there ever had been. Naturally the brokers preferred goods of high value and of small bulk, like jewellery, watches and silverware, amongst the most mobile of all Victorian things.

The pawnshop could attract the very rich as well as the very poor, and it was as much frequented by women as by men. In his chapter on the pawnshop in *Sketches by Boz*, published one year before Queen Victoria came to the throne, Dickens explicitly chose to concentrate on the penury of poverty, but he referred in passing to pawnbrokers who called themselves silver merchants and who would have spurned brass for the three balls displayed outside their premises. There was an informative journal for pawnbrokers, too, little read by historians – *The Pawnbrokers' Gazette and Trade Circular*, which first appeared in 1838, a whole generation before *Exchange and Mart*. Its second editor, Alfred Daniel Keeson, who worked on the paper for fifty years, was a witness before the Committee on Pawnbroking in 1870 which explored the many ramifications of pawnbroking into the world of crime as well as the world of trade.

There is far more to say of burglary and theft – and locks – than I have had space to say in this book. Criminal statistics amongst all statistics are notoriously difficult to interpret over long periods of time and there is continuing argument about the origins and role, even the existence, of a 'criminal class', a class which most Victorians were sure existed. Changes both in the law and in the organization and operations of the police force affected statistics and attitudes. Yet a Victorian as devoted to statistics as Edwin Chadwick could write unequivocally a few days before his death in 1890 that the police had made it possible for people safely to possess things that would have been in jeopardy early in the century. Working-class families on the eve of Victorian England could 'hold in safety no personal property of any sort ... They had no silver spoons, nor any other article of that kind. The possession of such property at that time endangered their lives.'

Chadwick would have doubtless approved also of the 1849 comment of the Chaplain of Preston Gaol, the Rev J. Clay, who was well known to him, that it was 'not manufacturing Manchester, but multitudinous Manchester' which gave birth to 'whatever criminality may be imputable to it'. A late-Victorian decline in violent crime and in juvenile crime did not mean, however, that middle-class families in the 'multitudinous places' were entirely secure during the 1880s and 1890s. Indeed, Sunday newspapers – and Sherlock Holmes – could make almost as much of theft as of murder. By then the categories of thieves might not be quite as colourful as those listed by Mayhew – he noted no fewer than fourteen categories of purloiners of 'goods, provisions, money, clothes, old metal, etc' from 'drag sneaks' stealing luggage to 'noisy racket men' who stole china and glass – but there was an organized market in stolen goods, which had its national network and its international contacts and outlets.

For this reason locks were among the most important categories of Victorian things. So, too, were the questions they posed. Was it possible to create a perfectly safe lock? In 1851 Alfred C. Hobbs, who exhibited a new American lock, challenged British lockmakers to let him test established British models, a challenge which generated as much argument as design in general and argument which many householders thought of as more pertinent. The Hobbs lock won the 1851 Prize Model at the Crystal Palace – it was deemed 'impregnable against every practicable method of picking, fraud or violence' – and Hobbs and Co of 76 Cheapside were even more prominent at the Exhibition of 1862 when large numbers of patent locks were on display. Hobbs locks, we read in the illustrated catalogue, 'possess a strong recommendatory quality to the owners and occupiers of house property, in their comparative cheapness to hand-made locks, combined with the nicety of the finish of the working parts, effected by the machinery, and their universal adaptability.' Nonetheless, Chubb and Son, of Wolverhampton and 57 St Paul's Churchyard, who in 1840 were producing the whole of their output without machines, continued to maintain their clientèle. 'No locks of inferior quality are made by Chubb and Son', we read in 1862. 'The whole of their locks sold to the public at large are exactly the same in security and excellence of workmanship as those supplied to Her Majesty.'

Collectors of things were particularly concerned about theft. Indeed, some of their critics suggested that they and criminals had certain features in common, notably the desire to possess something not yet your own and the will to realize it. One Balzac character spoke of the motivation of the collector being 'to desire what you no longer want and buy all the time'; and certainly some of the most interesting collections, passionately acquired, have far transcended want. If only for that reason, indeed, it is proper to refer to what Maurice Rheims called in his book title of 1959 *La vie étrange des objets*: the strange life of objects.

Books on collectors and collections and the deliberate acts of choice, even the 'pathology', that have lain behind them have often been written by museum keepers. James Laver, curious about every thing, spent nearly forty years as a Keeper at the Victoria and Albert Museum, where almost every collection provides source material for this book; and Sir Roy Strong, until recently Director of the Museum, wrote the introduction to the *Collectors' Encyclopaedia, 1851–1939* which appeared in 1975. Lord Clark, for eleven years Director of the National Gallery, told BBC listeners in 1946 how important it was to learn 'to look at things' outside museums as well as inside them – in railway stations, for instance – but he himself concentrated, unlike more recent guides to the public, on high art. It was left to the enterprising Director of the Ethnographic Museum at Neuchâtel to include in his book *L'objet témoin*: the object as witness, chapters with headings like 'The Object is a Sign', 'Photography considered as a Sign', and 'What are the Children of the World Playing with?'

Such a new approach to the function of the specialized museum, now widely shared by museum directors, is so different from the Victorian approach to the often small general museum, presenting stuffed birds, firearms, fossils, mummies and machines as well as 'works of art' – an extension of the schoolboy's museum – that we are in danger now of losing all our remaining specimens of museums of the Victorian variety. Yet the Victorians themselves did not always easily create museums. In Birmingham, for example, it needed Joseph Chamberlain to ensure that £1,000 was on offer in 1878 for the acquisition of 'examples of industrial art'. Ten years later, there were only 11,124 objects or 'groups of objects', most of them acquired abroad representing 'extinct civilization'. Nor were they always appreciated. A 'well-known, well-educated and prominent citizen' of Birmingham asked the Curator why money was wasted on the acquisition of 'earthenware platters', by which he meant majolica plates in the Italian Gallery.

The French Ministry of Culture, which would never have asked such a question, has recently produced a magnificent inventory of 'Victorian' (and older) artefacts in French museums, *Objets civils domestiques* (1984) with the sub-title *Principes d'analyse scientifique*. It begins with J. Baudrillard's question, posed in his *Système des Objets* (1968) and frequently asked by Victorians, as to whether man-made objects can be classified like flora and fauna. Accompanied by superb illustrations of particular objects, the text concentrates on typology, with sections on such subjects as food, toilet, medicine, care of the home, decoration and textiles, all described as elements in *le domaine du quotidien*, the domain of everyday life.

Clark had limited curiosity about many of these objects. He somewhat reluctantly accepted stamp collecting as a field of enterprise and even admitted that 'one can conceive a "great" collection of Rembrandt's etchings in which the stamp collecting element – the search for perfect specimens and the rare states' – would have been the inspiration. 'It becomes less easy to apply the word "great" to a collection of Baxter Prints', he went on, however, 'and impossible to apply it to a collection of matchboxes'.

The intimidating word 'great' had not deterred Pitt-Rivers or James Laver from being deeply interested in things which were not great, but it raises complex questions about the relationship between 'art' and the things described in my book, some, though not all of them, proclaimed at the time as 'art objects', Henry Cole's language, or more simply as 'art'. Indeed, the stimulating historian of architecture, Stein Eiler Rasmussen, who was as keenly interested in things as he was in buildings, noted, like Clark, that once delight in the brightness and order of inanimate objects, an impulse for the collector, was transferred to 'those mysterious communications of human experience which we call works of art, our difficulties begin'.

There is relatively little in this book about professed 'works of art', the market for which has been studied in detail by Gerald Reitlinger in his *The Economics of Taste* (1975). Some of the people who bought them had made their money from producing very different things, like the American collector of ceramics, furniture and paintings, Thomas Benedict Clarke, whose fortune was based on collars and cuffs. The Clarke sale of 1896 has been described as 'a benchmark in American collecting.' There is more to say about this kind of collection, but in this book I have been more concerned myself with 'the treasure trail' followed by Tony Curtis in *The Lyle Guide to Collectibles* (1983) than in the great collections and the great sales. I have noted, however, how the term 'art' was interpreted in radically different ways even by big dealers and how even small collectors of 'trivial objects' could make large claims – for example that they were reliving the experiences of the artist or craftsman who produced the things they were collecting. Nor have these been the only large claims made in the name of Art. At the time, the popular sculptor John Rogers of New York, who produced no fewer than 100,000 'groups' of figures between 1860 and 1890, was praised not for his craft but for his art, 'not high art', one critic admitted in 1873, but nonetheless, 'genuine art of a high naturalistic order, based on true feeling and a right appreciation of humanity.'

There are many difficulties in identifying 'works of art' in the 'universe of things'. What, for example, was the role within this context of replication, already mentioned in a different context? What happened when a 'great picture' was reproduced and circulated in large numbers? What happened when objects, including, for example, the Crystal Palace or the Statue of Liberty, were sold as models in glass or metal? This was an age of moulds, dyes and punches. Was Cole right to talk of 'wedding' mechanical skill and high art? Was photography necessarily a 'foe-to-graphic art?' Did Ruskin choose the right word when in his section 'the Ways of Truth' in *The Seven Lamps of Architecture* he spoke of 'deceits', like the painting of surfaces to represent some other material from that of which they actively consist? Could 'Art' survive 'deceit'? There was significant Victorian debate about all these matters, as there was about design and decoration.

*Pace* Clark, I have deliberately included in this book stamps, specifically single out by Marc Bloch as items worthy of serious historical study, and Baxter prints, viewed by Clark with such condescension. It is interesting that W. E. Imeson, who wrote a short pioneering history of *Illustrated Music Titles and their Delineators* before the First World War also wrote a 'philatelic phantasy' – *The Stamp-Fiend's Raid*.

I have included in my own chapters matches, too, an important new 'Victorian thing' which for a number of reasons captured the imagination of many Victorians and my own – and clusters of objects in metal, wood or paper, which were associated with matches. Humphry House mentioned matchboxes in his own list of 'collectibles', and *The Matchbox Collectors' Scrapbook*, published appropriately by Vesta Publications, has surveyed many of them in retrospect. A wonderful Bryant and May collection, first exhibited in 1927, included, for example, boxes combined with 'smoker's outfits' (1840) and boxes 'in the form of a church chest ... with on the lid St George spearing a dragon in relief' (1865). The girl producers of match boxes, some of whom made twelve gross of match boxes a day, showed that they could be as choosy as twentieth-century collectors: 'Miss O.' wrote, Annie Besant, their redoubtable protector, 'has preferences for some kinds of matchboxes. She does not like to do the smaller ones, which on the other hand, some workers prefer. She is in the fortunate position of being able to have what she chooses.'

Collectors always chose, although what they purchase in the way of surviving 'collectibles', like what consumers purchase at the time as 'objects of desire', usually has to be decided within a budget. They have turned increasingly to Victoriana since the 1950s for six main reasons. First, older antiques are scarcer; the Victorian plenitude, not all of it machine-based, was in some sense a plenitude for posterity. Second, for this reason Victorian things are on the whole cheaper than older things, although their price has risen significantly, but not always constantly or consistently. There really can be 'fortunes in junk piles'. Third, beyond those markets, although not entirely separate from them, is the market for Victorian art, and there, too, there has been a marked change in tastes reflected in auction sale prices as much as in the activities of the Victorian Society.

Fourth, there is a very wide range of Victorian things to collect, and since many collectors like to be specialists and dealers emerge ready to cater for them, there is ample scope for specialization, a feature which has always interested collectors; they can collect one category of objects, like Staffordshire figures or picture postcards or military medals or biscuit tins – there are always some 'rare' items – or theme objects in different categories like 'natural wonders', 'awesome experiences', 'sporting memorabilia', increasingly specialized, or more simply 'railroadiana'. There have been clubs and associations of collectors, sometimes sub-cultures in themselves, ranging from the Goss Collectors' Club to the Royal Philatelic Society. There have also been invaluable and easily accessible guides, notably the admirable and deservedly popular *Shire Album* collection, which includes guides to, among other things, thimbles and samplers, dry stone walls and tiles.

Fifth, a favourite category of Victoriana, 'collectibles', consists of 'souvenirs' or 'bygones': nostalgia can still cling to them in an age when nostalgia counts for even more than it did for the Victorians. There can also be a sense of shared enthusiasm, as Nicolette Scourse explained in her delightful book *The Victorians and their Flowers* (1983). 'The love of flowers', she began – and what she said applies to more than flowers – 'kindles rapport across the centuries. Shared enthusiasms, wonder and enquiry render the separation in time irrelevant.'

Finally, in large areas of the world, leaving on the side ancient cultures, explored in the nineteenth and twentieth century by archaeologists and anthropologists, most of the objects associated with pre-twentieth century cultural history are nineteenth-century objects. They have a very special place in the making of new societies, like Australia, Canada and the United States, where Victorian things could be produced as well as imported. There is added interest in that there are local variations within a common Victorian frame. Moreover, even in the 'ancient culture' of India, traditional handicrafts could be influenced by Victorian tastes and odd hybrids produced.

Not all the imports, whether prestigiously distinctive or meticulously prefabricated, were suitable for life on the frontier or even in the city. In Calcutta, for example, the Marble Palace, the home of the Mullick family built in 1835, still contains what Geoffrey Moorhouse has called 'vast quantities of Victorian bric-à-brac that look as if they were scavenged in job lots from Portobello Road on a series of damp Saturday afternoon in October ... bronze boys on chargers, plaster fruit and stuffed kingfishers presented under glass domes, gewgaws in papier-mâché and firedogs in cast iron ... There is a very old Queen Victoria in plaster standing large as life by the main stairway and a very young Queen Victoria in oak, somewhat larger, dominating a red marble room'.

There are other things in the Mullick house too, many of them pre-Victorian, like mirrors from Venice and vases from Sèvres, just as there are many such things in surviving Victorian 'mansions' in Melbourne or Toronto. The Victorians were, after all, great collectors themselves, not only of their own bric-à-brac but of old objects ransacked from different cultures. 'This is a collecting age', *The Graphic* proclaimed in 1869 eight years after Prince Albert, one of the most dedicated of collectors, had died. Some Victorian writers on collecting thought of it, like Clark, as the expression of a biological drive: others related it to the psychological urge, often through rivalry, always through pursuit, to possess a whole series of objects – books, coins, prints, Staffordshires, stamps. 'The popular amusement amongst young ladies for some time past', *The Bookseller* observed in July 1862, 'has been the collection of foreign postage stamps ... We fear that there are not many persons who have succeeded in collecting all'.

Collecting started at school and was encouraged. It usually began with shells on the beach or fossils from the moors or wild flowers from the hedgerows. The private museum was as familiar an institution, therefore, as the public museum, though usually shortlived. J. E. Taylor's *Notes on Collecting and Preserving Natural History Objects*, first published in 1876, began with the message, 'The great end of natural history reading should be the development of a love for the objects dwelt upon, and a desire to know more about them. This can only be brought about by such practical acquaintances as collecting and preserving them induces'. Yet the same might have been said – and was said – about books or even toys.

Those were not, however, the only values attached to the habit of collecting. In 1876 Loftie wrote of 'the prudence' collecting fostered. A university undergraduate had shocked his father when he spent £40 on two jars. (He would not have been shocked, Loftie added, if the boy had lost money on a horse race.) Thirty years later, the jars were sold at Christies 'at a price which paid interest on the original outlay of 20 per cent per annum for all the thirty years, and left a good margin over, besides, as a profit'.

# VII

There are some modern collectors of Victoriana – and some dealers in it, like John and Jennifer May – who, like me, have turned from the objects they assemble to contemporary writing about them. Yet one contemporary book which I came across late in my exploration, *Wonderland of Work* (1883) by G. L. Matéaux, has caught my imagination more than any other. The copy which I studied was a prize, presented by the Worshipful Company of

Clockmakers in London; and, not surprisingly, watches and clocks – and a Brussels carpet – figure prominently in it. Its author began not with artefacts, however, but with resources, in particular with coal, taking the reader on 'a breathless journey' underground before travelling back through a longer span of time than any watch or clock could measure, to the prehistoric forests from which the coal had first come: 'what a wonderful sight a flourishing forest ... would have presented had any mortal eye been there to view its marvels'.

Matéaux had his own angle on coal, 'Every three tons of coal is the ... equivalent of one man's life-long muscular activity – a fact which must make us feel a sort of wondering respect when we look at a solid lump of coal ... A block some twelve feet high, the base of which is only a yard square, has more "work" in it than many a man's life labour'. Thus was Man himself compared with a thing, just as animals, whether wild beasts or man's servants, could also be converted into things – Staffordshire dogs as well as stuffed birds and beasts kept in glass cages.

The titles of the various chapters in Matéaux speak for themselves:

| | |
|---|---|
| Old King Coal at Home and Abroad; | Furniture and Furniture-Makers; |
| The Lights of London; | Stock, Whip and Umbrella Making; |
| Striking a Light; | Our Clocks and Watches; |
| Concerning Iron and Steel; | Toys, Old and New; |
| 'The Toyshop of the World'; | Glass, and How It Is Made; |
| Our Knives, Forks and Spoons; | China and China-Making; |
| Tool, Chain and Nail Making; | Leather and Leather-Workers; |
| Forest Timber – Its Story and Its Uses; | Kid Gloves; |
| | 'Things that are Done With'. |

As I read the contents page of *The Wonderland of Work*, I was struck at once by the fact that the author had chosen to include among the 'things' listed in his book resources like coal and wood; man-made materials like glass and steel; what Dickens called 'household scenery' like carpets and furniture; 'everyday things' like knives, fork and spoons – for J. R. Green, pre-eminent among Victorian social historians, at the very heart of history; and 'pleasure objects', like jewellery and toys, which now figure in most accounts, popular and specialized, of 'Victoriana'. I was struck, too, by the title of Matéaux's last chapter, 'Things that are Done With', for this raises questions about the role both of 'ephemera' and of 'rubbish' in everyday life.

Printed materials among the ephemera were collected with loving care by John Johnson of Oxford long before it was fashionable to attach value to them, and they are now the province of an Ephemera Society, a lively society founded by Maurice Rickards in 1975. Rubbish, which includes 'waste', is the subject of a remarkable book by Michael Thompson, *Rubbish Theory* (1979), which takes the fate of 'Stevengraphs' as an example for detailed study of what has happened to what was once considered to be Victorian rubbish, but does not explore the ramifications of waste, including the profitable opportunities considered by P. L. Simmonds in his *Waste Products* (1862). It is in the spirit of Thompson that Victorian rubbish heaps are now ransacked by collectors most of whom have never read either Thompson or *Our Mutual Friend*, but they will be lucky to find much there that was deposited before the 1880s and 1890s. Already by then, many earlier Victorian things were being thrown on to the rubbish heap by the late-Victorians, just as the early-Victorians had consigned pre-Victorian things, including Chippendale chairs and Georgian carriage clocks, if not to their rubbish heaps, at least to their attics. What once had been treasure now became lumber. Thompson seeks to explain how, when and why the rubbish, as in the case of 'Stevengraphs', became or could become treasure again.

More recently Paris has celebrated the centenary in 1985 of the *Marché aux Puces*, the world's biggest flea-market, honouring the Prefect Eugène Poubelle, who introduced the metal dustbin with lid. At first Poubelle alienated the Paris rag-and-bone dealers, who had previously picked their rubbish from the gutters, but soon they were allowed to raid the new dustbins and to exhibit what they found provided they exhibited away from the centre. The result was the *Marché aux Puces* which offers browsers more variety than any provincial rubbish heap in France or in Britain.

The more imaginative Victorians had a somewhat different conception of the 'waste' element in rubbish, as Simmonds demonstrated, and this is how the Victorian author Matéaux dealt with such themes:

> 'Done with at last' – but when is a thing done with, much less destroyed, I wonder? Shakespeare wrote long ago that 'a good wit will make use of anything'; and Emerson tells us that nothing in nature is exhausted in its first use. Yet what *does* become of the masses of odds and ends that are daily thrust into the world's vast rag-bag, to be eagerly seized upon for some purpose or another by the numerous dealers in rags and bones, who offer so much a pound for all such dingy treasures? I do not, of course, mean cotton or linen rags – the merest child knows that they are transformed into paper – but the mixed remainder when these things are all routed out, the shapeless, colourless, unfragrant bits, wrecked shadows of old coats, torn jackets, worn-out dresses, scraps and cuttings, and tangled woollen rubbish of all sorts, which every household helps to accumulate yet never finds a use for, however thrifty it may be.

Matéaux had 'shoddy' in mind, the despised 'flock', the value of which had been spotted by Benjamin Law in Batley, who converted waste into usable cloth, by Samuel Jubb who published his *History of the Shoddy Trade* in 1862, the same year as Ruskin's *Unto the Last*, and by Leeds manufacturers, little concerned about what Arnold Shimmins, historian of the Leeds textile industry, called 'the unfortunate title of the material'. It was this concoction which William Morris picked out when he tried to give a name to the whole age, which he saw in a dialogue as an 'age of shoddy'.

'It is a shoddy age', I cried. 'Shoddy is King.
From the statesman to the shoemaker all is shoddy!'
I concealed my boots under the table . . .
'Then you do not admire the commonsense John Bull, Mr Morris?'
'John Bull is a STUPID UNPRACTICAL OAF.'

Whatever Benjamin Law was, he was not a 'stupid unpractical oaf': he
actually believed, as Ruskin and Matthew Arnold observed of many of his
fellow countrymen, in 'the Goddess of Getting On', 'making a fair fortune
out of the strange new invention he had suddenly stumbled upon', as
Matéaux put it. 'The rags of all nations', Matéaux went on, 'travel to us
English folk.' He also noted how 'the bones of dead animals yield the chief
constituent of our lucifer matches' and how 'the offal of the street and the
washings of coal gas reappear, carefully preserved in the lady's smelling
bottle, or are used by her to flavour blancmanges for her friends'. He might
have mentioned 'scrap' too, for the metal scrap heap offered far quicker and
more easily calculable returns than the waste on the rubbish heap.

Morris's 'intelligible universe' consisted only of beautiful things. 'Keep
nothing you do not know to be useful or believe to be beautiful', he advised.
He was prepared, therefore, altogether to dispense not only with 'shoddy'
and with 'scrap' but also with coal, most prolific of all products for its by-
products and its 'pure' forms described by others among his contemporaries
as 'black diamonds':

> I should be glad if we could do without coal, and indeed without burrowing like
> worms and moles into the earth altogether; and I am not sure but we could do
> without it if we wished to live pleasant lives, and did not want to produce all
> manner of mere mechanism chiefly for multiplying our own servitude and misery
> and spoiling half the beauty and art of the world to make merchants and
> manufacturers rich. In olden days the people did without coal, and were, I believe,
> rather more happy than we are today, and produced better art, poetry and quite
> as good religion and philosophy as we do nowadays.

There was nothing semiological about that. Nor was there about Robert
Louis Stevenson's plea *not* to introduce electric lighting in his *Virginibus
Puerisque* (1881) – 'Mankind, you would have thought, might have remained
content with what Prometheus stole for them and not gone fishing the
profound heaven with kites to catch the wildfire of the storm?' Electricity was
a 'lamp for a nightmare'.

There were many Victorian chains of connection with an element of
fantasy in them, as Lucinda Lambton demonstrated in her study *Vanishing
Victoriana* (1976), a book with a foreword by John Betjeman, admirer of
eccentric Victorian things, subtitled 'the curious side' of the Victorians.
After all, Victorian things could appear in a multiplicity of disguises –
pumping stations that looked like manor houses; vases that looked like
animals; tombs that looked like tents. There were mists, too, of private
associations as thick sometimes as London fogs. Thus, when the poet Robert

Stephen Hawker built a vicarage for himself with five out of six chimneys made as replicas of his favourite church towers, he admitted that the design of the sixth 'perplexed' him very much 'till I bethought me of my mother's tomb; and there it is in its exact shape and dimensions'.

The symbolism was usually explicit – in town halls, monuments, schools and churches. In 1894 the Rector (and Squire) of Bradfield wrote a letter to the Headmaster of Magdalen College School in Oxford. Stevens's black-smith had made an iron weather vane for the school, but Stevens was not content with that. He has to explain that this ordinary weather vane was really something more.

> The cross and vane in gilt are to remind the pupils of other bright rays that come down from the Cross. The vane spins round with the wind to show that the spirit bloweth where it listeth. An olive branch and other motifs are designed to reinforce the Christian symbolism. To those who look up high enough, whilst the cross will firstly represent all that is real in the schooling of life, the vane will tell also of what has been won by it; a crown to come after, when the schooling is over, and a bright star in the meantime to guide all along.

We are far from the twentieth century. There was at least one mid-Victorian who appreciated that later generations would have to learn to crack codes as semiologists now crack codes if Victorian things were to be made to speak for later generations. 'Suppose', he wrote, that

> a modern drawing room, with its sumptuous furniture of velvet, silk, glass, gold, china and rosewood, were to be hermetically sealed up and consigned to the inspection of our descendants some two thousand years yet to come. They would hardly understand its paraphernalia and appointments. It would require time and study to make out the use of this article and the meaning of that. Their minds would be discordant from ours, and the material substances upon which they employed themselves, or by which they signified their wishes, wants or desires, would, in process of time, have become so completely new and foreign that *we* could not understand them, not *they* us.

We are not yet two thousand years ahead, but already we require 'time and study to make out the use of this article and the meaning of that'.

The unnamed mid-Victorian was writing in an obscure periodical, *The Journal of Mental Pathology*, in the year of the Great Exhibition of 1851. He would certainly have understood why we have to choose things carefully when we decide what to put into time capsules. The future of things was a main theme in 1851. In almost every case, indeed, exhibitions, the theme of my next chapter, were planned to present future vistas, and it is paradoxi-cally for this reason that they immediately open up the lost vistas of the past.

# 2
# The Great Victorian Collection

I made my way into the building; a most gorgeous sight . . .
beyond the dreams of the Arabian romances. I cannot
think that the Caesars ever exhibited a more splendid
spectacle.

LORD MACAULAY, letter of 1851

Its grandeur does not consist in *one* thing, but in the unique
assemblage of *all* things. Whatever human industry has
created you find there. . . . (Yet) it seems as if only magic
could have gathered this mass of wealth from all the ends of
the earth.

CHARLOTTE BRONTË, letter of 1851

The shortest way to do many things is to do only one thing
at once.

SAMUEL SMILES, *Self-Help*, 1859

When the [Melbourne] Exhibition was shut, we wandered
forlorn. . . . We were spoiled for a humdrum life.

ADA CAMBRIDGE, *Thirty Years in Australia*, 1903

# I

When the young William Morris visited the Crystal Palace in 1851, he found it and the objects inside it 'wonderfully ugly'; and since he was to devote so much of his life to the making of 'beautiful things', as he called them, his judgement must be taken seriously. There are additional reasons, however, for so treating it. The 'things' that Morris made or praised sometimes point in their design to the 'modern movement' of the twentieth century; the ostentatious 'things' of 1851, whatever their inspiration, belong unmistakably to the mid-nineteenth century.

Yet that is not the end of the matter. Three other points must be taken into the reckoning. First, it was widely acknowledged in 1851 itself that there was a lack of a truly distinctive 1851 style; and a very different critic from Morris, Ralph Nicholson Wornum, in an essay which won him a hundred guinea prize offered by the *Art Journal*, complained that in at least one part of the Exhibition all that you could find were 'copies of old ideas', 'old things in an old taste', while in others there was 'a want of individuality' in the 'gorged designs' on display. The fairest general description was a 'medley'. Wornum was to be appointed Keeper of the National Gallery in 1854, and two years later was to publish a book called *Analysis of Ornament*.

Second, as far as Morris himself was concerned, for all his bitter contempt for the techniques, tastes and values of his age, expressed in a comprehensive indictment of the whole of it, many of his own 'things' look as unmistakably 'Victorian' in restrospect as his clients were. The adjective Victorian can be applied with equal justice to his wallpapers and to his tapestries, to his books and to his stained glass. Collectors of Victoriana in the twentieth century, who may share none of his values, love to collect them. They think that they know what is 'Victorian' whatever its disguise.

Third, Morris and his disciples did not spurn exhibitions as such. The Arts and Crafts Exhibition of 1888, the first of an annual series organized by the Arts and Crafts Exhibition Society, was deliberately designed to reform design and to encourage simpler and less derivative styles: Walter Crane, illustrator, writer, teacher and socialist, its first President and an admirer of Morris, stated that the Society – 'the movement' he called it – represented 'in some sense a revolt against the hard mechanical conventional life and its insensibility to beauty (quite another thing to ornament)'. In 1851 itself Henry Cole also had had the reform of design in mind, and he too had the experience of previous exhibitions to fall back upon.

It was because of its sponsorship, its scale, its successful organization and its public impact that the 1851 Exhibition pointed the way to other exhibitions, local, national and international. It must be seen, therefore, not only as an event in itself but as one exhibition among many – albeit the key one – in an exhibition sequence in which there were different impulses behind the schemes of their projectors. There were also different impacts in different countries and in different cities within England itself.

Most visitors to the Crystal Palace in 1851, if not most historians, were impressed rather than repelled by the biggest possible display of a very wide range of things, new and old, domestic and foreign. This was the *Great* Exhibition, and the adjective has stuck. Moreover, the Crystal Palace itself, with its 293,655 panes of glass, its 330 standardized iron columns and its 24 miles of guttering, was the biggest and most extravagant of all the things on display, not just a building to house exhibits but in itself a symbol. The 'regularity and severity' of its design, Peter Conrad has rightly noted, separated it from 'the disorderly growth about it'.

An attempt was made also to impose internal order on the multitude of exhibits on display, objects which were classified, catalogued, illustrated, commented upon (even by people who had not seen them) – often controversially, sometimes satirically. Classifying, itself controversial, was a favourite as well as a necessary Victorian preoccupation, like naming and listing, if only because it made 'general propositions possible', and by identifying 'grand divisions' it drew attention to 'gradations' within them. For Dr Whewell, philosopher and Master of Trinity College, Cambridge, 'suitable gradation was the *felicity* of the classifying art.'

Prince Albert, the President of Her Majesty's Commissioners for the Exhibition, which met for the first time in January 1850, had strong opinions about classification himself. He wanted there to be only three main sections on display in the Crystal Palace – 'the raw materials of industry; the manufactures made from them; and the art used to adorn them'. The pattern seemed too philosophical – drawing necessary dividing lines between the three sections was deemed to be impracticable – and an alternative scheme of classification, thought of as more 'practical', was suggested by the 33-year-old Lyon Playfair, one year older than Albert. There should be eight divisions, he proposed – Metallurgy; Chemical Manufactures; Vitreous Ceramic Manufactures; Textiles; Organic Manufactures; Engineering and Machinery; Architecture, Fine Arts and Music; and Agriculture and Horticulture.

This alternative proposal had wide implications. 'Philosophers', dear to Albert, were already giving way to specialists in particular branches of industry and of the sciences; and in time, if not then, there were to be 'experts' in the understanding and management of each sub-division. Playfair himself was to live long enough – until 1898 – to see specialists, not least chemists, become increasingly professionalized in their own organiz-ation; and long before that, in 1858, he was able to advise Prince Albert that the Prince of Wales should attend a special course of lectures in Edinburgh on the chief manufactures of the kingdom and the 'scientific processes' involved in them. (The Prince was also to be invited to visit 'some mill or factory' in order to see one of the specified processes in operation.) That was the kind of education Playfair always favoured. Nonetheless, there remained a strong general educational thrust of a 'philosophical' kind behind the idea of exhibitions; and at the last great exhibition of the century, that in Paris in 1900, when there were eighteen 'divisions' and 130 'classes' of objects, 'education and instruction' were to come first in the list of priorities. They even took precedence over 'works of art', which had a strictly limited place in London in 1851, but which were prominent in all French exhibitions.

Playfair's practical approach to classification was accepted in 1851 although, following argument, particularly with the French, who then and later had a philosophical approach of their own, different from that of Albert, the system became rather more complicated than Playfair had originally hoped for. Eventually five major divisions of exhibits were agreed upon – Raw Materials: Machinery; Manufactures – textile fabrics; Manufactures – metallic, vitreous and ceramic; Miscellaneous; and 'Fine Arts' – and within this broad classification there were to be thirty classes, each of them with a separate jury not only to award prizes but to report on the state and prospects of the class in question. The first 'class' covered 'Mining, Quarrying, Metallurgical Operations and Mineral Products', and the last 'Sculpture, Models (in Architecture, Topography and Anatomy) and Plastic Art.' All other fine arts were explicitly excluded. Among the other items listed in the classes were 'Substances used for Food'; 'Decoration, Furniture and Upholstery, including Paperhangings, Papier-mâché and Japanned Goods'; and 'Manufactures in Mineral Substances, used for Building or Decoration, as in Marble, Slate, Porphyries, Cements, Artificial Stones, etc.' Large masses of some of these substances were on display in the open air outside the Exhibition galleries.

It is said that the French Commissioner's handsome walking stick settled the choice of classification. It did not easily fit into the kind of 'philosophical' system of classification which he favoured, and the first winner in the exhibition was Playfair's approach, supported by English 'philosophers', among them Whewell and in the background Charles Babbage. (See below, p. 409.) Playfair, using the word 'clothing' with exceptional comprehensiveness and not without a sense of humour, thought that the stick fell naturally into his own Class XX, 'Miscellaneous Objects', among 'Articles of Clothing for immediate Personal or Domestic Use'. For the French Commissioner it would have been exhibited among 'Machines for the Propagation of Direct Motion', a group eventually placed in Playfair's Class V – 'Machines for Direct Use, including Carriages, Railways and Naval Mechanisms', a broad class which was to include landaus, broughams, *droitzschkas* and sledges.

Happily, for all *Punch*'s interest in the statistics of walking sticks (see above, p. 36), none of them seems to have been submitted for exhibit to the Commissioners, although among the exhibits there was a pocket umbrella submitted by Samuel Plimsoll, who was to press for load-lines on ships, and a 'medical walking-staff', containing 'instruments, medicines and other professional articles'. 'Would not a small tin case have answered the same purpose far better?' Henry Tallis asked in his contemporary *History and Description of the Crystal Palace*. Playfair's comprehensive Class XX was subdivided relatively simply into 'Hats, Caps and Bonnets; Hosiery; Gloves; Boots, Shoes and Lasts; and Under Clothing and Upper Clothing'. The first of these sub-groups is the subject of my Chapter 7: the class as a whole included 'a life-preserving elastic cork jacket capable of being worn unobserved under a coat', 'bisunique' or reversible garments, a 'bachelor's shirt of peculiar construction without buttons', and 'Anaxyridian trousers'.

Class XXIX – 'Miscellaneous Manufactures and Small Wares', the most comprehensive class of all – chafed ambitious exhibitors like the wig-maker who had wished his exhibits to be placed in Art (Class XXX) and had objected indignantly to their being relegated to 'Vegetable and Animal Substances chiefly used in Manufacture, as Implements, or as Ornaments.' There was certainly diversity in the miscellaneous section. One South Lambeth firm exhibited 'writing fluids, seidlitz powders, marking ink, culinary essences, hair-oil and perfumes etc.', while another firm from Lambeth exhibited 'artificial peas, made from white muslin'. The last named British exhibit in this section was 'a collection of stuffed birds and animals.'

Clearly, 'Nature' – or at least *nature morte* – was not excluded from the Crystal Palace, and a remarkable stuffed elk from the zoological museum at Turin was hailed as a model of 'the art of representing the living animal'. Nor was animal nature, sentimentalized as it so often was, the only kind of nature on display. You could turn from a pair of stuffed Impeyan pheasants, entitled 'Courtship', and a sleeping stuffed orang-outang, labelled 'Repose', to the impressive 'Trigonometrical Model of the Undercliffe, Isle of Wight', one of the exhibits discussed at length in Robert Hunt's *Handbook to the Great Exhibition*: it attracted almost as much attention as a model of the docks at Liverpool, complete with 1600 fully rigged ships.

Of course, Joseph Paxton, who produced the design of the Crystal Palace building on what quickly became the most famous piece of blotting paper in history, was a custodian and developer of nature who had in mind a lily house in the Chatsworth garden over which he presided as the Duke of Devonshire's 'confidential gardener': his great lily, introduced into Britain in 1837, had been named *Victoria Regia*. A greenhouse had set a fashion for glass, and although Ruskin could write

> The earth hath bubbles, as the water hath:
> And this is one of them

most people shared the opinion of the author of a children's picture history produced at the time, *The House that Paxton Built*, based on *The House that Jack Built*, which included the up-to-date lines:

This is the Iron, the Wood and the Glass
Which all other Building Materials surpass.

Certainly Paxton's design, which triumphed over 233 designs, submitted as
his had not been, in a competition without prizes, was a remarkable
achievement, converted into finished drawings in nine days. It would be
misleading, however, in dealing with Paxton to move direct to the Crystal
Palace from Chatsworth (where he built a 'Great Stove'* as well as a Great
Conservatory) as so many twentieth-century historians do.

He had already planned Birkenhead New Park in 1843 – which was to
influence Frederick Law Olmsted in his work on Central Park, New York –
and he had devised much admired Coventry Cemetery in 1846. Edwin
Chadwick was one of the admirers. Paxton had also begun work in 1850 on
the design of a great Rothschild house, Mentmore, (see below p. 422) before
the Great Exhibition opened. Like Playfair, his life had been active and
purposive long before 1851. And he was fully prepared for such remarks as
'mathematicians have calculated that the Crystal Palace will blow down in
the first strong gale.'

Playfair was equally prepared for such remarks as 'the galleries will crash
in and destroy the visitors as well as the objects', although it was difficult for
him or for anyone else to chart in advance the 'intelligible universe of things'
before the Exhibition actually opened. Statisticians could easily tot up with
precision the number of exhibitors – 13,937, of whom 6,556 were 'foreign' –
but the number of exhibits, many of which, according to the *Official Catalogue*
arrived late, was described simply as 'over 10,000'. Their classification in
terms of countries, which determined the layout and topography of the
exhibition, was devised not by Playfair but by Cole, who had worked with
Albert on the Council of the Society of Arts and had organized an industrial
exhibition for the Society in 1847. In practice, Cole's display of exhibits by
country was doubtless of greater interest to most of the visitors than
classification by category: it also allowed for decentralization of decision
making. Foreign exhibits were placed in the eastern half of the building and
classed under their respective countries: appropriately enough, British
exhibits filled the western end. More than sixty 'local committees' were free
within the British section to display their products as they wished.

Statisticians, who were busy in 1851 calculating 'tremendous arrays of
figures' concerning the decennial population census taken on March 31st
1851, collected as many statistics about the building as about the objects on
display inside it. It was proudly proclaimed, for example, that it was 1,848
feet long by 408 feet wide, with the amount of space occupied by exhibits
amounting to 338,714 square feet (horizontal) and 653,143 square feet

---

* It proved too expensive to heat after the First World War when it had to be demolished by
dynamite since the structure was so sound.

(vertical), and that the total floorspace was 772,824 square feet. The weight of iron used, it was estimated, was 4,500 tons (700 wrought), 3,800 (cast), and there were 900,000 square feet of glass, it was claimed, in the 293,655 panes.

It needed engineers to get behind such global statistics, just as it needed juries to get behind the number of entries and to settle questions of quality. Charles Downes in his book *The Building Erected in Hyde Park for the Great Exhibition of the Works of the Industry of all Nations* (1852) added force to interpretation when he noted that there were no 'large pieces' of any material employed, nor was any scaffolding necessary during the erection. The heaviest pieces of cast iron were the girders, which were 24 feet in length and none of which weighed more than a ton, and the wrought iron consisted chiefly of round and flat bars, angle irons, bolts, screws and rivets. The panes of glass produced by Chance Brothers of Birmingham were the biggest yet manufactured.

The speed of manufacture and construction – the building was erected in six months – rightly impressed non-expert contemporaries as much as the quantities. Dickens, who declared that he had 'a natural horror of sights', extolled in *Household Words* not only 'boundless resources in materials' but 'the marvellous arithmetical skill in compiling at what cost and in how short a time they can be converted to a special purpose'; while Paxton himself was deeply impressed when he watched a few men erect three columns and two girders in sixteen minutes.

The choice of primary colours – blue, red and yellow, with the cast iron columns, a feature particularly abhorrent to Ruskin, variegated in colour with a yellow stripe – immediately impressed many visitors too. Yet the colour scheme, devised by Owen Jones, a Welsh architect and since 1844 an employee of De la Rue, the printers, was scarcely less controversial than the materials and the scheme of classification. The Royal Institute of British Architects needed convincing, and *The Times* had qualms that it might involve 'a huge vulgarity'. The *Art Journal*, however, as always willing to be critical, believed that Jones, who was to publish his classic *Grammar of Ornament* in 1856 and was to be known to contemporaries as Alhambra Jones for his delight in Moorish architecture, had 'produced a result which has met with very general approbation'. By experimenting with his colours on the spot, by calculating the effect of a long perspective on them, and by being willing to tone them down when necessary he had won over his critics.

The *Journal* did not add that the ribs of the building might have been adorned not only by columns but by texts. Fortunately, there were not enough funds to allow for them. There were other interesting features to which the *Journal* did not attach as much importance as twentieth-century commentators were to do – the use of standard sign boards and standard lettering throughout the building, the uniform crimson colour prescribed for hangings and stall coverings, and the display of everything that could be possibly shown vertically rather than horizontally, like carpets.

'The first impression conveyed to the mind of the visitor experienced in the science of architecture', the *Art Journal* went on to report, was 'a sense of insecurity' conveyed by the building itself and 'arising from the apparent lightness of its supports as compared with the vastness of its dimensions'. But the feeling was soon dissipated when the visitor was 'informed that the strength of every separate part has been tested'. In relating visual impression to verbal information the *Art Journal* was characteristic of the time if limited in its perceptions. It did not mention, for example, Charles Barry's brilliant idea of flying the flags of all nations from the long flat lines of the stepped-up roofs – Barry, too, was a Commissioner while his Houses of Parliament were still in course of construction – but it paid general tribute to his 'judicious suggestions' and said of the central court that it 'flashed on the eye more like the fabled palace of Vathek than a structure reared in a few months by mortal hands'.

The building, like the exhibits inside it, provided ample material for both poets, theologians, scientists, and engineers, and it was 'one of the marvels of the age'. 'The building should be as original as its object', W. Bridges Adam had written in an article of 1850 before Paxton's scheme was accepted. 'It should not be suggestive of the ideas of a pyramid, a temple or a palace; for it will not be a tomb, a place of worship nor a mansion of royalty'. Another contemporary, the civil engineer, Thomas Page, who had designed part of the Thames Embankment, had suggested – even earlier in 1849 – that the building should be 'so constructed that it could be taken down and refixed at any other place or at any other time'. In fact, Paxton's building was immediately thought of as a 'palace', not only as a glittering crystal palace or as Vathek's palace, but as a people's palace, 'a palace of the nations', open to all. Dostoievsky found it 'astonishing'. 'You gasp for breath.' 'It is like a Biblical picture, something out of Babylon, a prophecy ... coming to pass before your eyes.'

The term 'crystal palace', coined by Douglas Jerrold, former editor of *Punch*, made its way from London round the world in the nineteenth century. So, too, did Baxter prints, described in my next chapter, samplers, Beard and Mayall steel engravings, and photographs, among them William Henry Fox Talbot calotypes, all of which pictured it. The *Reports of the Juries* contained photographs also. However, it was after the Palace – with elaborate and expensive new extras – was moved in 1852 to a 200 acre site in Sydenham, where it was to have a long new life ahead of it, that Phillip Henry Delamotte published his remarkable 1855 portfolio of albumen photographic prints called *Photographic Reports of the Progress of the Works of Crystal Palace and Gardens*, some of them showing the building in the course of reconstruction. Appropriately, a rare copy of Delamotte's portfolio is now held by the Corning Museum of Glass in the United States, which had its own 'crystal palace' built in 1852 for an 1853 World Fair.

The idea of an American exhibition had been mooted by many American visitors to London in 1851, among them Horace Greeley, journalist and politician, who told his fellow-Americans that 'the Crystal Palace, which covers and protects all, is better than any one thing in it'; and the Corporation of New York, having leased a site, laid down as the first of its conditions that 'the building should be composed of iron and glass'. A design which Paxton submitted was turned down because it did not fit the site, and at least one historian of exhibitions, John Allwood, has unfavourably compared the successful design – that submitted by Charles Gildemeister and his partner George Carstensen – with that of an Observatory and Ice-Cream Parlour built by a New York businessman opposite. Nonetheless, Gildemeister and Carstensen, who had laid out the Tivoli Gardens in Copenhagen, won considerable acclaim. Their building, like London's Crystal Palace, was hailed in superlatives:

> ... A Palace,
> Loftier, fairer, ampler than any yet,
> Earth's modern wonder, History's Seven outstripping
> High rising tier on tier, with glass and iron facades.

In retrospect, at least, one particular exhibit on display there was more interesting than the building and was to revolutionize the future layout of exhibitions and of much else – Elisha Grave Otis's 'safety elevator' which he demonstrated himself.

The name 'Crystal Palace' has survived in Britain as a topographical name and as the name of a football club, long outliving the building itself, which was to have a far longer life than its American counterpart which was destroyed by fire in 1856. There was a great fire at Sydenham as early as 1866, when the North Transept was destroyed, but it was not until 1936 that final disaster fell. A spectacular fire on November 30th of that year seemed to mark the end not only of a building but of an age: the flames could be seen over eight counties.

By that time, a new generation was finding fun rather than romance in the building itself: and in an introduction to a new 1950 edition of Christopher Hobhouse's *1851 and the Crystal Palace* which had first appeared in 1937, Osbert Lancaster described how for several decades before the 1936 fire the Crystal Palace had been regarded as 'the funniest of all the Victorian jokes'. Its fate had often been uncertain, and Lancaster quoted a *bon mot* of the architect Sir Edward Lutyens: when asked what should be done with the Palace, he had replied that 'it should be kept under glass'.

Such comments now seem even more out-of-date than the Palace itself, which won new admirers even when the objects in it continued to be treated almost entirely as jokes. For example, both John Gloag, prominent at the Festival of Britain in 1951, and T. C. Rolt, a railway enthusiast and a knowledgeable historian of technology, contrasted the 'clear functional beauty of line and proportion, unmarred by any excess', of the outside of the

Crystal Palace building and the vast lumber room inside, where 'a jetsam of miscellaneous objects' had been assembled, 'some pathetic, some ludicrous, but all representing a prodigal misuse of labour and ingenuity'. They quickly dismissed contemporary comments like those of Thackeray who wrote of the 'miscellaneous objects'

These England's triumphs are,
The trophies of her bloodless war

or of Queen Victoria herself, who when she first looked down on 'all sorts of objects of art, manufacture, etc' from the gallery thought that they had 'quite the effect of fairyland'.

Tallis in his profusely illustrated *History and Description of the Crystal Palace* had gone further. Quoting in his opening sentence the Keats line 'a thing of beauty is a joy for ever', he had associated himself with one of his contemporaries who had written eloquently of the objects on display that they demonstrated how Englishmen 'would have everything in a house touched by the divining rod of the poet. An inkstand, instead of being a literal glass bottle, or a fine piece of ormolu or bronze, significant of nothing but costliness, might be fashioned to represent a fountain, with a Muse inspiring its flow.' After such words it seemed a descent when Tallis himself urged that 'every effort to perpetuate the remembrance' of the contents of the Exhibition 'should be regarded as conducive to the general development of taste'. Yet there was to be a further descent in the twentieth century when Gloag decreed that Tallis's *History* itself was 'badly illustrated by indifferent steel engravings and packed with information conveyed with the utmost tedium'.

Gloag missed much. The rhetoric that went with the objects was always as revealing as the objects themselves and sometimes as interesting as the criticism which Gloag also ignored. Thus, not uncharacteristically, the article on the Great Exhibition of 1851 in the *Journal of Psychological Medicine and Mental Pathology*, which ended in the semiological conclusion quoted on p. 51, ranged widely in time and space. It began with the 'lost past', the past represented in museums, before turning to the 'advanced' present, as it recalled the 'ruins of Djerash' and the 'caves of Elephanta and Ellora'. It then turned to contemporary cultural juxtapositions, like 'the flight of omnibuses' regularly 'plying the eighty-two miles between Cairo and Suez with the names of Cairo and Suez painted in large letters on their panels'. It noted also how at St Stephen's Hotel in the Egyptian capital you could find 'English crockery, with Sheffield ware'. It was a matter of pride for the writer of the article, just as it was for almost all commentators, that the Exhibition included objects from 'all the nations', young and old. Their geographical spread – and their place in time – were as interesting as their functional variety. 'Here in a great Open Book', wrote the *Illustrated Exhibitor*, 'we read of the industry of our brethren of the north, the south, the east and the west'.

There was an acknowledged place in the Crystal Palace, therefore, as there was not to be in New York in 1853, both for tradition and for invention; and many people associated with the exhibits made much of it. For example, Owen Jones, who observed that in the works contributed by the various nations of Europe there could be found little but 'a fruitless struggle after novelty, irrespective of fitness', looked outside nineteenth-century Europe for the secrets of traditional design – 'construction should be decorated: decoration should never be purposefully constructed' – just as Pugin in his dark Medieval Court, contrasting sharply with the rest of the exhibition, looked back to the middle ages. For Owen Jones, 'if we would return to a more healthy condition we must be as little children or as savages: we must get rid of the acquired and the artificial.'

Not everything British in 1851 was modern, therefore. When the Whig Prime Minister, Lord John Russell, making much of anti-Popery themes in 1851, protested against the presence of 'papal wax-works', Albert replied that he could not eliminate 'crucifixes, rosaries, altar plate, etc', adding (and it would have pleased Jones) that 'those who object to their idolatrous character must be relieved to find Indian Pagodas and Chinese Idols in other parts of the Exhibition'.

The Indian section, assembled by the East India Company and much admired, not least by the Queen, 'derived its momentum', as the historian C. R. Fay has written, 'from a crumbling past'. Yet a French writer on the Exhibition, a Member of the Institute of France, could claim that it carried its visitors back to the 'heroic age' of human history: after all, India, 'the glorious glowing land', had been 'the golden prize contended for by Alexander the Great'. The United States section, by contrast, seemed somewhat disappointing to this writer, as it did to many other visitors, although not to the Americans themselves. They had commissioned too much space and found difficulties in filling it, so that *Punch* could dwell complacently on the 'glaring contrast between large pretensions and little performance' – 'a few wineglasses, a square or two of soap, and a pair of salt cellars!'

There were, in fact, among the American exhibits stuffed black-eyed squirrels and six thousand fossils. Nonetheless, for those with eyes to foresee the future was there also. A McCormick reaper, a Hobbs lock, a Colt revolver, and two tiny sewing machines, worked by one small girl, who could turn 600 stitches a minute, were among the most interesting entries. Singer sewing machines were absent, but of the reaper the author of *Dickinson's Comprehensive Pictures of the Great Exhibition of 1851* (1854) could write enthusiastically that in agriculture this and similar machines 'will be as important as the spinning jenny and power-loom in manufactures'.

France also could be forward-looking as well as fashionable, and in one of the five French courts you could see a French sewing machine which was 'adapted for coarse cloth'. There were pointers to the future, too, in French photography, in a French calculating machine, and in the presence in

London of a French prototype submarine which had submerged at Calais and surfaced at Dover. Despite all this, the *Art Journal* concentrated in its own reporting on French 'articles of *virtu* and ornamental furniture . . . plate, bronzes and china . . . carpets, and jewels'.

Canada, according to Fay, achieved 'one of the pictorial successes of the Exhibition' by 'sheer simplicity', the simplicity of maple sugar, canvas, fur and sleighs, but it, too, included six elaborately covered chairs of Canadian timber 'in the style of the fourteenth century' along with a fire engine from Montreal. Its entry was singled out by one commentator on the grounds that while its busy inhabitants were paying 'more attention to the useful than to the ornamental', there was an intermixture in the goods it displayed between 'the works of a savage population' and 'the clearest evidence of English civilization'. Canada was, after all, 'a vast field for emigrants from the mother country – a giant river flowing from a placid lake'.

Thackeray himself was interested, like most writers on the exhibition, not only in artefacts, but in resources: they were subdivided into four classes which included not only coal and iron but peat and ivory tusks. Class II, 'Chemical, Pharmaceutical Processes and Products Generally', was itself subdivided into two classes – 'chemical substances for the use of the scientific chemist' and the rest – but who would be able to draw a convincing division at that point or to justify the allotment of dyes to Class IV, 'Vegetable and Animal Substances'? It is interesting that it was the most 'natural' resources that some visitors preferred. Thus, for one knowledgeable visitor at least, the geologist Gideon Mantell, the only objects inside the Crystal Palace that impressed him were 'a splendid piece of opal, and a fine mass of quartz rock, with rich veins of gold, from California'.

Just outside the Great Exhibition you could see a small engine-house in which Armstrong boilers supplied power to 'machinery in motion' inside, and alongside anchors and obelisks large masses of raw materials, including a huge aristocratic block of coal, weighing 24 tons, from a Staveley mine owned by the Duke of Devonshire, Paxton's patron. This block of coal, symbol of power, was placed for effect alongside Baron Marochetti's colossal equestrian statue of Richard Coeur de Lion, symbol of courage. The latter hero figured too – and more light-heartedly – in the *Journal of Psychological Medicine* article:

Over the billows and over the brine;
Over the water to Palestine!
Am I awake or do I dream?
Over the ocean to Syria by steam, . . .
Godfrey of Bolloigne, and thou,
Richard, lion-hearted king,
Candidly inform us now,
　　Did you ever –
　　No you never
Could have fancied such a thing!

63

The writer of the article went on to hail the invention of printing, 'the turning point of the intellectual world', while observing that communications were still in their infancy. There was no display of the great *Times* printing machine, 'the Leviathan of Printing House Square' inside the Crystal Palace, but 'the alphabet of the electric telegraph' was there for all to see, as messages were sent out 'to Manchester, Edinburgh etc' and replies received in only a few seconds. The alphabet suggested, the writer claimed, that 'a more facile language . . . than the one we at present employ awaits the schooldays of our more fortunate posterity'.

There seemed to be prospects also, as Prince Albert himself recognized, of a more facile system of work in the future, with human beings liberated from the most oppressive forms of physical toil. The point was emphasized by Robert Hunt in his *Handbook to the Official Catalogue*, where he referred to machines that would 'efficiently represent hand labour in the harvest field', and by the Queen when she wrote of 'what used to be done by hand and take months' now being accomplished in a few instants. Nevertheless, much physical toil was still taken for granted in 1851, not least in the raw materials section, which included from Cumberland 'a good collection of specimens of blacklead', symbol of women's physical toil in the home.

Significantly, the image of the hive was popular, at least among writers, in 1851, and there was great public interest among visitors in 'Mr Milton and Mr Neighbour's glass beehives' in Class IX, where insects were said to be setting an example to human beings. 'Her Majesty and Prince Albert,' we read, 'frequently bestowed their notice on the wonderful operations of the gifted little insects, whose undeviating attention to their own concerns in the midst of all the various distraction of sound and sight that surrounded them, afforded an admirable lesson'. There was no sense of liberation there.

Might there then be liberation through paper as a medium of knowledge? In 1851 it was already as much a basic resource as coal, although, unlike coal – or glass – it was still taxed at $1\frac{1}{2}$d per pound. Much of it came from cotton rags, but esparto was being increasingly used. At the exhibition itself the presence of paper was ubiquitous – in the form of catalogues, tickets and wallpapers, most of them to be thrown away, as well as in the exhibits, some designed to last for ever – among them Queen Victoria's favourite De La Rue envelope-making machine, folding and gumming 60 envelopes a minute. There were also wallpapers, some of them since 1841 machine-printed and considered evidence of 'a manufacture of considerable importance'; playing cards (137 different designs had been produced by Owen Jones since 1844); papier-mâché chairs and tables, including work-tables; papier-mâché trays and boxes, some inlaid, as was some of the furniture, with mother-of-pearl or pearl-shells. A gem-inlaying process had been patented in 1847.

Books were there mainly for their bindings, not for their contents, but there was a special collection in the Austrian section, a gift from the Emperor to Queen Victoria, housed in a huge carved-oak Gothic book-case; and one of the medals in Class XV went to F. A. Brockhaus of Saxony for 'his collection of 356 volumes, the whole printed at his own establishment in the year 1850'. There was also a prize-winning catalogue of 'all the books published in Egypt'. The jury regretted that 'neither of the great universities of Oxford or Cambridge took any part in the Exhibition', but praised the 'high merit' of the Clarendon and Pitt Presses. Less genially the British and Foreign Bible Society was criticized by Cole for showing their Bibles not as 'specimens of printing' but as a demonstration of their 'religious enthusiasm in spreading knowledge of the Bible. All forces were employed to get their own way, contrary to rules'.

One of the most bizarre objects at the exhibition was a garden seat for Osborne made from coal, and one of the discussed objects was the 'Day Dreamer' easy chair in papier-mâché with buttoned upholstery. It was designed by H. Fitz Cook and made by Jennens and Bettridge of Belgrave Square, London, and Birmingham; they also exhibited a papier-mâché piano, 'seven octave, semi-cottage', a music stool, a work-table and a 'Victoria Regia cot'. At its top the Day Dreamer chair was decorated by 'two

*A papier-mâché village – for Australia:* The Illustrated London News, *1853*

winged thoughts' – the one with bird-like pinions and crowned with roses, representing happy and joyous dreams; the other with 'leathern bat-like wings – unpleasant, and troublesome ones'. Fortunately, the top of the chair also incorporated Hope in the guise of the rising sun. It is a chair which perhaps deserves to be compared with Morris's equally famous 'Sussex chair' made of ash with a rush seat according to a traditional pattern. This was first produced by his firm fourteen years after the Exhibition.

When Thackeray's thoughts took wing in 1851, it was of steam power that he first thought, just as writers on the great Paris Exhibition of 1889 – with its towering Eiffel Tower symbol – were to think first of electricity. The Crystal Palace belonged, of course, to the great age of steam, as the writer in the *Journal of Psychological Medicine* agreed; and the great British engineer, I. K. Brunel, whose huge hydraulic press was on display, wished to keep out all electric machines on the grounds that 'as yet' they could 'only be considered as toys'. 'The history of the steam engine is the history of all enterprises and ingenuity for the last seventy years', *The Illustrated Exhibitor* proclaimed. Nasmyth's steam hammer, 'so high and so gentle', was to suggest to Samuel Smiles that the right God for Victorian England was a god with a hammer in his hand; and for less imaginative visitors, who were prohibited from buying alcoholic drinks at the Exhibition, there was always the steam brewery.

Farmers, who were well catered for, could see not only double-action turnip cutters, horse seed dibblers and portable mills for grinding and splitting produce (all these came from 'backward' Oxfordshire) but also agricultural steam engines from 'progressive' Lincolnshire. The latter were boosted with the thought that 'whoever goes into the farmyard of a real, practical, go-with-the-time agriculturalist will hear the rattle and observe the smoke of stationary or locomotive steam engines'.

The locomotives, part of the same class as the carriages, included Crampton's 'Liverpool', said to be the most powerful locomotive in the world, and Crampton was one of the winners of a Council medal. So also was J. Cockrill of Belgium for a group of exhibits, including a pair of 140 horsepower vibrating cylinder engines for river navigation. Because steam was being applied in so many contexts and for so many purposes, there were steam engines of every kind in evidence at the exhibition, including one made by James Watt and Company of Soho, Birmingham, a massive engine with 'the collective power of seven hundred horses'. Some engines were 'fat and bulging': one required sixteen real horses 'to impel its course towards the park'. Some were in borrowed 'architectural styles' – Greek, Gothic and even Ancient Egyptian, like the architecture of Marshall's mill in Leeds. Once installed, engines were kept in action inside the Palace:

> The engine roars upon its race,
> The shuttle whirrs along the woof,
> The people hum from roof to roof
> With Babel tongue.
> The fountain in the basin plays,
> The chanting organ echoes clear
> An awful chorus 'tis to hear
> A wondrous song!

For Thackeray there was music – Victorian music – in all this movement, just as there was in some of the objects themselves; and the Queen herself listened enthusiastically to pieces of music which were specially written for the occasion, including Martin Tupper's Exhibition Anthem, set to music by the organist Samuel Wesley and with the words translated into thirty languages. There were also popular exhibition ballads with appropriate music covers. Nonetheless, most visitors to the exhibition, including the Queen, were aware of the noise as well as music, including the 'bewildering' whirring sound of the steam press. After admiring the 'myriads of beautiful and wondrous things' in her diary just before the Exhibition opened, she noted that 'the noise was overpowering, for so much was going on everywhere, and from seventeen to twenty thousand people engaged in arranging all sorts of things.'

Behind all the objects on display there was energy and restless activity – for 'hands' as well as for machines. Mid-Victorian technology depended on people: it was not robotic, whatever might be said about bees. Appropriately the motto for Cole's biography was 'Whatsoever thy hand findeth to do do it with all thy might.' And the same kinds of people who worked the machines, often dismissed as 'hands', were also part of the crowd. In Henry Mayhew's *1851, or the Adventures of Mr and Mrs Sandboys*, illustrated by George Cruikshank, for many of the 'working men who visited the exhibition as "shilling people"', the Exhibition was 'more of a school than a show'. Mantell, by contrast, was impressed more by the ignorance of the visitors than by their desire to learn. He would like to have been able, he said, 'to petrify the living, and to animate the marble. Perhaps a time will come when this fantasy will be realized and the human breed be succeeded by finer forms and lovelier features, than the world now dreams of.'

There was scope for more than one kind of fantasy in 1851, even for what Walter Benjamin, the German philosopher of things, was to call 'phantasmagoria – residues of a dream world'. Thus, appropriately, perhaps, in the Prussian pavilion, there was an iron stove designed by Edward Baum in the form of a knight in full armour, and among the sculptures there was an 'expanding man' capable of being increased in size from 'that of the Apollo Belvedere to that of a colossal statue'. The phantasmagoria was there outside as well as inside the Palace, for there were 'panoramas' and 'dioramas' of various kinds, favourite Victorian 'ways of seeing' taking visitors on the 'Overland Route to India', 'A Trip up the Nile', 'Jerusalem and the Holy Land', and 'The Overland Route to Oregon and California' which included the gold rush.

The fantasy extended to animals as well as to human beings. Indeed, the role of animals in Victorian Britain – real or imaginary; alive or stuffed; in gingerbread (as Nathaniel Hawthorne pictured them in his *House of the Seven Gables*, published in 1851) or in metal – deserves a book in itself.

From Hamburg came a suite of stag-horn furniture, bristling with horns, and from Würtemberg an even more fantastic Hermann Ploucquet collection of stuffed animals, 'comical creatures' much admired by the Queen: they included a frog shaving his companion, 'really marvellous', 'the kittens at tea', 'longtail teaching the rabbits arithmetic', and another much

Elevation of stove.        Side of stove.        Section of stove.

*Stoves in disguise: for an entrance hall, 1868*

admired stuffed frog carrying an umbrella. The animals were placed in Class
XXIX – 'Miscellaneous Manufactures and Small Wares' – and for the
commentator in *The Illustrated Exhibitioner* the 'humorous' attempt to
represent them as 'actuated by human motives and passions' – as in the case
of the Impeyan pheasants and the sleeping Orang-outang – was so
impressive that 'it would almost be worth a journey to Studgardt [*sic*] to be
able to have a chat with such a genius' as Ploucquet, who had spent twenty
years preparing his collection. Among his other exhibits was a taxidermist's
version of *Reynard the Fox*, complete with bear, lion and hare, a story
described by Thomas Carlyle as a 'universal best companion ... lectured on
in universities ... thumbed to pieces on the bench of the artisan'.

Hawthorne, far away from the Crystal Palace, revealed somewhat similar
attitudes to things, which he carefully listed, as can be traced in the

68

catalogue of the Great Exhibition. In Hepzibah's shop in his new novel a 'curious eye' could discover things ancient and modern, the latter 'of a description and outward form . . . hardly known in ancient times'. Alongside 'soap in bars' and 'white beans and split peas', you could see 'a party of leaden dragoons galloping along over the shelves in uniform of modern art', and 'a pickle jar, filled with fragments of Gibraltar rock; not indeed, splinters of the veritable stone foundation of the famous fortress, but bits of delectable candy, neatly done up in white paper'. There were also camels and elephants in gingerbread.

Another phenomenon in the window, still more strikingly modern, was a package of lucifer matches which, according to the author, would have been thought in 'old times . . . actually to borrow their instantaneous flare from the nether fires of Tophet'. Voltaire, introduced by a writer into the Crystal Palace from the eighteenth century, thought of them with quite different associations in mind, but his wonder was just as great. In one of the most extraordinary articles on the exhibition, which appeared in *Blackwoods* and which described an imaginary visit Voltaire had been able to make to the Crystal Palace, the 'great philosopher' is depicted as being unimpressed by both the machinery and by the art, but fascinated by 'common matches', articles which were not on display. He had never before seen anyone strike a match, and having seen a passer-by strike one, he asked for 'the experiment to be repeated'. He also asked for an old flint and tinder box so that 'he might make comparison between them'. 'They smiled at him. Such a thing did not exist.' 'Here is a real invention', Voltaire exclaimed, 'which as a real contribution to the comfort of life, far surpasses anything I have seen. Oh Lucifer! as they call thee, thou son of the morning, if I had had thee in a box beside my bedside, how many hours should I have saved! How much anger and impatience shall I have escaped?'

Some of the marvels of 1851 still retain their glamour in an age when glossy monographs can now be devoted to pocket and table lighters. Brian Moore's list (see p. 13) singled out for special attention the great 27 feet high crystal fountain, containing four tons of glass, which his hero recognized as the work of F. and C. Osler, 'a marvel of casting, cutting and polishing of faultless blocks of glass, erected originally in the transept as the centrepiece of the Great Exhibition of 1851'; and for the *Art Journal* this at the time was 'the most striking object in the Exhibition', admired by all the visitors for its 'lightness and beauty, as well as the perfect novelty of its design'. 'Never before', it was noted in the *Catalogue*, had a piece of glass-work been executed 'involving the treatment in casting, cutting and polishing of blocks of glass of a size so large (4 tons) and a purity so uniformly faultless.'

The fountain was deliberately placed in the middle of the transept, its glittering jets of water introducing intricate patterns of what looked like lacework. In retrospect, as at the time, it is 'difficult to imagine a central ornament more appropriate for the Palace of Glass than a glass fountain'.

There were five chandeliers too, including one by Apsley Pellatt hung to a length of 24 feet. For Hobhouse it was 'in the running for the most beautiful individual object in the building'. But, then, he believed that 'it is almost impossible for a chandelier to be really bad and that the Victorian passion for elaboration was sublimated in the chandelier'. It was one of the few objects in which elaboration became virtue itself.

'In plate-glass, we have no equals, as the mirrors at the Exhibition clearly show', boasted the *Illustrated Exhibitioner*, even if it picked out for highest praise in painted glass *The Ideas of Dante Illustrated* by Bertini of Milan, not mentioned in the *Art Journal*. There was an entire stained glass gallery in the Palace, where there was a pervading sense of permanence, but, like paper, much of the glass was soon to be thrown away, as were the more than a million bottles which had contained soft drinks sold to visitors. Most were to be used again, of course. Nor were the windows vandalized: 'people who live in glass houses should not throw stones.' Fortunately there were almost no vandals in the Palace in 1851, where everyone or almost everyone behaved well, to the delight of the Queen – and of the Police Commissioners. 'Appoint someone to act as leader,' the *Official Popular Guide* had advised parties visiting the exhibition, 'and if possible one who *has* visited it, and if a little higher in station or influence than the rest, the better'. More democratically, it also stated that 'objects that attract attention will be readily found, and may easily be ascertained by asking questions of the by-standers'.

Thackeray tried to be funny as well as serious both about the objects and about the people. If *The Journal of Psychological Medicine* could treat Richard Coeur de Lion lightly, almost in the later mode of W. S. Gilbert, Thackeray could write not only his Exhibition ode, but *Maloney's Account of the Crystal Palace*, 'a sublime Musayum', in the current mode of *Punch*:

> There's taypots there,
> And cannons rare;
> There's coffins filled with roses;
> There's canvas tints,
> Teeth insthrumints
> And shuits of clothes by Moses,
> There's lashins more
> Of things in store,
> But tim I don't remimber;
> Nor could disclose
> Did I compose
> From May time to Novimber.

There was, in fact, as much comic writing as there was serious writing about the 'Fresh Wondthers' of the exhibition and much eclectic comic/serious writing too. For one of Mayhew's characters the whole exhibition was simply 'the great eggs and bacon, for I hope it will bring us that sort of grub.' Was that the opinion, one wonders, of the 'three poor working men', real Irishmen from Lisburn, County Antrim, who submitted a 'sculptured and perforated armchair, from the antique mode ... expressly for the Exhibition, of Irish black bog oak, found in Moyntagh's Moss'?

## II

According to Pevsner, 'the buoyancy and showiness of so much of the Crystal Palace' marked 'the final flourish of a century of greatest commercial expansion. Hence the amplitude and lavishness of the style.' Leigh Hunt said much the same when after noting that the exhibition was 'full of surprises', he called it essentially a 'bazaar'. Nonetheless, the objects on display were essentially not for selling but for seeing. 'No article is allowed to be sold directly in the Building', the *Guide* stated, 'except the Official Catalogues, the Medals struck at the Press, refreshments, and bouquets of flowers.' The exhibition was not a trade fair and there were no price tags.

In his contemporary *History and Description of the Crystal Palace*, Tallis made the most of this point. The exhibition 'was undertaken solely for the display of excellence', he insisted, 'and for the encouragement of every effort towards the attainment of it ... Exhibitions of goods, merely considered as marketable commodities, assumed to be the best of their kind, were common enough in all countries pretending to civilization ... but exhibitions in which the perfecting of the articles exhibited should be the primary object, and the commerce to be afterwards derived from them merely secondary, have only taken place among us, during the latter half of the preceding century to the present time.'

*The Times* took the same line. At first, it had been critical both of the idea of the exhibition and of the design of the 'palace', and it had complained that 'by the stroke of a pen our pleasant park is to be turned into something between Wolverhampton and Greenwich Fair'. It changed its perspectives, however, on the day of the opening. 'There was yesterday witnessed a sight the like of which has never happened before', its reporter wrote. 'They who were fortunate enough as to see it hardly knew what most to admire, or in what form to clothe the sense of wonder and even of mystery that struggled within them ... There were many there who were familiar with magnificent spectacles ... but they had not seen anything to compare with this.' The exhibition gave its visitors a unique opportunity of seeing things of every variety which were 'the best of their kind'.

There were difficulties, nonetheless, in determining what things were 'the best of their kind', difficulties which were as apparent to the 34 panels of jurors, 'the supreme heads of wisdom', as they were to the critics; and *The Times* itself in a most interesting leader on July 1st 1851 complained of an 'imitative rage' which influenced pottery and carpets. 'Our potters have sent contributions which illustrate every known style of the manufacture': 'the

English section of carpets has imitations of India, of Brussels [*sic*], of French, of parquetrie and tesselated pavements and of the mediaeval style of manufacture.' England was particularly, if not exclusively, bad: 'the sins committed against good taste are confined to no single people, but as we send to the Crystal Palace the largest number of contributions in each section, our faults and shortcomings are unavoidably the most glaring ... Whether we shall ever have a school of design incorporated with our manufactures, original, characteristic and meritorious, it is impossible to tell, for the Exhibition throws no very hopeful or decided light upon that subject ... The power of cheap production and the advantages of excellent material turning the scale of the market blind our eyes to defects which would not otherwise escape notice if competition pursued us more closely.'

The juries were concerned with competition, and their reports, which have been neglected by most twentieth-century writers on the exhibition, are revealing evidence in themselves. The idea of the jury was French, first put into effect in 1798, but in 1851 it incorporated a genuinely international ideal: as Cole put it, 'for the *first* time in the world's history, the men of Arts, Science and Commerce were permitted by their respective governments to meet together to discuss and promote those objects for which civilized natures exist.' In fact, each jury consisted of an equal number of British subjects and of foreigners, and they could call on the service also of 'associates'. The juries in each group met in joint sessions before finalizing their awards. The procedure seemed almost as interesting to Cole – and others – as the decisions themselves, and Albert himself referred to the 'singular harmony' the juries had demonstrated.

The design of the medals which were awarded in lieu of money prizes was left to the Society of Arts which included a Frenchman, Bonnardel of Paris, among the three designers chosen. The other two were William Wyon and G. G. Adams. All the medals were in bronze and the 170 large Council Medals were distributed among 13,937 exhibitors, with the 6,861 United Kingdom exhibitors securing 78 of them, 52 of them for machinery. France won 54, other countries the rest. The Council Medals were offered for some 'important novelty of invention or appreciation, either in material or process of manufacture, or originality combined with great beauty of design'. Smaller Prize Medals were presented to exhibitors who had demonstrated 'a certain standard of excellence in production or workmanship', and still smaller commemorative medals were given to jurors, exhibitioners and others for services rendered.

To take a few examples of jury decisions, in Class I – 'Mining, Quarrying, Metallurgical Operations and Mineral Products' – more Council Medals and Prize Medals went to foreign entries than to British entries. It was French firms which secured Council Medals for 'a process for washing and purifying coals' and for presenting 'brass of a superior quality', and it was the Prussian Krupps enterprise which won a similar Medal for 'cast steel of superior quality'. In Class VI, however, 'Manufacturing Machines and Tools', Britain secured seventeen Council Medals out of twenty-four. Here it had big names like W. Fairbairn and Sons, Maudslay and Sons, and Whitworth and Company. William Fairbairn not only made everything from girders to boilers, but sat on the Council of almost every Manchester scholarly institution; Henry Maudslay, founder of his business, had died in 1830, but his Lambeth firm was renowned for its industrial skills until it closed in 1900; Joseph Whitworth, to be made a baronet eighteen years after the exhibition, was a member of the Society of Arts and a friend of Cole, who often stayed with him at his Derbyshire home. He received his medal for 'a large collection of engineers' machine tools of all kinds, screw stocks, standard gauges and a knitting machine; also his machine for measuring less than the 200,000th part of an inch.' In an exhibition which made much of size, this was the great exception. There was only one American Council Medal winner in this group.

In Class XV – 'Mixed Fabrics, Including Shawls, but Exclusive of Worsted Goods' – the only Council Medal awarded was to a French firm 'for a new and important process in the production of elaborate designs', while in Class XVIII – 'Miscellaneous Fabrics Shown as Specimens of Painting or Dyeing' – no Council Medals were awarded at all, and of the forty-two Prize Medals only sixteen went to British firms. The two Council medals in Class XIX – 'Tapestry, Floor-Cloths, Lace and Embroidery', a composite group – went to Britain and France, the latter represented by the national Gobelin Factory, and the British winner was commended *inter alia* for 'imitation Valenciennes lace'.

The greater the design element, the more likely it was that Britain would not win a major award, although Elkington and Company received a Council Medal in Class XXIII for 'artistic application of the electrotype' and R. W. Winfield a similar Medal in Class XXII for 'brass foundry work and metallic bedstead with taper rolled pillars and chandeliers'. In Class XXVI – 'Furniture, Upholstery, Paper Hangings, Papier-Mâché and Japanned Goods' – the French won four of the five Council medals and Austria one.

Many, indeed most, of the objects illustrated in Pevsner's *High Victorian Design* won no prizes. Indeed, in his choice of illustrations Pevsner seems to have been more impressed by 'ingenuity' than the juries were, for they ignored, as he did not, Taylor and Sons' 'Steamship Furniture Converted into a Raft', a sideboard of gutta-percha made by the Gutta-Percha Company, an invalid bedstead 'capable of being converted into an arm-chair, with wash-stand, table and reading desk', all the entries of the American Chair Company, which the *Art Journal* believed 'increased the luxury and convenience of this necessary article of furniture', and even the Jennens and Bettridge Daydreamer Chair. The only Jennens and Bettridge award was given for 'a Japan inlay pianoforte case'. One of the few 'surprise objects' mentioned by Pevsner which may have won a Prize Medal was Rogers and Dear's (not as he says Dean's) 'Ottoman Coal Sarcophagus, answering the purpose of an ottoman and coal receptacle', but neither the catalogue nor the jury used this description and the jury referred only to a 'bedstead'.

Contemporary comments, including jury comments, on furniture do not justify Pevsner's conclusion that 'a universal replacement of the straight line by the curve', a feature of mid-Victorian design, won universal approval. For example, in the comments on bedsteads, for example, there was obvious disagreement. Smee and Company's mahogany 'Canopy Bedstead', singled out by the *Art Journal*, did not win a prize. Nor would the *Art Journal* have won a prize for its comment on it – 'there is sufficient ornament in this object to constitute it an elegant article of domestic furniture, but the manufacturers have not aimed at producing an elaborate work of industrial art.' The jury wrote more sensibly of the whole of Class XXVI that 'a popular taste must be greatly influenced by those things which are ever before the eye as household companions' and that 'it is important, both for the strength and good effect of furniture, that the principles of sound construction be well carried out, that the construction be evident, and that if carving or other ornament be introduced, it should be by decorating that construction itself, not by overlaying and disguising it. It is not necessary that an object be carved with ornament or be extravagant in form to obtain the element of beauty.' Surely Pevsner should have quoted this key passage in a book called *High Victorian Design* along with the following sentence from the jury's report, 'Articles of furniture are too often crowded with unnecessary embellishment which interferes with their use, purpose and convenience.'

The *Art Journal's Illustrated Catalogue* was no more successful in picking out in advance all the winners than Pevsner was long after the race was over. Contemporaries could be more percipient. A comment before the event on an iron bedstead by Messrs Cowley and Jones, which did win a prize in Class XII – 'Iron and General Hardware' – is interesting for the light that it sheds on some contemporary tastes at least: 'we prefer it to much of the overwrought and highly-elaborated articles, which we are not infrequently called upon to notice'. Similarly, the jury in a general comment regretted that there had not been 'more specimens of ordinary furniture for general use.' 'Few have the means of purchasing such beautiful works as the sideboard of M Fourdinois or the cabinets of M Ringuet le Prince, which came almost under the head of fine art than of manufacture; and it is much to be desired that attention be directed towards improving the taste of those more ordinary objects that come into daily use by the many.'

How much decoration there should be – and of what kinds and on what objects – were major themes for public discussion in 1851, even if they had been raised earlier (often within an ideological frame) not only by Pugin, in relation to furniture, household goods and buildings, but by protagonists in the often bitter debate about the role of Schools of Design, new institutions created in the aftermath of the Select Committee on Arts and Manufactures, appointed in 1835 (see p. 20).

Ralph Wornum, who was prepared, like the jury, to take economics into account when discussing aesthetics, believed firmly that 'the best shapes remain Greek', and like the painter, Richard Redgrave, who was closely associated with Cole and edited the *Journal of Design and Manufactures*, Cole's organ which first appeared in 1849, he objected to naturalistic decoration or rather to 'mere imitation of nature'. As the *Journal* put it in 1849, 'whilst the spirit of nature should guide ornament, ornament should be a new creation maintaining an originality of its own.' 'Every article of use has a certain size and character defined for it by the very use it is destined for', Redgrave argued, 'and is wholly independent of ornament in its primary condition of a mere form of use ... But it is upon this skeleton that the designer must bring his ornamental skill to bear ... and he is a poor designer if he can do nothing more than imitate a few sprigs or leaves wherewith to decorate it.'

Dickens was to make fun of Cole, but fun could be made also of the kind of designers Cole and Redgrave disliked. Thus, *Punch* in 1842 had described a house painter in New York who grained a door so exactly in imitation of oak that 'it put forth a quantity of leaves and grew an excellent crop of acorns'. Redgrave complained in 1849 of a flower vase that looked like a flower – 'Flowers in flowers! Sweets to the sweet' – and he objected too to mixtures of styles – 'Louis Quatorze' with Alhambra and 'the Italian School if any' – as 'forcible evidence of imperfect education in the designer.' By contrast, he described a candlestick by Pugin and Hardman exhibited in 1851 as 'honest' and 'useful', and paid tribute to the Mediaeval Court not because it was mediaeval but because the materials used in the making of its objects were 'correct' and the principles of decoration 'just'.

The *Journal of Design and Manufacturers*, which classified designers as carefully as the Commissioners classified objects, picking out no less than 75 ornamental designers divided into groups, itself tried hard to set standards in design. It entertained a hope that '... the Journal will become the *pattern* book of the decorative manufacturers', and it criticized in detail – and relentlessly – particular objects of every kind, including 'cups, bottles, shoes, boots, hats ... boxes and simple chairs'. Wallpapers should give a 'proper impression of flatness' (Pugin had led the way here, encompassing carpets also, as did Redgrave and Cole); ironwork should be treated in harmony with 'the material and its manufacture' (Ruskin might not have gone so far); 'ornament is not ... principal ... it must be secondary to the thing decorated' (compare Pugin – ornament should be no more than 'enrichment of the essential composition'). For Redgrave, 'the absence of any fixed principle in ornamental design' was 'most apparent in the Exhibition'. 'The taste of the producers in general' was 'uneducated'.

For Matthew Digby Watt, architect, author of the lavish folio volume *The*

*Industrial Arts of the Nineteenth Century* and later first Slade Professor at Cambridge, the only way to educate was to surround the pupil with 'every attainable example of general beauty of form': 'his sense of enjoyment will teach him selection'. Complexity of design should rest on simplicity. Yet Wyatt recognized that there were Victorian complexities in the social context. 'The endless diversity of men's tastes, and the ever-changing conditions of their education and association of ideas, demand for their productions a variety almost as incessant as that which pervades creation. Whenever that craving after variety has been justified, irrespective of *fitness*, novelty has degenerated into frivolity, design into conceits [compare Ruskin's 'deceits'] and style into mannerism and vulgarity'. 'The public' could no more be left out of the picture than the manufacturers. For the *Journal*, 'the restless demands of the public for constant novelty are alike mischievous to the progress of good ornamental art as they are to all commercial interests'.

How could 'indefinite development' be achieved? Wornum maintained in his Prize Essay on 'The Exhibition as a Lesson in Taste' that the first thing to do was to separate the good from the bad, recognizing that 'generally the English side does not betray that great inferiority of taste which has so long been prognosticated of it'. While condemning the makers of silverware, therefore, for being 'under the absolute control of trade conventionalities' and while finding the wood workers represented in the exhibition 'very inferior to the French and German carvers', he praised the Wedgwood stall, 'where we find only exquisite shapes only sufficiently decorated to enhance their effect'. In fact, it was not Wedgwood but Minton and Company, the firm with which Cole and Redgrave had been associated, that won the Council Medal in Class XXV – 'Ceramic Manufactures, Chairs, Porcelain, Earthenware etc.' – sharing it with the Sèvres Manufacturing Works in France, representing 'High Art'. Herbert Minton had won a medal at the first Society of Arts Exhibition in 1846, when Cole himself, under the name of Felix Summerly Esq., won a prize for his subsequently famous tea-service, made for sale by Minton's with the hope of reviving 'the good old practice of connecting the best art with familiar objects in daily use'. The two men had met Wyatt in Paris in the summer of 1849 when they decided to try to make the 1851 exhibition genuinely international 'with contributions from every nation.' 'The earth is the Lord's and the fulness thereof,' and all that dwelt within it should have their chance to compete and to compare.

After the exhibition was over, Cole went with Minton to Vienna to deliver in person a dessert service made by Minton and bought by the Queen as a present for the Emperor of Austria (in return for his bookcase); and Minton was one of the first to congratulate Cole when a month later he was given charge of the management of Schools of Design as General Superintendent. He also congratulated Redgrave, who knew Cole well but was often the butt of his humour, when he was made Art Superintendent of a new department of the Board of Trade, the Department of Practical Art.

Cole was to stay in his new post until 1873, and Redgrave, a talented painter, who became Surveyor of the Queen's Pictures in 1857, was to survive him by several years. There was no longer any need for a *Journal of Design and Manufactures*: a different network was at the disposal of the reformers offering opportunities for encouraging 'indefinite development'.

At the centre of the network was a Museum of Manufactures, housed first in borrowed rooms at Marlborough House, a royal residence, and later moved in 1857 to a new structure in glass and iron in South Kensington, designed by C. D. Young and Company, a firm that specialized in exporting prefabricated iron buildings to the colonies, and known by its critics and even to its administrators as the 'Brompton Boilers'. It was officially described as being 'of a plain and economical character' and Cole, who used the engineer Sir William Cubitt as a consultant, himself called it 'that unlucky iron shed'. A large corps of gas attendants were responsible for the gas lighting points which had to be tended by hand, and a detachment of Sappers and Miners of the Royal Engineers instituted a Museum Fire Brigade.

The gallery included the scientific objects later to be transferred to the Science Museum along with what were described as 'culinary curiosities' including birds' nests, sharks' fins, sea slugs and 'other edible dainties'. Playfair determined their classification. Cole, however, may have been more interested in food than Playfair. He wanted to improve food as he wanted to improve taste ('God provided the food, the Devil the cooks') and he set up a National Training School for Cookery. One of his daughters, Rose, wrote a cookery book.

It was at Cole's insistence that the gallery included a collection of objects designed according to 'False Principles'. It was known to one of its critics, writing in Dickens's *Household Words* as 'A House full of Horrors', 'a gloomy chamber hung round with frightful objects . . . curtains, carpets, clothes, lamps, and what not.' Cole himself believed that the object of this permanent exhibition was not to entertain but to instruct in the correct principles of taste. It was to be no 'lounge for idleness' but an 'impressive schoolroom for every one', including the general public. The *Household Words* correspondent was 'ashamed of the pattern of my own trousers, for I saw a piece of them hung up there as a horror'. Cole wanted 'Correct Principles' to reach beyond London to 'Coketown' and elsewhere. There were to be 'circulating collections' of objects, therefore, which would be carried in horse-drawn wagons and displayed at provincial Schools of Design, and there was to be an extensive use of photographs for educational purposes.

Since their foundation, the promoters and organizers of the Schools of Design had argued passionately and relentlessly, almost violently, about the place of art in the education of designers and on modes of instruction and management; and Cole, who had the strongest possible views on such subjects, had already been drawn into the argument four years before the

Great Exhibition opened. Under his influence the *Journal of Design* declared boldly in 1849 that it would 'best prove itself to be the friend of the School of Design by helping to accomplish a complete reformation of it.' And it stated equally boldly that it ought to have 'politics of its own'.

Minton urged Cole in 1852 to be 'more mild or gentle than you usually are ... not so obstinate and dictatorial', but Cole was always a man with a mission, determined that under his direction from the National Training School in London the number of Schools of Design would be multiplied, even outside England, and that their mode of instruction should be above all 'systematic'. As he put it later, he wanted to remodel 'twenty tiny Schools of Design into one hundred and twenty flourishing Schools of Art in all parts of the United Kingdom and other schools like these in the Colonies and the United States.' He appreciated as a good Utilitarian that the Schools had not been set up originally for 'aesthetic purposes', although the National Training School's first commission was the Duke of Wellington's funeral bier, designed by Redgrave and Gottfried Semper. Like Wornum, Cole appreciated also that his 'age', whatever one thought about its achievements, was 'so essentially commercial that it hardly looks to promoting anything ... except for commercial purposes.'

In 1851 itself it was Wornum above all others who insisted most clearly on the differences between British and French approaches to art and design, while Semper, born in Hamburg, brought German ideas also into the debate. 'While England has been devoting nearly all its efforts to the mere [*sic*] comfort of the millions', Wornum wrote, 'France has expended its energies for the most part over luxuries for the few'. The *Journal* had put it more succinctly: 'if the French beat us in art we have the palm for cheapness.' In Wornum's view, it was 'an amalgamation of the two' which the country required, 'fitness and elegance combined; recreation for the mind as well as the comfort of the body ... single works of great cost and magnificence' *and* replicated objects in general supply. In both cases a 'surfeit of means' was a danger to design. For Semper, who may well have published his *Wissenschaft, Industrie und Kunst* in November 1851 at Albert's request, 'only in products in which the seriousness of their use does not allow anything unnecessary, that is in coaches, weapons, medical instruments, etc, can one occasionally see a sounder way of decorating and improving form'.

Neither Wornum nor Redgrave would have disagreed. Nonetheless, as Sir Ernst Gombrich has suggested, in his own buildings and designs Semper was as confused as the age from which he emerged, as indeed was Redgrave in many of his own designs. It is interesting to note that Wornum also, while anxious to escape confusion, did not succeed in doing so. 'The time has perhaps now gone by, at least in Europe', he wrote, 'for the development of any particular or national style, and for this reason it is necessary to distinguish the various tastes that have prevailed throughout the past ages, and preserve them as distinct impressions; or otherwise, by using indiscriminately all materials, we should lose the expression, and the very essence of ornament, the conveying of a distinct aesthetic expression, would be utterly destroyed. For if all objects in a room were of the same shape and details, however beautiful these details might be, the mind would soon be utterly disgusted.' What could have been more Victorian than that?

There was a clear Victorian note in Whewell, too, when somewhat insensitively he compared British approaches not with those of the French nor of the Germans but with those of 'less developed civilizations'. 'There the wealth of a province is absorbed in the dress of a mighty warrior; here the gigantic weapons of the peaceful potentate are used to provide clothing for the world.' Whewell was prepared to go further than Wornum at his most optimistic when he claimed – in far too complacent a tone of voice – that 'we perceive that in advancing [from earlier ages of history] to our form of civilization we advance also to a more skilful, powerful, comprehensive and progressive form of art'.

On this matter, Owen Jones, along with Cole and Redgrave one of the first editors of the *Journal*, flatly contradicted Whewell. The 'science' in the Exhibition, he believed,showed Britain in the van, but when 'art' was considered 'far from leading the van we must fall into the rear ... In the employment of colour we were not only behind some of our European neighbours, but, in common with them, were far outstripped by the natives of the east ... We have no principles, no unity; the architect, the upholsterer, the paper-stainer, the weaver, the calico-printer and the potter, run each their independent course; each struggles fruitlessly, each produces in art novelty without beauty or beauty without intelligence.'

## III

There was one critic in 1851 who was out of sympathy with all the ideas to which Cole and his supporters subscribed – John Ruskin. For Quentin Bell, historian of the Schools of Design, Ruskin's protest against Cole's 'system' was necessary if only on 'instructional' grounds: the Schools of Design, as they developed under Cole's direction after 1852, were dangerous places to study. Even if successful, they would fashion students from a mould, the mould that Dickens made fun of in *Hard Times*, where in his second chapter he turned Cole into a school inspector, 'a mighty man at cutting and drying ... always in training, always with a system to force down the general throat like a bolus'. When Ruskin denounced not only 'system' but 'machine', he was rebelling both against false instruction (Wornum, too, himself drew what became a familiar contrast between 'education' and 'training') and against 'mechanical standards of excellence' which inhibited 'invention'. Students were not only being moulded: they were being turned into machines. Art teaching was being corrupted into 'a state of distortion and falsehood'.

79

Nevertheless, Ruskin's approach had its own weaknesses, as Gombrich has pointed out, for his strong distinction between 'mechanical precision' and 'organic rhythm' was a gross over-simplification – as was his claim that the habits of the 'Old Venetians' accounted for their ability to make attractive glass. He was more convincing when he turned to the problems of workers in his own time. Indeed, his probing political economy, developed during the 1850s and set out in *Unto this Last* (1862), had more depth – and clarity – than his moralizing historical aesthetics. It was not quite enough to ask simply 'regarding all ornament' whether or not it was done with enjoyment – 'was the carver happy while he did it?'

For Cole it was plainly a fact that, in mid-Victorian Britain, consumers as well as producers counted: 'the crafts and even the "status symbols" of the wealthy now appeared to be within reach of almost anybody'. Yet for Ruskin this was not a starting point but a matter to be debated. Nor was the evidence entirely on Cole's side when he dealt with production. As Bell shows, provincial manufacturers in towns and cities where Schools of Design were located were often completely uninterested in the promotion and development of arts and crafts through education. Sometimes, indeed, there was hostility, as in the case of a manufacturer of printed fabrics who had told Sir Robert Peel in 1840 that an 'outrageous' specimen of his wares might be deemed to be in 'bad taste by a man who had "perfect taste", yet when offered for sale could do "better than highly commended articles of one particular class" '. The remark recalls Mr Crumpet's exclamations after visiting Cole's museum of unacceptably designed objects that they were just like those in his own house. Mr Crumpet was more 'confused', however, than the manufacturer of unacceptable printed fabrics, and seeking to console himself with a cup of tea he added to his confusion when he looked inside his cup. 'A butterfly inside my cup! How horrible.'

An 'unqualified' Birmingham manufacturer was described in *The Builder* in 1865 as an 'anomaly'. Yet even the qualified might have had economic reasons for complaint about the way Cole's system worked. It is interesting that in the Potteries Messrs Minton – for all their earlier links with Cole – told a Select Committee of 1864 that they had withdrawn their support from the School of Design in Newcastle-under-Lyme on the grounds that 'there was no just claim upon them to pay for the artisans of the Potteries, because when they had educated the young men in their own works they had no power over them; they might go away and they were sought by other manufacturers and paid higher wages than Messrs Minton would give them after educating them.'

It was partly because of the complexities of such circumstances that Ruskin was drawn more and more deeply into the study of political economy, for him a study of values more than of facts. Long before then, his first critique of the Great Exhibition, as set out in his short study *The Opening of the Crystal Palace Considered in Some of its Relations to the Prospects of Art* (1854), published when the Crystal Palace moved to Sydenham, had had its 'melancholy' side. Yet while it mentioned *en passant* the 'relations of each Dives and Lazarus', it had been more concerned with the building than with products which had been on display in 1851, 'petty arts of our fashionable luxury', or with the processes of work which he had already considered in his *Seven Lamps of Architecture* (1849). 'There is assuredly as much ingenuity required to build a screw frigate, or a tubular bridge, as a hall of glass,' he conceded – though it was scarcely a concession – but 'mechanical ingenuity' was 'not the essence either of painting or of architecture.' Was 'our Doric and Palladian pride' to be 'reduced' at last to being fascinated by 'the lustre of a few rows of panes of glass?' Was 'this little Europe . . . this narrow piece of the world's pavement worn down by so many pilgrims' feet' to be 'swept utterly and garnished for the masque of the future?' Was not the new America 'wide enough for the elasticities of our humanity?'

It is in Ruskin's other works that he considered within his own historical context the questions raised by Cole, Wornum, Redgrave and Semper. Thus, when he made his first appearance in Bradford in 1859, he told his mixed audience, as Cole might have done, that 'design is not the offspring of idle fancy'. Without 'observation and experience', he went on, 'without peace and pleasurableness in occupation', all 'the lecturings and teachings and prizes and principles of art in the world' were of no use. Yet even these pre-conditions were not enough. You had to 'surround your men with happy influences and beautiful things'. Thereafter, Ruskin diverged further and further from Cole. In 1864 on a return visit to Bradford, when he was invited to lecture not on design but on architecture, he talked of the false religion of the goddess of getting on; and a year later he explained to the Institute of British Architects that he himself was so much under the pressure of 'mechanization and the fury of avaricious commerce' that he had been forced to 'secede' from the study not only of architecture but 'nearly of all art'.

Ruskin approached the relationship between art and industry, as he approached the relationship between nature and culture, in a different way from Cole or from Albert, whose first public task in England – in 1845 – had been to serve as head of a Royal Commission, of which Charles Eastlake was secretary, 'to inquire whether advantage might not be taken of the rebuilding of the Houses of Parliament to promote and encourage the Fine Arts in the United Kingdom.' In 1851, therefore, it was perhaps as well for Ruskin that there was no section on 'high art' in the exhibition except for Class XXX – 'Sculpture, Models and Plastic Art' – although it was possible, doubtless to his horror, to submit paintings to illustrate 'improvements in colours', to be regarded as examples not of the skill of the artist but of the preparer of the paints.

The Royal Academy seems to have made no protest, although one journalist complained that 'at a time when furniture, dress and utensils for the table all come in for a share of the improved taste of an age ambitious in art, it seems an act of fatuity . . . to exclude from the lists that very branch of art which affords the highest resources for decoration': instead of 'the ample breadth of canvas . . . the disappointed artist was obliged to substitute such sorry materials as tin, glass, plate-iron or pieces of Dresden or French porcelain'.

Later exhibitions, including that at Dublin in 1853, were to include sections on 'Art', and in 1852 Dr Gustav Waagen, who had first visited Britain in 1835 in order to inform his fellow countrymen of the state of art in Britain, published his *Treasures of Art in Great Britain* with Albert's blessing. Meanwhile, the sculptures of 1851 forced some topical consideration of the role of taste and of the relationship between original art and reproduction.

The statues on display in the Crystal Palace included some near life-size of contemporaries or near-contemporaries, like Lord Eldon and his brother Lord Stowell, seated side by side, the Duke of Rutland and the Marquis of Bute, patron of William Burges, the architect. There were many also with strong historical or mythical references, among them 'King Alfred taught by his Mother', 'Cupid and Psyche', 'Lord Ley', the horses from the *Niebelungenlied*, and 'Una and the Lion' to which the title 'Purity' was given. Many of the pieces appealed to the worst elements of Victorian sentimentality and prurience; all were widely commented upon. Some, indeed, like 'Dorothea' by John Bell, a friend of Cole, were immediately copied in popular Parian ware, bearing Cole's Summerly label. Others had a more complex fate: one, as Pevsner states, was converted, with the addition of some highly realistic lilies and some dockleaves, into a gas bracket.

There were some art critics, however, like the editor of the *Journal of Design*, who believed that it was a mistake to 'Parianize' Hiram Power's much admired Greek Slave, since 'the merit of the original' consisted 'more in its exquisite finish in the marble than in its sentiment or composition'. As for *The Times*, it made fun of all such kinds of 'reproductions'. 'No sooner is Parian introduced for modelling statuettes', it observed, 'than cupids and other juvenile indelicacies are perpetually smiling at us under glass shades, or sitting uncomfortably upon projections of dishes, or balancing themselves miraculously upon the summits of lids'.

Fortunately for the sculptors, Ruskin had little to say about contemporary sculpture, tastes in which were to change much by the 1870s: Bell, for example, went completely out of fashion. Yet when Ruskin was to write later, as a historian, that 'the state of sculpture in modern England, as compared with that of the great Ancients, is literally one of corrupt and dishonourable death, as opposed to bright and fameful life', his use of the word 'fameful' raised contemporary as well as historical issues. Some nineteenth-century sculptors, like Hiram Power, had undoubtedly won fame. The *Art Union Journal* would itself write of J. H. Foley's 'The Youth at the Stream', the models for which have survived (the statue was eventually to find its way to Stratford), that 'had such a figure been dug up in Rome, or near Naples, somewhat mutilated, it would have been pronounced a valuable specimen of classic art'.

Some 'sculpture' was exhibited in 1851 in classes other than Class XXX. Thus, Bell's *Eagle Slayer*, first exhibited at the Royal Academy in 1837 and cast now both in bronze and iron, was displayed by the Coalbrookdale Company under an iron canopy, as was his *Andromeda*. The former is now exhibited, *pace* Ruskin, outside the Bethnal Green Museum: the latter was bought by Queen Victoria and was displayed, as Albert wished, at Osborne.

Albert always had his own ideas on art. They were formed before he married Victoria and they shaped his tastes as an active collector. After 1851 he gave unqualified support to the most interesting collection of 'art treasures', including paintings as well as sculptures, ever exhibited. It was organized in 1857 not in the metropolis, but in Manchester, where smaller exhibitions both in the arts and in science had already been on show.

When the idea of a Manchester Exhibition was mooted, there were sceptics inside and outside the city. 'What does Manchester want with pictures?' some asked. 'Which possessors of the richest works of art' others asked, 'would be so improvident as to send them into the neighbourhood of the tall chimneys of Manchester?' 'Why can't you stick to your cotton spinning?' the Duke of Devonshire is reputed to have demanded. Yet Albert's patronage, assistance offered concomitantly by the Manchester Chamber of Commerce, the perseverance and enthusiasm of Thomas Fairbairn and of other industrialists, like the calico printer Edmund Potter, and the backing of the *Manchester Guardian* won over most of the sceptics. Thereafter, indeed, the rhetoric of enthusiasts prevailed in the industrial North as it had prevailed and continued to prevail in Kensington. One long-term result was the Hallé Orchestra formed after Sir Charles Hallé, one of Manchester's highly talented refugees, had been invited to contribute music for the Exhibition.

Twenty-five designs for an exhibition building were received, including one by Owen Jones, yet while it was claimed that no expense was spared, there was to be no opportunity on this occasion for a new Paxton. The winning design was one submitted by C. D. Young and Company on the basis of a preliminary estimate received before that of any other firm was considered. The cost was £33,933, but when the buildings were taken down at the close of the exhibition, they realised only £7,000.

*The Builder* described the design as 'a repetition of the three steam boilers, side by side, with which Brompton is disfigured', but Manchester opinion about the product was less scathing. There were regrets that the new specially built 'edifice', linked by corridor to a railway station, might not 'rival the Vatican in its stateliness and solidity or the Louvre in its gorgeous interior', but in one respect, it was felt, it would be 'more wonderful than either'. 'The Vatican is the depository of the accumulated treasures of ages;

the Louvre displays the trophies of warfare, and the purchases of an Imperial Exchequer; but this Exhibition would furnish proof to the world of the unselfishness of Englishmen, when appealed to for the proved purposes of developing a good and ennobling design'. After such talk, it was something of an anti-climax to have the building compared with Sydney Smirke's new Reading Room at the British Museum or the City of Manchester as a whole with Venice and Florence.

More than a million visitors viewed the Manchester Exhibition, among them Napoleon III, Prince Frederick William of Prussia, Dickens, Tennyson, Hawthorne, Morris, Florence Nightingale – and children from poor districts sponsored from an Alpha Fund. Thomas Cook, appealed to by the organizers, is said to have multiplied the numbers more than even he expected when he was asked to arrange excursions from near and far. It needed no such appeal, however, to inspire the many publications that were specially devoted to the contents of the Exhibition – not only paintings and sculptures but 'exhibits made of glass, enamel, metal clay, porcelain and other materials', no longer considered 'inferior to the fine arts'. The display of engravings was hailed as the 'first attempt in the history of engraving to . . . show to the public generally, at one view, a complete chronological series of prints from the commencement of the art up to the present time.'

The paintings spanned the years between mediaeval art and Turner and beyond, and there were certainly enough interested members of the local public to challenge any sceptics. There were, in fact, no fewer than 156 people described as painters in Manchester at the census of 1851, and there was an active local art market. Yet there were blind spots. Constable was thought 'plashy' and 'weedy' as well as monotonous, and some of the latest paintings on display provoked laughter rather than respect. Fairbairn advised his friend Holman Hunt, from whom he had commissioned *The Awakening Conscience* in 1854, not to use the adjective 'pre-Raphaelite' in relation to nineteenth-century paintings 'when talking to Manchester people . . . since the term has become one of such confirmed ridicule that they cannot accept it calmly'. Three years later when an exhibition was held in Bradford Old Exchange there was such suspicion too, although the pre-Raphaelites had several enthusiastic local patrons.

Outside Manchester, art enthusiasts were encouraged after 1857 to press more strongly for a large National Gallery – the *Quarterly Review* was in the lead – while after the exhibition closed, Cole secured the collection of Jules Soulage, a Toulouse lawyer, mainly of decorative utilitarian objects, to add to his Museum newly-housed in South Kensington. The *Athenaeum*, however, remained uneasy about the prospects for the future. 'Who would educate a race of apprentices who will admire – and buy?' Nineteenth-century art had 'broken from the patron's drawing-room' and appealed to 'the crowd'. Yet 'everything was to see' and 'nothing to sell'. There was criticism of a different kind. Long after the exhibition closed, Morris was more concerned about the visitors who were excluded from art because they had had no money to buy. The public had been encouraged 'to do its art as it does its religion – by deputy'. It paid a certain number of 'what I should call art persons to perform certain mysteries of civilization.'

With or without such sentiments, 'fine art' figured prominently in the next large-scale exhibition to be held in London, in 1862, even if John Hollingshead in the *Illustrated Catalogue* dwelt very simply on other themes: 'we may or may not be more moral, more imaginative, nor better educated than our ancestors, but we have steam, gas, railways and power looms, while there are more of us, and we have more money to spend'. This time there was no great symbolic building. The *Art Journal*, one of its many critics, called it a 'wretched shed'. It had been designed by a Cole protégé, Francis Fowke of the Royal Engineers, who had made many specifically Victorian things, like 'a portable bath to pack up like a book' and a 'collapsing camera'. The building might have been redeemed had Cole's dream of using artists like Rossetti, Hunt and Millais to paint large coloured mosaic murals been realized.

The objects on display in the exhibition were in many respects more interesting than those of 1851. No fewer than 9,862 applicants sent in claims for space of whom all but 2,000 were in the 'industrial' department. One applicant's request for space was described as it had been in 1851: he wished to submit a dear penny loaf of 1801, 'the oldest piece of bread in the world'. One applicant who secured space and had hated 1851 was Morris, whose furniture could be seen along with a firegrate depicting the Rape of Proserpine, an elaborate cabinet designed by William Burges, coconut matting 'covered with brilliant patterns that one could hardly have expected from so coarse a material', and Japanese exhibits on a stand of their own, which for aesthetic reasons attracted the attention of Arthur Liberty and led Hollingshead to meditate on the future of 'the competitive power of production of the Japanese.'

There were many inventions also, including bread and biscuit machinery, a steam winch, 'traction engines for common roads', a travelling crane capable of lifting 24 tons and Ramsbottom's 'self-feeding fender to supply water to express engines without stopping'. Perkin displayed his dyes, and it was proudly claimed that 'hardly a name of any eminence was missing in any branch of chemical manufacture, from magenta and borax down to matches and blacking.'

Significantly, perhaps, although 'coal specimens were abundant', the great 1851 block of coal was replaced in prominence by a 'gold' obelisk nearly 70 feet high, constructed from wooden poles, canvas and gold leaf and designed to show the massive volume of gold sent from the Australian colony of Victoria to England between 1851 and 1861. And although there was aluminium on display too, 'much lighter than ordinary metals', it was not clear 'what to do with it'. It is significant that it was recognized at the time that 'the most defective parts' of the exhibition were those concerned with cotton manufactures and calico printing.

The exhibition, somewhat neglected by historians, had been originally planned for 1861, and many of the same people were involved in the 1862 venture as in that of 1851, including Cole, this time given the position of 'Consulting Officer', and John Scott Russell, Secretary of the Commissioners in 1851, who had subsequently become a ship designer as well as director of the Crystal Palace Company at Sydenham. Albert, however, was missing. His last public appearance was in June 1861, when he opened new gardens at the centre of the 87-acre estate of the Royal Commission for the 1851 exhibition, originally 'fields intersected by narrow lanes', which had been purchased out of a handsome surplus of £186,000 left over when the Great Exhibition closed.

Albert had hoped to convert the site into a great cultural centre with a Palace of Arts and Science at the centre, but the learned societies and the National Gallery had been strongly opposed to his ambitious plans. He was just as disturbed as Cole was by such reactions. Indeed, he had told the citizens of Manchester in 1857 that they had done well 'not to aim at a mere accumulation of works of art and objects of great interest' but to 'give your collection by a scientific and historical arrangement an educational character – thus not losing the opportunity of teaching the mind as well as gratifying the senses'.

This message was the real legacy of 1851 as interpreted by Albert, by Cole and by Playfair, and it was to be represented, it was hoped in perpetuity, in Aston Webb's 'Lombardic Renaissance' Victoria and Albert Museum, the foundation stone of which was laid by Queen Victoria in 1899, at her last public function, in Waterhouse's Natural History Museum, and in the Science Museum, planned by a Committee headed by Sir Hugh Bell, the Middlesbrough industrialist.

Built in red brick and terracotta to reflect the Germanic tastes of Albert (and Semper), the 'V and A' still perpetuates many of the ideas of Cole. It also contains decorative work commissioned by him and features still appropriately named after him, including his loggia overlooking Exhibition Row, now part of the Museum, and a glazed ceramic staircase with tiles produced by his friend Minton which had been displayed in Manchester. It was sad, however, that Cole was not mentioned in any of the speeches at the official opening of the Museum in 1909. King Edward VII, who made one of them, was no Albert, although he had been elected President of the Society of Arts back in the mid-Victorian years in 1863 and he had opened the Bethnal Green Museum in 1872. This alas, had not been an architectural gem. It was the Brompton Boilers building removed from west to east, but this time clothed in brick rather than corrugated iron.

The objects displayed included Sir Richard Wallace's collection of paintings and works of art, furniture from the 1862 Exhibition, for a time the

Pitt-Rivers collection, and the Animal Products Collection and the Food Collection from Playfair's science museum. Three years earlier in 1869 when he resigned from his Chair of Chemistry at Edinburgh University (which he had occupied for twelve years) in order to become a Member of Parliament, the Senatus of the University thanked Playfair more generously than Cole was ever thanked for his help in 'guiding the general education of the people'.

Albert's reputation was to survive through different associations. In 1871 the Royal Albert Hall, another of Cole's dreams, was opened by the Queen. Devised at Cole's behest by Fowke and planned after his death by Lieutenant Henry Young Darracott Scott, it echoed Semper, contained many Cole features, and has been described as 'the most conspicuous example of the South Kensington style'. It was intended as a 'Hall of Arts and Sciences' to house conferences as well as concerts, and its huge roof, a triumph of engineering, was as remarkable as its huge Willis organ. Cole had written music criticism in his youth, some as a deputy for Thomas Love Peacock, had tried to include music in the 1862 Exhibition, and had once claimed that 'music unites in the highest degree both Science and Art'.

Opposite the Hall is the Albert Memorial, mooted almost as soon as Albert died (Cole would have liked an Albert University as the most fitting memorial) and completed in 1872 in Gothic style with the help of many hands as a kind of open shrine. The Sir Walter Scott Memorial in Edinburgh had shown what might be done, and another Scott, George Gilbert, born eight years before Queen Victoria, had won the competition for the new Memorial. Cole did not approve of it, but the features of the Memorial were supremely Victorian, and it must surely figure, however briefly, in any book on Victorian things.

Prince Albert is presented at the centre of the shrine, surrounded by emblems of the continents: Bell sculpted America, William Theed Africa, Foley Asia and Patrick MacDowell the Europe Albert most wished to serve. An upper group of sculptures represents Manufacture, Agriculture, Commerce and Engineering (complete with steam hammer, blast furnace and the Britannic Bridge); and there is a podium frieze depicting 169 poets, sculptors, painters, including Turner, who for Ruskin would 'stand with the great of all time', and musicians (surprisingly Monteverdi was among them). There were architects too, including Vanbrugh and Palladio along with Pugin and Barry, and, discreetly, at the Queen's request, Scott himself. Finally, but not least, there was abstraction in the niches of the spire of the Memorial where Faith, Hope, Charity and Humility are displayed, and at the angles of the niches Fortitude, Prudence, Justice and Temperance.

If all this was reverential, contemporary comment on the Memorial could be as barbed as any twentieth-century judgement. Thus, *The Architectural Journal* declared that 'the superstructure . . . seems more in the style of that which gave birth to the Lord Mayor's carriage than anything else'. Albert himself had not wanted his own likeness to figure in any Memorial 'as it would both disturb my quiet rides in Rotten Row to see my own face staring at me: and if (as is very likely) it became an artistic monstrosity, like most of our monuments, it would upset my equanimity to be permanently ridiculed and laughed at in effigies.' The one feature in the Memorial that might have restored his equanimity was the fact that in J. H. Foley's gun-metal effigy of him he is bearing a Great Exhibition scroll.

# IV

In retrospect, as at the time, it was not Britain, but France, the country where the idea of exhibitions had emerged in the eighteenth century, that organized the most interesting late-nineteenth-century exhibitions before and after Napoleon III, a very different character from Albert. There was a strong French contingent in London in 1862, determined on their return to arrange a great new exhibition in Paris, just as the British who attended the Paris Exhibition of 1855 (among them Fowke, then Secretary to the British Section) had been determined to arrange 1862.

The fascinating and at times curious interplay of ideas between the two countries had gone back even before Napoleon III, for in the late 1840s it was a French Minister of Agriculture and Industry, Buffet, whose name has subsequently figured more at parties than in exhibitions, who first conceived of an exhibition that would be international, not national in scope, the idea that was taken up by Cole and Minton. In 1851 itself, parties of French workmen had been sent across the Channel at official expense to see the exhibits of all the nations in the Crystal Palace, some of which were bought and placed in Paris in the *Conservatoire des Arts et des Métiers*. Moreover, four years later against the background of the Crimean War, when Paris had organized its own 'Exposition Universelle' staged ironically in 'a temple of peace', interest in the *Palais de l'Industrie* had inspired the British Government, which had provided no money for the Great Exhibition of 1851, to give £50,000 to support the British section. It was then, too, that Thomas Twining, a member of the Society of Arts, introduced to the French the characteristic British idea that there should be a section of the Exhibition devoted to cheap objects of practical everyday use, an *exposition économique* which would interest ordinary visitors. Napoleon III was strongly in favour.

The most French of the ideas of 1855 had nothing to do with cheapness. The classification of wines, called for by the Commissioners and demanded with authority by Napoleon III himself, was to lead to the naming for posterity of the four great wines of Bordeaux – Haut-Brion, Château Margaux, Château Latour, and Lafite and Mouton Rothschild. The Chamber of Commerce of Bordeaux had been reluctant to comply with the request but the classification, which entailed naming and listing the different *crus* – the last of them *bourgeois ordinaires* – survived the fall of most other Victorian schemes of classification. Characteristically, when Gladstone secured a lowering of the duties on claret in 1860, it was the *bourgeois ordinaires* which were uppermost in his mind.

There was a touch of extraordinary luxury in all the Paris exhibitions in and after 1855 – in 1867, 1878, 1889 and, above all, 1900. Thus, of 1855 *The Times* noted how it glittered with 'gold and silks and satins: "the simple" had been put aside for the costly and the gaudy'. In 1867 the Exposition was visited by no fewer than eighteen monarchs. Yet a thematic section on 'the history of work', devised by the sociologist at this exhibition Frédéric le Play, extolled art, science and industry, and there was one section dealing with 'social and moral problems' associated with the rise of factories. For Le Play as for Playfair, considerations of prestige were less pertinent than consider-ations of education. 'The very poorest student in the poorest school, the most ignorant, the least gifted', one of his closest colleagues wrote, 'has the capacity to recognize the truth, to understand it and to live by it'.

Things were there to teach, and you could see aluminium (Napoleon III ordered a dinner set to be made out of it); petroleum; a large-scale model of the Suez Canal complete with ships passing through it; a huge 50-ton Krupps steel cannon; artificial limbs displayed by the Surgeon General of the United States; and a patented and much admired American rocking chair. The Art Gallery, more brilliant than any in London, excluded Cézannes and Monets, but Manet, also excluded, ran a private gallery just outside the entrance where he conceived his painting *A Panorama of the Paris Exposition* while collecting 50-centime entrance fees. You could also see the main sights of the Exposition for yourself from a raised balcony in the Machinery Gallery, or more ambitiously from a tourist balloon.

The ingenious grid design of the 1867 exhibition was said to have been influenced by an article in *The Builder* published in London in 1861: 'manufactures and products of cognate natures' were 'to be arranged in concentric bands, with a garden in the middle', and 'the articles of the different nations' were to 'intersect the bands by transepts or avenues radiating from the centre'. Outside in the grounds there were to be national pavilions, many with national restaurants, as there were to be at most subsequent exhibitions.

In 1878 medicine and hygiene figured in the classification, and pho-tography, as at London in 1862, had a section to itself. *Savants* with an international reputation were invited, too, to confer together and to mingle with the 'very poorest students'. The exhibition, designed to prove that France had recovered after the fall of Napoleon and defeat in the Franco-German War, was not a financial success, although it made its main political point. One visiting English journalist, G. A. Sala, was worried not by the politics but by the economics. He regretted the absence of the kind of 'naive specimens of individual ingenuity and labour' which had been present in

1851 and in 1867. 'Individual man', he felt, had disappeared 'save in a few instances' and was being replaced by 'great companies and great firms solicitous of orders'.

In 1889 the great *Exposition Tricoulère*, held to celebrate the anniversary of the Revolution, placed the Revolution itself within a far larger time span. It focused on an evolutionary process leading man back to the paleolithic and neolithic ages, and it included a section designed to illustrate the role of institutions created 'to alleviate the moral and material condition of the workers.' Above all else, however, it offered the Eiffel Tower to the world. This was designed by Gaston Eiffel, who had also designed the 1867 Exhibition building, and it was far more controversial than the Crystal Palace or even the Brompton Boilers. 'Is this the horror that the French have created in order to impress us with their vaunted taste?' a group of shocked French writers and artists, among them Alexander Dumas and Guy de Maupassant, asked the Minister of Commerce, adding that they loathed the prospect of a 'dizzily ridiculous tower dominating Paris like a gigantic black factory chimney.'

Eiffel was not intimidated. Nor was the Minister. Paris accepted the Tower at once, and in time it was to be thought inconceivable that it would have been complete without it: 'Old abandoned towers, no one listens to you now,' it seemed to say. 'Don't you now see that the poles have shifted and that the world now turns on its iron axis?' Ruskin would have shuddered to hear talk of 'the transformation of the techniques of architecture, the substitution of iron for stone.'

The Eiffel Tower contained no exhibits, but from a travelling platform, also designed by Eiffel, you could see at the 1889 Exposition all the other transformed things that had been assembled in Cotamin's huge 'palace of machines'. You could also hear voices and music through a telephone and phonograph, while electricity lit up the fountains at the Champs de Mars. The lighting created almost as much of a sensation as the Eiffel Tower itself. Once again Londoners, many of them 'packaged' by Thomas Cook, flocked to see it. 'Then why did you marry him?' Cousin Jack asks Effie in a *Punch* cartoon of 1890, 'Oh well, I wanted to see the Paris Exhibition, you know', was the reply.

Cook could organize longer Exhibition journeys. At Vienna in 1873, where there was an obvious Victorian presence, there was a huge rotunda complete with a dome twice the size of that of St Peter's dome in Rome, and there was also a Machinery Hall, almost as impressive as those in Paris in 1878 and 1889, in which the exhibits from different countries were arranged geographically according to Mercator's projection. 'It may well be doubted', wrote H. C. Sweny in his appendix to the official British report on the Vienna Exhibition, 'whether the practical and the picturesque, the modern and the mediaeval, the East and the West will ever mingle again in one harmonious whole, with such equal aid from art and nature, as on the Prater of 1873, in the Buildings in the Park'.

The rotunda and dome had been designed by John Scott Russell, Secretary to the 1851 Commissioners, while Francis Philip Cunliffe-Owen, who, after serving as Cole's Deputy Director, was to succeed him as Director of the South Kensington Museum, was one of the most prominent personalities present in Vienna as he had been in Paris in 1855. He was also to be an honoured guest at the great Bicentennial Exhibition in Philadelphia in 1876, and for his work in connection with such exhibitions he won many foreign decorations: indeed, his obituarist in *The Times* suggested that these were *his* favourite things. Yet Cunliffe-Owen was prepared notwithstanding to organize smaller British exhibitions at home, among them a Fisherman's Exhibition in South Kensington, held in 1883, into which he is said to have introduced such an effective 'element of amusement and popularities' that the exhibition became 'the fashionable lounge of London for the summer.'

Another popular exhibition in late-Victorian London was a Colonial and Indian Exhibition held in South Kensington in 1886. Sydney had already held an exhibition in 1879 and Melbourne had followed in 1880; and now in 1886 as proof of changing British preoccupations there were lavish displays both of things and in retrospect most disturbingly of people – of cheap trinkets and rich carpets, of New Zealand wool and Australian wines – and of Kaffirs and Bushmen from the Cape (*inter alia* they were shown washing diamonds). Free trade was given less emphasis than empire. Lord Tennyson, the Poet Laureate, wrote an ode, set to music by Sir Arthur Sullivan, and Professor Max Müller translated the second verse of 'God Save the Queen' into Sanskrit. Not everyone was impressed by diamonds. 'The excitement incidental to diamond fields and other speculative undertakings', the official report stated, 'no doubt tends to the neglect of purely agricultural and horticultural pursuits.'

An increasing element of diversion, even of escape, was common to most late-nineteenth-century exhibitions. It had always been there – even in 1851, where there were as many sideshows in London as there were stalls – but it had usually been subordinated to economics if not to science. Nor did it appeal greatly to those businessmen (and journalists) who feared that with every successful new foreign exhibition the supremacy that Britain had held in 1851 was being steadily lost. For them foreign exhibitions increasingly seemed to be providing warnings. They were heard already at the time of the Paris Exhibition of 1867: by 1889, James Burnley in his *The Romance of British Industry* chose to begin his study with the words 'industry and romance have long been regarded in the popular mind as a "thing apart", or at all costs, as having their kinship only in a remote past.' How long ago, it might have been asked, was 1851?

# V

By 1900 two other countries were 'forging ahead' faster than Britain – Germany, which in 1851 had undergone no industrial transformation, but after 1870, now united, was industrializing rapidly, and the United States, which after its Civil War ended was able to develop its huge resources on a continental scale. There were few international exhibitions in Germany: indeed, for reasons outside the scope of this book, Germany does not figure directly in *The Anthropology of World's Fairs*, edited by Burton Benedict in 1983, although the King of Prussia and Bismarck had attended the Paris Exhibition of 1867 and German exhibits were prominent at most international exhibitions. Perhaps Germans were less interested in arranging 'the rituals of competition' than in actually competing in events arranged by others: and certainly what rituals they followed at home were military rather than economic. The United States, by contrast, with great economic and social *élan*, played a leading part in the exhibition sequence, and Benedict's book, the only one of its kind, was written there: it has particular reference to the Panama Pacific International Exposition held at San Francisco in 1915, but it looks back far into the nineteenth century.

After New York in 1853 came many smaller American exhibitions during the late-Victorian years, like the Cotton Centennial Exhibition staged at New Orleans in 1884/5. By far the most interesting and important landmarks in the nineteenth-century exhibition sequence, however, were the Philadelphia Exhibition of 1876, celebrating in 236 acres of parkland the centenary of American independence, and the world's Columbian Exhibition in Chicago in 1893, celebrating, a little late, the fourth centenary of Columbus's discovery of America. Both were well attended and extremely well-documented and photographed; both created imposing buildings, some of them to survive; both displayed a plethora of things, new and old; both introduced new systems of transportation; both had circuses and theatricals, ice cream and soda; both generated new activities and institutions for the future; both have had their historians.

A selection of the 1876 exhibits is still on display – in Washington, if not in Philadelphia. They were carried to the Smithsonian Institute in seventy-eight wagons after the closing of the Philadelphia Exhibition, which had been ceremonially opened by President Grant and the Emperor of Brazil on May 10th. When Grant had signed the legal documents making possible the Exhibition (in face of substantial opposition in Congress, which had twice refused subsidies and only offered one after Japan had contributed $600,000), he had used a pen made from the quill of an American eagle. There was less of a flourish in his final speech, which was felt to be far too short.

One young visitor to the 1876 Exhibition, George Eastman, who was to pioneer photography, was determined to see for himself everything which had been submitted by almost 14,000 exhibitors. 'I intend to traverse every aisle', he wrote. 'The ingenuity that exhibitors have displayed in arranging such things as tacks, cables, soap, hardware, needles, threads, pipe and all such apparently uninteresting articles is something marvellous – and they command the attention of the observer even against his will.' There were, of course, many things which at once captured the imagination and the will. There was also a Photography Hall, the first building ever designed specifically for this purpose.

Prominent in the Machinery Hall was a great Corlis steam engine with a 56-ton flywheel which revolved without noise: the twenty steam boilers were in a different building. The engine, a thing of beauty in itself even if for the *Scientific American* it had 'not many points of actual novelty', provided power for all the other machines on display. Less prominent was a Brayton internal combustion engine which used crude petroleum: ironically it was designed by an Englishman living in Boston. There was also a giant organ which provided music, and it was musical metaphor to which one of the foreign Commissioners resorted when he wrote that 'the numerous separate exhibits harmonize with the principal halls [there were no less than 15 national halls] like movements of a mighty fugue in which every voice intones the melody anew.'

The system of classification of the Paris Exhibition of 1867 was followed at Philadelphia in 1876. Indeed, one of the Members of the Centennial Commission had been present both at Paris in 1867 and Vienna in 1873. Not surprisingly, there were many European echoes, and one genuinely new piece of European music, a ten-minute Wagner march to supplement Beethoven's sixth symphony and Handel's *Hallellujah Chorus*. There was American music, too, including a very American Sousa rendering of Offenbach, the composer closest to the spirit of nineteenth-century exhibitions; a *Centennial Hymn* with words by Whittier; and a cantata with music by Dudley Buck – *The Centennial Meditation of Columbia*. None of the music escaped criticism. Nor did the awards, although *The Times* in London acknowledged that 'the products of the industry of the United States surpassed our own, more often than could be explained by the fact that the exhibition was held in Philadelphia: 'they revealed the application of more brains than we always have at our command.'

There was only one level of award, accompanied by a written report and a bronze medal, and over 13,000 awards were presented. They went to makers of many different kinds of things, among them a typewriter, a telephone, a sewing machine, three internal combustion engines – and a gas meter. There was even a statue in the grounds of the inventor of the lock-stitch sewing machine, Elias Howe, while Alexander Graham Bell, inventor of the telephone, himself attended the exhibition for one day and demonstrated three of his devices before a committee of judges headed by the Secretary of the Smithsonian. One other innovator was not impressed by the system of classification. George Pullman found that his exhibits, including a gold and silver model of a railway sleeping car, were displayed not together but in several different sections.

In 1893 at Chicago, which had been suggested as an ideal site for a Columbian exhibition eight years before, there were even more articles on display and you could visit Pullman's model community. The huge exhibition spaces, planned by America's most famous landscape artist, Frederick Law Olmsted, were designed to make the visitor feel, as the President of the Exhibition put it, that he was present in Athens 'during the age of Pericles', and Charles B. Attwood's 'Palace of Fine Arts' was declared the 'greatest achievement since the Parthenon'. Daniel H. Burnham supervised the architects, sculptors and painters, and the monumental *beaux-arts* buildings associated with him were officially described in rather less ambitious language as 'neo-classical, Florentine'. For the innovatory American architect Lewis Sullivan, such judgements merely demonstrated how 'architecture had died in the land of the free and brave', a land declaiming democracy; inventiveness; unique, daring enterprise; and progress. 'Thus ever works the pallid academic mind', he went on, 'denying the real, exalting the fictitious and false'. There was as much argument in Chicago in 1893, therefore, as there had been in London in 1851.

Most of the objects in the 'White City' Exhibition were 'real' enough, however, and Sullivan himself with his partner designed one remarkable building, that devoted to Transportation: it had a magnificent 'neo-Byzantine' gold and silver arched portal, built at 'prodigious expense', and it was described in *The Dream City: A Portfolio of Photographs* (1893) as 'Wagnerian' in its polychrome 'effects'. Another unusual building designed by a Chicago architect, Henry Ives Cobb, depicted in its sculptures 'all the creatures of river and sea'. Separate buildings were devoted to leather (Napoleon's riding boots were displayed there), to mines and mining, to electricity, and to the Singer Sewing Machine Company.

Between the buildings there was a narrow gauge railway with an elevated section, and there was also a gigantic revolving Ferris wheel, 250 feet in diameter, carrying 1,440 people around every ten minutes in thirty-six 'gondolas', as big as small railway cars.

The dome of the Administration Building was exceeded in size only by that of St Peter's in Rome – and the Vienna Dome of 1893 – and in keeping with the style was a 75-foot high statue of 'The Republic' by Daniel French, holding in its right hand the pike of the Revolution and wearing on its head a Liberty cap, at the outer end of what Olmsted called the 'great basin'. 'The feet of the goddess (of 'The Republic')', wrote one French writer, 'are bathed by the tranquil waters of the great basin'. At night the illumination was stunning: 93,000 incandescent lights represented three times the electrical power then used in the entire city of Chicago.

Both in Philadelphia and in Chicago people received attention as well as things. At Philadelphia there were ten 'classes' of exhibits devoted to the 'Physical, Social and Moral Condition of Man' and a Women's Pavilion, 'erected by money raised through the exertions of women of the United States [by then almost 20 per cent of the American labour force] and devoted exclusively to the results of women's labour.' Even the steam engine in this Pavilion, which powered six looms and a printing press, was worked by a woman engineer. The President was a great-granddaughter of Benjamin Franklin.

A similar pavilion at Chicago was three times as large: the last nail, a golden one, was presented 'by the ladies of Montana' and was driven in by a hammer from 'the ladies of Nebraska'. 'It will be shown', the organizers of the Pavilion stated, 'that among all primitive peoples, women were the originators of most of the industrial arts,' and that it was not until these arts became 'lucrative' that they were 'appropriated by men, and women pushed aside'. Thirty-one special sessions were devoted to a congress on 'Women's Progress'. Mrs Haweis was one of the enthusiastic participants.

'Woman's Progress' was only one of the messages of 1893. 'We know the bringing together of men is more than the bringing together of things', one speaker put it. 'In these contacts are formed the circuits which constitute the currents of progress'. Yet sessions on labour demonstrated how limited that progress still was in a city where large numbers of unemployed were tramping the streets and where in August a mass labour demonstration gathered together 25,000 people on the lake front. For once there was more peace on the religious front as a 'World Parliament of Religions' was held. 'We are come, not as Baptists and Buddhists, Catholics and Confucians, Parsees and Presbyterians, Methodists and Muslims', the Chairman of the Planning Committee declared in his opening address, but 'under the banner of love, fellowship, brotherhood'. W. T. Stead, who reported the Conference, felt that one person was missing. His book *If Christ Came to Chicago* was produced, with Stead's usual sense of timing, in Exhibition Year.

The potential of exhibition conferences had been appreciated in Paris in 1878, where an air-conditioned hall was built for symposia on subjects as different as 'the unification of measures', 'mental medicine' and 'the protection of literary property'; Victor Hugo, who in 1867 had produced in exile a manifesto 'To the People of Europe' at the previous exhibition, presided over the last of these. Two years earlier, the President of the Centennial Exhibition in Philadelphia had told his large audience at the closing session in November 1876 that 'the Exhibition has been a great educator'. Now in Chicago in 1893 Stead did not hesitate to speak of a 'new Divine impulse'. A Brahmin visitor spoke of 'universal bliss'.

Of the many different impulses behind the different late-nineteenth century exhibitions few were, in fact, divine. Business drive was one impulse: Ferris made a fortune from his Wheel, which was subsequently sold to Pullman to power his machinery. Rivalry was another: the Manufacturing and Liberal Arts Building at Chicago had a central span which was deliberately designed to be seven feet greater than that at the 1889 Paris Exhibition. National pride was a third impulse: 'we had a nation to show', General Hawley explained after 1876. A fourth impulse was taste: 'as wealth and European travel have increased', Professor Walter Smith claimed in Philadelphia, 'a taste for the skilled handiwork of foreign craftsmen has been rapidly developing among our people, and the desire to become the possessors of elegant objects to make the home attractive has amounted almost to a passion'.

There was always, it seemed, and always would be a place for nature and for art in the grand design, though art could by now transcend nature. The botanical collection in Philadelphia's Horticultural Hall was a favourite *rendezvous*, and in Chicago it was entirely appropriate that there should be a Live-Stock Building. Yet in Philadelphia the giant hand of Bartholdi's 'Statue of Liberty', exhibited there to raise funds to complete the whole statue, dwarfed any human hand (the head was to be displayed at the Paris Exhibition of 1878) and French's gilded statue of 'The Republic' was hailed as 'the best colossal effigy' ever created on the grounds that 'the eye could never guide the sculptor who made this figure'. Nor, it might be added, could the mouth or stomach have coped with a fifty-foot obelisk of bottled olive oil from Santa Barbara or a thirty-two foot tower of oranges from Los Angeles. The Live-Stock Building itself was situated next to a Roman-style Agriculture Building which had been designed far from the country by architects in New York.

The main impulse on which the organizers of the American exhibitions depended was curiosity, curiosity about the strange as well as about the new – or the very old. Many 'oddities' could be found inside and outside each exhibition. At Philadelphia, hailed as 'the acme of progress', you could see, for example, outside the Exhibition a five-legged cow and inside the Exhibition a bust in butter of a beautiful young girl presented by a woman exhibitor from Arkansas: the artist happily produced another such bust on the spot in one-and-a-quarter hours before the exhibition closed. At Chicago – on the Midway (so named for the first time) – you could view Algerian, Dahomey, Javanese and Lapland villages, not to speak of an Irish market town, a Bedouin camp, a Persian harem and a whole street from Cairo, complete with (highly controversial) belly-dancing. (There had been 'scorpion swallowers' at Paris in 1889.)

Nevertheless, curiosity was not all, and an attempt was made both in Philadelphia and in Chicago to take 'ethnology' more seriously. At Philadelphia there was a large display of American Indian artefacts, and both there and at Chicago there was a separate anthropological building. Even the odd animals were taken seriously. At Philadelphia there were 'learned pigs' and 'educated horses' that could count.

The seriousness – and learning – of the judges (as they were now called) at the Centennial Exhibition was such that their reports, like those of the Paris Exhibition of 1867, are essential reading for economic as well as for cultural historians not only of the host country but of Britain. Indeed, they touch on almost all aspects of Victorian things.

Selecting one only out of their general reports as an example – that on Group XXV, 'Instruments of Precision, Research, Experiment, and Illustration including Telegraphy and Music' – we are left with an impression of immense care to get things right – and fair. One of the judges in this Group was the distinguished British scientist, Sir William Thomson, later Lord Kelvin, although he arrived at the exhibition late and left early. The Americans included John Fritz from Bethlehem, home of the great steel works, and H. K. Oliver from Salem. The report was written by an elected Chairman, J. E. Hilgard, who had a gift for generalization. 'The United States possesses an immense territory, almost as large as Europe', he remarked in one of his first sections – on surveying – 'which requires to be surveyed and divided into properties, and where rapidly increasing population is occupying new lands and building new houses and towns. It is not surprising, therefore, that the fabrication of surveying instruments should be a flourishing branch of industry.'

One of the most interesting sections of the report dealt with clocks and watches. In an age when exact time took on a new significance, the manufacture of clocks in the United States, Hilgard noted, had become 'a distinctive branch of our industries': they were 'constructed on a uniform plan, with interchangeable parts made by machinery, and the rivalry of the manufacturers' was 'almost wholly in the direction of cheapness of production'. Indeed, the prices of American brass clocks were so low 'as to open for them a market in every country of the world'. By contrast, the German clockmakers were exhibiting attractive clocks which would remain in demand as toys 'long after they ceased to be sought after for the purposes of marking the hour', while the French clockmakers were exhibiting 'beautiful specimens of ornamental clocks with artificial singing birds'. The Swiss had one electric clock which was taken out of the Group and assigned to the judges dealing with electrical apparatus.

It was in relation to watches, however, that the American achievement seemed most conspicuous in face of strong Swiss competition; and one single company, the American Watch Company of Waltham, Mass., exhibiting for the first time, was by far the largest contributor. Even in relation to precision watches, the judges wrote, the Swiss could no longer 'expect a monopoly', for the American Watch Company had perfected since 1850 what was commonly called 'the American system' on scientific principles: inter-changeability had now become such an important part of the production of 'many American machines' that it was 'barely necessary to allude to the fact'.

Interchangeability lowered costs, but not the least important of its features was that it facilitated repairs and saved the owner of the watch from the 'ignorant manipulations' of untrained repairers. 'It had only one genuine innovatory element as far as processing was concerned, although this was fundamental – the elimination of fusée and chain', and this greatly reduced the size and complexity of the watch.

The Swiss had already learned the lesson, the judges wrote, but the British had not. They were displaying incredible 'tenacity' in still adhering to old notions. The report did not mention the innumerable solid gold watch presentations to long-serving and faithful British servants of industry, but it noted that British watches had long since ceased to be sent abroad 'as in olden times'. 'The conservatism of most of the English watch-makers', Hilgard concluded, 'has resulted in a steady decline of the watch-making industry in Great Britain, and especially for export to other countries.'

The French were not paid much of a compliment either: 'the French watches shown at the exhibition were ostensibly by Paris makers, but an examination – and this was meticulous – showed that they were in most cases of Swiss manufacture'. There was less point in such subterfuge since statistics appended to the report showed the decline in the numbers of Swiss watches imported into the United States in face of a growing American industry.

There were other comments on international competitiveness in the report. In general, both British and German machinery won less praise than American. 'All that Great Britain and Germany have sent,' wrote T. R. Davis in *Harper's Weekly*, 'is insignificant in amount when compared with our own contribution. The superior elegance, aptness and ingenuity of our machinery is observable at a glance.' And Sweden and Belgium were no more spared than Britain and Germany. It was not just Americans who were of this opinion. Thus, from London *The Times* praised 'the mechanical imagination' of the Americans: 'the New Englander mechanizes as an Old Greek sculptured, as the Venetians painted, or the modern Italian sings.' The experience of Chicago in 1893 confirmed the verdict. It also brought what A. M. Schlesinger called 'the westward march' into the picture also, 'the new significance of the interior country in the nation's life'.

Within this changing context Britain seemed an even older and more traditional place than it had been before. At Philadelphia the British pavilion in Tudor style had appealed to some Pennsylvanians: at Chicago 'Victoria House', 'an elegant cottage such as one sees everywhere at the seashore' (a French verdict), was said not to have 'commended itself favourably either to the taste or the pride of the Americans'. It was perhaps symbolic that one of the British paintings on display inside it was Sir Frederick (later on his deathbed, Lord) Leighton's 'The Sluggard'.

# VI

At the Paris Exposition of 1900, 'the great world's fair', which was hailed as '*the* exhibition of the century', the British pavilion, one of 23 official pavilions, was placed on the 'Rue des Nations' between the Hungarian and the Belgian, in a coveted spot by the side of the river. The Americans had to fight hard to secure such a privileged place for themselves.

The pompous-looking American Pavilion was in the style of 1893, that is to say in a derivative *Beaux Arts* style which was used for most of the other buildings: there was 'nothing for sale' inside it, 'no peddlars, no fakers, no nuisances'. The British Pavilion recalled a different heritage: it was a faithful reproduction in stone of the Marquess of Bath's 'old manor house' near Bradford on Avon, complete with ivy, and the *Golden Book of the Exposition* devoted almost as many words to the Bath family's genealogy as to the objects on display inside it. It noted, however, that 'the young architect Edwin Lutyens' had been in charge of its construction, that it incorporated Burne-Jones pictures and tapestries, the latter woven by the Morris firm, and that Queen Victoria had sent portraits of two of her daughters. There was also a bust of the Queen by Onslow Ford.

There was no reference in the *Golden Book* to British industry. Nor at a time when there was considerable European interest in British *art nouveau* and, indeed, in British architecture, was there evidence within the Pavilion itself of any sensitive British response to that interest. Paris had sent 'art objects' to Chicago which heralded *art nouveau*, and there was no shortage of *art nouveau* in the Paris of 1900, not least in the Hungarian and Belgian pavilions adjacent to the British. Yet for British examples of *art nouveau*, which was to be seen in retrospect as a main constituent in what came to be called 'le style 1900', a style that had its origins in the decorative arts, you had to visit Samuel Bing's private pavilion on the Esplanade des Invalides or his shop in the Rue de Provence. The things purchasable there included Walter Cranes, Aubrey Beardsleys and C. R. Mackintoshes along with Emile Gallés, prominent in the exposition itself – there was a touch of Gallé everywhere – and ingeniously fashioned René Laliques. These were the art objects of 1900, very different from Cole's art objects of 1851. Significantly, Bing had started by selling Japanese art.

From one point of view, the Paris Exposition was not *nouveau* but *fin-de-siècle*, a climax rather than a beginning. At the opening ceremony on April 14th President Loubet (the President who was to grant a pardon to Dreyfus) referred to the nineteenth century as 'this noble century', continuing as optimistically as Albert might have done half-a-century earlier that 'soon, perhaps, we shall have completed an important stage in the slow evolution of work towards happiness and of man towards humanity'. Characteristically the orchestra went on to play *The Hymn of Victor Hugo* by Saint-Saëns.

There were hints in the exposition of problems – and of opportunities – to

THE GREAT VICTORIAN COLLECTION

come in the twentieth century. Japan, for example, sent guns as well as art objects. Nations bickered about sites as they were soon to fight about boundaries. The Germans showed a retrospective exhibition of German uniforms. 'The people crowded round the military exhibits', wrote one French pacifist observer. 'They stood spellbound before the plumes and gold lace, the tinsel and uniforms. Poor creatures!' Nonetheless, the rhetoric of 1900 was usually optimistic, and when compared with other exhibitions in the nineteenth-century exhibition sequence the 1900 exposition stands out as the most ambitious of the attempts to display every thing that could possibly be displayed from the intelligible universe of things.

It was clearly becoming almost impossible, however, to classify or to summarize, and there were no fewer than 46 volumes of reports by the juries on the 18 categories (and 120 classes) within which the objects were grouped, while the official French report on the exposition ran to eight volumes. Educational things came first, but you had to be well educated to understand the official catalogue, which ran to 20 volumes. There were some national catalogues also, like the German, bound in muslin, and illustrated in *Jugendstil* fashion: they were published in German, English and French.

There was more popular reading, however, and you could turn to *Le Livre d'Or de l'Exposition de 1900*, massive successor (in two volumes) to a similar volume for the exposition of 1889, or more immediately to the pages of the enthusiastic Henri Gautier's bimonthly *l'Exposition Universelle 1900*. *Le Livre d'Or* of 1889 had pointed out that the colour of that exposition had been blue: in 1900 there were many colours, from plain red and yellow paint on the Swedish pavilion to gold itself. There were more social colours also. Before describing the new gilded Alexander III bridge, *Le Livre d'Or* offered details of a workers' restaurant, *le restaurant ouvrier*.

It is a difficult task, given the mass of surviving verbal evidence, to picture the whole panoply of things on display in 1900, beginning with steam turbines, dynamos and the innumerable electrical objects, and going on to include bicycles, automobiles and 'theatre-phones'. Display was a general feature in 1900. It ranged from cinema shows (though the equipment broke down) to demonstrations of X-rays. At every point the organizers directed attention to the range of knowledge that lay behind technology and set out to educate the more than 50 million visitors to understand it. The knowledge, however, was by then as hard to grasp as the plethora of objects was confusing. As a writer in *Le Livre d'Or* put it, 'the Exposition, unlike that of 1889, will not leave a clear impression. It abounds in interesting details, but it lacks great lines'. After travelling on the moving sidewalk (Chicago had had one too) the visitor usually left without any sense of the whole. There were too many categories. For the British sociologist Patrick Geddes, who wrote a fascinating article on the exposition in the *Contemporary Review*, 'no man has been actually able to see ... this vast, indeed too vast, labyrinth of labyrinths, this enormous multitude of collections, this museum of museums

... Despite the 350 acres ... twice the space would not have been too much.'

Ideas and their communication could be confusing also in 1900, as was demonstrated at the conferences held in association with the exposition on publishing, on copyright, on libraries, on medicine (the biggest), and on the care of the handicapped. Meanwhile, one especially perceptive solitary visitor, the American historian Henry Adams, who spent hours, in his own words, 'haunting' the exposition, described himself as 'aching to absorb knowledge and helpless to find it'.

From what he saw – and he compared what he saw with what he had seen at Chicago in 1893 – the twentieth century, an age which would 'call electricity its god', was not going to be a 'noble century': 'the fellow who gets to 1930 will wish he hadn't'. There was no trace of President Loubet's message in his thinking. While Adams turned to prophecy, however, the organizers remained content with allegory. Indeed, it was within an allegorical rather than a chronological framework that many of them related the present to the future and to the past – 'Inspiration guided by Knowledge', 'Immortality conquering Time', 'Harmony destroying Discord'. The American pavilion, which paid no attention to Adams's Virgins and Dynamos, was not exceptional in its approach when it displayed at its entrance a sculptured group of naked males and females restraining four wild horses pulling 'a Chariot of Progress in which appeared the Goddess of Liberty'. *Art nouveau* was not allegorical, of course, yet in most of its manifestations it was self-consciously non-historical. Chronology was out of fashion.

To some critics the strong sense of 'pleasure', so evident in 1900, constituted a kind of worship of the present, and the opulent art on display seemed to have about it a touch of the decadent. 'The Republic is enjoying itself', wrote *l'Aurore*. 'There are Chinese lanterns, dances, and brass bands everywhere. The Republic amuses itself as it dies.' The best-named pavilion of all for such critics was the Palace of Illusions. Theirs was a very different mood from social critics of England's Crystal Palace in 1851 or of France's Eiffel Tower in 1889. Meanwhile, leaders of the Republic, facing political crisis, made the most of the *attractions* of the exposition: they included a *Grand Guignol*; Sarah Bernhard performing in *l'Aiglou* a performance that could be picked up by 'theatre-phone'; and a Japanese artist, 'an Asian Sarah Bernhard, bringing Japanese prints to life'.

It is true that some of the attractions failed to make money – and that there was a small loss on the exposition as a whole – and it is true also that those of them which incorporated an educational element were at least as successful as the rest. A drop of Seine water magnified a thousand times was described by one observer as a terrifying sight, while a stroll in a reconstructed Andalusian village at the time of the Moors or in *vieux Paris* could bring back selected aspects of the past, particularly if you found actors dressed in historical costumes strolling beside you. For Paul Morand, who was terrified by the magnified drop of water, a 'new and ephemeral City of Paris had been created in the midst of late nineteenth-century Paris', a Paris 'in fancy dress'.

When all the arguments had been stilled, and when all the electric lights had gone out, much was, in fact, left to survive in a Republic which itself was to survive long into the twentieth century. A post-1900 complex, more grandiose than the South Kensington complex, created out of the 1851 surplus, included the Grand Palais and the Petit Palais, which were to remain as galleries and museums, and the Alexander III bridge over the Seine. In time 'Le Style 1900' could come back into fashion too. In a little booklet with that title published in Paris by Marabout Flash in, of all years, 1968, one of the last sentences was headed 'Dans votre living, l'angle 1900'.

It is revealing to compare this booklet with the 1900 catalogue called 'A Consumer's Guide' which was distributed by the American mail order business Sears Roebuck and which was reprinted 'in miniature' in 1970. Sears Roebuck had begun by selling watches and had not issued a first full catalogue until 1891: in 1900 they seemed, like Harrods in London, to be selling nearly everything. They divided their goods into 18 'departments', beginning with drugs and ending with baby carriages. The items included an ice box and a tombstone. Unlike the great Paris department stores of 1900, *Printemps* and *Bon Marché*, which had their own pavilions on the left bank of the river, Sears Roebucks' first word to their readers was 'Now we can undersell all other concerns.' At the end of a half-century of exhibitions they were confidently offering something more – and less – than the various versions of the great Victorian collection.

# 3
# The Philosophy of the Eye: Spectacles, Cameras and the New Vision

Spectacles are incontestably the most universally useful gift which optical science has conferred on mankind .... It is remarkable also, that, unlike most other productions of art and science, cost can add nothing to their perfection.

DIONYSIUS LARDNER, *The Museum of Science and Art*, 1855

You cannot say you have thoroughly seen anything until you have got a photograph of it.

EMILE ZOLA, interview of 1901 in *Photo-miniature*

Photographs will give you nothing you do not work for.

JOHN RUSKIN, *Lectures on Art*, 1870

These things, these things were here and but the beholder Wanting ...

GERARD MANLEY HOPKINS,
'Hurrahing for the Harvest', 1877

# I

When 'the learned and philosophic' Dr Whewell delivered a lecture in 1851 for the Council of the Society of Arts on 'the general bearing of the Great Exhibition on the progress of Art and Science', he claimed simply that he was 'representing the views of an unconnected spectator of the great spectacle.'

Much in the nineteenth century, culminating in Paris, 1900, had the sense of a 'great spectacle', particularly for the curious and entranced eye. Moreover, although Whewell himself went on to refer to the exhibition as 'great and grand drama', it was not just a 'tournament of industry' but a dream drama with images, objects and music of the kind conjured up by Offenbach and later analysed by Benjamin, 'a big peep show'. There was far more lavish theatrical spectacle during the 1860s than ever before, and the 'spectacular', like the 'sensational', was even more lavish a generation later during the 1890s.

Coincidentally, however, the word 'spectacles' in the plural was applied increasingly during the nineteenth century not to 'great and grand drama' but to a category of 'common things'. They might be popularly known as 'glasses', and successive editors of the *Encyclopaedia Britannica* might consistently refer readers interested in them to an article called 'eye glasses', which changed with the advancement of knowledge, but inside and outside exhibitions they usually figured as 'spectacles'. Indeed, it was under the general label 'common things' that the Reverend Dionysius Lardner classified 'spectacles worn on the nose' in his *Museum of Science and Art* published four years after the Great Exhibition.

'More wonderful [optical] instruments abound', Gardner went on, describing as marvels 'philosophical instruments' like microscopes and telescopes. Spectacles, however, while both useful and ubiquitous, were unmarvellous. There were too many of them, and 'in the palace of the monarch and in the cottage of the peasant' their 'beneficent influence' was equally diffused. Gardner said nothing of monocles or of lorgnettes or of *pince-nez*, of 'spy-glasses' or 'quizzing glasses' (with mirrors, not magnifying properties) and of 'opera glasses' or of 'captain's glasses' worn at sea. Nor, of course, did he mention 'goggles', not a new Victorian word, but a word which was given far wider currency after cyclists – and later motorists – demanded them during the last decades of the century.

Gardner left photography for a different section of his museum. Cameras in his time were certainly not 'common things'. Indeed, looking back from the vantage point of 1902, pioneers in their use could be called by a Japanese-German writer 'those valiant knights of Daguerre'. And although the numbers of all cameras in use increased dramatically particularly after the first Kodak camera was placed on the market in 1888 – 'You press the button, we do the rest' – the next great development, photographing the moving image, was still deemed 'marvellous', and the showman Georges

Meliès, born in 1861, was known as 'marvellous Meliès.' The cinema, unlike spectacles, had its origins in a universe of toys, pastimes and magic.

Accounts of nineteenth-century progress that were published near the end of Queen Victoria's reign took spectacles,though not cameras – nor for that matter glass – for granted. A. R. Wallace, for example, in his *The Wonderful Century* (1898) did not mention them either in his list of nineteenth-century inventions – they did not fall into this group – nor in the far shorter list of earlier inventions which he drew up for purposes of comparison. Yet he devoted a whole chapter to photography, 'new marvel of a marvellous age' – with a sub-title 'new applications of light' – and his own photograph which appeared opposite the frontispiece of his book showed him wearing steel-rimmed spectacles. Wallace left out from his list the opthalmoscope also, an instrument for examining the inner structure of the eye, although one of the best-known of nineteenth-century inventors, Charles Babbage, designed one in 1847. It is fair to add that Wallace also left out Babbage's remarkable 'calculating machine', the ancestor of the computer. (See page 409.)

Much the most interesting article on spectacles to appear in Victorian England was published in *Fraser's Magazine* in December 1876. It was written by Henry Hengist Horne, who, while in his late thirties, had collaborated, a generation earlier, with the young poet Elizabeth Barrett Browning. While for Horne the microscope was ' wonder-showing' and the telescope was 'sublime', 'the rich second sight of modern man' was 'a good pair of spectacles'. They were at once 'the rejuvenescence of the eye, the preservative of that most important organ, the means of making darkness visible or of turning night into clear-faced day'; and when the eyes were 'young in years, but defective in power, the optical magic of spectacles' so accommodated 'discrepancies'that their lenses 'brought the world of vision into a proper focus and put eccentric nature to rights.'

In a late-twentieth century age, when two out of five people in the population wear 'glasses' – by now the most familiar contemporary term for spectacles – it is difficult to conceive of a time when they were not available for more than a tiny fraction of the population. Indeed, they are worn in the late-twentieth century not through choice, but by what is thought of as necessity; and they are worn, as individually prescribed, by people of every social class. Yet Carlyle's father, writing to thank his son for a gift of silver spectacles, told Thomas that 'a pair of silver spectacles is a thing I have often looked at and thought of, but never could call any of them my own before', and even in 1876 Horne could write that he had recently secured a pair of spectacles with 'different glass for each eye' as if this were a novelty. He was testing them, and the result would be known 'only after I have worn the spectacles some time'. Horne generalized freely that most classes in the community did not need to wear glasses. With the exception of engravers, 'who destroyed their sight over copper and steel', jewellers and 'those artisans and mechanics whose peculiar work demands a constant, and therefore, injurious strain (particularly when it is night work) upon the eyes', Horne wrote, 'it will be found that near-sightedness is extremely rare among operatives; while among the great mass of outdoor labourers, and the whole of the agricultural class, such a thing is scarcely known.'

Direct evidence from 'operatives' themselves is limited, although in the United States the *Atlantic Monthly* noted in 1893 that 'ordinary people are in the habit of regarding with some misgivings the constantly increasing use of spectacles' and when school inspections of eyesight began to be made in the early twentieth century only a minority in many cases were deemed to have 'normal sight'. One militant North Eastern coal-miner, Edward A. Rayner, who published his interesting study *The Martyrdom of the Mine* in 1898, discussed the subject of eyesight with particular interest because when he was a boy he had an accident to his right eye in a fire and thereafter was forced to face 'horrible sufferings and dangers . . . through defective sight in and out of the mine.' It was not until 1907, however, that W. M. Beaumont published a book on *Injuries of the Eyes of the Employed and the Workmen's Compensation Act*. Even without accidents miners were prone to nystagmus, not identified until the 1860s. The chief symptom and physical signs of this was a rotary oscillation of the eyeballs which prevented the miner from 'accurately fixing anything towards which his vision is directed.' It might involve 'photophobic' fear of the light.

There is ample direct evidence from politicians, poets and artists. Robert Lowe was an albino, and little could be done for his eyes. The aged Gladstone suffered as much as Queen Victoria herself from what he called 'increasing blindness'. During the 1890s the Queen could not find spectacles to suit her – she suffered from cataracts too – and her secretary had to use blacker and blacker ink. Already years before, when Tennyson saw the Queen in 1883, they had agreed about the 'darkened' state of the world. Neither was in any doubt that seeing or not-seeing and feeling were closely related. Nor was Richard Redgrave, almost blind in the latter years of his life, or Gladstone's Boswell, Lionel Tollemache, who stated simply in his *Who's Who* entry under 'recreations' – 'debarred by extreme near-sightedness from ordinary amusements'.

Horne tried to trace back 'near-sightedness' in old age, extreme or otherwise, to childhood, although he was on no stronger ground when he generalized about the children of the upper and middle classes than he was when he generalized about artisans and mechanics. 'Near-sightedness', he maintained, 'when [sufferers] are not born so [he did not seek to estimate the influence of heredity] is probably in a great measure attributable to a premature straining of the optic nerves by minute and intricate toys, difficult puzzles, too early lessons in reading and writing; also to sleeping in over-heated and unventilated rooms, or bedroom windows throwing a glaring light upon the face, or a want of sufficient out-of-door exercise; and atmospheric influences'.

Much the same kind of 'reasoning' was employed in Victorian warnings about masturbation. Nor was there anything distinctive in Horne's way of presenting the case for control of children. Nearly a quarter of a century after Horne, *Cassell's Family Magazine* (1889) was telling its readers, 'young and old', to 'sit erect in your chair when reading, and as erect when writing as possible. If you bend downwards, you not only gorge the eyes with blood, but the brain as well, and both suffer.' The same warning applied to users of the microscope.

'Want of bodily exercise' also tended to age the eyes. The writer – 'A Family Doctor' – went on, 'So, too, do indigestion, however caused, intemperance in anything, whether in eating, drinking, working, or thinking, a disposition to the formation of adipose tissue, and neglect of the skin'. It seemed an anti-climax to add that 'of course, these are only a few of the causes of early dimness of sight and senile long-sightedness.' The writer offered special advice to readers and to authors. 'Do not read much in a railway carriage. I myself always do, however, only in good light, and I invariably carry a good reading lamp to hook on behind me.' He also selected the kind of paper he used scientifically. 'Authors should have *black-ruled* paper instead of blue'.

Like most writers in magazines, Horne, who admitted that he was near-sighted, was prepared to draw on his own experience. Indeed, he presented an autobiography of seeing. As a boy, he recalled, he had not understood his complaint, even when 'objects on the opposite side of a street which other boys appeared to see clearly I could see only mistily'. Yet while at Sandhurst he had actually won a medal from the Society of Arts for a copy of an etching by Rembrandt. Unfortunately, he went on, despite this and other successes, he continued to strain his eyes 'at scenes on the stage, girls' faces over the way, picture galleries etc.' and this eventually led him to an optician from whom he bought 'a handsome single glass', unfortunately 'of the wrong focus'. Having speedily discarded it, he managed without any glass for twenty years until he found that 'the second or smaller type of newspaper could only be deciphered with an effort'. More specifically, he found that he was incapable of reading easily the copy of the third edition of 'a battered, ragged and otherwise unsaleable book' published in 1816, which he bought for 6d at a second-hand bookshop in Marylebone High Street.

The title of the book was providential, if protracted – *The Art of Preserving the Sight Unimpaired to an Extreme Old Age; and of Re-establishing and Strengthening it when it becomes Weak: with Instructions how to proceed in Accidental Cases which do not require the Assistance of Professional Men, and the Mode of Treatment proper for the Eyes during and immediately after Small Pox: to which are added Observations on the Inconveniences and Dangers arising from the Use of COMMON SPECTACLES &c &c, by an Experienced Oculist.* For Horne, in retrospect, this battered book seemed 'one of the best books of the kind ... ever published in England or elsewhere.'

As he recalled its contents, Horne revealed that many of his earlier ideas about sight and spectacles, were, in fact, like so many ideas concerning health in Victorian times, pre-Victorian and that they had been derived from sources like the 'Experienced Oculist' who proved to be a 'kind, excellently benevolent' man. It was he, for example, who had warned about the dangers of 'the common practice' of suddenly drawing back curtains and raising blinds on first getting out of bed, who had suggested that bedroom curtains should not be of 'very red or other bright colours' but of a 'sober hue', advice to be repeated in *Cassell's Family Magazine*, and who had advised the use of wax and never of tallow candles. 'Never,' he urged, 'hold a book or other writing behind the candle.' It was he, too, who made Horne feel that he had spent too much time studying as a child and that one of the silliest practices at Sandhurst had been that of locking up insubordinate cadets in a 'black hole' where they had to grope about like men who were blind.

Horne learned about two more topics from the book – first about 'squinting' and second about the differences between the eyes of 'boys and girls'. 'It appears that we all, as babies, have, more or less, a tendency to squinting', a point made not only by the 'Experienced Oculist' but by Buffon and Dr Priestley. Nurses – and relatives – were told, therefore, to be sure to position babies in their cradles in such a way that both eyes were treated 'in the same way in relation to external light' and not to place at one side of the cradle any 'highly polished object of plate, brass or cut glass.'

As for gender, it was not only that boys were commonly more near-sighted than girls because they were kept too long each day doing work that taxed the eyes – he knew that already – but that girls at school, despite being expected to indulge in 'the nonsense of fancy needlework', were 'vigilantly watched when they were "on parade" lest they use their eyes by looking about them'. It was a subsequent misfortune, of course, that when they were a little older they were unwilling to wear spectacles 'or even simple eye-glasses' for reasons of beauty. Horne himself recalled that he had known a young lady in Canada, 'very handsome and well educated', who refused ever to wear glasses even though she was so near-sighted that 'she often could not find her partner in the movements of a quadrille'.

That boys might suffer as much as girls – though in a different way – is proved by the experience of Rudyard Kipling, who was the only schoolboy in his school to wear glasses: glasses with pebble lenses framed in dark blue steel. The other boys called him 'the Beetle', a nickname later changed to Giglampo, a word used by the odd-job man, and shortened later to 'Gigs' or 'Giggers', and his form master, according to one of Kipling's contemporaries, was equally sarcastic: he disliked confronting Kipling's 'four eyes'.

There were few people who were prepared to believe, as the author of the *Atlantic Monthly* article of 1893 believed, that a more general use of spectacles by girls and boys was 'the result not of any increase of eye disease or degeneration of vision' but rather of 'the application of physical science to the relief of a widespread very ancient series of troubles arising from defects which have always existed but which are now far more readily tested and remedied.' They must have been embarrassed, however, when the President of the Opthalmological Section of the British Medical Association told a meeting in Manchester that the day would dawn when 'a man who goes about with his eyes naked will be so rare that the sight of him will almost raise a blush'.

Horne was never embarrassed. From perusing the advice of the 'Experienced Oculist' he was led cheerfully if very belatedly, to the 'scientific opticians' of his own day and to the purchase of a pair of spectacles with different lenses for each eye, to be worn, not all the time, but only when he needed them. He proceeded not by trying on various pairs but by having his eyes examined. Next he began to examine what writers on the eye had had to say. The first modern book which he examined was concerned, however, not with 'common things' but with alarming occurrences. White Cooper's *On Wounds and Injuries of the Eye* (1859) demonstrated that 'the human eye could bear the deepest incisions done with cutting instruments without any serious detriment to the sight'. Cataracts, therefore, *pace* Queen Victoria, were more easily treated than 'squinting'. So, too, were fist blows and 'flying morsels of metal and stone'. From another book by White Cooper, *Near Sight and Impaired Vision* (1847), which seemed to him altogether the best book on the subject, Horne moved on to J. Z. Lawrence and R. C. Moon's *A Handbook of Opthalmic Surgery* (1866) and the American Walter Adler's *The Human Eye* (1866), which argued *inter alia* 'with no small degree of moral courage' that 'smoking affected the eye seriously'.

Every detail of the eye seems to have fascinated Horne, and after briefly mentioning 'astygmatism', considered a curiosity before its prevalence was established by F. C. Donders of Utrecht in 1864, he devoted much of his attention to colour blindness, *achromatopsy* or 'Daltonism': males, he claimed, were nearly ten times more frequently affected by it than females. Sir George Biddell Airy's invention of sphero-cylindrical spectacles in 1825 to deal with his own astigmatism had never been exploited in Britain either by himself or others – although he turned back to the subject in 1846 – and it was left to others outside Britain, notably in Vienna, to develop the practical optics of spectacles rather than of microscopes, telescopes and cameras.

As far as colour blindness was concerned, however, there remained a continuing thread of interest in Britain, as there was also in 'eye strain', with myth playing its part in the story as much as fact. Horne himself, who had written a book on Australia in 1859, described a 'small squatter' near Melbourne who had told him that while his shepherds often suffered from sore eyes, 'no gentleman ever did'. The reason he claimed was that a gentleman often washed his eyes with cold water. 'Those fellows never do.'

Horne's anecdotes were not quite exhausted, one feels, when he turned to his own severely practical advice:

A method of discovering whether spectacles will be a benefit to you is thus given us in his lectures 'On Preservation of Sight' by Dr David Smith. Take a thick card, and pierce a little hole in it, of about the size of an ordinary pin's head. Hold this up towards an object, first to one eye and then to the other, covering the eye not employed. 'If the dimness of sight which exists arises from such a defect of the humour of the eye that normal refraction can be re-established by the use of spectacles of any kind whatever, vision through the aperture ought to be rendered clearer.' By this process, you will also discover if there is a difference in the power of the two eyes.

In choosing glasses, 'the first general rule' for Horne was to remember that 'good glasses ought never to magnify the object very much, but merely to show them to us *clear*, simple and exactly such as they are'. In choosing an optician it was essential never be deceived by 'great names or royal arms: go for the practical, educated man'. And reverting to the point made by Lardner, 'it was a 100 to 1 bet,' Horne stated, that you would suit yourself and he would suit you 'with a pair of steel-framed spectacles for two shillings as well as if you paid sixteen shillings or a guinea.'

Not surprisingly, Horne was at pains to add that he himself was not 'an optician or an oculist in any professional sense' and that he did not 'deal in spectacles', British or American. He had come to admire greatly the skill of professionals, however, including the surgeons who sometimes worked with them and he considered, as they did, that there had been real 'progress'. It was certainly no longer true, as Sir Ashley Cooper had once stated, that 'many a man destroys a hatful of eyes before he becomes an expert operator as a surgeon-scientist'. Indeed, it was now possible to carry out hitherto impossible operations. Meanwhile a healthy balance was slowly being achieved in guidance about the care of the eyes, culminating in Dr Lytton Forbes's statement in 1882 that 'the great point to attain in spectacle-glasses is the happy mean of a maximum of improvement with a minimum of strain on the eye', almost a Benthamite proposition.

It was not until 1880, four years after the publication of Horne's article, that the Opthalmological Society was founded by 'a few gentlemen in London' who had invited 'a large number of the leading Opthalmic Surgeons and others likely to be interested in the three kingdoms'. It built up a library which Horne, who died in 1884, would have envied, and published volumes of transactions, often placed on shelves alongside the *Opthalmic Review* which first appeared in 1882. (The invaluable library of the British College of Opthalmic Opticians was not to be set up until 1901.) Germany and the United States had already led the way in such professional development before 1880, although the Worshipful Company of Spectacle Makers had been in existence in London since 1629. From 1898 onwards, following in the wake of the newly-founded British Optical Association, it organized examinations for opticians. In the words of *The Optician* it was seeking 'to advance the status and knowledge of the optician'.

There were the seeds of institutional rivalries here, yet since it was still possible for anyone to set up as an optician, the good advice given by Horne about how to choose spectacles retained its validity. Reporting in July 1899 that spectacles could be bought for one penny a pair in the open market of one of the large towns in the North of England, *The Optician* ran out of words:

'The mere fact that spectacles can be retailed at 1d. is lamentable ... But that a public exists who will buy such –!'

The exclamation mark suggests that times were changing in the 1890s, but not fast enough. In the seventeenth century Lord Ferrers had written to his half-brother in Ireland asking him to procure two pairs of the best spectacles. 'You know my age', he wrote, 'and therefore want no further directions.' Two hundred years later, as C. S. Flick has reported in his absorbing anthology *A Gross of Green Spectacles* (1951), Lord Buckinghamshire could request Mr Dixey of Bond Street in only slightly more specific language 'to send him down to Sidmouth a pair of spectacles such as he thinks will suit a youth of 16 years of age, who has never worn any, but is so short-sighted as to be obliged to hold his face down close to his plate when he takes his meals'. They were wanted for one of Lord Buckinghamshire's sons.

At least, the mid-Victorian poor, who might buy their spectacles from a cheapjack – Dickens described the process vividly – did not usually have to secure them by post – although the Sears Roebuck Catalogue of 1900 advertised them – and some of the more respectable among them may have read Charles Knight's *The Penny Encyclopaedia*, prepared for the Society for the Diffusion of Useful Knowledge, which warned that the choice of spectacles 'should not, where it is possible to avoid it, be delegated to another'. Even making your own choice on the spot had its problems, of course. As late as the late 1880s in the United States, visitors to an optician, J. C. Bloom has reported, would often be simply asked their age, given boxes with 'appropriate' spectacles mounted in it and asked to choose. The price was between £1 and £30. Such boxes can still be found in New York antique shops.

Between the date of publication of Horne's article and the death of Queen Victoria there was a continuing pressure on both the rich and the poor to buy more carefully. Yet the dictates of political economy continued to influence the demand for spectacles more than *The Optician's* sensitivity to the demands of science. The great change was not to come until after the founding of the National Health Service in 1947, when between 1948 and 1951 nearly 20 million pairs of spectacles were to be supplied: at one point in July 1949 over three million pairs of spectacles requested were outstanding. The strain on production and later on finance – the proportionate share of expenditure on 'eyes' in National Health Service expenditures had risen between 1948 and 1951 from 1.2 per cent to 5.4 per cent – proved at least as great as the strain on eyes.

The idea of the state's being responsible had been slow to develop, and even in the twentieth century was quickly subjected to qualification. Yet as early as 1842 William Kitchner in his book *The Economy of the Eyes* had argued that there should be an institution where poor people could obtain suitable spectacles at cost price or less – 'There could not be a more useful charity'. Of course, charity by its very nature could be odd. Thus, in 1898 the Empire Bible and Spectacle Institution of Tiverton, a voluntary organization, was offering to send out to all parts of the country a 'Philanthropist's Parcel' containing '1 dozen good spectacles, ages assorted [note the mode of classification], 1 dozen cases, 1 dozen Gospel Books and 3 copies of the Gospel in 3 dozen foreign languages, all post paid in wooden cases, for 36 penny stamps to any address in the United Kingdom'.

Sears Roebuck, acting on strictly commercial lines, were more responsible in their catalogue. 'We particularly caution our customers', they began, 'against buying the very cheap grades of spectacles or eye glasses. The lenses of these cheap goods are made of very poor material, and improperly cut, and are almost certain to do untold injury to the eyes.' They went on to print 'type for testing the eyes' – in the miniature form of the republished catalogue this is peculiarly testing – and to give 'instructions for ordering spectacles or eyeglasses'. Yet there were limits to knowledge if not to responsibility. The first question was 'What is your age?' The last was 'Do you desire lenses especially for reading or for distant objects?' 'Gold-filled' spectacles cost $1.90 and were warranted for ten years, and there were 'riding bow' spectacles and 'cable riding spectacles', difficult now to envisage, which were cheaper. There were also bifocals.

## II

In his own article Horne had listed lovingly various kinds of spectacles, and each item in his list demands a gloss. 'There are the ordinary shapes of spectacles', he began, 'rounds, ovals, oblongs and of different sizes, up to the grotesquely large circles worn by the Chinese.' Oval and rectangular lenses had been patented as early as 1797, although the former had been more popular, it had been claimed in 1818, among people 'who want to appear half-blind as is required by fashion.' By contrast, some Victorian opticians recommended 'large and round glasses' which they did not consider 'grotesque': they were to cover 'not only the globe of the eye but also a part of its vicinity.'

Monocles certainly did not have this property, and they figured prominently in cartoons, like that of Lord Dundreary, a character in *Our American Cousin*, who seemed to establish a type which lasted until later in the century (see page 266). Yet not everyone relegated monocles to cartoons. Bismarck was often depicted unsatirically with a monocle attached to a ribbon worn around the neck, while Joseph Chamberlain when being photographed made as much of a point of showing his monocle as he did his orchid.

'There are the half-eye spectacles, the upper half being cut off', Horne went on, 'but these have been superseded by the pantascopic, or far-sighted glasses, the frames of which are so arranged that the lenses are thrown obliquely under or before the eye.' There were also the K-shaped or French spectacles, with no comfortable bridge for the nose, 'which some people prefer and all the rest detest', and 'the double-focus or split spectacles, the lenses in the upper halves being of a weak focus for distant objects and the lower halves of a stronger focus for reading &c.' The latter, he said, had been invented by Benjamin Franklin, although the terms 'bifocal' and 'trifocal' had not been introduced until the 1820s. Horne had once known an old Royal Academician, he added, who wore three pairs of spectacles at the same time, an anecdote corroborated in other sources. Obviously the Academician contrasted sharply with Henry Cole who, doubtless on grounds of vanity, refused to wear his spectacles when he was being photographed.

Finally Horne turned to 'protection glasses' – mentioning 'goggles' and *coquilles* or shell spectacles 'covering the eye as with a neutral-tinted cup' – and 'spectacles for special purposes', such as those which Mr Cooper devised for the Polar and other expeditions 'likely to cause snow blindness'. He did not add, as Pitt-Rivers would have done, that when explorers went on such expeditions they would find that 'the rude skill of the untutored Esquimaux' was expressed in eye shades made in bone or pinewood. They were at one end of an evolutionary scale, it seemed, with 'the gigantic telescopes of a Herschel' at the other.

Horne said little about coloured spectacles. Yet *Good Society*, a book on etiquette published in the previous decade, had recommended 'blue or smoke coloured spectacles' for people with weak sight and had described green spectacles as 'detestable'. Blue spectacles were sometimes called 'conservative spectacles'. The use of sunglasses in hot sunny climates was not mentioned by Horne. Nor was the wearing of 'dark glasses' for effect.

At every Victorian exhibition some of the more unusual kinds of glasses were on display, and it is not surprising that at the Centennial Exhibition in Philadelphia in 1876, the year Horne published his article, Franklin's famous spectacles were recalled with affection. The 30th sub-section of Class 324 at Philadelphia – 'Optical and Thermotic Instruments and Apparatus' – was labelled 'spectacles and eye glasses, field and opera glasses, grapho-scopes and stereoscopes' – with the 31st labelled 'cameras and photographic apparatus', the 32nd microscopes, and the 33rd telescopes. 'Pebble lenses are greatly superior to those of glass', the jurors remarked – in complete agreement with Horne, who complained only that they were more expensive – although they praised the exhibits of the Spectacle Makers' Society of

Paris, 'lenses ground with remarkable precision' and sold 'at extremely moderate prices'.

The British were congratulated in 1876 for their microscopes and telescopes more than for their spectacles, which do not seem to have been on display, although the Dollonds, from whom the firm of Dollond and Aitchison derive, had won medals in 1851 and at exhibitions in Paris and in Sydney. There had not been one British exhibitor of lenses and prisms even in 1851, and America, well ahead in spectacle production by 1876, was even more ahead by 1893. Indeed, one of the few learned historians of spectacles, Professor Moritz von Rohr, mentions that a bias in favour of sophisticated optical devices had 'held back the development of spectacles in Britain in the early nineteenth century'.

Certainly costs were relatively high in early and mid-Victorian London. The cheapest pairs in single-jointed steel frames were selling in the 1830s for 18 pence; and an 1854 price list of Horne, Thornthwaite and Ward of Newgate Street, London, offered pantoscopic spectacles in 'best standard gold and pebbles' for 'older long sight' at £4 4s and 'blue or yellow steel and best glasses' at 10s 6d. For short sight the cheapest glasses cost 7s 6d and the most expensive £4 10s. 'Solid gold spring-open eye glasses with chased gold cases, very handsome' £10 10s. Of course, travelling cheapjacks, with a gift for patter which Dickens felt was faster than even that of gun salesmen, were selling spectacles at a fraction of these prices; and by the end of the century, while the price of the cheapest spectacles had fallen, there was an even wider range of prices than there had been when Dickens wrote. It could be already claimed by 1880 that with improved modes of manufacturing glass 'for all practical purposes glass lenses were quite as good as pebbles and much cheaper'. By 1900 Sears Roebuck were claiming that 'our crystalline lenses are the best in the market'.

Materials may have been better than the quality of service, or so Charles Forshaw, the secretary of the Yorkshire Optical Society, believed. In 1899 he composed appealing verses about an advertisement for a female 'optical assistant' to run a stall selling glasses: she had to have 'a knowledge of sight-testing' and 'good personal character' and was to be paid 21s a week:

She knew little of testing
The optical orb,
Her method was destined
Your cash to absorb.
What with smile so bewitching
And pince-nez so neat,
She brought down the gallants
In crowds at her feet.

Forshaw's 'Spectacle Girl' was selling the frames of the glasses as much as the lenses, and the jurors at Philadelphia in 1876 were already showing an increased interest in the frames of the spectacles they were called upon to judge. It is interesting, however, that they singled out for comment the magic lantern before they turned to spectacles, describing it as 'an almost indispensable part of the apparatus of instruction in nearly every department of human knowledge'.

When they turned to spectacles, they selected for special tribute T. A. Wilson and Company of nearby Reading, Pennsylvania, who unusually made both lenses and frames, and two firms in New York, one of them Bausch and Lomb. 'In the methods of constructing the frames', the jurors said of the former, 'are secured the advantages of simplicity, economy of material, elasticity and strength.' Steel was the only metal used. Again, Horne would have approved of this, since he liked 'blue steel' and objected to 'the injurious dazzle of gold, silver or any shining substance'. Yet one other American manufacturer, recommended by the jurors, used rolled gold and silver, and another shell, rubber and celluloid as well as steel of 'an excellent temper'. There was no reference to horn or tortoiseshell, although these materials were already in use. So, too, were rimless spectacles. Contact lenses had been conceived of in London as early as 1845 by Herschel, and the first versions of them, in glass, along with the name, were introduced in 1887 by Dr A. E. Fich, a Swiss physician. Materials mattered here, however, and it was not until much later in the mid-twentieth century, when plastics had been developed, that they came into more general use.

It was not until the twentieth century, too, that the first major book was published about the form as distinct from the function of eyeglasses, although this was far earlier in the century – 1911. Nonetheless, it would be a mistake to ignore altogether the role of fashion in relation to spectacles in the Victorian years. While as late as 1900 a writer in the *Optical Journal* could generalize that 'wearing spectacles or eyeglasses out of doors is always a disfigurement', wearing certain kinds of eyeglass indoors was thought by some to be an adornment. In Dickens's *Little Dorrit* (1855–7), for example, the worldly Bar carries a double eye glass, young Clarence Barnacle carries a single eye glass, which he does not know how to hold in his eye – 'it kept tumbling out against his waistcoat buttons' – and the enriched Edward Dorrit acquires a single one, which he holds perfectly. Meanwhile, Mrs Mardle, 'moving in Society, knew exactly how to use her glasses in looking at persons of lower rank.'

A reader of *Answers*, one of the new popular magazines of the late-nineteenth century, found different reasons for wearing glasses, particularly during discussions at home or at a debating club. 'While I am fumbling with them I gain several valuable seconds in which to collect my thoughts.' (Compare pipes.) And 'through glasses you can look a man full in the face, when without you would from pure nervousness avoid his glance.'

Conan Doyle's Sherlock Holmes had yet another reason for interesting himself in glasses. He deduces from 'a golden pince-nez with two broken ends of black silk cord dangling from the end of it' first that its wearer had 'a puckered forehead, a peering expression and probably rounded shoulders' and, second, that she had probably been to the optician at least twice during recent months. 'It would be difficult to name any articles', he told Watson, 'which afford a finer field for inference than a pair of glasses, especially so remarkable a pair as these'.

What would Sherlock Holmes have made of the most exotic category of Victorian things relating to the eye – 'artificial eyes'? London was one centre of production, with William Wolford's workrooms exporting artificial eyes throughout the world. Another centre was Birmingham, where a successful firm manufactured for trading purposes artificial eyes 'that portray every disease to which the human eye is liable'. A writer in *Pearson's Magazine* in 1897 surely made the most of the subject. 'Thirty years ago the cheapest eye obtainable cost not less than two guineas, and for the best as much as five guineas was demanded'. Now the price of a 'hospital eye' was 10s 6d and of a 'best eye' two guineas. Wolfords, who were making a hundred eyes a week, found grey eyes most in demand. They had noted too that 'the sclerotic or the white is never the same shade in the eyes of two individuals'. Like opticians, they were more interested in the effects of smoking than most of their contemporaries. In children's eyes the sclerotic was a pale china blue: 'in people from hot countries, and in great smokers' it was dirty yellow.

The author of the article, Diorben Griffith, could not avoid melodramatic literary flourishes. Since visiting the workshop he had been haunted, he said, by 'eyes on whose glittering balls is recorded a life-time of crime; leering, cunning eyes that make me creep; others faded, dim and sometimes pathetic, that speak of unselfish toil and a fixed, stony stare as to those who have passed into a world of eternal silence whose secrets they dare not reveal.'

# III

There were many Victorian writers and artists who had much to say about eyes, spectacles, telescopes, microscopes and cameras, sometimes echoing past sentiments, sometimes contemplating new aspects of perception. 'Never believe anything you hear and only half of what you see' was one Victorian motto which echoed a less pithy ancient Greek reference to 'the modest witness of the eye and the vague report of the ear'. In Henry James's novel *The Bostonians* (1886), for 'heroic' and 'sublime' Miss Birdsey – or so she appeared to Olive – 'the whole moral history of Boston' was 'reflected in her displaced spectacles'.

The remark could not have been made in a previous century, although the then Secretary of the Royal Society of Arts, H. Syer Cuming, quoted 'moral lines' from Shakespeare's *King Lear* in an article on spectacles in 1855. 'Come if it be nothing', Gloster exclaims, 'I shall not need spectacles.' Cuming offered four other Shakespeare quotations concerning spectacles. The drama of spectacles was offered to Victorian audiences at a very different level by the playwright Sydney Grundy, whose comedy *A Pair of Spectacles*, an adaptation from the French, was first performed in 1890. The actor-manager John Hare, who wore and broke the spectacles of the title, was remembered for this role for the rest of his life on the stage.

The play was about seeing as perceiving; and when in the early 1890s Gladstone was being interrogated by Tollemache, he contradicted his interrogator who had described the eye as 'the organ of sight' telling him that 'strictly speaking it is the carrier of sight'. Ruskin would have agreed. 'The eyes of man are of his soul, not of his flesh'. 'You do not see with the lens of the eye. You see *through* that, and by means of that, but you see with the soul of the eye'.

There was bound to be argument in the nineteenth century about different ways of seeing, about what to see and what to choose not to see, about whether what the eye saw was the same as what the camera 'saw' a matter involving the relationship between science and art, and even more fundamental about the relationship between the seen and the unseen, and about 'mechanism' and 'soul'. Horne was naive, therefore, when he claimed that the right spectacles enabled you to see things 'exactly as they are'. That begged all the questions. So, too, across the Channel did Hippolyte Taine when he said 'I want to reproduce things as they are or as they would be even if I did not exist.'

It was appropriate that one of the new books in 1837, the year when Queen Victoria came to the throne, was called *The Philosophy of the Eye*. It was written by Dr John Walker and was sub-titled 'A Familiar Exposition of its Mechanism and of the Phenomena of Vision with a View to the Evidence of Design'. On his opening page Walker described the eye as 'the most beautiful of all the organs of the senses', adding that it was 'likewise the most important and the most valuable'. It may have been a coincidence that Walker, a surgeon, lectured on the eye in the Manchester Royal School of Anatomy and Medicine and carried out operations at the Manchester Eye Institution. What 'evidence of design' could the unassisted eye see in that great city? It was perhaps as well that the Mancunian surgeon John Leigh, Manchester's Medical Officer of Health, insisted that 'the eye fails to appreciate any but large differences.'

When in *Sketches from Boz*, completed in the same year as Walker's treatise, Dickens's Mr Tickle displayed a pair of '*new-invented*' spectacles, which enabled the wearer to 'discern, in very bright colours, objects at a great distance, and rendered him wholly blind to those immediately before him', he told the sceptical President of the Mudfog Association for the Advancement of Everything, that the invention was firmly based on an understanding of 'the principle of the human eye'. Surely, the President could not fail to be aware that 'a large number of most excellent persons and great statesmen

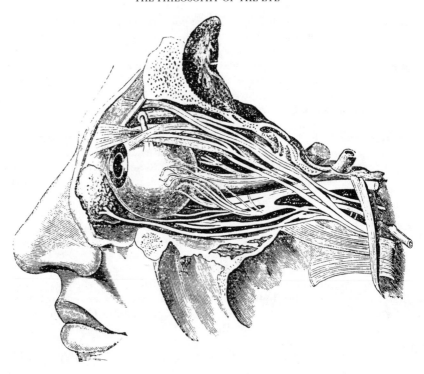

*'The Phenomena of Vision', 1837*

could see, with the naked eye, most marvellous horrors in the West Indian plantations, while they could discover nothing whatever in the interior of Manchester cotton mills'.

The co-founder and first President of the *Opthalmological Society*, William (later in 1884 Sir William) Borman, was a Cheshire man who was a member of the Manchester Philosophical Society, and he had worked not in Manchester but in Birmingham before moving to London's Moorfields Opthalmic Hospital. He was a friend of Florence Nightingale and would have understood just what Dickens meant. In *Pickwick Papers* (1836) Dickens had on one occasion presented Mr Pickwick, 'a philosopher', standing in the main street of an 'illustrious town' and gazing 'with an air of curiosity, not unmixed with interest, on the objects around him'. Yet as the novel proceeded it was impossible to treat Mr Pickwick's eyes as if they were a camera, an object with which he was not acquainted; and the novel describes how through 'perplexity and bewilderment' and much 'confused consciousness', Pickwick discovers what the world is like. At times in his vision everything seems 'restless and troubled; and the people ... crowding and flitting to and fro like shadows in an uneasy dream'.

Such images were to recur frequently in Dickens, with the flittings of objects as well as of people adding to the 'delirium'. That is how *Edwin Drood* begins. Long before, in *Dombey and Son*, when the removal men were taking away the furniture from the bankrupt Mr Dombey's house, which had once seemed so settled and so rich, 'chaotic combinations of furniture' appeared before the house settled into silence. When Mrs Clennam emerged from her confined bed in *Little Dorrit*, she had no time to consider 'the unexpected changes in half-remembered objects and the want of likeness between the controllable pictures her imagination had often drawn and the overwhelming rush of reality'. Dickens himself saw clearly that different people, and indeed the same person, see the same world and the objects in it in different and often disturbing ways at different times. In his Memorandum Book he wrote once about 'representing London – or Paris, or any other great place – in the light of being actually unknown to the people in the story, and only taking the colour of their fears and fancies and opinions'.

Horne knew Dickens, and in his 1876 article about spectacles he told his readers how 'the late Charles Dickens had very peculiar eyes. They took in all objects, within more than a semi-circle, at a single glance; but I never saw him use glasses except on one occasion.' This was on a foggy night when after dinner Dickens had driven Horne home in his American buggy rather than trust groom or coachman. He wore a special pair of spectacles for the journey and achieved 'a good pace' while chatting all the time. Not surprisingly, this led Horne to ask 'what sort of glasses Dickens could have found to effect any clearing in a London fog'. Unfortunately he did not put the question to Dickens himself.

No Victorian writer except one made more of fog metaphors than Dickens or understood more clearly all metaphors of the eye, including spectacle metaphors. The exception was Ruskin, who was as much disturbed by polluted cloud ('The Storm-Cloud') as he was by fog and who deliberately pitted himself against most of the assumptions of his time when he talked and wrote about eyes and eyeglasses and light and colour. J. D. Rosenberg in a fascinating 'portrait of his genius', *The Darkening Years* (1961), has called him 'eye-driven, even photo-erotic'; Elizabeth K. Helsinger in her *Ruskin and the Art of the Beholder* (1982) has emphasized how from his childhood Ruskin was interested in patterns, including books on patterns; and Jay Fellows in a very different book *The Failing Distance* (1975) has been concerned with the autobiographical aspects of Ruskin's seeing, beginning with 'the desire of the eyes', continuing with 'the camera lucida and the optics of intervening space' and 'the moral retina and the optics of attention', and ending – after a journey as difficult as Ruskin's own – with his autobiography *Praeterita*.

All three books abound in relevant Ruskin quotations, some of which seem very close to Dickens, although more usually critics have drawn comparisons between Ruskin and Wordsworth. 'My entire delight was in observing without myself being noticed', Ruskin wrote in *Praeterita*. 'If I could have been invisible, all the better. I was absolutely interested in men and their ways, as I was interested in marmots and chamois, in tomtits and trout.' There are forward links, too, between Ruskin and Proust, who admired Ruskin's approach to places and to things and began by trying to see things through his eyes. The titles of two of the critical studies of Proust reveal the affinities – Howard Moss's *The Magic Lantern of Marcel Proust* (1962) and Roger Shuttock's *Proust's Binoculars* (1964).

'Seeing' for Ruskin was the most basic of all activities. It began for him as a child when he 'stared' at patterns in the carpet or on the bedcovers and at all the objects in his room, and later in his life, for him it was a sign of his own sickness, physical or mental, when his eyes felt 'weak' or 'swimming'. The vistas closed: the vision did not simply darken, it became blurred. Likewise, seeing 'badly' was for Ruskin a collective national affliction. 'Hundreds of people can talk for one who can think, but thousands can think for one who can see' was one of his best-known phrases: for him, 'to see clearly is poetry, prophecy and religion – all in one.'

'In old times', Ruskin wrote – without saying when the 'old times' were – 'it was not thought necessary for human creatures to know either the infinitely little [that, in particular he did not like] nor the infinitely distant; nor either to see, or to feel, by artificial help.' A drop of Seine water under a microscope would have been as abhorrent to him as a drop of Thames water. Yet he knew that the first spectacles were medieval – they figure in a portrait of 1352 – and that the Venice he acclaimed, while still in its Gothic age, was a major centre for the manufacture of optical glass.

Those Victorians who were more interested than Ruskin was in the detail of even 'older times', or in places in the world beyond Venice, liked to trace back the use of spectacles to Pompeii or to the Chinese: they noted also how there were several spectacled faces among the sculptured figures from Henry VII's chapel in Westminster Abbey, later to be placed in the Victoria and Albert Museum. Yet Ruskin was in agreement with most of his contemporaries when he displayed as much of an interest in the eyes of animals and insects as in those of men. 'There are many insects which have a very much larger field of vision than we have', the author of an article on 'chit-chat about eyes' wrote in *Chambers's Journal* in 1891, and Ruskin himself, drawing metaphor out of fact, referred more than once to the 'rattlesnake retina' and 'the deadly cleft in the iris of a rattlesnake's eye'.

Some of the questions Ruskin raised about seeing and knowing had been raised in the seventeenth century, when there were fundamental developments in optics – the first reference to a portable box *camera obscura* dates back to 1657 – and it was Alexander Pope who had asked and answered an important Ruskinian question in his *Essay on Man* (1734):

Why has not man a microscopic eye?
For this plain reason, man is not a fly.

Yet in dealing with specifically nineteenth-century questions Ruskin was always prepared to look back beyond the seventeenth and eighteenth centuries to the middle ages. Magnifying glasses were medieval, and of these Ruskin was prepared to approve. He once told a girl correspondent to use a magnifying glass in looking at crystals, adding 'I send you one for yourself, such as every girl should keep in her waistcoat pocket always handy'. Ruskin concluded, however, by warning her, as Pope might have done, never to use a microscope. 'Learn to use your own two eyes as God made them, to see His works as He made them'.

Spectacles were 'common things', but in the light of such discourse, it is difficult in retrospect to treat them entirely as such. Cameras – and photographs – were obviously far more difficult to dismiss quickly. There are many links between spectacles and cameras. They were often made – and exhibited – by the same manufacturers, and it was opticians who first sold cameras. When Louis Daguerre's invention of his camera became public news in 1839, 'all the opticians' shops' are said to have been 'besieged'. Moreover, there were critics of photography, a word invented by the astronomer Sir John Herschel, who spoke about cameras as trenchantly as Ruskin spoke about microscopes. Thus, one German journalist claimed in 1839 that 'to fix fleeting images is not only impossible ... it is a sacrilege: God had created man in His image, and no human machine can upturn the image of God.' Baudelaire, too, used the word 'sacrilege' in relation to photography, adding for good measure that 'the vile multitude known as Society' was not shocked, but was rushing 'as one Narcissus to contemplate its own trivial image in the metal plate'.

Whatever Ruskin thought of microscopes, telescopes or spectacles – or the relationship between nature and art – he did not hesitate to use a camera himself very early in the history of photography. 'John is going to have some daguerrotypes taken of the churches as long as they are standing', wrote Effie to his parents on their ill-fated voyage in 1849.

In 1854 and 1856 Ruskin produced other daguerrotypes in Switzerland, including one of a glacier, and in the preface to *Examples of the Architecture of Venice* (1851) he wrote that he regretted that 'artists in general do not think it worth their while to perpetuate some of the beautiful effects which the daguerrotype alone can seize.' Ruskin did not claim, however, that the collection of photographs which he assembled represented 'art', since he maintained that 'each great artist conveyed not so much the scene as his own originality of mind.' There was no way of seeing things 'exactly as they are', as Horne believed. Turner alone demonstrated this. Emerson put it more crudely. 'The work of Art, it cannot too often be repeated, appeals to a man's emotional side; it has no wish to add to his knowledge – to his science.'

Many nineteenth-century artists, among them Delacroix and Courbet in France and in England William Powell Frith, were prepared to use photographs – Frith collected them before he painted his famous 'Derby Day' – and although Paul Delaroche when he first saw a daguerrotype is said to have exclaimed dramatically 'From today painting is dead', Delacroix maintained that 'the photograph is a demonstration of the true idea of nature, something of which we otherwise have only the vaguest notions'. It took time to realize that the eye of the camera was itself not an 'impartial eye', whether it was dealing with places or with people, and that, as Gisèle Freund was to put it in her *Photography and Society* (1974), it actually permitted 'every possible distortion of reality': 'the character of the image is determined by the photographer's point of view and the demands of his patrons.'

There was certainly an artistic dimension to the early history of photography, leading back through the silhouette and the miniature, and while some of the first photographers thought of themselves as 'men of science' 'reproducing Nature', as Delacroix hoped that they would, others proclaimed themselves as 'artist photographers'. Some, of course, proclaimed themselves as both. Lady Eastlake, wife of Sir Charles Eastlake, was closer to understanding their role, however, when she wrote in 1855 that the invention of photography was 'neither the province of art, nor description, but of that new form of communication between man and man'. It was made, she felt, for the present age, 'in which the desire for art resides in a small minority, but the craving for cheap, prompt and correct facts resides in the public at large. Photography is a purveyor of such knowledge to the world.' The word 'facts', of course, raised as many philosophical issues as the word 'eye'.

For the historian of Victorian things there is obvious interest in the convergence of science and art. The scientific foundation of photography lay not only in optics but in chemistry, in the first instance the chemistry of silver salts. This was first fully explored during the eighteenth century and early-nineteenth century with Watt, Wedgwood and Humphrey Davy among the British explorers. The relevant science of optics – and the *camera obscura* – was far older. Nonetheless, a Latin verse on 'photography' by Pope was not translated into English until Victorian times, and it was done then on the suggestion of A. R. Russell, author of *The Wonderful Century*, who emphasized that the application of the knowledge of silver salts to the promotion of pictures 'belongs wholly to our time'.

Reversing Pope, Oxford University set the subject of photography – *Sol Pictor* – for the Chancellor's Prize for Latin verse in 1876 when it was won by Francis Paget, a future Bishop of Oxford. It was in Oxford, too, that Lewis Carroll, drawn to photography as early as 1855, took many of his most interesting amateur photographs, at first in a rented studio and later in his rooms at Christ Church. He also on one occasion made the Archbishop of

Canterbury's great house, Lambeth Palace, his photographic headquarters for three weeks. All his photographs were carefully numbered, placed in albums and indexed. One of the most famous of them, that of Alice Liddell, was placed at the end of the *Alice* manuscript now in the British Museum. Eyes figured prominently in the whole philosophy of *Alice*. He had written *Alice in Wonderland*, Carroll stated, so that she could one day 'gather round her other little children, and make their eyes bright and eager'.

No spectacles there, no 'weak and sore eyes', described in the *Girls' Own Paper* in 1880 as a girl's complaint. There was a deep seriousness in all this. Yet Carroll could also see the fun in photography and wrote a delightful parody of Longfellow's *Hiawatha*, 'Hiawatha's Photography', which began

> From his shoulder Hiawatha
> Took the camera of rosewood;
> Made of sliding, folding rosewood . . .

There were cross references to Ruskin: thus, of the son of the sitter, an aesthete, we read:

> He suggested curves of beauty
> Curves pervading all his figure . . .
> He had learned it all from Ruskin,
> (Author of *The Stones of Venice*,
> *Seven Lamps of Architecture*,
> *Modern Painters* and some others);
> And perhaps he had not fully
> Understood his author's meaning.

Clearly the son of the aesthete knew well enough how 'the character of the image is determined by the photographer's point of view' – Gisèle Freund might have added the ambience of the studio and its 'props' – 'and the demands of his patrons'. Hiawatha's patrons – father, son and daughter, were unhappy about the result:

> Really any one would take us
> For the most unpleasant people.

There must have been many Victorians who felt the same.

# IV

The first fixed photographs, 'heliographs' or 'sun drawings', had been made in France by Joseph Nicéphore ('bringer of victory') Niépce during the 1820s, but it was left to his compatriot and from 1825 partner, Louis Daguerre, a born impresario, both to perfect his methods and to publicize them. Details of his photographic processes were released in January 1839, and in August the French government acquired – and immediately renounced – a right to a monopoly. The invention was now 'open' in France, a decision which captured the imagination of the public. Indeed his *Handbook* was translated into eight languages in 1839/40 and appeared in 72 editions. He also dedicated some of his daguerrotypes to famous foreign persons like Metternich. Yet the 'openness' of Daguerre's invention was restricted in one significant way. He had quietly patented it in London five days before the French Government eloquently donated it to the world.

The daguerrotype, employing silver iodide as a light sensitive substance, was a great success both in France and across the Atlantic. Positive pictures on a metal plate, copper coated with silver, could be produced after a minimum exposure of several minutes; soon considerably reduced, as was the size and weight of Daguerre's first huge camera. Meanwhile, in Britain, the only country where Daguerre's patent rights were enforced, a competitive photographic process had been introduced with interesting results. William Henry Fox Talbot, using silver nitrate, had produced fixed photographs, negatives on paper, in 1834, although it was not until after Daguerre had announced his discovery that Talbot announced his. The 'calotype', described as 'a mode of drawing', was patented from the start, and its inventor fought hard and long to keep his monopoly. He needed retail outlets, however, and the first person to advertise his 'new Heliographic Camera' was an optician, Francis West of 83 Fleet Street, who also advertised 'Photogenic Drawing Paper and Fixing Liquid'.

The year 1839 was a remarkable year in London as well as Paris, for Talbot's demonstration of 'photogenic drawing' to 'lovers of science and nature' in the Royal Society was not the only memorable event in August. Sir John Herschel announced in that same month the fixative properties of 'hypo' – sodium thiosulphate – and two months earlier Hippolyte Bayard, a long neglected pioneer of photography had held a photographic exhibition, the first of its kind, in Paris. Bayard refined a technique for making and fixing photographic images on paper, and long after his death he was to achieve another first. His 'Study of Items of Statuary', a direct positive on paper made in 1839, was the earliest photograph to be sold by auction at Sotheby's – in 1984. It fetched £7,150.

During the 1840s the daguerrotype and the calotype processes were compared scientifically and artistically, particularly for their results. The daguerrotype image was deemed 'pinsharp' and 'mirror-like': the calotype image seemed softer. The daguerrotype was a unique object – the technique did not allow for multiple reproduction, and if you wanted more 'copies' you had to have more sittings, as with a miniaturist painter: the calotype could be reproduced by means of paper negatives. Both could be treated as 'art', although the uniqueness of each daguerrotype – and the often handsome case and frame which contained it – gave it a special appeal: so, too, did the propaganda, often sentimental, of 'a mirror with a memory'.

Propaganda, however, was scarcely necessary. An American magazine called the first daguerrotypes 'the most remarkable objects of curiosity and admiration in the arts that we ever beheld', and asked the reader to judge simply on the basis of his own experience. 'Let him suppose himself standing in the middle of Broadway, with a looking-glass held perpendicularly in his hand, in which is reflected all the street, with all that there is in it, for two or three miles, taking in the haziest distance.'

There were hints of the distant future, too, in the early history of the daguerrotype. As early as 1840, a Swiss, Johann Issenig, is said to have discussed a method to colour daguerrotypes with 'chemical powders'. There were many techniques of tinting, some of them very popular, and while colour photography was slow to develop, in 1861 the great physicist James Clerk-Maxwell produced the first true colour photograph which could only be viewed through a projector. The next great invention in three-colour photography was arrived at independently eight years later by Charles Cros and Louis Ducos du Hauron. Experiments continued on both sides of the Atlantic, and were recorded by L-P. Clerc in 1898 in the first history of colour photography.

Victoria and Albert bought their first daguerrotypes early in 1840, and later in the year daguerrotypes of London and of 'figures from the living model' were on sale at Antoine Claudet's shop at 89 High Holborn. Claudet, who had previously sold plain and painted glass and glass shades or domes for 'the Covering and Presentation of Statuettes, Wax Flowers, Alabaster and other Articles of Vertu', held the British Daguerre patent. He soon had a rival, for in March 1841 a businessman from a very different background, Richard Beard, formerly a coal merchant, opened the first professional photographic portrait studio in London on the roof of the Royal Polytechnic Institution: it was sufficiently popular to be caricatured in a Cruikshank woodcut. Beard made much of the fact that 'the Photographic Principle' could be applied not only to 'expressions of countenance', but to 'drapery in elaborate patterns, carved furniture, articles of vertu whether of marble or silver, indeed for every description of still life', and he was careful to stamp all the gilt mounts of his daguerrotypes, well marketed products, with the words 'Beard Patentee'.

The fierce legal struggle which ensued between Beard and Claudet was only one of many such struggles in the early years of photography, as of many other Victorian things. It ended in Beard's bankruptcy in 1850, to be followed three years later in Claudet's appointment as 'Photographer-in-Ordinary to the Queen'. Meanwhile, Talbot's patents caused bitter resentment also until they were partially relaxed in July 1852 following overtures by Sir Charles Eastlake and Lord Rosse, the President of the Royal Society, both of whom appealed directly to Talbot's patriotism – 'Although England continues to take the lead in some branches of art, yet in others the French are unquestionably making more rapid progress than we. It is very desirable that we should not be left behind by the nations of the continent.' Two years later, in 1854, the Talbot patents were completely freed.

In the long run, economics mattered more than science or art or, for that matter, patriotism, in the history of photography, which, as Lady Eastlake recognized, came to a society that was ready for it. This indeed, has been the main French emphasis in André Rouillé's *L'Empire de la Photographie, 1839–1870* (1982) which is sub-titled *photographie et pouvoir bourgeois*. Nor was there anything special about the basic economics. They rested, as did so much of the economics of the Victorian period, on an extension of the market through a lowering of prices both of equipment and of products. Things soon went 'down market', although even in the smart 'age of the daguerrotype', when Paris was driven by *daguerromanie* and New York had hundreds of daguerrotypists, there was already a significant lowering of price. Further improvements went with market extension. Thus, Daguerre's first huge camera costing 400 francs, soon gave way to lighter equipment which by 1841 was costing 250 to 300 francs. During the same period the price of the light-sensitive silver plates was halved.

In the Britain of the mid-1840s a complete daguerrotype outfit, including lens, cost between eight guineas and £26 and hypo cost 8s. a pound, but by 1851 the prices had been halved. Meanwhile, German competition from Voigtländer further reduced the price of the lens and introduced the first completely metal camera. It is remarkable how Peter Voigtländer's so-called 'system' exploited every aspect of the new camera economics, so that in 1862 he was able to sell his 10,000th lens. The United States was to push such economics further during the 1880s: George Eastman, bank clerk turned photographic manufacturer, was born in 1854.

One of the most revealing literary sketches of a daguerrotypist – there were 10,000 of them in America by 1853, among the first of them Samuel Morse, inventor of the Morse code – is to be found in Nathaniel Hawthorne's *The House of Seven Gables* where we are introduced to Clifford, 'artist as well as daguerrotypist', a man of whom 'Hepzibah did not know what to make': he himself said that he was making 'pictures out of sunshine', and when he was accused of presenting 'unamiable' likenesses, he said simply that the reason was that the originals were so. He believed that people should live in new houses and use new things, and he had no use for the 'moss-grown and rotten Past'.

Oddly enough, it is daguerrotypes themselves which now seem to belong to the 'mossy', if not to the rotten, past. Indeed, by the end of the nineteenth century, Hartmann, a pioneer essayist on photography, already conceived of the daguerrotype, whatever its theme, as a quintessentially Victorian thing:

> There it lies in its case among old papers, letters and curios. A frail encasement of wood with black embossed paper. We cannot resist the temptation to open and glance at it. The clasp is loose. What a strange effect this silvery glimmer and mirror-like sheen ... The image of some gentleman in a stick or some lady in a bonnet and puffed sleeves appears like a ghost-like vision.

Hartmann rightly began his evocation not with the picture but with the case, for in the United States in particular, 'Union cases', often ornate, began to be manufactured during the 1850s from various materials – often with engraved relief patterns, with landscapes, or perhaps with a portrait of Daguerre himself: they were to become collectors' items. Yet as far as the content of daguerrotypes themselves was concerned, there was a note of caution in Hartmann's account. 'How truthful they are to nature', he wrote, 'it is difficult to say'. Daguerre himself is represented in the Louvre by an ivory miniature, said, however, to be one of the largest ever made.

There is certainly much to say about calotypes, even those calotypes in which, according to *Punch*, both the style and content had already faded as early as 1849. Some did not fade, and those taken by the painter/photographer David Octavius Hill must be included in any collection of outstanding Victorian things, among them a set of calotypes of the members of the Edinburgh Synod of 1843 which led to the founding of the Free Church of Scotland. It was fortunate that Talbot's patent, which was to be extended to the United States in 1847, did not cover Scotland, and that Hill, who had been commissioned to record the Synod in a monumental painting, already knew enough about photography to make use of it. The painting itself, 'The Signing of the Act of Separation and Deed of Demission', is of little interest: the calotypes of the ministers are. They not only record individual traits, but catch the collective values – and atmospheres – of Edinburgh society.

Later in his life, Hill brought the fishing village of Newhaven to life as much as the Church Synod. He was collaborating then with Robert Adamson, the first person to set up a photographic portrait studio in Scotland – in Edinburgh. It is interesting that artists in paint themselves liked to be recorded for posterity in photographs, and Jeremy Maas has assembled large numbers of calotypes in his *The Victorian Art World in Photographs* (1984). Few of them could have been described in Balzac's language as 'spectres of the dark room'.

Nor was there anything sinister in those Victorian visual records of the successes of technology which have survived, like the photographs of each class of locomotive produced at the Crewe works from 1865 onwards by the London and North Western Railway. While technological achievements were far more popular with photographers than with painters, particularly in the case of waterworks, gasworks, ports and villages, it has rightly been pointed out by the Royal Commission on Historical Monuments that for every photograph of a textile mill there must be a hundred photographs of 'ruins'. Already four years before Queen Victoria died, the National Photographic Record had been established 'to obtain photographic records of all objects and scenes of interest in the British Isles, and to deposit them with explanatory notes in the British Museum, where they may be safely stored, and be accessible to the public under proper regulations.'

The South Kensington Museum had had a resident photographer from the beginning – Charles Thurston Thompson, who photographed the 'Brompton Boilers' (see page 77) – and from the 1860s onwards manufacturers began to make photographs of their premises for their letter heads: some deliberately included smoke, some deliberately not. Some great engineers and some great engineering events were photographed too. Thus, Isambard Brunel, photographed by Robert Howlett in 1857, is shown standing near the anchor chains of the *Great Eastern*, and Francis Frith left an imposing photograph of the opening of the Manchester Ship Canal in 1894.

Meanwhile, many hospital and prison photographs had been taken – among them a remarkable series of photographs assembled during the 1850s in the Female Department of Surrey County Asylum by Dr Hugh Welch Diamond. Sander L. Gilman in his *The Face of Madness* (1976) has set in context Diamond's fascinating paper 'On the Application of Photography to the Physiognomic and Mental Phenomena of Insanity' read to the Royal Society in 1856. It is more about the face than about the eye. Yet Diamond had written an earlier paper for the Photographic Society on 'The Simplicity of the Calotype Process', and saw at once how valuable the camera would be in presenting 'types of insanity' which hitherto had been elaborately engraved. The photography is more remarkable than the psychiatric deductions drawn from it, although *The Lancet*, which did not then know of Diamond's work, had high hopes of its future in medicine as a whole. 'Photography', the editor wrote, 'is so essentially the Art of Truth ... that it would seem to be the essential means of reproducing all forms and structures of which science seeks for delineation,' Charles Darwin, a fine photographer, would have concurred.

Diamond's photographs were of people who were out of the ordinary. There were, in fact, fewer earlier photographs of ordinary people, however, than the social historian would like – although there is one of the great Chartist demonstration at Kennington Common in 1848, and from 1868 onwards Thomas Arren recorded the slums of Glasgow for the City Improvement Trust. Even later in the reign there were fewer photographs of ordinary people at work than there were of ordinary people at play or of extraordinary people in their wards or in their cells. There were probably fewer photographs of new buildings also than there were of old ones: the Society for Photographing Relics of Old London was founded in 1875, and ten years later had produced 120 carbon prints. Occasionally in 'play pictures' and in street pictures, like those of the wood engraver, Paul Martin, taken in the 1890s, we get rid of the 'poses' that usually froze Victorian individuals and family groups for posterity. Yet although there was an increasing eagerness to catch people unawares, we know far less from Victorian photographs of the interiors of factories than of photographers' studios, many of them portrait factories where derivative and restricted techniques were normally employed.

*I  Australian grandeur: house and garden in Melbourne*

*IIa)   The pull of the past: the Medieval Court at the Great Exhibition*

*b) The lure of the future: the Columbian Exhibition, Chicago 1893*

*III  Art, Economics and History, 1846: a Repeal of the Corn Laws jug featuring a not very life-like Cobden and, on the reverse, Peel*

*IV Art for the home: John Gibson's 'Narcissus', reproduced in Parian ware by Copeland and Garrett for the Art Union, 1846 ( $12\frac{1}{4}$ inches high)*

*V Popular panoply: a Friendly Society Membership Certificate*

*VI  Henry Mayhew's 'Lucifer Match Girl' (from a photograph)*

*VII  The Strike Committee of the Matchworkers' Union, 1888*

*VIII Commerce and Empire: 'Britannia Welcomes the Great New Cocoa Mazawattee'*

Talbot himself, who concentrated on buildings, landscapes and 'compositions' like 'The Chess Players' or 'The Open Door', is said to have made £25,000 within three years, and he, too, was the subject of a Cruikshank cartoon. He talked of the 'Pencil of Nature', the title of the first photographically illustrated book (1844), as did the twelve founding members of the Calotype Club formed in 1847. All of them were amateurs, and most were well placed in society. One was a civil engineer, one a miniature painter. Roger Fenton, who was to make his name with Crimean War photographs (see page 162), was one of them.

In Britain the reign both of the daguerrotype and of the calotype was short lived. A new 'wet glass plate era' began in 1851, the year of Daguerre's death, when Frederick Scott Archer, one of the first twelve members of the Calotype Club, invented a new 'collodion process'. Collodion was guncotton dissolved in ether, and although Archer made no money out of his invention and died in financial straits in 1857, thereafter photographic images were as clear as those of the daguerrotype. An era of continuing technical improvement followed, however, beginning with George Washington Wilson's accelerated developer in 1856 which made 'quick exposure' (onetenth of a second) pictures possible. Improvement was stimulated not only by a sense of opportunity, but by the hazards of the new wet glass plate process, and it is recorded faithfully, sometimes excitedly, in the pages of early photographic magazines. There were 25 of these by 1864, one of the first of them *The Photographic Art Journal*, published not in London but in New York, another the *Journal of the Photographic Society* of London which held its first meeting in 1853. Sir Charles Eastlake was President, and Victoria and Albert attended its first exhibition in 1854. Later, the Queen and her Consort had a dark room at Windsor, and they were sufficiently enthusiastic photographers for the Queen to present the King of Siam with a photographic outfit in 1857. In the same year, Lady Eastlake noted how 'slight improvements in processes' and 'slight variations in results' were being discussed 'as if they involved the future of mankind'.

The making of negatives on sensitized glass plates was a messy business, particularly when carried on in a dark room or a portable 'dark tent', and there was an element of discomfort, too, if not of danger, for the sitters, whose necks might be fitted into neck clamps to keep them still. Nonetheless, the hardships could often seem worthwhile:

You see yourself within this frame,
And, in a looking glass, the same.
The glass, though, must reflect your eyes,
Or straight the charming image flies;
But fixed you have your shadow here,
So that it cannot disappear.

This portrait as it is will last
And when some twice ten years have passed,
Will show you what you were;
How elegant, how fresh and fair.
I wonder what the mirror will,
Compared with it, exhibit still!

*Punch*, for which these verses were written in 1862, regularly included cartoons about photography and photographers, though it was serious enough in its own style on Archer's death when it suggested that his 'dark chamber' would light up wonderfully if his friends offered even a deposit of silver: 'gold', it added, 'will do', and 'answers must not be negatives'. If photography was a language, it carried with it a verbal vocabulary also. Fortunately there was never any shortage of caricaturists dealing with photography in pictures. One of the best collections of caricatures is Cuthbert Bede's *Photographic Pleasures* (1855), written by the author of *The Adventures of Verdant Green* (1853): his real name was the Rev Edward Bradley.

Bevis Hillier has drawn attention to the most delightful of photographic satires, J. Thompson's *Public and Private Life of Animals*, published in 1876. It introduces a Brazilian monkey, Topaz, who comes to Europe to study portrait painting. He quickly realizes that he will never succeed, steals a purse, buys a camera and returns to Brazil, where he sets up a studio in 'an elegant hut of branches beneath an ample shade of banana leaves'. It bears the sign 'Topaz, painter after the Parisian fashion'. His first customer is a boar: a prominent Liberal politician, who is willing to pay double the price and is delighted with the result. 'The little image seemed to reduce his bulk in every way, while the silvery grey of the metallic plate replaced with advantage the sombre monotony of his dark coat'. Thompson shows Topaz the photographer at work, but he implies throughout that the camera was no substitute for easel and brush. He compares Topaz's purchase of his 'photographic camera' with the purchase of a barrel organ by a musician who has sold his piano and flute.

At the census of 1851, 51 photographers declared themselves, certainly an under-estimate. In 1861 there were 2,534; and at the exhibition of 1862 it was reported that in London 'scarcely a favourable spot for the practice of the art is left untenanted'. By then there were said to be over 30,000 people in Paris making a living from photography and its allied trades, appealing by now to a broad clientèle. 'Photographic portraiture is the best feature of the fine arts for the millions that the ingenuity of man has yet devised', wrote *The Photographic News* in October 1861. 'It has ... swept away many of the illiberal distinctions of rank and wealth.' 'Blessed be the inventor of photography', Mrs Carlyle had written two years earlier. 'I set him above even the inventor of chloroform. It has given more positive pleasure to poor suffering humanity than anything that has 'cast up in my time.'

Not surprisingly, there were traditional artists – in paint or print who were both critics and victims of photography – painters and engravers who saw their livelihoods endangered and thought of photography as a 'foe-to-graphic' art. For them it seemed an omen that photography was admitted in 1859 to the Annual Fine Arts Salon in Paris and that for the first time in the same year no miniatures were shown at the Royal Academy Exhibition in London. It made matters worse for them that the so-called 'high art' photographers, repudiating science, were usually on the offensive, seeking, they said, to serve 'higher purposes than [photographers] have hitherto done'. They included Julia Margaret Cameron, photographic illustrator of Tennyson's *Idylls of the King* and a friend of the painter G. F. Watts, the brilliant Oscar Gustav Rejlander, prominent at the Manchester Art Treasures Exhibition of 1857 (Queen Victoria bought his remarkable set-piece, 'The Two Ways of Life', for Prince Albert), and Henry Paul Robinson, who in the name of idealism could sentimentalize ordinary life as systematically as Julia Cameron sentimentalized allegory.

Mrs Cameron did not take up photography until she was 48, and she used her coal house as a darkroom and her chicken house as a studio. Yet she was in search of beauty and has been described as 'the Rembrandt of the English photographic art'. Hers was photography with models. Rejlander, who was born in Sweden and studied painting in Rome, before turning to photography, achieved a greater element of mystery, and in retrospect seems to anticipate the surrealists. Robinson was an author as well as a photographer, and in his *Pictorial Effect in Photography* (1869) explained cogently how and why there were as many 'individualizing' features in a good photograph as there were in a drawing or painting, a point taken up by George Bernard Shaw in his note on 'the unmechanicalness of photography'.

Rejlander, too, though he could capture the dream, was always capable of highly intelligent argument to dispose of muddled philosophies of the eye. He had delivered a paper to the *Journal of the Photographic Society of London* in 1858 in which he discussed his motives for producing 'The Two Ways of Life' ('Industry' and 'Dissipation') and the techniques he had employed. Long before the century was through, *The Photographic News* in 1886/7 had already attempted to assess the significance of his works and in 1901 Robinson himself claimed that 'the limits of photography as an art have yet to be precisely defined.'

Even then, the mid-century argument was not in any way settled. While a new generation of art photographers, some of them associated in the Brotherhood of the Linked Ring, founded in 1892, had chosen 'artistic themes' for their hand-crafted photographs and at the same time responded technically to the challenge of photogravure [see page 137], it was still possible for influential supporters of 'fine art' to compare them con-temptuously with 'artist tailors' and 'artist barbers'. It was not merely that it was felt that they could not vie with portrait painters, a diminishing group. There was a more fundamental problem with the camera itself. Joseph Pennell could write in the *Contemporary Review* as late as 1897, 'the senseless lens of the camera will never record the vital, characteristic qualities of great architecture', while other critics, unimpressed by Robinson's pleading, felt that it was even less well equipped to probe the depths of personality or of passion. Art photographers had to fight on more than one front, challenging 'realists' and at photographic exhibitions condemning instantaneous photographs for lack of 'composition'.

'High art' photography remained at one end of the spectrum: at the other end during the mid-Victorian years were *carte de visite* photography and for a time stereoscopy. For a time, indeed, the makers of *cartes de visite* and stereoscopic photographs were far more popular than any other photographers. There was money in what *Le Monde Illustré* in Paris called the 'delightful and quite absorbing' *carte de visite* 'mania', which had quite 'supplanted autograph mania, porcelain mania' and other manias. Yet there could be more than money in stereoscopic photography: there could be a direct appeal also to a 'philosophy of the eye'. 'If two images were set side by side and viewed simultaneously but co-dependently, they would recreate the sense of depth of image seen through the naked eye in "real life". The two would become one and produce effects unknown to art.' For some photographers that was Science.

Sir David Brewster's 'lenticular' stereoscopic viewer was on display at the Crystal Palace in 1851, and in the years that followed it became as prominent a feature of a number of well-off Victorian homes as a twentieth-century television set might be – and sometimes, if made in highly decorated papier-mâché or mother of pearl, far more 'handsome'. There are interesting connections in the history of this development. Brewster, a Fellow of the Royal Society, had been consulted by his friend David Octavius Hill before the latter produced his calotype of the Church of Scotland General Assembly. However, he owed much, too, to Sir Charles Wheatstone, inventor of the telegraph, who has been called 'the father of stereoscopy', and who himself consulted Richard Beard before producing stereoscopic pictures of Charles Babbage.

The London Stereoscopic Company, with its mottoes 'no home without a stereoscope', and 'no family or school should be without one', provided ample 'software' for the customers of the 1850s, some of the stereo-photographs straightforward (the cheapest cost half a crown for three), like stereo-photographs of the Alps or the Pyramids, some of them full of tricks, like double exposure stereo-photographs to convey not representations of 'reality' but 'dreams'. Twelve family portraits cost 10s, twenty-five in two positions, £1.

At the exhibition of 1862, for which the company paid £1,500 for exclusive rights to take photographs, a 'megalothoscope' was one of the favourite stereo exhibits: the photographs were viewed by reflected light to present daytime scenes and by transmitted light to present scenes by night. Nearly 300,000 stereoscopic slides were made: their ingredients included 200 gallons of albumen, made from 32,000 eggs, and 35 ounces of gold.

Stereo-photography dropped out of fashion within the next five years when *cartes de visite* portraits, first popularized in France by André Disdéri, *arriviste* son of an Italian clothier, became the rage on this side of the Channel too after J. E. Mayall produced a 'Royal Album' of portrait *cartes* in 1861, and for a time there were even some stereoscopic *cartes de visite*. Disdéri, who had reduced the size of the portrait photograph, had mounted it on a card, and – even more important – had sharply reduced the cost, made and lost a fortune. His *cartes* (usually around $2\frac{1}{2}$ to $3\frac{1}{2}$ inches) record social types rather than individuals, and even at the time they were collected in albums, like autographs or postage stamps, but with more of a family flavour. They could also be assembled in *pot-pourris*, pasted into Victorian scrapbooks, or exchanged with friends.

In retrospect, the Disdéri *cartes* constitute a rich visual archive in themselves. They illuminate the Paris of the Second Empire – he was the official photographer at the Exhibition of 1855 and photographed the Emperor in 1859 before he departed for Italy at the head of his army – but with the Republic: that particular phase was over. Other *cartes*, however, can be equally revealing, including the *cartes* of 'celebrities', some from the stage, some from the pulpit; and for the social historian even contrived *cartes* of ordinary people have their interest. There were some makers of them who offered far better bargains than Disdéri – 'your likeness and a cigar for sixpence'.

At the production end of one popular British line in landscape *cartes* was Francis Frith, born in 1822 and a founder member of the Liverpool Photographic Society in 1853. After returning to Britain following a period spent exploring and photographing abroad, he went on to photograph scenes of 'almost every town and village in the country', happy to be back:

I think with a sigh I'll abandon the rest
For a home in old England, the last and the best.

His photographs, processed in and distributed from Reigate, went to over 2,000 shops in different parts of the country. 'Brought up-to-date', as they were from time to time, they constitute an indispensable record for the social historian both of the city and the countryside. They anticipated picture postcards described below in Chapter 8.

With the introduction and evolution of dry plates and improvements in developing, photography from the mid-1850s onwards was changing yet again. In 1864 the first workable photographic emulsion was introduced; in 1871 a London doctor, R. L. Maddox, successfully experimented with a gelatin dry plate process; and in 1873 John Burgess moved beyond experiment to practical success with an announcement of 'dry plates equal in sensitiveness to the best wet plates.' In 1877 Sir John Swan's company began selling them and two years later the famous 'Ilford' plate was introduced. Within a decade dry plates passed into general use: they could be employed without any chemical preparation on the spot on the part of the photographer, and they were far more sensitive to light than older plates; indeed, they could be exposed in a fraction of a second. Photography now became in the enthusiastic, if exaggerated, words of the Archbishop of York, President of the Dry Plate Club, 'almost a child's toy', neither science nor art.

The switch from the use of albumenized paper to emulsion paper came more slowly, but there were important changes in printing, with their origins in the United States, by the end of the century. The term 'instantaneous photograph' was now brought into use, and there was even a photo-automat at the Paris Exhibition of 1889. Cameras were now being mass-produced, too, with many varieties like 'magazine cameras', 'reflex cameras', and more imaginatively named, the so-called 'detective cameras', which were capable of being concealed in walking sticks or even in buttonholes. The term 'detective camera' was coined six years before the first Sherlock Holmes story appeared, and popular articles, for example in the *Strand Magazine* which published Conan Doyle stories, had included articles about the 'curiosities of modern photography' telling, for example, of its use in solving crimes.

It was George Eastman who invented the name that would stick – 'Kodak', though his first Kodak was described as 'the smallest, lightest and simplest of all detective cameras'. It cost only $25, and 90,000 Kodaks were sold within five years. As compared with later cameras, it had no focusing apparatus and only a single speed on the shutter, but it had an exposure time of only one-twentieth of a second, incorporated a roll holder, and was sold ready loaded with a roll of negative stripping paper film sufficient to produce a hundred pictures $2\frac{1}{2}$ inches in diameter. Most important of all – for this, not the camera itself, was the real innovation – an untrained photographer could now take pictures without having to bother about developing and printing. When the hundred pictures had been taken, the camera was packed up and shipped to Eastman's factory in Rochester, where it was unloaded, charged with fresh film, and together with the developed film returned to the customer in ten days.

Eastman appealed in his early advertisements not only to the 'general public' but to particular groups. Thus, he told artists that they could use the Kodak 'to save time in sketching', surgeons that they could acquire a 'record of their cases', and 'lovers of fine animals' that they could record their pets. Nonetheless, even in the short run, the Kodak exploited universal 'human' appeal. One early pictorial advertisement, not a photograph, shows Jack asking his mother 'Do you think baby will be quiet long enough to take her picture, Mum?' to which the answer comes as quick as the click of the camera,

'The Kodak camera will catch her whether she moves or not: it is as "quick as a wink"'. The' fleeting moment' could be captured 'at home', and of the camera it could be said quite simply 'anybody can use it: everybody will use it'. Not every one approved. Thus, the *Weekly Times and Echo* in 1893 applauded the formation of a 'Vigilance Association with the purpose of thrashing cads with cameras who go about in seaside places taking snapshots of ladies emerging from the deep'.

Among early British box cameras the most remembered name is still the Brownie camera, named after Frank Brownell, Eastman's camera maker, which was launched along with a Brownie Camera Club in 1900. In the last year of Queen Victoria's reign over 100,000 'Brownies' were sold, nearly half of them in England. Meanwhile, celluloid invented in 1861 (see above p. 20) and registered as a tradename by John Wesley Hyatt, the son of a blacksmith, in 1873, had been introduced into photography in 1888, in the form of 'Carbutt's flexible negative films'. John Carbutt, an English photographer who had emigrated to the United States, had worked with Hyatt at his Celluloid Manufacturing Company in Newark, New Jersey, to produce 'the most complete and perfect substitute for glass yet discovered'. The two men had rivals, however. In 1886 the Rev Hannibal Goodwin had also applied for a patent for his 'photographic pellicle', a transparent roll film made of celluloid: he cared little for photography as art, science or hobby, but wanted a material that would be even better than glass for the photographic illustrations of Bible stories which he told with the help of a magic lantern.

The magic lantern was a favourite device in Sunday Schools (and in temperance societies) on both sides of the Atlantic (see page 137) and was often thought of as a marvel. The Kodak, however, was a device for the home, the garden, and the holiday and 'click, click, click' became the music of a new 'age of the snapshot', only just beginning in the last years of Victoria's reign. The 'snapshot' was to reflect a more relaxed approach to the photograph, and thousands of snapshots were to be collected in treasured family albums that were very different both from the old *cartes de visite* albums and the new picture postcard albums (see pages 364 ff). Yet many of the new amateurs who had eagerly bought Kodaks also joined photographic societies: there were 14 of them in 1880, 256 in 1900. In this activity Britain led the way, for according to the British journal, *Photographic Almanacs*, quoted by H. and A. Gernstein, there were only 23 such societies in continental Europe in 1900 and 109 in the United States.

An old amateur tradition of 'expert photography' continued also, not least in Oxford and in Brighton, and it found new outlets as travel, including foreign travel, became easier; and the buildings and scenes that Ruskin had recorded in his daguerrotypes were now recorded by travellers who spent most of their holidays behind a camera. Back at home, there were still many dark rooms in middle-class villas, and many families who liked to display photographs on their crowded walls above their fireplaces or on the tops of their pianos. Few amateurs were as enterprising, however, as Lewis Carroll: at the sale of his effects in Oxford in 1898 there were several photographic lots, including 'fancy costume for photographic purposes'.

Carroll's own techniques were, of course, 'professional', as were those of several other Oxford dons, but he would have hated the word 'professional'. Nonetheless, the number of professional photographers making a living out of their 'art' was still increasing sharply. At the census of 1881 there were 7,614 of them (1,606 of them women); at that of 1891 12,397; and at that of 1901 17,268 (4,933 of them women). In Carroll's Oxford one of them, Henry Taunt, collected pictures of the city and of the countryside as well as of people and events. Some were taken on commission, like his collection of 1890s pictures of every process in a Witney blanket factory and, rather later, of Frank Cooper's Oxford marmalade works.

In 1890 Henry Paul Robinson, whose first book had been on *Pictorial Effect in Photography*, had published his *Photography as a Business*, to be followed a year later by his *The Studio and What to Do in It*, but there were quite different ways of carrying on the photographic business or of planning photographic studios. Provincial studios, dealing largely in weddings, funerals and family groups, usually used standard equipment purchased from catalogues, and some of them had links with London photographers. Yet in London there were also exotic studios furnished in eccentric individual taste and fashionable salons incorporationg the very latest styles in furnishing. Earlier in the century there had been 'temples of photographic art'. Now, later in the century, it was possible for a London studio, like that of Alexander Bassano, who had moved from Regent Street to Old Bond Street in 1877, to display expensive oriental carpets and plaster busts by Bassano himself to enhance his favourite photographs. There was a huge panoramic background in his principal studio.

# V

Most studios were confined in space. The camera, however, could rove through space and gave new significance to the nineteenth-century idea of 'panorama' which had been proudly proclaimed in 1842 in the first issue of the *Illustrated London News*. The new readers had been told then that the periodical was 'determined to keep continually before the eyes of the world a living and moving panorama of all its activities and influences.' (See p. 145.) They were soon told also that they should not throw away their copies for there was permanent as well as present interest in them. Although there were no photographs in the *Illustrated London News* during Victoria's reign – like *Punch*, it continued to provide useful employment for other and older kinds of illustrators – the German essayist Dolf Sternberger was surely right to entitle his interesting study of nineteenth-century culture (1938: English translation 1977) *Panorama of the Nineteenth Century*. 'Oddly', he wrote in a characteristically long footnote, 'the first appearance of panorama painting occurred almost exactly in 1800, its decline being sealed around 1900'.

The word 'panorama' was used then and later to describe 'a pictorial representation of a whole view visible from one point by an observer who is turning around looking successively at all points of the horizon'. This was what Mr Pickwick had set out to do, and now in 1894 a panoramic camera was patented in Paris – by Damoizeau – capable of taking photographs at a 360 degree angle.

English journalists preferred Pickwick's spectacles, and in 1899 Clement Shorter, then editor of the *Illustrated London News*, could still maintain confidently that there was a basic difference between illustrated newspapers bedecked with engravings and 'photographic journals' and that a 'large part of life, and particularly of public life, cannot be depicted by the camera'. Technically, at least, other countries were 'ahead' in this respect as in others as they were to be in photo-mechanical printing in the late twentieth century. *Illustrierte Zeitung* reproduced a half-tone photograph as early as 1883, and in 1896 *Paris Moderne* produced photographic essays on Paris. In England, the advent of the photogravure process in the 1880s offered more possibilities to publishers of books than to editors of newspapers, and in this field of enterprise there were some superb volumes like *Pictures of East Anglian Life* (1888).

Before the end of the nineteenth century there was to be the biggest of all the technical changes when the techniques of the moving image were introduced into photography to present a genuinely 'living and moving panorama'. There was a pre-history here, too, but the richest history was still to come. There was the same interplay also of art and science, instruction and entertainment.

The first moving images had been mechanical and belonged to the world of toys. Thus, during the 1830s a revolving magic disc or 'wheel of life' had released a succession of painted human figures or animals into apparent movement, and the word 'illusion' had been used to describe the resulting performance when it was watched in the theatre. The devices had some odd names, far odder than the name 'Kodak': they included the 'Zootrope', the phenakisti[s]cope', 'the ph[f]antascope', the 'zooproxiscope', and after photographs began to be used, not paintings, the 'kammatograph'.

Magicians made as much use of optics as opticians, and some of them, like the famous John Maskelyne, co-founder in 1873 of London's 'Egyptian Hall', 'a Hall of Mystery', had started life as watchmakers. Moreover, as Erik Barnouw has realled in his *The Magic and the Cinema* (1981), magic lanterns were used secretly by magicians before they were used didactically by Sunday School teachers or temperance lecturers: the word *phantasmagoria* had emerged in this context. The Royal Polytechnic Institution, where

Beard opened his first photographic studio, was the setting for regular magical performances, and there were often untidy frontiers between magic and spiritualism. It was not only that old faces would be seen again, but that familiar things could be made to move. The author of the most interesting book on the techniques of 'ghostly' projection, *The Ghost!* (1864) was a civil engineer, Henry Dircks.

The first successful use of a camera sequence to suggest movement was in 1872, when Eadweard Muybridge, an Englishman, born at Kingston-upon-Thames, whose real name was Edward Muggeridge, prepared a chronophotographic series of horse photographs for the horse-loving Governor of California, Leland Stanford: his *Animal Locomotion* appeared in 1888 and his *Animals in Motion* in 1899. Before 1872, however, the idea of such or similar photography had been put forward by others, including Alfred Pollock and L. A. Ducos, Pierre Jules, César Jansen and Étienne Marey in France; and after 1872 Muybridge was far from alone in his experimenting. Marey, in particular, presented pictures of girls in 1882 and of flying birds a little later: he, too, was an author, and his study *Le Mouvement* (1894) is now treated as a classic. Meanwhile, the Prussian Ottomar Anshütz had produced a sequence of 120 photographs illustrating the life of a family of storks including the building of their nest. It has remained more popular than his sequences of soldiers on parade. Muybridge is the most fascinating figure in the story however, for his private life as much as for his achievement, which impressed artists as different as Watts, Degas – and Francis Bacon. In 1874 he shot dead the lover of his wife, was arrested, charged, imprisoned, brought to trial and finally acquitted. Nineteen years later he was to open a 'Zoopraxographical Hall' at the Chicago Columbian Exhibition.

A different approach to the simulation of movement was apparent in techniques for 'dissolving' from one picture to another first with two magic lanterns, later in the 1870s with one, and this is interesting not least because the spell of the magic lantern rested, of course, on what was seen in a darkened room on a screen. The history of 'the screen' itself is as complex as the history of 'the track' before the history of the locomotive. Many people in the mid-Victorian years, including Queen Victoria herself, had kept photographs not only on the walls or on the tops of tables and desks but on screens. There were many screens in the home, therefore, before there were screens in the cinema or screens in the home again in the days of television.

The counterpart of the locomotive appeared in the 1890s, a decade of 'new things' and of predictions about how they might be used in the future. There were links with the history of entertainment and of exhibitions. Thus, at the Chicago World Fair of 1893, only three years before the first regular cinema shows were presented in London, Ottomar Anshütz's 'Electrical Tachyscope' – displaying leaping horses and gymnasts – was a greater popular attraction than Muybridge's Zoopraxograph, and in 1896 itself Walter

Woodbury's *Photographic Amusements including Tricks and Unusual or Novel Effects Obtainable with the Camera* (1896) appeared: it was to go through ten editions by 1931.

In 1894 Thomas Edison and his colleagues – one of them an Englishman, Dickson – introduced the Kinetoscope [see Chapter X]. Edison, who said later that he had first been inspired by the zootrope, had been visited by Muybridge in 1886, and his first 'continuous strip' patent was filed two years later: in 1889 he was buying transparent celluloid film from Eastman. His first intention was to make 'sound pictures', but the kinetograph gave way to the kinetoscope, billed in New York, Chicago, Baltimore and Atlantic City, where kinetoscope parlours were opened in 1894, as 'the wizard's latest invention'. 'There is not and has never been any motion picture film machine ... that is not descended by traceable steps from the kinetoscope', Terry Ramsay was to write in his *A Million and One Nights: A History of the Motion Picture* in 1926, when sound was at last just around the corner.

Louis Lumière, born sixteen years later than Edison, would have insisted rightly on his own special place in the line of descent. He had managed a photographic factory in Lyons and on 28th December 1895 he introduced his 'Cinematograph' '*le nouveauté du jour*' at the Grand Café in Paris to 35 spectators. Lumière claimed that it was during one single night in 1894 when he could not sleep that he settled all the technical problems of his own invention.

Edison did not see the possibilities of the kinetoscope, which he conceived of, at best, as a peephole, with one person at a time looking at the pictures; Lumière was more percipient, and quickly introduced the 'cinematograph' to London at the Empire Theatre in Leicester Square in 1896, a remarkable first year of cultural convergence in the history of what were to be called in the twentieth century 'the media'. In the same year Harmsworth launched his new *Daily Mail*, a landmark in popular journalism, and the first motor race was organized between London and Brighton on Motor-Car Day, 14th November – of the thirty cars that set out for Hyde Park, only 17 arrived safely, the first of them a steam car.

Lumière belonged indubitably to the age not of steam but of electricity, recognizing that there was a potential global market for 'films' and that the general public in no matter what country would be more interested in the cinema than magicians or their sponsors. This, indeed, was to be the most important line of descent. Yet old links were not broken as new ones were forged either on the road to Brighton or in the history of the cinema. One unauthorized English maker of kinetoscopes was an optical instrument maker, Robert William Paul, only 27 years old in 1896, who also designed a projector, the Theatregraph, and produced what may have been the first British fiction film *Soldier's Courtship*. In Germany Oskar Messler, 'the father of German cinema', came from a family of optical instrument makers who had established their reputation with microscopes and opthalmoscopes.

Maskelyne, grandson of John, became a cinema actor: many old theatres became cinemas, like the New Oxford Theatre of Varieties in Brighton, opened in 1854 as Wright's Music Hall and later to be called the Coliseum. There was, in fact, a 'Brighton School' of the cinema that actually exported films to the United States. One of its pioneers, George Albert Smith, inventor of kinemacolor, was a lecturer in astronomy with an impressive knowledge of optics; he turned to the cinema after a visit to the Empire Theatre in Leicester Square on Lumière's 1896 visit.

There were many ghosts around in 1896. Among the titles in the *British Film Catalogue*, which begins in 1895, are *Photographing a Ghost*, which shows a photographer trying in vain to take a picture of a ghost, and *Faust and Mephistopheles* (1898), which refers back to still older themes as Satan conjures up the vision of a girl to induce Faust into signing his pact. One of the first films of Georges Méliès was called *The Vanishing Lady*: in it a skeleton suddenly becomes by a time reversal a living woman. Lumière had tried running a film backward through the projector in *Charcuterie Mecanique* (1895).

The media as they developed were to offer many new kinds of magic, not all of which were to be taken as magic by their often uncritical audiences. Indeed, the problem of the relationship between 'reality' or 'the truth' and what you saw on the screen after the 'universal eye' of the moving camera had done its work was to be posed most controversially not in the late-nineteenth century but in the late-twentieth century. The ramifications of the 'philosophy of the eye' had certainly not been fully appreciated by 1900.

Queen Victoria herself, the subject of more photographs than of paintings, had kept pace with her reign. Nor was she only in this respect a highly suitable subject worthy of a 'biography in word and picture' by Helmut and Alison Gernsheim. She was an actor in the story too. She sketched, painted, and etched, of course, tried her hand at lithography, and took photographs; and she and Albert had a dark room at Windsor Castle under the supervision of Roger Fenton. She collected snapshots avidly and assembled no fewer than 44 albums of 'Portraits of Royal Children' between 1848 and her death. Lord Salisbury received a photograph when he gave way in 1886 to Gladstone: the Prince of Wales had long before that been given a camera. Some royal children and relations had been sent to the London Stereoscopic School of Photography. Victoria knew more, therefore, about the 'philosophy of the eye' than most of her subjects. Moreover, bad though her eyesight was in later years, she greatly enjoyed a private performance of Sydney Grundy's comedy in three acts *A Pair of Spectacles* which she saw at Windsor in 1891. She doubtless appreciated the climax when the confused Mr Goldsmith got his old spectacles back. 'You look yourself again', his wife tells him.

He may or may not have been lucky, for after Queen Victoria's death it was difficult for most people to get their old spectacles back again. Things were never to be quite the same again. Nor after 1914 was 'the great spectacle' itself.

# 4
# Images of Fame

Royalty first . . . Murderers Galore.
JOHN BEDFORD, *Staffordshire Pottery Figures*, 1964

Tho' music old may lose its charm
And long neglected lie,
Attuned not to the modern ear,
It yet may please the eye . . .
With Fashion's list of fickle types
That pass man's wit to name,
Musicians – poets – statesmen swell
Song-Titles' roll of fame.
The World of Travel, Sport and Art
Within its wide scope fall,
For – be the subjects what they may –
The 'Cover' covers all.
W. E. IMESON, *Illustrated Music Titles*, 1912

'Shall Smith have a Statue?'
COVENTRY PATMORE, *Principles in Art*, 1889

A brass never can be an architectural decoration.
It must always be treated as a memorial.
*Ecclesiastical Art Review*, March 1878

# I

The idea of photography offering not just representation but record was well established by the end of Queen Victoria's reign. As early as 1855 the Ordnance Survey had begun to experiment with photography in producing maps, and by the end of the century anthropology was being influenced by photography at least as much as geography was. 'Photographs, I find', wrote the director of the Pitt-Rivers Museum, 'are so important an adjunct to a museum that I try to buy all I can.' Here, it was felt, was new evidence to set things straight and it could even be used in politics. Thus, *The Times* reported in 1888 how Gladstone had produced two photographs of Ireland as a historical record in a speech delivered at Birmingham on home rule; they were offered to his audience in order to show that official accounts of violent incidents at Mitchelstown were wrong.

During the early part of the reign the idea of a historical record had been concerned primarily with documents, and it was in 1838 that the Public Record Office was created with Henry Cole as one of its Assistant Keepers. Indeed, Cole had played a prominent part in its creation. During the mid-Victorian years the process of acquisition and cataloguing continued, and routines were established after the new Public Record Office building was completed in 1866. Nor was acquiring and collecting confined to the P.R.O.: the Camden Society was set up in the same year as the P.R.O., the Early English Texts Society in 1864 and the Royal Commission on Historical Manuscripts in 1869. During the last years of the reign, however, it was beginning to be appreciated that pictures, including at the very end of the reign moving pictures, were essential evidence for the record, even if the provision of adequate archival facilities was to be long delayed. One of the most distinctive features in the 'marvellous' early cinema work of Georges Meliès was his reconstructed news reel. Not on the spot but in his studio he filmed simulated history – scenes of the Greco-Turkish War of 1897 and of the American intervention in Cuba a year later.

As far as the 'real' historical record was concerned, Victorian historians asked questions that concerned not merely the nature of evidence about people and events and how to use it but about values. What was worth recording? What stood out? One of the favourite contrasts drawn by J. R. Green, author of the popular *Short History of the English People* (1874), was that between 'common things' and 'great events'; and in his view social history, to which he gave new life, had to concentrate on the former, not the latter. His preference would have amazed Meliès, who wanted history to entertain, but it would have strongly appealed to Pitt-Rivers, who wanted anthropology to instruct.

According to Green, history of all kinds had to deal not only with 'English Kings or English Conquest' but with the 'common people' and how they lived. Wars should not dominate the story. Swords had to be beaten into ploughshares. For him, therefore, the best kind of museums to open were not military or waxwork museums but folk museums. Green wanted his *History* to be 'interpreted and illustrated by pictures which should tell us how men and things appeared to the lookers-on of their own day, and how contemporary observers aimed at representing them'. He died, however, before he could realize this 'favourite wish', and it was left to his wife, who shared his interests and values, to produce a new illustrated edition of his *History* in 1892.

In re-assessing English history Green, a Victorian liberal, born in the year when Queen Victoria came to the throne, was pointing to the future, for during the early and mid-Victorian years themselves there had been a growing rather than a declining interest in 'great men'. Thomas Carlyle's *Hero-Worship* appeared in 1841. History, Carlyle believed, was 'nothing but the biographies of great men'. Fifteen years later, Ruskin, who knew much about lesser men, singled out 'men who feel *strongly* and *nobly*.' 'One man is so little,' a lecturer in London's Exeter Hall told his audience in 1851, 'that you see him a thousand times without caring to ask his name. Another man is so great, that if you ... possess a "hair of him" when dead, it is something of which you are proud.' If you could not get 'a hair of him', you could often get an image. Indeed, a year later, more images of the dead Duke of Wellington were in circulation than there had been in his lifetime.

By a 'singular coincidence' Wellington died on the same day as Pugin, and there was more than a touch of Pugin in a lithograph showing his lying-in-state in Chelsea Hospital. There was nothing Puginesque, however, about the memorial for Wellington designed in 1857 after competition by Albert Stevens, 'a man of the Renaissance', and placed in St Paul's Cathedral, a cathedral unfashionable with all Gothic revivalists and abhorrent to William Morris. The monument, unfinished after many tribulations when Stevens died in 1877, has been described as the finest piece of nineteenth-century sculpture. It was certainly as worthy a tribute to the great Duke as Tennyson's magnificent ode on his death. An earlier memorial to Wellington had been less lucky. One of the City's two monuments to the Duke, designed by Francis Chantrey in bronze, was also unfinished when Chantrey died. It was displaced in 1883 and almost melted down before finding safety in Aldershot. The choice of safe place was ironical. The monument did not commemorate a great Wellington victory in the field but his assistance to the City of London in getting a bill passed through Parliament for the rebuilding of London Bridge.

The other great hero of the struggles against Napoleon, Horatio Nelson, had had his statue displayed on the ground – *terra firma*, the *Illustrated London News* called it – at Charing Cross in 1842, before it was moved to the top of the column in Trafalgar Square. It seemed to have 'the great merit of likeness and character', and '100,000 persons' are said to have examined it in two days. The only regret of the *Illustrated London News* was that 'more than thirty years had elapsed before so 'obvious a duty to Nelson's renown was accomplished'. His monument, it claimed, was far more than 'a national tribute to his fame: it was a funeral record ... raised in a sacred spot and consecrated by religion'. The *News* descended from the column to *terra firma* itself, however, when it remarked that 'the sacred spot' was not the finest open space in the metropolis, but 'the commonplace ... front of the National Gallery'.

Images, large or small – and Nelson's statue weighed eighteen tons – evoked sentiments as well as memories. Recalling the whole Victorian period, early, middle and late, in 1918, Edmund Gosse wrote without exaggeration that 'the Victorians ... carried admiration to the highest pitch. They marshalled it, they defined it, they turned it from a virtue into a religion', while Samuel Butler, even more of a rebel than Gosse, wrote in his notebook, 'He is greatest who is most often in man's good thoughts'.

As the readership of newspapers and periodicals grew, the idea of a kaleidoscope of 'great events' took shape alongside the idea of a gallery of 'great men'; and although newspapers were as slow to produce images as *The Annual Register*, an indispensable national record, as early as 1843 the *Illustrated London News*, bedecked with wood engravings, had been designed to offer a whole 'living and moving panorama' to be enjoyed and 'museum-preserved' in 'the drawing room, the portfolios or the library'. There was the same conception of the panorama in the *Graphic*, founded in 1869, by William Luson Thomas, although there was no daily illustrated newspaper until the *Daily Graphic* appeared in 1890.

The artist employed to illustrate these periodicals could indicate 'a passing scene', it was claimed, by a few strokes of the pencil, 'a kind of pictorial shorthand which is afterwards translated and extended in the finished drawing'. Yet the requirements of the machine press changed the character of wood engraving. A key figure in the story was Ebenezer Landells, who was a principal in many publishing ventures, as well as a successful engraver.

The perception of the 'passing scene' that they and their editors fostered left a place not only for great men in war or politics, the kind of men who inspired 'good thoughts', but for great names in sport or in crime, who might inspire the very reverse. It was not just that Lady Hamiltons were as much in demand as Horatio Nelsons. There was a place, too, for the brutal and the nasty.

The *Weekly Dispatch* had made its reputation with vivid descriptions of prize fights and always sold large numbers of extra copies after a particularly brutal murder; while it was not until 1872 that it could be said of *The Observer* that it was 'one of the safest contemporary papers that could be put into the hands of ladies' and was consequently to be found 'in families where only two or three others of its weekly contemporaries could find admission'. Moreover, at that time, thirty years after the death of the popular broadsheet printer James Catnach, there were still four 'ballad presses' in active operation, dealing in contemporary sensations, the most successful of them Henry Disley's press in the midst of the notorious Seven Dials district.

Throughout London and the provincial cities, embellished with many new statues of local and national heroes, there were still wall posters and almanacs and image-objects of all kinds as there had been long before Queen Victoria came to the throne. Louis James has described them in his *Print and the People* (1974) which begins in 1819, the year Queen Victoria was born, and ends in 1851. Yet such ephemera did not disappear with the building of the Crystal Palace. At the time of the notorious violent Northumberland Street murder of 1861, for example, one of the many 'sensations' of a decade that made the most of them, a habitual dealer in popular prints was brought before the Magistrate's Court for obstruction. 'Had you been there before?' the magistrate asked him. 'Yes, sir,' he replied, 'only for sellin' some of these here things', pointing to the prints which the police had confiscated. 'They were remarkable', it was purported, 'for consistent inaccuracy in the main features and in all the details.' But this had not stopped them from selling.

Throughout the reign, while the 'common people' were encouraged to acquire national mementoes of political leaders who were in the news, particularly at times of stress or celebration, they also without prompting were choosing their own heroes and heroines – and villains – as they always had done. They might be the kind of people who found a place in Madame Tussaud's wax museum, not least in its Chamber of Horrors. But they could also be radicals who challenged the authorities. The *Weekly Dispatch* was thought to be a public nuisance in respectable circles not just because it dealt in crime but because it sometimes focused on Chartist leaders and because it once declared that there was no more harm in being an infidel than in being a clergyman.

Stone or paper or wax were not only materials used to register people and events. There were objects also in wood, metal, silk and glass, with the range of commemorative objects varying in size and shape and, from time to time, in range. There might be small plaster models of huge future statues, and one well-known statue, Gibson's the *Tinted Venus*, was not only reproduced photographically by the London Stereoscopic Company in 1862 but became the subject of a 'farcical romance' in 1885.

Fashions influenced production as much as more long-lasting cultural factors. Thus, most stereoscopic images had been relegated to the rubbish dump long before the end of Queen Victoria's. Near its beginning, when the demand for wooden snuff boxes declined from the 1830s onwards, the famous Mauchline 'box factory' in Perthshire began to turn out a very wide range indeed of wooden things, with varying finishes. In an age of increasing travel most of them dealt with places rather than with people but, not surprisingly, Sir Walter Scott figured as well as the monument erected after him in Edinburgh. So, too, did Sir Rowland Hill, pioneer of penny postage.

Hill's own statue, designed for a competition by a young sculptor Onslow Ford in 1882, was an impressive, even subtle, work in bronze. It was worthy of the man who commissioned the penny black (see page 338) with its image of images.

From the very beginning of their production during the early 1860s Thomas Stevens's mounted silk woven pictures and bookmarks, known as 'Stevengraphs', exploited the potential of popular portraits in silk: they might even be given away as Sunday School prizes or sent as Christmas presents. They were in demand at exhibitions, too, where Stevens sometimes exhibited his loom at work as well as his productions. His 'Dick Turpin's Ride to York on Bonny Black Bess' was issued at a York exhibition in 1879.

The subject matter of Stevengraphs included both heroes of sport and politics, and both religious and political leaders. There was a place in the collection, too, for one trade-union leader, Joseph Arch, organizer of the Agricultural Workers. This was a very simple image compared with the often magnificent trade-union and friendly society emblems, printed or woven, which were commissioned by the unions themselves and which concentrated more on 'solidarity' than on 'leadership'. They often incorporated not only pictures of workers in their places of work, but inspirational mottoes, like 'In All Labour There is Profit' (the Stonemasons, 1868) or '8 Hours Labour' (The Gas Workers, 1890). There was elaborate allegory, too, employing traditional as well as historic figures.

Between 1870 and 1900 100,000 such trade-union emblems were sold. One of the finest of them was produced by the Amalgamated Society of Lithographic Printer in 1889, although one of the best of the late lithographers, Alexander Gow, is not listed among the members of the Lithographic Society. Very few new emblems were produced in paper in the years after Queen Victoria died. Trade-union banners continued to be carried, however, at big events in the history of the labour movement – strikes as well as galas.

Commemorative artefacts for the home, including the working-class home, were for the most part decorative rather than functional objects, to be placed over the chimney-piece, on a window sill or in a glass cupboard. There were some functional pieces, however – among them jugs and plates, tobacco jars, inkwells, and, not least, money boxes and chamber pots, sometimes in Sunderland pink lustre: (Henry Doulton of Lambeth is said to have been the first potter fully to appreciate the significance of Chadwick and the 'sanitary' idea.) Heroes and heroines might also be depicted on food tins, on pot lids, (the latter the subject of a detailed study in 1972 by C. Williams-Wood), and on match boxes; and in 1897 W.D and H.O. Wills produced their first set of fifty cigarette cards called 'Kings and Queens'. They went back to Alfred and ended with Victoria.

There was a direct relationship between pictorial prints and pottery images through the simple crafts of transfer printing. As early as 1756, a

Liverpool potter, John Sadler, and a Liverpool painter, Guy Green, had developed a method of transferring printing to earthenware. Hitherto each piece had to be decorated by hand: now one man could do the work of fifty. The nature of this process would not have appealed to Ruskin or to Morris, Nor would the transfer process developed in Mauchline woodware by the early 1850s. Nonetheless, such processes forged new links between the pottery trade and the press, with the *Illustrated London News* providing illustrative copy for commemorative plates and jugs. And there were other links, too, between different modes of presenting images. Thus, the *Illustrated London News* noted in 1856 how a statue of Franklin recently erected in Boston bore 'a close likeness to the Staffordshire portraits'. The face on a medal of General Gordon was taken from a photograph.

The new techniques of production coupled with enterprise in distribution laid the foundations both for huge expansion of the home market in the nineteenth century and for the rise of a substantial export market. Canada and Australia were particularly welcome customers. One Staffordshire potter incorporated the beaver and maple leaves into a Canadian design bearing a favourite nationalist motto in French '*Nos Institutions, Notre Langue, Nos Lois*', and Canadian views were presented at a distance. Thirty years later Mauchline was producing views of Melbourne.

In Europe there was often an active market in France and Italy for national heroes and heroines. Indeed, what Surgeon-Captain P. O. Gordon Pugh, author of *Staffordshire Portrait Figures* (1970), considers to be the 'tallest and finest Staffordshire patent figure ever made', that of Napoleon, 24 inches in height, was produced for the French market. There were no religious inhibitions in the export business either. While some of the images designed for Britain were aggressively Protestant – Ridley and Latimer as a pair were paired with a figure called 'Protestantism' – there was no hesitation in producing Roman Catholic images for Roman Catholic countries or even Islamic objects (not, of course, images) for Islamic countries. This was trade, and English Roman Catholics could be catered for, too. Two untitled pairs, showing a friar and nun, were produced at the height of the anti-Popery campaigns and have been identified as Sister Margaret Mary Hallahan and Father Bernard Moulaert, well-known figures in the Catholic communities of the Midlands.

Stevens was equally versatile in offering both the great Baptist preacher C. H. Spurgeon ('We preach not ourselves but Christ the Lord') and Cardinal Wiseman. He also had a Protestant 'Jesus died for all' and a sentimental *Mater Dolorosa*, not to speak of a more simple 'I believe in God'. Appropriately the *Journal of the Society of Arts* singled him out for his business acumen in 1873. 'It is gratifying to note that every part of the work, mechanical and artistic, is English', his admirer wrote. 'Mr Stevens cannot see any reason why, in the name of competition, England should not be well up to the goal. Mr Stevens is a staunch advocate of perfect freedom of trade ... "A fair field and no favour".'

Staffordshire potters were as tolerant as he was. Thus at the time of the Franco-Prussian war of 1870, with a proper sense of neutrality, figures were produced of the King, Queen and Crown Prince of Prussia and leaders like Bismarck and Von Moltke on the German side and of Napoleon III and Marshall MacMahon on the French. In relation to Italy they moved with the *Risorgimento*, however, and after 1848 they had produced a Louis Kossuth which may or may not have reached Hungary.

As far as the British market was concerned, fashions had been set long before 1851. Images in pottery of the Queen and Prince Albert proliferated after their wedding in February 1840, and there are ten Staffordshire portrait figures of Sir Robert Peel and more than a score of Wellington, whose death in 1852, like that of Peel two years earlier, was recorded in many different objects, including jugs. One of Peel in green smear glaze included the words 'Farewell great statesman. Long will thy honest worth be missed in the Councils of the Nation. And when the time of England's difficulty comes, Then will the people truly feel the Patriot they have lost in Robert Peel.' One Wellington jug shows the Duke in an oval cartouche topped by a ducal coronet and surrounded by standards emblazoned with his victories. Unlike the first London statue of him erected in Westminster Abbey, which showed him dressed as a classical orator, the potters dressed him as he dressed himself. Gibson, the sculptor, had considered that 'the human figure concealed under a frock coat and trousers' was not 'a fit subject for sculpture'.

Boxers – and criminals – frequently depicted by the potters but not by the sculptors, included John Carmel Heenan and Tom Sayers, who drew a great boxing contest in 1860, watched by 12,000 spectators: it pitted the 6' 2" American boxer Heenan, who weighed nearly 14 stone, against the 5' 8" English Sayers, who weighed under 11 stone. Later heroes were the cricketer Frederick William Lillywhite, the celebrated round-arm bowler, and Captain Webb, the first man to swim the Channel unaided in 1875: he was to meet his death in 1883 attempting to swim across Niagara.

From the world of crime the murderer James Rush and his housekeeper were represented among the Staffordshires in 1848/9, along with models of Stanfield Hall, the site of the murder, Potash Farm, where the murderer lived, and Norwich Castle, where he was executed. Rush is depicted clutching a bag of money: his housekeeper wears a white mob cap: Potash Farm has roses round the door. Stevens avoided murderers, but picked up a later generation of sportsmen, among them R. Howell, bicycling 'Champion of the World', and W. G. Grace, the cricketer, on the occasion of his century of centuries. Grace and Spurgeon were Staffordshire figures also.

Actors and musicians always had their popular audiences, in the home as well as on the stage. Sir William Macready, for example, was depicted by Staffordshire potters both as Shylock and as Macbeth, and there were at least eighteen figures of the 'Swedish nightingale', Jenny Lind. Some

Staffordshire pottery seems to have been sold outside theatres and music halls. Other pottery was sold at holiday resorts or at fairs. Indeed, the name 'fairing' was invented to describe one category of knick-knacks, few of them directly political (courtship figured more than cabinet making) and many of them manufactured in Germany, free trade in reverse. Dealers' names for such products included Bed Pieces, Cottage Mantelshelf China, and, in Lancashire, Valentines.

Fairings, which might be prizes or which might be bought, made few artistic pretensions. There was one category of ware, however, that did and still does – Parian, a development of biscuit porcelain, which is often quite wrongly described as marble. The mid-Victorian formulae for making it included 'frit', a vitreous mixture of silica and alkali, china clay and felspar: adulterated versions included ball clay and even flint glass. The colour of the objects made from it depended on the amount of iron silicate in the mix. The art depended in part, therefore, like photography, on chemistry, in part on technology.

In 1844 Benjamin Cheverton patented a 'three dimensional pantograph' which enabled 'exact' alabaster (or wax) models of busts to be made that were said to be far more 'lifelike' than Staffordshire portrait figures made from moulds; and in the same year the sculptor Gibson returned to England from Italy to produce Parian ware. He was probably not the inventor of the process which, when perfected, involved the assembly of parts and joining of the seams. There has been prolonged argument both about his claims, as there has been too about claims made for the first industrial manufacturer. Was it the firm of Copeland and Garrett, formerly Spode, who called it 'statuary porcelain', or Thomas Boote who said that he had invented it, or Minton's, who from the first used the name 'Parian' in their advertisements? The claims were examined in a Dutch book on the London Exhibition of 1862 published by order of the Government of Holland in 1864.

Whoever first made Parian soon found that he had rivals, all encouraged by the Art Union and directly or indirectly by Henry Cole. Copeland is said to have been encouraged to experiment with 'statuary porcelain' by the editor of the *Art Journal*. 'We attach very great importance to this material', the *Journal* wrote in 1846, 'as offering a valuable medium for the multiplication of works of a high order of art, at a price which will render them generally available.' Gibson drew attention to the artistic claims of Parian when he approved of a reproduction in the new medium of his marble statue of *Narcissus*, sculpted in 1838 and recreated on Christmas Day 1845. So also did John Bell, whose *Dorothea* was made by Minton for Summerly's Art Manufactures and the Art Union and exhibited in 1851. Pugin himself designed a Madonna in 1847, known in the Minton Factory Book as 'Pugin's Pedestal'.

Politicians and other 'great men' – and women – soon figured prominently, however, alongside Narcissus, Dorothea and the Madonna. Thus before long Minton was presenting Hannah More as well as Queen Victoria, Copeland Jenny Lind as well as Wellington, Wedgwood a 'Carrera' George Washington and a George Stephenson, the latter 'reduced' from an E. W. Wyon statue, and Robinson and Leadbetter a Tennyson. In the first edition of *The Ceramic Art of Great Britain* (1878) Llewellyn Jewitt wrote of the last of these enterprises, Robinson and Leadbetter, which produced nothing but Parian ware, that it specialized in 'statuary groups and figures in large variety: and statuettes and busts, both classical, portrait and imaginative' along with 'vases of endless form, variety and size ... brackets and pedestals ... and a considerable variety of fancy articles'. It was also exporting large quantities to the United States, which produced its own Parian between 1847 and the late 1850s at Bennington, Vermont and Greenpoint, New York. Among the Bennington products was a double-sided Charles Dickens spill-holder, fitting tribute not only to Dickens the novelist but to Dickens the journalist: he had written an article in *Household Words* (1852) which saluted 'the delicate new material called Parian'.

Much Parian ware – and not only Pugin's models – lent itself to display on pedestals, doubtless as many of the historical characters represented would have wished: indeed, Copeland and Garrett specialized in items that could be placed on columns. Parian was less homely than 'Staffordshire', therefore, and more expensive. Robinson and Leadbetter, it was claimed by Jewitt, had 'studied excellence of body, originality of design and cleverness of workmanship' more than 'marketable cheapness'. Marketing may well have depended, indeed, on the fact that the products were not cheap. A Montreal auctioneer was not alone in 1864 in advertising Parian figures along with 'Crimson Damask curtains' and a 'what-not' as desirable furnishings of a 'comfortably furnished residence'.

Parian ware – and later Goss ware, designed for a broader market – figure along with 'Staffordshires' among the most characteristic of Victorian things. Indeed, for many twentieth-century collectors, these are the essential Victoriana. Staffordshires were little collected before the 1950s, however, and it was not until 1951, the year of the Festival of Britain, that Thomas Balston published his first illustrated article on them in the *Country Life Annual*, to be followed seven years later by his authoritative book *Staffordshire Portrait Figures of the Nineteenth Century*: Bryan Latham's *Victorian Staffordshire Figures* had appeared in 1953. Interest in other items of Victoriana came even later. W. S. Bristowe's *Victorian China Fairings* did not appear until 1964, and Austin Sprake and Michael Darby's *Stevengraphs* was published in 1968 to commemorate the ninetieth anniversary of the first mounted silk pictures in 1879. The first big private collection of Staffordshires had been offered for sale in 1962, and twenty years later Christie's had produced its first special catalogue on the subject. None of these books could be seen clearly in the perspectives of this chapter, however, before Benedict Read wrote his *Victorian Sculpture* in 1982.

Appropriately the first piece of Victorian Staffordshire Balston had bought before the First World War was called 'The Fortune Teller', and Michael Thompson was to use the peculiar statistics of the graph of Stevengraph prices as main evidence in propounding his rubbish theory. Those Stevengraphs which had not been consigned to the rubbish heap and which had miraculously survived acquired a value far higher than would have been anticipated when the objects were first produced. Already in 1968, however, Austin Sprake, a keen collector, had made the modest claim that the prices of Stevengraph portraits, less popular in the twentieth century than other thematic Stevengraphs, would catch up 'when a few more collectors appreciate their superb delicate weaving which reproduces the facial expressions, the whiskers and wrinkles as faithfully as the camera'.

'Staffordshires' had humble origins, although their twentieth-century collectors are not all quite as humble. As late as 1829, Simeon Shaw in his *History of the Staffordshire Potteries* could concentrate on the story of aristocratic orders potters received, including an order to Messrs Daniel from the Earl of Shrewsbury in 1827, twice the value of many previous orders. By the late 1840s, however, there were more than thirty 'toy' or figure manufacturers in the Potteries, most of them 'humble potters', working in what one of George Hood's highly articulate employees, Colin Shaw, called 'rusty and grim premises'. By 1851, two years after the opening of the 112 miles of North Staffordshire Railway (with 39 stations), there were 165 manufacturers of china and earthenware manufacturers of all kinds.

Already, therefore, a new popular market had come into being, described by John Bedford as 'a new and vigorous folk art – except that it had a strong flavour of the new urban populations rather than the peasant countryside'. As early as 1929, Herbert Read, unlike other twentieth-century critics of Victorian aesthetics, had recognized the 'unconscious artistry' of Staffordshires. Unlike Stevengraphs they could make little claim to verisimilitude. Staffordshire images had nothing in common with photographs.

The most sensitive account of their production is that of Anthony Oliver in his *The Victorian Staffordshire Figures* (1971). Like Reginald Haggar before him, he noted how small children were paid about two shillings a week and were expected to produce up to 400 small images in unhealthy conditions in a long and uncontrolled working day. Leisure activities of adults and children not surprisingly included dog and cock fighting.

In fact, we know more of the ways of life of the potters than we do of the skills of the designers: in 1843 one pottery manufacturer, whose father employed 'about ninety hands', told the Commissioners on the Employment of Children that he did not think that 15 hours a day was 'too much' and that if 'there were evening schools the children are so tired when they get home that they would not attend them.' Nonetheless, art classes had been held in the Mechanics Institutes as early as 1834, and in 1845 the Mechanics Institute of Henley applied to Somerset House for aid in establishing a

School of Design. Class instruction began in 1847. In 1851 J. A. Hammersley, who was to become Superintendent of Art Treasures at Marlborough House, was lecturing the workers there on 'The Aesthetic Theory of Ornamental Art.'

Because of late-nineteenth century and early twentieth-century changes in fashion, tracing back the history of particular designs in detail has become almost a sporting activity. There is a sense of discovery in the dealer John Hall's account of the surviving moulds in the possession of William Kent (Porcelains) Ltd, founded in 1878, which it has been shown belonged originally to the Parrs of Burslem, 'toymakers', from at least 1828 onwards. We can, of course, trace back the origins of many pottery designs to the *Illustrated London News* – the Peel on Horseback, for example – and to comic song covers a number of portraits, like that of actress and singer Rebecca Isaacs. 'I want to be a Bloomer', a reference to the dress reforms of Mrs Bloomer, was another song, appropriately illustrated, which inspired a piece of pottery.

The cheapness of the Staffordshire products was one of their great attractions, a point fully realized by one large manufacturer of Staffordshires, Sampson Smith of Longton, who had already established his name and reputation before he moved to a new factory in 1859. Sampson Smith was responsible for some of the best-known designs of popular Staffordshires, some of which were still being reproduced at the end of the century. 'Garibaldi at War', for example, was still selling as late as then at £8 per dozen, as were Gladstone and Disraeli, and 'Garibaldi on Horseback' was selling at £30 per dozen. Early wholesale prices had been much cheaper: the first copies of 'Garibaldi on Horseback' for example, cost only 60s a dozen when they left the factory.

The figures stood in their own right, made of whiter clay than earlier types and usually with flat-back design. Some were heavier than others, some more translucent. Some figures were far more ambitious than others. They also varied in size, from huge almost to miniature. As the reign went by, any attempt to imitate porcelain figures – some early royal figures had been produced both in earthenware and in porcelain – were abandoned. There was no real copyright in the figures, and they were – and subsequently often have been – pirated. Few bore marks of factory origin, and the collector realizes at once that some were well finished and others were not.

Colour was important as an attraction, and among forgotten Victorian inventors F. W. Collins and A. Reynolds patented in 1848 a process for affixing three colours – blue, red and yellow – from a single transfer with a single firing. There are some remarkably colourful mid-Victorian Staffordshires, therefore, with cobalt blue (a cheap product) applied as a favourite shade under the glaze. Later in the century, however, figures became paler, and the underglaze blue virtually disappeared after 1860, possibly for reasons of economy. Underglaze black (or enamel black) used for dress coats and trousers of politicians like Gladstone and Disraeli and preachers like Spurgeon – or duller overglaze black – did not provide an adequate substitute.

The quality of the gold deteriorated, as did much else, during the 1880s: so-called 'bright gold', a liquid preparation of gold filings in *aqua regia* was harsher, if more stable, than 'best gold', (a highly toxic mixture of gold and mercury) had been, and 'best gold' continued to be used in more expensive pieces. 'Lustre' could 'improve' even dull designs, it was thought, and in 1852 John Ridgway patented a means of lustring ceramics in silver and copper using the electro-deposit method invented by George Elkington (see page 25).

Decisions as to what particular pieces of image pottery to make were doubtless difficult, and some lines were soon discontinued. It is interesting that some politicians do not figure in the Staffordshire gallery of fame, whoever the potter. Thus, there was no Palmerston, although there were no fewer than fifteen places for Garibaldi. Later in the century, the Irish nationalist Parnell found a place, as William Smith O'Brien, transported to Australia, had done, decades before. Parnell figured also among the Stevengraphs, as did his enemy, the English radical Joseph Chamberlain. Yet there was no Staffordshire figure of Chamberlain, only a picture on a plate.

No Whigs were ever included in the gallery of fame: there was no Lord John Russell, no Duke of Devonshire. Similarly, while there were fifteen Nonconformist ministers, some prepared for the thriving Welsh market (Mauchline in Scotland had one scene of an actual Welsh market), there was only one Anglican clergyman. Pio Nono, Pope Pius IX, found a place as did Cardinal Manning. The Tory Evangelical, the Earl of Shaftesbury, was included doubtless because of his concern for the poor, and so was the Tichborne claimant in the Tichborne case, Arthur Orton, who won the sympathy of the poor. The prosecutor's favourite question in the Tichborne case 'Would you be surprised to hear?' was turned into the title of a popular song, while the Shah of Persia, unrepresented in pottery, was the subject of another music hall song 'Have you seen the Shah?'

If there were no inscriptions on early and mid-Victorian figures or other printed evidence relating to them, it would often be more difficult to recognize many of them, including Victoria and Albert, than to date them. There were, indeed, some extraordinary features about the images which have subsequently been pointed out by twentieth-century dealers and historians. The first Victoria, for example, modelled in the style of Obadiah Sherratt (1775–1846), is identical with an earlier figure of the opera singer Maria Felicity Malibran, who died in Manchester after falling from her horse the year before Victoria came to the throne. The only visual differences in this rapid reincarnation were the title and an added crown.

There was nothing new, however, about such cavalier treatment. What is said to be the very first royal commemorative piece, a mug celebrating the coronation of Charles II in 1660, had been originally intended for a different event and the body is that of Oliver Cromwell. Perhaps this was no more remarkable than the stories of the same mould being used for Wellington's nose as for the teats on cow milk jugs, of Gladstone and Disraeli emerging from the same mould, or of using the mould of the Duke of Clarence after his death to create Robert Baden-Powell, complete with a new slouch hat. Poses were copied, too: that of the Prince of Wales in 1874 is identical with that of the King of Prussia.

Animals seldom required precise representation, and Staffordshire dogs, hounds, poodles and whippets, 'white and gold, black and white, and red and white', were not only produced in greater numbers than people but continued to be made in large numbers and sold by the gross after the fashion for portrait figures had declined. So, too, were hens. Yet there were 'individual' animals of fame also, like 'Master McGrath', the black greyhound owned by Lord Lurgan, which won the Waterloo Cup three times, the last time in 1871, and 'Jumbo', the African elephant, obtained in 1865 from the Jardin des Plantes in Paris by the London Zoo. It is not clear whether or not Jumbo gave his name to the stuffed elephants of the nursery or the other way round. He certainly made his way into the Law Courts and into music when in 1882 the Fellows of the Royal Zoological Society decided by a substantial majority to sell him to Phineas T. Barnum for $10,000. A minority of Fellows tried unsuccessfully to seek a court injunction to prevent his leaving the country. The *Daily Telegraph*, rousing public protest and offering to collect £100,000 to outbid Barnum, was unsuccessful also.

Jumbo himself was equally unsuccessful, for when on his way to the docks he sat down and refused to budge, Barnum, who referred to him genially as 'the biggest brute walking the earth', considered this the best possible advertisement. Nor was Barnum completely disconsolate when three years after being taken to the United States Jumbo was killed at Ontario charging a railway train. In his place he then introduced 'The Great Jumbo's Widow'.

Some of the best known music of Jumbo was 'anti-Yankee': ('I love the dear old British flag, of it, my boys, I'll always brag') but there was also a popular 'Jumbo and Alice Quadrille' by Henry Klein:

> Jumbo said to Alice 'I love you',
> Alice said to Jumbo 'I don't believe you do',
> If you really love me, as you say you do,
> You wouldn't go to Yankeeland and leave me at the Zoo.

There had been an earlier C. W. Marriott Alice Quadrille based on *Alice in Wonderland* and called *The Wonderland Quadrilles*: it won the approval of Tenniel, whose monograph appeared on the title page. There was also a 'Jolly Dog's Galop' drawn in 1863 by Alfred Concanen.

The fame of Master McGrath must have been as great as that of Jumbo or of *Alice in Wonderland* in the Potteries. Yet in an area with a strong minority interest in popular education there was a secure local place also for Shakespearean pieces, including the seven models derived from Tallis's *Shakespeare Gallery* in 1852/3, well modelled, painted all round and more expensive than other pieces, which have given their name to a category of statuettes. Other pieces were made for the Shakespeare tercentenary celebrations in 1864. Surprisingly, however, there was no Dickens in the Staffordshire figure collection and perhaps less surprisingly no Tennyson.

Stevengraphs, made in Coventry and praised for 'excellence, skill and resource' by no less a person than Gladstone in 1870, included both 'Ye Lady Godiva' and 'Ann Hathaway's Cottage' in nearby Stratford, and three Shakespeare tercentenary ribbons, not intended as bookmarks but as three parts of a 'favour' to be joined together by the customer. 'They are marvellously worked', wrote the *Derby Mercury*, 'and are undoubtedly the best specimens of weaving we have seen'. Stevens was shrewd enough to go on selling the ribbons long after 1864 with the words 'Shakespeare's Tercentenary' omitted. He sensibly included also a Shakespeare bearing the words 'He was not for an age but for all time'. Dickens figured in his collection, but there was still no Tennyson. Nor was there a Tennyson in Doulton salt-glazed stoneware, first made at Lambeth and later at Burslem. There was a Shakespeare and a Dickens, however, along with a Burns, an Albert, and a Victoria.

In Parian ware you could find a Dickens bust as well as the Dickens spill-jar, and you could also find a Thackeray (if mis-spelt as Thackary) – and a Tennyson, not to speak of a Palmerston. Obviously the customers for Parian ware were better-off. And while some firms producing Parian ware concentrated on objects rather than figures, like the fine-tracery open work basket produced by the Belleck Factory at County Fermanagh, opened in 1863, even the Belleck factory produced a Dickens along with a Parnell and a Wesley. There had never been any doubt about Wesley's popularity in the Potteries from the eighteenth century onwards, and there is one Enoch Wood bust made after Wesley himself had given a sermon in Wood's house. Once again, there were oddities of treatment. It is said that when Wesley visited Wednesbury, effigies were made of him in haste by painting the cervicles of horses to resemble the preacher with a cravat.

One well-known nineteenth-century potter, W. H. Goss, known to thousands of collectors, some of whom were to form a league, later to be called the International League of Goss Collectors, was born not in the Potteries but in London in 1833, and on his mother's side he was of Huguenot descent: he is said to have studied at the Government School of Design in London and to have learnt pottery from Alderman Copeland: he was also a friend of the editor of the *Art Journal*. Goss, who established his pottery at Stoke-on-Trent in 1858, specialized in small portrait busts in 'ivory porcelain' along with tobacco and scent jars, bread platters and 'heraldic china', including many commemorative items, which were to continue to be produced well into the twentieth century. The first printed *Goss Record*, the brainchild of J. J. Jarvis of Enfield, Middlesex, giving a list of agents who sold Goss porcelain, was not published until 1901. Goss died in 1906, but his firm survived to benefit from the First World War when there was a great demand for commemorative pieces. It finally disappeared after takeovers in the Second World War in 1940.

Goss had left Copeland's factory in 1858 and was soon using a family crest and producing in terra cotta as well as in pearl, china and 'modified Parian' ware. His first bust was probably that of Palmerston – both Gladstone and Disraeli were to follow – and in 1862 he won a bronze medal at the London Exhibition, for his 'ivory porcelain': in the same year the *Art Journal* called his pieces 'generally of a cheap order, frequently for "the masses"'. His modeller and general manager, William Bromley, was induced to leave him in 1863 to go to Belleck, taking with him many of Goss's workmen. One of the most accomplished of them, William Gallimore, lost his right hand in an accident, but learned to model with his left before migrating to the United States. 'He never seemed to take care', wrote Jewitt, 'but a perfect portrait would appear to grow out of a series of hurried and apparently careless dabs at the wet clay'.

Goss's later range, manufactured in large quantities from 1865, included 'jewelled porcelain after the manner of Sèvres', egg shell porcelain, the thinnest and most delicate ever made', a Lady Godiva riding her horse, 'Little Red Riding Hood', Napoleon I, bearing of all things the arms of the island of St Helena, and, of course, Queen Victoria in many versions and bearing many legends. One 1887 design showed the Queen inside the Garter Star, but this had to be withdrawn because of official protests over illegal use of the Star. Another in 1897 showed national emblems, including the rose, the leek, the thistle and the shamrock round an imperial crown. It bore the words 'liberty, loyalty, legality'. The first heraldic pieces, in themselves not a new idea, were produced in large quantities from the 1880s onwards and proved a great business success when the market for bigger Staffordshire figures was declining.

## II

For all J. R. Green's distaste for heraldry, for the history of royal families, and for war, neither he nor his fellow citizens, among them potters like Goss, could ignore any of these themes. Victoria's long reign was registered not only on her coins and stamps but on much else besides, and her jubilees were public landmarks. Other monarchs, even other régimes, came and went. She stayed. There were always official medals too, and in the early years of the reign one William Wyon, who died in the year of the Great Exhibition, produced a medal of the Queen which was directly used both for coins and for stamps. His son, Leonard Charles, who died in 1891, and his cousins dominated British medal making until the last years of the reign.

The Queen's most recent biography by Stanley Weintraub begins not with the events but with the things of 1887, including the Jubilee inkstand given to her by the Prince of Wales. Its lid was a royal crown, and in the privacy of her diary she described it as 'very pretty and useful'. This, of course, was a very special object. The Queen's loyal subjects, who sent her more than 2,000 illuminated addresses, could acquire Jubilee medals (ten times as many popular medals were produced for the Jubilee than for any previous occasion in history) and be given, particularly if they were children, mugs and plates or buy glass dishes and Staffordshire figures. There was even a souvenir clay pipe.

An 1870s figure of the Queen, standing crowned, with veil, ermine-edged cloak and multi-flounced skirt was reissued for the Jubilee, now bearing the words 'Year of Jubilee'. The same figure was to be used in 1901 at her death, this time with the date of death added. In between there had been one new figure of the Queen on a pedestal. It was the only recorded 'portrait' of the Queen during the last twenty-five years of her reign other than those made from earlier models. Yet there was one realistic gold medal issued in 1887, that of the Art Union which did not seek to hide the age of the Queen. The City of London's medal, designed by Anton Scharff, and produced by Elkingtons, was sent abroad to 39 libraries, museums, societies, including Leeds and Sheffield libraries and the Imperial Library in Vienna.

By 1901 there were, of course, statues of Prince Albert everywhere – not to speak of the Albert Memorial – and his name, like hers, had been given also to streets, parks and public houses. Even when he was very young, *Punch* had observed that 'we are charmed to see in the shops a new portrait of Prince Albert. It was very much wanted and makes, we think, the forty-fifth of the year.' The Queen, venerable by 1890, had appeared in her time in many youthful poses: thus, in one delightful Staffordshire figure she is shown mounted on a chestnut horse and wearing a tight-fitting riding habit and a low round crimson hat. This was before she had turned completely to bonnets (see page 263), and there was need for only one single word as an inscription – 'Queen'.

Cartoonists made more of her vulnerability at the beginning of her reign than of her prowess. Thus, John Doyle in a well-known cartoon 'Susanna and the Elders' showed her riding between Melbourne and Palmerston, and the *Observer* produced (exceptionally) a crude engraving of her Coronation in 1838. In *Punch* in 1841 she is depicted as 'Little Red Riding Hood' with Peel as the wolf. Not surprisingly, the first Victorian Staffordshire noted by Thomas Balston was the wedding of Albert and Victoria, and he noted too how very soon after there were figures showing the Queen holding a baby in long clothes. Already by 1846, however, Balston remarks, it seemed as if the public were losing its interest in royal babies or children: there are no figures of the seven younger children in childhood. Marriages, of course, were to remain interesting: thus the Princess Royal reappeared on the occasion of her marriage to Prince Frederick William of Prussia in 1858.

Albert was unrecorded in pottery during the Crimean War, or later during the 1850s, but when he died in 1861, one moulded jug issued in commemoration looked back to the Great Exhibition in the background. A large and still imposing Albert tazza, showing the 'Island Palace Home' at Osborne – and yet again the Exhibition – was commissioned from Copeland by the Art Union and distributed to subscribers by ballot after his death, and in 1887 a new Albert plate bore his portrait encompassed with a wreath. It is doubtful if the Queen would have approved.

The Prince of Wales, who had first appeared (after a painting by the royal family's favourite painter Winterhalter) in a sailor suit and as a Highland boy on a Shetland pony, was depicted skilfully a year after Albert's death in civilian dress following his engagement to Princess Alexandra. There was a reissue of an old medal of the Prince in 1890 with the name Prince Alfred on it. The potter had confused two sailors. By then the Prince of Wales looked completely different, and there was only one late new model made by Sampson Smith during the 1870s before his Coronation images in 1901 and 1902.

There were two other late-nineteenth century royal figures, however, the second of whom was to become an indefatigable collector. The Duke of Clarence, who died before he could marry Princess May, was paired with her in 1891: she was wearing a pearl necklace and carrying a large ostrich fan, ostrich feathers being treasured status objects. May married the future George V instead (himself a collector of stamps) and was to be known to posterity as Queen Mary. No Staffordshire figure could have quite done justice to Queen Mary or to her collecting habits. Nor did the crude figures of Edward and Alexandra which were prepared for the delayed Coronation.

Foreign royalty received ample attention also during the mid-Victorian years, particularly Napoleon III and Empress Eugénie – in many guises. During the Crimean War Britain and France were allies, and a half-allegorical figure piece of 1865 shows the Emperor in uniform being transported on a roaring British Lion. This was a time for flag waving, and there was an inevitable patriotic vein in the products of the Potteries during the Crimean years just as there was in the pictorial music covers of Victorian songs.

During the year of the Great Exhibition there had been songs and dances of peace, like 'the Crystal Palace Quadrille'. Now artists of pictorial music covers turned enthusiastically to action themes which could be more dramatically illustrated. A. Hyatt King has noted in a brief pioneering study published in 1950 how it was during the 1850s that decorative black and white music title pages gave way to chromolithographical covers. It was not that chromolithography had not been employed before: Louis Antoine

Jullien, conductor and impresario of Crystal Palace fame, used it for the covers of polkas and quadrilles, and Nelson and Jeffreys had issued their musical annual *The Queen's Boudoir* with 'illustrations in chromolithography' as 'specimens of fine art' in 1840/1. What happened during the Crimean War was that chromolithography began to be considered almost essential for the illustrations. It went well with the text. Thus, Augustus Butler, 'a Bohemian of Bohemians', who nonetheless specialized in military song covers, produced 'The Cardigan Galop' and 'The Guards Quadrille', while Alexandre Laby, whose masterpiece was a painting called 'The Death of St Joseph', produced the cover for a song version of Tennyson's 'The Charge of the Light Brigade', with music by John Blockley.

Pathos might go with patriotism, however, as the century proceeded: 'Now what will become of poor old Ireland?', and 'Brighter Days Will Come'. Yet *pace* Green, who was writing after the Crimean War, Victorian historians could no more avoid the topic of war even than in peacetime Victorian boys could avoid toy soldiers. 'War', Henry Vizetelly told the proprietor of the *Illustrated London News*, was 'the food on which picture newspapers thrive best'. In the middle years of the century the images left behind at the end of the Crimean War provide almost as valuable evidence for the historian as the millions of words. There are, indeed, almost as many surviving 'Crimean things' as there are things directly associated with the Crystal Palace. Whole galleries of commemorative pottery – and other memorials of fame – were produced in 1853, 1854, 1855 and 1856. There are, for example, at least eleven Staffordshire figures of Field-Marshal Lord Raglan, the Commander-in-Chief, and three of his successor, Sir James Simpson. Divisional Commanders on display included General Sir George Cathcart, killed in a cavalry charge, and General Sir William Codrington. There were figures of war heroes, too, like Colonel Sir George de Lacy Evans, who threw back a group of Russians from Sebastopol, itself the subject of many models.

In Parian ware there was less to offer, but in the plethora of Crimean prints and Crimean music covers, every kind of technique was used – etchings, woodcuts, lithographs and zincographs – and every kind of typographical art exploited. Some of the prints were as ephemeral as the pictures in the *Illustrated London News*, one of which was said to have been sent to London by an artist whose friend had his horse killed in the very square where the artist was producing his sketch. Some, however, were to have a very long life, among them eighty hand-tinted lithographs by W. Simpson which survive in a group called *The Seat of War in the East*. The rarest of them today is one showing Florence Nightingale ministering to the wounded.

There were many private memorials, too, after the Crimean War was over, like the statue of the horse, Sir Briggs, kept by Godfrey Morgan, Lord of Tredagar and hero of Balaclava: he also maintained a menagerie. At the Green Jackets Museum in Winchester you can see not only water colours of the Crimea by Brevet-Major H. Clifford V.C., but 'a lady's slipper and embroidered scarf taken out of a Russian lady's bedroom' by a Captain Wilkinson in February 1854. There is also a Russian necklace presented to a British Soldier by a Russian soldier after peace was signed. Such Crimean private things are to be found in many places. I have in my possession a remarkable hand-illustrated record of the war battles of the Crimea with the signatures of officers and men arranged geometrically to form an ingenious pattern.

I also have several Florence Nightingale 'Lady of the Lamp' pictures and Florence Nightingale Staffordshire portrait figures. The lamp image, surprisingly never used by the Staffordshire potters, was only one of several Florence Nightingale images of fame. Nightingales themselves could figure in cartoons – and music covers – all of which stimulated voluntary effort from the unknown millions. Another nurse who attracted popular attention, the Jamaican Mary Seacole, figured prominently as 'Our Own Vivandière' in *Punch*: over the headstone of her tomb in Shepherds Bush, one of many Crimean memorial tombs, she was described as 'a notable nurse who cared for the sick and wounded in the West Indies, Panama and on the battlefields of the Crimea'. Florence Nightingale, the subject of a striking 1856 photograph, was to live until 1913. Her own favourite Victorian thing was a brooch presented to her by Queen Victoria in 1856: it bore the words 'Blessed are the Merciful'.

The Crimean War was an extremely unpleasant, if popular war, and since it was fought at a great distance it tested the strengths and weaknesses of the communications system as much as military – and medical – organization on the spot and the personal qualities of the generals taking part in it. News about it was precious. So was family news in the opposite direction: one transferred pottery design shows the much awaited 'Arrival of the Post in the Army before Sebastopol'. 'Many thanks for the stamps, paper and pens that arrived so timely', wrote one soldier, 'my pens and paper were quite done.'

The *Illustrated London News* did not hesitate to describe the horror: 'It was impossible to pass along' after Inkermann, we read, 'without treading on the wounded or the dead, so thickly was the ground covered with them.' And it catalogued an inventory of 'relics' left on the battlefield – 'Russian cartridges not yet broken – ramrods – Miniéballs – Russian pouches – belts – old gun barrels – fragments of clothing'. There was a litter both of things and of people. W. H. Russell, the famous *Times* war correspondent, described in *Victorian People*, looked behind the litter to expose and to explain as well as to describe.

Because the War entailed heavier casualties from disease than from combat, medicine had to be considered as critically as action, and Florence Nightingale, herself deeply preoccupied with the inadequacies of military organization, was a necessary romantic heroine, depicted in many paintings which did not do justice to the grim realities of the horror which she experienced far away from home. Distance had much to do with attitudes. Gaps in communication were generally associated with failures in organization, and while many of the images of war left out the fact that heroism and folly often went together, as they had at 'the unfortunate murderous' Charge of the Light Brigade, they could never completely leave out the plight of the wounded. Thus, the 'Royal Patriotic Jug', black-printed and gilded and advertising a 'Royal Patriotic Fund', shows wounded soldiers on one side and on the other an angel who is surely related to John Bright's powerful 'angel of death' whom he invoked in one of his most famous speeches. (See *Victorian People*, Chapter VIII.)

This was genuinely a war of crutches as well as swords and of words. Of course, swords and words went together. The picture on a rare uncaptioned Kertch mug showing the 10th Hussars in action and the Cossacks retreating – with a Hussar impaling a retreating Russian on his sword – was based on an illustration with commentary in the *Illustrated London News*, and a group of invalided soldiers returning from the Crimea was based on an illustration in *Cassell's Illustrated Family Paper*.

It is remarkable that many of the images of war, including one series of 'incidents of the war', appeared on children's plates, some in black and white, some in colour, and it seems equally remarkable now – though it would not have seemed so then – that many of them were probably made by child potters, who had figured so prominently in the *Report of the Royal Commission on Children's Employment in Industry* in 1843. Their own work carried with it danger, for processes like dipping usually led to lead poisoning, and there must have been many child potters in the 1850s who were aware that not all wounding was wounding in war.

Nor was all the wounding a wounding of people. The children's plates sometimes showed animals, particularly horses, around their borders, and the shot horse of the Victorian artist of the *Illustrated London News* was by no means a unique creature. There was an educational element in iconography for children, but it is not always clear what the lessons learnt really were. This was an age when schools were not managed by the state nor by local authorities and when schooling was not compulsory – many of the people who made the pottery of images could neither read nor write – and as far as sick children were concerned there was no children's hospital in Britain until the opening of Great Ormond Street in 1858.

Photography was more prominent by then than it had been in 1851, partly because of the war work of the solicitor, Roger Fenton, first Honorary Secretary of the Photographic Society (see above p. 129) who had been born in the same year as Queen Victoria and who was sent out to the Crimea in March 1855 with letters of introduction from Prince Albert. He took no fewer than 360 Crimean War photographs. Yet unlike the influential words of Russell, Fenton's photographs conveyed none of the horrors of war, so that the historian has to turn to other sources for war in action.

The nature of visual evidence concerning war was raised explicitly in the *Illustrated London News* in November 1853. 'The historian of the war in future years', the reporter stated, 'will be seen bending over these memorials, and comparing them with the *literae scriptae* of the correspondents of the journals, in order that, before setting himself to deck out his epigrammatic paragraph, or to roll his sonorous period, he may be well "up" in the fortunes of the country and the bearing of those who fought on its soil.' Fenton inspired 'sonorous periods' rather than repudiated them.

Characteristic Fenton titles – and they were noticed as much in Paris as in London – included 'The Cookhouse of the 8th Hussars' or 'A Quiet Day at the Master Battery', and even 'A Cantonière tending a Wounded Man' gives no sense of the agonies of the wounded nor, indeed, of the filthy conditions within which Fenton himself had to work. Yet Fenton saw the same sights as Russell and could write himself in one graphic passage of how 'we came upon many skeletons half buried. One was lying as if he had raised himself upon his elbow, the bare skull sticking up with still enough flesh left in the muscles to prevent it falling from the shoulders.' Perhaps in retrospect the most interesting feature of his art was that his 'studio of battle' was an ingenious transportable tent which took the place of a dark room.

Fenton, approved of by the Queen, was certainly as much interested in images of fame, however, as any maker of prints or pots, and one of his best-known photographs, 'Council of War', a typical set group, shows Lord Raglan, General Pelissier and Omar Pasha (all subjects of Staffordshire portrait figures) in solemn deliberation. Fenton soon learned that in this as in all wars lesser men wanted to be remembered too. 'Everybody is bothering me for their portrait to send home', Fenton complained, 'my hut seems to be the *rendezvous* of all the colonels and captains in the Army.'

When the War was over, the colonels and captains were remembered, dead or alive, in long lists on military memorials, sometimes ornately decorated. Winchester Cathedral is rich in them: one of them, that of the 97th Regiment, refers to the fruitless assaults on the Redon battery in which Campbell was killed. There is a memorial to the 7th Royal Fusiliers also, and their colours hang in the south transept with the names of their battle honours – Alma, Inkerman, Sebastopol. The memorial notes honestly, however, that more than half of the Royal Fusiliers' original strength died in 'action or disease', and the memorial to the 97th Regiment is even more specific. One hundred and twenty-two men died of cholera in Greece on their way out to the Crimea, one 'died of dysentery brought on by exposure in the trenches', and another was 'suffocated by the fumes of charcoal' possibly given off by a brazier in an ill-ventilated dug-out or tent.

Such monuments reveal, like Mary Seacole's tomb, that the war experience they record was not restricted to the Crimea. Personal history, like regimental history, might cover a variety of campaigns. Thus, the Winchester memorials relate, often vividly, the Crimean War to the 'Indian

Mutiny' of 1857, the Afghan Wars, the Ashanti Wars, the South African Wars and, as a terrible climax, 'the Great War'. There are also many memorials recording deaths at sea.

Official medals tell the same story. In 1854 the Queen had commanded that a medal bearing the single word 'Crimea' should be struck and that bars from Alma and Inkerman should be awarded to those who had taken part in the battle. Further bars were added later for Balaclava and Sebastopol. The medals were issued promptly while the battles were still in progress. The bars have been described by Augustus Steward as 'the most ornate of the whole series given with British medals', but the obverse side of the Wyon design was the same as that on the Peninsular and India General Service medal.

While the nineteenth-century memorials and medals are mainly concerned with so-called 'little wars', in retrospect at least the Crimean War, which involved the Great Powers for the first time since 1815, might well have been a 'great' one, and certainly when it ended no one who had expected it to produce 'great' results – and there were many who had – was really satisfied. Nonetheless, there is one Staffordshire piece called 'The Victory', based on an illustration in *Cassell's Illustrated Family Paper* with the caption 'The Real Peace Negotiations', which shows ordinary soldiers, not officers. There is also a well-known 'Peace Jug' produced not in the Potteries but at Kirkcaldy in Scotland, showing on one side returning soldiers, and there is at least one local peace beaker commemorating a Peace Festival held at Worksop on May 25th 1856.

Much commemorative pottery, like the popular medals, was made not for national but for local events, and it is important to recall that as far as war was concerned local origins and local loyalties determined the pattern of Army organization. According to Major-General R. F. K. Goldsmith, author of a pamphlet 'The Military Memorials of Winchester Cathedral', 'In moments of crisis, the British soldier, true to the national character, draws his inspiration more from his membership of a regimental family with its comradeship and identifiable traditions than from higher but more intangible ideals.'

While the Crimean War lasted, war themes as expressed in things were of two kinds – those dealing with particular events, like the Battles of the Alma or of Balaclava, and those incorporating more general war *motifs*. 'May they ever be united', were the words often to be found on plates, plaques, mugs, jugs and even on chamber pots: the pictures might be of Victoria and Napoleon III or of British and French soldiers. Sometimes, when there were no pictures, there were clasped female and male royal hands or crossed flags. Other designs introduced the third ally, Turkey, and some of the symbols of the enemy, most prominent the Russian eagle. The Turks, like the French, had issued a special medal. So, too, had the Sardinians.

It is not so much these memorials of the Crimean War that have lingered longest, however, but rather three words related directly to things which entered the vocabulary for the first time – the raglan overcoat, named after Lord Raglan; the balaclava, the knitted helmet worn to stop frostbite; and the cardigan, named after the colourful general who led the charge of the Light Brigade. The haughty Cardigan, it has been said, was for years the best hated man in England. Yet not only did he give his name to a humble knitwear garment, but when he talked to the Queen on his return from the Crimea he concentrated not on glory but on common things. There had been 'no hammers, nails, bill-hooks etc, so no wood could be obtained, and they could not construct anything. The things never came . . .'

Memories of the Crimean War had not faded when in 1857 news came through of the Indian 'mutiny'. Before the public had had time to buy handsome jugs celebrating the centenary of the battle of Plessey, 'the battle which won Bengal', the shock of the 'mutiny' was almost as great as that of the Crimean War. As the Meerot mutineers marched on Delhi and besieged it for three months, cholera, dysentery and fever were once more in the news along with military glory. In Winchester Cathedral one tablet shows Colonel Chester, 'a good man, a brave soldier, a sincere friend', who was killed in a skirmish with the mutineers during the march on Delhi, while another shows Lieutenant Rivers who died of cholera during the siege.

Staffordshire figures of General Sir Henry Havelock, Commander-in-Chief of the Army in India who died in 1857, were widely circulated, and on this occasion too there was a heroine – 'Highland Jessie' as she is called on the Staffordshire figures. She, too, was a nurse, and she was the first person to hear the sound of the Highlanders' Bagpipes as Sir Colin Campbell's force approached to relieve Delhi. (A flamboyant piece of piano music called 'The Battle March of Delhi' recalled the event.) In one of the Staffordshire figures Jessie's left hand rests on the shoulder of a soldier dressed in Indian tropical uniform and sitting, appropriately enough, on a powder barrel. The 'Highland Jessie' remains a more popular piece of Staffordshire than the Campbells. Indeed, the collector/dealer John Hall rescued his Campbell from a Burnley dustbin.

At the end of the decade there was a burst of patriotism in 1859 and 1860 when volunteer riflemen were mobilized to present a show of force against Napoleon III, and one Staffordshire pottery piece shows a rifle range with a tented camp in Wimbledon Common in the background. There were also plates showing drill positions both of riflemen and bayoneteers, based on a publication of the School of Musketry at Hythe, *Manual Exercise*. *Punch* lent a touch of satire at the moment of 'crisis', but there was a touch of romance when R. J. Hammerton anticipated later music illustrators with his cover for 'My Beau in the Rifle Brigade'.

Napoleon's annexation of Savoy and Nice in 1860 aroused not only riflemen but the many armchair lovers of Italy who bought their Garibaldis with enthusiasm. Indeed, in the same year, the *Illustrated London News* provided the pictorial source for a pair of Staffordshire figures of Garibaldi and Victor Emmanuel, who ten years later was to become the first king of united Italy. When Garibaldi visited London for ten days in 1864 to the delight of the crowds and a Workingmen's Garibaldian Fund Committee, founded four years earlier, he went to the Crystal Palace twice. Doubtless many images were sold on this occasion as they also must have been on the day when a great procession, led by the Cordwainers and bearing the most colourful trade-union and friendly society banners, made its way from Elm Street station to Stafford House to salute the Italian hero. (John Bright watched from a balcony in the Board of Trade.) There were a few red-shirted Englishmen who had actually fought with Garibaldi, and Colonel Peard, paired in pottery with him, was known to the public as 'Garibaldi's Englishman'. Another pair, this time on a mug, consisted of a Garibaldi and a Havelock.

Thereafter, Garibaldi's famous red shirt could be seen in more English homes than Abraham Lincoln's cloak, but the figures of both men were popular. As Bryan Lethem pointed out in an excellent little book on *Victorian Staffordshire Portrait Figures*, published in 1953, interest in such figures was often greater than knowledge, and more than one Benjamin Franklin figure is labelled General Washington. There are also some interesting home-produced American Civil War pieces, like a pottery platter made by the Edwin Bennett Pottery Company of Baltimore, depicting a Civil War battle, but this was made not in 1861 but in 1901.

During the 1860s, American potteries for the most part could not compete with the British in producing either figures or more useful articles for the table, and there is an element of irony in the cultural history of the two countries in that while Englishmen were buying Lincolns and character figures from *Uncle Tom's Cabin*, the Confederate Government in the South was ordering useful china from England. The table service used on board the *Trent*, the ship which, when seized, provoked the international crisis in 1861 in which Albert successfully intervened just before his death – he changed the wording of a Foreign Office dispatch – had been bought from a Burslem firm in the Potteries.

During the 1870s and 1880s, the Staffordshire potters, sensitive to shifts in mood, favoured war less than religion as a subject for their artefacts; and this seemed natural enough given that the Potteries area remained as renowned for its Methodism as for its pots. Surprisingly they did not produce any figures of their own first early-nineteenth century revivalist Hugh Bourne, founder of Primitive Methodism, but they took particular pride in the figures of the American revivalists Dwight Moody and Ira Sankey who made two highly successful evangelistic tours of Britain in 1873–5 and 1881–3. The potters also produced an outstanding head and shoulders of General Booth, founder of the Salvation Army, wearing his hat and uniform and carrying a device with the words 'Blood and Fire' stamped on it.

None of the war figures produced during the Egyptian Wars (1882–5), the River War (1896–1898) or the Boer War (1899–1902) are comparable in artistry with this religious figure (nor with an allegorical Band of Hope figure), although the four portraits of General Gordon, killed at Khartoum, are historically interesting, and in metal there is an Afghanistan Medal issued in 1880 which is crammed with an immense amount of interesting detail. Melton Prior's drawings of the Ashanti War and of later 'little wars', which were published in the *Illustrated London News*, which he had joined in 1868, are fascinating too. The sketches had added point in that Prior carried a double-barrelled shotgun and had actually fought in one battle; and on his return, he liked to appear in military jacket and wide-brimmed hat when he gave popular lectures. Once the Prince of Wales was in his audience. When the Boer War drew Prior out to South Africa, another illustrator produced a full page sketch of him at work on the spot, 'the sketcher sketched'. Yet another illustrator, Frederick Villiers, was as romantic a figure as Prior. His memoirs were called *Villiers: His Five Decades of Adventure*.

The Boer War produced two official medals and more bars (26) than had ever been issued before, but there were few popular medals. It inspired a final burst of activity in the Potteries during the very last years of the century and the beginning of the twentieth.

'No artist' in the words of the *Art Journal*, attempted to depict a scene of actual carnage although the photographer Horace Walter Nicolls, who had worked in Chile during the 1880s, produced outstanding photographs, preserved in the Imperial War Museum, which he hoped 'would appeal to the artistic sense of the most fastidious' and would at the same time have 'the enhanced value of being truthful'.

Violence was certainly far removed from a medal produced by the Austrian Emil Fuchs, an *art nouveau* designer, while Staffordshires, which came into fashion again, mainly represented officers in equestrian poses and left no place for the wounded. They were all of soldiers – Lord Kitchener, the subject of an earlier figure produced at the time of the Battle of Omdurman in the Sudan; General Sir Redvers Buller; Lord Roberts of Kandahar, who after three months of war succeeded him as Commander-in-Chief; General Sir John French, with a long military career ahead of him; Colonel R. S. S. Baden-Powell, who in 1908 was to found the Boy Scouts; Major-General Sir Hector Macdonald, 'Fighting Mac' who had risen from the ranks; and Lord Dundonald.

By then there had been a marked decline in artistry in Staffordshire making, and the headdress of the officers varied more than the horses they rode. Indeed, it was more expressive than their faces. One figure of Kitchener in Sudan shows him wearing not a peaked cap but, like Gordon, a fez: one of Macdonald, also a hero of Omdurman, shows him wearing a busby: Sir John French wears a helmet in one figure and a cocked hat in another: Baden-Powell wears his famous – and more appealing – slouched hat. Surgeon-Captain Pugh in his study of Staffordshires has traced back some of the designs to figures on a music cover called *Siege of Ladysmith* and subtitled 'Grand Divertimento'.

There was one Staffordshire piece, too, which brought in symbolic rather than real figures. It was hastily and messily prepared for the Peace of Vereeniging which brought the war to an end in May 1902. Significantly, perhaps, it was a modification of an earlier piece produced in 1882 when the Kilmainham Treaty brought together Gladstone and Parnell in a short-lived Anglo-Irish Deal. In its 1902 form it shows a bearded Boer and John Bull in a Union Jack waistcoat shaking hands – in both cases new heads had been substituted since Kilmainham – and it bears words which in the light of later events both in South Africa and in Ireland were to acquire profound irony in the twentieth century – 'Peace on earth, goodwill towards men'.

# III

Gladstone and Parnell were paired at the time of Kilmainham, the subject of cartoons very different from the piece of Staffordshire. Both men had their disciples, and both men repelled as well as attracted. There was a break in Parnell's career, and because of Gladstone's longer, if often equally controversial, political career, it is interesting to trace how he, in particular, was associated at various times of his life with a wide variety of Gladstonian things, not least the Gladstone bag and the Gladstone collar. Most of them became named objects relatively late in his life, however. He had long been known for his zeal as an axeman in chopping down trees, but it was when he was already old that visitors to Hawarden used to carry away with them some of the wooden chips left from the choppings. Lord Randolph Churchill made fun of the habit when he deliberately tried to destroy Gladstone by calculated irreverence. He did not succeed. Gladstone's daughter described 'the mountain of things' left for him at Hawarden on his 80th birthday – 'flowers, blankets, gingerbreads, pocketbooks, sausages, crumpets, pillows, books, lamps, vases, rings, cushions etc, etc'.

An early free-trader and a confirmed supporter of Peel at the time of the repeal of the Corn Laws in 1846, Gladstone would have found no place then in any Staffordshire gallery. Cobden did, of course, as did a lesser-known repealer, Colonel James Perronet Thompson, and Peel himself, a subject for teapots as well as plates. Bright, Cobden's closest colleague, was not depicted at that time and had to wait until later. There is only one known transfer of a print of him – on a mug – and on that he is in late-Victorian dress. His portrait was often paired with Gladstone in prints, however, and like Gladstone and Lord Randolph Churchill he appeared on Stevengraphs.

The Anti-Corn Law League, which was led by Cobden and Bright, is interesting in the history of political images since it made the greatest possible use in a pioneering fashion not only of tracts but of *memorabilia*. It also made the most of dreams of cornucopia. A seaport scene on a mug suggested that if British manufactures were exchanged for foreign corn every port would thrive. Another plate proclaimed the power of commerce – 'The Staffordshire Potteries and free trade with all the world.' There was the same approach to cornucopia in the great bazaars held at Manchester in February 1842 and, to the sounds of Jullien's music, at Covent Garden in May 1845. There, according to Harriet Martineau, 'the porcelain and cutlery exhibitions, the mirrors and grindstones, the dolls and wheat-sacks, shoes and statuettes ... made a curious and wonderful display, which was thought to produce more effect on some Parliamentary minds than all the eloquence yet uttered in the House of Commons'.

The League has subsequently passed down to posterity not only through publications like the *Antibread Tax Circular* or through trade and revenue statistics, but through anti-monopoly scarves and pincushions, free-trade tea and breakfast sets, table-cloths and handkerchiefs, and ornate engraved membership cards. One of the cards showed the opposite of cornucopia. On one side was a picture of a starving family with the caption 'Give us this day our daily bread': on the other there was a picture of Bethlehem. Religion and politics were one.

When Cobden went on in 1860 to negotiate successfully with the French for a free-trade treaty, subscribers to a fund collected for him included many of the makers of the most Victorian of Victorian things. Pilkington Brothers, the glass-makers of St Helens, subscribed £500, as did George and John Crossley, carpet makers of Halifax, and Titus Salt, textile manufacturer of Saltaire. Yet even at that relatively late date Gladstone as a Peelite Chancellor of the Exchequer had still not been finally converted into 'the People's William'. He seemed to be a supporter of the South during the American Civil War, and it was not until 1865 that he was 'unmuzzled' when after eighteen years as a Member of Parliament for Oxford University he moved to a popular constituency. In 1864 as a lover of Italy he had welcomed Garibaldi to London, and in the same year he publicly supported the extension of the franchise to working men. Yet the famous spy cartoon 'The People's William' did not appear in *Vanity Fair* until July 1879.

At that time Gladstone, who had been Prime Minister from 1868 to 1874, was in opposition, and Disraeli was at the helm, and it was during their years of rivalry that the first significant Staffordshire pieces dealing with domestic politics since the 1840s began to appear. Gladstone was paired at least twice in pottery with Disraeli, and both figured in Parian ware. The fact that the Staffordshire Disraelis bore the words 'Beaconsfield' shows that they were issued after Disraeli was given his title in 1876. Another Disraeli bust in Goss ware can be dated 1879 from a description in *The Reliquary* which also referred to a bust of the future Prime Minister Lord Salisbury. He and Disraeli were depicted against the keystone of an arch and were described as 'the Keystones of the Kingdom'.

Between 1878 and 1880 Gladstone was throwing stones rather than serving as a keystone. Returning to politics after the brief retirement which followed his defeat at the general election of 1874, he stumped the country, first attacking Disraeli's foreign policy and then the whole of his policy. He became known in the flesh during these years and not just as an image to far bigger audiences than Disraeli had ever assembled. Yet the universal demand for images of both men shows that while offering what seemed to him and to many of his supporters to be a moral choice Gladstone had at the same time given both a prize-ring flavour and a theatrical flavour to the struggle for political power. It was he, not Disraeli, who had a special chair when he visited the Lyceum Theatre (it was specially upholstered for him in very old age), and it was his house at Hawarden rather than Disraeli's house at Hughenden which was turned into a place of popular pilgrimage: 26,000 people were to visit a flower show there in 1896. Finally, there was more than a touch of the preacher in him, and he was shown in one Staffordshire figure standing bare-headed in a pulpit with his right hand on the turban of a Turk who stood against its front. The Turks, old allies of the Crimean War, had never won Gladstone's praises. Given such an approach to politics it is ironical that before and after Disraeli's death Gladstone was to accuse his rival of revelling in 'display'.

Unfortunately there are no details of the relative shares of sales of Gladstone and Disraeli Staffordshires which might tempt us to measure the strength of public reactions to the two parties without resorting to all their manifestos or to the printed election ephemera.

Gladstone, however, was associated with far more images than Disraeli, partly, of course, because he lived seventeen years longer, dying fittingly on Ascension Day in 1898, but partly, too, because he enjoyed addressing crowds all over Britain and because people who heard him in person wanted to have a keepsake of him. At Longton, one of the Potteries' six towns, 'the living and working museum of British pottery' which traces the history of British ceramics is called 'The Gladstone Pottery': it was so named after a visit from Gladstone to Potbank Yard, one of the many visits he paid to industrial locations, another of them Middlesbrough, described in *Victorian Cities*. In Arnold Bennett's *The Old Wives' Tale* one of the Potteries characters describes him as the 'semi-divine Gladstone'.

During the busy years after the early 1880s, when Gladstone had already begun to be called 'the Grand Old Man', or just the G.O.M., he was frequently depicted with Mrs Gladstone, whom he had married in 1839 and who was to outlive him by two years. There are many pictures, including photographs, of the two of them at Hawarden, and there is one excellent photograph of her alone just before her death. There is no Stevengraph of her, but she is paired with him in Staffordshire pottery and shares with him matching plates. They are sometimes surrounded with flowers.

Primroses, Disraeli's favourite flower, were not the only flowers, therefore, which were depicted on Victorian things including, not least, song covers. Yet Disraeli was a powerful enough personality with or without flowers to inspire the production of Disraeli things even after his death. There were Disraeli jugs and octagonal plates, complete with primrose decorations, and there were memorials of what he considered to be scenes of triumph, like the Congress of Berlin in 1878. One year after he died, Primrose Day was inaugurated in his memory, and thereafter real or portrayed primroses figured prominently for new generations in Conservative memorials and celebrations. Primroses decorated his statue in Parliament Square and gave their name to a new Primrose League. Only the poppies of the First World War were to linger longer in the public mind. Music covers once again caught the mood. One 'patriotic conservative' song entitled 'Primrose Day' was dedicated to Lord Randolph Churchill and was recommended for Conservative banquets.

Other flowers depicted on Victorian things included a spray of white lilies for Bright, and for Joseph Chamberlain, who broke with Gladstone on home rule, his favourite orchids. Gladstone in one Stevengraph was decorated with a spray of thistles and roses, Parnell had clover leaves and a yellow harp, and Lord Salisbury was surrounded by roses – red, bright yellow, and orange. By the 1880s the borders of music covers showed increasing numbers of domestic objects as well as flowers – china, glass and furniture.

There was no national agreement about party colours in the nineteenth century, when local political leaders, more immediately known to their audiences, often demanded their image of fame also – in the form of commemorative mugs or medals as much as statues in the parks. There was in fact a wide range of things, some of them Goss things, associated with local 'great men', some of whom were by any criteria outstanding. There were many local Stevens products also, like the bookmark made for the Fine Art and Industrial Exhibition at Coventry in 1867 which incorporated a view of the city and a bust of a local 'great man', Lord Leigh, the President of the Exhibition, with his coat of arms underneath.

More than one local 'great man' was a collector and more than one was a benefactor. An outstanding example of both is the jeweller Joseph Mayer, a collector of antiquities, who was born in the Potteries in 1830. Before he presented his collection to Liverpool in 1867 to form the basis of the City's Museum Collection he had been concerned with many contemporary local Liverpool things, including a Royal Mersey Yacht Club Challenge Cup in 1845, a model silver cradle presented to the wife of the Mayor of Liverpool in 1848, a seal, also of 1848, designed for the curator of the Historic Society of Lancashire, a trowel which he made for the laying of the foundation stone of St Peter's Church in Everton in 1849, medals to commemorate the centenary of the philanthropist William Roscoe in 1853 and the opening of the free Public Library and Museum in 1860, and an elaborately carved Roscoe chair which he also designed and which was made from timbers acquired when Roscoe's house was demolished. It comes as no surprise that Mayer left an unpublished manuscript *Materials Towards a History of the Arts*.

The trowels used in the laying of church and chapel foundation stones have often survived the churches and chapels themselves. Sometimes, too, they have survived the Victorian objects to be found in those churches and chapels, including memorial brass and stained glass. One church in Leicester, St Mark's, which exceptionally included stained glass of Labour leaders, as interesting as the trade-union banners to be found in the Museum of Labour History in London, is at present on the danger list. Statues, of course, have always been vulnerable, proving how fickle images of fame can be. For example, Thomas Attwood's statue in Birmingham, like John Fielden's in Todmorden, were moved from their first places of honour to public parks. Coventry Patmore was not unduly worried about this. 'It should be remembered', he wrote, 'that, in our haste, we may be placing an awful and easy vengeance in the hands of posterity; which might choose, not to pull down such monuments, but – to let them stand.'

# IV

Within the compass of the arts dealt with by Mayer, printing became more important during the Victorian period than it ever had been before, influencing and being influenced by other arts; and the delineation of 'great men' on the printed page was a favourite pursuit. 'Books', the *Manchester Guardian* proclaimed in 1852, 'are the cheapest luxury, the most rational enjoyment, within the reach of all the classes, that in this nineteenth century can be presented to mankind', and for Carlyle they were 'like scouts ... penetrating the whole habitable globe'. Newspapers shared the same acclaim (see page 324). 'The cheap daily press will do more than any other agency to form the public opinion of this country', wrote Cobden, for once echoing Disraeli who had declared in his novel *Coningsby*, published in 1842 before the telegraph had established itself, that 'opinion now is supreme, and opinion speaks in print'. At Gladstone's Hawarden, where newspapers were always in demand and where journalists were amongst the most regular visitors, books were treated more tenderly than trees. Indeed, the Grand Old Man devised a mobile storage system to save precious library space.

Yet despite the rise of publishing and changes in the technology of printing associated with the machine press, Victorians also felt that print had its limitations, partly because there was a substantial, though declining, illiterate population, partly because even at the end of Queen Victoria's reign, when the 'number of people who can read' was 'enormous', the printing press, 'following the law of supply and demand', seemed to be now appealing to 'the uneducated mass of all classes'. One anxious observer who made this particular judgement in the *Nineteenth Century* in the year that

Queen Victoria died was the young historian G. M. Trevelyan. By the time that *he* died, equally anxious observers were complaining that 'the uneducated mass' was beginning to live in a world not only of words but of pictures. It had broken, it was suggested, with Victorian cultural traditions.

In fact, there were significant changes in the way in which the Victorians themselves handled pictures before the coming of the cinema. The woodcut which in the eighteenth century had been largely relegated to the chapbook came into its own in an age of cheaper books, periodicals and newspapers, and there was a growing interest in other modes of illustration, particularly wood engraving, and photography, which for W. S. Ivins in his *Prints and Visual Communication* (1953) brought with it a major breakthrough. 'Up to that time', he wrote, 'very few people had been aware of the difference between pictorial expression and pictorial communication of statements about fact. The profound difference between creating something and making a statement about the quality and character of something had not been perceived ... Photography and its processes quietly stepped in and by taking over one of the two fields for its own made the distinction that the world had failed to see.'

Ivins commented on the changes in the graphic arts before photography, although he did not cover much of the relevant evidence, such as the reminiscences of the radical engraver W. J. Linton who emigrated to the United States in 1866. Nor did he mention one range of specifically Victorian things – Baxter prints, which have been collected as eagerly as Staffordshire portrait figures, often by the same people. They frequently offer images of the same people also, setting out to represent not to satirize. They were deemed free from 'objectionable features' which Thomas Wright in his *History of Caricature* (1864) had associated with pre-Victorian cartoons, and they had none of the political edge of Charles Knight or of the early *Punch*.

Interest in collecting Baxter prints preceded interest in collecting Staffordshire figures, however, and as early as 1908 C. T. Courtney Lewis produced a 'manual for collectors', to be followed three years later by his *George Baxter, Picture Printer of the Nineteenth Century*. For Lewis, Baxter was 'in his way a historian' who 'depicted the events of the early Victorian days in which he lived as graphically by means of the pencil as any writer with his word pictures', a comment that recalls Thackeray's description of John Leech as 'the social historian of the nineteenth century.'

George Baxter was born at Lewes in Sussex in 1804, the son of a local printer and publisher, who learned engraving at a time when copper engraving was still the main engraving process, very soon to be largely replaced by steel engraving. The engraver's instrument was not a pencil but a burin or engraver which was moved across the surface of the copper or steel plate to follow a desired line. Baxter's main interest was in providing colour, as much of a challenge to him as the provision of colour was to be in the development of twentieth-century television. Very soon after beginning business on his account in 1829, he was experimenting with pictures in polychromatic colours, starting with birds and butterflies (as Mass Observation was to start in the twentieth century) before turning to people. When in 1836 he produced a print called 'the Conqueror [*sic*] of Europe', the title did not refer to Napoleon – or to Louis XIV – but to a flower, the auricula, and it appeared in the *Horticultural Journal*.

Baxter had obtained his first patent a year earlier, and in the year when Queen Victoria came to the throne he published his fascinating *The Pictorial Album* or *Cabinet of Paintings* which included a print of Cleopatra holding the asp to her bosom. The first contemporary great person depicted in his gallery of fame was, not surprisingly, a very different Queen – Victoria – and his first print of her appeared in Sir Harry Nicholas's *History of the Orders of Knighthood* in 1842. Thereafter, many familiar contemporary figures, like Albert, Peel, Wellington, Napoleon III and the Prince of Wales, took their place in Baxter's albums alongside Victoria. Jenny Lind was there too. Yet Baxter was less interested in worldly fame than the makers of Staffordshire were. Before Victoria he had produced a series of missionary prints – his first portrait was of a Congregationalist missionary, the Rev John Williams – and before the missionaries he had chosen as subjects people of whom J. R. Green would have approved – 'Bohemian Peasants', 'Hungarian Peasants' and 'Southdown Sheep'.

Present at Queen Victoria's coronation in 1838, Baxter was given special facilities there, but it took him almost three years to prepare his splendid print 'Her Most Gracious Majesty Queen Victoria receiving the Sacrament at her Coronation', complete with a key to the *dramatis personae*. It was bought, according to one contemporary account, not by the 'common people' but by 'patrons' and by 'people of quality, present at, or much interested in the ceremony' and it was 'dedicated by command to the royal Family'. The work was set in a maple and gold frame with the royal arms in gold at the top. It came in two sizes – $21\frac{3}{4}'' \times 17\frac{1}{2}''$ and $17\frac{1}{2} \times 13\frac{3}{4}''$: the larger size cost 5 guineas, the smaller size 3 guineas, and there was also a sepia print. Yet the prices asked were not standard, and some people paid as much as 10 guineas. A further related picture was published in 1841 – that of the Queen opening the first Parliament of her reign.

All Baxter's earliest works had been designed for books and had no signatures: from 1835 onwards, however, they often bore markings like 'Baxter's Patent Oil Colour Painting' or 'Printed in Oil Colours by G. Baxter, Patentee', and they were designed not for the pages of a book, but to hang on walls, like oil paintings. The great wood engraver Thomas Bewick, born in 1753, whose *Memoir*, published in 1862, thirty-four years after his death, had anticipated this in one prophetic passage: 'Prints', he judged, 'might with good effect be made from wood blocks printed in colours like paper hangings, of subjects fit to embellish every house throughout our country'.

Already before 1862 there had been a proliferation of other Baxter objects also – including Baxter pocket books, music covers and needle-box prints. One box-print dealt with 'The Year of the Great Exhibition', another with the Allied Sovereigns and the Commanders of their Forces during the Crimean War, and a third with 'the Queen and the Horses of India', including, surprisingly, in the collection the Duke of Cambridge, Napoleon III and his son the Prince Napoleon. Baxter was deliberately appealing now not to a handful of patrons, but to 'the million', and his prints were advertised as 'cheap artistic pictorial illustrations'. Yet he continued to stress high quality. 'By no other means can such extreme detail, such truthful colouring, and such unlimited numbers be produced'. He made the same point in relation to his Crimean War prints, which included 'The Siege of Sebastopol' and on a more homely plane 'The Soldier's Farewell, The Parent's Gift.'

Baxter's techniques were painstaking. He began by engraving the picture he wished to publish on a sheet of soft steel (or copper) and went on to take impressions of the key plate he had prepared and to cut wooden or copper blocks, based on it, the numbers of the blocks depending on the number of colours he wished to employ. The different blocks were then used in succession, each printing one colour, and as one block dried another was carefully superimposed. The key plate was used to complete the picture. It was an 'expensive process', Baxter declared, based on step-by-step improvements which produced coloured impressions of a high degree of perfection, 'far superior to those which are coloured by hand'. Perhaps his biggest leap ahead came early in the story when he used oil rather than water colours.

Such techniques, which to Baxter were arts not crafts, can be related to more general trends in the history of printing, just as the appeal of his finished products can be related to more general trends in the history of society and culture. As far as both arts and techniques were concerned – and there were other step-by-step 'improvements' in both – useful and now familiar distinctions were being drawn by the Victorians. Relief techniques, associated with wood engraving, went back to the medieval wood cut, and were sharply distinguished from *intaglio* techniques, associated with line engraving from copper or steel plates. The distinction was drawn picturesquely by Ruskin. 'In metal engraving you cut ditches, fill them with ink, and press your paper into them; in wood engraving you leave ridges, rub the tops of them with ink, and stamp them on your paper.' A more important distinction affecting use was that with woodcuts printing-type, text and illustrations could be printed together on the same press, while *intaglio* techniques demanded a separate press. Illustrations had to be printed separately or when they had to be integrated with the text called for double printing, once for the text and once for the illustrations.

There was a third way into nineteenth-century print making – lithography, discovered at the end of the eighteenth century and based on the simple fact that grease repelled water. The design for a lithograph was drawn with a greasy crayon or ink on a block of limestone – or later of zinc or aluminium – and the block was covered with water which was repelled from the greased surfaces. Paper was then applied to the block in a flat bed press and the print was made. Much of the success of the lithograph depended on the skill of this last operation.

The challenges in such processes – and in the logical development of the third, chromolithography – were fully appreciated in an age when there was an increasing demand – and a different kind of demand – for such a product; and Baxter had to cope both with rivals, like Abraham Le Blond, to whom he subsequently sold his licence, and his former pupils, Gregory Collins and Reynolds, whose work could be seen in the *Art Journal*: Reynolds later went to join Minton. Baxter also had to cope with critics, some of whom were enemies. Thus, the *Illustrated London News*, not without its own vested interest, dismissed the best of Baxter's own Exhibition prints as 'pretty and pleasing' and called the rest 'inartistic' and based on 'very bad drawing'. For a recent critic, Ronald Russell, 'No matter how one defines "artistic merit",' Baxter prints 'cannot be claimed to have any'. In his view, at their best they do no more than 'exude a period flavour'. The same could have been said, of course, of the prints issued across the Atlantic by Currier and Ives, founded in 1834. Their 'cheap and popular' hand-coloured lithographs, pictures with no pretensions, sold in huge quantities at far cheaper prices than Baxter prints – from 15 cents to 25 cents retail. The firm opened a London office. Its catalogue listed among the categories of paintings 'Catholic Religious', 'Patriotic' and 'Family Registers' along with 'Horses', 'Kittens and Puppies' and 'Ladies' Heads'.

Baxter's attempt in face of competition to combine cheapness with quality was evident in all his comments on his own work, many of which stressed, as did Courtney Lewis, the 'honest grit' which he put into his productions. He was remarkably consistent too. As he stated in the preface to his *Guide to the Great Exhibition*, the most topical of events, he was determined to reproduce 'artistic pictures' which were not simply topical, and which would be within the reach of everyone. There were some contemporaries who acknowledged his achievement. Thus, for the pro-Palmerstonian *Morning Post* in 1859 – in full agreement with the liberal *Daily News*, which had been founded in 1846 under the editorship of Dickens – 'Baxter's printing in oil colours is really one of the most beautiful and ingenious inventions of our time'. Lord Brougham, who believed in diffusing everything, words even more than pictures, had long ago concurred: Baxter's invention, he claimed in 1849, was 'of public utility, because whatever makes good coloured prints . . . of easy access to the common people, to the cottagers and labourers, is of great use to them in every respect. It is a pleasure to them and now it is made a cheap pleasure.' Brougham, whose head had once appeared on a stoneware gin flask, did not talk about Baxter's gallery of fame: already by 1849 his own fame had greatly diminished and there must have been few people who knew what he looked like.

It seemed likely that Baxter's own fame would be just as short-lived, for although he dreamed of wealth, he was a complete failure as a businessman. Nor did he have admirers, as Linton, 'Patriarch of the Art of Engraving' did: 'hero worshippers bowed down before him as a genius'. In his early years Baxter could not interest publishers based on Paternoster Row, and in 1835, the year when he took out his unique patent, he was already in serious financial difficulties. The London Missionary Society briefly saved him as it might have saved an aborigine, but a member of his family described him in 1840, when he was working on the Queen's Coronation, as 'desperately poor'. The first prints said to have made a profit for him were those of the Queen and Albert. In 1854 he lost his patent, and although he won a prize at the Paris Exhibition of 1855, where, as in 1851, he had a stand of his own, in 1857 he quarrelled with his family, and in 1860 he was forced to retire from business. All his plant, plates, blocks, 'drawn, engraved and highly finished by the patenter himself', and over 100,000 prints, were now put up for sale in London. Yet even this sale did not save him – nor did further sales in the provinces – and five years later he was adjudicated a bankrupt on his own petition. Towards the end of 1866 he was struck by a horse-drawn omnibus and died early in 1867.

It would be a mistake to attribute Baxter's business failure entirely to his personal qualities, although he was not of the stuff from which Victorian entrepreneurs were made. Engraving of all kinds was to go through a Victorian crisis, while the intricate work of a chromolithographer of the calibre of J. B. Waring seemed redundant when the Germans introduced cheaper techniques later in the century. Waring's *Masterpieces of Industrial Art and Sculpture at the International Exhibition* of 1862 had used three thousand stones to produce three hundred chromolithographs. It can not be said, however, that the final challenge to the kind of work Baxter did – photography – was unappreciated by him. The work of early photographers greatly interested him, and in 1858 he actually took out a patent himself for 'colouring photographic pictures'.

The late-Victorian story after his death is complicated. During the last decades of the Queen's reign, 'pictorial art' was left to the Royal Society of Painter-Etchers and Engravers, founded in 1880, to a few artist-engravers using wooden blocks to reproduce in colour, to Walter Crane and to Kate Greenaway, and, not least, to the art photographers (see page 131), none of whom were conspicuously interested, as Baxter had been, in furnishing galleries of fame. There were many cross currents, however. Thus, when Joseph Lundall wrote his *Brief History of Wood Engraving* in 1895, six years after Linton's *The Masters of Wood Engraving*, he observed that 'owing to the invention of various mechanized processes, and the perfection to which photography has risen, the art of wood engraving must seem to be in danger

of becoming extinct.' Yet with William Morris and 'arts and crafts' in mind –
and with developments in the United States – he was quick to add that 'this is
by no means the real case'.

Baxter's own lost reputation began to recover surprisingly soon – after
Frederick Möckler had acquired Baxter's plates from Le Blond, had
produced a portfolio of reprints and in 1893 a catalogue, had created a
Baxter Society (with Lord Leighton, Britain's first painter-peer as President), and in 1896 had organized a Baxter exhibition. When Courtney
Lewis published his *The Picture Painters of the Nineteenth Century* in 1911, he
paid generous tribute to Möckler, whom he interviewed. He added that
'cheapness' was still an asset as far as Baxter prints were concerned: collectors
'of moderate means' would be able 'to spare from time to time the
comparatively small amounts that are needed for the accumulation of these
prints'. They would have the extra satisfaction, he concluded, of gathering
not 'puerile things', 'the craze of the hour', but things with abiding interest,
which had been 'growing in public estimation and value for nearly twenty
years', and which were 'destined to take a very much higher position'. There
was no rubbish theory here.

As one of his illustrations Courtney Lewis included without comment
Baxter's 'The End of Time' (1835) which portrayed the Angel from the *Book
of Revelation* proclaiming the Creator not only of Earth and 'the things that
therein are' but of Heaven and of all 'the things that therein are' also.

Heroes might get a little nearer to Heaven than their worshippers, but the
millions for whom the images described in this chapter were intended had to
be content with the things of Earth, among them the most common things
that J. R. Green most prized, and among these were now photographs.
Conotone's photograph albums in *The Old Wives' Tale* preferred 'an
astonishing menagerie of unknown cousins and their connections, and of
townspeople' to heroes local or national. 'Nothing will open the memory,
evoke the past, regain the deed, rejuvenate the ageing, and cause both sighs
and smiles', Bennett commented, 'like, a collection of photographs gathered
together during long years of life.'

Heroes came and went, and great empires might fade like Nineveh and
Tyre, but 'ordinary families' remained. Fame, Green was not alone in
insisting, was not the most important aspect of life. Nor was 'doing good'.
'Any one who knows what the worth of family affection is among the lower
classes', Green wrote in 1871, 'and who has seen the array of little portraits
stuck over a labourer's fireplace ... will perhaps feel with me that ... the
sixpenny photograph is doing more for the poor than all the philanthropists
in the world.'

# I

'Common things' however new are usually quickly taken for granted. This, however, did not prevent Victorian authors from frequently describing in detail in magazines and books where and how they were found or made. The authors set out to entertain as well as to instruct, but there was undoubtedly a moral dimension to the message. At the end of the century, Archibald Williams, author of *How It Works*, observed in his supremely practical book *How It Is Made* that at exhibitions people who were 'increasingly specialized in their own occupations' were always curious to cluster round 'to watch the creation even of an article which may not be interesting in itself'. And Williams did not conceal either his own curiosity or his conviction that learning how things were made was itself a 'good thing'. 'Wordsworth has confessed to being deeply moved by the sight of "the meanest flower that blooms". Might not a match, a pin or a needle – worth but a fraction of a penny – also stimulate a poet who has seen it in the making?'

The chapter on 'pins' in Williams's book comes between 'screw making' and 'twine and rope', and not surprisingly it begins not with a real Victorian pin-making factory but with Adam Smith's classic account of the division of labour in the pin business which appeared in the first chapter of his *Wealth of Nations* (1776). Smith was writing before there was any sense of an 'industrial revolution', and it was only in 1838, one year after Victoria came to the throne, that the first practical pin-making machine was introduced in Birmingham. By the end of the century, however, about 500 million tons were being manufactured weekly, most of them in Birmingham. 'Where they all go is a mystery', wrote Williams. 'We should doubtless be greatly surprised if we were suddenly gifted with the power of seeing clearly all "the lost and strayed pins" [note the Biblical allusion] that litter the Earth's surface.' Among them were 'safety pins', 'a real blessing to mothers', patented by Charles Rowley in 1849 and made out of a single piece of wire.

Needles, known since prehistoric times, were described by Williams in a chapter called 'In Needle Town', which focused the spotlight not on Birmingham but on Redditch, 'till recently scarcely more than a village'. By then there were said to be no fewer than twenty-two distinct operations in needlemaking, the last of which was called 'needle polishing'. Birmingham figured in this story too, however, for while pin-makers were usually their own wiredrawers, needlemakers procured their steel wire ready drawn from Birmingham. The most controversial process, at least as far as the workers were concerned, was 'pointing' (what was a needle without its point?) and as late as 1854 a pointing machine at Redditch had been ceremoniously destroyed by the hand pointers. The fact that there was no such controversy in Germany, to which the inventor of the machine, Colin Banks, had taken his invention – and there had been earlier English patents, including one granted to Daniel Ledson and William Jones in Birmingham in 1833 – was described in 1876 as 'one of the reasons which enables Germany to compete with English needles in markets all over the world.'

Williams placed his chapter on matches, the third in his book, between chapters on paper making and the building of a piano, and his chapter on pens followed immediately after 'the cradle of a locomotive'. The juxtaposition of great and small was characteristic. In the case of matches and pens, however, two of the most common things in increased use in Victorian England, there were special reasons for detailed treatment. Nor did it need a returning Voltaire (see page 69) or an omniscient Herbert Spencer to appreciate them: the latter called matches 'the greatest boon to mankind in the nineteenth century'. Probably the most eloquent nineteenth-century statement about the pen was made by the pioneer of Zionism, Theodore Herzl, in his will. 'I know that I have used my pen like a man of honour', he wrote. 'I have never sold my pen, never committed a dastardly deed nor courted friendship with it.'

Both matches and pens created images. Matches were associated with the need for and the power of fire. 'A friend of man and teacher of all arts', the pen was usually associated not with honour but with literacy. It had long been deemed mightier than the sword. Mythology reinforced symbolism, particularly in the case of matches. Prometheus, the light bringer, seemed to have been devised for the matchmakers: after all, it was pointed out, Shakespeare had made Othello say:

> I know not where is that Promethean heat
> That can thy light relume.

Vesta, the virgin goddess of the hearth and of fire, came into her own again, too, when vest matches were made from wax, not wood: for whatever reason they were said by the *Encyclopaedia Britannica* to be especially popular 'on the continent'.

Of course, metaphors of matches related less often to virgins than to marriages. 'Everyone is connected more or less intimately with the great industry of matchmaking', wrote *London Society* in 1890 in a laboured article which ended with an account of the scene in Bryant and May's London factory. 'Some make their own matches in secret; others have them made by scheming mothers and provident fathers, with a degree of undisguised publicity that imparts a lively commercial spirit to the transaction. Whether treated as a mere pastime or as fine art, matchmaking, in an inflammatory sense, is indulged in by peasant and prince, by dairymaid and duchess; in a combustible way its votaries are somewhat restricted as regards class and locality. Yet in their way the matchmakers of East London are more interesting than their fellows in the service of Hymen.'

Ian Hay was to handle such themes more lightly – and effectively – in his novel *A Safety Match* (1911) which began with a chapter called 'the striking of the match' and which after dealing with a marriage – 'a match is struck' –

included an account of an industrial 'strike'. One of the most famous incidents in the Victorian history of Bryant and May had been the match girls' strike of 1888, yet at the time of the strike itself, most match metaphors, of which there were almost as many as there were pictures on match boxes, were still dwelling on harmony, not on conflict. 'Why do Bryant and May use the Ark as their Trade Mark?' ran a riddle advertisement of 1890. 'Because', ran the answer, 'the Animals went into the Ark in pairs, therefore it must have been full of Matches.'

Unlike animals, children figured in the literature rather than in the advertisements; and the German story of Struwelpeter, the little boy who burnt himself – and his parents' house – because he played with matches, made its way on to packs of cards as well as the pages of books. Bryant and May prided themselves that they had protected children against their own worst instincts. 'Before the safety match was introduced', the *City Press* told its readers, also in 1890, 'children were continually being burnt and poisoned.' The safety match was almost as much of a blessing to mothers as the safety pin.

There were other tales about children, however, which were less inspiring. Mayhew included in his gallery of 'disaster beggars' a group whom he called 'lucifer droppers', 'impostors to a man – to a boy – to a girl.' 'Men seldom, if ever, practise this dodge', he went on. 'It is children's work' –

> A boy or girl takes up a position on the side of a busy street, such as Cheapside or the Strand. He or she – it is generally a girl – carries a box or two of lucifer matches, which she offers for sale. In passing to and fro she artfully contrives to get in the way of some gentleman who is hurrying along. He knocks against her and upsets the matches which fall in the road. The girl immediately begins to cry and howl. The bystanders, who are ignorant of the trick, exclaim in indignation against the gentleman. The result is that either the gentleman, to escape being hooted, or the ignorant passers-by, in false compassion, give the girl money.

Mayhew had a surprising punch line, however, 'White peppermint lozenges are used more often than lucifers'.

## II

Those authors who made the most of matches were conscious that they were writing with pens that had a far longer pedigree than matches. Indeed, the word pen was derived from the Latin word for a feather, *penna*, and for generations before the Victorians the quill pen had changed little in its appearance. The quill itself, sometimes straight from the bird (goose, turkey, even crow) linked nature and culture – with the 'penknife' as the indispensable intermediary – and as late as 1869 a writer in *Leisure Hour* was describing 'office pens' as 'close battalions of feathered troops'.

Birmingham was once more in the lead in introducing steel pens, that is pens with steel nibs. Dr Priestley is said to have acquired one in 1780; and in 1820 it was claimed that you could buy a hand-made steel pen for the same price as 'the writing master's fee for teaching the art of cutting a quill'. Yet despite their undoubted existence steel pens were said to have been 'almost unknown' in 1830. The great change came during the next ten years with the development of machinery, and when the British Association visited Birmingham in 1839 almost every member of the Association used one. A generation later, when every child in the new post–1870 Board Schools was equipped with a steel pen, George Lindsay of Birmingham could generalize that 'the modern implement for writing with a fluid is a very different thing to the pen of former times'. It had made its way into offices too, while there were few writers who could now claim

With one sole pen I wrote this book
Made of a grey goose quill:
A pen it was when it I took
A pen I leave it still.

Pens might well have come immediately after pins, therefore, in Williams's *How It Is Made*, and they had, indeed, figured together in the autobiographical account given by Josiah Mason of Birmingham, a pioneer of the Birmingham steel pen, who sold cakes and fruits and made boots and furniture before he made pens. In the late 1820s he was employed by the man who had supplied Dr Priestley with pens. It was 'about 1829', he wrote later, when he saw in a bookshop window in Bull Street, Birmingham, nine 'slip' pens on a card, marked 3s. 6d, and 'the novelty', he recalled, induced him to go in and try to buy one so that he could 'improve upon it'. At first, the bookseller Peart said that he would only sell the whole card; but eventually 'he consented to sell me the one he was writing with, and so I bought the "pin" for 6d. I returned home, and made three pens that evening'. The name stamped on the pen was 'Perry, Red Lion Square, London', and Mason sent the best of the three pens he had made to London, in a letter, 'for which I paid 9d postage – what a change now, to only a penny!' (see Chapter 9) to ask whether he might be employed to make pens for sale. 'Remarkably, this brought Mr James Perry, proponent of a Perryman system' to Birmingham the following day but one, 'by eight o'clock in the morning' and 'from that moment I became a steel pen maker.'

Mason's account is so vivid that it does not sound legendary. Indeed, it is recorded in detail how in 1831 he made pens worth £1,421 for Perry in London. We read also of 'Patent Perryman Pens' in an advertisement in *The Polytechnic Review* in 1843, although it did not refer to Mason as a manufacturing source. 'Prices rendered accessible to all writers', the advertisement went on, offering them with fine or medium points in cases containing 'a quarter hundred'. Mason's biographer, local newspaper editor

*Pens for sale – 'for the most fastidious writers', 1885*

John Thackray Bunce, who also wrote a *History of Birmingham*, described how the demand for steel pens subsequently grew with reduced prices. 'Increased machinery and a larger number of workpeople were provided to meet it', he continued, 'until Sir Josiah Mason [he was knighted in 1872] became the largest pen-maker in the world.'

Unlike needlemakers, Mason obtained his steel wire not from Birmingham but from Sheffield: one ton of steel yielded about $1\frac{1}{2}$ million pens. By 1874, seven years before his death, Mason was producing 32,000 gross of steel pens each week and employing over a million workers. He introduced rolls to reduce the steel to the required thickness, and had special presses made which slit the pen nibs rather than cracked them. Characteristically, Mason made the dies and punches required for the slitting with his own hands, and was so jealous of his 'secrets' that the machinist who made the special presses for them never actually saw them in operation.

There was another Birmingham steel pen maker, however, who also used presses to slit pens and whose name for long was far better known to the British public – Joseph Gillott, also the founder of his own firm, operating at the very properly named Victoria Works in Birmingham. 'The Patentee', Gillott declared flatteringly in an advertisement of 1840, which was written in the style of an epitaph, 'is proud to acknowledge that a discerning public has paid the most gratifying tribute to his humble though useful labours, by a demand for his Pens far exceeding his highest expectations.' Between October 1839, and October 1840 he had produced 44,654,702 pens – he was precise about the number – and between December 1840 and December 1841, 62,126,928. From April 1840 onwardly he had been producing them 'by royal command'.

Gillott did not meet Mason until both had already established their businesses, but thereafter they were friends as well as rivals. Indeed, Gillott suggested when they first met that they should go into partnership. Another and more famous person to offer Mason a partnership more than once was the armament manufacturer Baron Krupp of Essen, who visited Birmingham when he was trying to sell his earliest patent. There was one partnership, however, which Mason welcomed, and he was far better known during his lifetime for his part in it than he was for making pens – that with the Elkingtons in the electroplating business. Elkington, Mason and Company advertised their products: Mason's pen nibs were never known as such. After his death Mason was to be remembered mainly for his educational initiatives, particularly the founding of the Mason Science College in 1879 which was to provide the stimulus for Birmingham University: Joseph Chamberlain, who had made screws in Birmingham, was to be its first Chancellor. Yet Mason had figured prominently also in the history of many other new and common Victorian things, including 'India-rubber rings', and he was praised by Dr C. W. Siemens for his keen interest in electricity before most of his contemporaries were aware of its potential.

As far as pens were concerned, the nibs, of course, were not all. 'Holders' allowed for more variety, if far less ingenuity, than nibs. They could be made of wood or of gold, of ebony or of glass, and they could carry personal inscriptions as well as trademarks. They could bear names like the Waverley or the Pickwick – in the words of an 1880s jingle:

They come as a boon and a blessing to men,
The Pickwick, the Owl and the Waverley Pen.

Another pen called the Phaeton, made by MacNiven and Cameron, the same manufacturers as the Waverley and the Pickwick, was said to be particularly well christened, since it could 'literally fly all over the paper'.

Mason was the first pen manufacturer to make holders out of cedar wood, with metallic receptacles for the 'slip' nibs: in 1840 Gillott bought £300 worth of them. A generation later, so-called 'ball-pointed' pens – very different from late-twentieth century ball-point pens – were on sale: they held more ink, 'lasted longer', and had been submitted by Sir Henry Ponsonby to the Queen herself. By then, too, some pen holders were very ingenious products – one incorporated a monthly calendar – and many of them, although not those used in the Board schools, were attractive objects in their own right. Some of them were well adapted also to the art of calligraphy which became a fashion during the 1880s and 1890s and even influenced printing types. Some pens were even called 'stylographs'.

Meanwhile, 'fountain pens' of all colours, shapes and sizes were being widely advertised during the late-Victorian years: they bore familiar names like 'Swan' and 'Waterman'. Surprisingly, although the thing – a fountain pen – was new, the word was not: the *New Oxford Dictionary* gives the date 1710 for the first use of the expression 'fountain ink horns or fountain pens'. It was not until 1835, however, that John Joseph Parker, another of the still familiar names in the pen-making business, secured a patent for 'certain improvements in fountain pens' – at that time they were more often called 'reservoir pens' – which permitted self-filling. By the end of the reign you could usually buy a fountain pen for as little as 3d. There were even some which cost a penny.

Parker was only one, if the best-known, of a large number of inventors who discovered radically different ways of feeding the pen with ink. Increasingly the ink as well as the pen was trademarked. Ink for the quill pen was not suited for the steel pen; it corroded the nib, and Henry Stephens chose the right moment to set up his first ink factory in 1834. Very soon 'Stephens' ink' became the best known of all inks, with Waterman's coming second. Stephens' ink was advertised grandiloquently at first as 'a carbonaceous black writing fluid which will accomplish the so-long desired and apparently hopeless task of rendering the manuscript as durable and as indelible as the printed record'. Yet soon it became a household necessity. Meanwhile aniline dyes changed the composition of ink which could be sold also in the form not of fluids but of powders, and it was these that were used by the new School Boards after 1870 in order to save money.

Teachers in these and other schools called, of course, for ample supplies of red ink as well as black-blue. Centuries earlier – and in the history of ink as much as in the history of pens the Victorians liked to look far back in time – 'red letter days' had been picked out in the calender when they had been marked in red ink, and the term now became fashionable. As for black ink, Victorian historians noted that according to Pliny the Romans had made their ink out of soot taken from the furnaces of their baths. One of the late-Victorian advertisers in the *Illustrated London News* (1885) introduced a more topical element. 'Dresden Inks' he claimed were, 'the best': they come from 'the oldest and largest establishment in Germany'. 'Beware of imitations.'

# III

The long history of experimental development in the story of matches and pens – and ink and fireworks – fascinated the Victorians just as much as the mythic force of fire or the practical power of literacy, and in both cases there was, they knew, a prehistoric prelude. Matches, for instance – and they are dealt with first in this chapter – made possible instantaneously what always must have been prayed for by 'stone age' rubbers of dried sticks. It seemed perfectly appropriate, therefore, when Bryant and May not only brought out regularly new lines in matchboxes but acquired a historic collection of 'firemaking appliances', including specimens of fire drills, fire screws, fire pistons and, of course, tinder boxes, the kind of collection that would have appealed to Pitt-Rivers.

After the prehistory and the history came the chemistry, late in the story, a missing element in the Victorian story of the needle or the pen. Although wooden splints had been tipped with sulphur to produce fire in the sixteenth century and in 1699 a German alchemist in his search for the philosopher's stone had by accident produced phosphorus, the Greek word for 'light bearer', it was not until the late-eighteenth century that chemical firemaking devices were marketed, among them 'philosophical' and 'ethereal' matches offering 'an immediate light on the road or in the chamber'.

'Phosphoric tapers' (1781), 'phosphorus boxes' (1786) and 'oxymuriated ignitors' (1806) made their appearance next, and in Britain, Samuel Jones's 'Promethian' glass beads containing acids, the outside of which was coated with an igniting substance: they were supplied with two pairs of pliers, one to grip the bead, the other to fracture the glass. Patented in 1828 with the challenging health warning 'If possible, avoid inhaling the gas that escapes from the black composition', they were highly tempting but highly dangerous novelties: the tempted sometimes tried to fracture the glass with their teeth. Equally dangerous were 'Congreves', appropriately named after the inventor of the military rocket. At one time they were known as 'German tinder' and their smell was as unpleasant.

The first British friction matches, non-phosphoric 'lucifers', were not patented. This was because their North Country maker, John Walker of Stockton, a chemist and druggist who lived on until 1859, the year of publication of Samuel Smiles's *Self-Help*, believed mistakenly that it was not worth doing so 'considering the simple and trifling nature of the article'. He is said to have invented matches by accident around 1827 two years before Mason began to make metal pen nibs. A match dipped into some lighting mixture, which he had prepared for his own use, fell on the hearth and took fire by accidental friction.

The town of Stockton was better known then and in the later years for another 'first' which was very much not an accident: only eighteen months before Walker began to sell his 'friction lights' in 1827, the first public railway between Stockton and Darlington had been opened. At first, however, the promoters were as modest as Walker and gave more publicity to horse traffic on the railway than steam trains. Until 1833 locomotives were used only to haul freight.

Walker, a keen mineralogist as well as an experimental chemist and more of an amateur than a businessman, was enough of a businessman, however, to start selling his three-inch long 'friction lights' in tin boxes to customers at a price which soon fell from 1s 2d a hundred to 2d for a tin: 1,836 tins were disposed of in 1827 and over 12,000 in 1830. The boxes were made by a bookbinder, and the tin included a piece of doubled sandpaper to set the lights in flame 'by pressure of the thumb and a sharp pull'.

Walker carefully recorded all his business transactions too. There are 168 entries listing sales in his day book – 23 in 1827, the first (in Latin) for a sum of 1s 2d to a Mr John Hixton – how rare such a detail is in the history of businesses – 70 in 1828, and 69 in 1829. Some of the sales were to 'young men', who are said to have bought his matches to ignite and throw at the feet of ladies 'in order to startle them'. The fun quickly disappeared, and in 1832 Richard Bell and Company set up the first match manufacturing company in Britain in Wandsworth, soon acquiring other factories in Basing Lane and Bow.

Recounting the details of the early story, James Clapham, born in Stockton and for a time editor of the *Gateshead Observer*, looked back across the years in the style of Pitt-Rivers to describe how Captain Cook had seen the Australian aborigines making fire – 'light by collision' and 'light by attrition'. He noted too how when 'Locomotion' first made its way along the Stockton to Darlington railway no one had a light, and a 'navvy' had to produce one from a burning glass. Outside Stockton, however, other people were working on the same lines as Walker, one of them Sir Isaac Holden, Yorkshire textile manufacturer and pioneer of industrial education.

The word 'match', which came to England from France was said to have been derived not, like the word 'pen', from the Latin, but from the Greek; and the first definitions of a match were as long and complex as the definitions of a postage stamp (see page 328). For Webster, a match was 'a thing used for catching and sustaining a communicating fire, made of some substance which takes fire readily, or which, on being lighted remains burning a long time, especially in a modern usage, a splinter of wood dropped at one end in a preparation of phosphorus, sulphur or the like, and ignited by rubbing.'

Phosphorus matches, far easier to strike than Walker's friction matches – indeed they were known as 'strike anywhere matches' – were not introduced commercially until the 1830s, despite the fact that yellow phosphorus, which glowed in the dark, had first been discovered in the seventeenth century. There were various claimants for the discovery of the new phosphorus matches in different countries, yet wherever the matches were made they were not safe. The chemistry in the phosphorus match-making process was to be greatly developed and refined by the time that T. E. Thorpe dealt with it in his invaluable *Dictionary of Applied Chemistry* (1876), the first chemical dictionary to introduce the adjective 'applied' in its title. Even then, however, the process could be almost as crude as the colour of the synthetic magenta then applied to the tips of the matches or as the recipe for one of the first chemical powders used in match-making before the introduction of phosphorus itself – pyrophorus, three parts alum and two parts honey, flour or sugar.

*Phosphorus mirabilis* was a dangerous substance, and to work with it was from the start an even more perilous occupation for the match-workers than 'striking' some of the first non-safety matches was for the customers. Yellow or white phosphorus carried with it a terrible disease, *phosphorus necrosis*, a destruction of tissues, which defied all attempts to treat it. The main symptom was a decay of the jaw bone caused by fumes of slowly oxidizing phosphorus entering through carious teeth. Ironically, as a medical doctor noted, 'beautifully clear' phosphorus sticks were as 'innocent looking and as pretty as so many sticks of barley sugar rock', and even when phosphorus was produced in large quantities it was moulded into what were termed also in the language of delight as 'cheeses'.

Most of the phosphorus in Britain was made at Oldbury, near Birmingham. The well-named Arthur Albright, who at the age of sixteen had been bound apprentice to a Bristol chemist and druggist in the same year as Walker sold his first friction matches in Stockton, had concerned himself with his chemistry since the 1840s, working at first in partnership with the Sturges, Birmingham Quakers, who dealt in dyes before they began to make phosphorus from bone ash in 1844. Ten years later Albright set up on his own.

Already phosphorus had ceased to be imported, and at the 1851 exhibition, when Spaniards from the Estramadura displayed natural phosphorus, Albright exhibited 'amorphous phosphorus' or red phosphorus, a non-toxic product with different properties from yellow phosphorus: it had been discovered in 1845 by an Austrian Professor, Anton von Schrötter, who four years later had been Albright's guest when he attended the second meeting at Birmingham of the British Association. At the Paris Exhibition of 1855 Schrötter was to win a gold medal and Albright a silver one. By 1863 there were 27 blazing furnaces in action at Oldbury, using 648 retorts and masses of cheap coal to which Albright attributed his competitive international strength.

Demand for Albright's material came from matchmakers producing 'strike anywhere' matches, the tips of which did not contain any combustible material easily ignited by friction, and which had to be struck on a specially prepared surface on the match container. The first person to produce them in Britain was the Manchester match manufacturer, Elijah Dixon, but it was a dangerous exercise, and the mixture on one occasion exploded so dramatically that Dixon is said to have thought that his head had blown off. 'It's on, it's on!' he is reported to have cried when he discovered that it was still there. Albright, too, and his workers, were familiar with explosions at Oldbury itself. The Swede Carl Lundström was one of his main customers. He visited Britain for the first time in 1850, and he sold matches to William Bryant and Francis May, grocers and blacking manufacturers in Tooley Street. They too were Quakers as, of course, were many mid-Victorian manufacturers, the best-known of whom, the Rowntrees, the Cadburys and the Frys, dealt not in phosphorus but in chocolate.

Lundström made the first safety matches for sale in 1852, having included potassium chlorate in his match heads and amorphous phosphorus on the rubbing surface of the match box. The fact that he also used wood rather than cardboard for his match boxes, adding to transport costs, and the further fact that the Swedish business could not supply anywhere near enough matches to satisfy British customers encouraged Bryant and May to enter the matchmaking business themselves. In 1885 they acquired Lundström patent rights for the modest sum of £100, and after having begun by importing Lundström's matches – one box was presented to Prince Albert – they opened their own factory five years later in Bow. At that time, 8,000 million boxes of matches were being sold each year, of which two-thirds were made in 29 factories in London, some of them no more than rooms in private houses. None of the home-produced matches, however, were safety matches. The 'Exhibition lucifers' displayed by the old firm of Bell and Black of Bow at the Crystal Palace in 1851 had been made, like those of their competitors, with yellow phosphorus, not red.

More British imagination was displayed then and later in devising match boxes than in improving the chemical processes for making the matches themselves. Already matches bore such tempting names as 'Gas Camphorated Lights' and 'Fixed Stars'. Later, Bell and Black were to produce

'Red Heart Wax Vestas' and 'sporting match boxes' which showed pictures of football, bicycle and boxing contests (one variety bore the text 'Let 'Em All Come'). Others showed eagles and wolves. A generation after the exhibition, Bell and Black were to take over in 1881 Elijah Dixon's Manchester business, with its Eddystone Lighthouse symbol, and the business of John Battersby and Sons of Leeds, with its St George and the Dragon symbol, before they themselves were taken over by Bryant and May in 1885.

Bryant and May modelled their Fairfield Works in Bow, not far from the London docks, on Swedish match factories; and by the end of the century, after many amalgamations, they had a dominating position in the trade. There were by then only 25 match factories in Great Britain and Ireland, giving employment to 4,311 workers, most of them (3,298) females, many of them (1,405) 'young persons', and Bryant and May employed no fewer than a quarter of them. The firm concentrated on patent 'special safety matches', but also produced other 'chemical lights'. Bow and Oldbury were inter-dependent, therefore, and it was the *Oldbury Weekly News* which in 1884 quoted the verse:

> The safety match, the safety match,
> Oh! that's the match for me;
> Let others praise the common sort,
> With them I can't agree.

The Lundströms looked to Oldbury too – and when in 1892 they chose as their motto 'the torch of light', they added with acknowledgment to Albright's Quakerism that the match-making business was concerned solely with 'peace and the enlightenment of mankind'. For twenty years Oldbury had possessed something more impressive than a symbol – a huge chimney stack 252 feet high, built out of half-a-million bricks.

Sweden remained ahead of Britain in techniques, and the United States soon moved ahead too. A continuous process match-making machine was introduced in Sweden as early as 1864 – it could deliver 570,000 matches an hour – and later in the century a similar machine was being mass produced in the United States by the Diamond Match Company. In Britain much was being made of the fact that a skilful 'dipper' could handle 400,000 splints a day. Much was made too of 'quality'. The dip had once included brimstone – a logical constituent of a 'lucifer' – but by the 1890s brimstone matches were rarely seen except in the company of 'sailors, lighters and cabmen'.

The reason for this was logical enough too, and might have been noted by Sherlock Holmes. Sulphur had a low igniting point, and brimstone matches were not so readily extinguished by the wind as 'ordinary lucifers'. The fact that 'imperial' timber, usually Canadian pine, was used in the splints was a matter of pride in itself, and match boxes could have explicit imperial themes too: thus, S. J. Moreland and Sons of Gloucester, produced matches called 'Hope and Glory'.

Bryant and May's safety matches, 'Brymay matches', offering not only fire but 'protection from fire', were sold in four sizes in wooden slide boxes almost three inches long, each box bearing two separate yellow labels printed in Nottingham by Alfred Goater, draughtsman, engraver and die-stamper as well as 'ornamental printer', and they won a first prize in the 1862 Exhibition, the first of many such prizes and medals. 'No careful house-keeper who ever looked at [Fire Brigade] returns', wrote *The Times*, 'would ever allow any but safety matches inside their doors.'

Yet they were not the only Bryant and May product in mid-Victorian England. Among other lines introduced before the 1880s in a period of steady growth were 'ruby matches', the first label Goater handled (in 1862), 'tiger matches' (1864), 'elephant matches' and 'Victoria matches (1870), 'runaway matches' (1864), not to speak of 'Sultan matches' (1871), doubtless for export, 'Cleopatra flamers' (1878), and 'Pillar Box Vestas' (1878). Some of these brands were registered at Stationers' Hall in London.

The boxes have all become collectors' pieces, as have the Captain Webb match boxes, registered in 1876 by Collard, Kendall and Company of Liverpool, who also produced a 'Drunkard's Match' with a chemically treated splint that would not burn below mid-point. The Captain Webbs showed the head and shoulders of Webb, the greatest swimmer of his time (with a swim suit buttoned to the neck), from a portrait painted by George Phoenix, and on the other side Webb swimming the breast stroke. The portrait might have been used on Stevengraphs or medals. The same images of fame could become ubiquitous.

The firm of Collard, Kendall and Company is important for another and more important reason, however. When Bryant and May showed little interest in continuous process match-making machines, the American Diamond Match Company took over Collard, Kendall and Company in 1895 and built a large, new, up-to-date factory, equipped with sixteen of the new machines and capable of producing 92 million matches a day. Bryant and May, which had become a limited liability company in 1884, immediately felt the competition, for Captain Webbs sold at one shilling per gross of boxes as against Bryant and May's ruby and tiger matches at 1s 7d and 1s 6d per gross. Not surprisingly, therefore, the firm threw its weight behind a 'Buy British' campaign during the late 1890s.

The eventual result, as was so often the case in business history, was a merger of two very different enterprises in the last year of Queen Victoria's reign. Bryant and May, which had an original capitalization of £500,000, purchased the good will, assets and rights of the British Diamond Match Company for £480,000, and the American Company acquired 54.5 per cent of the share capital of Bryant and May. There was a touch of imperialism, however, even in this agreement, for the American Company undertook not to manufacture or sell matches in any part of the British Empire or the West Indies.

# IV

Matches had stolen the headlines twice during the 1870s and 1880s. On the first occasion, Gladstone's Chancellor of the Exchequer, Robert Lowe, the fascinating subject of Chapter IX of *Victorian People*, had tried and failed to impose a stamp tax on matches in 1871. Thirty years earlier, *Punch* had humorously suggested imposing a window tax on spectacles: for many there was humour too in Lowe's thwarted effort in 1871 which was, nonetheless, described seriously by the *Annual Register* as 'the great failure of the session'. The second occasion when matches had stolen the headlines was in 1888, when the girls employed by Bryant and May went on strike, one of the most surprising, most publicized, and most remembered strikes of the late-nineteenth century.

In 1871 Lowe, faced with the biggest budget deficit since 1841, described with exaggeration as 'formidable', proposed a tax of a halfpenny per hundred on wooden matches, whether made in Britain or imported, and a tax of one penny on a box of 100 vestas because the latter were in his words more 'aristocratic'. Together, he estimated, the taxes would yield £500,000 annually.

Comparing Lowe's position in 1871 with that of the Chancellor of the Exchequer a generation earlier, when *Punch* had suggested a spectacles tax, *The Spectator* noted how much more fortunate Lowe was than his predecessor had been. In between there had been 'progress'. People had got richer. Nobody felt 'the smallest real anxiety', therefore, at his declaration of inability to make both ends meet 'without fresh resources'. There was the sort of 'grumbling' expected from both Radicals and Conservatives, the first wanting still cheaper government, the latter less liberal government, but the only real complaint concerned not the tax itself but the purpose for which one large item in government expenditure, the Army estimates for the year, was required. Lowe's speech was said to be 'quite dull and lame' compared with Gladstone's Budget speeches, yet the first Parliamentary reaction to the match tax, which Lowe, no lover of American democracy, copied from across the Atlantic, was described as one of 'hilarity'.

This was only the first reaction, however, and that of a limited, if decisive segment of opinion. *The Times* at once attacked the 'reactionary' idea of a tax which would fall on everyone in the population and told Lowe in fighting language that he should have raised the money instead from a 2d tax on tea, no less 'reactionary' though this would have been. Lowe's proposal, it thundered, was at the same time 'a tax upon a necessity of life' and a tax upon a branch of manufacturing that gave 'remunerative employment to a great number of poor children', most of them matchgirls. Should this most extraordinary imposition become law, 'the result to hundreds of families in the East End of London will be simply ruin'. Meanwhile, 'a great proportion of the home trade' in matches would 'drift into the hands of foreigners', a foretaste of the argument that was to become far more popular twenty years later.

Queen Victoria, who complained to Gladstone about Lowe's proposed tax at least as eloquently as *The Times*, concentrated characteristically only on the first objection. 'It is difficult not to feel considerable doubt as to the wisdom of the proposed tax on matches which is a direct tax and will be at once felt by all classes to whom matches have become a necessity of life. Their greatly increased price will in all probability make no difference in the consumption by the rich; but the poorer classes will be constantly irritated by this increased expense and reminded of the tax by the stamp on the box. Above all, it seems certain that the tax will seriously affect the manufacturer and sale of matches which is said to be the sole means of support for a vast number of the poorest people and little children . . . so that this tax which it is intended should press on all equally will in fact be only severely felt by the poor.' This, she concluded, would be 'very wrong and most impolitic at the present moment'.

The moment was a moment of national prosperity, for this was the height of the biggest mid-Victorian boom. Yet the Queen's appeal for compassion – and she was thinking of the sellers of matches in the streets, the girls vividly described by Mayhew, as well as the makers of matches and matchboxes – is a necessary reminder that prosperity was not universally shared. When the 'matchgirls' themselves protested vigorously against the tax, encouraged or even organized by their employers, they were rehearsing their independent militant strike action in 1888. The year 1871, after all, was not only a boom year, but the year of the Commune in Paris and of the demonstration there of working-class intransigence.

English positivists like Frederic Harrison, who sympathized with lowly paid workers, could approve of the girls' protest on ideological grounds, but the reactions of the employers were based primarily on self-interest. As *The Spectator* pointed out, one argument that they used – that the tax would hit exports and would also be difficult to levy – was not a very substantial one. In 1868 the computed real value of the export of matches was 'less than a third of the sum that Lowe expected to accrue from his tax'. In any case, the Chancellor was not proposing to raise the stamp tax on exported matches just as he was not proposing to raise the existing stamp tax on exported playing cards, on which the home duty was six times as high as his suggested tax on matches.

It is important to add that the match tax was the subject of a sophisticated paper by the economist W. S. Jevons, *The Match Tax: a Problem in Finance*, not published until after Lowe had decided to withdraw it, and that the idea had won the support of what *The Spectator* called Gladstone's 'Cabinet of financiers', which included 'men like Dr Lyon Playfair', all firmly committed to the gospel of free trade. 'The country', they claimed in complete opposition to *The Times*, 'wants nothing so much as tax on some article of necessary use.' It had to be a tax that would 'be felt universally', while not involving a diminution of bodily strength and health in 'hard times'.

*The Economist* under the direction of Walter Bagehot, whose approach to political economy was different from that of his ex-fellow student Jevons, made the same point, as did the radical Henry Fawcett. 'Every proposal which makes the more numerous class of society – collectively a very wealthy class – pay any part of the taxation, is in the present day most valuable ... If by a tax on matches, which the poorer classes buy as well as richer, something can be extracted from the immense body who escape so easily, every sound financier will rejoice.'

Gladstone treated Bagehot as a 'spare Chancellor of the Exchequer', an independent-minded man who would always give good advice and to whom he was closer in feeling than his own Chancellor, Lowe. He must have noted, however, that while not quarrelling with the argument that had led Lowe to propose his match tax, Bagehot did not consider that the tax was practicable. 'The actual operation of it is sure to create many vexations which no one could forestall, and the tax is therefore sure to be more unpopular than any one would imagine.' 'What', after all, Bagehot went on to ask, 'is "a match?" Is a piece of wood with igniting matter at both ends one match or two? If one, what is a *fusée* [they were to bear the same rate of tax as the vestas] which has many igniting parts? If it is two, how can you ever know, except by accurate counting of the number of matches in a box? How could the Chancellor's minions decide what a hundred matches were?'

Jevons, less worried by such questions than Bagehot, had statistical questions of his own to ask. How many matches were currently being manufactured in Britain? How many matchmakers were producing them? 'The Census Tables [and 1871 was a Census year] are wholly astray on this point, giving the number as 532, not a tenth part of the truth.' All calculations as to the likely return of the revenue if the tax were to be implemented were 'of a very uncertain character'. 'I do not find that any accurate information on the subject exists', Jevons complained, 'and even manufacturers can only make rude guesses.' One estimate (in Kopp's *Chemical Technology*) was that the English people 'consumed' on an average eight matches per head per day. The estimate seemed too low. Jevons concluded, nonetheless, that the tax would raise substantial sums for the Exchequer, 'half of the abandoned corn duty, the whole of the assessed tax on carriages, nearly as much as the railway duty'.

For Jevons, whose publishers printed a picture of the proposed match stamp on the title page of his pamphlet, 'calm and impartial examination' would make it abundantly clear that the match tax fell upon 'the consumption rather than the production of wealth' and no one would 'in any appreciable degree' be hindered in his business 'because his wife or servants use a few less matches, and pay a few pence more for them'. As for 'the poor', it was true in their case also – and in other places Jevons showed that he did not lack compassion for them (see page 316) – that 'the price of a commodity which forms a very small part of a person's expenditure has not a great effect upon its consumption'. In any case, since 'the poor' were wasting 30 per cent of their money by buying matches in 'driblets' – in farthing boxes rather than in 'large penny boxes . . . containing 250 matches', over six times as many for the price, the end of the farthing box for tax reasons would actually prove a blessing in disguise. It would actually be in the interests of the poor themselves!

There was a late-twentieth century ring to Jevons's further *riposte* to critics of the tax who had argued that match workers would be thrown out of employment. 'Men, women and children are not born specifically to be matchmakers, and if by the wise organization of our finances we can promote the general prosperity of trade and industry, it is no matter of regret that a few hundred or a few thousand children have been transferred from one occupation to a more healthy and useful one.'

The children, most of them girls, who worked in the trade were like Queen Victoria in one respect: they had not been trained in political economy. At a mass meeting held in Victoria Park near Bow on the very day that the Queen wrote her letter to Gladstone, April 24th, they decided, therefore, to demonstrate, gathering in 'orderly fashion' in the Bow Road with the intention of carrying a huge petition from the East End to Parliament. Many of them carried banners also, some of them bearing home-made slogans. They had not marched far, however, when in Mile End Road the Metropolitan Police barred their passage and broke up their procession into smaller sections. Excitement grew when some of them reached Westminster, by river as well as by land. There had been scuffles on the way, and there were more serious and more violent skirmishes outside the Commons, where the girls' banners were confiscated by the Police and thrown into the Thames. The few girls who managed to break through and get into the Commons 'set up a "shrill shout" when it was discovered that their petition was safe and had not been destroyed'. All entrances to New Palace Yard were then blocked, and Lowe himself had to get into the House of Commons by an underground passage.

The following day Lowe dropped his proposal. He must have felt that the noisy nature of the demonstration more than justified the bitter *critique* of working-class collective action which he had made during the debates on the Reform Bill of 1867. Lack of logic was most dangerous, he consistently maintained, when it carried with it a resort to force. The same lack of logic was plain enough also, he thought, in a letter from Bryant and May published in *The Times* on the same day as the demonstration in which the employers argued (as Jevons observed, with little evidence to support them) that one effect of the match tax would be to discourage the use of safety matches and thereby increase instead of diminish the risk of fire. In fact, relatively few safety matches were being used by 'the poor' in 1871: they were too expensive when compared with other types.

For Lowe political fire was the most dangerous form of fire, and it was Bryant and May who were playing with it. There was irony, therefore, as well as folly, he believed, in their stress on 'security'. Moreover, as they well knew, the main reason why Lowe was wishing to impose the tax was to find revenue to meet the demands of national security. He was responding to an appeal by his Army-reforming colleague Edwin Cardwell to make England 'unassailable even if our fleet were decoyed by a ruse to a distance, as Nelson's fleet was decoyed to the West Indies before Trafalgar'. Any pecuniary sacrifice would be fully justified, Cardwell argued, if the continental powers in Europe could be convinced that 'a successful invasion of England would be a hopeless dream'. That would be real security. Whether Lowe, who was uninterested in military and naval matters, really believed that there was a need to strengthen security, was immaterial. He had to make the case on behalf of his colleagues.

If Bryant and May were unimpressed by Lowe's rhetoric, so, too, were most Members of Parliament. Indeed, after Lowe had given way on the match tax, he had to give way also to the pressure of his own backbenchers, representatives of the counties, and abandon his proposed legacy and succession duties, thereby completely wrecking his budget. 'The Budget is Down', *Punch* crowed. 'Matches, Succession, Percentage Rate are swept away.' Moreover, the succession duties were withdrawn, as *The Spectator* pointed out, 'not in deference to any *popular* outcry' of the kind represented by the match girls and their employers, but as a 'flight before the county members' who objected to any governmental tampering with property rights, and the freedom 'to leave or to inherit'.

'No sooner did the middle and upper classes perceive that they were likely to obtain a victory for the poor man by defeating the match tax', *The Spectator* went on, 'than they resolved, while running before the wind of popular favour, to do a little job on their own account as well.' The claims of one's own things obviously mattered more than the claims of the nation, although the price (announced by Gladstone, not by Lowe) was an increase of 2d in the £ in the income tax, a tax which Gladstone himself would have dearly liked to abolish.

Lowe's rapid surrender to his critics did not save him from ridicule in 1871. At an exhibition of fire-making appliances held in 1926 in the Bryant and May Museum, a display of 'Lowe exhibits' included several cartoons, mainly from now forgotten satirical magazines. The first, which appeared in *The Hornet* in May 1871, was accompanied by the caption 'The Naughty Boy who played with the Lucifer Matches and burnt his Fingers'. It showed Lowe as a small boy sucking his fingers: he had just dropped a flaming torch, encircled by a scroll inscribed '*Ex Luce Lucellum*', a characteristic Latin pun the classicist Lowe had used in his speech, 'out of light a little profit'. On the floor was an open box of Bryant and May's matches with many loose matches scattered on the floor.

Another cartoon, 'Lucifer and his Match', also from *The Hornet*, showed a boxing ring with John Bull in fighting attitude (and labelled 'Public Opinion') at the centre; he had just knocked out Lowe, who was depicted in the character of Lucifer. In the background there was a banner inscribed Bryant and May, accompanied by their Noah's Ark trademark, the word 'Security' and, for good measure, the *Arc de Triomphe*.

*Punch*, in perhaps the best-known of the Lowe cartoons drawn by Tenniel, displayed Lowe in the guise of Lo-Lo, named after Lu-Lu, a female contortionist and acrobat popular at the Holborn Circus, where each night, by mechanical means, she was shot upwards in 'a blaze of light' from a trap-door in the stage. The trap in the cartoon consisted of a box labelled 'Fusées' and there were accompanying verses:

But if up Lu-Lu go
Like arrow from bow,
What's Lu-Lu to Lowe-Lowe ...
No light person, we know
Such a somerset throw.
Turn his back on himself,
And from match-box – light elf –
Bound to Income-tax shelf.

Meanwhile, Bryant and May, who had proved themselves as interested in words as in things in 1871, decided to produce a 'Chancellor Match' bearing the facsimile of a halfpenny stamp and an unflattering portrait of Lowe. In fact, it was never issued.

All satire spent, there was a note of Victorian earnestness in the firm's official commemoration of its victory. Its 'high character and reputation' as a firm having been established – and it was always worried about this – a subscription was raised to erect outside the railway station in Bow Road a commemorative drinking fountain 'of early Gothic character of Venetian type'. It was officially opened by the Lord Mayor of London on October 5th 1872, with the Band of the Honourable Artillery Company providing the music and the Rector of Bow offering a prayer. George Cruikshank, the cartoonist, was among the party on the platform.

As a confirmed teetotaller, William Bryant preferred water to wine, although as Patrick Beaver, the official historian of Bryant and May, has written, the places where Lowe's defeat had generated most rejoicing were the public houses of Bow and Bethnal Green. The 1872 commemoration was not, however, the first pre-eminently Victorian celebration staged for or by Bryant and May. In 1858, three years before the opening of their Fairfield Works, they had held a great workers' party for visitors from Sweden at which 52 bags of coffee and, despite teetotallism, 67 bottles of port had been consumed.

It was left to the *Annual Register* to print in a footnote details of the provisions of the 'Match Bill' for the study of those 'curious' about 'defunct bills'. The provisions included the clauses that matches should be contained in a 'box', a term wide enough to include every other kind of 'enclosure', including tins; that stamps should be affixed to the boxes in such a way that they could not be opened without tearing or destroying the stamps; that the police could arrest any person selling matches without a stamp on the box, a threat to Mayhew's match girls; that offenders found guilty could be sentenced to one month's hard labour; and that the penalty for selling stamps without authority was £20 and for forging or counterfeiting them penal servitude for a period of from three years to life or imprisonment not exceeding two years. They were to be treated like postage stamps (see Chapter 9). All these provisions implied tough controls, and the Treasury, which had already printed stamps in anticipation of Lowe's budget being passed, would doubtless have pressed for the rigorous enforcement of the law by the Police and the Courts.

When the Treasury stamps were destroyed, there were suggestions that Lowe's pun *ex luce lucellum* should become Bryant and May's company slogan. 'To waste-paper dealers', a *Punch* mock advertisement read, 'to be disposed of: an immense quantity of unmatched classical literature, the writer having no further use for it ... This is an opportunity that will never occur again, as Mr L-L Brimstone, Budget Office, Somerset House, has resolved in future to get his tax first and consult the classics afterwards.' The advertisement may have done justice to Lowe's political economy, but it did less than justice to his abiding love of the classics, for he himself is said to have composed in relative tranquillity after the event the lines:

*Ex luce lucellum*, we all of us know;
But if Lucy can't sell 'em, how then Mr Lowe?

Later still, in 1880, there was another opportunity for Lowe to revert to Latin, anticipated by *Punch*, when in 1871 it raised Lowe to the peerage as Lord Marathon de Matchbox. When Gladstone returned to power in 1880, he decided to give Lowe a place in the House of Lords and insisted on a viscountcy in face of the Queen's opinion that a barony would be 'ample' for him and that anything more would be 'objectionable'. Lowe himself had no illusions. Aged 69, he knew realistically that with his viscountcy he was at last moving into the limbo from which *Victorian People* was to help to rescue him, and he could not resist yet another Latin quotation: 'I feel very much as if I had got again into the company of the four neuter verbs of the Latin grammar – *Vepulo*, I am beaten; *Veneo*, I am sold; *Exulo*, I am banished; *Fio*, I am done.'

## V

Bryant and May were certainly not 'done' in 1880, even though they were to face tough business opposition twenty years later before their merger with the Diamond Match Company. The years from 1871 to 1883 have been described by their historian as years of 'steady growth'. Their share of the home market substantially increased, and during the mid-1870s they were producing 1,728 million boxes of wooden matches a day, selling retail at 7½d. per dozen, and 500,000 boxes of wax vestas. They were also increasingly involved in export markets which *The Spectator* had claimed did not exist in 1871. The match boxes and tin and other containers in which the matches were contained were cleverly designed to meet the demands of different export markets, and in Melbourne alone, one of the cities described in my *Victorian Cities*, sales of Bryant and May matches in the mid-1880s were said to be 1,000 cases per month. Australians were said to have been impressed by dryads sitting by gurgling brooks and ships sailing for distant ports, and the Chinese by bright pictures. For the Indians or for the Raj there were 'Bengal lights', a 'striking novelty', and in Britain itself there was lavish advertising.

Many tin boxes were made, as were tin boxes for Seidlitz powder or for blacking, by tinplate machinery installed at the Reading works of Huntley, Bourne and Stevens, designed in the first place to meet the local demand from Huntley and Palmer, the biscuit manufacturers. Wooden boxes were often made and packed, however, in crowded East End homes, 'poor and in ill repair'. The girls who made them were often very young: one, aged six, was said to be making four gross a day. Parents found such 'manual dexterity' a 'constant temptation', for they too were victims of the economic system. One Irish match box maker, proud of her own dexterity, had worked in a lead factory before lead poisoning compelled her to move home and make match boxes instead.

There was certainly a continuing danger of poisoning in the match making trade, for the use of yellow phosphorus was not proscribed by law. The danger of workers suffering from phosphorus necrosis was an inevitable feature of match production, therefore, until 1898, when phosphorus sesquisulphide, first discovered in 1844, was patented as an ingredient in the match dip. As W. H. Dixon, a former employee of Bryant and May, wrote in 1925 in a useful little book, *The Match Industry*, published in Pitman's Common Commodities and Industries series, 'It would at the present time appear strange that in spite of the ravages of necrosis, the usefulness of this material was not appreciated until so late a period.'

A Factory Inspectors' Report, supplied with evidence from the client T. E. Thorpe and other experts, noted as late as 1893 that many match works, though not the biggest, were 'old and lent themselves with difficulty to the improved structural arrangements found in the more efficiently equipped factories'. Moreover, in most of them 'methods now shown to be obsolete' were in use, 'involving unnecessary risk to the work people employed.' 'It cannot be said', the report concluded, 'that due diligence has been generally exercised, either in observing the letter and spirit of the existing rules, or in introducing the improvements and precautions which have been brought forward, to some extent, in this country, but more extensively abroad, since the rules were framed.'*

Among the bigger firms one was believed to be exceptional. The girls employed by Bryant and May in their Fairfield Works, where safety and non-safety matches were made, were, supposedly, better paid and better treated than girls in most other factories, and the firm, converted after 1884 into a public company, had the reputation of being a caring employer. It was possible, indeed, for a girl to earn by piecework 12s. a week, a substantial wage by contemporary standards, particularly in London's East End where 'sweated trades' predominated. Moreover, when the public company had been set up, shares had been allotted to long-serving employees, including travellers, as well as to heads of departments.

Nonetheless, there were serious labour troubles in store. The dividend of 23 per cent paid to shareholders was high in relation to the wage rates. Nor were most girls able or willing to earn the piecework wages which potentially they were capable of doing, let alone to acquire shares. As the statistician Charles Booth noted in his massive *London Life and Labour*, they were 'irregular' in their attendance. Seasonally, too, there were 'irregularities in the demand for their labour': the demand for matches fell off regularly during the summer months. Like the nearby dockers, most masculine of labour groups and different from the match girls in almost every respect, they were a vulnerable group in an unregulated labour market. They could earn money from hop-picking or fruit-picking during the summer and early autumn, but their extra earnings then depended on the weather.

In 1871, when Lowe had tried to introduce his match box tax, England was in the middle of the great Victorian boom. The 1880s, however, were years of trade depression. Indeed, this was a decade of social conflict and of political propaganda, with the spotlight often focused on the East End, its homes as much as its workshops. The little known socialist magazine *The Link*, the journal of the Law and Liberty League, had emerged, like the League, from riots in Trafalgar Square in 1886 and exclaimed in 1888: 'Would that some easy going shareholders would come through some alleys in Bethnal Green and Shoreditch, and see the sources of their wealth'.

The weather was bad, too, in 1888, when the Bryant and May girl match workers found it difficult to obtain extra work at a time when there was a fall in basic work; and since the firm decided to share out piecework rather than lay off workers, take-home incomes fell. In such circumstances *The Link*

---

*The report includes interesting international comparisons, for example with Sweden, where the match industry was said to employ 'one twentieth of the artisan population' and represented 'about one thirtieth of the total value of Swedish industrial production'. One big factory, called the Vulcan factory, had a Hall of Recreation and an Educational Institute. In Denmark legislation had been passed as early as 1876 totally to prohibit the use of yellow phosphorus.

focused attention on the match girls and their 'plight' in a series of articles, the first appearing on June 23rd. Its exposure of conditions in the Fairfield Works was forthright, but in the view of the company greatly exaggerated. Certainly the charge had as much to do with politics as with economics, and it showed how politics was changing. All Bryant and May workers, it was claimed, had had a shilling a week deducted from their wages to pay for a statue of Gladstone commissioned by Theodore Bryant and erected in Bow Road.

Other journals took up the match girls' theme, as did socialists of different persuasions, far more of them in numbers in 1888 than there had been in 1871, and Members of Parliament of all persuasions were canvassed as actively as they had been in 1871, but this time from two sides – the company defending itself as vigorously as the protagonists of the match girls attacked it. There was drama too. Thus, on one occasion a procession displayed a giant match box bearing the words 'Thirty-eight per cent Dividend' and showing a picture of a clergyman praying for higher dividends.

Few people expected a strike, however, particularly since the dismissals were withdrawn following protests. Yet a strike is what happened after two girls were dismissed for insubordination on July 5th. Nearly 700 girls left work in a remarkable display of solidarity, and the Fairfield Works were closed. Significantly it was not to Westminster but to Fleet Street that the first group of strikers made their way.

The strike did more to publicize matches – and the way they were made – than any of the many advertisements placed by Bryant and May during the 1870s and earlier 1880s. This was partly because of the genius of the extraordinary agitator Annie Besant, then living the fourth of her nine lives as a socialist and a trade-unionist. She and W. T. Stead, outstanding amongst even the greatest publicists, had chosen the title *The Link* for the new magazine and had sub-titled it 'A Journal for the Servants of Man', a phrase of Victor Hugo. Mrs Besant, however, was more interested in mobilizing women, and earlier in the year, before writing an article on 'White Slavery in London', had heard Clementine Black lecturing at a Fabian meeting on 'Female Labour' and urging the formation of a Consumers' League.

During the match girls' strike Mrs Besant's closest collaborator – Herbert Burrows, a member of Henry Hyndmans' Social Democratic Federation, which represented a different strand in Socialism from hers – shared her objectives and methods. The special touches, however, were her own. Thus, she was said to have been greeted with delight when she carried a bunch of roses to the match girls in the Fairfield Works: they 'literally danced for joy'. Victory was won mainly, of course, because of the vigour and determination of the match girls themselves. 'It went just like tinder', one of them declared, to be quoted later in *Toilers in London*. Other trade unions were actively concerned, among them the Operative Bricklayers, the Society of Compositors and, nearer in interest, the Cigar Makers' Society.

The fact that the girls were able to secure middle-class as well as working-class support was commented upon throughout the Press, as was the fact that George Bernard Shaw was cashier of the match girls' fighting fund which collected £400 in subscriptions in a few days. Less noted was the presence of the Fabian intellectual Graham Wallas, who handed over shares of the still inadequate funds to the girls on strike after Burrows had registered them, or the poem by J. A. Elliot, 'The Matchmaker's Complaint' which appeared in *The Link*. Later in 1888, when Mrs Besant addressed an International Trade Union Congress, she irritated many of her colleagues when she complained that British trade unionists had left it to her, 'a woman of the middle class', to organize 'the oppressed match girls'.

Such words were soon forgotten, and the strike has passed down to history much as it was described by the militant 'new trade unionist', the engineer Tom Mann, in his *Memoirs*, a classic text of its kind, first published in 1923:

> During 1888 the years of propagandist effort on the part of Socialists [with William Morris prominent among them] ... were beginning to show results. The first considerable movement came from the women and girls employed at Bryant and May's factory at Bow. Kindly-disposed persons had written about the awful conditions under which many of the girls worked, resulting in the terrible disease known as 'phossy jaw', and other serious troubles, it being argued that better methods might be applied that would materially minimize these evils. In addition, the wages were shamefully low. No response to appeals from the workers was made by the firm. Lists of shareholders were publicized showing that a considerable percentage of these were clergymen: but nothing brought any change for the better until the women and girls went on strike. This immediately attracted public attention, and Mrs Annie Besant – at that time devoting her whole energies to the Socialist movement ... at once gave close personal attention to the girls on strike ... Ably assisted by Mr Herbert Burrows, the girls were soon organized in a trade union. Their case was conducted with great skill. A club was formed, which was used as an educational and social centre, and a spirit of hopefulness characterized the proceedings. The girls won. This had a stimulating effect upon other sections of workers, some of whom were also showing signs of intelligent dissatisfaction.

Mann did not describe how the strike was settled on terms which Mrs Besant stated 'far exceeded her expectations'. The London Trades Council was brought in to arbitrate, and the company made important concessions, including a promise that there would be no reprisals. The announcement of the settlement was received with 'great and enthusiastic cheering' by a crowd of 'match girls' in the Assembly Hall in Mile End Road. Mrs Besant was made honorary secretary of a new Matchmakers' Union, and *The Link* urged some Shavian philanthropist to provide it with a 'match girls' drawing room' which would incorporate a library – and a piano.

During the strike which Mrs Besant was to describe in her autobiography as a 'pretty hubbub', she did not hesitate to use the most emotive language in appealing to a middle class audience:

Do you know that girls are used to carrying boxes on their heads until the hair is rubbed off and the young heads are bald at fifteen years of age? Country clergymen with shares in Bryant and May's, draw down on your knee your fifteen-year old daughter; pass your hand tenderly over the silky beauty of the black, shining tresses.

Perhaps when she said this, she had her long estranged husband, the Rev Frank Besant specially in mind, but she certainly had Stead in mind when she became sentimental. Her phrases appealed more to the radical *Star* and the *Pall Mall Gazette* than to the socialist *Justice*, which had doubts about her, and *Commonweal*. When the company threatened legal action for libel, it added to her middle class appeal when she said that she awaited it 'placidly'.

Years later, she had not greatly changed her language, although there was no element of contrivance in her memory of what happened to the worst sufferers of all, the matchbox makers, thrown out of work by the strike and hard to reach. 'Twopence farthing per gross of boxes, and buy your own string and paste, is not wealth, but when the work went, more rapid starvation came. Oh, those trudges through the lanes and alleys round Bethnal Green Junction late at night, when our day's work was over; children lying about on shavings, rags, anything; famine looking out of baby faces, out of women's eyes, out of the tremulous hands of men. Heart grew sick and eyes dim, and ever louder sounded the question, "Where is the cure for sorrow, what the way of rescue for the world?" '

Patrick Beaver has described Annie Besant as a 'Fabian reformer', and so she was in 1888, having turned from secularist humanism to socialism. Yet the strike scarcely figures in Edward Pease's early *History of the Fabian Society* (1916). Nor was *The Link*, Annie Besant's weekly journal, a Fabian paper. Moreover, the quintessential Fabians, the Webbs, in their *History of Trade Unionism* which first appeared in 1894, only six years after the strike, while acknowledging that it was Mrs Besant's 'indefatigable energy' backed by Burrows, that 'aroused public opinion in a manner never before witnessed', included only three references to her.

Already by then Mrs Besant had moved on into her fifth life – into theosophy – and the pages on the strike in her autobiography are headed 'through storm to peace'. She had represented the match girls at the International Trades Union Congress and been elected to the London School Boards, but her remarkable personality soon became involved in quite different matters – with a Blavatsky Working Women's Club in Bow as a link when *The Link* passed out of circulation.

The match girls themselves carried on their work in what were now described as 'the most healthy conditions', and it was claimed in *The Nonconformist and Independent* that 'on most mornings, on going up the Fairfield Road, Bow, one may meet a crowd of women, girls and boys, returning disappointed at not obtaining an engagement at Messrs Bryant and May's extension works'. In the opinion of *The Morning Advertiser* in 1889

'Socialist agitators' would 'find it difficult in future to influence Messrs Bryant and May's workers.' Yet the *Star* drew attention to further phossy jaw cases at Fairfield Road in 1892 and in 1898, and there were prosecutions and further official enquiries before the century ended. 'Lucifer in the East' was one new headline. These events were forgotten until recently. No historian however, could forget the year of the great dockers' strike, 1889, and the Webbs, among others, acknowledged that the match girls had set a precedent for what the dockers were to achieve in their still more famous fight for 'the dockers' tanner'. Francis Williams, doubtless with matches in mind, was to call their strike 'a beacon fire'.

# VI

There was no such beacon fire in the history of the needle. Earlier in the reign in 1844, however, there had been a three-month strike at Redditch, the needle-making town, and the official history of the Union of Tailors and Garment Workers has as its title *The Needle is Threaded*.

Needles figured prominently in the Victorian imagination, largely because so many of them were in use in comfortable homes where mother, daughters and maiden aunts pursued the gentle arts of needlework, including crocheting and embroidery and making quilts and samplers, today some of the most coveted of Victorian things. As late as 1912 the editor of *The Girls' Own Paper* could write that 'the cult of the needle' was not dead. *Beeton's Housewifes' Treasury* included sections on 'domestic and fancy needlework, dressmaking and millinery', and while noting that 'the invention of the sewing machine has threatened to make hand-needlework one of the lost arts', it devoted many pages to the fancy varieties and to embroidery, 'working in silks, wools or cotton, upon a more or less elaborate ground', with one kind of embroidery singled out by the French as *broderie anglaise*. (See page 216.)

There was another more specialized Beeton publication, *Beeton's Book of Needlework*, published in 1870, which could be set alongside Coulfield and Saward's *Dictionary of Needlework* (1882). They looked back to the very beginnings. 'Needlework is as old as Eve: fancy needlework, probably not quite so old'; and they quoted the Countess of Wilton, who wrote that while needlework was 'twin-born with Necessity', she had quickly left 'this stern and unattractive companion' to become 'the handmaiden of Fancy'. 'She adorned the train of Magnificence; she waited upon Pomp; she decorated Religion; she obeyed Charity; she served Utility; she aided Pleasure; she pranked out fun . . . such is the important part the little needle plays in life.'

The relationship between 'Necessity' and the rest was not quite seen in this light by those who could not escape this 'stern and unattractive companion', although the most publicized of the 'necessitous' were more involved in fancy needlework than in plain. Cassell's *Compendium of Victorian Crafts* (1978), based on four volumes of *Cassell's Household Guide* (1875), leaves out basic needlework and knitting altogether, but includes sections on point lace work, ornamental button work (including the making of 'tea cosies') and 'work-box furniture'. Yet the editors, Marjorie Henderson and Elizabeth Wilkinson, noted correctly that while the daughters in a well-ordered Victorian household might spend long hours doing plain sewing, 'it was the visiting seamstress who did the complicated fitting and sewing required for their elaborate *toilettes*'. Bachelors were sometimes presented with a set of needles, including darning needles and 'buttons of many sizes' along with a verse that ended:

> Each with these pins helped to complete your store
> Leaves you but wanting just one item more,
> Oh Bachelor if you are fond of life,
> Resolve to take at once a loving wife.

Provincial seamstresses, like Mrs Gaskell's Mary Barton, might prefer working at home for a milliner or dressmaker to working in a factory or working as a domestic servant. So, too, indeed, might provincial girls who travelled to London to become apprentices. Even though it could be claimed in 1864 that 'no slavery is worse than that of the dressmaker's life in London', there were, of course, women's trades where wages and conditions of work were worse, including sections of the clothing industry.The plight of seamstresses was never unique. The second reason why needles figured prominently in the Victorian imagination – because consciences could be pricked by revelations of working conditions – has to be related to the whole structure of society, to different strata of exploitation.

Sometimes the exploited could speak for themselves. Tailors had been encouraged to do so by Francis Place, 'the radical tailor' who died in 1854: he had been a specialist in 'button-holing' Members of Parliament, although he was out of politics for the last years of his life. Shoemakers, who used their own special needles, required little encouragement: they were notoriously independent and, overseas as well as in Britain, often radical – articulately radical and far more radical than Place – in their politics. Saddlers, to be found in large numbers in every country, were a far more dependent and deferential group. Dressmakers largely depended on other people to make their problems known. 'We are often so ill', one of them is quoted as saying in 1863, 'that nobody takes much notice of it'. The quotation came in an article called 'Living – and Dying – by the Needle' in *The Englishwoman's Domestic Magazine*.

Notice of their plight depended on the Press (and on official inquiries), and the Press usually focused on the makers of dresses for the rich who might never be known to their wearers: they might meet only their employers. An 1842 enquiry on child labour by the Inspector R. D. Grainger had concluded that there was 'no class of persons in this country, living by their labour whose happiness, health and lives were so unscrupulously sacrificed as those of young dressmakers'. They were in a particular degree 'unprotected and helpless'.

Mayhew told the same story, dividing milliners' establishments into four – 'first rate', 'more like mansions for a nobleman than milliners' establishments'; second-rate, for the wealthy middle classes, like the first 'putting out most of their routine work'; and third-rate and fourth-rate for the less well-off'. There was less deference in the last two, more cotton and less silk. There were also lower wages as there were in establishments which had introduced machinery.

Thomas Hood's 'Song of the Shirt', a lament for the exploited, first published by *Punch* in 1843, had already passed into 'literature' by 1863: it made the most of contrasts of condition and set patterns of response.

> With fingers weary and worn,
> With eyelids heavy and red,
> A woman sat, in unwomanly rags,
> Plying her needle and thread –
> Stitch! Stitch! Stitch!
> In poverty, hunger and dirt,
> And still with a voice of dolorous pitch, –
> Would that its tone would reach the Rich! –
> She sang this 'Song of the Shirt'.

The song was still being sung when John Everett Millais's picture 'Stitch, Stich, Stitch' appeared in 1876.

Mark Lemon, the editor of *Punch*, had published Hood's poem, although his colleagues would have preferred him not to do so – it seemed to them out of place in a comic journal. Yet Lemon, a good judge of the tastes of his readers, knew that it would appeal to them, and throughout the whole of Queen Victoria's reign the different editors of *Punch* who succeeded him frequently reverted to the theme. One of the most remarkable cartoons appeared in 1863 – 'The Haunted Lady – or the ghost in the looking-glass'. It followed a correspondence in *The Times* about the death of a dressmaker, Mary Anne Walkley, and showed a lady of fashion looking into a mirror and seeing there behind her own image that of her dead dress-maker. The caption put into the mouth of the dressmaker's employer read 'we would not have disappointed your Ladyship, at any sacrifice, and the robe is finished *à merveille*'.

There had been a dispute about the facts, and the dressmaker's employer had written an irate letter to *The Times* in response to the charges. *Punch* parodied it with the words 'there are no slaves in England ... It is true that we make our milliners work fifteen hours a day, and twenty-four upon emergencies, but then of course you know their labour is quite voluntary'. Other periodicals were drawn to the case also. Thus, *The Englishwoman's*

*Domestic Magazine* claimed that the lace in fashionable Regent Street windows was now 'pointedly suggestive of shroud trimmings'. A later *Punch* cartoon of 1888 showed 'The Modern Venus Attired by Three Dis-Graces'.

Dickens often struck this tone, notably in an article 'The Iron Seamstress' in *Household Words* (1854) where, after quoting Hood, he described the needle as 'a horrible little instrument of torture ... to thousands of poor Englishwomen': 'soft-notioned people have wept abundant tears over the pictures of misery drawn by this sharp little instrument'.

Yet he could strike other tones, too, for example in a memorable earlier article of 1851, where he suggested that 'people who use such articles as needles must have a good deal in common, however widely different they appear. How many wants and wishes, designs and plans, efforts and achievements must be common to the minds of all sorts of persons who sew things together to make garments and do it by means of some invention – of an instrument which shall pierce the material and draw a thread after it, to the two edges together?' There were such people 'all over the known world' using English needles 'wherever exchange of commodities is going on'. Two years after Dickens died in 1870, Gustave Doré produced the first known picture of a Shetland sweater, which had a new touch of romance about it. In an exhibition on the history of knitting, held in 1976 it was introduced with the words, 'In the foreground ... stands the fisherman with mouth open, dazzled by the early morning scene at Billingsgate Fish Market. Is it the first authentic illustration of a Fair Isle Sweater?'

The needles themselves were of many sizes and kinds, at least as many as the people who used them, and Victorian writers describing and, as was their wont, classifying them, seldom overlooked the sharp-pointed surgical variety, curved needles, thin and flat for four-fifths of their length. 'The delicate purposes to which these needles are applied', we read in *British Manufacturing Industries* (1876), 'the necessity which exists for sparing unnecessary pain to the patient, requires them to be made by hand with the greatest possible care, and each ground and polished separately'. Other varieties which now stand out as curiosities were 'double needles for seamstresses troubled with imperfect sight', where the eye of the needle was made to open at one side 'to facilitate easy threading', 'magnetized needles [and thimbles] to prevent the needle being lost' and 'golden needles', gilded in a solution of gold in *aqua regia*.

The statistics of needle production, imperfect though they are, are fuller than the statistics of thimbles which were made in even more varieties, some of them highly decorative, some very expensive, than the needles themselves. They have become favourite twentieth-century 'collectables', made as they were from materials as different as pearl, bone, horn, ivory, tortoise-shell, silver, rolled gold, pottery and porcelain. Some were rubber-lined. No one seems to have studied the thimble-makers. The match box makers – and the makers of biscuit tins – have fared better.

Eleanor Johnson, who has dealt in general with 'needlework tools', divides thimbles into 'workaday thimbles' – one of the best known was called 'Dorcas' – 'thimbles for the accomplished lady', 'milady's thimbles' and 'novelties and oddities', the last category including souvenir and commemorative thimbles, of which there were many, and small thimbles specially made for children. Thimbles could be toys too, and even measures for drinks and medicine ('a thimbleful'). Advertisers used them to proclaim the merits of salt or biscuits or even corsets, and a silver thimble was thought of as a desirable present. Thimble cases have become 'collectables' also. Some were made to look like barrels, others like animals. They were among the specialities of the Mauchline works.

There has been little point in collecting needles, although Victorian needle-cases complete with needles have survived and have been collected. Huge quantitites were produced, some of them very elaborate. In his *History and Description of Needlemaking* (1854) M. T. Morrell noted that by the middle of the century the output of needles from Redditch alone was fifty million a week, and a generation later the author of an article on needles in *Chambers's Journal* claimed that the hundred manufacturers and workmen engaged in the trade in Redditch were turning out double that quantity. At the end of the century, around 1,000 million needles a year were being produced in the country as a whole.

Among the needles were so-called 'Whitechapel sharps', but the geographical reference to London's East End home of milliners and dressmakers as well as of match girls was misleading in this context. The 'sharps' had acquired their name because a German needlemaker Elias Krause had settled at Whitechapel in the sixteenth century.

Thoughout the Victorian period the needlemaking business remained proud of its ancient pedigree. The Worshipful Company of Needlemakers of London had been incorporated by a charter granted by Cromwell in 1656, and its coat of arms referred back to the most ancient pedigree of all, this time bringing in Adam as well as Eve beside the tree of knowledge with the motto 'They sewed fig leaves together and made themselves aprons'.

Many Victorian sermons must have been delivered on this theme (had not Dr Johnson, with bachelor in mind, remarked that 'many a man has committed suicide for want of knowing how to darn a stocking'?) and Dickens introduced a sermonizing note into his *Household Words* article. It was most prominent in his description of the needle pointers of the generation just before his own, perhaps the most publicized of all the needle craftsmen, who lived where they worked in 'an atmosphere thick with stone dust and steel-dust [Sheffield steel was deemed to be the best], generated by the dry grinding of the needles upon the wheel, just under their noses. They would go out about once an hour and rinse their mouths.' 'Grinders' asthma' had been as serious an occupational disease as 'phossy jaw'. Nor had eyes been safe from the brilliant stream of sparks which followed the abrasion of the wire when the needles were being pointed. 'We wonder', Dickens added, 'how any seamstress ever dared to break an eye or turn the point of a thing which had cost so much pain' at a time when 'every needle that was pointed helped to shorten some man's life' and when, if boys tried the work, 'they were gone before twenty.'

Nor did the *Household Words* sermonizing end there. Partly because of this 'sacrifice', the article went on, needleworkers, unlike match girls, had been well paid and they preferred wealth to health: 'some men earned a guinea a day: none less than two guineas a week.' They had settled willingly, therefore, for long hours.

> A short and merry life they'd lead
> And of the future take no heed . . .
> Saturdays brought them no enjoyment
> They stayed till six at their employment.

They refused to take safety precautions, like wearing wire gauze masks which would have prevented steel dust entering their mouths, or using canvas cylinders brought down close over the grindstones to contain or carry away the dust.

Dickens was writing, as he did so often, about the generation just before his own, and he stressed, as he so often did, how things had changed. Yet *Chambers's Journal* said much the same a generation later, adding for good measure that when the grinders went on strike in the 1840s 'the masters were resolute in holding their ground'. It was only after the strike was over that 'Dr Holland's fan for blowing away the particles of dust from the workshops' was introduced, and 'the ignorant prejudices of those whom it was designed to benefit' were finally overcome. For Dickens, forgetting for once the sermon, the needlemakers, unlike the match girls, returned to work 'very hungry, very sad, and very humble', and as safety devices were gradually introduced, so, too, were machines: 'We saw, the other day, hooks and eyes made by a machine which gave us a very strong impression of being alive (someone said that it could do anything except speak).' Another stamping machine to give needles their eyes and their 'guttering' channel allowed a machine to strike five thousand needles an hour. For *Chambers's Journal* this was a victory of 'spirits of the present' over those of the past. There were Dickensian echoes here.

For all the strictly limited mechanization, Victorian needle-making still rested on the same time division of labour which had impressed Adam Smith when he contemplated his pin factory. 'Simple operations', highly specialized, tended by 'needle magic (Sala's phrase) to produce 'successful results'. There was also increasing reliance on cheap labour for the simplest operations. *Household Words* described John James's Victoria Works at Redditch, 'well off for air, light and cheerfulness', where no children under ten were employed, but James, most of whose workmen still worked at home, admitted that he could not prevent 'some of his people from hiring the help of children under that age'. At a factory just outside Redditch, half of which was used for grinding not needles but flour, a seven-year old boy had established a reputation for 'spitting' needles before they were heated, tempered and polished, under the direction of a woman 'whose wrists and arms were obviously of unusual strength'.

Workmen at that time paid for their own tools, and when they carried out any work processes in the mill also paid mill rent. They were sometimes expected too to meet part of the costs of improvements introduced to 'cut the sacrifice of life'. As the century went by, bringing with it further, if still limited, technical change, control of working conditions and school education, the earlier wage differentials fell without breaching older craft traditions. Aspects of the story can be traced in detail in 3,600 letters and the papers of the firm of John English and Company, needle manufacturers of Feckenham, which cover the period from 1788 into the twentieth century. They were presented to the Worcestershire Record office in 1961.

There was still a marked separation of work processes at the time when *British Manufactures* was written. Work began with the cutting up of bundles of steel wire drawn to gauges for various sizes of needle, and this was done by hand with shears. In the penultimate process, final polishing, done by hand with the help of a 'bob' (a revolving cylindrical piece of wood of small diameter covered with thin buff leather) a good polisher could deal with a thousand needles per hour. Intermediate processes had once included 'hard straightening' – making the crooked way straight – but the need for this had been eliminated (or greatly diminished) when oil was substituted for water in the trays in which the needles were hardened or tempered. It was still the case, however, at the end of the century, that the required elasticity or rigidity of the needle depended on the knowledge of the hardener, generally gained only by practice and experience.

Not the least interesting point in the elaborate production process came after the needles had been passed on to the warehouse. This, indeed, was the final process, and it was well described in *British Manufactures* in a section on counting and wrapping of the finished needles.

> The paper selected was of dark slate colour, and dried carefully (damp paper would rust and injure the brilliant colour of the needles) and then cut into the proper sizes by means of a bookbinder's guillotine knife, a great number of sheets at a time. The folding was done by two rolling machines, one of which determines the length of the 'envelope', the other its breadth; and a clever wrapper-up (generally a woman) could count and wrap up 120 papers containing twenty-five needles each, in all 3,000, in the brief space of one hour. It was next the turn of boys who pasted and attached small labels, bearing the number of the needle and the manufacturer's name or that of the retail dealer. For export the small packets were made up into larger packets (in dried papers) and frequently contained ten, twenty, or even fifty thousand needles, these packets being packed into tin boxes and hermetically soldered.

'A recently introduced feature in the needle trade', the author went on, 'was the sale of packets of needles in ornamental cases of brass of various devices. Some of these elevated the needles on being opened, by simple ingenious mechanical arrangements, which, on closing, withdrew them into its interior. The cases, however, not being made by the needlemakers (though an adjunct to their trade), do not call for further notice.' They have called for further notice, however, from twentieth-century collectors of Victoriana who have treasured them along with thimbles, thimble cases, match boxes and match tins.

It is interesting that they already called for further notice from Dickens. The piles of 'gay boxes' which were to be filled with 'an assortment of needles for presents of foreign trade' were, he observed, 'a branch of industry in themselves, with their portraits of the Queen and Prince, and their copies of popular pictures from popular painters, such as Raffaelle's "Madonna in the Chair".' As so often, there was a romantic ending to his story. 'They are probably to be seen on the walls of many a log cabin in America, and chalet in Switzerland, and bungalow in India, and home of exiles in Siberia. It seems as if all the world of needlewomen, of every clime, were supplied by England.'

# 6
# Hearth and Home

Between the Home set up in Eden, and the Home before us
in Eternity, stand the Homes of Earth in a long succession.
... Every home has its influence, for good or evil, upon
humanity at large.

JULIA MCNAIR WRIGHT *The Complete Home,*
*An Encyclopaedia of Domestic Life and Affairs,* 1881

This is the true nature of home – it is the place of Peace, the
shelter, not only from all injury, but from all terror, doubt
and division.... So far as it is a sacred place, a vestal
temple, a temple of the hearth watched over by Household
Gods.... roof and fire are types only of a nobler shade and
light – shade as of the rock in a weary land, and light as of
the Pharos in the stormy sea.

JOHN RUSKIN, *Sesame and Lilies,* 1864

We in England have decorated our churches sometimes
perhaps a little too much. And it is surely time we turned to
that second church, the temple in which even the old
heathen placed a family altar, and would give our homes a
little more of the beauty which comes of order and purity.

W. J. LOFTIE, *A Plea for Art at Home,* 1876

I have often observed that the men who left home very
young have, many long years afterwards, had the tenderest
regard for it.

CHARLES DICKENS, letter of 1856, quoted by
Samuel Butler in his *Notebook*

# I

Common things were 'everyday things', and they were gathered together inside the home. Yet for the Victorians the home was more than a house and the objects, common or distinctive, to be found inside it. 'Theirs was the first generation', wrote G. K. Chesterton of the Victorians, 'that ever asked its children to worship the hearth without the altar.' There had already been many Victorians who stressed how closely hearth and altar were related to each other, one of the most assured of them American, not British. 'Remember', wrote Julia McNair Wright in her *Complete Home* in 1879, 'that the Home is an institution of God himself; it is his ideal of the life of humanity.'

There was a strongly pervasive and, by present standards, repelling moral tone in this imposingly large book, although Aunt Sophronia, the most active and omniscient of the moralizers in it – she is introduced as 'an Oracle' – had little use for those often equally fervent moralists who spurned religion and trusted in 'humanity'. The home for Julia McNair Wright, a staunch advocate of temperance, should not only be a moral centre: it should be 'garrisoned by Family Faith'. The worst homes were 'fountains of bitterness', not 'wells of strength'. The best homes were 'sanctuaries'.

The English writer, W. J. Loftie, insisted in similar fashion in 1876 that 'a working view of Christianity would include an ideal of heaven as a home', while Ernest Newton told the Architectural Association fifteen years later that 'belief in the sacredness of home-life is still left to us, and is itself a religion, pure and easy to believe. It requires no elaborate creeds, its worship is the simplest, its discipline the gentlest, and its rewards are peace and contentment.'

Of course, the kind of Protestant piety which Julia McNair Wright proclaimed was very different from Chesterton's Catholicism – even if the idea of a sanctuary was a pre-Protestant conception. It was reinforced also from non-conformist teaching in which the altar had no part. More than ten years before *The Complete Home* appeared, the Reverend James Baldwin Brown, Minister of Brixton Independent Church in London, had published on this side of the Atlantic his book *The Home Life in the Light of its Divine Idea*, the kind of book which Chesterton particularly abhorred; and thereafter the home remained at the centre of his teaching. All great human institutions had 'divine originals', and one function of the home was 'to develop the Divine image in parent and child'.

In a sermon of 1871, with the title *Young Men and Maidens, a Pastoral for the Time*, Brown had urged women, in particular, to 'pray, think, strive to make a home something like a bright, serene, restful, joyful nook of heaven in an unheavenly world', and he had equally firm, if significantly different, guidance to offer men. 'Man learns his lessons and practises his art and power in the little world of the home before he goes forth to the great battle.'

In 1883 Brown published a second book on the home, his *The Home in Its Relation to Man and Society*, in which one of the nine chapters was called 'The Sacred Burden of the Home'. The book began and ended with Biblical quotations. It noted *en passant* that '*Home, sweet home* is almost our national melody'.

There was, indeed, as much verse, most of it solemn, that centred on domestic life as there was prose. It ranged from Coventry Patmore's *The Angel in the House* (1854) to S. W. Partridge's *Upward and Onward: A Thought Book for the Threshold of Active Life* (1851), which included a poem called 'A Home', written with would-be husbands in view:

> ... with care,
> Prudence and forethought, first prepare thy home.
> For 'tis not manly to allure a girl
> From peace and comfort, and sufficiency,
> To a sad cheerless hearth and stilted board.

There seems to be some considerable distance between such verses and sermons and two of the best-known books of the 1860s – Isabella Beeton's *Book of Household Management* (1861), which had first appeared in monthly instalments during the two previous years in *The Englishwoman's Domestic Magazine* and sold 60,000 copies in book form in its first year, and Charles Lock Eastlake's influential *Hints on Household Taste in Furniture, Upholstery and other Details* (1868). And there seems to be an even more considerable distance between what Mrs Beeton and Eastlake had to say and what actually happened in practice in Victorian homes.

In fact, distances were bridged, if not always very securely. Mrs Beeton herself began with a quotation from the *Book of Proverbs* (xxi, 25–28), and Eastlake borrowed the word 'hints' from a host of familiar publications, which included moral treatises, recipe books and even *Hints on Husband-catching; or a Manual for Marriageable Misses* (1846). There was a wide-ranging literature, some of it periodical literature, relating to real homes which was more concerned with practical matters than with morals. Yet periodicals were often interested in the ideal house, too, as they were interested in the ideal city.

For Sir Arthur Conan Doyle, inventor of Sherlock Holmes, there was 'more wisdom to the square inch' in Mrs Beeton's *Book of Household Management*, than in 'any work of man'. And there seemed to be the same sense of wisdom in Eastlake, who was as certain about art and taste as Julia McNair Wright's Aunt Sophronia was about religion and economy. 'There is a class of young ladies', he observed, 'who are in the habit of anticipating all differences of opinion in a picture gallery or concert room by saying that they "know what they like". Whatever advantages may be derived from this remarkable conviction in regard to music or painting', Eastlake went on, 'I fear it would assist no one in furnishing a house – at least in accordance with any established principles of art.' Like Samuel Smiles, neither Mrs Beeton nor Eastlake would have been drawn so successfully into writing had Victorian practice followed precept.

Books like *Mrs Beeton*, for this is how the book has come to be thought of after going through more than sixty editions in a hundred years, and Eastlake's *Hints*, are often taken on their own, like Matthew Arnold's *Culture and Anarchy* (1868), and subjected to detailed textual exegesis. They should be considered in context, however, which means comparing them with other books in a similar genre, earlier and later, and, equally important, comparing different editions of their own text. In the case of Mrs Beeton, too, it is necessary to take account also of a companion volume *Beeton's Housewife's Treasury of Domestic Information*, a work of over a thousand pages offering 'every requisite devised to secure the comfort, elegance and prosperity of the home'.

When Mrs Beeton began to write her *Household Management* she had at her disposal shelves full of earlier books like Thomas Webster's *An Encyclopaedia of Domestic Economy* (1844), Eliza Acton's trail-blazing *Modern Cookery for Private Families* (1845), Alexis Soyer's *The Modern Housewife, or Ménagère* (1849), and his *A Shilling Cookery for the People*, which appeared in the same year (1855) as *The What-Not: or Ladies' Handy-Book*. The first biographers of Alexis Soyer, who had been appointed Chef of the Reform Club in 1857, complained that 'the world is full of cookery books', but while their own book *The Economy of Cookery for the Middle Class, the Tradesman and the Artisan* (1860) is forgotten, Soyer himself had had to wait only two weeks for the second edition of his *The Modern Housewife* to appear, while Mrs Beeton had to wait for eight years.

Married to a publisher, Samuel Beeton, who had published *Uncle Tom's Cabin* in Britain, the real Mrs Beeton was only 25 years old in 1861 and died, a mother of four, before she reached the age of 30. It is necessary to note also that Samuel Beeton had published the first number of *The Englishwoman's Domestic Magazine* in 1852 three years before he met Isabella (the Crystal Palace was one of their *rendez-vous*) and that in 1865 she followed up her own *Household Management*, which cost 7s. 6d. with a cheaper book 'in serviceable binding' which cost only 3s 6d, *Mrs Beeton's Everyday Cookery and Housekeeping Book*. It was described as the first in a series of 'All About It' books, and its first section was entitled 'philosophy of housekeeping'. Less than two pages on children were followed by more than one page on chilblains and more than four pages on spring cleaning.

Unlike Mrs Beeton, Eastlake, whose tenth edition appeared in 1878, lived long enough (until 1898) to see complete changes of taste, recorded in books like C. J. Richardson's *The Englishman's House* (1870), Loftie's *A Plea for Art at Home*, one of a series, R. W. Edis's *Decoration and Furniture of Town Houses* (1881), Mrs Haweis's *The Art of Housekeeping, A Bridal Garland* (1889) and Rosamund Marriott Watson's *The Art of the House* (1897). Only six years after Eastlake's death, Hermann Muthesius, who had been attached to the

German Embassy from 1896 to 1903, was to write his enthusiastic study *Das Englische Haus* (untranslated until 1979) which stressed that 'the recent revival of the applied arts, [including] the work of William Morris ... began quite specifically in the house'.

There seemed to be far less reason to change the recipes in *Mrs Beeton* (and it was her *Everyday Cookery* which more than anything else made her 'the guide, philosopher and friend of countless happy homes') than there was to change advice on furniture, wallpapers and carpets; and Mrs Haweis included no section on cooking in her book on the sensible grounds that Mrs Beeton had said all there was to say before her. Eastlake himself began the preface to his fourth edition by explicitly acknowledging the beneficial effects of 'the remarkable change which has taken place within the last few years in the character of domestic furniture, especially of cabinet-work, textile fabrics and pottery'. The number of 'artistically appointed houses' was steadily increasing. Nor had it been necessary 'to sacrifice the refinements and comfort to which we are accustomed in the nineteenth century in order to secure simplicity of style'.

Books figured prominently in the 'comfortable' home as books about the home multiplied. 'This is emphatically an Age of Books', we read in a chapter in *The Complete Home* exclusively dedicated to them. An article on 'Furniture Books' in *Fraser's Magazine* in 1853 dealt with books as furniture, where the author quoted approvingly Bagehot on Edward Gibbon – 'the best way to reverence Gibbon is not to read about him at all, but look at him from outside, in the bookcase, and think how much there is within'. Yet as in the case of writers on furniture – or food – the author felt that he was writing to help readers who might be drawn into doing the wrong thing: he was appealing to a similar public as Dickens had been in *Household Words* a year earlier when he had observed that 'most people amuse themselves at one time or another ... by fancying what sort of house they would like to live in'.

For the *Fraser's Magazine* author, 'the whole domain of art and of decorative furniture' had fallen, not surprisingly, under the control of 'a parcel of dealers, who make their market out of the foolish vanity of that large section of the public which is stimulated to extravagance'. Another cause of trouble was 'the imperfect knowledge picked up in museums and the infinite babblement about art manufacture with which we have been stunned for the last few years: even the world of books had not escaped 'the prevailing contagion'. For the author, who liked long sentences, the most appropriate Latin tag was not *caveat emptor* (let the buyer beware) but *Populus vult decipi et decipietur* (the public wants to be deceived and will be).

# II

Three main secular themes dominate books with 'hints' or 'home' in their title – how to start: how to manage: and how to improve – and by their very nature these three themes were calculated to appeal to a primarily middle-class public. *Mrs Beeton's Everyday Cookery*, might be given away, like Samuel Smiles's *Self-Help*, as a Sunday School Prize to working-class girls, but books or magazines specifically for working-class readers fall into as different a category from those devised for middle-class readers as working-class homes did from middle-class homes with servants. It was only towards the end of the century that the idea of a mass readership covering all sections of the population began to emerge in works like *Cassell's Book of the Household* (1897), although during the fifty years before, aspiring working-class readers might turn to works not specifically addressed to them.

Starting 'properly', to take the first theme, meant more than acquiring the right *trousseau*. 'House hunting' usually came first. 'Which of you intending to build a tower, sitteth not down first and counteth the cost?' Counting the cost might well mean the male initially 'deferring' marriage until what William Cowper had called 'the proper time', the most important example of a broader range of 'deferring' which was held up for admiration as a middle-class quality: its significance in relation to population studies was established more than thirty years ago by J. A. Banks in his *Prosperity and Parenthood* (1954). Indeed, one of the most fascinating sections of that pioneering book – to be followed up a generation later by his *Victorian Values* (1981) – dealt with the lively correspondence in *The Times* in 1858 as to whether it was, or was not, possible to marry on £300 a year. Obviously for many correspondents, what Tennyson was to describe as 'debtless competence' was not easy to achieve. It was a 'problem' that had only recently been examined in a very practical fashion by J. H. Walsh in his *Manual of Domestic Economy* (1857) which presented details of four appropriate scales of domestic expenditure for incomes of £1000, £500, £250 and £100 a year.

Once married – or about to be married – the female came into the picture too, of course, for at least in the 'literature', and particularly in the American literature, she seems to have been directly involved in the choice of furniture as well as in housekeeping: for Julia McNair Wright, 'it was the duty of the husband to make money and of the wife to spend it judiciously: to save as far as you can, without sacrifice of comfort and decency', and for Mrs Beeton, who praised American women as 'wonderfully clever buyers', the housewife was 'the steward of her husband's property. It is not enough to have plenty of money: one must become a very clever buyer.'

Wives alone or husbands and wives together were not, however, the only agents involved in 'starting' homes. For *The Times* in 1861, the main trouble in getting things right was that newly married couples, both husbands and wives, expected 'to begin where their fathers and others ended'. They wanted the same range of things, inheriting 'stupid prejudice', while at the same time acquiring houses 'replete with ... all the paraphernalia of a drawing room of fashion'. And when Fashion came into the picture they were under the spell, most contemporaries believed, of persuasive salesmen in the shops. Eastlake, in particular, made much of this point. But he took the makers of goods into the reckoning also. 'So long as a thirst for novelty exists independently of all aesthetic considerations, the aim of Manchester and Sheffield [it is strange that he left out Birmingham] will be to produce objects which, by their singular form or striking combination of colours, shall always appear new.' He would like to have been able to reject all forms of veneering on moral grounds, but could not quite do so.

The 'morals' of housekeeping centred not only on 'taste' but on the relationships between 'starting' and 'continuing' and between 'acquiring' and 'aspiring'. What was chosen in the first place influenced patterns of choosing later, and Banks in his study was rightly just as much concerned with aspirations as with standards of living or 'quality of life'. Like the Victorian authors on whose work he drew, he very quickly, therefore, had to put children into the home. There were often so many of them (morality came in there too) that they were expected to be seen and not heard. A key section of his book dealt with the 1870s when, he claims, the cost of children began to be directly related in people's minds to the cost of things. The subsequent 'vital revolution' was supported by birth control – and new conceptions of morality began in the home.

How to manage, the second theme in the literature of home, was perhaps the major one, even when there was relatively little financial pressure, for 'order in the home' ('a place for everything and everything in its place' and 'a regular time for everything') preceded 'economy in the home'. Disorder, it was argued, was 'the slowest worker in the universe': an orderly worker, like an economical worker, had to pay attention to 'little things'. 'There was neither honour nor advantage in the neglecting of little things.' But there was an even more important dimension to such advice – the belief, well expressed by Julia McNair Wright, that 'managing the objects in the midst of which we live is establishing between us and them bonds of appropriate-ness or convenience: it is fixing habits without which man would tend to the savage state'. This Victorian judgement must lie at the very heart of any study of *Victorian Things*. It might have been inscribed in gold.

It is significant that Mrs Beeton, a young bride, claimed that she was moved to write her own book in the first instance by 'the discomfort and suffering which I have seen brought upon men and women by household mismanagement. I have always thought that there is no more fruitful source of discontent than a housewife's badly cooked dinners and untidy ways.' For Mrs Haweis also, it was not the beginning but the continuation of married life which was 'the real *crux*'. There was a contrasting strain of rhetoric in H. Southgate's *Things a Lady Would Like to Know Concerning Domestic Management and Expenditure* (1878). 'Wise economy and management of things will tend, with God's blessing, to secure the permanent happiness of the little kingdom in which she [the young Mistress] reigns and light up with brightness of content and satisfaction the face she most loves to see.'

Prosaically, managing the world of things had to start with a knowledge of the things themselves. 'I have a mop for the dishes', Aunt Sophronia's niece Miriam, a good manager, tells her sister Helen who was not, 'and a high-handled scrubbing brush for pots and pans, and a cork two inches high for polishing the knives – and I use gloves when I sweep and dust, and whenever else I can'. She also knew how to use ammonia ('nothing is like it'), flour paste and muslin. Managing things meant managing money too. 'Keep accounts.' 'Pay ready money if possible, regularly if the tradespeople will let you.' Then came the rhetoric again. 'Practise economy as a Fine Art', Aunt Sophronia tells Helen. 'Make a duty and a pleasure of it; it is the mortar wherein you lay up the walls of home.'

Mrs Haweis provided full details of just what should be retained in a kitchen store and when the items should be bought monthly (like most groceries), weekly (like matches), or daily (preferably for everything!). She also advised those of her readers with servants 'never to replace utensils, cloths &c without viewing the worn one'. Some of the reviewers of Mrs Haweis felt even at the time that many of her views on economies were 'quixotic'. But other writers, like Mrs Caddy, provided full details also. 'A good thick dormat' was 'a great temptation to people to rub their boots with'. Indeed, a mat – or two – was far better than 'one of those delightful indoor scrapers all set around with brushes, which are seldom used after the first two weeks of their introduction'.

The reason often given at the time why books like *The Complete Home* have a great deal to say about 'household management', part of the title of Mrs Beeton's book, was that 'modern systems of education may tend less than formerly to the thorough equipment of women in this respect'. A more important – and more convincing – reason, however, was that there were 'difficulties in the way of housekeeping, and many modern demands upon it, with which our grandmothers and even our mothers had not to contend'. One of the difficulties, of course, not spelt out, was the increase in the number of things in the home and the number of things about which the housewife had to know (and tradesmen had their lists as well as housewives). Yet there was a different and more positive final reason. Husbands as well as wives were now felt to be more interested in what was going on in the home than they ever had been before. In this connection, John Stuart Mill's somewhat stilted words in *The Subjugation of Woman* (1869, written 1861) have often been quoted: 'The improved tone of modern feeling as to the reciprocity of duty which binds the husband towards his wife – has thrown the man very much more upon home and its inmates, for his personal and social pleasures.'

The conclusion now was that if either 'side' failed to make the home attractive, or if the 'atmosphere' was wrong, there would 'come a longing', as Mrs Haweis observed tartly – and she knew this from experience – 'for the old homes [before the marriage] where everything moved by clockwork and where there was no visible responsibility'. The mothers and fathers – and the servants – were usually still there, and it was as easy to become sentimental about them as it was about 'the old school'.

The same tendencies in home-making and home management were apparent on both sides of the Atlantic.The editor of *Cassell's Book of the Household* (1890) had obviously not read *The Complete Home* – or many other American books – when he (or she) wrote that 'it is a striking fact that in the great nation of America, with all its advantages in many respects, there is a widespread cessation of old-fashioned, housekeeping, home-life; and the fact is a most melancholy as well as a striking one, for it cannot be other than an evil thing to substitute boarding-house publicity for the sacred privacy of the domestic household'.

The United States was not like that. Eastlake had been even more influential there than in Britain. 'Not a young marrying couple who could read English', *Harper's Bazaar* reported in 1876, 'were to be found without *Hints on Household Taste* ... and all its dicta were accepted as gospel truth'. It was one of Eastlake's greatest admirers, Mrs M. E. W. Sherwood, a regular contributor to *Appleton's Journal*, a rival of *Harper's Bazaar*, who wrote succinctly that 'the soothing influence of an Eastlake bookcase on an irritated husband has never been sufficiently calculated'. Another American woman writer, Mrs Ella Church Rodman, believed that there was 'no reason, either in prose or rhyme why a whole house should not be a poem'.

The prose of home in all its range demands careful exegesis. The contents page of *Cassell's Book of the Household* recalls the sub-title of Julia McNair Wright's *The Complete Home*. It was not the publisher's first venture in this field: *Cassell's Household Guide to Every Department of Practical Life; Being a Complete Encyclopaedia of Domestic and Social Economy* had appeared in a new and revised edition – for subscription only – in 1875.

The adjective 'complete' was obviously as much of a selling point as the adjective 'practical'; and significantly both adjectives appeared in the sub-title of Ward, Lock and Company's ambitious *The Young Ladies' Treasure Book*, published during the early 1880s, when the market for such books was at its height – 'A Complete Cyclopaedia of Practical Instruction and Direction for all Indoor Occupations and Amusements suitable for Young Ladies'. Ward, Lock and Company made the most of the market, with Samuel Beeton serving for a time as their literary adviser after disposing of his copyrights to them in 1866 when on the verge of bankruptcy. He was to break with them after litigation in 1874.

The market did not provide sources of authority, however, and Mrs Beeton in her *Book of Household Management* was at pains to insist that her chapters on the diseases of infancy and childhood had been written by 'a surgeon', and that her 'legal memorandum' had been written by a solicitor: they were both 'gentlemen', Mrs Beeton noted in her preface, 'fully entitled to confidence'. Without acknowledging such debts, other writers preferred to sound encyclopaedic. Thus, Julia McNair Wright was even more comprehensive than Mrs Beeton, for her sub-title ran 'The Household in its Foundation, Order, Economy, Beauty, Healthfulness, Emergencies, Methods, Children, Literature, Amusements, Religion [note how religion appeared low in the list in the sub-titles, although not in the book], Friendship, Manners, Hospitality, Servants, Industry , Money and History: a Volume of Practical Experiences Properly Illustrated.'

Later in the century, the introduction to *The Book of the Household* emphasized that although 'the home was one', there were many 'divisions' in its study. 'Furniture, food, clothing, health, and disease', 'household mechanics' and 'servants' had their place, but so too did 'family life' and the 'relation between different members of the family, beginning with 'master' and 'mistress' and their 'duties and responsibilities'. 'The Children' had to have a series to themselves: 'We must treat of their Rearing in Infancy, their Childhood, their Education'.

There was just as strong a managerial stress throughout *Cassell's Book of the Household* as there was in *The Complete Home* and an increased stress, too, on 'the important subject of Income and Expenditure', the main theme of Mrs Caddy's *Household Organization* (1877) which stated boldly that 'every family might be its own Economical Housekeeping Company (Limited), comprising in itself its shareholders and board of directors, realizing cent per cent for its money, because £200 a year would go as far as £400'. By then, there was much talk of the new strains on middle-class finances even in a period of falling prices. Mrs Beeton herself, often accused of extravagance, had written so earnestly about management (before price levels fell from the 1870s until the late-1890s) that she felt it necessary, given what she had said, to remind her readers that 'to be a good housewife does not necessarily imply the abandonment of proper pleasure or amusing recreation'. 'We think it the more necessary to express this', she added editorially and royally, while still in her twenties, 'as the performance of the duties of a mistress may, to some minds, perhaps seem to be incompatible with the enjoyment of life.'

It is fascinating to list the qualifications Mrs Beeton chose to make in her 'argument', the warnings she uttered, and, not least, the references she made to previous periods of history. While Julia McNair Wright quoted Plato more than once, Mrs Beeton told her readers about 'handsome, well-regulated Greek dinners' – with symposia to follow – and the Roman art of dining, before going on to quote from Milton, Byron, Keats and Tennyson. Her anthropology was more suspect than her history: 'Creatures of the inferior races eat and drink; man only dines'.

The Reverend Baldwin Brown chose a different period of history to spotlight in his 'analysis'. Pushing the Greeks to one side, he claimed that 'as far back as we can trace the history of the Teutonic peoples' it was 'the German capacity for a noble home-life' and 'the sacredness and purity of the German home' that had to be considered most relevant to Victorian experience. He did not note, however, that the word 'home', which has no precise counterpart in the Latin or Slavic European languages, goes back to the Old Norse 'heima' and that the Dutch had made much of 'the home' (*hejm*) in the seventeenth century.

Baldwin Brown included one chapter on 'Christian Education' in *The Home in Its Relation to Man and Society*, but he had nothing to say in it concerning the third secular theme in the 'hints' literature – how to improve the home – the theme on which Eastlake concentrated. Eastlake, who told people how to lay their carpets, paper their walls and choose their furniture to make their homes more 'tasteful', was, above all else, an educator, a 'taste-maker'. But he was writing for a public large sections of which *wanted* to be educated. 'In these days of general comfort', wrote H. Southgate in *Things a Lady would like to Know*, 'we expect to find some degree of refinement as well as comfort in the domestic arrangements of persons in the middle class of English society. A cultivated mind will by a touch add embellishment to common things.'

Neither *The Complete Home* nor *Cassell's Book of the Household* left 'improvement' out. The former included a chapter called 'Home Adornment' and the latter dealt at length on home furnishing and how to improve it, while offering a far greater freedom of choice than Eastlake had suggested. 'Houses would be much more furnishable, as well as inhabitable', it claimed, 'if we had a few feminine architects.' An earlier male writer, the Canadian engineer Henry Rutton, had claimed in 1862 that 'amid the blaze of light which in this nineteenth century has so illumined the world, architecture alone lies motionless, covered by the dust of the ages. Not a single new idea . . . has been suggested by the profession within the memory of man.' Perhaps women could do better.

As far as improvement was concerned, the main message of all writers at all times – and it was deliberately a reassuring one – was that neither 'elaboration' nor 'costliness' constituted beauty. An expressive house was not necessarily a beautiful house. 'Fanciful quilting would not make the quilt warmer, nor make it better, but it would make it *fine*. A million times better spend that time in the garden raising flower-seeds.' 'Costliness' was an unnecessary luxury inside as well as outside. 'Many people seem to think that we can secure beauty only by profuse money outlay – that beauty is largely dependent on expense. On the contrary, beauty is largely independent of expense.' 'The least handsome parlor that I ever saw', wrote Julia McNair Wright, 'was a very expensive one – not a book or engraving to be seen . . . It was early summer and the garden had plenty of flowers, but not one was in the parlor; instead, silver vases of wax monstrosities and porcelain baskets of waxed fruit: a gaudy assertion of superabundant dollars.'

## III

How does Eastlake's *Hints on Household Taste*, recently reprinted like so many Victorian books, look within the Victorian context? Eastlake, who was to write *A History of the Gothic Revival* in 1872, has been described as reacting against the tastes of the Great Exhibition and certainly in more than one passage he referred to the 'dangerous labyrinths of rococo ornament'. Yet such a description is far too vague, for [see Chapter 2] there had been many different attitudes to design, colour and decoration in 1851 itself, and Eastlake was at one with many other people in 1851 when he disclaimed the 'mawkish simplicity' and 'insipidity' of eighteenth-century architecture. Moreover, before he talked as he always did of 'art furniture', he could have found a precedent in Henry Cole's talk of 'art objects': he was like Cole, too, in abhorring garlands and bouquets in carpet design. Both men talked of 'improving taste' and both men were subjects of satire. Eastlake was accused, unlike Cole, of 'mediaeval predilections', but he greatly admired the elaborate objects of the sixteenth and early seventeenth centuries, which were as highly ornamental as any of the elaborate objects in the Crystal Palace.

It is interesting to compare him with writers very different from himself. Thus, he and Julia McNair Wright were in agreement in disliking the demand for 'novelties' which, Eastlake wrote, 'may be as remarkable for ugliness as beauty'. Nor, he claimed, was he any more interested than she was in 'examples of refined workmanship which are only within the reach of the wealthy'. In the preface to his 1872 edition he stated explicitly that it was 'strange to say' that there was no warehouse in London 'in which the public can be sure of finding articles of ordinary household use, *ready-made*, of uniformly good design and as cheap as those usually offered for sale'. Yet he was prepared to praise not only Jacobean-style furniture but medieval gas furnishings and to urge the claims of 'picturesque internal fittings'.

Eastlake was writing from London, but his book, as we have seen, sold well across the Atlantic – the first edition appeared there in 1872 – and, as far as can be judged, well enough in the English provinces. His hope that architects and interior designers would work more closely together was shared more generally across the Atlantic than in London. Nonetheless, in the 1878 edition of his book Eastlake complained that 'American tradesmen' were 'continually advertising what they are pleased to call "Eastlake" furniture, with the production of which I had nothing whatever to do and for the taste of which I should be sorry to be considered responsible'.

For Eastlake, like Pugin before him and Morris after him, 'improving' taste involved a recognition of the fact that things had got worse in the nineteenth century, not better. 'It is to be feared that instead of progressing ... we have gone hopelessly backward in the arts of manufacture.' And this was true not only with respect to the character of design, or to such procedures as French polishing – like Ruskin he referred to 'structural deceits' – but often in regard to the actual quality of materials employed. 'It is generally admitted, by every housewife who has attained a matronly age that linen, silk, and other articles of textile fabric, though less expensive than formerly, are far inferior to what was made in the days of our grandfathers. Metal-workers tell us that it is almost impossible to procure, for the purpose of their trade, brass such as appears to have been in common use a century ago. [Eastlake left out iron at this point, but brought it in later.] Joinery is neither so sound nor so artistic as it was in the early Georgian period.'

The reality for Eastlake was – at least during the 1860s – that 'commonplace taste', sentimental when it considered pictures, was tawdry when it considered things. Such taste 'crosses our path in the Brussels carpet of our drawing rooms; it is about our bed in the shape of gaudy chintz; it compels us to rest on chairs and to sit at tables which are designed in accordance with the worst principles of construction ... It sends us metal-work from Birmingham which is as vulgar in form as it is flimsy in execution ... It decorates the finest modern porcelain with the most objectionable character of ornament. It lines our walls with silly representations of vegetable life ... It bids us, in short, furnish our houses in the same fashion as we dress ourselves, and that with no more real sense of beauty than if art were a dead letter.'

It is obvious not only that Eastlake felt as much reverence when he spoke of art as Julia McNair Wright felt when she spoke of piety, but that he would have been as disturbed by journalistic talk of 'infinite babblement about art manufacture' as she would have been about agnosticism. National art for him – and he was writing as a future Keeper and Secretary of the National Gallery, who had published his aunt's *Journals and Correspondence* – was 'not a thing which we may inclose in a gilt frame and hang upon our walls, or which can be locked up in the cabinet of a collector. To be genuine and permanent it ought to animate with the same spirit the blacksmith's forge and the sculptor's atelier, the painter's studio and the haberdasher's shop. In the great ages of art it was so.' Now painters know nothing of jewellery, jewellers of painting. Every branch of manufacture was 'inclosed within its own limits'.

Eastlake drew no boundaries between appreciation of pictures and appreciation of things. 'Articles of household use', including clothes, revealed the same limitations as works in the Royal Academy. And there were far too many knick-knacks (advertised as 'articles of vertu') and 'fancy things' from glass shades and paper weights to wax flowers and scrapwork screens. There were also too many 'what-nots', specially carved for displaying them.

At this point the 'improving' Eastlake found his role, starting not with furniture, but with clothes. The crinoline, *pace* James Laver, who was to find profound reasons for its existence (see page 26), had been a 'wretched invention' forced on women by fashion makers to such an extent that any lady appearing without one would be thought a 'fright' and that even children 'must have grown up in the belief that it actually lent a sort of charm to the skirts of their mothers'. And though fashion had now displaced the crinoline, it was still true that 'ninety nine out of every hundred English women who had 'the credit of dressing well' depended entirely upon their milliners for 'advice as to what they might, or might not, wear'.

From clothes Eastlake passed to carpets. 'When *Materfamilias* enters an upholsterer's warehouse, how can she possibly decide on the pattern of her new carpet when bale after bale of Brussels is unrolled by the indefatigable youth who is equal in his praises of every piece in turn?' Shall it be the 'House of Lords' diaper of a yellow spot upon a blue ground or the 'imitation Turkey' with its multifarious colour; or the beautiful new *moiré* design; or yonder exquisite invention of green fern-leaves tied up with knots of satin ribbon? In this dilemma the 'shopman', using words like 'striking' and 'unique', came to the rescue and stated his firm opinion as to which was 'most fashionable', and this at once carried the day. 'The carpet is made up, sent home, and takes its chance of domestic admiration together with all other household appointments. It may kill by its colour every piece of *tapisserie* in the room. It may convey the notion of a bed of roses, or a dangerous labyrinth of rococo ornament – but if it is "fashionable" that is all-sufficient. While it is new, it is admired, when old, everybody will agree that it was always "hideous".'

The role of the carpet, singled out in Eastlake's attack on 'fashionable' furnishings, had been much discussed, along with the role of wallpapers, before he wrote. Statisticians like Porter treated it as the symbol of comfort, and designers treated it as a symbol of taste. It had figured, of course, in the much quoted second chapter of Dickens's *Hard Times* (1854). 'Suppose you were to carpet your room – or your husband's room ...' the 'third gentleman' (usually taken as Cole) asks, 'would you use a carpet having a representation of flowers?' The chorus of No was very strong, and when Sissy Jupe, under pressure, said that she was 'very fond of flowers', and 'fancied' that flowers on the carpet would not crush and wither, like real flowers, if they were trampled on with heavy boots – they were pictures of 'what was very pretty and pleasant' – she was told firmly – and twice – by the 'third gentleman', 'You are never to fancy'.

Whatever the point was for the 'third gentleman' – or for Cole in real life – that was not quite the point for Eastlake. People who bought 'fashionable' flower carpets did not have too much fancy, they had too little. In their 'thirst for novelty' they were copying others. He was like Cole, of course, in believing that they had lacked 'instruction'. 'Even the simplest and most elementary principles of decorative art form no part of early instruction, and the majority of the public, being left completely uninformed by them, is content to be guided by a few people who are themselves not only uninformed but misinformed on the subject.'

Just because carpets were symbols, even more because their choice affected the appearance of everything else in the room, it was particularly unfortunate that carpet merchants could so easily lead people by the nose. 'They fancy they are choosing chairs, and rugs and crockery – in reality they only look on while their tradesmen select for them. The young couple will probably be told that a Turkey carpet and a dark paper are proper for a dining-room, while a light paper and a Brussels carpet must adorn the drawing room.' The atmosphere of the house was already being set before they bought any things besides carpets. 'What is the prevailing tint on your carpet?' 'Crimson.' 'Then you must have crimson curtains, crimson sofa, crimson everything.' Mrs Wright was to see other dangers in carpets. She did not believe that the role of the carpet was over once it had been bought and admired. Indeed, *she* would have banished carpets from her house altogether: they harboured dirt, and fear of their fading kept out the sun. 'If I could not have the carpet and the sun, I would give up the carpet.' And that was after the carpet sweeper had been introduced into the house during the 1860s.

Wallpapers were almost as important to Eastlake as carpets. As he explained in an anonymous article, much noticed, on 'The Fashion of Furniture' in the *Cornhill Magazine* in 1864, the saleman in this case would explain to newly-weds which wallpapers were 'elegant', 'genteel', 'neat' or, most frequently, 'in much request'. 'They may have rose sprigs interlaced with satin ribbon,' he might go on, or crimson 'flock' designs in panels of sham perspective, or 'Mooresque intricacies' surrounded by a border of wild flowers. By 1872, Eastlake noted an improvement of tastes in wallpapers. 'There is a growing impatience of paperhangings which would beguile the unwary into a shadowy suspicion that the drawing room walls are fitted up with trellis-work for training Brobdignag convolvuli; and portraits of the Bengal tiger no longer appear on the domestic hearthrug.'

After dealing with chairs – 'unstable, rickety sticks of walnut or rosewood, inlaid perhaps with mother-of-pearl which no one sees, or twisted into "fancy" backs which torture the sitter or break beneath his weight' – Eastlake declared himself even less happy about sofas. 'It is difficult to conceive anything in the whole range of upholstery uglier than the modern settee or couch.' Not surprisingly, given the choice of reclining on a settee or couch or of going to bed, people generally preferred to go to bed. Then came another generalization which linked Cole and Eastlake. 'It is not too much to say that there is hardly an article to be found for sale in a modern upholsterer's shop which will bear evidence of even the commonest principles of design.' On another occasion Eastlake wrote disparagingly of 'the upholstering mind', anticipating Giedion, who from his twentieth-century vantage point was to describe the nineteenth century as the reign not of Victoria but of the upholsterer.

'Rude and unsophisticated' people (like Maoris and North American

Indians) fared better, Eastlake felt, with simple objects. Indeed, 'one of the few speciments of honest English manufacture which remains in this country' was 'the ordinary Windsor chair, some very pretty types of which may be sometimes seen in our cottages or round a kitchen fire'. Invented not by urban cabinet makers but by rural craftsmen, the Windsor chair, usually made of beech, had survived industrialization and was to pass in the future into almost every book on design. It seemed to belong to the same universe as trees and flowers. And Eastlake, for all his Jacobean propensities, liked to go back to that universe too. 'We are more likely in our present state of civilization to rightly appreciate the grace and loveliness of nature than to form (untaught) a just estimate of the artistic value of human handiwork.'

If there were contradictions in Eastlake's approach, there were also explicit qualifying notes, like his recognition in 1872 that if drawing room furniture remained *in statu quo* there were some signs of 'improvement in the way of carpets and paper hangings'. Some later historians have forgotten this, being far too willing to generalize, as Ralph Dutton did in his *Victorian Home* (1954) which followed his books *The English Interior* (1948) and *London Homes* (1952). Well aware as he was of the twists and turns of fate which were to lead to Eastlake's own style being parodied during the 1890s, Dutton stated comprehensively – and wrongly – that Eastlake's advice was 'ill-advised and that in many [Victorian] rooms there would be nothing to be seen which would now be worth more than a few pounds, if subjected to the cold test of the auctioneer's hammer'. Susan Lasdun is more trustworthy when in her delightful and beautifully illustrated *Victorians at Home* (1981) she writes of Victorian homes that 'the variety of the individual pieces is endless . . . and pieces with characteristics thought of as typical of one period have disconcerting ways of turning up in another.' One of her groups of pictures relates to the house of the bachelor antiquarian and artist George Scharf (1868–9) which 'demonstrated precisely the sort of popular taste which Charles Eastlake and his friends condemned'.

Dutton was prepared, however, to refer to 'unusual' interiors like that designed in elaborate taste by Owen Jones for the industrialist Alfred Morrison in Carlton House Terrace – it was thought to brighten up a dull Nash building – and to note generally 'many subtle changes . . . almost imperceptibly creeping into the way of life in the Victorian home'. It is necessary to add that many of the changes (like the shift to blue and white or to Japanese, including 'japano-bethan') were far from 'subtle'. They were certainly much commented upon – not least by Victorian taste-makers – and were seldom 'imperceptible'. Thus, for example, as Dutton himself noted, the poet W. E. Henley could write in 1882 that 'the Japanese dado has become almost a household word, and the Japanese fan a household essential'. That was not the end of the Victorian story. The architect Charles Voysey, born in 1857 and designer of door handles and of fire grates as well as of houses, expressed disgust in 1895 with 'the motley collection of forms and colours with which most rooms are crowded' and asked his readers – and his clients – to 'try the effect of a well-proportioned room, with white-washed walls, plain carpet and simple oak furniture, and nothing in it but necessary articles of use, and one pure ornament in the form of a simple vase of flowers'. Two years later, Rosamund Marriott Watson in her *The Art of the House* attacked 'stuffy passages', 'swollen table legs', 'hippopotamus-like sofas', lumber of all kinds, and 'art colours which simulate the hues of corruption'.

Dates matter in all judgements about Victorian taste, and Giedion was right to call them 'the historian's yardstick': 'conceived in interrelation, that is vertically and horizontally connected within the network of historical objects, they delimit constellations'. Surprisingly, therefore, Dutton does not date a fascinating quotation which he offers from 'the sculptress Mrs Freeman', whose works were described in the *Magazine of Art*:

> Her studio is full of delightful models for rendering home surroundings elegant and practical. Her model for a chimney-piece has on the entablature a frieze of babies representing the Happy Hours and [there is] another frieze of Household Genii on the marble fender.

Compare Rosamund Marriott Watson: 'Our forefathers' fenders were beyond compare superior to ours.'

Fortunately we can date the gable-ended Guest House described in Morris's *News from Nowhere*, 'the drawing room in cardinal red hung from the middle of the ceiling and looped up to give the appearance of a tent' described in George Moore's *Confessions of a Young Man* (1888), and the increasing appeal in the 1890s of the *Old Cottages and Farmhouses in Sussex* described in Guy Dawber's book of 1900. They were praised just because they were different from Moore's tent. The exotic and the simple were back in fashion. The farmhouses never pretended to be anything but what they were. 'There is as a rule nothing fantastic in their outline, nor frivolous in detail.'

It is impossible to deal with furnishings and decoration without bringing in William Morris, who himself made things which were sumptuous as well as things which were simple. He once wrote in 1879, however, that he had 'never been into any rich man's house which would not have looked the better having a bonfire made outside it of nine-tenths of all that it held' and he refused to consider as 'civilisation ... more studded chairs and more cushions, and more carpets and gas'. Some of the things that Morris made himself were very simple. Thus, his rush-seated 'settles', which sold in the early 1880s for £1 15s, were as different as possible from the sofas described in the *Cornhill* article of 1864, although scarcely more comfortable.

Dutton used adjectives like 'rugged', 'robust', and 'forceful' in the account he gave of Morris's work and influence, but these are quite inadequate to reflect Morris's remarkable range. The Burne-Jones eighteenth-century Fulham home, The Grange, for example, was papered with Morris papers and furnished by the Morris firm – it also included Dürer engravings given to Edward Burne-Jones by Ruskin – but, as Susan Lasdun demonstrates, much of the Morris represented in the house was early rather than late Morris, and there were considerable differences between the two. A more fascinating house furnished in Morris taste was Wightwick Manor three miles from Wolverhampton and built in 1887 for Samuel Theodore Mander, a Wolverhampton manufacturer. Mander turned to the firm of Morris and Company and to other craftsmen influenced by Ruskin and the pre-Raphaelites. The house survives, complete with Morris wallpapers, silk and woollen textiles, carpets and books from the Kelmscott Press, along with de Morgan tiles, W. A. S. Benson metalwork, Rossetti, Ford Madox Brown and Millais paintings, C. E. Kempe stained glass windows, and a grand piano made for the Great Exhibition, the only English piano to win a prize at the Paris Exhibition of 1878. And these Victorian things cohabit easily with Jacobean furniture, a Queen Anne walnut marquetry cabinet, Chinese porcelain and Persian rugs.

Morris started not with furniture but with a house – Philip Webb's Red House, which he first began to build in 1859 – and he always regarded architecture as the master art. Yet after he had set up his 'Firm' in April 1861, he left his own main mark as a designer on what were thought of as 'lesser' or 'minor' arts. Between 1876 and 1883 he prepared at least 11 designs for wallpapers, 22 for chintzes, and 24 for machine-made carpets. (At Wightwick Manor there is a 'Pomegranate Passage' and one room is called Acanthus Room after another Morris paper. There is also a Honeysuckle Room named after a Morris printed linen.)

Morris chose the 'lesser arts' as the subject of his first public lecture in 1878. They constituted, he claimed, 'that great body of art, by means of which men have at all times more or less striven to beautify the familiar matters of everyday life'. In his own century they had become 'trival, mechanical, unintelligent, incapable of resisting the changes pressed upon them by fashion or dishonesty'. And Morris set out with enthusiasm and organization to redress the calamity. In the beginning he and Webb produced the 1862 trellis wallpaper, the trellis devised by Morris and the birds by Webb, and although another early Morris partner, Rossetti, complained when Morris turned to textiles that 'Topsy has taken to worsted work', such complaints never deterred him. In 1877 he opened an impressive show room in Oxford Street, and he advertised in circulars and newspapers 'the personal touch' that he could offer to clients seeking advice on internal decoration.

Morris's clients, once his Firm produced many things, were many also, and some of those known to him, including the biggest, have been studied in detail. They were often rich, a fact that troubled Morris even before he became a socialist, but his independent, sometimes eccentric, attitude towards them seems to have attracted rather than repelled them. He certainly proved himself a shrewd businessman, looking for openings, manufacturing and distributing, and carrying out research, notably in dyeing; so that to two recent business historians, Charles Harvey and Jon Press, he was a man 'very much of his age, who played an active part in shaping its identity; and a shrewd and vigorous participant in the commercial world, who came to terms with its pressures and restrictions to create a uniquely colourful and successful enterprise'.

Linda Parry in her study of Morris textiles has noticed how it became a fashionable imperative for all self-respecting London households to possess at least one item of Morris manufacture; and there is ample evidence concerning a diffusion of the 'Morris look' that was far wider than the market for his things. Indeed, other designers benefitted in the process, as the 'hints' literature of the 1870s reveals. Thus, Mrs Orrinsmith in her book *The Dining Room* (1889) described the 'style of colouring employed by Mr Morris and his school' as based upon 'scientific calculations analogous to those which obtain in the sister art of music. It is in no way connected with the caprices of fashion.' Agnes and Rhoda Garrett's *House Decoration* (1875), written in collaboration with Owen Jones and singing Morris's praises, had gone through six editions by 1879.

Morris's disdain for fashion could not prevent him from being fashionable, and although when during the 1880s he turned to 'scientific Socialism' in a search for the same kinds of moral certainties that Mrs Orrinsmith discovered in his colours, his socialism was very much of his time.

Eastlake never crossed Morris's river of fire which led him towards revolution. Yet he too faced the same contemporary problem in relation to his judgements. Hating as he did the 'caprice of fashion', he would have shuddered to read a caption in *Furniture and Decoration* (March 1877), written one year after Morris's death. Besides the picture of a 'quaint' Eastlake-like sideboard, it said that while it 'would have been regarded as cranky a few years ago', now it seemed 'original, if nought else be conceded in its favour': 'it certainly bids fair to prove itself an inexpensive and somewhat effective production'. Fashion had won, although by the end of the century Eastlake was out of fashion while Morris never lost his admirers, some of them disciples.

*Furniture and Decoration*, a periodical founded in 1890, had absorbed the *Furniture Gazette* founded in 1872. And from its pages it is possible to glean much about the changing fashionable attitudes to clutter and display and to function and form, just as it is possible to glean much about houses and othe buildings from the pages of *The Builder*, a periodical which has been more fully used by historians. The very first number of the *Gazette*, which included 'carpet notes', a retrospect of the second Arts and Crafts Exhibition and a 'chapter on easy chairs', showed how remarkable the vagaries of fashion could be, for there was also an article on eighteenth-century French furniture which noted how 'the gradual and steady appeal of the Louis

Quinze style' had now reached the point where 'the taste for French furniture is fast becoming more popular among middle-class people'. 'A glance at the windows of any of the first-class furnishing houses will convince the most patriotic observer that there is, at the present time, a decided wave of fashion in favour of French art.'

It is not easy to see how the things illustrated in this first number could have fitted into the houses Eastlake himself admired. And from the start Eastlake had been as much interested as Webb or Voysey in houses as in their contents. 'Most of us are obliged to accept the outward appearance of one abode as we find it. In London it is sure to be irretrievably ugly.' Eastlake started, of course, from a Gothic premise: Gothic architecture – and here he followed Pugin – did not depend on the 'whims of a clique or the blind passion of an antiquary ... but on the sound artistic principles of early tradition'. LIke Ruskin, however, Eastlake appreciated that 'many monstrous designs have been perpetrated under the general name of Gothic, which have neither in spirit or letter realized the character of medieval art'.

# IV

When Eastlake turned from interiors to houses, he was as suspicious, therefore, as Ruskin was of 'vulgarities of design', and he would have agreed with Morris that stucco was 'invented in an evil hour'. Indeed, the stuccoed terraces of outer London spoke for themselves outside and inside. Most of the ornament – and there was exaggeration in this – was 'meretricious'. Plaster brackets supported plaster pediments, and floorboards came up 'unexpectedly after separating from the skirting'. Doors shrank so that they could not be securely fastened, and window-sashes warped and became immovable. The houses were often built by 'speculative builders', and they would continue so to be built 'as long as people of humble means will insist on assuming the semblance of luxuries which they cannot really afford'. Legislation was necessary to eliminate abuses. 'An Englishman's house was formerly said to be his castle. But in the hands of the speculative builder and advertising tradesman, we may be grateful that it does not oftener become his tomb.'

Mrs Haweis in her *Art of Housekeeping* (1889) dedicated to her daughter, offered a different remedy in a chapter called 'Houses for the Happy'. She first recommended newly-married couples not to live in newly-built houses – she herself had moved from 16 Welbeck Street to St John's Wood Road and from there to Queen's House, 16 Cheyne Walk, Rossetti's old home, in 1883 – and she went on next to tell them how to safeguard themselves if, quite unlike her, they could not find 'a handsome little old house, well-seasoned and capable of adaptation to modern needs with little outlay'. 'Have a surveyor of independent reputation, and independent of the building (and the *undertaking*) interest, to warrant the condition of the new house *in writing* before you sign the lease of a term of years longer than the walls may stand'.

When Mrs Haweis quoted the doggerel

He who takes a house ready wrought
Gets many a pin and nail for nought,

she was doubtless thinking of the thousands of fashionable 'Queen Anne' houses which had been and were being built as she was planning her book and which were much praised on both sides of the Atlantic: J. J. Stevenson, author of *House Architecture* (1880), did much to popularize it under the name 'Free Classic', and what Vincent Scully has called 'Shingle Style' was an American counterpart. It was one of Eastlake's many admirers, George William Curtis, who had described the 'epoch of Queen Anne' in 1886 as 'a delightful insurrection against the monotonous era of rectangular buildings and the divorce of beauty and "use"', the theme too of William M. Woollett's *Old Homes Made New* (1878).

Eastlake had a more varied range of houses in mind when he wrote *Hints on Household Taste*, including those built in 'the so-called Italian style – now understood to include every variety of Renaissance design which prevailed in Rome, Venice and Florence from the sixteenth to the eighteenth century'. Whatever their 'aesthetic merits' and 'practical advantages', they were in his view completely unsuited 'to the age, to the climate, and to the country in which they are reproduced'. The leaden skies of London, as Ruskin with his love of light well knew, were quite inappropriate for them. 'Bold and sturdy features' which would hold their own against wind and rain and would 'defy the smoke and traffic of our busy coal-burning towns' were essentials.

It was within this context that what Muthesius called 'the English house' was developed, fortunately, he thought, with 'no startling exhibition pieces ... and ... thank heaven ... no trace of art nouveau'. Everything breathed 'simplicity, homeliness and rural freshness'. 'Queen Anne houses' – the description was a misnomer that stuck – had become fashionable at the same time as the revival of the traditional garden, and gardens were to play an important part as adjuncts (or something more than adjuncts) to the domestic architecture which Muthesius so much admired. Believing as he did that 'the Anglo-Saxon race has been denied the gift of building cities', everything, including 'the powerful sense of the individual personality', depended on the home. Norman Shaw had designed Albert Hall Mansions in 1880, but his houses were to be copied, like those of Voysey, more in the suburbs and the villages than in city centres, for there, as Muthesius saw, however grey the skies, the garden could 'extend the house into the midst of nature'.

It is interesting to compare the comments of Muthesius and of Eastlake earlier, with those to be found in trade catalogues of homes for sale, just as it is interesting to compare Richardson's *The Englishman's House from a Cottage to*

*From a Cottage to a Mansion: advice on taste from C. J. Richardson*

*a Mansion* (1870) or J. J. Stevenson's *House Architecture* (1880) with earlier books like John Claudius Loudon's *Encyclopaedia of Cottage, Farm and Villa Architecture and Furniture* (1843), A. J. Downing's *The Architecture of Country Houses* (1850), published in America – and above all Robert Kerr's *The Gentleman's House or how to plan English Residences from the Parsonage to the Palace* (1864). Kerr listed no fewer than eleven styles from which a client could choose – Elizabethan, Palladian, Italian, Revived Elizabethan, Rural Italian, Palatial, Italian, French Italian, English Renaissance, Medieval and Gothic – and certainly clients existed who might for whatever reasons choose any one of the eleven, if not for a whole house, at least for additions to an existing one.

The fact that 'new wealth' had to find either old houses of the kind which the aristocracy or the gentry inherited, if necessary 'Victorianizing' them, or to build new houses led them more to the country than to the cities where the wealth was made. Although there were imposing new Victorian houses of every style in most cities, they were seldom as numerous or as imposing as their American 'Victorian' counterparts; and new country houses, brilliantly described by Mark Girouard in *The Victorian Country House* (1971), were less popular, if only for economic reasons, by the end of the reign, when some of the largest new American houses were being built. There was still a rural bias, however, expressed in the village 'residence', in the suburban garden, and even in the 'model' working-class housing estate like that planned at New Earswick, York by Raymond Unwin, and begun in 1902.

Downing, like Loudon, had been a landscape gardener, and like Richardson after him, he produced copy books of sketches of desirable residences in which a rural bias was clearly present. Richardson's numbered versions included not only 'gingerbread houses', complete with sketches that suggest dolls' houses, but a 'double suburban villa' in the 'domestic style of the reign of Henry VII' and 'a small country retreat or French *maisonette*'. While Eastlake was uneasy about clients' tastes, Richardson was confident. 'Where for example, can be found superior specimens of art-choice than exist in their [his countrymen's] mansions, villas, or cottage *ornés?*'

Kerr's history was more systematic. He devoted one whole section, more than 70 pages of his book, to a historical 'sketch' going back to 'the Saxon time' and to 'building among the Gothic nations'; and in his third part he dealt, like Loudon and Downing, with choice of site and 'arrangement of grounds', including sub-sections on the rosery, the pinetum, the fernery (John Smith, Curator of the Royal Botanic Gardens at Kew from 1841 to 1864 enumerated more than 900 species of British ferns) and the 'American garden'. Richardson, like Mrs Haweis, who actually wrote a book called *Rus in Urbe: or Flowers that thrive in London Gardens and Smoky Towns* (1886), liked 'greenery' too, in and out of the home. More than any 'invention' of friezes, stucco, paint or other 'outward adorning', he wrote, 'does nature's greenery (how different from carpet or wallpaper greenery) decorate the house'.

Yet there was also a realistic – and urban – note in Richardson, as there was in Mrs Haweis. A surprisingly large section of his book was taken up not only with fireplaces, dealt with at greater length later in this chapter, but with the menace of coal smoke as it polluted both houses and cities. He had written earlier on this subject in a study called 'The Warming and Ventilation of Buildings', and it was clear that he intended to write on it again. A comment he quoted from the *Echo* in 1868 might well have stirred Ruskin:

> The most sad and remarkable circumstance about the fog of yesterday was that the newspapers and people in the streets spoke of it as a 'visitation', a 'gigantic pall' as if, indeed, the black darkness was something as strange and unaccountable as a fall of frogs or fishes from the sky. Of course, it was nothing but our own familiar coal smoke which stopped the way of the sunlight.

Back to *Victorian Cities*, to the long rows of working-class houses, and to the slums over which the sun never rose. Yet there were great differences even in such places in the quality of construction and finish, along with status frills like an extra elevation or a slightly bigger yard or garden at the corner; and there could be pride even in houses with no frills – in the scrubbed doorstep, the polished window sill and the blazing hearth.

# V

Richardson's chapter on 'The Fireplace' was subtitled 'Flue Construction and Smoke Prevention', yet its first sentence read 'An especial love for home comfort has always been an English characteristic'. The fireplace, Richardson observed, suited the English climate. It was a 'favoured spot' where

> ... Social mirth
> Exults and glows before the blazing hearth.

Later in his chapter Richardson claimed that 'the preference or rather prejudice, in favour of fireplaces [in England] is so great that a revolution of the nation in political matters could be more easily brought about than the abolition of the firegrate'. 'The common fireplace has held its own, and will continue to hold its own, against the best-contrived stove that can be introduced in lieu of it.' Not surprisingly, Muthesius was to observe that 'to an Englishman the idea of a room without a fireplace was simply unthinkable'. The fireplace had 'ethical significance'.

Nine years before Richardson's book appeared, similar claims had been made for the English hearth in Dickens's *All the Year Round* (October 1861), although the article 'On The Chimney Piece' dwelt more on the past than on the present, looking back to times when there were fireplaces without chimneys, to the introduction of the movable reredos or screen, and to the first canopies, 'one of which had been adopted', it was pointed out, by Mr Pugin, in 'the house he built at Ramsgate''. There had been a particular 'splendour', the article claimed, in the reigns of Elizabeth and James I. Grinling Gibbons was given his due, therefore, while there was no reference to the Adam brothers. This was long before Voysey, like Lutyens after him, was to build new homes with very tall chimneys.

Dickens's article had ended, where many Victorian books on fireplaces began, not with the symbolic, but with the functional – 'the ingenious and benevolent' Count Rumford, American (loyalist) soldier and inventor, who just before the end of the eighteenth century, in the name of science, had made 'a simple but useful improvement in grates, by contracting and sloping off the sides of the fireplace, thus giving it an oblique instead of a square shape; by which means great waste was avoided and the appearance of the chimney rendered more sightly'. 'Grates were now become fixtures', the article continued, 'and when thus altered were said to have been Rumfordized.' And here progress took over. 'This may be regarded as the forerunner of the register grates which have gone on improving until they have reached their present high state of finish and beauty.'

While many patents had promised improvement during the 1840s, there was more than a touch of complacency in this judgement. It was true that some fireplaces had been 'Rumfordized', but F. Edwards, an authority on the subject, could still write in 1865 in *Our Domestic Fireplaces* that 'remarkable little progress has been made on the most primitive methods of warming apartments by open fires, and that the elementary principles explained by Count Rumford ... are very far from being generally understood and applied'. The reason, according to Edwards, was that neither the 'vast emporiums' in London which supplied builders with 'the most inexpensive productions in metal' nor country ironmongers (in the twentieth century to become creatures of nostalgia) had any interest in improvements. Like Eastlake, Edwards wanted to get behind the sellers to the customers, in his case customers of all types and of all pockets, identifying for them 'principles that are of general application, that may enhance the content of the labourer in his cottage, of the studious man in his library, and of the lady in her drawing room'. 'It would give me much satisfaction', he added, 'if anything I could say would call attention to the helpless condition of the poorer classes on the subject of their fireplaces.'

It was not until the second half of the nineteenth century that many of Rumford's 'philosophical' principles were generally applied and iron-framed grates with fire-brick linings became common, but even then they did not solve the problems of heating or pollution. They kept room temperature higher, but there was still a great waste of heat. Indeed, so long as fires were open to the chimney, most of the heat would be drawn upwards, and it would be impossible to sustain what Richardson called 'an equable and pleasant temperature'. As far as 'the poorer classes' were concerned, there were still grave limitations. J. C. Buckmaster, writing in 1874, complained that they still wanted cheap fireplaces 'at which a woman can cook without being suffocated with smoke'. 'Science has not yet produced a good economic fireplace suitable for the houses of the working classes.'

Slow combustion grates were introduced in middle-class homes around 1870: they had a solid base of firebrick which cut off the supply of air from below. Later improvements, common by the end of Victoria's reign, were the addition of hoods or canopies, some of them adjustable, the insertion of close-fitting ash-trays or ashpans below the fire, and the increasing use of air regulators. In these ways a greater measure of control both of the rate of combustion and of room temperature became possible. It was left to Mrs Caddy and a few enthusiasts to suggest that 'a gas fire, built with pumice and asbestos, lasts without needing a touch for three years, and though less delightful than wood or coal, is infinitely cleaner and gives no trouble at all'. For good measure, she added that the gains were greater than that – 'if one considers the saving of labour in carrying upstairs heavy scuttles of coal, besides the original cost of the scuttles, with the ludicrous inappropriateness of the ornamental varieties'.

Aesthetics as well as economics came into other people's arguments also. *The Young Ladies' Treasure Book* and *Cassell's Book of the Household* had much to say about fireplaces in dining rooms and drawing rooms. 'Nothing is considered too costly a material upon which to paint or embroider a mantel-valance', the former told young ladies, going on to mention a recent wedding present consisting of 'white velvet, decorated with a wreath of orange blossoms and leaves in oils, intermingled with fronds of that most exquisite of ferns, the "maiden-hair"'.

For *Cassell's*, more than a decade later, there was far more to say about tiles and marble. Tiled hearths were then in fashion. So, too, were wooden chimney-pieces, often combined with over-mantels, sometimes in marble. 'There are artistic souls', the writer of the piece claimed, 'who will be glad to know that marble will take paint; and a grey one may thus be converted into a blue or terra-cotta.' He did not add that there were other 'artistic souls' then and later, who would not be so glad: for Dutton Victorian marble chimney pieces were of 'unparalleled horror and elaboration'. The tiles and the over-mantels could be as elaborate as the canopies, some of them decorated by the time that *Cassell's Book of the Household* appeared with art-nouveau patterns. There were few art-nouveau houses, and for consistency even of art-nouveau patterns you had to go to Brussels, Paris or Vienna.

Particular kinds of English fireplaces were thought suitable for particular English rooms – for example, for the sitting room the 'country parson's grate', which combined 'in a thin vertical fire the largest possible heating power with the least possible consumption of fuel', or for the bedroom 'George's Calorigen' which ventilated as well as heated. The former, however, had the disadvantage that it went out easily without regular attention, and the latter that, in Mrs Haweis's opinion at least, it looked 'extremely hideous'.

For many, perhaps most, Victorian writers of books on home management and improvement it was the kitchen hearth which was the most important hearth in the home. 'The comfort of the cook and *en revanche* of the whole house', wrote Mrs Haweis, 'lies with the kitchen range'. Mrs Caddy waxed lyrical about it. 'Near a nice bright stove, placed in a recess glittering with Dutch tiles or Minton's *artistic plaques*, surrounded by burnished pans and pots of well-lined copper or brass and neat enamelled saucepans, the genius of the hearth presides over the mysteries of Hestia.' *Cassell's Book of the Household* was more prosaic. 'What place is more cosy on a cold winter's night', it asked, 'than the kitchen fireside?'

By the end of the nineteenth century, the open kitchen fire in middle-class homes seemed almost as old fashioned as the stage coach. Yet its merits could still be sung with greater fervour than ever before – and on different grounds. 'Many epicures maintain', Mrs Haweis wrote, 'that the old-fashioned system, by which sweets and joints were not cooked simultaneously in one receptacle, and the roasting joint was guarded by a meat screen hung before the fire and laboriously basted is by far the best.' Certainly, even at the end of Victoria's reign, more people disliked cooking by gas than warming themselves in front of a gas fire.

Mrs Beeton had had relatively little to say on the subject of gas. She noted its 'cleanliness' and the fact that with gas 'culinary operations' were 'reduced . . . to something like a certainty', but she was afraid of gas bills. By contrast, *Cassell's Book of the Household* tried to keep a balance. After praising the merits of roasting a joint in front of a large open fire – and pointing to the prestigious example of Trinity College, Cambridge – it recommended gas stoves for convenience. 'They save an enormous amount of time and trouble, especially early in the morning. A servant can slip on a dress, or the master of the house his dressing gown, when, perhaps, the proper person has overslept herself [note the gender], turn a tap, light a match and go back to his room, and by the time he has finished dressing, there is a large kettleful of boiling water ready for the use of the house.'

Whether coal or gas – or oil – was used, the major development in early and mid-Victorian England had been the improvement of the highly versatile, but often temperamental, 'kitchener', a word coined by William Flavel of Leamington during the 1820s; and while the word is now largely forgotten, the thing itself has been described by Giedion as being 'as characteristic of the nineteenth century as hydraulic power and electricity are of ours'. The kitchener was a closed (or semi-closed) piece of kitchen apparatus, sometimes fitted with a second oven. (Mrs Beeton claimed that closed ranges were first used in Devonshire to make clotted cream.) By now, the word 'flue' is largely forgotten too, although flues figured prominently in the lives of servants, in the expense accounts of 'masters' and of 'mistresses', and in the operations of ironmongers and above all of chimney sweeps, small boys until philanthropic legislation controlled their work.

The kitchener flues were controlled by dampers which made it possible to divert the heat of the fire to any part of the range, and the range itself always included a boiler heated by a separate flue. Coal consumption and costs of repairs were high. 'Balancing the sink on one side of the stove', wrote Mrs Caddy *en passant*, 'is the fuel box containing a quarter of a ton of coal'. As for repair bills, 'should you possess a really good stove', *Cassell's Book of the Household* remarked, 'you are to be congratulated'. Many households, it observed, were dependent on outside assistance.

Kitcheners were advertised in 'almost endless variety', many of them with brand names like the Leamington, 'Constantine Treasure' and, simplest of all, 'The Mistress'. The main differences lay in the arrangement and capacity of the boiler, the size and placing of the oven or ovens, and, main point of trouble, the flues. Among the many patents there was a closed range, invented in 1866 by William Carter and Company, which was convertible into an open type. The first designs of the gas ranges were based entirely on that of the coal range – as was that of the first gas cookers – and it took many years before 'science' was applied to their construction.

One kitchen range was far more popular in the United States than in Britain – the portable range, known as the American range after the Great Exhibition of 1851, where one such range was shown. In fact, a similar type had been patented in London as early as 1815 by an ironmonger, Thomas Deakin. Portable ranges stood on four legs and could be moved to different parts of the room. Some stood within the fire of an old open fireplace: others were moved to the middle of the room, never a popular English location. Beside a portable stove it was difficult to read in the right mood *The Fireside Companion*, *The Hearthside Treasury* or *Home Words for Heart and Hearth*.

It was not a recommendation, moreover, for the middle-class customers that at the Great Exhibition the portable stove had been thought particularly appropriate by the Society for Improving the Condition of the Labouring Classes and had been fitted into Prince Albert's Model Dwelling Houses. It might even have been fitted also into the first working-class flats to be built in Old St Pancras Road, London three years earlier by the Metropolitan Association for Improving Dwellings of the Industrious Poor. By the time, however that the Peabody Trust's first group of flats was constructed in the 1860s, even in working-class homes the hearth was prominent, and working-class families were prepared then and later to spend considerable sums on the appearance of the fireplace. The first chapter of Gertrude Jekyll's *Old English Household Life* was to be called 'the evolution of the fireside'.

# VI

The 'comfortable', 'decorated', well-locked Victorian house, very different from any Model Dwelling Houses, attractive though some of these may now look, might spurn Rumford's 'science' or the kind of advice given in Webster's Encyclopaedia, but it was always a house of many mansions. Often, indeed, it could be 'detached': sometimes it would be turreted, suggesting visually, even if there was no drawbridge, that the Englishman's home was his castle. 'The apartment house has disadvantages', wrote the *Building News* in 1900, 'among them the gregariousness of the occupants. It is doubtful, we think, whether the English will ever abandon their own small castles.'

Within the castles, big or small, there were many very specific allocations of space and function as particular rooms were dedicated to particular purposes. The bell pull was an essential element in the well-off, well-regulated household, therefore, but even in households without bell-pulls – or servants to answer the bell – space could be dedicated too. Thus, in superior working-class homes the parlour was a very separate place. So, also, was the American 'parlor' to which Julia NcNair Wright was anxious to attibute a Norman origin (*'parlor* or talking place'). There was, in fact, nothing new about such apartness: Washington Irving could write of the good Dutch households of 'ancient New York' that 'they kept a parlor apparently sacred to nothing but a weekly ceremony of cleaning'. Nor was the only echo of seventeenth-century Holland: there were echoes in Britain itself.

During the mid-nineteenth century, gentlemen's smoking rooms could be set apart too. As Kerr put it in 1864 in his book *The Gentleman's House*, 'the pitiable resources to which some gentlemen are driven to be able to enjoy the pestiferous luxury of a cigar have given rise to the occasional introduction of an apartment specially dedicated to the use of tobacco'. Later in the century, after smoking had tended to become de-segregated with the advent of the cigarette, itself a Victorian thing supplemented by (but not supplanting) the cigar, Mrs Haweis still recommended in smaller houses a husband's 'smoking den' set apart, this time for feminine rather than masculine reasons. 'Tobacco smoke soon spoils pretty covers and ribbons, and yesterday's smoke hanging about curtains and carpets is worse than disagreeable.'

Mrs Haweis found other reasons also for encouraging the setting apart of the 'den'. 'A smoking-room should not banish the female element, but it should be kept sacred from discordant household affairs, accounts "warnings" and such like plagues, that are best discussed in kitchen or morning room.' The 'seamy side of domestic life' should have no place there, 'Away from the World and its Toils and its Cares'. It should be reserved for 'the husband's books and ancient belongings, photographs of the inscrutable people who were his early friends, gifts from unknown quarters which he still fancies he values'.

Mrs Haweis moved direct from the den to the bedroom which, as the French had long realized, need not, she felt, look 'bedroomy'. Mrs Caddy, like Eastlake, started more characteristically with the entrance, and the 'good thick doormat' which she considered better than 'those delightful indoor scrapers set all around with brushes'. 'It was not a healthy practice', she added, 'to heat the passage of a house.' For Eastlake, the most important thing in what was often a gloomy place (even with or because of its aspidistra) was to treat the floor with encoustic tiles.

Tiles, encoustic or otherwise, introduce a whole category of Victorian things which do not figure as prominently as aspidistras in most general books on Victoriana. Yet a great firm like Minton, which pioneered majolica glaze, could specialize in them, and a highly skilled and imaginative arts-and-craft potter like William de Morgan could found his reputation on them. The only general history, placing Victorian developments in perspective, was written by Anne Berendson and others in 1967, although Julian Barnard produced a fascinating study of the whole British ceramics industry between 1830 and 1900 in his *Victorian Ceramic Tiles* (1972).

Julia McNair Wright had health, not aesthetics, in mind when she concentrated on the cellars, where the products of the ceramics industry often played a minor role. She was uninterested in the possibility of gentlemen keeping wine there, but deeply concerned that cellars could become sources of many domestic dangers. 'Cellar cleaning' was necessary to make a house healthful. So also was the regular cleaning of the garret and the attics. 'Don't leave any shut-up rooms and corners in your homes to breed pestilence.'

In many Victorian middle-class homes cellars, attics, and odd rooms and corners were relegated to the servants (in upper-class homes they were usually kept segregated and were further segregated for men and women) or to the children or to both. Yet there were more of such spaces in Victorian homes than there had been in Georgian houses. There were, of course, cellar dwellings, too, in some of Britain's industrial cities, and at different times in Victorian England the middle-class spotlight was cast upon them.

Within the artisan's dwelling, apart from the parlour, which could be a very distinct place even in the long streets of standardized working-class homes which were built during the 1870s and later, the specialization of space was far less marked than in middle-class or upper-class houses; and although this may even have added to the sense of house as home, it was all too easy to sentimentalize its attractions within the national context. There was more than a touch of patronage in most middle-class talk of the simple spell of the 'respectable home', whether it was a house in a town street or a cottage in the country, and there was more than a touch of whitewash when more was made of its cleanliness than of its limited amenities or of its meagre contents. Nonetheless, Seebohm Rowntree in his study of York was precise, as always, in offering inventories of what could be found in working-class homes at the end of the century, and sometimes working-class wills, with few objects to dispose of, were just as carefully drafted as middle-class wills.

Skilled workers' houses in York usually consisted of five rooms and a scullery. The sitting room often contained a piano and an over-mantel 'in addition to the usual furniture'. It was mainly used on Sundays or as a 'receiving room for visitors who are not on terms sufficiently intimate to be asked into the kitchen'. 'The real living room', Rowntree noted, was 'the kitchen, rendered cheerful and homely by the large open grate, and the good oven, unknown in the south, but familiar in the north of England where coal is cheap, and where the thrifty housewife bakes her own bread. A sofa, albeit of horsehair or American cloth, an armchair, a polished table and china ornaments on the high mantelpiece, add the subtle touch of homeliness.'

Rowntree tried hard not to be sentimental. So, too, did many of the writers of middle-class 'hints' literature. Indeed, some of them tried hard to be frank. Thus, for Mrs Caddy in 1877 it was essential to avoid 'the great black beetle-trap cellar and to take pains to make the kitchen the most picturesque and cheerful room in the house'. Mrs Haweis mentioned black beetles, too, even in the kitchen. 'The mistress', she said, 'is responsible for them': they were 'the mere result of dirty wasteful habits and stupid neglect'. Everybody pretended to hate them, but few people intelligently 'combatted' them.

It was best for the kitchen to be level both with the dining room and the front door, Mrs Caddy stressed, and while a larder or 'store closet' might be partitioned off from it, it should be complete in itself, without pantry or scullery. The tables and chairs should be of unpainted wood, 'plain but of good form', but if a 'Swiss style' was followed, there could be 'mottoes in old English character' as 'an appropriate decoration to the cornice'. 'There is no more need to overstock the kitchen than any other room', Mrs Haweis insisted, while going on to catalogue a long list of utensils (and products), some of which a modern housewife would find it difficult to identify. A fish and egg lifter cost 8d., a gridiron anything from 6d to 2s 3d. Four distinct brushes and brooms were recommended. Branded utensils were coming into fashion, and Mrs Caddy mentioned, for example, Kent's patent knife-cleaner. Unlike Mrs Caddy, Mrs Haweis favoured a separate scullery for the sink and drainer.

The best possible sink for Mrs Caddy had to be of marble, but the cost of this, she recognized, would preclude its use in an 'economical household'. Beside the sink should stand a 'neat towel horse, and above it a well-chosen plate rack'. Mrs Caddy was prepared to indulge in the cult of the 'picturesque' as Richardson had been in his description of houses – Blenheim and Castle Howard he thought the most picturesque houses in England – but in her case the picturesque was represented by small rather than large things. 'Souvenirs of travel, such as the quaint wooden pails seen at Antwerp or the brass frying-pan-shaped candlestick at Ghent, should be eagerly sought, as they add much to the picturesqueness and piquant liveliness which are so desirable.' Not surprisingly, she believed that in every room it was 'well to exercise individual tastes'. So, too, did Mrs Haweis. 'Taste varies: some people liking pale, light-built and gaily-painted chairs, brackets, screens, and the endless nick-nacks falsely supposed to be Queen Anne; others preferring plain, quiet, rather dowdy goods. Some people have a passion for tying Liberty handkerchiefs to every object within reach.'

Like Mrs Caddy, Mrs Beeton had begun her book with the kitchen, even if she had a great deal to say about the dining room and even though she felt it necessary to remark of the drawing room that it was not 'admissible at any time to take a favourite dog into another lady's drawing room ... There is always a chance of a breakage of some article occurring through their leaping and bounding here and there, sometimes very much to the fear and annoyance of the hostess.' For Mrs Haweis it was equally necessary to insist that 'in furnishing a drawing-room, the guests are the principal part of the furniture'. For the contributor to *The Young Ladies' Treasure Book* the dining room had to come first. 'We enter it', she remarks, 'and everything breathes of comfort and that repose which acts so beneficially upon the digestive organs when they are summoned into active service.'

There is an interesting chapter on the dining room in Mrs J. E. Panton's *From Kitchen to Garret* (1888) which is more concerned with 'impecunious' than with well-endowed households: 'I am not writing for votaries of fashion', she explained apparently frankly, 'or for rich people, who could tell me doubtless a great many things that I do not know.' Notwithstanding – or more likely because of – this stance, she was obsessed with status. 'In starting to buy the furniture for our modest dining room', she maintained, 'let us consider not what is handsome or effective or taking to the eye, but what is suitable to Edwin's position, and what will be pleasant for Angelina to possess, without having unduly to agitate herself and worry herself in nervously protecting her chattels from wear and tear.'

There were some distinctive touches, down to minute detail. The door panels and shutters, Mrs Panton suggested, should be of 'good Japanese leather paper' or, if that was too expensive, 'one of Pither's papers with a bold frieze in a good floral design'. Window seats were recommended, along with a desk, complete with a bunch of flowers, a good blue and white china inkstand, costing 6d at the Baker Street Bazaar, and a blotter. (There was also a recommendation for Stephen's blue-black ink, 'nothing like it'.) The clock on the mantlepiece, which was a more prominent feature of the room than the unmentioned dining-room table, might well be 'a very charming Oetzmann of the Hampstead Road', selling at 25s. Clocks were always thought of, and still are, as a subject in themselves.

Mrs Panton's book, based on articles in the *Lady's Pictorial*, a new magazine of 1881, is particularly interesting in that she actually gave advice on decorating for a fee to 'ladies in their houses'. She had correspondents 'in

New Zealand, India, America and all parts of the Continent –

Forced from their homes, a melancholy train,
To traverse climes beyond the western main,

– some of them happy in a society free from many of the restraints of London
or the provinces.

She was looking, Mrs Panton admitted, for other ladies with 'a quick eye',
to share in her labours, 'provided that they were of sufficient social status to
be above the suspicion of taking commission or bribes from tradespeople to
advertise their wares'. She had actually started a Women's Guild at 11
Kensington Square.

The dining-room table twenty years before would have been as much of a
status symbol as a grand piano. Yet one of Mrs Panton's many sharp
observations was 'If you do not all of you remember the dining room of the
past, I do; but never without a shudder'. There had similarly been relatively
little emphasis on the table in *The Dining Room* (1878) by W. J. Loftie, author
of *A Plea for Art in the House*, although he began by quoting Thackeray's
dictum that 'the dinner at home ought to be centre of the whole system of
dinner-giving'. He, too, like Mrs Panton, started with the fireplace and
sandwiched the table between sideboards and chairs in his Chapter 3. In his
first chapter on 'feeding rooms in general' he cast an eye on the French, who
were more interested in the menu than the fittings and who were 'in no ways
troubled at being obliged to eat in what is merely the passage to the *salon*'.
One of his more interesting suggestions was that 'in every dining room there
ought at all times to be the possibility of boiling water, heating soup, or
making coffee, by fire, spirit-lamp, or gas'. There were too many people with
'few servants' who were unprepared to adopt such 'little inventions'.

*Cassell's Book of the Household* had something to say about dining-room
table and chairs, though what it said was very different from what has come
to be the conventional pattern in later general histories which focus on the
massive mid-Victorian mahogany table – and the huge sideboard or
chiffonier. For *Cassell's* there was 'no kind of dining table so sociable or so
easily made pretty as a round or oval one'. 'The sight of bare polished
mahogany is a thing of the past.' Deal was acceptable. And dinner waggons
were preferable to a huge 'elaborate' piece of furniture, 'yclept a sideboard'.
A dining room did very well without a sofa, but if a sofa had to be bought it
should be 'wide, roomy, substantial and comfortable'.

*The Drawing Room*, written by Mrs Orrinsmith and published a year
earlier – with many acknowledgements to Loftie's *Art in the House* – for once
treated the fireplace coolly. The author referred to 'the cold, hard,
unthinking white marble mantelpiece', to 'the inevitable mirror', and to the
fireplace itself as a 'marvellous exhibition of the power of iron and blacklead
to give discomfort to the eye'. Mrs Orrinsmith wholeheartedly condemned
'the withdrawing room, to which because of its showy discomfort nobody

withdrew'. 'The encouragement of original ideas', she wrote, 'has been throughout the motive of this book.' Yet the ideas were all related to a wave of new fashion, and in her critique Mrs Orrinsmith was attacking the kinds of drawing rooms which were already out-of-date, associated with a time not very distant, when 'all things' in a room seemed to have been chosen 'on the principle of unfitness for the fulfilment of any function' with 'everything in pairs that possibly could be paired'. It was mid-Victorian England which was under attack as the author explained that 'bad taste, though sometimes apparently intuitive, is mostly perverted taste, depraved by long habituation to evil models'.

Mrs Orrinsmith wanted to let in more light and air literally as well as metaphorically, eliminating Venetian or roller-blinds from the drawing room along with the 'superstructure of curtain poles and valances' and 'as abundant a display of curtains as possible'. She objected strongly 'from an aesthetic point of view' to 'coal scuttles ornamented with views of Warwick Castle', 'hearthrugs with dogs after Landseer in their *proper* colour', and screens graced by a representation of 'Melrose Abbey by Moonlight'.

After reading such a passage, which is paralleled in the Misses Garret's book on *House Decoration*, it comes at first as something of a surprise that Mrs Orrinsmith actually liked ornaments. In her drawing room there were to be 'shelves with delicate carving on side and edges, tiles and plates on the lowest, and Venetian bottles, old Delft vases or old Nankin cups arranged on the upper shelf'. 'What shall be added next?' ought, she said, to be 'a constantly recurring thought'. The answer was another 'object of taste'. 'To the appreciative mind, not spoiled by the luxury of wealth, what keen pleasure there is in the possession of one new treasure: a Persian tile, an Algerian flower-pot, an old Flemish cup ... an Icelandic spoon, a Japanese cabinet, a Chinese fan; a hundred things might be named.' While Mrs Orrinsmith wanted to let in light and air, she by no means, therefore, eliminated clutter. She was shrewd enough, however, to observe that 'those who have the ordinary cheap Japanese fans of a few years back will do well to consider that in Japan, as elsewhere, purity of natural art is gradually being distorted by acquired fashions and tastes'.

Mrs Orrinsmith had strong opinions about carpets – their size as well as their colour and design – and offered advice like 'no carpet should entirely cover a floor', in this case drawing on Dr Richardson as an authority. 'The only effective way to keep a carpet clean is to shake it frequently.' 'No heavy pieces of furniture, such as bookcases, pianofortes or china cabinets ... should stand upon the carpet.' 'The old flowery carpet, bravely discarded, will form an excellent lining for a simple substitute more gracefully gay.' 'The formed judgement which discreetly chose the carpet would find relish and enjoyment in the beauty of the rug.' Like many other late-Victorian writers, including Loftie, Mrs Orrinsmith strongly approved of parquet floors – and inlays.

That this was reaction, not revolt – was apparent in the sections of Mrs Orrinsmith's book which relate to ornament and in phrases like 'the able rules for choice and purchase given by Mr Loftie'. 'The best art education is to be found in recourse to approved examples of decoration and constant familiarity with fine qualities as to which there cannot be two opinions.' Loftie himself went further back in time in repudiating Pugin and Ruskin. 'Furniture in his [perpendicular] style', he said of Pugin's chairs and tables, 'has the singular property of looking bad' alongside furniture in any other style. This was simply because it was an 'extreme style'. 'I do not believe they really used furniture like it', he went on, 'when the perpendicular houses and churches were first built.' As for Ruskin, he was repudiated because he had failed to understand the merits of Dutch painters: yet 'Mr Ruskin cannot write them down if he would'. 'Taste', Loftie noted, 'spreads with wonderful rapidity.'

Not surprisingly, Loftie, like Mrs Orrinsmith – had something to say about pictures – and photographs – in the home. He approved of portraits, even badly taken family portraits – 'people who have family pictures do not have them taken down because they are ill done' – and of well chosen landscapes. Whether photographs could be considered 'decorative', however, was 'a matter of some controversy'. He felt sorry to condemn them outright, although 'the vulgar staring portraits produced by many photographers should obviously have no place'. Mrs Cameron and others might yet redeem the day, (see page 132) and photographs of buildings and places were admissible even if they did not live easily with watercolours. 'It is pleasant to lean back in one's chair and be transported to distant countries at a glance.' Television might have changed his perspective.

Whatever the decoration – and its conceived purpose – drawing rooms had little variety, and by the end of the century *Cassell's Book of the Household* would observe that 'the furniture of the modern drawing room is of the kaleidoscopic order. The individual pieces are of all sorts and sizes, and are always capable of fresh combinations.' It was thought desirable, however, that every article of furniture should be 'useful and comfortable as well as pretty' because 'the drawing room is eminently an apartment to be lived in peacefully after the rush and hurry of the day is over'. Like Mrs Caddy, the writer felt that it should look 'used'. And he – or she – went on to dispose of books like that by Loftie which were by then as out-of-date as the furniture that Mrs Orrinsmith had criticized. He had no use, he said, for 'a certain school of writers who . . . call everything Philistine which does not conform to certain rules of their own'. 'All true artists smile at this', the comment continues, 'and apply the term to people who have things so-and-so merely *because other people have them so.*' He used the word 'Philistine' himself, however, to describe those people who were prepared to sacrifice pianos in the drawing room 'for the sake of improving what they are pleased to call the decorative effect of the room'.

The piano, sold in increasing quantities in mid- and late-Victorian England – in 1890 more than twice as many were being produced in England than in 1850 – remained something of a sacred object, 'a household god', and in this connection it was not Mrs Haweis but her eloquent, if wayward, husband, the Rev J. R. Haweis, who left behind some of the most memorable comments. As Latin grammar strengthened a boy's memory, so 'the piano makes a girl sit upright and pay attention to details'. Moreover, 'a good play on the piano has not infrequently taken the place of a good cry upstairs'. It would be a mistake, however, to conclude that use of the piano was determined primarily by sex – or class. A South Yorkshire miner who told the Select Committee on Coal in 1873 that 'we have got more pianos and perambulators in recent years and that the piano was "a cut above the perambulator"' was not exceptional. 'What is a home without a piano?' was one of the advertisements noted on a wall in London's poorest East End by Charles Booth.

It was middle-class homes where most doubts were expressed about the presence of the piano. There, indeed, it might be draped to hide its very existence: Mrs Panton, for example, found the piano an often 'very ugly piece of furniture' and, revealing her own taste, made 'a very pretty frame for hers out of sage-green silk worked with rosebuds'. She might have chosen instead, she said, 'a turquoise-blue material worked in pale yellow campanulas'. 'Piano manufacturers', she complained, might be selling more and more pianos, but they 'resolutely' refused 'to march with the times'.

In the late-nineteenth century there were many enthusiastic housewives who in the same spirit as Mrs Panton were willing to expound their own preferences about many other objects besides pianos. There were many women, Mrs Panton admitted, who did not like things to last, while Mrs Haweis, who wanted to get rid of 'crowds of cheap gimcracks which come to pieces in five years', extolled the benefits of 'do-it-yourself', a term she actually used. In different, but equally individualistic, vein an anonymous writer in *Cassell's Family Magazine* in 1889 began her account of how she had furnished her house with the sentence 'of all the rooms in this house the drawing room is my favourite. I generally feel happy in it. It is furnished in no particular style and there is nothing valuable in it, but I cannot help knowing that it is a very pretty room.'

It was the wallpaper, 'a magic paper for men', which seemed to 'make' the drawing room and, *pace* Eastlake or Loftie, she had seen it first in an exhibition and felt that she 'must have it'. Having bought it, she then had 'to think seriously about what colours would go' with it. 'I covered the floor with plain China matting', she went on, 'and in the centre had a soft Axminster carpet in tints of yellow and dull red; it is very lovely and cost five and elevenpence a yard, so it ought to last for a long time'. The curtains were made of 'Capucine satin' in a design called 'Honduras': again, *pace* Eastlake and Loftie, they incorporated 'woven strawberry blossoms in colours of crushed strawberry, yellow and brown'. The curtain blinds were of pale blue Indian muslin. The colours multiplied. So, too, did the patterns of the furniture, which included a couch (7 guineas), the most expensive item in the room, a 'Thoresby settee' with a rush seat, two armchairs, one called 'Eugénie' (£1 4s), a plain wooden rocking chair (2s 6d), two cane 'little church' chairs (2s each), a rattan cane chair (8s 6d), two low wicker chairs in white straw (6s each) and an 'ebonised writing table'.

The 'lady of the house' did much of the painting of the chairs herself, as Mrs Haweis would have done, and she also oak-stained and painted a tea table and a corner cupboard before applying French polish 'to give the effect of inlaid wood'. In addition, she had covered the couch and two carpet foot stools in serge 'for which an outline pattern was worked with tapestry wool', and had made a suitable decoration for the over-mantel. 'I drove a nail into the centre', she went on, 'upon which to hang a pretty old looking glass with a cut-glass frame, below which was arranged a row of miniatures in ivory. I also fastened on some very pretty silver sconces, which looked well with two old silver plaques.' Eastlake had obviously lived in vain. It should be added that the couch and chair coverings were all made with 'petticoats', 'deep flounces not quite touching the floor, but hiding the legs', that below the seat of a shilling 'camp stool' a deep frill of white Valenciennes lace was sewn with a bag 'tied with ribbon to match the velvet', and that there was also 'a dear little spherical pouffé which looks like a big round ball on casters'.

When she came to the library, the 'lady of the house' was equally self-indulgent, describing in detail the oriental-patterned Brussels carpet and the curtains made of Madagascar maps, yet she approached simplicity in her accounts of the bedroom and of the nursery. There was, in fact, a considerable change in the interior of bedrooms in Victorian England, although at any time they might vary in many of their furnishings almost as much as drawing rooms. They could be austere or lavish, bare and scrubbed or squalid and cluttered. In working-class families, of course, they could be both bare and overcrowded. Once when Canon Bernett of Toynbee Hall took a group of Whitechapel women and children to a great country house, as was his wont, and they were invited to go to a bedroom to leave their outdoor clothes, one child exclaimed, 'Look, mother, here's a room with a bed to itself'.

One problem, described in *Notes and Queries* in 1860 as a 'generally tabooed subject', and more common than has been subsequently recognized, was the presence of bed bugs which, according to Queen Victoria's own bug destroyer, 'bit all persons the same'. In 1877 the *British Medical Journal* recommended 'bug-traps' of a kind used in Indian hospitals: they were sold for almost two centuries by a London firm, E. W. Scott and Sons of Tower Street, who also sold mousetraps along with coal tubs, maps, firescreens and travelling clocks. The grim theme was well handled by L. O. J. Boynton in the first volume of the journal of the Furniture History Society in 1965.

The bed, more often double than single, was a *sine qua non*. Old 'sarcophagus-like' fourposters disappeared even when the wardrobe remained massive, and were usually replaced by brass or iron bedsteads. They could be simple or ornate, plain or painted. (Iron was often painted green or at a later date enamel.) Until the last decade of the century the beds were commonly of a 'half-tester' variety, with tall, upright posts at the head supporting a curtain rail for the hangings. The hangings could be intricate. The mattresses were less so: feather mattresses were placed on wood or iron lattices. When wire and spring mattresses were introduced, they did not always prove as comfortable as their buyers hoped – or, as *Cassell's Book of the Household* put it, while they were 'comfortable enough for one person they are most uncomfortable for two'. 'Eiderdown quilts are great luxuries to chilly people and the majority of ladies', the article went on, sticking to the same theme, 'but many gentlemen find them far too hot'. The writer referred also to new types of 'cellular' fabrics, but not to home-made patchwork quilts, now greatly prized, no to new types of wooden beds which became popular only after 1900.

For Mrs Haweis the 'sleeping room, in which nearly half of one's life is passed, ought to be as pretty as a sitting room'. She devoted only one long paragraph to it, but concluded eloquently 'Bachelors – why not brides? – sometimes disguise and adorn the bedroom, where space is precious, with sofa-beds, Chippendale or old French closed washstands, palm-plants and gipsy-tables, that it may serve as a thoroughfare without a suspicion that anybody but a canary ever sleeps in it.'

One specialized room which did not figure prominently in the 'hints' and 'tastes' literature until the end of the century was the bathroom. Even though Robert Kerr stated firmly in 1864 that 'no house of pretensions will be devoid of a general bathroom', many 'pretentious' houses were still being built without them during the 1890s, two early Lutyens houses among them. A writer on plumbing, S. Stevens Hellyer, stated in 1864 – although he provided a qualifying footnote – that 'one may as well look for a fountain in the desert as for a bath in any of our old English houses'. There were certainly ancient prejudices, not least in the oldest, largest, and most prestigious houses, many of whose stately owners would have agreed with Mrs Haweis, when after calling a bathroom 'a convenience', she added that 'the only real *bain de luxe* is one fitted in your bedroom or dressing room'.

In mid-Victorian England taps for hots and cold water even in the bedroom were rare – so also were plugs – and water had to be carried considerable distances. When there were servants, this seemed natural enough, but for Mrs Caddy it was not good enough to take carrying water for granted. 'Men will do much for glory and vainglory', she wrote, 'even to using cold shower-baths, in winter, and boast of breaking the ice in them; but I never yet heard of a man who took the trouble to empty his bath after using it.' The subject was obviously thought to be important enough for another author to write that 'When a man likes to have his bath regularly, he should think of the labour that half a dozen or more baths entail, and in the evening prepare his can of water for tomorrow's use, place his own bath on his piece of oilcloth, enjoy his tub to his heart's content, pour away the water, put up his tub, and say nothing about it.'

Hippolyte Taine in his *Notes on England* described a washstand in his bedroom 'furnished with one large jug, a small one, a medium one for hot water, two porcelain basins, a dish for toothbrushes, two soap dishes, a water bottle with its tumbler, a finger glass with its glass'. Underneath it was a very low table with a sponge, another basin, and a large zinc bath for early morning bathing. Beside it was a towel horse. This to Taine was 'luxury' – 'An Englishman spent the fifth of his life in the tub' – yet *Mr Sponge's Sporting Tour* (1856) by R. S. Surtees describes a bedroom of a different kind at Hanby House: it was lavishly furnished with 'every imaginable luxury', including 'hip-baths and foot-baths, a shower-bath, and hot and cold baths adjoining and mirrors innumerable'. Already there were people who preferred showers, some of them very ingeniously contrived, to baths, just as there were people who preferred, usually on moral grounds, 'tubbing' in cold water to relaxing in hot. There was also a market for sprays, douches, sponges and 'jets of all descriptions'.

Metal baths, in cast iron or zinc, many of them with mahogany surrounds, became more common later in the century, when mahogany also made its way into the 'lavatory'. Yet Mrs Caddy, for all her propensity to lay down

*An adaptable Patent Lavatory – with a wash hand and foot range, 1862*

rules, did not mention chamberpots or night commodes. Nor did *Punch* which often included cartoons by John Leech and others showing the perils of plumbing. *Cassell's Book of the Household* referred, however, in 1890 to 'the objectionable practice of placing a w.c. in the bathroom ... common to suburban houses', calling it 'very bad and disagreeable'.

The water closet, sometimes called the 'wash-down closet', has not been without its historians, the latest of them Lawrence Wright, whose *Clean and Decent* (1980) provides a history both of 'the bath and the loo'. The water closet was, of course, a pre-Victorian invention, yet for most of Queen Victoria's reign there were far more earth closets than water closets and many of the new water closets were placed in basements or in backyards. Until sewerage systems were improved, middle-class homes with indoor water closets still depended on cesspools, and even after miles and miles of drains and sewers were laid, working-class families were often expected to share outdoor 'privies'. Nor even then did they always have easy access to water. The first middle-class water closets were often ornate – not only with polished mahogany seats, but with painted cisterns, china grips and iron brackets. By 1900, when sewerage systems had improved, the closets had become less interesting as Victorian things.

Plumbing remained a backward craft, and drains could still be news. 'They are now so fashionable a study', Mrs Haweis had written in 1889, 'that I need say little about them here ... A sanitary inspector is a great help, but the greatest help to health is understanding the drainage of your own house yourself.' *Cassell's Book of the Household* noted that water closets needed 'constant attention' and recommended housewives 'to arrange that two or three pailfuls of water should be thrown down the pan every day to clean the pipes'. They were also urged to keep a regular stock of spirits of salt.

Five years earlier, Hellyer in his *The Plumber and Sanitary Houses* had urged the government to deal with bad plumbing and bad drainage as if it were waging war: it was better to pay drain-diggers than grave-diggers. Values were wrong. 'A man made strong objections, not long ago, to the writer to having his drains put right, and directly afterwards made an offer of nearly a thousand pounds for a very little table to stand in one of his drawing rooms.'

When Mrs Panton dealt with bathrooms and bedrooms, she had only one thing to say about drains and nothing about tables costing a thousand pounds. Instead, she recommended bargains like 'charming' brass hot water cans at 7s 6d and basins at 5s ('Maple's white Beaufort ware was', she admitted, 'much prettier'). She had also a sentence about 'bath blankets' to stand on the floor above a piece of oilcloth: they could be made at home from 'the old-gold and dark brown blankets one buys of Mansergh and Sons, Lancaster'. There was other specific advice. 'I always keep on my washing-stand one of Parry's invaluable sixpenny sticks of ink-erasor.' A soap dish should always be supplemented by a sponge dish: the latter, 'like a great many other expensive things, saves the whole of its cost in the long run'. And then she approached what to most people was unmentionable. 'Slop pails should all be of white china, and intense cleanliness should be insisted upon ... They should be scalded out every day with hot water and a little chloride of lime being kept in any separate place, ready for use when there are any drains.'

'Given the blessed refuge of a nursery, with its appealing cupboard', Mrs Panton remarked near the end of her book, 'very little other furniture is required'; and the anonymous lady of the house writing in *Cassell's Magazine* in 1889 would have agreed with her. Her nursery, she explained, was of 'the usual nursery kind – two good deal tables, a toy-cupboard, a work-cupboard, an armchair on rockers, children's high chairs etc. The doors of the cupboards are decorated with large bunches of blue cornflowers and ox-eyed daisies, painted on the deal and French-polished furniture.' 'A tiny dresser stands at the end of the room, upon which the blue willow-pattern cups and saucers shine. The lower shelf is covered with a blue-and-white sideboard cloth, which I bought for two and sixpence.'

For Mrs Panton the cupboards were basic. 'The lower shelves can be used for rubbish – the delicious rubbish that is so much nicer than expensive toys.' (The latter require a study in themselves.) There was a contrast here, however, with Julia McNair Wright, who after rightly explaining that the infant mind usually received less attention than the infant body – or 'the eccentricities of a cooking stove' – had nothing at all to say about rubbish, surely a necessary ingredient of any nursery. For her, however, as for many others, including Ruskin, it was almost obligatory to say that children in the home were better served by a museum. 'Have Mark put up two or three low shelves in the back of the hall, and encourage Tom to make a museum there of his wonderful curiosities; if you talk with him about them, you may make a philosopher of him.'

It should be added that Julia McNair Wright believed that before anybody made a philosopher of him, his mother should not leave him to the servants. 'If you can afford any sacrifice of luxuries or finery even, to keep a nurse-maid, do so', she advised. 'Always bathe, dress, undress, and feed your own child: no one else will exercise such tender care.' A little later in life, too, it was the mother who should lay down rules, like 'Boys and girls who go to school should make their beds before they go'. As Sir Arthur Helps had put it, 'These seem little things; and so they are unless you neglect them'.

# VII

There were many Victorian children of well-off parents in English families who would have wished that their mothers had followed Julia McNair Wright's advice when they were young, although there were some, of course, who felt that it was their nannies who really loved them, and others who loved their nannies more than their parents. There were many children too, who found being sent away to boarding school at a very early age more difficult than Tom Brown did.

Profound psychological questions may be raised here, but they are outside the margins of this book. What is not outside is the dependence of many British (and American) nineteenth-century homes on domestic service. 'The home never dies', proclaimed Julia McNair Wright. Guests came and went, and things wore out, but the home abided without end. Yet in most cases it could not have lasted for a single day without paid servants.

The care of the hearth itself depended to an exceptional extent on the duties of domestic servants. It was they who fetched the coals in scuttles from the cellar, cleaned the grates and surroundings, did the blackleading, laid the fires, burnished the fire irons and polished the fenders. In respect of domestic service, of course, the hearth was typical of the home as a whole, and, allowing for many exceptions, the bigger the house the more hearths (not least in the bedrooms and the 'sick rooms') and the more servants.

One of the few duties that were sometimes, but by no means always, reserved to the householders themselves – not, of course, in aristocratic households – was the making of beds. 'Many ladies make beds of their own choice', we read in *The Young Ladies' Treasure Book*. 'Servants are not to be depended upon always even to give us the same number of blankets every night.' 'We spend at least a third of our time in bed, and the care spent upon making them comfortable is far from being thrown away when it results in procuring an added measure of "tired nature's sweet restorer, balmy sleep".'

Most servants did *not* spend at least a third of their time in bed. Their working day began early – by candlelight – and often ended late, nor was it subjected to the kind of legislative controls that Eastlake advocated for buildings. The better-off the 'master', again allowing for exceptions of temperament and attitudes, the more specialized the domestic staff: indeed, they could be as specialized as – or even more specialized than – the rooms. They were concerned both with services to people from cradle to grave (nannies, valets, butlers, nurses) and with the care of things, often requiring great patience and attention, like the cleaning of silver, often sheer drudgery.

They were also concerned with the movement of people (there were no perambulators before the late 1850s, and carriages survived after 1900) and with the movement of things, the latter activity often requiring great physical strength, when coal or water or furniture were being moved. For their own well-being they depended on their 'masters' and 'mistresses' or, when they were working in large households with servant hierarchies, on other servants. In the latter circumstances they might never see their masters or mistresses at all.

Their income accrued to them in kind ('keep') as well as in cash or perks. Books on domestic economy, including *Mrs Beeton*, usually set out details of what they should be paid with or without 'livery', the costs of which were also set out, and what else they should expect as income in kind. For the most part, in their sections on management such household books, far more extensive than any books on industrial management, told masters and mistresses to treat their servants well: they were people, not chattels. 'The kitchen is made of flesh and blood as well as the parlour.'

In her *Home Scenes and Influences* (1866) Mrs Arthur did not find it surprising that her Mrs Jones could not keep her servants since even in the parlour or the dining room she apparently never spoke to them except in a tone of command or reproof. 'Never be afraid to praise your servants', wrote Mrs Panton. 'They are far more likely to remain where they are appointed and cared for than where they know they are only looked upon as so much necessary furniture.' The last article Mrs Haweis wrote (in 1898) on 'Servants' (for the *Contemporary Review*), combined advice with warning. 'We are practically at the mercy of our servants every hour of the day', she stated in her usual realistic manner. 'It would be wise to abstain from abusing them therefore: as a class, they are respectable, worthy, honest, and rarely come on the rates unless they marry unwisely.' 'We sometimes think them ungrateful, but more often than not it is the mistress, not the servant, who is ungrateful.'

In America, Julia McNair Wright, just as explicit, began at the beginning, pointing out, as many writers did, how haphazard the process of obtaining servants usually was. 'If we take a young girl into our house for a servant, and find her ignorant, careless, untidy, generally the first impulse is to discharge her and find better help. But stop a moment. Do we not owe this girl something – owe common humanity?' Mrs Haweis made the same point in a different way. 'Perhaps the chief thing to remember is that what servants (or we might as well say human nature) value most is freedom. This makes shop service, with all its oppressive hardship ... popular.' A wise woman would avoid, therefore, terms like 'flunkey', 'slavey' and 'drudge' and would 'learn the art of leaving her servants alone'. With excellent servants, another writer put it, the master could 'live at ease among his household gods, waited on, in some respects it seemed, by unseen hands. But supposing the servants are not excellent?' The master shaves 'and he can get no hot water ... The housemaids are neglectful, the waiters supercilious, the cook impossible.'

Wisdom, however, was often in short supply, on the side of the masters and mistresses, as was efficiency on the side of the servants, and there were often problems of communication, by no means unique, of course, to masters, mistresses and servants, which made Mrs Haweis insist that servants 'as a class' were 'no more like the gentry than dogs are like cats'. 'They also know a great deal more of us than we know of them – and perhaps it does not lead them to respect us – That depends.'

There were other problems too – not the least of them a clash between the kind of advice given by people whom Mrs Haweis, the wife of a clergyman, considered wise and the kind of advice which clergymen could and did present both from the pulpit and in tracts, backed by well-chosen texts from the Bible – 'Exhort servants to be obedient unto their own masters, and to please them well on all things.' (*Titus*, II, 9) Or, 'Servant, be obedient to them that are your masters.' (*Ephesians*, VI, 5, 6) It was not always easy to distinguish between the servant of Mrs Jones and the servant of the Lord. And the word 'things' figured prominently in the ultimate epitaph. 'Well done, thou good and faithful servant: thou hast been faithful over a few things, I will make thee ruler over many things.'

Just because so many different kinds and qualities of people were involved and there were so many different domestic situations in which servants found themselves, it is almost impossible to generalize. Perhaps, however, two generalizations can be made safely. First, if houses were dependent on servants, servants in turn were dependent on their masters and mistresses, not least if they sought to change jobs when they were dependent on the 'references' given them. Second, when treated *en masse* statistically, servants were a very substantial element in the population, numerically larger than at any time before or since and at that time larger than any other occupational group in the country. In 1851 there were 751,541 indoor domestic servants, in 1901 1,285,075. The proportion of women domestic servants within these totals increased, and in 1901 one in three girls between the ages of 15 and 20 was a domestic servant. Both then and in 1851, 28 per cent of the total female servant force was aged less than 20. The composition, size and attitudes of this 'class' were bound to be matters of public as well as of private interest.

There was little in common, however, between servants working in large households, where there might be a real lord, and maids-of-all-work employed in a single household, where anybody might be master or mistress. 'It's only in second-class houses', we learn from a servant's lips in 1889 (*Toilers in London*), 'that they treat servants without consideration. But it isn't everyone can get into a big house.' There were obvious exceptions to this generalization, but it was widely believed in.

The biggest aristocratic households might employ forty or fifty servants with a relatively high proportion of males. At the head of the formidable hierarchy was the house steward, not the butler, at the base the page or foot-boy – and there were many ranks between. In the 1880s *Beeton's Penny Guide to Domestic Service* (note the price) set out a table of wages for thirteen categories of male domestic servants and thirteen categories of female servants, with separate figures for those males 'found in livery' and those who were not and for those females given 'an extra allowance for tea, sugar etc' and those who were not. (These were not, of course, the only possible categories, titles or rates of remuneration.) The males included, in order of incomes, if not necessarily of status, the house steward, the valet, the butler, the cook, the gardener, the footman, the under-butler, the coachman, the groom, the under-footman, the page, the foot-boy, expected to do anything asked of him, and the stable boy. Members of the first category earned from £40 to £80 a year and did not wear livery; members of the last category earned from

£6 to £12. Each category had its own codes, learning them not so much through training as through doing. For example, footmen who were chosen for their looks and were often expected to powder their hair, learned more about one pre-Victorian thing – powder – than any other Victorians. Like much else in Victorian England, the powder could be adulterated. The groom of the chamber learned as much about ink and paper, candles and protocol as the stable boy learned about horses.

The females included the housekeeper (from £20 to £45 a year), the lady's maid, the head nurse, the cook, the upper housemaid, the stillroom maid, the nursemaid, the under laundry-maid, the kitchen maid and the scullery maid (£5 to £9 if there were no extra allowance for paper etc; £4 if there were). At the head of this female hierarchy, always with more women in it than there were men in the male hierarchy, the housekeeper could be a more formidable figure than the steward or the butler or even the masters and mistresses themselves. Mrs Beeton compared her role with that of the First Officer on board a ship: since she had to present the captain each day with a going concern, she had also to keep 'an accurate registry of all sums paid for any and every purpose ... periodically balanced, and examined by the head of the house' along with the keys of all the cupboards, store-rooms and household chests. She was often involved in – or even responsible for – the engagement of maids as well as being their supervisor.

The sense of hierarchy began below stairs. 'His Lordship may compel us to be equal upstairs', J. M. Barrie was to write in *The Admirable Crichton*, 'but there never will be equality in the servants' hall.' The far older popular comedy 'High Life Below Stairs' (1775), wrote Mrs Haweis, 'shows how the servant class is riddled through and through with differences of grade – as the servants are represented in the farce as calling each other "Sir Charles" or "My Lord" according to their master's rank and treating each other accordingly'. The rigid lines of work demarcation, more rigid even than the dedication of the Victorian room to particular uses, were made fun of in cartoons and jokes in periodicals as much as on the stage, but they were serious enough in 'real life' in households where there were many servants and where there were often demarcation disputes.

Sometimes, of course, there was a kind of inverted fun, as in *The Greatest Plaque of Life, or the Adventures of a Lady in Search of a Good Servant* (1847) by the Mayhew brothers or in *Punch* cartoons like:

*Lady*         'Why, Parker? You came here only yesterday.'
*Lady's Maid*: 'I've been looking over your drawers, ma'am, and I find your things are not up to the mark and the lack would not do me credit.'

*Punch* was sensitive to every change in servants' attitudes and claims, although there is little evidence that servants themselves read it.

The demarcation of servants' rooms and what things should be placed there was a matter discussed by writers on architecture like Robert Kerr, who devoted a whole 'division' of his book – complete with 'maxims' – to 'the domestic offices', including servants' private rooms ('privacy conditional', he added). It was also a topic of discussion in books like Mrs Panton's which were concerned with smaller households. 'Notwithstanding the School Board and the amount of education given nowadays to the poorer classes', she wrote, 'I am continually astonished at the careless disregard of the simplest rules of health and cleanliness shown by girls . . . who will keep their kitchens etc beautifully, yet will heedlessly allow their bedrooms to remain in a state that *ought* to disgrace a resident, nowadays, in Seven Dials.'

There was no recognition of the fact, appreciated by Mrs Haweis, that it must have been a relief to get away from the order of upstairs or from the detailed instructions about things set out in the kitchen or the pantry, like 'Lower the gas if not required' or 'Breakages not mentioned within the day must be made good'. There was certainly much to know. The things a housemaid was expected to have at her disposal were listed by Mrs Caddy in a characteristic Victorian list of things – 'a well-stocked housemaid's book, black lead, red, if liked, blue starch (a very little lasts a year), matches, hammers, pincers and nails, carpet tacks, and a riser, emery cloth, Turks'-head, feather brush, mattresses and other brushes, lamp-wicks, haber-dashery. She will want one or two dozen dusters well-softened, three to six chamber-cloths, two hearth cloths, from two to six dust-sheets, one ironing blanket, plate leather if she does the plate, twelve glass-cloths, twelve tea-cloths marked pantry, a window-rubber, lamp cloths and sponges.'

This housemaid was a member of a household which also employed a cook and a butler. There were, of course, far more households where there was only one servant – the maid-of-all-work. For Mrs Beeton she was 'perhaps the only one of her class deserving commiseration: her life is a solitary one, and in some places her work is never done . . . She starts in life, probably a girl of thirteen, with some small tradesman's wife as her mistress, just a step above her in the social scale; and although the class contains many excellent, kind-hearted women, it also contains some very rough specimens of the feminine gender, and to some of these it occasionally falls to give our maid-of-all-work her first lessons in her multifarious occupations . . . By the time she has become a tolerable servant, she is probably engaged in some respectable tradesman's house, where she has to rise with the lark, for she has to do in her own person all the work which in larger establishments is performed by cook, kitchen-maid and housemaid . . .'

Mrs Beeton carefully described the daily routine of the maid-of-all-work, beginning with the opening of the shutters and (weather permitting) the downstairs windows, with the clearing and lighting of the kitchen-range, with the clearing-out and just as carefully the lighting of the dining-room fire, with the dusting of the dining room (not forgetting the furniture legs) and with the laying of the table for breakfast, which she was then expected to cook after having swept the hall and front doorstep, polished the knocker, and cleaned any boots required early. Later in the day there was further cooking and washing, sewing and mending.

Given all these duties, Mrs Beeton believed that 'a bustling active girl' should nonetheless manage 'in the summer evenings' to sit down for two or three hours, and for a short time in the afternoons on 'leisure days'. There were many girls, however, who were not so 'bustling and active' or who found that domestic service offered them no real escape from daily routine, and by the end of the century their voices were more often heard. There were others, too, who were thought of as 'treasures', and there were appropriate Biblical texts for them also.

A few commentators recognized that such treasures would not always be there. Mrs Caddy was clear about this in 1877, when there was more talk than usual of a 'servant problem': it was not just that servants were not what they used to be in the golden age, but that you could not get them. With her regular stress on economic enterprise Mrs Caddy tried to make a virtue out of what others thought of as necessity. 'If we save the money we now spend upon keeping servants to do our work for us, we shall have more to spend on our holidays, and so should feel all the more refreshed by our respite from work.'

The Reverend Baldwin Brown concurred. 'The progress of society is a progress in the limitation of numbers and the dependence of the class that supplies our servants: the cultivated class will do well not to fix too firmly on the axiom that it has a right to be waited upon.'

There were other lines of thought. H. G. Wells put his trust in robots – or machines, and in *Kipps* (1905) he was to present a critique of the kind of home where servants were forced to be drudges. 'Some poor girl's got to go up and down, up and down, and be tired out', Ann complains, 'just because they haven't the sense to give their steps a proper rise – and no water upstairs anywhere – every drop got to be carried! It's 'ouses like this wears girls out. It's 'aving 'ouses built by men, I believe, makes all the work and trouble.' 'The Kippses', Wells added in a comment that stretched time far beyond the universes of Victorian things:

The Kippses, you see, thought they were looking for a reasonably simple little contemporary house; but indeed they were looking either for dreamland or AD 1975 or thereabouts, and it hadn't come.

# 7
# Hats, Caps and Bonnets

The hat is, beyond all doubt, one of the strangest vestigial anomalies of the nineteenth century.

*Blackwood's Magazine*, 1845

We protest against the 'monstrous regiment' of Hatters. Their power has increased, is increasing, and ought to be diminished. Britons, countrymen, and brothers, let us no longer bow the head to them.

*Chambers's Journal*, 1889

Hats and hair ... are very much more susceptible to influences of the day even than dress.

JAMES LAVER, *Taste and Fashion*, 1937

There is much philosophy, as everybody knows, or should know, in the wearing of hats.

*All the Year Round*, 1892

# I

Mrs Haweis was as much interested in women's dress as she was in domestic servants or in furniture. Indeed, her book *The Art of Beauty* (1878) was her first and was followed by *The Art of Dress* (1879): it preceded *The Art of Decoration* by two years. All these books were illustrated by her, and although her advice alienated her own daughter, who objected when grown up to being made to wear 'Kate Greenaway clothes', what Mrs Haweis had to say clearly exerted an influence on readers far outside her own family circle. She offered firm advice, too, based on firm principles. 'We can hardly find a modern dress which is not throughout in the worst taste and opposed to the principles of good art.' 'No Artist, no Art.' 'Much ornament is imbecile.' 'No detail ought to be admitted in a dress that is not indispensable there.' 'Some dresses tire the eye as much as a wriggling kaleidoscope.' 'Tight lacing is mischievous: it is a practice more culpable than the Chinese one of deforming the foot.' 'It is not wicked to take pains with oneself ... We have begun to think of the mind almost to the exclusion of the body.' 'Dress bears the same relation to the body as speech does to the brain.'

Like most writers on dress, Mrs Haweis had much to say about 'the hair' which she considered 'a source of torment to most of us – both our own and other people's'. The trouble of arranging it in an elaborate form drove many ladies 'to the expedient of cutting off their own "glory" and wearing a wig': this always seemed to her a 'tristful holocaust to the Moloch of Fashion'. Hair was meant to keep and 'to touch': 'One should be able to run one's fingers through it, and shake it into form again.' If you had 'a wealth of hair', one hairpin ought to be enough with which to fasten it – 'no maid, no gum, no wig, no forest of pins and pads and ties.'

Not every woman had a wealth of hair, however, and hair could always be improved by 'dainty head gear'. While a woman's head-dress might not be so important as her head, there could be no doubt that what she chose to wear on her head, and the way in which she chose to wear it, 'vastly affected' the impression she made on others. A head-dress had to be – 'first, becoming; second, beautiful; and third, useful.' Utility came third in the order for Mrs Haweis because 'we have long quitted the primitive idea of what a head-dress should be.' Most women now wanted 'to attract'. At the same time, they made a mistake in putting too much trust in Fashion. The fashion in hats changed too often, and their wearers were too easily tempted to say 'What a change, how delightful!' not pausing 'to think whether the old fashion became them better.' Mrs Haweis did not dwell on hats with a history, hats which had been retrimmed or even reshaped to respond to changes in fashion, but rather related the hat exclusively to the psychology of its individual wearer.

'A head-dress', she maintained, 'should set off, and should draw the eye towards the noblest portions ... of the face ... It ought, of course to be a pretty object in itself, and made of handsome materials.' It held 'a place of honour in the whole toilette', and was not like the skirt 'liable to collect the dirt of the ground' nor, like the bodice, 'apt to be hidden under a bushel'. It was always 'conspicuous' and had 'a character to keep up'. 'With propriety', however, it could be 'useful and comfortable'. That was 'just as well'.

All head-dresses, Mrs Haweis went on, sprang from two primitive forms – the hat and the cap – an ancestry that applied to men's headwear also. The choice might have social (and economic) as well as aesthetic implications, particularly as far as choices were concerned, but in the naming of the head-dress there was something of a paradox in that it was the humbler 'cap' that as a word had a Latin origin: the ecclesiastical 'cope' was another, and in this case dignified, derivative. Copes came back into fashion in the nineteenth

*Hats on parade, 1896 and 1897*

century among the vestments of the Oxford Movement: one designed in 1901 by G. F. Bodley was worked in two shades of gold thread and incorporated the letter P, pineapples and fleurs-de-lis.

By contrast the word 'hat' had an Anglo-Saxon origin, *haet*, and it had cognates in all the Teutonic languages. Its etymology was hidden, however, as the hat rose in the world. The socialist Keir Hardie created a sensation when he appeared in the House of Commons wearing a cloth cap, not a silk hat, and long before that the cap of liberty had been worn with pride. It was thought Bohemian when the great women's couturier Charles Frederick Worth, who had devised both elegant hats and rakish hats for women, chose to appear in a photograph taken during the last decade of his life wearing a beret.

The distinction between men's hats and men's caps was a more interesting social distinction than that between women's hats and women's bonnets, for red or white 'caps of liberty' had a longer history than silk hats. Far back in the year of Peterloo, the year when Queen Victoria was born, the *Manchester Observer* had written that the cap had already been 'the symbol of the free man' in classical times because it was venerable: it was triangular because it indicated that freedom rested on 'the broad base of the people', a pyramid because it symbolized eternity, and woollen in order to prove that 'freedom belongs to the shepherd as well as the senator.' There was no suggestion then, however, of Andy Capp. As far as women's hats and bonnets were concerned, there was an apparent paradox in the fact that Queen Victoria greatly preferred the bonnet to the hat. Indeed, at her Jubilee in 1887 she refused to wear either the crown or the robes of the State and chose a new bonnet instead, a special bonnet though it was, gleaming with white lace and diamonds. Lord Rosebery might exclaim that the empire should be ruled not by a bonnet but by a sceptre, but the Queen, supreme in these matters, issued printed orders ordering her ladies to wear 'bonnets and long high dresses without mantel at the service in Westminster Abbey.' By that time, young ladies of fashion were favouring hats: bonnets were coming to be associated with the old.

For Mrs Haweis there was no question that hats were, 'as a rule', more beautiful than bonnets. 'An artist often introduces a hat on the grass or on a chair – never a modern bonnet.' The reason was that a hat was generally of a definite shape, while a bonnet was not. It was, she felt, a great fault of 'the bonnets of the present day' (1878) that they were – and looked – 'so temporary'. Nonetheless, Mrs Haweis believed that there was much to be said in winter both for caps and for hoods. 'It is a pity that caps are so entirely forgotten for young people,' she observed when discussing head-gear for 'indoors'. 'They seem to be considered fit only for servants and great-grandmothers.' And among hoods she recommended the Russian *bashlyk*. She also noted how 'the entire display of the hair in the public streets is a very recent fashion, and is significant of the safety of modern cities.'

The constituents of the hat had aesthetic as well as economic value. 'When jewels, furs and lace were being worn on every other part of the person', there was no purpose in 'decking' the head and crown with 'a mass of rubbish'. 'The artificial flowers in bonnets and hats are generally execrable: indeed, artificial flowers, except when quite deceptive should never be worn, and all who can afford it should wear real flowers.' In another place Mrs Haweis had similar things to say of feathers: 'Concoctions of feathers, chopped and tortured into abnormal forms, odious alike to art and nature, should be rejected with contempt.'

Nonetheless, Mrs Haweis did not anticipate critics of all feathers, the members of the Society for the Protection of Birds, founded in 1889, who pointed out how in an age when taxidermy flourished ostriches and other birds like the osprey and the egret might suffer in the course of feminine adornment and who strongly objected to birds' heads or even whole birds becoming parts of a woman's plumage. Instead for Mrs Haweis 'one fine black or white ostrich feather, nay one ostrich-hen plume' was worth 'a hundred false wigs, tinsel and abominations and muslin flowers'. She had a good punch line, although it was buried away before the end of a paragraph. 'Before women put sensible, not to say beautiful, things outside their heads they will have to put a little more inside them.'

Mrs Haweis was as anxious to prevent women being at the mercy of their milliners as Eastlake was to prevent their being at the mercy of furniture salesmen. She would have agreed with Robert Louis Stevenson that public taste was 'a mongrel product out of affection by dogma'. Yet she made an attempt to trace back the vagaries of fashion, as she saw them, to even more powerful figures than the working milliners. Behind them were 'secret rulers', as another writer on clothes called them, 'mute inglorious Alexanders and Bismarks, who conquer and rule the world of clothes.' 'You might change a man's whole nature by changing the nature of his dress,' the same writer claimed, although he conceded that men's dress changed far less in the nineteenth century than women's dress so that the proposition could never be adequately tested.

Meanwhile, perhaps, women retained or acquired their 'traditional reputation for instability', because 'the variations in their fashions' were 'too radical, as well as too frequent' for them to maintain 'a settled disposition'. As an earlier writer had claimed, with more than a touch of what would now be called male chauvinism, the only way to describe women's 'instability' – or volatility – as he called it – was in terms of metaphors derived from nature – rainbows with changing colours, the wind in the month of March.

It was women, nonetheless, not men, who produced the rebels, the clothes reformers, bursting forth from 'the fetters of Valenciennes and ribbons', very different in temperament and tactics from the 'dear creatures' who were said to perpetuate 'petticoat government'; and although Mrs Bloomer won few converts – and much ridicule – with her plea for 'rational dress' in 1851, nonetheless, as Fiona Clark has observed, her wide straw hats were 'essentially the same as appeared on entirely conventional heads at the English seaside four years later.' Holland produced the most memorably named group of women dress reformers – the five Vs – Vereeniging Voor Verbetering Van Vrouwenkleeding – sounding less memorable when translated as the Society for the Improvement of Women's Clothing. Yet these and other reformers were fighting against the corset more than against the hat.

Both the beach and the pew were places for the display of fashion, and in both settings status counted. *Punch* made more of the first setting than of the second. Indeed, we learn more in private letters and diaries about church and chapel than we learn from any published source. As C. Willett Cunnington has written in his massive *English Women's Clothing in the Nineteenth Century* (1937), 'the bonnet sufficiently gay for the Park would be flippant in Church.' The conventions in both places were many. Certain materials might be worn up to Easter, but not after; and at the close of the season there were 'special modes adapted for Cheltenham and Harrogate, for it seems one took the waters in subdued tones.' Brighton was always different. 'It is a Piccadilly crowd by the sea – exactly the same style of people you meet in Piccadilly – but freer in dress and particularly in hats', wrote Richard Jefferies, for once abandoning nature for art. He lived for several years in Hove not in Brighton.

The whole rhythm of dress conventions could be disturbed by funerals which did not obey the dictates of the calendar. 'The finer shades of mourning', we learn, 'were a test for the Perfect Lady.' Even at weddings, where only brides wore veils, many wedding dresses were grey or lavendar coloured, not white, as a sign of half mourning. The weather set its own tests of convention too. Both Cheltenham and Brighton gave their names to waterproof coats during the 1870s.

The perfect gentleman was bound by conventions at all times, wet or dry, funerals included. He was allowed, however, to make the best of *his* hair. Men were expected to be proud of their hair, and some of them dressed it with perfumed Macassar oil: hence anti-macassars. Luxurious locks went well with side-whiskers and beards in mid-Victorian Britain: late-Victorian Britain favoured the moustache. By then, however, the first safety razor had been patented in 1874 and star razors were widely marketed in Britain after 1887, with the first Gillette blade appearing in 1895. Soon words like 'hone' and 'strop' were to pass from the language.

There was always far more variety in hair – and in hair-brushes – than in hats, and the Hairdressers' Guild was founded in 1882. Shampoos became fashionable during the 1890s, with France leading the way. The term 'side-burns' was American in origin, derived from the general and politician A. E. Burnside: the British preferred 'mutton chops' and the Americans them-selves Dundrearies after Lord Dundreary in *Our American Cousin* (1858). (See page 112.) Napoleon III's 'Imperial' was said to have been devised by his barber who felt that he had too little hair on his chin to permit a great beard, while the Emperor of Austria's 'Kaiserbarb' was said to have been invented to hide his protruding Hapsburg chin.

George Bernard Shaw, known to the public by his own beard after the fashion for beards had long gone, was to make much of mid-Victorian beards, drawing attention to Wells's comment that Marx's beard was so godlike that it could not have been unintentional, and adding that William Morris's 'Olympian coronet of clustering hair and Düreresque beard were such as no man less great could have carried without being denounced as an impostor.' Henry Hyndman, the socialist in the top hat, only wore the hat, he added, because it went with his beard, and when he discarded his hat in desperation and replaced it with a broad-brimmed soft hat, this 'immediately became the hat of Wotan and made him more godlike than ever.'

Men's urban clothes had begun to 'go dark' before 1850: and Jane Carlyle has described how when she was reading her husband's *Philosophy of Clothes* in 1845, in walked the supremely fashionable Comte d'Orsay who was 'all in black and brown'. Five years before he had been 'as gay in his colours as a humming bird'. Where d'Orsay led others followed. Colours stayed dark throughout the Victorian years, except at weddings, so that Whistler, when he settled in England in the late 1850s, was conspicuous for wearing white duck trousers. The tall black hat, the 'topper', which had supplanted the three-cornered hat, became the indispensable symbol of good form. It might be made of black silk plush or, until beavers were in short supply, of beaver skin – one of the earliest references to silk dates back to 1799 – and although it might vary somewhat in silhouette from year to year in crown and brim and might be worn in revealingly different ways, the variations between 'stove pipes' and 'chimney pots' were merely variations of design within a genre.

Lewis Carroll's Mad Hatter was depicted by Tenniel wearing an out-of-date Wellington style hat to emphasize his madness. He had an advertisement outside his hat, too, not an uncommon place to put one in Victorian times, although for gentlemen it was the hatter's advertisement inside the hat that really counted. Lock and Company of St James's Street did not need to advertise: they had been in existence since 1765. At the end of the century the shape of the top hat was slim, neat and waisted, words which Fiona Clark has pointed out could also be used to describe the fashionable line in men's tailoring.

There was as little variation in the use of the hat in space as there was in time, for the etiquette of the hat was deliberately made as universal as possible. If you were a real gentleman, therefore, you knew precisely when and to whom to doff it and when to place it by your side, as in a *Carte de Visite* photograph. You had to carry it to the drawing room, of course, when you were visiting, for the caller, as books on manners put it, had to demonstrate that he was privileged in being able to pay his respects. As James Laver was to put it succinctly, 'the code of Pall Mall was thereby imposed on the pattern of Calcutta and Columbo'.

The code involved authority, and policemen, railway stationmasters, park keepers, postmen and cricketers were at first expected to wear top hats as a matter of course. Surviving three-cornered hats, once *de rigueur*, were left to coachmen, town criers, Chelsea pensioners, Bank of England officials and some, but not all, Lord Mayors. They recalled past times and perpetuated a sense of fading traditional ritual.

There were many working coachmen and grocers, however, who wore top hats with light-coloured bands, and there were collapsible hats for all occasions. A mid-nineteenth century invention was 'the conformateur', a giant hat which when placed on a man's head measured its contours to ensure a good fit. For those men who could not afford hatters' silk plush there were versions of tall hats in papier-mâché. At the Exhibition of 1851 builders on the Crystal Palace site wore top hats.

Nonetheless, before the end of the century, when the cricketing term 'hat trick' had passed into the language, there were many variations in hats – straw hats; soft and round felt hats; bowlers; trilbys (from the 1870s); and light-weight helmets based on the Indian 'topee' or 'topi'. These were not variations on a theme, but themes in themselves. Meanwhile, lounge suits were beginning to be worn by men as well as by boys, high collars were giving way to turn-down collars and cravats were turning into ties. There were 'Norfolk shirts' that came to be called 'Norfolk jackets' and other sports jackets too. Working men might wear tweed trousers and reefer jackets.

Straw hats were known during the 1840s, when the boy Prince of Wales was shown wearing a straw hat with sailor suit in a picture by Winterhalter, and when *Punch* depicted straw-hatted passengers on a steamer boat to Margate. Such hats deserve a book in themselves, fuller than that provided by the Luton Museum, then five years old, in 1933. It was called *The Romance of the Straw Hat*, and it traced the story back to an Egyptian tomb, bringing Luton into the story in the seventeenth century.

Straw hats in Victorian times were worn by women as well as men, and the book concentrated on women's wear. It noted, however, the early attempts to sew hats by machinery. The first machines were introduced from the United States, where straw hats were popular too: a '10 guinea' machine to sew straw plait was first used in 1875 and machine blocking was introduced during the same decade. The Luton guide does not note that also in the same decade the policemen of Luton adopted straw hats for wearing with their summer uniforms. By then, however, foreign straw plait was being imported at a quarter of the cost of English straw plait, and the local industry was doomed.

Felt hat making made its way to Luton during the 1870s, and in this industry also the first machines were devised in the United States, and had made their way into Britain by 1858. Rabbit skins were the basic material for 'fur felts', sheep's wool for wool felts. The former felt was deemed of a higher quality than the latter – out of the rabbit, without conjuring, came the hat – but there were many processes involved before fur or wool became finished hats. Brim shaping and trimming were the last.

Men's felt hats could be soft or hard, and some of the first of them were known as 'wideawakes', according to *Punch* because they had no nap. The hard version was known as the bowler after the hatter William Bowler of Southwark, and was popularized by Lord Derby who wore it at Epsom. It was narrow-rimmed and 'pudding basin' shaped and preceded the hat-making machine. Another later name for one specimen of the bowler, a contraction of the name of William Coke, who first wore it, was the 'billycock'. At the top of the social scale Lock's sold large numbers of 'Cambridge' bowlers named after the Duke of Cambridge who ordered a flat-crowned bowler in 1865. The trade unionist and future Liberal minister, John Burns, always wore a serge suit, a white shirt, a black tie and a bowler hat. In the words of a fellow trade unionist 'he looked the engineer all over'. Many of the bowlers of the 1880s had high crowns, but by the end of the century they had medium crowns and brims well curled up at the sides.

The soft felt hat became popular only after the introduction of the Homburg (of Tyrolean origin and named after the spa) during the 1880s and, above all, during the 1890s after the Prince of Wales had worn a soft felt hat in the right company. His father had told him in the 1850s always to dress 'with scrupulous attention to neatness and good taste', but the Prince's taste was more adventurous than his father's and he liked tweed knickerbockers and caps as well as soft hats. Artists, among them the pre-Raphaelites, had long favoured soft felt hats with wide brims, and Oscar Wilde, like Richard Wagner, was to choose velvet as his material: he went to Lock's for a velvet hat to wear on his first American tour. He liked velvet knee breeches too and supported the activities of the Rational Dress Society founded in 1881. Dr Gustav Jaeger argued the case for knickerbockers as well as for wool, as did George Bernard Shaw who joined another dress reforming society, the Healthy and Artistic Dress Union, founded in 1899.

Kenneth Morgan in his admirable life of Keir Hardie has suggested that the exact character of Hardie's 'cloth cap', which was to become a symbol for the Labour Party – and for Andy Capp – had a certain ambivalence about it. Although in his election leaflets and posters in 1892 Hardie had been shown with a miner's cap on his head, he usually wore a Sherlock-Holmes type of deerstalker in the House of Commons: 'Later, after 1900, a slouch hat bought in Philadelphia, backed by a red cravat, crowned his glory.' According to Morgan, Hardie was himself a Bohemian, an eccentric, who on entering Parliament wore clothes which were the last things that a Scots miner would wear. They were certainly clothes which could shock, very different from working men's 'Sunday best'. By a coincidence, Hardie first arrived in the House of Commons in 1892 at exactly the same moment as Gladstone, who was not amused.

It is significant, of course, that Hardie wore headgear at all. Schoolboys started life with caps or with various styles of hats, including the Etonian: they were as symbolic as ties. The City was to take up the bowler. Early photographs of football matches show very few hatless people of any age. Even beggars wore hats.

# II

Women's hats varied in style from time to time, more indeed than they had ever varied before, from place to place and from occasion to occasion, sometimes even when dresses did not. There was nothing exceptional, therefore, in a comment in an article on 'The Fashion of Dress', which appeared in the first number of the new periodical *The Lady* in 1855, that 'the most complete change will doubtless be in our headgear'.

At the beginning of Queen Victoria's reign, the poke bonnet of 1837, a remarkably persistent kind of close-fitting bonnet, was very similar to that of 1817, with a wide brim, and it had a downward curve at the chin edge. The ears were concealed as in the profiles of the Queen in her first coins. By 1841, however, the close-fitting bonnet with a brim closing round the face was smaller. Laver compared it with a coal scuttle. Others have described the face being served up as if on a plate. This was a year of thick corkscrew side-curls, reminiscent of the seventeenth century as little else was in 1840–42 except the mood of popular revolt, just as big sleeves, worn by women in the 1830s, had recalled the sixteenth century.

After the mood of political revolt had petered out in smoky provincial towns, where fashion often seemed irrelevant, curls and long ringlets remained fashionable, along with layers of petticoats and straw hats made not in Luton but in Switzerland. There was also a plethora of handkerchiefs. Modest bonnets in fashionable places, it has been suggested, implied a low profile – display was conspicuous during the 1840s, described by one historian of fashion, Angus Holden, as 'the most uninspired dress period in the nineteenth century' – although there was scope for ornamenting even the most modest bonnets with sprays of flowers or bird of paradise feathers. Inevitably, given the hair styles of the 1840s, hats were shorter at the ears and were worn more forward on the head. Some were very small, *petits bords*. One hat recalled Marie Stuart, and in 1846 there was a return to the eighteenth century in a fashionable hat *à la Clarisse Harlow*.

During the mid-1850's after side curls had gone, poke bonnets remained – along with bonnet strings – although they had begun to recede to the back of the head, a trend that was to continue: worn far back, they were sometimes elaborate, fashioned out of ribbons and lace, and they were often decked with artificial flowers, particularly roses. There was a fashion for wearing them in colours which contrasted with the dress. While there were some curiously wide and flat hats, some of them thought 'bold', bonnets became even more diminutive, almost like skull-caps, by the mid-1860s; and there was one small hat, the 'pork pie', which had appeared in 1859. It was made out of dark straw or velvet. In retrospect, such hats and bonnets seem to be out-of-keeping with the elaborate lace and silk trimmings of the crinoline dresses of the period or even the elaborate hair nets which were often composed of strings of pearls. Meanwhile, hat pins, first introduced around 1855 although they did not become popular until the 1890s, made it possible to tilt the hat further over the forehead. One hat was called the Garibaldi. Late-nineteenth century hat pins would have made worthy weapons for him: some were twelve inches long. Now there is a Hatpins Museum.

The popularity of the crinoline, already far enough advanced by 1858 to be described as 'crinolinomania', drew attention away from the head to the hoop; and although dress prophets predicted that its 'iron reign' – in fact, the hoop was often made of steel – would soon end, the crinoline continued to be worn until 1867. The most that happened to it was a change in its shape. When the crinoline was eventually discarded, there could still be equally awkward shapes. In 1866 a train a yard and a half long was not considered unusual in fashionable streets. Crinolines were never popular on the stage, or in the theatre stalls. They frustrated 'the spectacle'. They were never much

*'A Crossing in Love', from* Fun, *1866*

approved of by believers in traditional manners either. How could a gentleman take a lady's arm? There were more profound questions, less often posed. How could a crinolined lady hold a child's arm? How could she rock a cradle?

During the 1840s attention had been drawn in evening dresses to the bare neck and shoulders: now, given the smallness of the bonnets, when attention did not move to the crinoline itself, it might focus not on the figure but on the face. Everything else was concealed until the ankles, among the first of them those of the Empress Eugénie, came into view after 1860. *Noli me tangere.* Jewels were more profuse too, than they had been during the 1840s and the fabrics far richer, although they became lighter in weight during the 1860s. Shawls were worn in cashmere or China crepe: 'How to wear a shawl' – and it was not easy – was the title of an article in *Sylvia's Home Journal* in 1861. New fabrics included mohair and bombazine. Fans copied French master-pieces. Parasols were elegant, sometimes ingeniously combined with umbrel-las. After Albert's death black combs were popular. This time it was the French who copied rich Whitby jet, in what was called French jet, actually black glass.

During the later 1860s and 1870s bonnets were still the smallest part of the head-dress, and there was a variety of hair-styles ranging from large buns, projecting backwards, to hair worn loosely over the shoulders. Wave partings had been introduced in 1860, middle parting during the late 1850s. The *chignon*, which was to have a longer history than the *crinoline*, was a gathering of the hair (one's own or artificial hair, sometimes somebody else's!) worn on the back of the head often in a net: it was estimated that in 1863 chignon makers were using 100,000 pounds of hair a year and that ten years later one firm was turning out two tons of artificial hair each week. Hair, like hats or bonnets, needed decoration and there was a prominent place for strands of ribbon – for sprays of foliage and even for grapes and strawberries (*paniers à fruit*). Plumes, and even complete stuffed birds, became prominent mainly during the next decade, when hair styles were comparatively simple: one bore the name 'Unique'.

The names of the hats of the 1870s included Sailor, Shepherd, part of a 'Dolly Varden' outfit named after the heroine of Dickens's *Barnaby Rudge*, Gainsborough, which might be worn by 'aesthetes', Jockey, for those who preferred suggestions of the open air, and 'a chimney pot hat.' *Toques* were worn flat on the crown. Materials used ranged from velvet to straw and even to horse-hair. Of the style of wearing bonnets at the back of the head a fashion writer in *The Graphic* could write in 1875, 'few faces can fail to look either imbecile or impudent'.

During the 1880s, when there were marked changes in hair styles, including the widespread adoption of fringes, and when ostentatious hair ornaments went out of fashion, masculine models were increasingly copied. Thus, the Homburg, with birds on the brim, became the *Chapeau Jean sans*

*Peur.* The bowler was always the bowler, but it could be decked with feathers. During the 1880s, descriptions like 'Renaissance' and 'Directoire' recalled in appearance as well as in name the styles of earlier periods of history. Meanwhile, the 'dress improver' had followed the crinoline, had been discarded for a time and had returned again, reaching its most elaborate form in the large bustle of the 1880s, which gave a new sharpness to the skirt. For G. F. Watts, the painter, there was a 'persistent tendency to suggest that the most beautiful half of humanity is furnished with tails'. Heavy hair styles disappeared, but hats might be bedecked not only with flowers or feathers or birds, but with insects and leaves.

By the end of the 1890s hats had wider brims again and were placed flatter on the tops of heads. Flowers were still there, including artificial flowers of exaggerated size. There was a renewed place for jet decorations also, although Queen Victoria was not yet dead, and there was not enough natural jet to go round. Bonnets were on the way out. Spotted veils were common, particularly when the hats were small. One writer on 'household organization' was bold enough to recommend the lady of the house to wear a muslin cap in the home 'to keep the dust from falling on her hair'. They were 'prettiest', she said, when made in the shape of a large hair-net and 'might be made of Swiss muslin, trimmed with a frill border edged with Valenciennes lace'. Even in the privacy of the home, therefore, there was a place for finery. As James Laver has noted, as the end of the century was reached, there was 'as yet no sign of the revolution' which was 'to take place in women's clothes during the next twenty-five years'.

There was rather more 'informality' in men's clothes: after the bowler hat came the fishing-cap, after the Norfolk jacket the re-discovered knicker-bockers. An observer at Charing Cross Station in 1897 reported 'nearly two lounge suits to one morning coat and quite three lounges to one frock coat'.

Earlier in the century there had been a few men who had complained against the tyranny of the hat while not actually rebelling against it. Thus, *Blackwoods Magazine* as early as 1845 had described the top hat, whether of beaver or of silk, as an 'ungraceful' and 'misshapen canister', asking 'Does it set off any of the natural beauty of the human cranium? Are its lines in harmony with, or in becoming contrast to the expressive features of the face? Is it comfortable, portable, durable or cheap?' 'The least exposure to wet ruins it,' the author went on, 'a moderate blow will crack or break its form.' Yet, like Mrs Haweis later, the author did not believe that utility was the only criterion, even if for him it came first. 'The merely useful' might make the shape of a hat 'approximate to that of a Quaker or a jarrey's, but the beautiful has to elevate and modify it into the mystical proportions fit for a man of taste.'

The 'common hat' was as unbeautiful as the common nightcap. The latter was too familiar, the former too stiff. 'It gives us straight or nearly straight lines, going upwards like tangents from the oval of the face, and cut off above by another straight line. All such lines and angles are foreign to the face and head.' And then the author crossed the social divides, and while he rejected 'Highland caps' and 'all fancy-caps with whale bone, falling tops, angular projections etc', he praised above all other headgear the common foraging cap. 'Every man looks well in a foraging cap; it harmonizes with everybody's face; it makes the old look young and the young look smart; it is without pretence, plain in detail, and yet elegant in outlook.' Moreover, if you wanted to show rank, nothing so easily allowed for suitable ornament: 'a plain band – a golden one – or even a coloured one – makes it suitable to the various ranks and occupations of men'.

That rank could count was revealed after the Indian Mutiny when the old Persian curtain of white washable material to cover cap and neck was christened 'the havelock' after Sir Henry Havelock, the British general. Eight years later, when the 'havelock' had not quite established itself, a forgotten periodical called *Fun* included in June 1865 a verse 'Ode to my Clothes' in which the disadvantages of the hat in 'broiling' weather were singled out:

And, oh! How I hate my hat!
That box of roasted hair.

Fortunately for gentlemen, it was not in every year in London that you could complain 'Oh! Isn't it hot! Isn't it hot!'

And all is soft and clammy and damp
No need to moisten your postage stamp.

In India you might wear a *topi*, but even in Cheltenham this was rare.

# III

During the 1860s the language of fashion columns in the periodical press had become as colourful as many of the often violent colours that were in vogue, and great claims were being made for women's dress designers. 'A toilette', Hippolyte Taine had complained, was by then 'worth as much as a painting'. The language of fashion certainly was a necessary part of the fashion itself. The first number of *The Lady* in 1885 pointed out that with changes in headgear, bonnets worn with the hair piled up on the top of the head or with a close coil of basket plaits would become 'totally useless'. 'I have already seen a few new bonnets', the author went on, 'with close round crowns almost covering the back of the head, the fronts open, and framing the face, formed of frills of velvet, and trimmed with clusters of looped ribbons, holding an aigrette or a bird.' The knowing 'I' was to figure more prominently than the discerning eye in fashion literature.

Nearly twenty years earlier in 1866 the *Illustrated Times* had quoted a 'humorous' description from a newspaper of the way to make a fashionable bonnet:

'Take a piece of plaited straw of a round or oval form, and bend it into any shape you please so long as you can balance the article on the top of your head. Smother it with artificial flowers, or cover it if you like with puffed tulle, and add lappets at the side if you think becoming; but this I should add is quite unnecessary. Plant a full-blown rose in the centre, or encircle the whole with a wreath of roses, passion flowers, pansies, hyacinths, ivy, or lilies of the valley, or bunches of grapes, or some cherries or gooseberries. Then attach some glass beads around the rim, and strings of ribbon of the same colour as the predominating tint of the flowers or fruit framing the wreath, the end of which tie together across the breast. Next add, if you please, a second pair of strings of muslin or tulle; and you have a bonnet of the prevailing mode, which you can call *chapeau Lambolle, fanchon, Trianon, print axier, été, Marly*, or *mandarin blanc* according to your fancy.

Much fun could be made of fashion, particularly when it made large claims or expressed itself 'absurdly'. *Punch* made the most of it, and it was one of the staples of *Fun*:

Trust me CHIGNON OF HAIR,
Though Paris fashions woman apes,
Your great grandfather and his wife
Smile at the claims of bonnet-shapes.
Howe'er this be, it seems to me
'Tis fair to fascinate and flirt,
Your hair's worth more than coronets
And simple braids than Russian dirt.

One way of finding fun, popular nearer the end of the century, was to predict the fashions of the future, and in 1893 the *Strand Magazine* included a lively article on 'Future Dictates of Fashion'. While it got the twentieth-century history of fashion completely wrong, it was not far from the truth when it forecast that during the 1940s and 1950s fashion history might well assume 'the dignity of a science', studied in universities. Whereas in the nineteenth century fashion had been thought of as 'a whim', the author wrote, 'a sort of shuttlecock for the weak-minded of both sexes to make rise and fall'' during the 1940s and 1950s its movements would be 'explained' in terms of 'certain strict rules'. It was easier for him to predict Roland Barthes than Mary Quant.

One nineteenth-century development favours the university student of past fashion – the invention of photography. Fashion plates flattered. Photographs sometimes did, sometimes did not. Madeleine Ginsberg's *Victorian Dress in Photographs* (1982) and Avril Landsell's *Fashion à la Carte, 1860–1900* (1985) are invaluable sources for the historian not only of hats, caps and bonnets, but of clothes of all kinds. They show clothes being worn, not displayed. They reveal, too, something of the extent to which fashions in dress percolated – or could percolate – through the whole of the society. 'It is almost impossible to recognize working people when in their Sunday best', it was claimed in 1858, and Avril Lansdell believes that 'cartes-de-visite bear this out, for it is not always easy to place the figures in the photographs in their level in the social scale'.

A wider range of photographic evidence beginning with school photographs of children points to continuing social difference, as does verbal comment. Avril Lansdell herself quotes in her *Wedding Fashions, 1860–1980* (1983) the patronizing comment of Gertrude Jekyll on the photograph of 'a wedding party of the labouring class' at the turn of the nineteenth century. 'The bride had a veil and orange blossom, a shower bouquet and *pages*. The bridegroom wore one of those cheap suits aforesaid and had a billy-cock hat pushed back from his poor, anxious, excited face that glistened with sweat. In his buttonhole was a large bouquet and on his hands *white cotton gloves*. No more pitiful exhibition would well be imagined. Have these people so utterly lost the sense of their own position that they can derive satisfaction from the performance of such an absurd burlesque?'

The perception of social difference comes out in a different way in Arthur Munby's collection of pictures of the working-class women he admired, contrasting weekday trousers, shirts, aprons and bonnets with 'Sunday best'. Again verbal commentary from Munby's diaries is a necessary complement to Munby's photographic collection now in Trinity College, Cambridge. Many of the women he depicted had fashions of their own, but were complete strangers to the Paris fashions which dominated women's magazines – and even to an increasing extent popular advertisements.

# IV

It was during the decade of the Crimean War and the Mutiny that women's fashions, even those of the Empress Eugénie herself, seemed to be dictated by powerful figures hidden behind the scenes – if not 'mute inglorious Alexanders and Bismarcks', as Mrs Haweis suggested, Parisian *femmes entretenues*, as different as possible from Mumby's working-class girls.

Half-true or false, there is no doubt that Paris figured more prominently than London in the determination of fashionable mid-Victorian tastes and that Charles Frederick Worth, patronised by Eugénie, was just as influential among the tastemakers as Ruskin was in guiding tastes in buildings or Eastlake was in the determination of tastes in furniture and décor inside the home. After all, like Morris, he actually *made* things – or rather 'composed' them. 'We owe to the artistic grace of this great milliner, and to his intuition for aesthetic elegance', wrote a French admirer, 'the revival of grace in dress.'

Ruskin was referring to Worth without actually naming him when he told the citizens of Bradford, who had invited him to lecture there (see page 81)

275

that 'you hear of me, among others, as a respectable architectural man-milliner; and you send for me that I may tell you the leading fashion'. As a textile city, Bradford was expected to know with whom Ruskin was comparing himself. Yet, as Malcolm Hardman has written in his *Ruskin and Bradford* (1986), 'However hard they tried, Bradford could not compete with Paris, nor even Paisley, in the production of fine cashmeres or silks or velvets ... sense, as well as sensibility, suggested the cultivation of decency and delight, rather than flamboyance.' The best-known figure in the Bradford textiles industry, Sir Titus Salt, pioneer of alpaca and founder of Saltaire, had no desire to be a 'man-milliner', although he was always more than a millowner.

Worth was born far from the textiles districts at Bourne, Lincolnshire, in 1825, the son of a solicitor who lost his money in speculation. When young Worth moved to London one year after Queen Victoria came to the throne, he is said to have raised the necessary money by making ladies' Easter bonnets: if so, he needed his mother's help. When he got to London, he was apprenticed to Swan and Edgar at the Quadrant, Regent Street, still a new shopping centre, which, alas, was to lose its Nash colonnades ten years later. There he was near enough to the recently opened National Gallery in Trafalgar Square to study the costumes of the past. He was near enough too to shops of quality. The first shops there specialized in male fashions, but 'milliners', a general name for dressmakers as well as hatmakers, were soon to be found there, as were exclusive silk mercers, like Lewis and Allenby. John Swan and William Edgar had humbler beginnings: they had both started by selling haberdashery on stalls. Worth learnt much both from his early experience in retailing – he moved for a time to Lewis and Allenby – and from the collections, particularly the portrait collections in the National Gallery, to prepare him well for moving to Paris to find his fortune on the eve of his twentieth birthday. He was to stay there for the rest of his life.

He was soon selling fabrics, satins, brocades, cashmere shawls, and ready-made garments at Gagelin's, a fashion shop in the Rue Richelieu, and stayed there until 1858, getting to know how to deal with women customers without actually making dresses for them: at that time that would have been unthinkable. Nearby was a boutique once owned by Rose Berlin, who had dressed Marie Antoinette, but in the late 1840s women's dress in France (including the poke bonnet) was almost as 'demure' – or 'modest' – as it was in England. There was no place for a Marie Antoinette – or for a Eugénie. It was only after Napoleon's *coup d'état* in 1852 and his 'imperial marriage' in 1853 that Worth's move to Paris really began to pay off. He is said to have assisted the future Empress, still in her twenties, in the choice of materials for her trousseau.

Worth had certainly been picked out already by Gagelin's not only to sell goods but to talk to clients, some of them rich and influential, and to discuss with dressmakers the merits of different dress materials and accessories and of different shapes and colours; and, more important, although he had no training as a tailor, 'on the side' he was soon making clothes as well as selling or discussing them, benefiting from his direct relationships with textile manufacturers. His first client was a model, a *demoiselle du magasin*, Marie Augustine Vernet, two years older than he was, whom he had married in 1851 and whom he now began to dress in simple, well-fitting clothes; and it was in that year that Gagelin's, under new ownership, won a Gold Medal for 'very excellent embroidered silk, wrought up in dresses of elegant style' at the Great Exhibition in London. By 1853 Worths' hand-painted dresses were being advertised, and they were displayed at the Paris Exhibition of 1855, when another gold medal was won for Worth's court train, a *manteau de cour*, in watered silk, embroidered in gold, the style of which recalled the empire of Napoleon I. It was attached to the shoulders, not to the waist.

Worth's successes do not seem to have been fully appreciated by Gagelin's, although they had advertised his wares in *Le Moniteur de la Mode*, and in 1858 he set up business on his own at 7 Rue de la Paix, not far from the imperial palace, employing fifty 'hands' and attracting foreign as well as French clients. Forty years later, assisted by his two sons, he was employing about 1,200 workers at his 'Maison Worth', turning out between six and seven thousand dresses and between three and four thousand cloaks, and exporting model gowns and patterns to be copied, particularly across the Atlantic. By then his high-ranking foreign clients, some of them ordering clothes by telegram, included the Empress of Russia, the Queen of Spain and the Queen of Portugal, but not Queen Victoria.

By then, too, after many changes in fashions, Worth was as clear about his own ideas on Fashion in general as was Mrs Haweis. 'It is difficult to enter into all the details which influence changes of style', he told a correspondent of the *Strand Magazine* in 1893, 'but briefly I may say that, when a manufacturer invents any special fabric or design, he sends me a pattern asking if I can make use of it. That fabric may require a secure style of dress, or if light and soft, is adapted for draperies, puffings, etc. If the material pleases me, I order a large quantity, to be specially made for me and design my dresses accordingly. A purchase by a large firm of a great quantity of material influences other firms, and that material, and the style it is best suited to, becomes the fashion.' Worth had come to believe, although he did not tell this particular correspondent, that fashion had a life of about five years.

Worth was obviously giving away no secrets in his supply-side explanation of fashion. He added, however, that the stage, which provided him with customers, had 'a great influence over fashion' and that 'one of the most beautiful women' he had ever seen was Mrs Brown-Potter, who had just presented him with a large photograph of herself as Cleopatra in a dress he had designed for her. The Empress Eugénie, his main client during the mid-Victorian years, had by then long disappeared from the scene: but the Worth scenario would have been very different had she not for years been at the centre of it. The first dress he had proposed for her – an elaborate heavy brocade dress – did not appeal to her, but Napoleon III is said to have persuaded her to acquire it on the grounds that the material came from Lyons, where he needed political support, and that the dress would be worn there later that year. It proved a great success, and soon Worth was supplying a gown for each imperial occasion. Since Eugénie not only never wore the same gown twice but expected her ladies to change their costumes twice a day also, she was the perfect customer.

Moreover, given her patronage and such a policy, Worth did not need to advertize. He was not the Empress's only *costumier*: there were many 'purveyors'. Nor did he supply her hats – they came from Mme Vivot and from Mme Lebel – while her riding clothes came from Henry Creed, the Emperor's own London tailor – and d'Orsay's tailor – whom he had employed before Eugénie met Worth. Worth made all her grand clothes, and was always on call, however, and he must have been fascinated to see how, once discarded by the Empress, they often made their way into the theatre.

Eugénie, who loved masquerades off the stage and who believed in luxury, always set the tone for the ladies of the imperial court and for foreign hostesses in Paris, like Princess Pauline von Metternich, after whom Worth named a colour, a shade of green. The naming was deferential: after Bismarck, however, no friend to Napoleon III, Worth gave a different name to a colour – a Bismarck brown. It was for Princess von Metternich that Worth made his first hat, a tiny round hat, in 1860. Hitherto, he had allowed a bonnet-maker to work on the ground floor of his premises, and he had referred all his customers to her. In 1863 he produced his first 'rakish' hat, first worn by Marie. He wanted women to emerge from their bonnets. A later hat for the Pruniers was bolder than the first: it had a broad brim.

It was neither by styles – some thought that particular hat 'mannish' – nor by colours that Worth first made his reputation as a *costumier*. His *forte* was exact measurement. When he first made dresses out of white muslin for his wife-to-be, he insisted on exact fit. And this was one of the points taken up by Dickens, with an extra twist, in *All the Year Round* in 1863. 'Would you believe that, in the latter half of the nineteenth century, there are milliners – man-milliners, like Zouaves – who, with their solid fingers take the dimensions of the highest titled women in Paris – robe them, unrobe them, and make them turn backward and forward before them?' If cage crinolines, then at the height of their fashion – and size – were designed to keep men at a distance from women, the *costumier* or *couturier* was in an exceptionally privileged position to draw near.

Worth did not invent crinolines, although even before they were introduced he had put his trust in 'expanding skirts'. And after having sold large numbers of crinolines, he played an important part in switching fashion away from them after 1864 when he invented the flat-fronted crinoline. He produced his first advertisement in 1868, when he had many rivals, some of them, like himself, from England, and when there were magazines which showed his fashions without attributing them to him. He is said to have read all the magazines – one of the best-known, *La Mode Illustrée*, first appeared in 1864 – while knowing that he had no more depended on advertisement to sell his wares to English ladies, not all of them close to the court, as he did to French ladies at a court which contrasted sharply with that of Queen Victoria. 'When I see my respected friends the Boodles of Bangor clothing themselves at Worth's', wrote an English observer of the court of Napoleon III – his book appeared after Napoleon's fall in 1870 – 'I can only sigh for poor B's banker's book, and feel that the ladies would have been as well dressed, and half as cheaply, at home.'

Worth knew how to deal with all his customers, established or *parvenues*, in a shop that some compared with an embassy. The only thing that customers had to have in common was the ability to pay for his very expensive 'creations', the most expensive of which, he said, was a gown made of lace costing £5,000 at then current prices accompanied by a fur cloak costing £2,000. The best that was on offer was the most exclusive as well as the most expensive.

He was well aware that in Paris he had to dress himself and his premises in the fashion people wanted, knowing, of course, that his own costume mattered as much as the costumes he made for others. 'Black coat, white cravat and batiste shirt-cuffs, fastened at the wrist with gold buttons', wrote Dickens, 'he officiates with all the gravity of a diplomatist who holds the fate of the world locked up in the drawers of his brain.'

But Worth was never the only officiator. Paris had several would-be fashion dictators, each with his own wares to offer and each with his own privileged customers. There were even other Englishmen like Poole and Smallpage, while the Maison Creed continued to dominate male fashions. It was a sign of Worth's skills, and Creed's, that their business not only survived the fall of Napoleon and Eugénie, but became more independent as a result of it. 'Obtenir et tenir' was the motto Worth chose for a coat of arms, and like all successful Englishmen, he had to have a place in the country as well as in the city. Before the fall of Napoleon he acquired an imposing country house overlooking the Seine at Suresnes. There he could indulge in his acquired interest in interior decoration.

Losing the imperial court was not a tragedy for the 'man-milliners'. Creed's son became tailor to the Austrian and Russian Emperors and to the Kings of Spain and Italy, while Worth acquired an even more exotic court than Napoleon III's when Lady Lytton's husband became Viceroy of India in 1876, and all the vice-regal gowns made their way to Calcutta from Paris. 'Worth has sent me a lovely gown from Paris', Lady Lytton wrote in her diary in 1877 on the eve of a great Durbar. It was 'of dark blue velvet, and silk, let in at the sides and the front, stamped blue velvet on white satin ground ... and the bonnet to match, Marie Stuart shape, with pearls round and soft blue feathers.'

Lady Lytton's tastes did not draw her to the 'aesthetic movement', but Worth's did, at least for a time, and he actually escaped from history with some of his tea gowns of the late 1880s and early 1890s. As his biographer, Diana de Marly, has written, 'Aesthetic dress was about as close to timelessness as a costume could get'. Nonetheless, having invented the close-fitting 'Princess line' in 1875, named after Princess Alexandra, wife of the Prince of Wales, Worth returned in 1881 to the 'crinolette', a distinctive bustle, which horrified *Punch*:

> We'll not yield without a struggle, so, fair ladies, do not fret –
> Stick to fourteenth-century fringes and abjure the Crinolette.

Whatever he may have learnt in the National Gallery when he was a boy, Worth was living in the nineteenth, not in the twentieth, century and his views on the bustle triumphed over all opposition. He was successful, too, in establishing in Paris not only a Mourning Department but a Maternity Department. He also looked forward to the twentieth century in presenting spring and autumn collections.

It is appropriate that the last nineteenth-century words on Worth, flamboyant words, should be pronounced by G. A. Sala:

> It is in the Rue de la Paix where the veritable Temple of Fashion is situate, the *sanctum sanctorum* of feminine frivolity, over the more than Eleusinian mysteries of which the great Worth presides in person. The masculine eye has no more chance of penetrating its arcana than those of the *Bona Dea*; yet reports have from time to time reached me that the hierophant combines the suavity of a Granville, the diplomatic address of a Metternich, the firmness of a Wellington, and the prompt *coup d'oeuil* of a Napoleon; and that before him princesses discrown themselves, duchesses tremble, countesses bow their aristocratic heads in mute acquiescence, and citizenesses of the Transatlantic Republic humbly abnegate that self-assertiveness that is one of their most prominent characteristics.

# V

Sala was writing for the *Daily Telegraph*, which was interested in far more than whether or not the sale of *les articles de Paris*, fashion objects, had survived the fall of Napoleon and the Commune. Before and after 1870 news of the world of fashion was communicated through the Press and through an assortment of periodicals specially devoted to it, with fashion plates, which presented the ideal to be arrived at by fashionable women, even if the majority of the readers of many such journals were unable to afford such dresses or hats. News was also communicated, of course, through advertisements and later in the century through mail order catalogues. Worth himself read *Le Follet* (1846–1873), *Le Journal des Demoiselles* (1845–1873), *Les Modes de la Saison* (1873–1878) and *La Belle Assemblée* (1841–1870).

In Britain as early as 1845 *Blackwoods* had referred to 'all the *Recueils des Modes, Petits Couriers des Dames, Belles Assemblées*, etc' along with 'the poet-laureates of Moses and Son, Hyam and Co' and long before 1845 *The Galley of Fashion, The Ladies' Monthly Magazine*, and the *Journal des Dames et des Modes* had been founded in the 1790s. The *World of Fashion*, a profusely illustrated monthly magazine founded in 1824 and surprisingly left out of the *Blackwoods* list, began in 1850 to include in each month's issue a collection of patterns 'in order that ladies of distinction and their dressmakers may possess the utmost facilities for constructing these costumes in accordance with the most approved Taste in the Highest and most Perfect Style of Fashion'. Two years later it changed its title to *The Ladies' Monthly Magazine*.

There was a spate of new publications during the 1850s and 1860s. *Le Monde Élégant* appeared in 1856, *The Ladies' Treasury* in 1858, and *The Queen* in 1863, and many magazines, including *The Young Ladies' Journal* and *The Young Englishwoman* (a Beeton publication) emulated *The World of Fashion* in carrying free paper patterns. *The Graphic* often had 'fashions' columns during the 1860s and 1870s, but it was not until January 1901 that the *Illustrated London News* introduced a regular 'Ladies' Page'. It began appropriately with a reference to Mother Shipton's prophecy that the twentieth century would be the Century of Women.

Before the prophecy could come true there would be an end to many Victorian taboos. In Victorian Britain hats or bonnets had to be worn: underclothes, often lavish, particularly during the 1890s, never had to be mentioned. 'Anatomical facts', to which they drew attention, were 'not things, my dear, that we speak of', as one Victorian lady put it. 'Indeed we try not even to think of them.' Hands were hidden by gloves, and 'drawers' became 'an article of feminine attire, borrowed from the opposite sex'; Lady Chesterfield remarked in the 1850s that the latter were garments 'which all of us wear but none of us talk about'. 'All of us' was an exaggeration: it was not until the 1880s that working-class women began to wear them.

Nor were gloves worn in the same ritualistic fashion kept in papier mâché or leather boxes or stretched with wooden, bone or brass 'stretchers'. As for knickerbockers, originally boys' wear, when they came in for women with the bicycle there were complaints that they were 'horrible' and a demand that they too should be 'tabooed'. 'If I meet a girl dressed in that loud style I feel pleased when she is out of sight; not till then do the modest wildflowers seem to look skywards.'

With rituals, taboos and rebellions, there inevitably went jokes. Some of them centre on buttons, more of them on corsets. Throughout the whole tight-laced Victorian period, early, middle and late, corsets were as obligatory as hats or bonnets, and the adjective has survived them. In the very first years of the reign it was noted that 'women who wear very tight stays complain that they cannot sit upright with them, nay, are compelled to wear night stays when in bed', and in 1877, as James Laver noted, some ladies succeeded in reducing their waists to nineteen inches. In the very last years of the reign, tight lacing was more extensive than ever. *Décolletage* might shock: tight lacing did not. Indeed, one corset of 1901 was called 'the Duchess of Teck', another 'the Duchess of York'. Cunnington quotes Professor T. H. Huxley's terrifyingly non-scientific observation that women, unlike men, did not use the diaphragm in breathing, adding correctly 'in his day they could not'.

The introduction of the blouse – it was said to be derived from the earlier 'Garibaldi' – did not bring with it freedom. As for the older bodice, when it had a low-set sleeve it made it difficult to move the arms. During the late 1870s, when skirts were narrow and tight it was even more difficult to move the legs.

Nor did the move to ready-made women's clothes necessarily bring greater freedom. It was a gradual move: part-made dresses were available even before Queen Victoria came to the throne, but it was not until 1857 that the wholesale firm of Salincourt and Colman of Cannon Street in the City began to supply fashionable London shops with ready-made items. By 1866, Mrs Addley Bourne was advertising in the *Illustrated London News* 'a thousand crinolines at half price, commencing at 5s 11d.' The demand for ready-made clothes was, however, restricted. There were large numbers of poor people who continued to make their own clothes and large numbers of the poorest who, if they were lucky, had them given. The rich still went to their own dressmakers. They also gave their old clothes away.

Boys and men led the way in the move to ready-made clothes, as a larger proportion of income was spent on clothes. An official report of 1889 suggested that workingmen's expenditure on clothes had risen from 6 per cent of wages in 1845 to 8 or 9 per cent: a later report of 1904 put the new figure at 12 per cent. Women lagged behind, and servants, sometimes in the vanguard, were often obliged to wear secondhand clothes with few new things. During the 1890s the *Girls' Own Annual* published articles with titles like 'A Young Servant's Outfit and What to Buy for it': an initial outfit then cost very precisely £3 11s 4¾d.

In provincial Liverpool, where David Lewis was a pioneer of the British retail revolution and offered a wide range of newly-made goods in the department store which he opened in 1856, women's clothes were not on sale for eight years, and thirty years later his biggest department was selling not clothes but a material for making them – velveteen. In London the biggest department at William Whiteley's, the Universal Provider, who set up business in Westbourne Grove in 1863, the year of the Metropolitan Railway, was until 1881 silks: in that year millinery sales were only about a fifth of silk sales, although 'Wonderful Whiteley', as Sala called him, provided facilities for gentlemen 'to go in one attire and come out in another, instantly equipped for wedding, garden party, racecourse, funeral or evening party'.

Much was made of bargains. Thrifty ladies at Lewis's were told that by buying their velveteen at Lewis's they could save five shillings in the pound: less than a year later, the figure had been doubled to ten shillings. Hats were selling at Lewis's during the 1880s for 3s 11d each. They were bought direct from the manufacturers, Lewis claimed in his lavish advertising, and supplied to the public 'at less price than ordinary Hatters who have to pay the middleman for the same quality. This is a very good thing for the public but not so pleasant for the middlemen.' Sale prices were further reduced, as they were later in the century in London. Thus, Swan and Edgar had a 'Great Autumn Sale' in 1899 when a hundred chiffon blouses were offered at £1 1s 6d each – 'usual price £2 2s 0d.' Whiteley never advertised, but he was never short of publicity, and in 1885, soon after a great fire, he produced an *Illustrated Catalogue and General Price List* with twenty-five pages of contents.

Manchester supplied some of Whiteley's products and many of Lewis's, including velveteen. It was Leeds, however, which was the first big centre of the ready-made clothing industry. In the same year as Lewis opened his Liverpool store, John Barran opened his first small factory in Leeds to produce ready-made boy's clothes, a factory where he was to pioneer a new clothing technology, based on sewing machines and hand-cutting. The band-knife, as important an item in this context as the sewing machine, was invented by the engineering firm of Greenwood and Batley: it made it possible to cut through several layers of cloth at the same time.

Barran's business philosophy was as innovative as his technology. 'Our business does not depend on orders', Barran wrote in 1864. 'We make our goods in anticipation and send out our travellers to sell our work.' The Crimean War had given a boost to everything. And other manufacturers followed in Barran's wake. In 1871, 1,523 men and 483 women were employed in the clothing trade, including hat and cap making, which was already carried on in Leeds before Barran started in that city. By the end of Queen Victoria's reign the number of men had multiplied tenfold and the number of women thirtyfold. Some workers had been diverted from other older local textile industries. More were migrants. Many were girls who were said to be able to work the new machines 'with as much ease as a Samson could'. By 1901 more people in Leeds were employed in the clothing industry, including footwear, than in engineering. It was only during the last decades of the century that Leeds forged ahead not only of London but of Manchester, Birmingham and Glasgow. In one respect Leeds was genuinely innovatory. In 1883 the clothing manufacturers, Joseph Hepworth and Sons, set up their own first retail stores. Montague Burton was to follow. Meanwhile, Marks and Spencer had set up their first stall, precursor of the Penny Bazaar, in Leeds market.

Barran's factory was a large one, but there were scores of Leeds workshops also, many of them Jewish, some of them producing hats and caps. Conditions often left much to be desired, but it was claimed that they were better than in the small workshops of London's East End, where the problems of 'sweated labour' began to attract more and more attention, some of it anti-Semitic, during the 1880s and 1890s.

The ready-made clothing trade in London had developed on much the same lines as in the provinces during its early years, with Moses and Sons advertising as early as 1860 – again with men in mind – that they could 'make ready-made suits that Beau Brummel would have been proud to wear at prices that a mechanic could afford to pay'.

Yet Mrs Addley Bourne, with her headquarters in Piccadilly, struck a metropolitan (even an imperial) note in her 'Books of Illustrations', offering 'India outfits' for brides sailing out to be married overseas. Surprisingly, no hats figured in what was in effect an imperial trousseau. One pair of 'French wove corsets' did.

# VI

The advent of the sewing machine had promised a less arduous future everywhere for milliners and dressmakers, and *Punch*, this time with male readers in mind also, had noted in 1853 how 'shirts would feel more comfortable to wear when we shall be enabled to think to ourselves that their manufacture has been ground out of wheels and cogs at small cost, and not out of human nerves and muscles for miserable pay'.

In fact, from the start, machine-workers were paid less than hand-workers and were expected to produce far more in the same time; and already by 1862, long before the problems of 'sweated labour' received widespread publicity, *The Lady's Treasury* talked of the sewing machine itself being 'made chargeable with a weight of care and misery which, if it were human too, would overwhelm it'. In 1901, when there were complaints in the *Illustrated London News* that following Queen Victoria's funeral dressmakers were not preparing urgently needed gowns 'within a reasonable period', the periodical observed 'What with strappings, tackings, cordings, *appliqués* and insertions of lace, and rows of machine-stitching, every dress demands a length of time for its construction that must be as troublesome to the workwomen as it is certainly costly to the wearer'.

It is interesting to note that by then 'machine-stitching' figured as one of the irksome operations. It had certainly not made the lot of workwomen easier in the higher branches of millinery and dressmaking. They remained the hidden figures behind the display, 'fashion's slaves' as Richard Redgrave had perceived them in a remarkable picture exhibited at the Royal Academy in 1846. Already by 1842 there had been 15,000 of them in London alone, most of them under twenty. By 1862 there were 17,500. By the end of the century, as a result of the invention of the sewing machine, there seem to have been few more.

Human or not, the sewing machine usually had a name: one was called 'Golden Rule', a second 'Cottage Queen', and a third 'Dagmar' after Princess Alexandra's sister Dagmar, who married the Czar of Russia. Inside the middle-class home the sewing machine, which could be hired as well as bought, could be thought of as a beautiful as well as a useful object: inside the factory – or the home of the domestic worker – it could be an instrument of exploitation. By 1900 it was being used not only for dresses and hats but for boots and shoes (leather stitching was patented in the United States in 1858); for harnesses; for tents and sails; for books; and for umbrellas.

Charles Booth, who had discussed the subject of the clothing industry in earlier volumes, devoted the first part of Volume VII of his massive *Life and Labour of the People in London* (1896) to dress – with separate chapters on tailors and bootmakers; hatters; milliners, dress and skirt makers; makers of trimmings, artificial flowers, umbrellas, etc; and drapers, hosiers and silk mercers. At the 1891 census there had been more than a quarter of a million within these occupational groups – 90,126 men and 169,892 women – yet within this broad category there had been a contraction of the labour force in particular sections. Thus, while the number of tailors had increased in thirty years from 37,000 to 52,000, the number of hatters had fallen from 7,000 to 5,500. Booth recognized, of course, that much of the hatting industry was provincial. Felt hatting had long been concentrated in the area round Manchester and Stockport, and straw hatting in St Albans (men's) and Luton (women's).

The number of London shirtmakers and seamstresses had fallen too in thirty years from 28,100 to 18,500, while the number of people engaged in Booth's third category – trimmings, artificial flowers, etc – had increased, as had the number of drapers and silk mercers. Meanwhile, Whiteley was no longer unique. The retail revolution had created some very large establishments, among them Peter Robinson's at Oxford Circus, not far from where Worth had first been employed: it became a company in 1895. In 1901 the Robinson store was described – not in an advertisement – as a shop which contained everything for ladies' wear and much also for 'the rest of the family and the household'. There were 'a hundred different shops' there 'under one roof', where 'buyers whose means are modest' were catered for as willingly as 'the wealthiest of customers'.

As Alison Adburgham has written in her *Shops and Shopping* (1964), by 1901 the best London dressmaking and tailoring establishments, smaller and more exclusive than department stores, had acquired 'something of the status held by the couture houses of Paris'. She also drew attention to Lady Jebb's article on 'the ethics of shopping' in the *Nineteenth Century* in 1896 which directly related things to people. In shopping

We are not able to stand against the overwhelming temptations which besiege us at every turn ... We purchase something we want ... but when we get to the shop there are so many things that we never thought of till they presented their obtrusive fascinations on every side. We look for a ribbon, a flower, a chiffon of some sort or another, and we find ourselves in a Paradise of ribbons, flowers and chiffons without which our life becomes impossible.

Booth, who did not deal directly with shops, would not have liked this conception of Paradise. He was more interested in the making of things (and the ethics behind that) than in their advertising, their display and their sale. More and more money now seemed to be devoted to the latter. Thus, in the same year as Lady Jebb's article Whiteley undertook the decoration of Nelson's Column on Trafalgar Day, bringing a steeplejack from the North of England to entwine the column in laurel leaves.

Booth was always at pains to get at the attitudes of the people who actually made things, and he liked to compare. Thus, in boot and shoe-making, an industry relatively late to be mechanized, he noted how the boot and shoe-makers had retained their reputation for radicalism. There had been an employers' lockout in 1895 which was terminated only by intervention by the Board of Trade, and the National Union of Boot and Shoe Operatives, founded in 1874, had revised its rules in 1894 in 'a Socialistic direction'. Bootmakers were worse off, he observed, in terms both of wages and conditions of work than tailors in every part of London, including the East End, where 56 per cent of them lived and worked in crowded conditions. The hatters – 'body makers', 'finishers' and 'scrapers' – who were concentrated in seventeen factories in the neighbourhood of Blackfriars Road, had recently been on strike too, an unsuccessful one, but the best paid of them were paid considerably more than the bootmakers. Perhaps for this reason the apprenticeship system was tenaciously maintained.

According to Booth, the hatmaking trade was 'full of queer customs, chiefly connected with drinking': those hatters who broke with conventions were liable to be 'caulked' (compare undergraduate sconcing) and asked to redeem this offence by wiping it out in beer before any more work was done. (Another custom which Booth did not mention but which had been described by a writer in the *People's Magazine* earlier in the century in 1867 was 'wetting the bargain' when work began on a new order.) There were conventions of dress also. In the hot workrooms where they processed hats, hatters were allowed to discard their hats, waistcoats and ties, but outside the workrooms they were always expected to wear silk hats. One of the most spectacular features of a great 1884 reform demonstration in Hyde Park had been the presence of five hundred hatters all wearing glossy silk hats. Hatters had been prominent in the North of England in Cheshire and Lancashire in the politics of the 1840s, when they were rather patronizingly described to the Children's Employment Commission of 1843 as 'moderately intelligent, but not so much as the handloom weavers'.

NATURALLY THE FEMALE THINKS SHOPPING VERY TIRESOME.

*Superior Creature.* "FOR GOODNESS' SAKE, EDWARD, DO COME AWAY! WHEN YOU ONCE GET INTO A SHOP, THERE'S NO GETTING YOU OUT AGAIN."

*From the collection of* Mr Punch, *1842–1844*

There was a sharp contrast in the late-nineteenth century between the London hatters and the London capmakers, most of the latter Whitechapel Jews working in small workshops with less than twenty fellow operatives. In this case there was no system of apprenticeship and no guarantee of regular employment: indeed Booth thought it 'doubtful whether the workers could obtain more than eight months' employment in the year'. 'Needlehands were paid even when busy only a fifth to a seventh of the wages of hat shapers. Pay in every case, including factory work with machines, was by the piece.' The cap as a symbol, not least as a Jewish symbol, might well have symbolized the trade also.

The kind of comprehensive account presented by Booth enables the 'plight' of the young dressmakers, spotlighted by *Punch* and other periodicals to be examined in proper perspective. 'The condition and social standing of resident milliners and dressmakers', Booth stated, 'were similar to those of shop assistants' and that was where the first comparison had to be made. Factory girls, whose hours were regulated by the Factory Acts, a printed abstract of which had to be exhibited in every factory, came lower in status and in pay: residential milliners and dressmakers, those on whom the spotlight had fallen in 1863, came highest. By 1901 milliners in residence were in a still more superior position, fitters responsible for the work of others: each of them would have under her control a number of bodice or skirt hands, the former being the more skilled of the two.

Yet conditions of residence varied enormously, as they did for shop assistants also, among them the young H. G. Wells, who at the age of fifteen was apprenticed to a drapery emporium at Southsea, and who later embroidered the story in the fascinating opening chapters of his novel *Kipps*. In the West End of London dressmaking was carried on in regular workrooms with a fitter in charge of each room, but in the East End the workroom, showroom and living room were all in one. Conditions were often wretched, far more wretched than those at Southsea.

There was no substantial difference between such late-Victorian social constrasts and the contrasts drawn by Mayhew, although Booth was more precise than Mayhew when he noted, first, that there was always a demand for the 'more ordinary class of dress' in a trade where there were fewer seasonal fluctuations than there were in the trade for fashionable dresses and second, that 'some women prefer the smaller but less variable earnings to be obtained from local employers to the uncertain although larger sums that may be earned in a West End workroom'.

The most impressive workrooms could be as impressive as retail shops, although no workroom could have sounded as impressive as the shop John Barnes opened in Hampstead in 1900 or rather the shop which was opened in his name, for he was drowned in a steamer disaster off Guernsey one year before the opening. No expense was spared with the shopfittings nor with the pneumatic tube which carried the cash. Customers taking the central passenger lift could admire in all the fashion departments the rich Axminster carpeting on the floors. Comfort now meant carpets in the shop as well as in the home.

Yet comfort was not the word that could be most easily used in relation to dress, except in 'rational' dress circles. 'I tried to smarten up my few frocks and tied the strings of my bustle so tightly that it stuck out aggressively and waggled when I walked', the Hon Mrs Peel reminisced of a slightly earlier time in her *Life's Enchanted Cup* (1933). 'We wore high-boned collars which rubbed raw places on our necks; and stiff stays; and we skewered our hats through our hair with long bonnet pins, our gloves were tight and our boots buttoned.' The tailors' dummies in the costume room in Kipps had an easier time – 'lady-like figures, surmounted by black, wooden knobs in the place of the refined heads one might have reasonably expected'.

*IX Sentiment through the post: 'The First Letter'*

*Xa  Famous stamps: Cape of Good Hope triangles –*
*collectors' pieces, last auctioned in 1982*
*b )  A familiar stamp: a Penny Black posted on its*
*first day of issue, 6 May 1840*
*c )  A beautiful stamp: Joubert's Fourpenny*
*Carmine, 1855*

*a*

*c*

*b*

XI  Unissued stamps
a)  Victoria and St George
b)  Albert in his Great Year, 1851: surface-
printed stamps by Henry Archer, a few
experimentally perforated

*XII 'The Hall and Staircase of a Country House', Jonathan Pratt, 1882*

*XIII* '*Away from the World and its Toils and its Cares*', *Benjamin Spiers, 1885*

*XIV  Listening to the phonograph, 1880s (note the hats as well as the machine)*

*XV   The telephone celebrated in song, 1887*

# 8
# Carboniferous Capitalism: Coal, Iron and Paper

Coal alone can command in sufficient abundance either
... iron or ... steam; and coal, therefore, commands this
age.

W. S. JEVONS, *The Coal Question*, 1865

Paper is a material of almost boundless scope.... Whatever has fibre could with skill and enterprise ... be made available for the purpose of manufacturing paper ... and a person asked for information on the subject said, 'I could make beehives of paper, and panels of doors, and, above all, I look forward to build a carriage of paper when the duty is off.'

W. E. GLADSTONE,
House of Commons, February 1860

To a nation like England coal is only another name for gold; and we might even say that the presence of gold in Kent would be of far less importance to London than the existence of coal.

*The Standard*, 1878

The term 'ironmaster' has almost become a synonym in general parlance for a rich man.

J. STEPHEN JEANS,
*The Iron Trade of Great Britain*, 1906

# I

Annie Carey's *The Wonders of Common Things* (1873) did not include tailors' dummies. Yet she had a chapter on 'a Brussels carpet' and another on 'a bit of old iron'. Her book began with the autobiography of a lump of coal and ended with the autobiography of a sheet of paper.

There were no *isms* in her book, impregnated though it was with Victorian values. It was left to Lewis Mumford, writing in a very different vein in the twentieth century, to coin the memorable term 'carboniferous capitalism', a capitalism which depended until late in the reign on the technology of coal and iron – with steam as the agent of power. For Mumford, the colour of coal and iron, black, spread everywhere ... 'the black boots, the black stove pipe hat, the black horse and carriage, the black iron frame of the hearth, the black cooking pots and pans'. He might have added the black and white of the newspaper, now shortened in daily speech to 'paper', although paper came in many colours, including useful brown, as well as in many varieties, from silk thread to cardboard, and in many sizes, some named, like foolscap, after their original watermark. A current catalogue of 1860 listed 681 different kinds of paper, of which no fewer than 60 were forms of 'wrapping, packing' papers with names like 'mill wrappers' and 'sugar purples'. This was an age which demanded a greater and greater supply of paper, another key material, to sustain it.

Mumford made only one reference to paper in his *Technics and Civilization* (1934), but it was an eloquent one. 'A paper world came into existence' as its uses were appreciated, 'and putting a thing on paper became the first stage in thought and action: unfortunately often the last.' Paper, indeed, he believed, 'had a unique part to play in the development of industrialization as "a space-saver", a time-saver, a labour-saver'. Given that it was also the main communications medium (from stamps and stationery to books and banknotes), the demand for it as currency of all kinds was bound to increase dramatically with economic growth and social change. This was still the age of the golden sovereign, but as early as 1875 the *Graphic* commented that 'the germs are daily growing ... of a newer, better sentiment in favour of cheques.'

So, too, was the demand for paper for wrapping and packaging. More paper was thrown away than preserved. Yet it was also the main recording medium, for everything from printed diaries to business accounts, and from newspapers to photographs, and as the years have gone by the paper has aged so that the paper world of the Victorians, as we recover it now, is a faded world. The carbon copies – carbon paper was invented in 1872 – are as faded as the pressed flowers.

Many things were made out of paper, too, if not as many as were made out of iron; not only playing cards or wallpaper, already by 1837 sold in rolls, 'long Elephants', as well as in separate pieces, but trunks and saddles, innumerable articles in papier-mâché, including not only boxes or trays for articles as different as teacups and pens, but chairs, tables – and pianos.

The first papier mâché produced in England in the seventeenth century had been called 'fibrous slab' and in the eighteenth century, when the name of Pontypool was placed on the map, it was frequently associated with heavily glazed japanning. Before it became less fashionable in the late-nineteenth century at a time when the uses of paper were multiplying, a number of firms introduced new techniques, among them Jennens and Bettridge (see page 73), which was to close in 1864. Lampstands, candlesticks and parts of metal bedsteads could now be adorned in papier mâché. In 1852 George Goodman of Birmingham devised a means of transferring designs painted in oils onto paper from engraved plates, and ten years later, as one of the Victorian deceits, Alsager and Neville produced papier mâché that looked like malachite. Earl Granville, speaking in a debate on paper in the House of Lords in 1860, found it a positive merit that paper could be made to look like Moroccan leather and pigskin.

'The simplest form of producing a material for decorative purposes from paper is the best, however', wrote G. W. Yapp in 1878 in his *Art Industry: Furniture, Upholstery and Home Decoration*, 'namely the laying of sheet after sheet upon the object to be modelled, a coat of glue being given to each sheet.' And he took his example not from the home but from the theatre. 'In this way are produced toy masks and particularly those grotesque, gigantic specimens which figure in our pantomimes.' His chapter was called '*Papier-mâché, Carton-Pierre* [who now remembers this?], japan and lacquered ware.'

Like the production of iron and steel, the production of paper itself was radically transformed during the nineteenth century. Much of it was a new product. Yet David Landes has only one reference to it in his wide-ranging study *The Unbound Prometheus* (1969), which deals with technological change and industrial development in Europe 'from 1750 to the Present', and there is only one paragraph on the subject in the late-nineteenth century volume of the *Oxford History of Technology*. Already by the mid-century, the output of the hand-made branch of the industry, relying on vat mills, had fallen to a small share of total output, only 4 per cent in 1860, and machine output had soared ahead. There was a demand for completely different developments in the technology of materials. With increased demand, paper-makers found it difficult in mid-Victorian Britain to obtain adequate supplies of raw materials, including rags, the main source, esparto grass the latest material, and the most unlikely material, rhubarb; and the answer did not come until the processing of chemical wood pulp had been perfected by 1873.

Iron and steel technology and its economic implications have been the subject of many detailed studies. Henry (later, 1879, Sir Henry) Bessemer delivered his famous paper on 'the manufacture of malleable iron and steel without fuel' as early as 1856, and five years after that C. W. (later, 1882, Sir William) Siemens, a German who assumed British nationality, patented a new furnace designed to enable gases evolved during the coke-making process to be used to fire the furnace. But Bessemer's paper was treated 'rather as a good joke than as a reality', and Siemens too found it difficult to sell his ideas. The first of his improved furnaces was installed in a glass, not an iron, works.

This was still the age of wrought iron, and Bessemer seems to have thought mistakenly that the 'malleable iron' he was seeking to make was wrought iron. In fact, it was mild steel, a material which was to supersede iron, which was then used in almost as great a variety of ways, including decoration, as paper; and despite the initial scepticism of his audience, the merits of steel were obvious. The first steel rails were made in Sheffield in 1860 and were laid at Crewe station three years later. Also in 1860 the first Bessemer steel boiler was manufactured. Yet there were difficulties in the process and it needed further research to bring out the properties of iron and steel and to establish techniques of scientific control. Dr John Percy published his *Metallurgy of Iron* in 1864, which received far more attention at the time than the work of Dr H. C. Sorby of Sheffield in his private laboratory on the microscopical properties of the metals.

Because of lack of interest on the part of others, Siemens, scientifically trained unlike most early-Victorian British ironmasters, had to start his own 'sample steel works' in Birmingham, and then years later to found his own concern at Swansea to produce steel, using a new regenerative furnace to convert steel scrap and molten pig iron into steel at lower costs than ever before. His open hearth process did not replace Bessemer's, but it was more adaptable to circumstances. Moreover, the Bessemer process demanded the use of iron with a low phosphorus content, and it was not until it had been adapted by Sidney Gilchrist Thomas, a London police court clerk who studied chemistry in his spare time, that in 1879 the age of steel, during which British businessmen were to face many challenges, was really ushered in.

Thomas's first paper on the subject, describing how to eliminate phosphorus from the converter, had been rejected by the British Iron and Steel Institute in 1875, and although Bolckov, Vaughan and Company of Middlesbrough [see *Victorian Cities*, Ch. 6] at once took up the process under licence, it was Germany, which had a plentiful unexploited supply of phosphoric iron ore, that was to make more use of the invention than Britain, far surpassing Britain in production by 1900. The United States forged ahead also. In 1873 British steel production, 653,500 tons (more than ten times as much as in 1850), was double that of the United States. In 1900 British production was half that of the United States, where there were huge steel plants with fast driven blast furnaces. Iron was now in eclipse in all countries – no more iron rails were made, for example – and as a wide range of steel alloys was produced, Britain was forced to import steel. Both Germany and the United States could produce steel of better quality in a wider range – and at lower cost.

Given such substantial technological change, the paper world of the nineteenth century, itself revolutionized by technology, seemed increasingly separate from the world of iron, where technological change was less evident – and coal. Indeed, the separation seemed even greater than that between London and Birmingham, Swansea or Middlesbrough. By the end of the century, when a limited liability form of business enterprise had become more common and more managers had acquired scientific training, there were large numbers of holders of industrial equities and of City stockbrokers who knew nothing about the inside of a steel plant or of what happened down a mine. They might know a lot about the accounts, of course, and something of the statistics, those of coal being for some of them far more encouraging than those of iron and steel. There Britain seemed to have a lead: coal output in the United Kingdom had risen from 110 million tons in 1870 to over 181 million tons in 1890 and 225 million tons in 1900, while exports had increased four times. Yet because coal, unlike iron and steel, was produced in many different places, widely scattered on the map of 'the coalfields', they might have even less of a notion of its production than they had of iron and steel unless they were concerned with its distribution by rail or by sea.

For Bagehot, iron and paper were bracketed together almost as obviously as iron and coal, which were often produced in the same areas, sometimes by the same firm. 'If the iron trade ceases to be as profitable as usual', Bagehot wrote in *Lombard Street* in 1873, 'less iron is sold; the fewer the sales the fewer the bills; and in consequence the number of iron bills in Lombard Street is diminished.' For J. A. Hobson in *The Evolution of Modern Capitalism* (1894), the scene had shifted across the Atlantic to the Carnegie Steel Company and its control of the Lake Superior ores. Nonetheless, for both Bagehot and for Hobson there were fluctuations in coal and steel production which could not be explained in technological terms. Bagehot believed that it was part of the essence of 'carboniferous capitalism' that Lombard Street was 'often dull, sometimes excited', a sign that at a distance iron works and coal mines and even paper mills, little visited by London men of money, might be idle or busy and their workers unemployed or working overtime; and Hobson thought in terms of over-production and under-production. For Marx 'the superficiality of political economy' had shown itself in the fact that 'it looks upon the expansion and contraction of credit, which is a mere sympton of the periodic changes of the industrial cycle, as their cause'.

There were doubtless many people who mistook symptoms for causes, but most contemporaries knew just as well as Marx how much they depended, in particular, on real 'black diamonds' in good times and bad – not only on the 'Wallsend' in their own grates, but on coal of every kind in the factories. 'Coal alone can command.' All else, including iron, seemed to depend upon it. Even Whiteley set up a coal department in his store. It was in considering 'the coal question', for him the major national question, that the economist

W. S. Jevons, son of a Liverpool iron merchant and a keen student of industrial fluctuations, observed in 1865 how 'the momentous repeal of the corn laws [in 1846] throws us from corn upon coal. It marks the epoch when coal was finally recognized as the staple produce of the country. It marks the ascendancy of the manufacturing interest [and here he was both exaggerating and leaving out the bankers and the brokers], which is only another name for the development of the use of coal'.

At this point, Jevons, who had been drawn to the idea of investigating economics mathematically when he read Lardner's *Railway Economy* (1850), did not mention railways, although these were associated with the same 'epoch' and, because they demanded what seemed to be enormous quantities both of coal and of iron, had quickened the pace of economic growth. Nor did he mention 'railway paper' which had appealed to a wide group of investors. By contrast coal production and iron production had not appealed greatly to shareholders. Indeed, in the absence of limited liability they had not been organized for the most part in such a way as to depend on shareholders. *The Economist* was right to claim, therefore, in 1845, two years before a financial crisis created largely by railway speculation, that it was the railway which had 'introduced commercial feelings to the firesides of thousands'.

Jevons left out textiles too, and Lancashire millowners, committed to the claims of cotton, might not have concurred with his talk of 'corn upon coal' – particularly since it was the voice of Manchester, 'cottonopolis', usually a distinctive voice in national life, that had been decisive in 1846. Yet Manchester knew that textile production depended on steam – and on coal – far more, indeed, than the miscellaneous 'iron trades', and Jevons was a tutor at Owen's College, Manchester when he wrote his *The Coal Question*. In longer perspective than his, Landes was able to extend the Jevons' metaphors of corn and coal in his study of growth and call coal 'the bread of industry'.

A symbol of the new 'epoch', Jevons proclaimed, had been the new London Coal Exchange, opened in great state in 1849 by the Prince Consort. The royal party had arrived by river, the last such royal arrival in Queen Victoria's reign. The young Princess Royal, later – and briefly – to be Empress of Germany, had been a member of the party, hearing her father in his carefully prepared speech salute the advance of British industry and the place of coal in the economy. Unlike most other Exchanges, the Coal Exchange – with its inlaid wooden floor in the design of a mariner's compass and its handsome cast iron rotunda and dome – was open to the public. Described by the architectural historian, Professor Russell Hitchcock, as 'the prime city monument of the early Victorian period', the Exchange incorporated paintings by Frederick Sang of colliers, collieries, miners' tools and trees fossilized into coal, and it is sad that it was wantonly destroyed in 1962.

During its most active years, which preceded the dramatic development of railway trade in coal – only 55,000 tons of coal arrived in London by rail in 1849 – the Exchange conducted its bargains verbally on the basis of pit prices, and for even the largest contracts the only record was a note on a paper market slip of an entry in the dealer's book. Almost all the coal on offer was British, another difference between this and London's other commodity exchanges, which often dealt in produce originating in remote parts of the world.

The statistics of coal had been very carefully recorded since 1845 in, of all places, London's Jermyn Street by a Keeper of Mining Records who held the post for thirty-seven years, Robert Hunt, formerly Secretary of the Cornwall Polytechnic Society and Professor of Experimental Science in the Royal School of Mines: he was also editor of Ure's *Dictionary of Arts, Manufactures and Minerals*. The statistics of iron were far less well kept, and those of paper less well still. Yet it is recorded that the number of people employed in the paper-making industry had increased from less than 6,000 in 1841 to more than 13,000 in 1861, the year when the paper duties, which controlled newspaper prices, were finally repealed fifteen years after the repeal of the corn laws. And the number of people engaged in paper making, printing and publishing was to increase nearly three times between then and the end of Queen Victoria's reign, to reach a figure of 212,000. The newspaper with the largest circulation in 1861, the *Daily Telegraph*, which had reduced its price to a penny in 1856, claimed that repeal would 'benefit every class of literature'. It did.

## II

The history of publishing is still in its infancy, but there is often ample information about particular books. One of them, Annie Carey's *The Wonders of Common Things*, began as did many Victorian children's books, with four children sitting round the fire on a cold winter's afternoon. Arthur, aged 12, asks his sister Adelaide to tell them a fairy story. But first Edith, aged 11, tells 'Addy', 'Do break up that ugly lump of coal on top of the fire ... Make a blaze; I like to see the flames jumping about: they always seem to be alive.'

Addy is about to oblige when a voice from the middle of the ugly lump of coal asks if he might tell his own fairy story, the story of his own life, and the children, well used to what happens in fairy stories, are not unduly surprised. They settle down comfortably to listen as he explains that he comes from a far older family than any which they had read about in their histories. 'Ages and ages before the Conqueror's great grandfather was born, my family flourished.' There had been a time when instead of 'lying "a great ugly lump", I and my friends occupied large tracts of land, where we were lords of

*Fire gazing: 'A Lump of Coal', 1870*

the soil and enjoyed a most regal life' and where there were 'grand creatures about at my feet'. And then for centuries they had been in 'a sleepy state' – many fairy tales were invoked here – until the busy Englishmen of the nineteenth century 'sank mines ... came, saw, captured' and brought them up 'nolens, volens to the surface of the earth.' 'The place where I again revisited the outer world', the voice continues, 'is called, I believe, Wigan. It seemed to me a most dreary place, as unlike as possible to my reminiscence of my forest home.'

Not surprisingly, by the end of the story the lump of coal feels his constitution giving way, and he actually asks to be broken up to 'brighten the children's darkness' as Edith had asked. But before that he had made many telling points while 'smoking a little', an activity well understood by the children who had concluded that since their elder brother Reginald would never allow them to talk when he was smoking – he said he was busy – smoking and deep thinking must always go together.

The unnamed lump of coal carefully described *his* chemical composition and explained his economic value – 'I wonder where would have been your railways, your steamships, and the majority of your great inventions, if it had not been for our services'. When Addy told him knowingly that he was 'thoroughly destroyed' by his own combustion, he added a qualifying *riposte* on physics, what he called the operation of 'that wonderful chemist, *Heat*. I burn, and in burning I change into a number of different things ... Clever as your race is, there is one thing that none of you can do. No one can *destroy* the least thing that exists.' 'Not even', he went on, 'with a poker.'

This remarkable anthropomorphic children's fairy tale makes the very most of the anthropomorphism. 'I am black', the lump of coal tells Edith, 'but I think that you might have spared the adjective "ugly"' – he also objected to the word 'inflammable' – 'for if you will look carefully at me you will see that my blackness is not a dull heavy darkness, but that it shines ... That buckle at your waist, Miss Adelaide, is made of a relation of mine called "jet" [turned into jewels at Whitby in Yorkshire], and shows you what a real true polish some *black* things possess.' Like iron, which had many decorative uses, and like paper, which itself could serve as decoration, coal, too, had its aesthetics as well as its economics. Indeed, the lump of coal reminded Edith that for all his blackness it was out of his kind that 'those delicate [*sic*] colours, mauve and magenta, are formed.'

Annie Carey was fully aware of the didactic character of her fairy tale. Indeed, she emphasized it in her preface. All her statements, she declared, were 'in conformity with the "science of the day"', and she was seeking to lay 'foundations at an early age for the further pursuit of scientific knowledge to arrive at "the truth of things"'. Knowledge was 'progressive', and the acquisition of the right 'habit of mind' at an early stage – the power of perceiving clearly, discriminating carefully, and investigating patiently – would avoid 'surprise, suspicion, intolerance and general perturbation' in the future. 'Thanks to the clear teachings of many of our scientific leaders, the rising generation will not have to stumble and blunder into fuller light and broader paths, but may walk into them steadily and fearlessly.'

There was a superb optimism in such an expectation, as striking even then as the optimism of Macaulay. It was expressed for a different audience in the preface to the second 1887 edition of Robert Hunt's comprehensive study, *British Mining: A Treatise on the History, Discovery, Practical Development and Future Prospects of the Metalliferous Mines of the United Kingdom*, which was sold at a 'popular price' so that it might be read by 'young miners'. Meanwhile, throughout the country there were large numbers of children who were dreamily contemplating fire in the grate. In her delightful book *A Nineteenth Century Childhood* (1924) Mary MacCarthy, daughter of an Eton master, described how in the first house in which she lived 'at least twelve fires roared up before chimneys all day ... I can hear the coal being shovelled and shot and poured and heaped on by servants at intervals throughout the day. My mother even had two fireplaces filled with red-hot coal in her long bedroom, to muse by.'

Robert Louis Stevenson's 'Armies in the Fire' dwelt on the dreams or the nightmares:

> Blinking embers, tell me true
> Where are those armies marching to?
> And what the burning city is
> That crumbles in your furnaces?

Other writers, anticipating Gavin Stamp, dwelt on the realities, although even these could be deemed romantic. 'Coal contributes an important element to the character of the room as it is responsible for a fine layer of ash everywhere ... Dust ... is an integral part of the Englishman's room.'

Nonetheless, dust, if not ash, could suggest decay, and there was a note of pessimism about the coal industry during the 1860s and 1870s, when there were many economists who contemplated the possible exhaustion of Britain's indigenous coal supplies following an inevitable increase in costs. Annie Carey's lump of coal burnt out, but there were more coals in the skep. What would happen if there was no more coal in the national skep or if it could cost so much that firms would not fill their skeps with it?

The problem seemed more serious than the rhythms of the trade cycle: if capitalism in Britain, in particular, ceased to be carboniferous, how could it survive? Jevons, who was to develop his own theory of the trade cycle, estimated that in 1851, 57 million tons of coal were produced by 216,000 coal miners – 264 tons per miner: by 1871, 117 million tons were being produced by 314,000 miners – 373 tons per head. There had been more than a tenfold increase in production, he maintained, since the beginning of the century. Yet while man's increasing skill and efficiency seemed still to be triumphing over 'nature's reluctance' – a very different way of looking at the 'coal question' from that of a century later – it was already felt in many quarters that inevitably there would be 'retrogression'.

By the beginning of the last decade of the century, the statistics of growth seemed to substantiate such predictions, many of which looked to the distant future. By 1891, when 517,000 miners were producing 185 million tons of coal, there had been an unmistakable fall in the number of tons produced per head to 306. Beyond the limits of Queen Victoria's reign, the figure per head was to fall to 266 in 1913, the year when there was a record production of coal, 292 million tons. Then, and later, it was not 'limits to natural bounty', but man's declining productivity and/or the inefficiency of management that were to be blamed for the figures, more and more of them comparative statistics between nations, like those of iron and steel.

Jevons's *The Coal Question* had a striking sub-title – 'an inquiry concerning the progress of the nation and the probable exhaustion of our coal mines', and he gave it an even shorter label in 1864 when he wrote to his brother that he had been 'grinding up' the 'extensive subject' of 'coal exhaustion' in the British Museum. 'We cannot long continue our rate of progress', the author warned his readers in 1865, calculating that consumption in the previous ten years had been half as great as that of the previous 72 years. Unlike geologists, such as Edward Hull and E. W. Binney, founder of the Manchester Geological Society, Jevons, who was himself interested both in geology and in chemistry, did not concentrate on the physical supply of coal. As an economist of promise, who had studied gold before he turned to coal, he concentrated rather on the economics. 'It is not the exhaustion of the mines, but the period for which they can be profitably be worked, that merits earnest and immediate attention.' 'Should the consumption multiply for rather more than a century at the same rate', he went on to argue, 'the average depth of our coal mines would be 4,000 feet [no premonition of open-cast coal mining here] and the average price of coal much higher than the highest price now paid for the finest kinds of coal.' The *Daily Telegraph* was the main newspaper which echoed the 'note of alarm' that Jevons sounded.

Jevons was right about prices and costs, but wrong about both demand and output. Extrapolation might point to a coal consumption figure of 2,607.5 million tons in 1961 if the rate of growth in demand were sustained, and although Jevons did not suggest that so large an amount would be produced, he would have been amazed by late-twentieth century figures of output – for example, only 127 million tons in 1980. He was also wrong in foreseeing continuing large-scale exports of coal, as did his son, who in his large book on *The British Coal Trade*, published in 1915, concluded that they would go on increasing in the future at the same rate. His was still a Victorian vision. 'I cannot but think that our children's children will live to see a vast export trade in coal – much more than double the present figure.'

For Jevons, the father, who as we have seen in Chapter 5 was to argue the case in 1871 for a tax on matches, the idea of taxing coal exports also required discussion. The issue was, of course, far more serious, an issue of 'almost religious importance'. Matches struck light: coal provided heat as well as light. As Jevons put it in a letter to Gladstone, it had been a 'growing *power* for two centuries or more, and is now growing faster than ever, assisted by the improvement of the engine and of furnaces which render it a more economical agent.' It had also balanced Britain's accounts. 'Coal is to us the one great raw material which balances the whole mass of the other new material we import, and which we pay for either by coal in its crude form or by manufactures which represent a greater or less quantity of coal consumed in the steam engine or the smelting furnace.'

There were further human balances to take into account also. Without coal, 'we must either sink down into poverty – [Jevons referred to 'the laborious poverty of early times'] – adopting wholly new habits, or else witness a constant annual exodus of the youth of the country seeking employment prospects in lands which are better endowed by nature.'

Jevons no more foresaw late-twentieth century immigration than he foresaw open-cast mining; and he dismissed far too quickly a letter in *The Times* by an anonymous Welsh 'Coalowner', who pointed out that 'there are thousands of acres in the centre of South Wales' with coal supplies yet untouched and that the idea of our coal supply 'running out' was 'simply ridiculous'. Jevons did foresee, however, that the cost of foreign supplies would become relevant. 'We cannot now produce coal, even with the aid of the best engineering skill and of abundant trained labour, nearly so cheap as it can be had on the banks of the Ohio.'

He referred too to the Ruhr and to the inter-relationship between the production of coal and the production of iron there: faced by German competition, 'the crude iron manufacture' would be the first British loss, and before long 'our iron manufactures' would also be 'underbid by the unrivalled iron and coal resources of Pennsylvania'. Coupling coal and iron together as Germans were to do in their post-1870 industrial revolution, he looked back to Locke, who had written that 'he who first made known the uses of iron may be truly styled the Father of Art and the Author of Plenty', and referred to the first pages of Samuel Smiles's *Industrial Biography* where Locke was brought up-to-date.

Jevons also included digressions on machinery and machine tools and on the Britannia Bridge, 'our truest national monument', and a chapter on 'the iron trade' in which he estimated that the making and working of iron demanded between one-third and one-fourth of the current yield of coal. For this reason, given the pressure on coal supplies, 'as our iron furnaces are a chief source of our power in the present, their voracious consumption of coal is most threatening as regards the future. The iron manufacture must soon burn out the vitals of the country.' He had less to say about the domestic uses of coal, which already accounted for a fifth of British consumption, but he did note what for him was a revealing bracketing of coal and paper. 'A curious exchange had recently sprung up of Newcastle coal for Spanish or Esparto grass, a material much required for *The Times* newspapers and the vast masses of recent periodical literature.'

Jevons could be ponderous when he dealt with such economic linkages – he lacked Adam Smith's power to make them sound exciting – and he was rather too sure when he claimed that 'the reasoning' in his book was almost unanswerable, 'except when I have left the question open'. Yet, after all, he was to be appointed in 1886 to a new chair of Logic and Mental and Moral Philosophy of Owen's College in 1866, and there were times when he was prepared to change his style – back to the 'flowery' style which, in his own words, he once felt that he had outlived. Indeed, he did not see, as he put it in 1862, why 'one kind of writing and thinking may be inconsistent with other kinds'. Thus, when describing with enthusiasm the 'ice-machines' which had been exhibited at the Paris Exhibition of 1862, he could become lyrical. By such coal-using machines, he declared in italics, *'we may make fire in the hottest climate and produce the cold of the Polar regions!'* This was Jevons's fairy story, even if it was a story with a warning, a warning already delivered by the great von Liebig, who had written that England would inevitably lose its superiority as a manufacturing country 'inasmuch as her vast store of coals will no longer avail her as an economical source of motive power'.

Jevons concluded that an economic crisis in Britain would preclude any general energy crisis unless coal consumption were curtailed or a substitute source of energy found in Britain itself. He was not arguing that there were general 'limits to growth' but rather that Britain in particular should look to the need for 'economy of power'. As far as the general situation was concerned, he echoed the remark of Sir William Armstrong to a British Association meeting in Newcastle in 1863:

> The phase of the earth's existence suitable for the extensive formation of coal appears to have passed away for ever: but the quantity of that invaluable mineral which has been stored up throughout the globe for our benefit is sufficient (if used discreetly) to serve the purposes of the human race for many thousands of years. In fact, the entire quantity of coal may be considered as practically inexhaustible.

In dealing with possible substitutes for coal in Britain itself, Jevons was sceptical, even pessimistic, as was the author of an article called 'Coal and Smoke' in the *Quarterly Review* in 1866. A substitute for coal, they both thought, was 'chimerical'. Jevons admitted that there might be 'some wholly unlooked for discovery' but he pooh-poohed the 'high-sounding phrases' of Dionysius Lardner, who in his *Treatise on the Steam Engine* had prophesied that 'the steam engine itself, with the gigantic powers conferred upon it by immortal Watt, will dwindle into insignificance in comparison with the energies of nature which are still to be revealed'. Yet that was precisely what was to happen in the age of the turbine, already in use by the 1880s, and of the electric generator. (See page 404.)

Jevons maintained generally that there were more 'fallacious notions' in the air about the possibilities of electricity than about any other subject. 'Electricity, in short, is to the present age what perpetual motion was to an age not far removed.' As for petroleum – 'What', he asked, 'is Petroleum but the Essence of Coal, distilled from it by terrestrial or artificial heat?' Its natural supply was 'far more limited and uncertain than that of coal'. There was no intimation here of the future role of oil. Nor, for Jevons, could there be any return to the age of wood, wind and water, what Lewis Mumford was to call 'the paleotechnic age' – 'the forests of an extent two and a half times exceeding the area of the United Kingdom would be required to produce even a theoretical equivalent to our annual coal production'. Jevons was writing, of course, before forests were destroyed to produce newspapers and long before 'acid rain'. He included a brief note on solar energy, however – sun spots were to interest him when he tried to explain the trade cycle – but, having spent five years of his life in Australia between 1854 and 1859, he observed sensibly that 'this island would not be endowed as happily with the conditions of this new force [sunshine] as coal' and asked 'Why should not Russia or Africa or Australia happen to be endowed with the peculiar conditions of this new force just as this island is endowed with coal?'

As far as Britain was concerned, coal for Jevons was 'like a spring, wound up during geological ages for us to let down'. 'In our seams' – and here his language was not very different from Annie Carey's – 'we have peculiar stores of force collected from the sunbeams for us.' 'In burning a single pound of coal there is force developed equivalent to that of 11,422,000 pound weight falling one foot.' 'Coal is the naturally best source of power as air and water and gold and iron are, each for its own purposes, the most useful of substances and such as will never be superseded.'

For all the note of pessimism in much of the writing about Britain's reduced coal supplies – a fact welcomed by William Morris – Jevons in the last resort set out not to depress but to stimulate. Indeed, there was a challenge in his concluding and highly rhetorical reflections. 'The wish could surely never rise into the mind of any Englishman that Britain should be stationary ... rather than a growing and world-wide influence as she is.' Jevons was no Little Englander, and when he had visited the Great Exhibition several times in 1851 he had been just as much impressed as Morris had been shocked: he called it a 'place of all places'. His manifest enthusiasm then and later did not impress all his friends. Thus, when he sent a copy of his book to the astronomer Sir John Herschel, Herschel replied that he had given Britain's 'commercial and manufacturing supremacy' too long to run. The transfer of power to America was inevitable. '*Longe absit* – but it *must* come', Herschel claimed, 'and *I think you have been merciful in giving us another century to run.*' It would have been useful to have had a comment on Herschel's statement from another distinguished Victorian to whom Jevons sent a copy of his book – Lord Tennyson, who was interested in the run of centuries. He replied simply, however, that 'the question ... has great interest for me' and that he looked forward to hearing what Jevons had to say about it.

John Stuart Mill spoke on Jevons's 'admirable' book in Parliament in April 1866 in the budget debates, picking up Jevons's point that the country ought to reduce or to pay off the national debt 'before the time of exhaustion, and correspondingly the diminution of our national income arrives'. *The Times* in June 1866 was as grim as Herschel. If the British coalfields were exhausted, there would follow increasingly 'diminution of population, decrease in wealth, and declension in power. We may dislike to contemplate these gloomy consequences, yet come they will, as surely as sunrise tomorrow.' Britain would cease to be 'a great manufacturing nation', and as a consequence be no longer able to maintain its present position in the world. 'We may boast of the mental and bodily qualities which distinguish the Anglo-Saxon and glory in the valorous achievements of our forefathers ... we may delight in green pastures and golden cornfields, and, like a certain noble lord, look forward with satisfaction to the day when our soot-begrimed Manchester and Birmingham shall have crumbled into ruins and the plough shall pass over their sites ... but without great wealth (based on coal) we shall have remained in comparative obscurity.'

Jevons himself clearly recognized that 'in our Victorian age we may owe indirectly to the lavish expenditure of our material energy far more than we can really perceive', but he implied throughout his book that the expenditure had been worthwhile. Coal had provided '*the peculiar material basis* of our manufacturing supremacy'. 'In fearlessly following our instincts of rapid growth we may develop talents and virtues, and propagate influence which could not have resulted from slow restricted growth however prolonged.'

Herschel, who thought that Jevons made a mistake in appearing to disparage Francis Bacon's long-term vision – and apparently preferred von Liebig as an authority – took a different view. 'The enormous and outrageously wasteful consumption of every ... article that the Earth produces ... in two centuries, if it go in the present increasing ratio ... [and among] populations calling themselves civilized – but in reality luxurious and selfish ... would even make the Earth a desert.' 'A very ugly day of reckoning is impending sooner or later.'

The Conservative politician Edward Henry Stanley (later fifteenth Earl of Derby), addressing the British Association, refused to take sides between those who were 'sanguine' about coal and those who followed Jevons. Mill, however, thought and stated in Parliament that Jevons had 'exhausted' the subject – the right verb – while Gladstone, who thanked Jevons for sending him a copy of *The Coal Question*, was more on Jevons's side than on the side either of the 'sanguine', like Hull, or of the 'despondent', like Herschel. The country, he believed, needed – and would get – more and more coal, and it would be 'sheer folly' to constrain coal consumption by law. 'Until the great work of the liberation of industry was in the main affected' it would have been premature or even wrong 'to give too much prominence' to the coal question. 'Nor do I regard that liberation as yet having reached the point at which we might say that we will not cease to make a remission of taxes a principal element and aim in finance.' Yet Jevons, he admitted, had been right to draw attention to the question and his book was 'a masterly review of a vast, inlaid boundless subject'. Doubtless Gladstone was particularly pleased that Jevons had called one of the chapters in his book 'Taxes and the National Debt'.

Jevons, who like Gladstone and most economists was an undoubting free trader, returned to taxation later, objecting in 'the strongest terms' in 1865 to the idea of introducing an excise or export tax on British coal, a tax which had been deliberately prohibited in the Anglo-French commercial treaty of 1860, negotiated by the great free trader Richard Cobden. Such a tax was objected to also in the voluminous Report of the Royal Commission on Coal, headed by the Duke of Argyll, which was set up in 1866, on a motion of the Member of Parliament Hussey Vivian, welcomed by Jevons, 'to enquire as to the quantity of coal consumed in various branches of manufacture and to determine the probable duration of fossil fuel'.

There was a financial 'panic' in 1866, sparked by the banking failure of Overend, Gurney and Company. Yet by the time that the Commission reported – in 1871 – the greatest of all Victorian booms had followed, and coal prices, closely related to iron prices, were reaching record heights. Indeed, two years later a Select Committee of the House of Commons was set up to examine 'the causes of the present dearness and scarcity of coal'. Middlesbrough was one of the places which provided crucial evidence: 'There was not a single [business] house in Middlesbrough that had not six months' orders on hand at 45s to 47s a ton, when pig iron was selling at nearly120s; but as it was up to 120s, they were glad to give even 41s a ton for the coke in order to profit by the increase in the price of iron.'

The Committee accepted as a fact that coal prices would fluctuate, like any other prices, within the system of 'carboniferous capitalism' and that there would be booms and slumps: 'The coal trade has been no exception to the violent fluctuations which arise when the ordinary course of business is disturbed by unusually high prices, panic demands for the moment, and speculations for their rise and fall.' In the long run, moreover, it argued, the effect of high prices would be to stimulate economies in the use of coal. The German-born engineer Siemens, who pioneered the new open hearth furnace, had estimated that up to a half of Britain's coal consumption was wastage and believed that a rise in the price of coal would serve as 'the great incentive to economy in all cases'. Jevons himself noted that the French, who had far less coal at their disposal than the British, were more concerned about waste than 'we who are careless of it'. Indeed, an article in the *Journal des Débats* had welcomed the setting up of Argyll's Royal Commission.

Both the Commission and the Committee refused to indulge in 'speculative conjectures' about long-term trends, but they were in agreement with Jevons on two points – first, that the demand for coal was linked to the movements of the population, and, second, that output per man was falling. They illustrated their argument with statistical tables, some of them drafted by the Keeper of the Mining Records, and with forecasts of likely export demand, which they believed would continue to increase in the short run but not in the long run: 'The more effective working of the known coalfields of Europe will probably prevent any considerable increase in the future exportation of British coal.'

For this and for other and more general reasons, they were opposed, like Jevons, to an export duty. Such a duty would be 'imposed upon the assumption that England, having, in regard to coal, a home supply which gives this country an advantage over others, should seek by legislative means to keep it for herself and deprive other nations of its use in a degree proportionate to the assumed effect of the duty; but England, by the growth of its population, and the expansion of its industry, yearly becomes more dependent on other nations, not merely for the supply of the materials of industry, which are the indigenous products of other countries but for the supply of fuel for the people'. If Britain abandoned free trade, why should not others follow? In addition, much of the exported coal was carried in British ships or in foreign ships bringing useful produce, including raw materials, to Britain. Finally, in the recent years of price increase, if an export duty had been imposed, it would not have 'mitigated' the home demand for coal and the consequent rise in prices. It might, however, have seriously reduced overseas demand for British manufactured products.

It is interesting that Jevons's brother, then living in New York, favoured an export tax, and in 1872, when there was a shortage of British coal, wrote in a letter to his brother how there were signs of a shift in the export trade to the Americans: 'A great many vessels are now being loaded at Baltimore and Georgetown with coal for British steamers in Brazil and the East.' Jevons himself may have changed his mind on the idea of the tax by 1875. Before that, however, there had been one eloquent and well-known voice in favour of an export tax, for in 1873 Sir Rowland Hill, pioneer of cheap postage, discussed in the next chapter of this book, prepared a paper for the Statistical Society, succinctly presenting a five-point case:

1st It is universally admitted that the preservation – as far as practicable – of our coalfields is a matter of vital importance.

2nd It is established, on unquestionable authority, that there has hitherto been an enormous waste in the consumption of coal; and

3rd That the most efficient means of checking such waste is a higher price on the article.

4th Of course, however, as shown by recent experience [during the mid-Victorian boom] a high price – unmitigated by other measures – is itself a cause of much suffering.

305

5th It is thought practicable, however, so to modify other fiscal arrangements, that the present high price may be continued, and even increased, but with positive benefit to the community.

There was a fascinating addendum to the five points. Having stated them in his paper, Hill added that he had no longer 'the strength for controversy or even for correspondence'. Indeed, he had not had the strength to attend the meeting, and his paper was read for him by his son-in-law.

This was a very different Hill from the young Hill we shall encounter in the next chapter. Yet if Hill had hoped to avoid controversy, he was wrong. Immediately there was sharp criticism at the Statistical Society meeting, with one of the speakers, the formidable Professor Leoni Levi, regretting that Hill should have 'given the authority of his great name to a scheme so futile and erroneous as that advocated in the paper.' Jevons himself had been made a Fellow of the Statistical Society in 1866, but does not seem to have been present: as author of books on logic as well as political summary, he would have repudiated Hill's ideas on both logical and economic grounds.

Hill had suggested that a coal tax of 5s. 1d. per ton would justify 'the remission of all taxes save those on tobacco, spirits, wine and malt liquor and, further, as respects the last two, would warrant an abatement of the present duty by one half', while a coal tax of 10s. per ton might supersede all other imperial taxation whatever. The income tax, which Gladstone hoped would go, would be part of the remission. And Hill had an even more shocking suggestion. A duty of 6s 1d per ton would 'enable the legislators not only to repeal other taxes, but also in the course of fifty years to extinguish the national debt', the nation's great paper burden.

Hill, more interested in domestic consumption of coal than Jevons, framed his appeal directly to the domestic consumer of coal. He would not only save in taxes, but would be constrained to reduce his own bills for fuel. A rise in price would force him or her to use coal better: 'Dr Arnott's stove, one of the many excellent devices for which the public is indebted to its benevolent inventor, an apparatus obviously suited to halls and corridors, has been in use for nearly half a century. My own experience of its benefits extends over more than fifty years.' Railway charges and gas prices might have to go up, but the railways might obtain a 'special compensation' and the gas companies would be further encouraged to make money from the many chemical by-products of coal. Science would be stimulated as well as industry.

In the absence of Hill, his son-in-law elaborated the consumer theme which had been so effective in the campaign for cheap postage. Even an excise tax of 1s a ton would enable the Chancellor of the Exchequer to take off 'the taxes on tea, coffee, sugar etc and would give us a free breakfast table'. 'Who is there here, or how many are there in this Kingdom,' he asked, 'who would not gladly pay even 5s per ton extra on coal to be relieved of all taxes whatever, except those on spirits and tobacco and half those on wine and beer?'

The meeting was not convinced any more than the House of Commons had been convinced by Lowe's case for a duty on matches, and the knowledgeable and responsible Robert Hunt, who was present, questioned Hill's further argument that Britain's coal stocks were in danger of exhaustion, taking up the argument set out by 'Coalowner' in *The Times* in 1866. It was known that in South Wales alone there were seams of coal of a depth of nearly twice 4,000 feet. 'It would be a most lamentable thing,' Hunt argued, 'to check for a single moment, by anything like taxation, the produce of the great coalfields.'

Another member of the Society stated firmly that since he regarded the present high price of coal as 'a serious national calamity', he felt that 'a tax upon coal would be a tax on the very life and soul of our national industry. If it had not been for the almost unequalled prosperity of trade during the past two years, the high price of coal would have caused unspeakable hardship. Instead of endeavouring to maintain present rates, Englishmen should devote all their attention to the means which were likely to reduce the price, otherwise our manufacturing supremacy was likely to be taken from us.' A third member was equally forthright, adding for good measure that 'iron masters would be exceedingly glad if anyone would show *them* a means of encouraging savings in coal'. 'The proposed tax was one on a raw material and such taxes had been condemned by all political economists.'

The most interesting participant in the discussion was the social statistician, Dudley Baxter, best known for his statistical breakdown of the social composition of the British population. A tax on coal, he maintained, would 'engender great discontent among the poor: it would cause a general rise of prices, and English manufacturers would find themselves undersold in foreign markets'. And Baxter then moved back, as Jevons had done, to the corn/coal parallel. 'A coal famine was very like a corn famine. It came in peculiar ways and would be quietly endorsed as arising from natural causes, but a famine produced by legislative enactments was a different thing altogether and it would be an impossibility to maintain such laws.'

Baxter added sensibly that he did not think that Jevons's extrapolation of the figures of coal consumption was of much relevance: 'the present rate of increase' would not last very long. Likewise, Sir James Anderson did not believe operatives would leave Britain, as Jevons had suggested, 'no matter what became of our home supply of coal'. For Baxter 'the problem for this country to consider was not so much whether or not a tax shall be put upon coal, as how England shall maintain the supremacy of her manufactures'.

One point not made in the discussion at the Statistical Society, but sometimes made very strongly outside it, particularly towards the end of the century, was that, taxed or not, the export of coal was a sign of national weakness, not of strength. A nation which exported coal, it was maintained, was 'not really selling anything': it was 'draining itself of its life blood'. Again foreign comparisons seemed telling. For example, in actual coal production the United States was far ahead of Britain by 1913, but exported less than 6 per cent of its output. And while Britain was still ahead of Germany in total production, it too exported a smaller proportion of output than Britain – 24.79 per cent as against 32.96 per cent. 'Our own country', wrote Jevons's son in 1915, 'exports more coal than the four next largest exporting countries taken together, and is not far from claiming one-half of the whole of the world's foreign trade in coal.'

For the younger Jevons, there was still no writing on the wall. The reason for the rise in exports lay largely in 'the wonderful fall in freight rates' and in the supremacy of British shipping. The latter seemed impregnable. In his book *The Wonderful Century*, however, A. R. Russell took a radically different view of coal exports, introducing the theme in his last chapter, 'The Plunder of the Earth', which appropriately followed a chapter which he called 'The Demon of Greed'. 'The continual exhaustion of one of the necessaries of existence' expressed in the figures of coal exports was, he stated, 'wholly in the interests of landlords and capitalists, while millions of our people have not sufficient coal for the ordinary needs and comforts of life, and even die in large numbers for want of the vital warmth it should supply.' For Wallace, 'a rational organization of society would ensure an ample supply of coal to every family in the country before permitting any export whatsoever.' And then he brought in iron too. 'The operations of coal-mining and iron-making being especially hard and unpleasant to the workers, and at the same time leading to injury to much fertile land and natural beauty, they should be restricted within the narrowest limits consistent with our own well-being.'

# III

Many writers on things left the miners out altogether. Indeed, the title of Annie Carey's 'The Autobiography of a Lump of Coal' was more characteristic of the period than such a title as 'The Autobiography of a Miner'. Jack Lawson's warm and readable *A Man's Life* was not published until 1932. Born in 1883 and eventually, in 1950, to become Lord Lawson of Beamish (blessed location for all industrial archaeologists), Lawson started working in the mine the day before he was twelve years old. Before that, however, he had experienced the strike of 1892, known in Durham as 'the three month's strike'. 'Grim, desperate, savage, the men had fought for months.' 'Every wheel in the great coal-producing country was stopped, and the water was flooding the mines.' The fact that it was only the Durham miners who were on strike and that the rest of the coal fields were 'in full swing' produced a terrible isolation. 'It seemed as though we were forsaken by God and man.' Lawson's account is vivid: so, too, is his assessment of his own reactions. 'All unconscious of it, I had even as a boy of eleven become class conscious.' 'As the sense of defeat deepened, passions rose until women and children were as bad as the men.'

Such notes are not struck by Annie Carey, or by E. A. Martin in his book *The Story of a Piece of Coal*, which appeared five years after the Durham strike. There can be an even greater distance between the literature of things and the literature of people than there was between the paper world of the City and the 'real world' of Birmingham, Swansea and Middlesbrough; and it was a Leeds, not a London, newspaper which in 1860 reported the uncomfortably awkward words of a Leeds draper, John Holmes, President of the Leeds Corporation Flour and Provision Society: 'If the masters will but treat their men as human beings, who have interests, families and bodies, sensitive to injury, and will thus prove to the men that they are conscientious in their relations, we should hear less of strikes.'

Four years after Jevons published his book *The Coal Question*, miners' wages in Yorkshire were cut by $7\frac{1}{2}$ per cent and the South Yorkshire Miners' Association began its longest industrial dispute, which went on for eighteen weeks. The employers were determined to stamp out trade unionism, and the dispute began not as a strike but as a lock-out. There was a note of violence throughout as non-unionists were brought in by the employers, and the word 'riot' was used to describe the worst disturbance in January 1870. A journalist who visited specially built cottages inhabited by the 'blacksheep' described how everywhere 'broken furniture and crockery were strewn about in wild disorder, large stones covered the floors and everything seemed wrecked and destroyed'. George Dawson, a spokesman of the employers, who called the disputing miners 'very stupid', received one threatening letter which began 'Mr Dawson, you may think you are a bad Devil. People talks about how bad it is to shoot anybody, but I would sooner shoot you in the morning than shoot a pigeon.'

The dispute ended with the South Yorkshire Miners' Association weakened, and settlements on different terms were agreed upon in different pits. Yet in the most difficult pit there was a qualified victory for the miners: a shortened working day on Saturday was won, the employers did not insist that miners should cease to be members of a trade union; and there was little victimization.

In the boom years of the early 1870s the story was quite different. Wages in South Yorkshire were raised in September 1871 and raised again three times during the year that followed. Indeed, there was a rise as large as 5 per cent in January 1872. The demand for coal was so great at that time that the employers felt able, using the language of the miners, to 'comply cheerfully' with demands for such increases.

The human implications of the business cycle were never more clearly demonstrated. As John Benson has written in his social history of British coal-miners in the nineteenth century, the miner lived on a roller-coaster, not only cycle by cycle but week by week: 'Even if he stayed in the same job at the same pit and there was no change in wage rates, the miner could never know what he would be earning the following week.'

In West Yorkshire, where during the difficult late-1860s wages had been reduced, the West Yorkshire Miners' Association, founded in 1858, had almost disappeared. Yet the miners were in a strong enough position in 1872 to demand a rise in wages of 25 per cent and to add that if the demand were not conceded they were 'determined to take immediate steps to get it'. The employers offered 15 per cent and increased the price of coal by 3s per ton, declaring the miners responsible. More pertinent was the fact that at Leeds, according to the *Leeds Times* the coal yards were 'blocked with carts waiting to be loaded, and, in numerous instances, coal could not be had at one yard or another'. Another Leeds newspaper, the liberal *Leeds Mercury*, agreed with the employers, adding for good measure that 'we may say in plain language that the chief results of the greatly advanced wages now paid for coal getting have been a diminished supply of coal, and a terrible increase in drunkenness, idleness and dissipation on the part of the men'.

This was a familiar one-sided verdict, but the miners could be criticized for opposite reasons, too. Thus, there was criticism when John Dixon, Secretary of the West Yorkshire Miners' Association, 'admitted' to the Select Committee of 1873 that some miners had been 'thrifty' and had 'large banking accounts.' It did not help when he claimed that virtue had been rewarded, a claim that could have been substantiated from other evidence relating to miners' membership of friendly societies and their taking up of insurance.

Generalizations provided an essential part of the evidence both in the Select Committee, which itself pointed to the dangers of 'idleness' and 'dissipation', and at the meeting of the Statistical Society in London, also in 1873, when one of the members present stated that in his opinion the current high price of coal was due 'to a very large extent to the fact that the workers had found that if they limited the production they would get higher wages by working shorter hours. Probably two hours a day had been taken off from the time that the coal getters were at work, yet they could get double the amount of wages that they received before'. And the workers, he added, had had another weapon at their disposal: 'They would not permit stores of coal to be accumulated in the summer as a provision against the winter.' When Hunt spoke at the same meeting, by contrast, he was not content with such economic generalizations. Leaving his own subject, geology, on one side, he declared that 'the accidental circumstances which gave way to the present unnatural high price of coal' must in a short time 'give way to a better system regulating the relation between the master and the man, and between the coal men and the public'. It was what Holmes had said in 1860.

In West Yorkshire itself, the outcome of the events of 1873 was what Hunt hoped for – conciliation rather than conflict or rather conciliation emerging out of initial conflict. In May of that year when the coalowners, strengthened in their stand by large stocks of coal, proposed to reduce wages by 15 per cent – and the price of coal by 3 per cent – the men refused, as they also refused an invitation to submit the proposal for arbitration to the Mayor of Leeds. Instead, in June 1873 a Joint Committee of six coalowners and six miners was established 'to arbitrate on all matters of dispute arising between masters and men, similar in its scope and objects to that now in operation in the counties of Durham and Northumberland'. Both wages and 'the practice and mode of working' were to figure on its monthly agenda, and the meetings were to be held in the Queen's Hotel. The new system was to last for ten years, and it produced practical results, including the preparation and promotion of a standard set of colliery bye-laws.

Meanwhile, in 1872 there had been progress in a different form, not through conciliation on the spot but through national legislation. The Coal Mine Regulation Act of 1872 was the latest in a series of legislative interventions to influence working hours and conditions, which had begun just thirty years earlier in 1842 when Parliament prohibited women and children from working in the mines. In future it was to be informed of what was happening by inspectors, one of whom, the experienced H. S. Tremenheere, was to find women still being employed underground in Wales in 1851. In 1855 and 1860 the law was strengthened in relation both to inspection and notification of accidents, 'the curse of coal'; and the Act of 1872, introduced after a conference of employers and miners, was both the climax of a process and, as H. S. Jevons was to put it, 'the foundation of modern legislation to increase safety in mines'.

Mines were now to be inspected daily by 'firemen' or 'deputies' for safety, mine managers were to be required to have their 'competency' certificated, and more rigorous conditions were to be imposed on the use of safety lamps and of explosives for blasting. As far as the miners were concerned, there was an immediate gain in the provisions relating to 'checkweighmen'. As early as 1844, they had demanded in vain the right to appoint the men who measured their output, and the numbers of checkweighmen had increased during the 1860s. Now, all coal leaving the pit had to be weighed and paid for by weight unless the employers and miners agreed to payment by measure, and miners could appoint checkweighmen from amongst them-selves at their own expense. Moreover, in any conflict concerning the checkweighmen which reached a court of law, no coal owner would be allowed to adjudicate. It was a sign of progress that 64 new weighing machines were installed in West Yorkshire in 1874, although there continued to be complains that the Act was being evaded.

Not all trade unionists favoured such legislation, and the Select Commit-tee of 1873 itself saw limits to it, believing that 'it must be left to the general feeling of the worker, improved by education, to prescribe the proper limits for their labour'. Nonetheless, there were further Coal Mines Regulation Acts in 1887 and in 1900. The former laid down *inter alia* that no boys under the age of twelve were to be employed underground, that the employment of boys over twelve years should be regulated, that the privileges and power of checkweighmen should be extended, and that the grade of 'competency' of managers (first or second class) should be stated on their certificates: the latter restricted employment underground to males over thirteen years. It was not until after the end of the Victorian period, however, that there was a far-reaching further enquiry into mining through a Royal Commission on Mines, appointed in 1906, and a statutory Eight Hour Day, demanded by the Social Democratic Federation since 1883, was introduced in 1907. Not all coalminers supported it: the Durham and Northumberland miners were consistently opposed.

Jevons himself had been drawn into an argument with trade unionists in 1866 following an introductory lecture he gave in Manchester 'on the importance of diffusing knowledge of political economy', a pre-Victorian theme which now seems in the late-twentieth century to have added point. In the lecture, as newly-appointed Professor of Logic and Cobden Professor of Political Economy at Owen's College, Jevons criticized trade unions for being 'as pitiless as they were powerful' and claimed comprehensively that all strikes were a 'dead loss to the workmen, even more than to any class in the community'. Moreover, referring to recent events in Sheffield, where non-unionists in the Sheffield cutlery trade were assaulted and one man killed, he described such 'atrocities' as but extreme instances of 'the tyranny which at this moment is paralysing the trade of a large part of the country'.

The report of his lecture provoked two highly critical letters in the *Manchester Examiner and Times*, one signed by 'A British Workman' and one by 'A Cobdenite'. The writer of the first explicitly disclaimed all intimidation of non-unionists: 'In the trades' union to which I belong each member is expressly told upon entering that he is not to use any intimidation to induce men to join the union or comply with its rules.' The writer of the second felt that Jevons had produced arguments 'calculated to aggravate distrust of economical science amongst working men' rather than to diffuse it. He had talked of strikes, but had not mentioned lock-outs, and in referring to the ignorance of trade unionists he had overlooked the ignorance of employers. Indeed, his lecture had been 'essentially a plea for the employer, to the detriment of the employed'. Part of the funds for the lecture had been provided by subscribers to the Richard Cobden Memorial Fund: Jevons, the writer claimed, had taken Cobden's name in vain.

The same point was made even more strongly in a third letter by William MacDonald, a trade-unionist house-painter in Manchester, who was one of the 33 delegates from Manchester to attend the first meeting of the newly founded Trades Union Congress, held in the city in 1868. This was the first time, he stated, that the kind of sentiments Jevons had expressed had been associated with 'the name of the immortal Cobden'. After all, Cobden in winning the battle for cheap corn had created an organization to do it and had not relied on individual effort alone. Could the corn laws have been repealed without a League?

Jevons knew little about trade unions, MacDonald went on, and relied on 'second-hand descriptions'. 'He may have fathomed the depths of the coal question, be a profound geologist and an infallible mathematician, and be able to discern the flow and ebb of national wealth in its great ocean and minor channels. But the character, wants and aspirations of that class from whose brain and muscle all that wealth springs he does not so well understand.'

MacDonald wrote his letter after Jevons had replied to his first two critics. He denied that he had 'advocated the employers' interests' or had taken 'a partisan view of the question of strikes'. He cherished 'such liberalism', he insisted, as Mill had proclaimed in his 'great essay on liberty'. And he ended with a peroration that in the late-twentieth century has acquired a particularly topical ring:

> Every workman should, in my humble opinion, be more or less of a capitalist, and in every trade a considerable proportion of the mills, factories and works [he did not add 'mines'] should in time be owned by workmen and managed by their deputies. The workmen will thus have in their own hands the means of breaking up combinations or lock-outs of the masters, and of being informed precisely concerning the employers' side of the question as well as their own. It avails not to say that the men cannot save the money. [A new point] The large sums raised by unions to support strikes, and the loss of comforts endured by those engaged in them, show what vast funds could be raised if the men had half the perseverance and abstinence in making their own fortunes than they have in marring alike the fortunes of themselves and their employers. I think I am doing far better in pointing out these plain truths than in trying 'to propitiate the working class'.

These were obviously not 'plain truths' for MacDonald. He began his letter with a plain truth of his own. It arose out of a bakers' strike then in progress in Manchester, the capital of cheap bread. 'It seems almost a profanity to offer up that petition "Give us this day our daily bread" while our bakers are starving. The same Manchester that may be said to have fed the people of Britain [when it had pressed for the repeal of the corn laws] is permitting a large portion of her own industrious citizens to be ground to death by overwork or to find homes in our infirmary and workhouses. It is miserable policy to reduce men to the condition of patients and paupers, and then grant them in charity what was due to them in wages. The trades' societies and their council seem the only good Samaritans to lend a helping hand to the bakers in their struggle.'

Persisting arguments on both sides were just as clearly put in Manchester in 1866 as they have been ever since. Nor have they ever been resolved within the British economic – and political – system. Herschel in the same year drew his evidence not from Manchester but Middlesbrough. A strike in the Cleveland iron district against the reduction of wages was leading not only to commercial disaster for employers in a losing business, he argued, but to a national disaster. 'The French and Belgians have been supplying the continental demand for iron for the last two or three years; and have supplanted English iron almost entirely by their own lower prices. Our business with the continent has dwindled away to nothing.' Herchel's conclusion was tougher than Jevons's, but he had no recommendation to make. 'The working classes are now fast becoming the controllers of our most important manufactures by means of their combinations and unions, and with or without *votes*, are gaining enormous influence on the commercial interest of the country.'

They were to get votes in 1867 [for the story, see *Victorian People*, Chapter X], and in the same year a Conservative Government was to set up a Royal Commission, of which Thomas Hughes and J. A. Roebuck were members, to enquire into the trade unions at a time when they were under attack [see *ibid*, Chapter VII]. By the time that the Commission reported in 1869, however, Sheffield was quiet, Manchester bakers were thriving, and Cleveland ironmasters were facing an unprecedented demand for their product. The trade cycle had turned. For the Royal Commission trade unions, whatever might be said about them, were already a *fait accompli*:

> All legislation, and all discussion with a view to legislation, must therefore take as its basis this general fact – that a very great proportion of the skilled workmen of the country have for many years shown a strong and increasing disposition to unite themselves in these trade societies. The evidence leaves no doubt in our minds that the union as a rule consists of the superior class of workers; and we can see no indications that it is ever regarded as injurious by any body of workmen deserving attention either for their numbers or their character.

As W. Hamish Fraser has written, 'What was probably intended as a forum for indicting trade unions proved to be a show case for the large amalgamated societies' like the Amalgamated Society of Engineers and the Amalgamated Society of Carpenters and Joiners.

One of the witnesses before the Royal Commission was the miner's leader, Alexander MacDonald, the eldest of seven sons, who had taken part in a bitter Lanarkshire coal strike as early as 1842. Thereafter, his trade-union record was outstanding. He had created a Scottish Coal and Iron Miners' Association in 1855 with great skill, although it slumped after another strike against a wage cut in 1856. He had influenced the Mines Act of 1860, which *inter alia* allowed the election of checkweighmen by the miners themselves, and had put the trade-union case to many official enquiries and in the Press. Most important of all, he had organized the meeting at Leeds in November 1863 out of which had emerged the Miners' National Association and had gone on to become its President. In 1868 he stood for Parliament and in 1874 he actually won a seat at Stafford, far from his native Scotland. In 1870 he led a one-day strike in Scotland, which won the eight-hour day in Fife; and at a great gala, a favourite event in the miners' year, held a year later, he was presented with a purse of golden sovereigns. He was given a second purse in 1872 after the passing of the next Mines Act. MacDonald was the kind of trade-union leader Thomas Hughes and the Positivist spokesman Frederic Harrison had in mind when they drafted key sections of the Report of the Royal Commission.

Through trade unionists like MacDonald the public became more aware of what trade-union leaders were really like, although there was to be a new generation of trade unionists – gasworkers as well as match girls or dockers – emerging during the late 1880s who were to present completely different images. Yet to know what trade-union leaders were like was not quite the same as to know what the daily lives of ordinary coal miners were like. The latter came into view mainly at moments of drama, particularly mine explosions, which forced public attention on the perils of mining: the *Illustrated London News* published twenty engravings of mining disasters between 1843 and 1853, and there were at least four oil paintings of a mine disaster at the Hester coal mine in Northumberland in 1862. One of them – 'Unaccredited Heroes: A Pit Mouth' – won the acclaim of the *Art Journal*.

A poem on the subject has been included by Christopher Ricks, the editor of *The New Oxford Book of Victorian Verse* (1987) – James Henry's 'Two hundred men were killed'. Written in 1862, it described what happened when the great iron beam of the steam-engine which worked the pumps at the Hester mine snapped and a section of it fell into the shaft. The sides collapsed and the men were entombed – in Henry's opinion all 'for want of a second door' to protect them. His weapon was irony:

And what is it else makes England great
At home, by land, by sea,
But her cheap coal, and eye's tail turned
Toward strict economy.

The Queen, declaring that her heart bled for the poor people in the colliery, sent a telegram to the miners' families and arranged a 'decent interment', but Henry discerned irony in that also:

And burial service shall for us
In the churchyard be read,
And more bells rung and more hymns sung
Than if we had died in bed.

The last line of the poem was not about the men but about coal itself –

Not one whit worse the coal.

Jevons and his son after him showed that they were deeply concerned about accidents. The son devoted almost twenty pages to the subject: the father expressed his views very succinctly, following two dreadful mining explosions, in a letter to *The Times* in 1866 written soon after he had been in argument with 'A British Workman', 'A Cobdenite' and William

315

MacDonald. Jevons maintained, as his son was to maintain after him, that explosions could be explained in terms of the weather, just as he was to go on to argue, after elaborate research, that trade cycles were 'caused' through harvests by sun spots. But he did not conclude that it was nature that was responsible for particular outcomes. 'Coal owners are fond of assuring us that we need be under no apprehensions of a want of coal', he wrote in 1866, 'for they can easily sink to any depth, and work any number of square miles of country from a single shaft. Have they all of them clear consciences? Have they all of them adopted the latest and most efficient means for ventilating their mines and detecting danger? If not, I wonder that they can sleep in their beds at night for thinking of the heaps of blackened corpses in the burning pit, and the villages full of orphaned children and widows.' In fact the late-Victorian miner was four times as likely to die in an isolated incident – and 460 times as likely to be injured – as in a great explosion.

From his *Journal*, which he kept for fifteen years (there is only one entry after his marriage in 1867), Jevons showed that his own conscience was stirred when he was drawn into argument with the Manchester 'radicals' in 1866. 'I am often troubled', he wrote, 'and now more than ever to know how to reconcile my inclinations in political matters. What side I am to take, one – the other – or can I take both?' 'I wish with all my heart,' he went on, 'to aid in all that is good for the masses, yet to give them all they wish and are striving for is to endanger much that is good beyond their comprehension.' We are back to the 'ethics' that could seldom be completely relegated to Sunday sermons.


# IV

Whatever might be said about the limits of *their*, the workers', comprehension, there were limits of a different kind to the comprehension of most mid-Victorians – and late-Victorians – as to what was actually going on at the coal face. They know that it could be a place of danger, and they know too that scattered mining communities, each compact and isolated, constituted societies of their own with their own 'peculiar habits'. But that was part of the problem. Coal was exported everywhere, across every frontier, but the mining communities themselves seemed to have closed frontiers. As one writer put it in 1842, 'In the character of the collier population there are phenomena which demarcate it from every other class in the community.' Chimney sweeps you met in your own home and in the pages of Kingsley's book *The Water Babies* (1863). Miners were far away and out of print.

Observers of the mining communities usually preferred moralizing to domestic anthropology, and an article on the 'manners of the Northern coal miners', which appeared in the *Penny Magazine* just before Queen Victoria came to the throne, set the pattern for future comment, just as 'The Song of the Shirt' (see page 207) set the pattern for future comment on needlefolk and Lord Shaftesbury's successful plea in 1875 to abolish boy chimney sweeps set the pattern for future comment on chimney sweeping. There was hardship and danger in the miner's life, the author wrote, but in general miners were 'commonly strangers to poverty and want', and had not learned the lessons of temperance and foresight. They were abandoning their rough sports, however, and now participated in an increasingly wide range of lively community activities, including brass bands (a 'delightful pursuit') and Methodist classes. Unfortunately, however, their Horticultural and Botanical Societies had to struggle in an unfavourable environment 'where smoke and dust bedim the golden day'. 'The huge volumes of dense smoke continually issuing from the tall chimneys, and borne away in slow dismal pageantry on the wings of the passing breeze, render the atmosphere impure and unhealthy, the effects of which are very visible on the surrounding vegetation.'

More than twenty years later, in 1862, a writer in *The Cornhill Magazine*, J. R. Leifchild, also turned his attention to the miners of the North in an article called 'Life and Labour in the Coalfields'. Sixteen million tons of coal had been produced in the old established Northumberland and Durham coalfields in 1859, he stated, putting what Jevons was soon to say in longer term perspective. 'Should only the present rate of mining continue, the whole attainable coal might be exhausted in less than five hundred years' time.'

'No one, perhaps, would dream of making an excursion for pleasure to this great district of subterranean darkness and superficial blackness', the writer began; yet there was ample 'real interest', even excitement, for visitors in 'the extraordinary mechanisms ... for the extraction of coal and its delivery to other vessels', in 'the hundreds of tall chimneys' and 'the streaming barriers of smoke' and, not least, in the 'rough and begrimed human beings who throng all around and seem to belie the appellation of "white men"'.

Later in the article, Leifchild talked of the 'human moles' of different species, from 'putters' (pushers) to 'hewers', whose work was the most 'peculiar' he had ever witnessed. 'In a small corner-like recess, full of floating coal dust, foul and noisome with bad air and miscellaneous refuse and garbage, glimmer three or four candles, stuck in clay which adheres to wall and roof, or there may be only a couple of Davey lamps. Close and deliberate scrutiny will discover one hewer nearly naked, lying upon his back, elevating his small sharp pick-axe a little above his nose, and picking into the coal-seam with might and main.' Even the author and his fellow observers had to dress and equip themselves for the occasion in 'rough pilot-jackets, vests, and trousers, a round, hard, leather cap, a stout stick, a pound of pit candles, and a clay candlestick'.

Outside the mine Leifchild found the young miners 'a rough, roystering laughing, chattering, song-singing company', their elders either wildly intemperate or deeply religious. There was an increasing proportion of the latter, 'exhorting, preaching and teaching after their own fashion'. 'Men who may at any hour be buried alive in a dark pit which should prove their tomb, may well think of that other world into which two hundred of them entered recently without warning.' There was one virtue which all the miners, intemperate or religious, shared – 'deep sympathy for their brothers in misfortune': at a recent calamity at the Hester mine, that described in Henry's poem and in the *Illustrated London News*, they had manifested a remarkable 'courage and perseverance' in trying to reach victims buried when the coalface collapsed.

Their 'world of things' was more impressive than those of most other workers, as John Benson has corroborated. In nearly all their cottages 'and especially in all those tenanted by respectable families', the furniture was of a 'superior order'. 'The bedstead is pretty sure to be a mahogany four poster, with imposing patterns, clean white furniture and a quilted coverlet: it is placed in the best room as an ornamental piece of furniture, and beside it will frequently stand a mahogany chest of drawers, well polished, and filled with linen and clothes.' In the 'best ordered pit dwellings' the author had also seen, he said, 'good chairs, china, bright brass candlesticks and chimney ornaments; every one of these items being kept "scrupulously clean", for cleanliness was "the pride of the pitman's wife"'. Outside in the mining village, however, there was a mess, and the 'effluvia arising from the rubbish heaps' was 'disgusting'. Even the gardens looked grim: 'the plants appear to maintain a mere reminiscence of "green" under a prevailing shroud of coaly blackness'.

This was now becoming a stock account, which did no more justice to the variety of settings than many accounts of the industry did justice to the extraordinary heterogenity of the product coal itself. There was a sentimental Victorian conclusion, too, that 'the human heart can feel as warmly a thousand feet underground as in the most refined and cultivated circle of society'. Nonetheless, in the accounts the miners gave of themselves – and there are some late-Victorian oral accounts – similar notes were often struck. Frank Machin in the first volume of his history of the Yorkshire miners presents an interesting picture of attitudes during the prosperous years from 1871 to 1874, quoting a Castleford coal-manager who observed in 1874 how a little village, 'wretchedly poor and unproductive', had been converted within twenty years into a thriving town.

A tradesman living there had lately detailed the difference in his trade of ready-made clothes and furniture in the last five years. Five years ago, he could only sell the lowest cotton warps and second-hand furniture. Five shillings a yard for cloth, and 30s for a chest of drawers and a bedstead were the outside prices. 'Now he can sell no such rubbish. Cloth of 12s and 14s a yard and good French polished chests of drawers and a new bedstead of £5 and £6 each are the rule, and all else in proportion, both in quality and quantity. Miners' houses, children, wives and selves, are now pictures of comfort and prosperity as compared with the past. After a bonus day at Briggs' colliery [and the Briggses had introduced profit sharing in 1865] one shopkeeper alone took £120 in clocks and watches.' It would be a mistake, however, to think of spending entirely in terms of sprees, more popular with men than with women. There were women, indeed, who carefully watched every farthing.

The miners expressed themselves in symbols as well as in words, and they were as proud of their banners as they were of their uniformed brass bands. Their great gala days were, as George Howell put it in *Trade Unionism, New and Old* (1891), occasions for 'mutual congratulations and enjoyment', but they were also colourful demonstrations of their solidarity and of their spirit. Above the ground, miners liked to be on show. And this applied to the girls as much as to 'the lads' or to the men. The same point had been made by another knowledgeable friend of trade unionism, the Christian Socialist J. M. Ludlow, who addressed the National Association for the Promotion of Social Science in 1860. 'The mass do not reason, but feel strongly and instinctively: often their instincts are right when their reasons are wrong. Give them good wages and you will see them as busy as bees at work or at play, mining, betting, drinking, fighting.'

Those who laboured at the pit head – and they were a minority among the miners – were well described by an outsider in the *Edinburgh Review* in 1863. Theirs was 'heavy and dirty work', and when they were initiated into it they found it 'new and strange'. The darkness might 'almost be felt'. 'Hygiene was unknown and quite foreign', and while miners were carrying out their labours they looked 'sordid' in their 'shabby dresses' and 'their inverted bonnets stuck on the top of their heads'. Nonetheless, for the outsider, when they were 'out on Sunday' – 'we wish it were an equivalent phrase to say at church' – they were dressed in all the 'cheap finery which nowadays levels all distinctions of fortune':

> The pit-head girls are not less fond of holidays than their fathers, and much they enjoy the two days of saturnalia when, by immemorial custom, the field of labour is turned into a scene of general riot. On Easter Monday the men roam about the colliery in gangs, and claim the privilege of heaving, as they call it, every female whom they meet – that is of lifting her up as high as they can, and saluting her in descent. On Easter Tuesday the ladies have their revenge – and in their hands this strange horseplay acquires redoubled energy. Neither rank nor age are respected; not even the greatest of men, the manager himself, would be secure from attack.

That was very much an outsider's view. It was not only then that the manager might not be secure from attack. Nor did all the miners in all parts of the country engage in the same 'strange horseplay'. The writer was describing the Black Country. Mining had its different versions of folklore just as it had different practices in different parts of the country: it had produced regional and inter-regional diversity, as W. H. B. Court and other historians of coal have emphasized. As already noted, the markets were different too. 'For many industrial purposes the different sorts of coal are no more interchangeable than are the different kinds of steel. Household coal producers [the ones supplying Annie Carey's grate] have their own interests and special views of the world.'

The differences became even more apparent as the Welsh coalfields were developed in the late-twentieth century. In the early and middle decades of Queen Victoria's reign, iron was more important than coal in Wales and most of the coal was used in the iron works, but as coal boomed, few ironworks were left. Eight-and-a-half million tons of coal were produced annually in South Wales in the mid-1850s and nearly forty million tons in 1900. Moreover, the area by then had a near monopoly no longer of local markets but of the international market for steam coals. The most energetic owners believed in mergers: the miners developed an even more distinctive culture, the culture of Chapel and Working Men's Institutes, than that to be found in Scotland, in the old mining areas of Northumberland and Durham or in Derbyshire and Nottinghamshire, where D. H. Lawrence was born in 1885.

For Wales there are pictures as well as words to record changes, just as Thomas Bewick and Luke Cleamell had recorded changes in mining in early-nineteenth century Northumberland in drawings, engravings and water colours. The illustrated booklet *Coal Face*, written by Richard Keen and published in 1982 by the National Museum of Wales, presents very much an insider's view or rather a series of insiders' views of Welsh mining communities, a series since different cultures were represented in Wales itself – there were many immigrants – and since there were marked differences between different generations. The photographs in the booklet were the work of one man, William Edward Jones, born at Pontypool in 1890. He went to work in the pits in 1903 not long after Queen Victoria died, and left behind him 'tangible shapes and images', not snapshots but 'deliberate statements of the working political and social life within his community'. His father had presented lantern lectures: he himself had to use open flash magnesium powder when he took his photographs underground. These were not the first underground photographs of mines, however: J. C. Burrow had already taken photographs of the tin mines of Cornwall and the coal mines of Somerset.

It was in Wales that trade unionism established itself late in the century in forms that were to prove remarkably lasting. There was usually a political dimension, as there was in the life of Jones's father, who was an active member of the Independent Labour Party, pioneered by another miner, this time from Scotland – Keir Hardie, (see page 263) first returned to the House of Commons in 1892. (Old Jones believed that only donkeys went to the House of Lords.) The leadership of the Welsh miners was Liberal, however, and only in 1898 was the old trade-union leader, William Abraham, a

Liberal, best known by his Bardic title 'Mabon', toppled from favour after thirteen years as Member of Parliament for the Rhondda Valley.

Since 1875, miners' wages in South Wales, as in some other mining districts and as in the iron and steel industry, had been fixed according to sliding scale agreements between miners and owners, with wages automatically geared to the selling prices of coal. But the system had bitter critics, and the Miners' Federation of Great Britain, founded in 1889, was determined to get rid of it. The Welsh miners, like the Durham and Northumberland miners, about half the labour force, did not belong to the Federation, but when coal prices – and consequentially wages – fell after 1894, opposition to the scale grew, and in 1898 a burst of unrest culminated in a bitter 'strike of strikes'. The strike was, in fact, a lock-out, following a ballot decision by the miners to end the sliding scale agreement, and troops were called in and the Government urged to intervene.

The strike marked the end of a phase in the history of coal, for although the Welsh miners, without funds of their own, had to go back to work basically on their employers' terms, a new South Wales Miners' Federation emerged out of it and went on to affiliate itself to the Miners' Federation of Great Britain. Mabon's verdict might have been made by Jevons: 'The [1898] stoppage knocked everything on the head ... prices, prospects, agreements, amicable relationships, and everything necessary to create and maintain trade prosperity.'

It was difficult for anyone in Britain not to know that there was a Rhondda Valley in 1898 or that there were militant Welsh miners. And very soon the name of another Valley, Taff Vale, was to become even better known when during a strike on the Taff Vale Railway in Wales by the Amalgamated Society of Railway Servants in August 1900 an injunction and a claim for damages for picketing and molestation was brought in the Courts by the railway company's general manager. The 1898 strike of the South Wales miners had cost the Amalgamated Society of Railwaymen over £10,000, and once it ended the Taff Vale railwaymen, members of a moderate and a respected trade union, found it difficult to get the Taff Vale Railway Company to provide the guaranteed week which they had secured in an agreement of 1890. There was a direct link, therefore, between the miners' strike and the railwaymen's strike, although the latter was settled by mediation in only eleven days.

It was the aftermath that hit the headlines. The injunction was first granted, then reversed in the Court of Appeal, and finally restored in July 1901 in the House of Lords, which ruled that a trade union was liable to damages inflicted by its officials. The Amalgamated Society of Railway Servants was called upon to pay £23,000 to the Taff Vale Railway Company out of its funds, together with its own costs, another £18,000. The ruling not only hit the headlines: it entered the history books. It encouraged trade unionists to seek new legislation and it led many of them to support the

Labour Representation Committee which in 1906 was to become the Labour Party, although the Miners' Federation did not affiliate until 1909, when 13 miners were Members of Parliament. Meanwhile, of course, the Queen had died between the strike and the ruling, and labour relations were to be far more difficult in her successor's reign than they had been in hers.

# V

It would have been possible in this chapter to have demonstrated how trade unionism influenced – or failed to influence – the universe of Victorian things from the history not of the coal industry, but of a new and booming industry based on coal – gas: a militant new gasworkers' union was created in 1889 by Will Thorne, working at the great Beckton Gas Works at East Ham. The other industry associated with 'carboniferous capitalism' – iron – had more than one union and more than one brand of leader. The secretary of the Friendly Society of Ironfounders, Daniel Guile, had been active in the background of the Royal Commission of 1867, the report of which prepared the way for the two great pieces of trade-union legislation passed in 1871 and 1876, one by a Gladstone government, one by a Disraeli government, which seemed until the Taff Vale judgement to have given the trade unions a secure position from which to bargain and to act. Until then, indeed, it was believed, as the lawyer for the Amalgamated Society of Railway Servants claimed in 1900/1, that unions could not be sued in their registered names: they were not legal corporations.

In fact, an even more illuminating case study of the trade-union influence is close to the third industry considered in this chapter – paper. It is not the union of Paper Mill Workers which is most illuminating, but the Typographical Association, concerned with printing, an association the history of which has been studied in depth by A. E. Musson. It is illuminating because the origins of trade unionism in the printing industry lead the historian back to the customs and regulations of the craft guilds, which controlled the quantity and quality of things long before the Victorians cheapened and diversified them, long, indeed, before the advent of the factory system.

Even in 1851, the expanding printing industry was still small-scale and scattered: most 'master printers' – the term had survived – employed from one to six men: there were very few firms – and those were mainly in London – that employed a hundred or more. The wage earners were still 'journeymen', and it was relatively easy for an enterprising journeyman to set up on his own. Nonetheless, the same economic fluctuations that affected the fortunes of the ironworkers and the miners affected the fortunes and prospects of the printers too. Sometimes there was too much work, sometimes too little. There was a strong protective flavour, therefore, to the industry along with a strong sense of status.

The first number of the *Compositors' Chronicle*, which appeared in September 1840, declared that one of its objects was 'to maintain the claims of the profession to that rank among the industrious classes of Britain to which it is entitled, for its intellectual character and superior usefulness'. Yet printers were aware – and it made many of them uneasy – that in what contemporaries called 'an age of printing' new methods were being devised that were radically changing their art. Summing up in his chapter on printing in *British Manufacturing Industries*, Joseph Hatton was to write that while 'publishers had thrived, newspaper proprietors had prospered [not all of them], advertising agents had made fortunes as middlemen, with little or no risks and paper manufacturers had flourished, the printer *de facto*, the mere producer ... had frequently been worsted in the battle'.

The National Typographical Association, deliberately called an Association and not a Union, was founded at a time of relatively full employment at Derby in 1844 'to advance the interests of the typographical profession, and to improve the social condition of its members'. It did not include all journeymen printers in the country: the influential London Newspaper Compositors, for example, remained outside. When faced with economic recession, therefore, and a series of strikes, culminating in a bitter Edinburgh dispute in 1846, the Association collapsed.

It was during the mid-Victorian years that its successor, the Typographical Association, founded in 1849, alongside other print unions like the London Society of Compositors, was able to establish itself. There was, indeed, in this particular case, an obvious break between early and mid-Victorian history. Printing trade of all kinds, including the printing of ephemera, boomed in the years 1853–5, 1859–60 and 1865–74. The number of people involved in 'paper, printing, books and stationery' increased from 62,000 in 1851 to 94,000 in 1871, and 212,000 in 1901. There were technical changes too – among them the introduction of papier mâché stereotyping in the 1850s, which enabled newspapers to print as many copies as they wished, and the introduction of the linotype in 1886. There was also an increase in scale of plant, although there were still many small works engaged in local business and producing ephemera by old techniques which in themselves can be among the most interesting of Victorian things. A visit to the Johnson collection in Oxford will demonstrate this more effectively than any book could.

The Association firmly refused to admit women on the grounds that their admission would lower wages and increase unemployment. It had other limiting rules also. The number of apprentices was controlled. Seven years' apprenticeship was enforced. 'The opinion of the Executive' had to be elicited, it was laid down in 1867, 'before Branches initiate any movement for an advance of wages, reduction of hours, etc; and no memorial or other document bearing on these questions ... shall be issued to employers or the public without the knowledge and approval of the Board.' The object, also defined in 1867, was 'to adjust the balance of supply and demand and maintain a fair remuneration for labour.'

The Association and its predecessor had both demanded, like many other bodies and individuals (among them Dickens), the abolition of 'the taxes on knowledge', which until 1855 included a stamp duty on newspapers as well as a tax on paper itself. Earlier in the century, a recently much studied radical unstamped Press had thrived, and its organizers had been in the vanguard of the campaign to abolish the tax; so, also, had Richard Cobden and the heirs of the Anti-Corn Law League, who played an important part in the setting up of the Association for Repealing the Taxes on Knowledge in 1851 and in the creation of a Select Committee of the House of Commons to review the stamp tax under his friend Milner Gibson appointed in the same year. During the previous year the Exchequer had drawn in no less than £396,000 in stamp duty and £745,000 in paper duty.

The minimum price of the ten London dailies at the time of the Great Exhibition was fivepence, but it was not the free trade gospel of the exhibition but the hunger for news during the Crimean War, a war of which Cobden strongly disapproved, which led to the end of the stamp tax on newspapers. It also encouraged new forms of journalism, like the *Illustrated London Times* founded in 1855 with the object of being 'within the reach of everybody'. When the *Daily Telegraph*, which began publication on 29 June 1855, cut its price from twopence to one penny on September 17th, it deliberately appealed to the 'war party'. Soon it was boasting that it had the largest circulation of any newspaper in the world. Cobden's *Morning Star*, founded in 1856, was by comparison a paper for a small minority.

Both the *Morning Star* and the *Daily Telegraph* hailed the end of the paper duty in 1861 with different emphases in not dissimilar language: *The Times* said little. There had been setbacks in the persistent campaign to end the duty in which Milner Gibson played an important part, but it was fortunate that Gladstone, the Chancellor of the Exchequer in Palmerston's government of 1859, was a staunch advocate of repeal and that in 1861, the year of Albert's death, there was no danger of a budget deficit and of a consequential requirement to raise income tax. 'I trust', Gladstone said in his budget speech, that 'there is no one here who thinks this an improvident measure – who believes it to be what is called a sacrifice of the entire source of revenue and imagines that a tax of this kind on its repeal leaves behind it no reproductive powers.'

Some interesting points were raised in the debate, particularly concerning the 'burdens' on the British paper industry. The *Manchester Guardian*, which used a million pounds of paper annually, one two hundredth part of the paper manufacturered in the United Kingdom, was being supplied with paper made in Belgium. So, too, was the *Melbourne Argus*. Leveson-Gower said that 'with the exception of *The Times*, which stood by itself, he could not himself see any inferiority whatever in the penny papers to other newspapers' except that they were printed on 'atrocious paper'. Edward Baines of Leeds argued that the tax had hit very hard at two specific classes of publication – the privately printed Bible and school and illustrated books.

For the *Morning Star*, the day of repeal should 'henceforth be a red letter day in all English calendars'. 'This day', it went on, 'the chief obstacle to the dissemination of knowledge among the people is removed. This day the tax which was imposed with the direct object of putting fetters upon public writers who expose the abuses of government and of the governing classes, and which has been clung to with desperate tenacity by that class is swept away for ever.'

There was a sense of irrevocability as well as of triumph in 1861. 'Under no possible conjunction of circumstances', the *Morning Star* concluded, 'can the paper duty now be reimposed in this country'; while the *Daily Telegraph* traced the paper tax back to the reign of Queen Anne, proud that the production of paper would 'be governed henceforward exclusively by commercial rules and the emulation of energy and ability'. It would not only be newspapers that would benefit from repeal. 'Every class of literature' would benefit too – Shakespeare, Milton, and Shelley as much as the 'railway literature' available on W. H. Smith's bookstalls. It therefore opened up for writers 'a proportionately extensive field for the activity of genius and of talent which they never before enjoyed'. As for the newspapers – and in this respect its argument was identical with an argument that had been used by Cobden since the 1830s – in future 'a newspaper stands in fear of its readers – a far more formidable and trustworthy authority than any Attorney General or official censor of the Press'. As early as 1834, Cobden had declared that 'the influence of public opinion, as exercised through the Press' was 'the distinguished feature in modern civilization' and that 'this engine of good or evil can exist only by the breath of the public'.

The relationship of the Press to public opinion was to be far more complicated than such rhetoric, anathema to some Tories, implied: even in Cobden's own terms it was to be a vehicle of prejudice as much as of opinion. It was also to sell goods as willingly as either opinions or prejudices. Before the stamp duty and the paper duty had been repealed – and it was the repeal of the former which had the main effect on circulation – the advertisement duty had been repealed in 1853 (after the Chancellor had suggested that it should simply be reduced). No golden age of advertising was to follow, but by the end of Queen Victoria's reign many proprietors of newspapers were looking as keenly at their advertisers as they were at their readers. The tax as it operated had, indeed, been anomalous. Thus, the fifty-three pages of advertisements in the official catalogue of the Great Exhibition had all been tax free.

It is certainly possible to argue that one of the main roles of the Press as it developed after 1861 through both words and pictures was to shape the universe of things. Local newspapers had always advertised local sales, and continued to do so. National newspapers now drew increasing attention to national products, and these were increasingly branded products: in 1882 the *Daily Telegraph* devoted 63 per cent of its space to advertising, mostly small advertising, but increasingly large advertisements became more acceptable to editors and proprietors.

This was an age when 'mass consumption' became feasible with advertising as a necessary weapon. 'Any fool can make soap, it takes a clever man to sell it', Thomas J. Barrett, grandson of the founder of Pears' Soap, is said to have remarked. He became a partner in the firm in 1865 when he was 24, and when he finally took control he raised expenditure of advertising to between £100,000 and £130,000. 'Good morning! Have you used Pears' Soap?' one of his advertisements ran. Many people objected to the advertisement, but it sold Pears' soap. So, too, did the exploitation of art (Millais's *Bubbles*, 1887) and of all forms of pictorial imagery. W. H. Lever was to push advertising still further with his Sunlight soap after 1888. He used *inter alia* Frith's painting *The New Frock*. Not surprisingly there were to be soap wars as fierce as the Crimean War on which, of all historical events, one American Quaker Oats advertisement drew when it showed 'the Lady of the Lamp', a very different lady from Florence Nightingale.

During the debates on the repeal of the paper duties many speakers had dwelt on the uses of paper for purposes other than print; and in proposing their repeal Gladstone talked comprehensively about 'excise now payable upon or in respect of paper of any denomination and button board, mill board, paste board and scale board'. Paper, he said, was 'a trading industry', and he had to deal with critics who said that 'the working class' would have preferred to have the tea or sugar duties repealed rather than the duties on paper. One Member of Parliament referred to German competition in paper: they had no duties on it. And in the House of Lords in an earlier debate in 1860 Earl Granville, who said that 'there were a number of ingenious inventions in the production of paper waiting to come into action after repeal', referred to Japan and to 'the thousand useful as well as ornamental purposes to which paper was applicable in the hands of these industrious and tasteful people': 'it enters largely into the manufacture of nearly everything in a Japanese household'. Coal Japan might not have – and he was speaking before the opening up of Japan and the development of its industry. Paper it had in abundance.

One great supporter of repeal was Rowland Hill, the pioneer of the postage stamp made out of paper, and another great supporter was Thomas de la Rue, whose firm was already making surface printed stamps for foreign countries, including the Confederate States of the American South. If the newspaper was the symbol of the mid-Victorian communications revolution, as the railway had been of the early-Victorian communications revolution, the postal system was a necessary link between the two.

# 9
# Stamps – Used and Unused

Taxes, we know, are very wicked things –
They search our pockets and retrench our
    pleasures –
But 'tis the best of Ministerial measures
That wings the feathers of young Cupid's wings,
Father and mother, sister, brother, son,
Husband and wife, pronounce one benison.

HARTLEY COLERIDGE,
on the new Penny Post, 1840

Of all the events of which my career has been connected no
one I feel surpasses or, indeed, is equal in value to the world
at large as the adoption of uniform Penny Postage ... the
glory of England for all time.

HENRY COLE, *Fifty Years of Public Work*, 1886

When I ask for *timbres* [stamps] at my post-office window, I
am able to use that term only because of recent technical
changes, such as the organization of the postal service itself,
and the substitution of a little gummed picture for the
stamping of a postmark. These have revolutionized human
communications.

MARC BLOCH, *The Craft of the Historian*, 1940

There is, perhaps, no Department of Government the
business of which, if duly recorded, will furnish more
striking evidence of the prosperity, and progress of the
Empire than the Post Office; whether as regards the
increase of the general wealth, the growing importance of
the several colonies, the growing education and intelligence of some classes, or the stirring industry and energy
which is the national characteristic of all.

FIRST REPORT of the Postmaster General
on the Post Office, 1854–5

# I

Postage stamps, long taken for granted, were one of the first Victorian inventions. Before the first beautiful penny black stamps were sold to the public in May 1840, Rowland Hill, their chief but not their only begetter, had had difficulty in defining what was soon to become one of the most familiar Victorian things in use. At first Hill thought of a 'tell-tale stamp' as a stamp impressed by a clerk on a prepaid letter, rather like a rubber stamp, and, when he broadened his definition, a postage stamp was 'a bit of paper just large enough to bear the stamp [the older meaning of the word 'stamp'] and covered at the back with a glutinous wash which the user might, by applying a little moisture, attach to the back of a letter, so as to avoid the necessity for redirecting it'. Some writers called the glutinous wash 'cement'.

Hill himself believed that stamps would be used by the public less often than franked or stamped posted stationery which was issued at the same time. Indeed, when he appeared before a Post Office Commission of Enquiry set up in 1835, to consider reform of the postal system, his reference to separate stamps, 'small stamped labels', seemed, as several historians have put it, to have been 'almost an after-thought'.

A more vigorous and committed advocate of their introduction than Hill was a Dundee bookseller, James Chalmers, who used the word 'slip' to describe a stamp which he would affix to seal the pages of a letter. Chalmers had no use for specially prepared stationery nor for envelopes, a relatively recent innovation, now machine-made and selling in London in 1837 at 2s 6d a dozen, and he envisaged 'sheets' of 'stamped slips' being sold over the counter. Yet Hill, too, had £1 'sheets' in mind, with stamps arranged in rows of twelve, when he talked of 'a bit of paper just large enough to bear the stamp'.

Both Hill and Chalmers were more interested in the economic and social benefits of a postal reform based on a uniform, prepaid, cheap rate of letter postage than they were in the device of the stamp itself, the subject of this chapter, and they kept up sustained pressure for reform from outside Parliament, working through a Mercantile Committee of bankers and merchants. Joshua Bates, a merchant banker at Barings, was its chairman, and it had a new organ at its disposal, edited by Henry Cole, the *Post Circular*, a special number of which was cleverly bound into 40,000 copies of a part of Dickens's *Nicholas Nickleby*: because it was registered as a newspaper, it had to be carried by the Post Office for one penny before penny post applied to letters. This was perfect propaganda. Hill knew about newspapers: he had been an early advocate of the abolition of the stamp duty on them.

The fact that the drastic reform Hill envisaged was accepted quickly shows that it had won widespread and vociferous support both in London and in the provinces – with over 2,000 petitions being submitted in its favour. There had obviously been a marked evolution in opinion between 1835, when the Commission was set up to inquire into 'the management of the Post Office', and July 1839, when the Government decided to introduce a penny post bill. The Commission had not advocated a uniform penny postage in any of its ten reports, most of which led to sensible reforms in Post Office management, although Hill, one of its most important witnesses, had. And so, too, after studying Hill's proposals, had Robert Wallace, the pertinacious, if fussy, MP for Greenock, who was already a dedicated supporter of postal reform in 1835. The most striking conclusion of the Commission in its final Report published in 1838, was that 'postage duties must be looked upon ... not merely as a source of revenue, but as the price paid by the public for the performance of a public service.'

Hill, one of the six sons of a Birmingham schoolmaster, had produced his plan for prepaid, uniform and cheap postage in a remarkable pamphlet published in 1837 called *Post Office Reform: Its Importance and Practicability*. It was written while he was secretary to the South Australian Colonization Office. At first, it had been intended to be a 'private and confidential document', but it had soon become a much quoted public manifesto, arguing confidently that lower and uniform prepaid postage rates would actually increase Post Office revenue and lower the costs of management.

The pamphlet was one only, if the most important, of a number of declarations by Hill which were said to have 'exhausted' the subject: they included a May 1839 pamphlet *On the Collection of Postage by Means of Stamps* and a private letter to the Chancellor of the Exchequer in November 1839, written after the penny post bill had become law, in which he argued that 'the whole measure should be brought into operation as rapidly as is consistent with the mature consideration and efficient execution of each part.' By then, Hill, who had argued his case with great determination before a Select Committee set up at Wallace's instigation in 1838, had been appointed special adviser to the Treasury to guide and to supervise the implementation of the Whig reform plan, which started with a London trial scheme in December.

Hill took up his post in cramped premises on September 16th 1839, having started what was to become a much quoted journal a week previously: it caught the mood of excitement. The language, too, was the language of a gospel. Thus, when the penny post was introduced on January 10th 1840, Wallace wrote to him congratulating him personally on 'this wonderful day' when 'the innumerable friends of civil and religious liberty' were celebrating 'a signal triumph'.

There had been much activity behind the scenes and much public propaganda, including propaganda based on statistics, before the day of 'signal triumph', when the penny post was hailed at once as a measure that would offer 'a relief and encouragement to trade' and would be 'productive of much social advantage and improvement.' The repeal of the corn laws was already being campaigned for with as much vigour and with much the

*'Rowland Hill's Triumphal Entry into St Martin's-le-Grand'*, Punch, *1844*

same approach by the Anti-Corn Law League, and the success of postal reform seemed a portent. There was a sense too, in both cases, of Victory through Struggle. Similar arguments to those advanced by Hill concerning postal costs and receipts had been advanced with equal cogency concerning indirect taxes in Sir Henry Parnell's pamphlet *On Financial Reform* which had appeared in 1829. Now they were commonplace. The death, one year before Queen Victoria came to the throne, of the conservative Sir Francis Freeling, who had been Secretary of the Post Office since 1806 and who had bitterly opposed a reduction of postal rates, opened the way for a radical change in Post Office policy.

The reform was certainly one of the most radical changes since the seventeenth century, when in 1661 the Post Office began to stamp dates on letters – twenty-six years after Charles I had thrown open to the general public the services of the royal posts. Yet Freeling, 'a respected Tory of the oldest and most rigid school', was not alone in pooh-poohing the idea that a reduction in postage rates would lead to an increase in revenue. At first, indeed, the Whig Postmaster General, Lord Lichfield, echoing the kind of language his prime minister, Lord Melbourne, used, exclaimed that 'of all the wild and visionary schemes which I ever heard of, it is the most extravagant'. And Freeling's successor, Lt-Colonel Maberly, echoed Lichfield in calling it 'a most preposterous plan, utterly unsupported by facts and resting entirely on assumption'.

Lichfield soon changed his mind, however, and Maberly was forced to implement the scheme, so that Freeling alone is now remembered for the ironic gratitude that Thomas Hood bestowed on him in the first volume of his *Comic Annual* when he was thanked for his 'antiquarian care for DEAD LETTERS'. In fact, Freeling was not insensitive to the significance of the coming of the railways for the mail services, and is himself described in the *Dictionary of National Biography* as a 'postal reformer': it was his distaste for the then fashionable idea of 'economical reform', Parnell's guiding idea, of which changes in postal rates were one part that showed that he belonged to the past.

Given the preoccupation in 1840 with the need for a comprehensive scheme of postal reform, it was impossible to place the stamp as a thing in the middle of the topical picture. Indeed, Hill himself referred rather to letters, not stamps, as *primordia rerum*, the most important things to settle. There were no stamps on sale at all between January 1840 and May 1840, although the new charging system had been introduced. Local hand stamps continued to be used, and even after May 1840 there were not enough penny blacks to go round. Hill believed that the public would prefer to use stamped postal stationery to using stamps, and even unstamped letters continued to be accepted for cash over Post Office counters and were marked 'Paid' with a hand stamp. It was not until 1853 that the use of adhesive stamps was made compulsory, one year before the first perforated stamps appeared.

This was an important date in the history of the stamp as a Victorian thing as was 1840 itself. Chained scissors were no longer necessary objects in Post Offices, and the 'sheet' of stamps became easier to manage for the Postmaster or his staff. It was a belated date, however: in 1841 one of Hill's correspondents had quietly suggested that 'if in engraving the Postage Stamps, a deep line were cut between them, in the act of printing the paper ... each stamp might be readily parted from its fellows without knife or scissors'.

Summing up the significance of Hill's achievement in the mid-Victorian years, W. Lewins, the author of *Her Majesty's Mails*, who in his preface expressed his thanks to Samuel Smiles, called it 'a pleasant page in our national history', adding that 'the reform then inaugurated has since spread with such amazing rapidity, that its growth and progress may be said to belong not solely to English history, but to the history of civilization itself', while towards the end of the century A. R. Wallace singled out not the stamp, as philatelists, by then a very active group, would have done, but the 'conveyance of thought', what we would now call 'communication', as the great achievement. He identified as Hill's main contribution the introduction of a system of uniform charging for postage of letters irrespective of the distance they travelled, and called it 'one of those entirely new departures, so many of which characterize our century, and which not only produce immediate beneficial results, but are the starting-points of various unforeseen developments.' Wallace had the telegraph and the telephone in mind – and they are discussed in Chapter 10 – as well as the royal mails and letter box.

Such assessments were a little too rhetorical. In 1840 itself, it was the cheapness of the penny post – even more than the benefits that would go with it – that was its major initial attraction, although the poet Hartley Coleridge, persuaded by Hill, was by no means alone in concentrating on its other benefits. 'The multitude of transactions which owing to the high rates of postage are prevented from being done, or which, if done, are not announced, is quite astonishing', wrote Hill, going on to argue that lower postage rates would not only meet the requirements of every 'rank and class of person' but would actually increase revenue through stimulating a greater use of the mail.

Revenue, he observed, had not been increasing with the population, and as things were, 'bills for moderate amounts' were not being drawn; 'small orders for goods' were not being given or received; remittances of money were not being acknowledged; the expedition of goods, including corn and wine, by sea and land, and the sailing or arrival of ships was not being advised; printers were not sending their proofs; the country attorney was delaying writing to his London agent, the commercial traveller to his principal, and the town banker to his agent in the country. In all these cases, to which Hill attached the greatest importance, 'regularity' and 'punctuality' were being neglected 'in attempts to save the expenses of exorbitant rates of postage', for the most part paid on receipt of the correspondence and not in advance.

Hill needed only to have given the pre-1840 pattern of costs of letters from London to Birmingham – 9d – or to Liverpool – 11d – or even to Brighton – 8d – to have established his main point that the British economy, disturbed as it was by depression in 1838 and 1839, could not have expanded had it not been for cheap postage. He seems to have genuinely believed in 1837 that the penny post by itself could stimulate 'the general improvement of trade and commerce': as other people believed that the railways would. *Inter alia* it would enable the unemployed to find work more easily, he claimed, so that it would be in the economic interests of workers as well as their employers.

He believed too, of course, as did many radicals, including George Birkbeck, the educational reformer and founder of the mechanics institutes, and Dionysius Lardner, historian of the steam engine and much else besides, that commercial advantages would be accompanied by 'moral' and 'social' advantages, 'particularly acceptable and beneficial to the poorer classes' both as a group and as individuals. As the Select Committee had put it, 'Charitable institutions, unions for the establishment of Sunday Schools, Associations for the improvement of Education or the Diffusion of Knowledge had been greatly crippled by the limitations which the postage rates imposed.' Now they would be liberated.

Hill made the most of the point after 1840. 'The postman now has to make long rounds through humble districts where, heretofore, his knock was rarely heard', he observed, a comment echoed by Harriet Martineau and in more sentimental vein by many others, who had not scrupled to make the most of 'mothers pawning their clothes to pay for a child's letter', before the change took place. A late writer, Samuel Laing, in his *Notes of a Traveller* (1850–52) claimed that the penny post had done more for the poor than the new 'system of school education' had done for the poor in Prussia. 'This measure will be the great historical distinction of the reign of Victoria. Every mother in the kingdom who has children earning their bread at a distance lays her head on the pillow at night with a feeling of gratitude for this blessing.' Not surprisingly, G. R. Porter included a chapter on postage in his *Progress of the Nation* in his section not on economic but on 'moral progress'.

There were of course, dissentient voices at the time, like that of J. W. Croker in the *Quarterly Review*, who called penny postage 'one of the most inconsiderate jumps in the dark ever made by Parliament': 'the Gods must annihilate time and space before a uniform rate of postage can be reasonable or just.'* In an earlier number the *Quarterly Review* had pitted the railways against the Post Office and suggested that the more men travelled the less need would there be for letters.

By 1850–52, however, most of the hostile voices had not only been silenced but had been made to look foolish. Thus, while Henry Raikes had written in his *Diary* that the only effect of the measure would be 'to increase the number of idle scribblers', that it would be 'of little benefit to the lower classes, who seldom have occasion to write', and that it would only 'advantage the commercial houses and bankers, who can well afford to pay the postage', working-class people did write more letters after 1860 and industrialists and shopkeepers certainly benefited as much as traders and bankers.

As far as 'idle scribbling' was concerned, Dickens himself had something to say in *Household Words* in 1851 about the relationship not between letters and

---

* The remarks anticipated by nearly thirty years' criticism of Disraeli's passing of the Second Reform Bill in 1867 as 'a leap in the dark'. (See *Victorian People*, Chapter X.)

*'Britannia Presenting Rowland Hill with the Sack'*, Punch, *1844*

stamps but between letters and steel pens – 'While the national resources offer to every man incredible facility for the transmission of his bit of mind to a distance when he has written it, yet millions among us cannot grapple with a pen.'

In fact, weekly letter mail doubled in Britain between November 1839 and February 1840, as Hill proudly told the members of the Statistical Society of London two months before the penny black was introduced. And when he addressed them again in May 1841 he was able to tell them that the March figures for that year had further gone up by almost 50 per cent. Hill always preferred statistics to anecdotes, and he was fully content when after 1846, the year of the repeal of the corn laws, the blessings of cheap mail were almost inevitably compared with the blessings of cheap bread. Richard Cobden, the leader of the Anti-Corn Law League, who had given evidence to the Mercantile Committee, is said to have claimed that cheap bread itself had been secured two years earlier than it would have been had there been no penny post, for it was through a skilful use of the cheap new system of postage that League propaganda had been quickly disseminated to all parts of the kingdom.

Cheapness was the main object of reforms. The means of reform began not with the stamp, but with a new method of charging. The pre-1840 system of paying for letters on delivery at the door was open to abuse, and, above all, was time-consuming; each letter carrier (the word 'postman' was not generally used until later) was 'detained on the average two minutes at every house; and not only so, but check-clerks and check-accounts had to be kept at the Post Office of the amounts thus sent out'. Hill's pamphlet showed how 'a great economization of labour' might be secured by switching to prepayment. 'There would not only be no stopping to collect the postage, but probably it would soon be unnecessary even to await the opening of the door, as every house might be provided with a letter box into which the letter carrier would drop the letters, and having knocked, he would post on as fast as he could walk.'

Prepayment was not made compulsory until 1855, but by then unpaid letters accounted for only 2 per cent of the total, and 'postage due' penalties had been imposed either on the recipient, or, failing him, on the sender. The letter box in the streets of London came in the same year, following the success of an experimental letter box in St Helier, Jersey, three years earlier and soon to be copied everywhere. Its 'inventor' – Jane Young Ferrugia has shown it had a long pre-history – was one of the best-known Victorian novelists, for many years an employee of the Post Office, Anthony Trollope, who had first been appointed to a clerkship there because his mother knew Freeling's daughter-in-law. By Queen Victoria's death, there were over 30,000 letter boxes all with the initials VR. The essayist Ernest Raymond was to describe them as 'at first thought, perhaps the most supremely ugly thing that civilization has produced', yet one early box was designed by Cole's students at the Science and Art Department, and G. K. Chesterton was to find 'surpassing beauty' in them. Trollope, who knew that several years before his 'invention' there had been talk of placing 'strong iron boxes in the streets', characteristically pointed to doubts about them in one of his novels. Jemima Stanbury in *He Knew He Was Right* 'had not the faintest belief that any letter put into one of them would ever reach its destination'.

The number of Post Offices – and Jemima preferred posting letters there rather than in 'iron stumps' – increased also as the century went by – 515 were opened in 1854 alone – as did the number of deliveries. London had one each hour, twelve a day, during the mid-Victorian and late-Victorian years, and Birmingham which had three in the 1850s had six by the end of the century. Moreover, the postal system was extended to villages which in 1840 had been outside the network of 'post towns', and by the end of the reign there was a regular delivery for even the most remote places. Meanwhile, the letter weight covered by a penny stamp rose from half-an-ounce to an ounce in 1871 and to four ounces in 1897; and a parcel post, urged by Cole as early as 1839, in face of opposition from the railways, was introduced in 1883.

The Victorians liked to describe in set pieces or in pictures the bustle at St Martin's-le-Grand just before the newspaper window was closed for the day at six o'clock, and 'the cries of official policemen vainly endeavoured to reduce the tumult into something like post-office order'. They dwelt, too, on the intricacies of the sorting system, refined after 1857 when London was first divided into ten post districts:

> The letters when posted are, of course, found mixed all together, and bearing addresses of every kind. They are first arranged with the postage stamps all in one direction, then they are stamped (the labels being defaced in the process) and thereafter the letters are ready to be sorted. They are conveyed to sorting frames, where a first division is carried out, the letters being divided into about twenty lots, representing roads or dispatching divisions, and a few large towns. Then at these divisions the final sortation takes place, to accord with the bags in which the letters will be enclosed when the proper hour of despatch arrives.

'This seems a very simple process, does it not?' the author of *The Royal Mail, Its Curiosities and Romance* (3rd edn., 1889) remarked. 'But before a sorter is competent to do this work, he must learn "circulation", which is the technical name for the system under which correspondence flows to its destination as the blood courses through the body by means of the arteries and veins.'

Medicine, not geography, provided the metaphor. And the author was lost in wonder and praise, as were less knowledgeable writers who were thrilled by the travelling post office sorting system, if horrified by the many attendant accidents which hit the headlines – there were 28 between 1860 and 1867 in which TPOs (Travelling Post Office workers) were seriously injured or killed. Special mails introduced in 1885 ushered in a new phase. By then, Hyde would write that 'to imagine what our country would be without the Post Office as it now is would be attempting something quite beyond our powers; and if such an institution did not exist, and an endeavour were made to construct one at once by the conceits and imaginings of men's minds, failure would be the inevitable result, for the British Post Office is the child of long experience and never-ending improvement.'

## II

It is with this sequence of dates – and judgements – in mind that the history of the postage stamp is best considered, for as Marc Bloch put it, whenever he asked for stamps in a Post Office – and he was keenly interested in their history – he was able to use the term only because of 'recent technical changes, such as the organization of the postal service itself'.

Although the postage stamp was one of the first Victorian inventions, special sheets of paper bearing a mark or impression showing that postage had been prepaid had been used in Venice as early as 1608, and most recently in Prussia since 1823: indeed, one year after the appearance of Hill's pamphlet and before Britain introduced them, special envelopes carrying an embossed stamp were on sale in Sydney in Australia for the prepaid despatch of local letters. Their merits were canvassed enthusiastically by Charles Knight, the publisher of the *Penny Magazine* and the *Penny Cyclopaedia*, for whom paper was gold.

According to Hill, it was Knight, a fellow founder of the Society for the Diffusion of Useful Knowledge, a witness before the Post Office Commission, and a rival of George Baxter (see pages 173 ff), who interested him in the device, not James Chalmers, a friend of Wallace, whose claims to have preceded Hill were to lead to bitter nineteenth-century argument. Chalmers certainly had adhesive not embossed stamps in mind, but these too had been in use by the Stamp Office to record the payment of taxes on legal documents since 1711. In 1780 stamps in the form of tickets had been issued for the collection of an excise duty of 1d a mile levied on post-horses let out for hire.

In July 1839, the month before the penny post legislation was given the royal assent, Hill received a letter – via the radical MP Joseph Hume – from the Government printer Charles Whiting, who had produced revenue stamps since 1821, and in it the key issues relating to the making and use of stamps were clearly stated. Moreover, Whiting included examples or 'essays' of stamps to help the argument. 'A stamped cover or a small stamp like a medicine stamp', Whiting explained, 'a dozen or a quire at a time, if it please you, might in future be bought at any stationer's, post office or convenient shop, either for a PENNY if the letter weighs only half-an-ounce; or for TWOPENCE if it weighs one ounce ... and so on, one penny for each additional half-an-ounce.' 'It is believed,' Whiting added, 'that this stamp, though of simple appearance to an unskilled eye, alone presents mechanical difficulties in its construction of such a nature as of itself to give ample security against forgery, but ... such a stamp, which must be purchased for much less than a penny, could only be printed profitably by a machine which is very costly itself.'

This letter is interesting not only because it was so clear and avoided the kind of circumlocution to which Hill had resorted, but because it brought questions of security as well as of cheapness directly into the consideration of postal reform. Once brought in, they were never to cease to be a consideration in Victorian times. Whiting maintained that no forger could produce the kind of stamp which he had offered as an example if it were printed 'on paper like Mr Dickinson's' for less than an outlay of several thousand pounds, and even then he would need a safe market in which to dispose of them'. Not surprisingly, therefore, the contract for the first adhesive postage stamps in the world was offered to the British Government's security printers, Perkins, Bacon and Petch (from 1852 Perkins, Bacon and Company).

Jacob Perkins, its founder, who had emigrated to Britain from the United States in 1819, when the state of security printing was chaotic and forgery of banknotes was rife, has other claims to figure in *Victorian Things*. He was a born inventor, who in 1825 had produced a steam-powered gun capable of discharging no fewer than 1,000 bullets a minute. Later he invented a refrigerator. Things always interested him.

The appointment of Perkins, Bacon and Petch was by no means the end of the security story, however, for Rowland Hill recorded two early forgeries, both of them crude, one lithographical, of the penny black. Moreover, for a different reason of security, the penny black had to be converted into a less attractive penny red-brown as early as February 1841: it had proved possible to erase the red Maltese cross, employed to show that the stamp had been used, and start all over again with an apparently unused stamp, because the inks used in the stamp were not fugitive. Hill consulted the scientist Faraday among others before making the change. Later in the century, there were to be many other security scares, and one dramatic 'Stock Exchange' forgery of an 1867 green shilling stamp during the 1870s, not discovered until 1911.

The penny black, a genuine art object, emerged as the world's first new stamp, not as the product of one designer alone but of several – and only after a fascinating gestation process. It began with a Treasury competition, announced with the minimum delay on September 6th 1839 and open not only to 'all artists, men of science and the public in general' but, as Palmerston, the Foreign Secretary, put it, 'to people in any part of the civilized world'. The entrants, who included Whiting, were invited to submit designs for both stamps and postal stationery – letters and envelopes – with two prizes on offer of £200 and one of £100.

Ten days later, when Hill took up his Treasury post, one of his first assignments was to deal with this competition. Other entrants included Chalmers and Henry Cole, then 31 years old, who he had already proved himself in Hill's eyes by serving diligently – and imaginatively – as Secretary of the Mercantile Committee, closely involved with the production of the *Post Circular*. Chalmers's entry – circular in shape – has survived, Cole's has not. It is interesting to speculate what design Cole would have devised and how it would have related to his designs of other things.

All in all, there were 2,600 entrants, although only 49 of them presented designs for adhesive postage stamps. Only 19 of them appealed in any way to Hill, and none were deemed by him 'sufficient' in themselves. Three entrants, including Whiting and Cole – the third was Benjamin Cheverton –

won prizes of £100 – no £200 prize was given – and two joint entrants, James Bogardus, who had taken out a patent for a 'stamped wafer' in August 1839, and Francis Coffin shared £100 between them. Like James Chalmers, Bogardus and Coffin seem to have thought of the adhesive stamp being used to seal the pages of a letter rather than being placed on an envelope.

Whiting produced fascinating bi-colour essays and two circular stamps, one bearing the royal coat of arms, a prominent feature in some of the other entries. He also produced embossed essays, including the heads of the Queen (later he was to produce Prince Albert), Lord Byron, the Duke of Wellington, who had voted with no enthusiasm for postal reform, and Lord Brougham, who was a enthusiastic a supporter of it as he was of any other reforming cause, not least the Society for the Diffusion of Useful Knowledge.

It was the winning Cheverton entry which set the pattern for the future in one most important respect. Like Whiting, Cheverton presented essays of embossed stamps, but, unlike Whiting, he was interested in only one head, that of the Queen, 'a female head of the greatest beauty to be executed by Mr Wyon'. Moreover, he thought that representing this particular head would be the best guarantee against forgery. 'It so happens', he wrote, 'that the eye being educated to the perception of differences in the features of the face, the detection of any deviation in the forgery would be more easy – the difference of effect would strike one observer more readily than in the case of letters or any mere mechanical or ornamental device, although he may be unable perhaps to point out where the difference lies, or in what it consists.'

This was a very practical philosophy of the eye, as practical as Hill's philosophy of economics in his famous 1837 pamphlet. And it was a philosophy which prevailed. At no point in the Victorian age were British users of stamps to see anything else but the head of Victoria. There was, after all, only one side to the stamp, unlike the coin. Users of coins always saw the Queen's head too, but they had the chance of seeing something else on the obverse side – heads or tails. The continuity was to impress the young French historian of Britain, Élie Halévy, who contrasted English coins and stamps with the coins and stamps of France under contrasting régimes.

Wyon, an engraver as well as a medallist, had submitted an entry himself in 1839, a pen and ink sketch on a piece of paper bearing the uninspiring words 'Post Office One Penny Half Ounce'. He was a distinguished Birmingham man born into a family of medallists, who had been Chief Engraver of the Royal Mint in 1828 – the early Victorian coins bore his portrait head – and subsequently Engraver of Seals to the Queen; and it was natural that Hill (and Cole) should approach him after the competition was over to submit designs for postage stamps. Through his earlier roles he brought the history of the stamp into a relationship with the history of pre-Victorian things, and he was also a Fellow of the Royal Academy, which brought art into a new relationship with everyday things. It was the Government printers, Perkins, Bacon and Petch, however, who had decided before the competition to invite Henry Corbould, a skilful miniaturist born in 1787, to prepare water colour sketches of the Queen's head based on Wyon's City Medal of 1837 which commemorated Victoria's visit to the Guildhall on her accession.

Corbould's graceful drawings were subsequently used by a former partner of Jacob Perkins, Charles Heath, an engraver of repute, and his son Frederick, to produce the penny black stamp from a master die made of steel, costing 60 guineas and prepared by Perkins, Bacon and Petch. The older Heath was then at the height of his powers, and his work on the penny black should be compared with his work as a book illustrator, chiefly of annuals like *Literary Souvenirs* and *The Book of Beauty*. There he had more words at his disposal than the brief and well chosen ones which accompanied the head on the memorable stamp – 'Postage' at the top and at the bottom 'One Penny' or 'Two Pence', for a twopenny blue stamp was to be issued at the same time as the penny black. The name 'England' or 'Britain' or 'Great Britain' was not added, and thereby a distinctive tradition was established.

Since the stamps were for domestic use only, the tradition had a rational base, but it persisted long after penny and twopenny stamps were used on letters to be sent abroad. There was a rational basis, too, for the inscription across the margin of each sheet of stamps 'Price 1d. per label, 1s. per row of 12 [a figure which in a decimal age requires a note] and £1 per sheet. Place the Labels above the RIGHT HAND SIDE of the letter. In Wetting the Back be careful not to remove the Cement.' Long after the word 'cement' came to be used in a quite different way, there remained 240 pennies in £1.

Hill demanded also, as precautions against forgery, that in the two upper corners of each stamp, as on a banknote, there should be ornamental stars and that in the two lower corners there should be capital letters in sequence which would identify the location of every stamp in the sheet. The first stamp would bear the letters AA, the last stamp TL. No one had any idea at the time that these handpunched letters would be used to distinguish between the prices of penny black stamps in stamp dealers' catalogues. Stamp dealers belonged to the future.

The chronicle of the penny black has been well charted by Robson Lowe in his account of the R. M. Phillips Collection, the nucleus of the present National Postal Museum. The Chancellor of the Exchequer authorized Hill to give the order for the first stamps on December 11th 1839; Hill gave the order to Perkins, Bacon and Petch for engraving, die sinking and sieve making five days later; and on Boxing Day 1839 a Treasury Minute referred to four different kinds of preparations – stamped covers; stamped envelopes; adhesive stamps; and stamps to be stuck on paper of any description.

On January 1st 1840 Hill called on the Librarian of the House of Commons to make arrangements for the convenience of MPs to prepay their own postage; on January 6th he arranged with a not very cooperative Maberly for the printing of 500,000 notices explaining the use of adhesive stamps; on January 24th arrangements were made for the making of the paper under the direction of the Excise Office; on January 25th specimens of the proposed stamps were sent to Maberly; the master die of the engraved Head head was completed on February 20th; and on the last day of the month the words 'Postage' and 'One Penny', engraved by a separate engraver, William Salter, were added. Hill's brother Edwin was appointed Superintendent of Letter Stamps to supervise the printing and distribution arrangements.

The choice of paper, handmade paper, with each stamp to be watermarked with a small crown, was made in March after Hill had had difficult talks with John Dickinson, 'a most impracticable fellow' – Stacey Wise was to be the supplier – and in the same month methods of distributing the stamps and of offering discount to dealers were determined; on April 2nd Hill showed the Chancellor of the Exchequer a complete proof sheet of the penny black before the insertion of corner letters; and on April 15th final printing began. May 6th was chosen as the first day for the issue of the stamps to the public. In fact, the first penny black stamps could be bought in London on May 1st, and the first penny blues two days later. Immediately no fewer than 600,000 of the penny stamps were bought by the public.

Eleven different engravers' plates were to be used for the penny black – the first had to be withdrawn as early as April 1840 after showing signs of wear – but only two were needed for the penny blue. Because of the numbers of plates, the stamp collectors of the future were to find another reason for paying discriminatory prices to secure the particular plate numbers they were seeking; and at least one collector, R. M. Phillips, was to make a detailed study of the effects on the appearance of penny blacks of wear on the very first plate. No other studies of engraving have been quite so detailed.

We know something of the early costs of production from a variety of sources, including an interesting and informative report of a Parliamentary Committee of Enquiry set up in 1862 to examine the case of Henry Archer, the rather shadowy figure born in Ireland and involved in railway management, who had pioneered the idea of perforating stamps by machine. Archer had felt, as did a number of MPs, that he had not even been able to cover the expenses of his experiments which pre-dated the making of the first successful perforating machine for the 'semi-detaching of postage stamp labels' in 1847. The report dealt among other matters with the laying down of impressions on the plate and the costings of Bacon and Petch, who in face of competition from Archer in 1853, brought down their figure for printing, perforating and gumming stamps to that tendered by Archer – 5d for every 1,000. Britain was the first country to sell ready perforated stamps, although a mechanical device for separating stamps had been introduced on local carrier stamps in Boston, Massachusetts, in 1844.

Members of Parliament and civil servants did not obtain a special stamp in 1840 as they had hoped to do. It would have looked the same as the penny black except that it would have had the letters VR (*Victoria Regina*) in the top corners in place of the stars. There was justice in their failure to obtain one. Before the reforms MPs were the people who had benefited most from the *ancien régime* inside the Post Office, being allowed to send their letters free after 'franking', and there had been many complaints of their abuse of this privilege. The reason why special new official stamps were not issued in 1840, although over 3,300 sheets of them had been printed, had nothing to do with privilege, however. There had been little public demand for Hill's 'Postal Stationery' – envelopes and letter sheets – and such large stocks had been built up that it was deemed most sensible for MPs and officials to use them up first.

In consequence, unused copies of the non-issued special stamps were to be prized by collectors, and, despite the decision not to use them, there were even a few used copies as well, to be worth far more to philatelists. (There also survives a strip of four stamps cut from a sheet by Hill himself for experimenting with various cancellations.) Members of Parliament were never to get their own stamps, but several government departments were to get sheets of overprinted stamps in 1881, beginning inevitably with the Inland Revenue, and official adhesive stamps were issued a year later. Some initiative may have been shown by Treasury clerks when before perforation they had devised a means of wavy line separation called 'Treasury Roulette'.

The prize for designing the special stationery in which Hill, following in the wake of Charles Knight, had invested so many of his hopes had been won by the Royal Academician, William Mulready, an Irish-born painter of landscape, portraits and genre pictures. The designs, which he had produced as pencilled outline drawings, had been engraved in wood by John Thompson, an experimental engraver, who had engraved Britannia on the current one-penny coin. Other entries in the competition included a John Dickinson one-penny green envelope printed on Dickinson security paper with an embedded thread and an envelope in different colours submitted by James Wylie, Geographer to the Queen.

The Mulready envelopes were deliberately conceived of as art objects, 'pleased' the Chancellor of the Exchequer, and had Cole's somewhat dubious blessing. The reason why they did not appeal to the public may have been in part utilitarian: although envelopes were to pass into general use in the 1840s – stamps were complementary to them – there was little room on the Mulready envelope for the address. The main reason, however, was artistic. The Mulready designs celebrated the victory of the penny post through ornate emblematic figures. Thus, Britannia was shown with the British lion at her feet, greeting the peoples of the world, including Laplanders, Red Indians and Chinese, most of whom were extremely unlikely to receive any letters from London, at least in 1840:

Britannia is sending her messengers forth
To the east, to the west, to the south, to the north;

342

At her feet is a lion wot's taking a nap
And a dish-cover rests on her legs and her lap.

For once symbolism – or at least Mulready's brand of symbolism – was out-of-fashion.

The letters and their designer, W. Mullheaded or W. Mul-led-already, were immediately satirized – John Leech was one of the first cartoonists to do so – and the 1d envelope was withdrawn in January 1841 and the 2d envelope, printed in blue ink, in April 1841. Later in the year, the printing plates were destroyed by order of the Treasury, and in 1842 the whole of the remaining stock was destroyed. There was nothing unpopular about pictures as such on letters, for there were many pictorial letter sheets at this time, including letter heads showing the chain pier at Brighton, a subject that appealed also both to Constable and to Turner, and Sir Robert Peel's house at Drayton. Curiously enough, the failure of the Mulready envelopes may have given an impetus to the popularity of other envelopes bearing views of places and sketches of people and things.

Stage coaches were a familiar theme, and the future *Punch* artist Richard Doyle did sets on courting, music, dancing, hunting and racing as well as coaching. There is one 'Dickensian' set of six, too, with characters from *Pickwick Papers*. A serious and attractive Victoria and Albert envelope is said to have been used *inter alia* to send out invitations to a ball at Holyrood House in Edinburgh, and a satirical Victoria and Albert shows a pregnant Queen and a Germanic Prince Albert. The craze for such letters seems to have soon been exhausted, like other crazes, although it revived on more than one occasion later in the century.

Hill recognized that the Mulready stationery would have to be withdrawn as early as May 1840 when, in his words, it had been 'abused and ridiculed on all sides'. He already felt by then that it had been a mistake to reject 'established custom' and 'depart so widely [here it might have been Cole speaking] from the established Lion and Unicorn nonsense'. Mulready had been too fanciful, and there was no point in 'swimming against the tide'. Nonetheless, Hill did not regret 'our attempt to diffuse a taste for fine art'.

His use of the word 'fine art' stands out. According to his daughter, he had always displayed 'a strong bent towards art', having won as a boy of 13 a prize – a box of paints valued at three guineas – for the best original landscape. As a young man he had exhibited his drawings in Birmingham: he was also an accomplished architectural draughtsman. He believed that in rejecting Mulready the public had shown 'disregard and even distaste for beauty'. It was paradoxical for Hill, therefore, that many contemporary art critics, who were uneasy about Mulready envelopes, or hostile to them, accepted with enthusiasm the penny black stamp, which Hill cared little for, and that it figures prominently in most late-twentieth century histories of design.

A different criticism of public reactions in 1840 can be better justified than Cole's. Despite the fact that *The Times* claimed that 'from Sir Robert Peel down to the lowest kitchen maid' the Mulready covers had been laughed at 'by any one with a sense of the ludicrous', almost all the caricatures themselves revealed a somewhat limited sense of fun. So, too, did the cartoons in *Punch*. The jokes were laboured. Nor was the figure of John Bull, drawn by Richard and James Doyle, any less 'emblematic' than Mulready's Britannia. They, too, looked back with nostalgia to cows, horses and stagecoaches and not forward to looms, steam engines and railways. One particularly unfunny 1840 envelope included the words 'steam engines not exceeding a hundred horse power charged one penny! Eagles' feathers and bags of rice, if prepaid, carried free! No coffins except lead ones taken by post . . .'

Ironically, but not uncharacteristically, when the Treasury finally withdrew the unsold stacks of Mulready letter sheets in 1862, it chose a year when stamp collectors, a recently identified breed, were just beginning to show an interest in the envelopes and when across the Atlantic the Civil War was boosting them. The Treasury was responsible in part, therefore, for pushing up future prices in the interests not of the public but of stamp dealers, also a new breed. The stationery was not demonitized until June 1901 – in other words, it still could be used until the last year of Queen Victoria's reign; so that when in 1886 a London stamp dealer, J. W. Palmer, posted two unused Mulready envelopes to himself, subsequently and erroneously to be charged postage due, the postage due had to be withdrawn and a correction made to the envelopes that added still further to their value.

It was stamp collectors, not Post Office officials, who pressed most strongly in 1890 for a special pictorial envelope to celebrate the Jubilee of Penny Postage, held, as was now appropriate, at the South Kensington Museum. Doubtless with the memory of 1840 in mind, the envelope avoided all emblems except that of the crown. The theme was the favourite Victorian theme – contrast. On one side a postman of 1840 was shown, on the other side a postman of 1890. At the top there was a picture of a stage coach drawn by two horses at 8 miles an hour: at the bottom there was a picture of a railway train approaching Carlisle at 48 miles an hour. Even this envelope was satirized, by Harry Furness. This time it was the caricature which fell flat, while the official envelope sold over 150,000 copies. The proceeds went to Post Office charities.

Uniformed postmen were popular figures in 1890 and their work could even seem romantic. So, too, were the women employed by the Post Office:

Tinker, Tailor, Soldier, Sailor,
To Miss Smart of the GPO,
You are awfully proud, we all of us know
Because you're employed by the GPO.

Yet there was a warning

> Less mashing and giggling I think would be better
> Or your chance of a Husband will be a dead letter.

There were different kinds of warning to the Post Office itself as postmen became unionized. In 1890 the Post Office still resisted unions on the grounds that 'the public interest' required postmen to 'be regulated by authority as much as . . . soldiers and sailors', but a Postmen's Federation was formed in London in 1891 and by the end of the century moves were being made towards limited recognition. There was a complete contrast here with 1840.

There were other contrasts which did not figure on the Jubilee envelope. Postmarks were now precious. A young lady stamp collector who went to a Jubilee Exhibition at the Guildhall got an impression of the postmark on two pocket handkerchiefs and when told that the ink would wash out replied that she would never use the handkerchiefs again.

# III

By the year 1890, politicians and businessmen were re-examining many of the themes of 1840. In particular, there was a growing campaign for 'a penny post for the Empire, wherein lie the homes of so many of our kith and kin'. One witness before Wallace's Select Committee had actually favoured an imperial penny post in the 1830s, but instead colonial packet rates and printed slip rates were set in 1840 at twelve times and eight times respectively the domestic postal rates.

Hill recommended a reduction of the rate to 6d in 1853, when the first adhesive 6d stamp was designed, two years after Lowe, with his own Australian experience in mind, had argued that it was 'impossible to exaggerate the weighty political consideration as regards postal matters' in countries of the Empire: indeed, in his considered view it was more important to them than 'all the constitutions you can give them'.

The idealists of the 1850s and 1860s, led by Eliha Burritt, had urged 'Ocean Penny Postage' in the name of 'universal brotherhood', but when the first international agreement about foreign postal rates was reached in 1863 this idea had faded into the background. The late-Victorian imperialists, led by J. Henniker Heaton, MP for Canterbury – he had earlier emigrated to Australia and had brought back with him an Australian wife – were determined to win imperial penny postage, and were in no way appeased when in 1890 the Chancellor of the Exchequer, three years after the Colonial Conference on 1887, decided to reduce colonial postal charges to a uniform rate of $2\frac{1}{2}$d. For Heaton the Post Office was taking 'narrow and departmental views' on postal matters, and he quoted with despair the remark of

Cecil Raikes, the Postmaster General, that imperial penny postage was 'a bubble that merciless logic has burst'. He earnestly exhorted 'those who wish to secure for the Empire all the blessings of cheap postal communications' to disregard the allurement of the new rate, and to insist on 'the full measure of our rights in the matter'.

Hill at his most rhetorical could have done no better than Henniker Heaton in the *Nineteenth Century*. 'Trade between the United Kingdom and the colonies, and between colony and colony, would be powerfully stimulated', Heaton argued. 'The British merchant, provided with a postal service far cheaper than those of his rivals, would be able to communicate with his agents and customers and to canvas for new business, more than five times as often as is now possible without increasing his expenditure one jot.' The United Kingdom itself had shown the way. In the first year of penny postage 169,000,000 letters had been delivered: in 1889 the figure had been 1,558,000,000.

To forecast future imperial changes consequent on postal reform, Henniker Heaton went on, 'was a task for the poet rather than for the politician. The postage-stamp would become the symbol of Imperial unity, nay more, the symbol of universal Anglo-Saxon brotherhood.' Like so many other things, stamps were to be given an imperial halo. And the Dickensian sentiments of the sentimental 1840s were now recast in the language of empire. 'The poorest and humblest, divided from home and friends by oceans and continents might send his ill-spelt, blotted scrawl to father, mother or sweetheart, for no more than my lord pays when he sends an order to his tradesmen at the other end of the town. And, like my lord, he would for his penny obtain the best services of a great state department, with boundless resources, and an army of disciplined workers.' The last phrase ran easily from Henniker-Heaton's pen, yet despite uniforms, successive Postmaster-Generals were beginning to be concerned about 'discipline' and were noting with concern that the proportion of labour costs in total Post Office costs was rising. Having stood at a third in 1870/71, it had doubled by the end of the Queen's reign.

Such a shift in cost scarcely interested the energetic advocates of imperial penny post, and when it was introduced for most of the Empire (but not immediately for Australia and New Zealand) in 1898, following the Imperial Conference held to celebrate the Queen's Diamond Jubilee, they claimed that a great victory had been won 'at last' against both the proverbial Old Lady of Threadneedle Street [the Bank of England] and her more timorous sister, the Old Lady of St Martin's Le Grand [the Post Office]. Both institutions, like the pre-1840 Post Office, had *pace* Cecil Raikes ignored hitherto 'all systems of reasoning', and they had had to wait for Joseph Chamberlain, apostle of empire, to make a breakthrough.

Henniker Heaton, who was to go on to demand universal penny postage (and a colonial country, New Zealand, this time, led the way in January

1901) now called not for a poet but for a musician to peer into the future:

> Suppose we have a choice of nightingales, and that for years each bird were punished if he opened his mouth to sing; and that on some fine July evening all were turned loose in Kew Gardens: could Sir Arthur Sullivan set forth in advance their rapturous melody in one of his delightful compositions? I have seen lyrical utterances in the staidest of journals; there is a preliminary twittering in commercial circles; parted boys and girls, parents and children are breaking forth into snatches of old song, dear to both sides; soon we shall have a grand chorus; and what can it be but 'Home, Sweet Home!' and after that 'God Save the Queen!'

How much further could you go than that?

# IV

Long before 1898, Sir Rowland Hill had begun to be considered as great a national hero as James Watt. 'Father of the Penny Post' or 'King of the Penny Post', as Lyon Playfair described him, he had been honoured with a public subscription of £13,000 in 1846. When he died in 1879 he was buried in Westminster Abbey and had many memorials commemorating him in stone, including Onslow Ford's statue, unveiled in 1882 at the Royal Exchange and placed later outside the General Post Office in 1910. Yet after 1840 Hill's Post Office career had seldom been an entirely easy one. Within two years of the introduction of the penny post he had lost his adviser's post at the Treasury after the Whigs had given way to Peel's Tories, and when he returned to Government service under the newly restored Whigs in 1846, it was not in the supreme place there, but in the awkward position of Secretary to the Postmaster-General. Thereafter there was a continuing battle with Maberly until 1854, when Maberly, to Hill's relief, was moved to the Audit Office. That was the year when another outstanding public servant, Edwin Chadwick, was forced out of office, and it was the year also of civil service reforms associated with the Northcote-Trevelyan Report about which Trollope was sceptical (see *Victorian People*, Chapter IV).

Hill, who now became sole Post Office Secretary, never understood the nature of those reforms nor the relationships between political appointments and paid administrators. Moreover, he ran into further difficulties with a new generation of Post Office officials like John Tilley and Frank Scudamore, as he became increasingly authoritarian himself. Indeed, Hill was never without critics, if only because of his personality; and Trollope, who recognized the outstanding contribution that he had made to history, could write, notwithstanding, that he had never 'come across anyone' who 'so little understood the ways of men – unless it was his brother Frederic.' It was another of Hill's brothers who told him 'when you go to heaven, I foresee that you will stop at the gate to enquire of St Peter how many deliveries they

347

have per day, and how the expense of postal communication between heaven and the other place is defrayed.'

Chadwick might have asked similar questions of St Peter about drains and sewers as he did when he met Napoleon III, and certainly when Hill met Garibaldi in 1864 they were said to have talked entirely about postal matters. Nonetheless, unlike Chadwick, Hill found himself increasingly respected, receiving amongst his other honours the first gold Albert Medal for 'distinguished merit in promoting arts, manufactures and commerce' and an honorary degree at Oxford, 'where even the wayward and boisterous undergraduates forsook their frolics for one moment, to receive with becoming warmth the man who had helped them so largely to increase their social enjoyments.' Hill was knighted in 1860 – Chadwick had to wait until 1889 – and when he retired in 1864 he was paid special tribute in a Treasury minute and, even more felicitously, granted his full salary on retirement. Even more felicitously still, Parliament went on to agree to a special 'honorarium' of £20,000 on the motion of the prime minister himself, Palmerston, who had supported him strongly in 1839 and possibly in more than one later crisis.

Palmerston's speech proposing the honorarium is one of the many Palmerstonian speeches, most of them free from pretentious rhetoric, which itself deserves to be remembered. He referred in it to the simplicity of Hill's invention, the stimulus it had given to commerce and industry, and not least to the inestimable value of the measure in 'the cultivation of the domestic affections, especially among the humbler classes'. In a decade when the Police Act provided a very different framework for dealing with those classes, this was, indeed, a memorable tribute.

# V

There were few signs until the very end of that decade that collecting stamps would become more popular than collecting coins or rocks, indeed, that there would soon be talk of *timbromanie* or stamp mania. Later, the lasting word 'philately' was to be coined. A philatelist, it was then said, as it has been said so often since, was far more than a stamp collector. He had to study stamps at least as carefully as the numismatist studied coins or the geologist fossils.

One of the earliest philatelists was the Rev F. J. Stainforth of All Hallows, Staining, London, and it was in his rectory that the first philatelists gathered, among them Judge Philbrick, a founder member of the Philatelic Society of London in 1869. The first British journal with a word derived from 'philately' in its title appeared ten years later – *The Philatelic Record and Stamp News* published monthly, a sign that the transition from a mania to a persisting hobby and from a hobby to a serious study was by then complete.

Within the next twenty years philately became a pastime and a study even for the great. In 1895 the President and Vice-President of the Society were the Duke of Saxe-Coburg-Gotha, formerly the Duke of Edinburgh, Albert's son, and the Duke of York, later to become George V. The 'ordinary members' included one prince, two earls, and army and naval officers of the highest ranks. The first London Philatelic Exhibition to be held, in 1890, had been opened by the Duke of Edinburgh, when one of the winners of a gold medal was the Earl of Kingston, while the 1897 exhibition was opened by the Duke of York. One of the exhibitors on both occasions was E. D. (later Sir Edward) Bacon, who was to become Curator of the Royal Collection.

The word *timbromanie* points to a French or Belgian origin for philately, and Lewins among others had no doubt that 'the custom originated in France' in 'the Gardens of the Tuileries and the Luxembourg'. Certainly the first published catalogue of postage stamps appeared in Paris in 1861, containing details of 1,080 adhesive postage stamps and over 130 stamped envelopes. The biggest collector throughout the mid- and late-nineteenth century lived in Paris – the son of a Genoese Duchess, Philip von Ferrari, who in 1878 had bought for £3000 the collection of the first President of the Philatelic Society of London, Sir Daniel Cooper, an Australian who had been Speaker of the New South Wales Parliament before settling in London in 1861. Another Parisian collector was Baron Alphonse de Rothschild, founder of the *Société Française de Timbrologie*.

Philately would never have established itself, of course, had not stamps been printed between 1840 and 1860 by many other countries besides Britain, including France itself, which did not issue its first stamps until 1849 – with a symbolic head of Ceres, Goddess of Corn, soon to be replaced by Napoleon III. Australia produced its first stamps in 1850 with 'views' of Sydney Harbour and of immigrants. Brazil had been the first country in the Americas to issue stamps in 1843, and the United States did not follow with a general issue until 1847. In Europe two Swiss Cantons – Geneva and Zürich – had preceded France and Belgium. The first British colony to produce stamps was the island of Mauritius: they were engraved by a local engraver when stamps ordered in London from Perkins, Bacon and Company failed to arrive. By 1860 it was estimated that 2,400 stamps of various kinds had been issued, amongst them what came to be 'the world's rarest stamp', a British Guiana one cent black on magenta, which was not discovered until 1873 and then by a schoolboy who sold it for 6s 6d before it made its way – via a Liverpool dealer – into the Ferrari collection.

The first systematic handbook on stamp collecting in Britain was written by Dr J. E. Gray, Keeper of Natural History at the British Museum, who claimed to have anticipated Hill in conceiving of the regular use of adhesive postage stamps, and who with William Vaux, Keeper of Coins and Medals, started the first museum collection in 1864. Gray claimed that he had begun to collect stamps himself 'shortly after the system was established'. The first edition of his 54-page *A Hand Catalogue for the Use of Collectors* appeared in 1862 – preceded by articles in Journals – and the fact that the 1,000 copies printed sold out within twenty days was evidence of a very active demand. Four further editions appeared between then and 1875, the last of them, completely revised by Overy Taylor, running to 226 pages. The first English periodical on the subject, published both in London and Brighton, the *Stamp Collectors' Magazine*, appeared – some contemporaries said the date was appropriate – on April 1st 1863.

It, too, included a reference to *timbromanie* in an article of December 1865 which had more to say about political economy than philately. 'One of the greatest Maxims of Commerce', it began, 'is that wherever there is a demand there will be a supply.' 'Two years ago', the writer went on, 'the rising taste for collecting these little labels had scarcely a purveyor; now not only London and all the great provincial cities, but even the smaller towns, such as Hull, Dover, Hartlepool, and Ipswich contain dealers – many of them doubtless doing a good trade.' The expansion of the business, the article went on, had 'naturally induced a great fall in the prices'. It had also led to a demand for cleaner, even 'immaculate' copies of individual stamps. There was no reason, the author stated, why stamp collecting should lose its appeal once the 'mania' came to an end, and the first issues would then gain in value rather than fall in price. 'Who knows', he concluded, 'but that we may live to see Stamp Clubs similar to the Camden and Hakluyt Societies got up to reprint curious and obsolete stamps?'

There had been a far earlier use of the word 'mania' in relation to stamps, however, in 1842, when *Punch* reported 'a new mania' that had 'bitten the industriously idle ladies of England ... To enable a higher wager to be gained, they have been indefatigable in their endeavours to collect old penny stamps; in fact, they betray more anxiety to treasure up Queen's heads than Harry the Eighth did to get rid of them.' And *Punch* offered a few lines, attributed to Colonel Sibthorp, opponent both of all new fads and of all new ideas:

> When was a folly so pestilent hit upon
> As folks running mad to collect every spit-upon
> Post-Office stamp that's been soiled and been writ-upon?
> Oh, for Swift! such a subject his spleen to emit upon.

Sibthorp might have been equally aghast at the thought of Chadwick and drains and sewers or of Wellington and the Great Exhibition.

The ladies, abhorred by the likes of Sibthorp, were already collecting stamps – there were at that time only penny blacks and twopenny blues readily available – not to put into albums but to use as wall decoration. *Punch* did not make up the story. A *Times* personal advertisement of October 1842 proclaimed that 'a young lady being desirous of covering her dressing-room with cancelled postage stamps [note the past participle] has been so encouraged in her wish by private friends as to have succeeded in collecting 16,000. These, however, being insufficient, she will be greatly obliged if any good-natured person who may have these, otherwise useless, little articles at their disposal, will assist her in her whimsical project.'

The good-natured were invited to reply to her glover in Leadenhall Street or to her jeweller in Hackney; and one of the first dealers to advertise, William Diamond, was a tobacconist in Westbourne Grove, not far from where Whiteley was to set up his store. He started business at that address in 1859, and in one advertisement of 1863 in Beeton's *Boy's Own Magazine*, one of the ventures of Mrs Beeton's husband, he offered to buy, sell or exchange 'scarce foreign and colonial stamps'. Even at that date there were still people who were collecting stamps for 'quasi-ornamental purposes' just as there were people collecting stamp cases, like the Wonderland case, and miniature red post boxes. An article in *Leisure Hour* in 1859 'Something about Postage Stamps', later to be reprinted in the first number of the *Stamp Collector's Magazine*, talked of people 'papering a room with the deposed Queen's heads'. 'As there are collections of almost everything old under the sun – from old pots and pans, old metals, old stones, and old anything [see below Chapter 10] so also there are collections of old postage stamps.'

Diamond, however, was one of the new dealers who struck a new note, and he dealt in unused as well as in used stamps. 'Send a stamped envelope for list', he stated in what soon was to become the most conventional of philatelic advertisements. Another touch which was soon to become familiar was apparent in the publicity for the first stamp-collecting journal. Readers were offered one free stamp with the first issue they bought. Giving away in order to sell became a feature of stamp dealing.

The first meetings of stamp collectors took place in Birchin Lane in 1862, where, according to Lewins, 'crowds nightly congregated, to the exceeding wonder of the uninitiated': 'ladies and gentlemen of all ages and all ranks were busy with album or portfolio in hand, buying, selling, or exchanging'. This for Lewin was a 'new trade'. The first organized stamp auction in London did not take place until 1872 and there was no other such sale until 1888. There were said to be two thousand stamp dealers in Europe in 1864, when no less than £15,000 to £20,000-worth of stamps were sold under the hammer by three or four auctioneers. Von Ferrari's collection, about which he could be extremely reticent, was then said to be worth not less than £100,000, while the Topling Collection, treated more generously by the Trustees of the British Museum than the earlier Gray collection, was worth not less than £60,000. The price of stamps, like the price of Reitlinger's art objects (see page 44) was not to fall with the price level after the end of the Victorian boom years. Indeed, during the 1880s and 1890s the prices of the rarest stamps increased thirty or forty times.

The detailed early history of stamp collecting before collectors began to specialize is not easy to chart, as P. J. Anderson and B. T. K. Smith have demonstrated with great learning in their study of early English philatelic literature up to 1862. There were as many false or dubious claims as there were to be forged stamps – and these, too, were quick to appear and to pass into an increasingly lucrative trade.

Did collecting start with boys and move on to adults? In *Notes and Queries* in June 1860, from which date it is possible to be reasonably clear, S. F. Cresswell from Tonbridge School wrote how a boy in his form 'one day' showed him a collection of from 300 to 400 postage stamps, English and foreign, and that he had been told by no less a person than Sir Rowland Hill himself that at that time 'there might be 500 variations in existence'. And then Cresswell began to moralize, as so many writers on philately were to do after him. 'This seems a cheap, instructive and portable museum for young people to arrange; and yet I have seen no notices of catalogues or specimens for sale, such as there are of coins, eggs, prints, plants etc and no articles in periodicals.'

Beeton's *Boy's Own Magazine* offered advice to collectors to advertise in the *Daily Telegraph* provided that they did not expect to get stamps gratuitously – 'we know several collectors who have to pay for them' – and C. J. Armstrong, S. G. L. Harbourfield and E. L. Pemberton offered to 'effect exchanges with stamp collectors by post'. The introduction to *The Stamp Collectors' Guide*, published in 1862, stated clearly that while 'two or three years ago ... collectors were to be numbered by units', they were now to be numbered by hundreds.

Like Gray, Pemberton became a well-known collector and a prolific writer on philately, who published a book on *Forged Stamps and How to Detect Them* in 1862 and who edited the *Philatelical Journal*, founded in 1872. Another former schoolboy collector – at Harrow – Thomas Keay Topling MP, Vice President of the Philatelic Society from 1881 to 1891, left his stamps to the British Museum. They included Mulready envelopes and other posted stationery and Sydney views, the history of each of which Topling had studied in detail. He was said to have been 'in active correspondence with the principal stamp dealers throughout the world concerning the acquisition of individual specimens'. Throughout almost all of his short life – he died at the age of 36 – he was one of the first British collectors to acquire a number of other collections – all of unused stamps – in the process of building up his own.

One of them was that of W. A. S. Westaby, who had published with Judge Philbrick a pioneering history of British stamps in 1881, and who was to produce his own *Penny Postage Jubilee: A Descriptive Catalogue of all the Postage Stamps of the United Kingdom ... Issued during Fifty Years* ten years later, complete with 148 woodcuts for the jubilee of the penny black. By the year 1887, when he acquired a great French collection, his own collection had grown 'to such an extent that the stamps spread over both sides of the leaves of his albums, and the specimens ran an undoubted risk of damage from overcrowding.' For this reason, therefore, he changed over to the French albums and later remounted his stamps 'each stamp hinged and mounted upon a white card with a red line around it'. He also reconstructed entire sheets of stamps.

That collectors of far less status and wealth than Topling were becoming more sophisticated in their own management of their collections is evidenced from the numerous stamp-collecting journals: there were six of them in 1890 and sixteen in 1901. Even as early as 1879, one of them observed that 'a fair proportion of English collectors have taken to collecting upon more intelligent principles: to mounting their stamps properly, instead of gumming them down, in albums; and to paying some attention to paper, watermarks and perforations.' Critics of philately – and there were many – might think it absurd that it could become 'necessary to provide oneself with a "stamp measure" which splits an inch up into twenty-five sections, or with a "perforation gauge"' – but they were never allowed to have their own way. *Stanley Gibbons Monthly Journal*, founded in 1890, saw to that. The first Stanley Gibbons Catalogue of Stamps had appeared in 1865, and the only surviving copy is in the British Museum. Later editions were much advertised.

As early as 1866, *The Stamp Collector's Magazine* had faced the 'often repeated' question 'of what use is stamp collecting?' replying rather negatively – with the words:

> The writer is ready to admit that it is not the most beneficial occupation of time, but still believes it may claim the merit of being instructive and that as an evidence of the advance in civilization of the nations using them, postage stamps are not without interest.

Gray, quoted approvingly by Lewins, had been far more positive:

> The use and charm of collecting any kind of object is to educate the mind and the eye to careful observation, accurate comparison, and just reasoning on the differences and likenesses which they present, and to interest the collector in the design or art shown in their creation or manufacture, and the history of the country which produces or uses the objects collected. The postage-stamps afford good objects for all these branches of study, as they are sufficiently different to present broad outlines for their classification [a point made about many things]; and yet some of the variations are so slight, that they require minute examination and comparison to prevent them from being overlooked. The fact of obtaining stamps from so many countries, suggests [to the collector that he should] ask what were the circumstances that induced the adoption [of stamps], why some countries (like France) have considered it necessary, in so few years, to make so many changes in the form or design of the stamp used; while other countries, like Holland, have never made the slightest change.
>
> The changes referred to all mark some historical event of importance – such as the accession of a new king, a change in the form of government, or the absorption of some smaller state into some larger one; a change in the currency, or some other

353

revolution. Hence a collection of postage-stamps may be considered, like a collection of coins, an epitome of the history of Europe and America for the last quarter of a century; and at the same time, as they exhibit much variation in design and in execution, as a collection of works of art on a small scale, showing the style of art of the countries that issue them, while the size of the collection, and the number in which they are arranged and kept, will show the industry, taste, and neatness of the collector.

Much the same was being said at the end of the nineteenth century, for example, in E. B. Evans's *Stamps and Stamp Collecting* (1894). Philately trained the powers of observation, induced 'habits of neatness and accuracy', and encouraged the understanding of geography, of history and of printing.

What was usually left out, however, was design. The rarest stamps were certainly not the most beautiful: on the contrary, as a critic put it in the *Fortnightly Review* in 1894, 'they are almost as ugly and inartistic as it is possible for such things to be.' The British Guiana 1850 stamp, of which so few copies were known, was 'the most clumsy' stamp ever issued. It had been produced in haste, so that the Governor's wife, having seen the British penny black, could use her own new stamp on invitations for a ball. It was quite different with books. 'A book may be of the greatest rarity and yet have no commercial value, for rarity is only one of the several attributes which give a definite value to a volume.' The Philatelic Exhibition of 1897 might be held in the galleries of the Royal Institute of Painters in Water Colours in Piccadilly. Yet the view that 'there is anything great or ennobling about a lot of dirty and useless postage stamps' seemed to the *Fortnightly Review* critic 'simply nonsense'.

In the same year as his article appeared, an article in *The Strand Magazine* suggested that there were still stamp collectors who were in no sense philatelists, but who were prepared to use stamps entirely for decoration on screens or plates as 'the industriously idle ladies' of the early 1840s had done. The article was illustrated with a map of England and Wales made entirely from stamps – 2,139 of them – and was made by a man, not a woman. Another illustration, that of a 'Jubilee screen', this time made by a woman, showed butterflies, lilies and palm trees made out of the right colours of stamps, not to speak of a 'patriotic' crown, trident, rose, shamrock, thistle and a VR. Meanwhile, the article pointed out, the stamp dealer J. W. Palmer of 281 The Strand had entirely papered a room with 70,000 forgeries and 'reprints', which if genuine would have been worth more than a million pounds.

# VI

There were some philatelists who had been sceptical about the beauty of the penny black, which they thought dull; and when they chased the essays for the stamp which bore the letters VR in the top corners they were interested only in rarity and not in beauty. Indeed, it was a philatelic journal, *The Philatelic Record*, which argued forcefully in its foundation year, 1879, the year of Hill's death, that it was time to change the head of the Queen on British stamps, still essentially the same in outline as that on the penny black, and for good measure the shape of the Queen's head on British coins also.

Could not at last 'the mythic effigy' going back to the Wyon medal be cast into oblivion? the *Record* asked. 'Surely the likeness of our Queen as she is – of the sovereign who has earned our love and esteem by over forty years of beneficent rule, of the lady whose joys and sorrows as wife, mother, grandmother and great-grandmother, have been shared in by her faithful subjects – should have greater attractions for us than that of the untried girl but lately called to the throne.' Turning in equally forthright language from the front of the stamp to its back, the *Record* 'fondly hoped' also that 'we may be given something not only nicer, but less unwholesome to lick [red lead coming through?] than the atrocious compound which at present serves for gum or mucilage.'

The complaint about the quality of the gum was not new, for there had been talk of a 'Great British Gum Secret' in the early years of the stamp until Perkins, Bacon and Company revealed that on 'ill-conceived grounds of economy' the authorities had insisted on the use of potato starch to dilute the gum. There were complaints also during the 1850s of a chemical interaction between gum and ink. The question of the head was new.

While there was eventually to be a change on the Queen's head as displayed on coins – an 'old head' of the Queen wearing a diadem and a veil was introduced in 1895 – no change was made in British stamps. And for some this remained a matter of pride. Thus, in 1889 Westaby noted that 'stamps of no other country in the world save Great Britain will be able to show an unbroken line of representations of its sovereign during fifty years from their first issue.'

Abroad, however, in some parts of the Empire, there had been a different head, even in the early years of the stamp, based on an 1837 painting of the young Queen in her robes of state by Alfred Edward Chalon. It had been used on the first Canadian stamps in 1851, with Newfoundland, the West Indies, New Zealand and Saint Helena following. Later in the reign, too, there had been a decisive change, also in Canada, when a full-length painting by Heinrich von Angeli and a photograph by W. D. Downey were used to depict a elderly, coroneted and very dignified Victoria: she first appeared alongside the Chalon head in an 1871 Diamond Jubilee issue. The same 'old head' was used also on British East African stamps in 1896, on Indian and Ugandan stamps in 1898, and in Southern Nigeria in 1901.

In Canada, which printed its stamps in the United States, there had even been an Albert sixpenny stamp among its first issue in 'Albert's year', and in Britain also, Henry Archer and the engraver Robert Branston had produced trial Prince Albert stamps, experimentally surface printed and perforated, in red and blues, in 1850. They were never issued. Whether the Queen saw these stamps is not known, but Albert's was, after all, a very special head. Without fuss New Brunswick was not encouraged ten years later, in 1860, when its Postmaster-General, Charles Connell, chose to show his own head on the 5 cent stamp. A Chalon head of the Queen quickly replaced it.

Although the head of the Queen remained basically the same in Britain, there was a big technical and aesthetic change in 1855, when engraved stamps gave way to surface printed stamps, to be followed by a further change in June 1881 with the introduction of the first 'unified' stamp, the penny lilac, which was used both for postage and for inland revenue purposes and bore the words postage and revenue. Both changes were carried out through new printers, De La Rue and Company, who must figure prominently in any study of Victorian things. Unfortunately, although their history has been written, and there has been a detailed study of the British stamps that they produced, there is no correspondence in their archives before 1866.

Thomas de la Rue, who arrived in London from Guernsey at the end of the Napoleonic Wars, had begun as a straw-hat manufacturer before turning to bookbinding and, providentially, although it did not seem so at first, to playing cards and stationery. His son Warren was a friend of Hill, and although De La Rue's did not print any British stamps until 1853, when they were given the contract for fiscal stamps by the Inland Revenue, they had already produced half-anna embossed postage stamps for Sind in India, more like seals than stamps, in 1852.

As early as the mid-1840s, when the company was getting through 45,000 reams of paper a year, *Chambers's Journal* was already describing with relish the De La Rue works with their steam engines and machinery (including the envelope making machine displayed, to the Queen's delight, at the Crystal Palace: (see page 64), 'nestling in a cluster of old edifices' and complete with 'an apparatus called a "lift".'

Dickens was equally enthusiastic when he wrote an article in 1853 in *Household Words* called 'A Pack of Cards', still De La Rue's most profitable invention, although they had found a good line in railway tickets too. The increasingly prosperous business had been strengthened by the appointment as designer of playing cards of Owen Jones (see page 58), and when in 1855 Joubert de la Ferté became their engraver of stamps, they had access to very special talent. Meanwhile, Warren De La Rue, already a member of the Royal Chemical Society, had become a Fellow of the Royal Society in 1850, one year before the Great Exhibition, when his father was Deputy Chairman of Class XVII, Paper Stationery, Printing and Bookbinding.

In April 1853, when the De La Rues were awarded their first contract for making inland revenue stamps at a time when the stamp duties were reduced, they used the same typographical process – surface printing – as that employed earlier in the making of playing cards. The new stamps would be easier to perforate, the De La Rues claimed, and because of special fugitive ink impossible to use twice after cancellation. Inevitably Rowland Hill was interested – above all, in the lower cost – and with the warm approval of Cole, he contemplated a new Post Office contract with De La Rue in place of the old contract with Perkins, Bacon and Company. The penny black and the penny red that succeeded it had been line engraved: every sheet had been hand printed at high cost. The arts of the miniature were fully deployed. Now De La Rues offered a far cheaper process, involving contrasting techniques, a process which involved a further challenge to the role of the engraver and possibly to aesthetics as a whole.

There was undoubtedly great beauty, however, in the first postage stamp produced by De La Rue during the middle of the Crimean War, when the Chancellor of the Exchequer was pressing Hill to increase Post Office revenues. This was the famous fourpenny carmine – the 'purest carmine' – designed by de la Ferté, who had been commissioned directly by the Inland Revenue, in a colour worthy of the Crystal palace itself. Between 1855 and 1877 he was to design no fewer than twenty issues of postage stamps, all those of Britain being of higher denominations. Interestingly the only surviving 'head' of Joubert himself is a photograph taken about 1860 and 'burnt in on enamel for permanence' by a process that he himself invented. Photogravure was not to be used for British stamps until 1934.

The first lilac (or violet) stamp was not a penny but a sixpenny (along with a shilling green) which appeared in 1856. Hitherto, stamps of the higher denominations had been embossed, the first of them a shilling stamp, required on letters to the United States and for some of the colonies and as a receipt for the payment of a registration fee. It was issued in 1847. Why the first high value stamps were embossed is not certain. Perhaps Perkins, Bacon and Company did not have enough machines or spare capacity to produce more line engraved stamps. Certainly, as always, security reasons must have entered the argument, and it is significant that the embossed high value stamps were produced in conditions of strict security by the Inland Revenue at Somerset House.

Line engraved penny and twopenny stamps continued to be regarded, as Westaby put it, 'as a class distinct from those primarily issued for foreign postage, not only by philatelists but by the public'. Meanwhile, De La Rue specialized, as before, in surface printed stamps for the Crown Agents to the Colonies, while the line engraved stamps were produced, as before, but in face of increasing competition, by Perkins, Bacon and Company. In 1879, however, there was the first premonition of change. Perkins, Bacon and Company were not only warned by the Board of Inland Revenue that obliterations could be removed from their stamps 'with very little trouble' – a security threat – and forced to experiment with new inks, but told that there would be a tender for the next set of British stamps. Seven firms took part, and once again cheapness was a main criterion.

Perkins, Bacon and Company submitted both line engraved and surface printed stamps, the latter a new departure for them, but it was the De La Rue Company, now serviced by an excellent Chief Chemist, Hugo Miller, who had been recommended by von Liebig, that won the contract and went on to produce first a series of four values from one halfpenny to fivepence.

This was a 'watershed in British stamp production', as the postal historian A. G. Rigo de Righi has put it, and while cheapness, besides security, undoubtedly figured in the policy decisions leading up to it, De La Rue did not offer the lowest price. As usual, gum could not be left out either. 'In a department of the public service regulated with so dedicated an appreciation of small savings as the Post Office', wrote *The Globe* sarcastically, 'perhaps a liability to come off in letter boxes may be welcomed among the peculiar merits of the penny stamp.'

The tender for the new seven-year contract awarded to De La Rue stipulated that stamps should be surface printed, that the inks should be highly fugitive, and that the gum should be of a special character. The paper was dealt with differently, however. 'The sort of [watermarked] paper on which the stamps will probably have to be printed' was to be supplied to the seven tendering firms. One of the firms, Charles Slipper and East, offered by way of design a draped head of a 'mature' Victoria, identical with that struck on the campaign medals for the Maori Wars and the Abyssinian Expedition of 1868–9, the work of another Wyon. Perkins, Bacon and Company in their tender produced designs which in the opinion of G. B. Robertson, the Controller of Stamps for the Inland Revenue, were indistinct and wanting in relief. De La Rue, who offered what they thought were 'very good designs', dwelt on their business record, pointing out that 'the number of stamps we have supplied could be counted literally by billions, and yet in no case have we had a complaint of forgery, or of the stamps being cleaned for use a second time, when once they have been properly cancelled.'

'We trust we may be excused in expressing surprise', their statement went on, 'that the 1d Postage Stamp had been for so long allowed to hold its own', adding for good measure that while 'we have, of course, assumed that the Queen's head must be the leading and essential feature of the stamps ... should this not be the case ... we respectfully claim to have an opportunity of reconsidering the whole question.' The head stayed, but the corner letters went: they were felt to be no longer necessary on security grounds.

The new De La Rue penny red was 'assimilated' with 'the colour of foreign stamps of the same denomination' as recommended by the International Bureau of the General Postal Union set up, with Britain as a founder member, in 1874, but it did not last long. In 1881 came the famous one penny lilac, printed in double fugitive ink, a far better known stamp than the penny black, if only because it had a long life – for over twenty years – and because it was printed in far larger quantities. And since it was a 'consolidated stamp' used for both postal and non-postal purposes – to be followed by a 2s 6d – also in lilac – it is still found on surviving documents, including wills, as well as on envelopes.

Sixty to sixty-five million penny blacks had been issued between 1840 and 1841 before they gave way to the penny browns: no fewer than 1,000 million penny lilacs were sold between 1881 and the end of the reign in over 140 million sheets. Yet, as W. A. Wiseman has said, they cannot be regarded as 'popular stamps' with collectors, 'either general or specialist'; and only limited interest has been shown in the fact that more than 130 plates were prepared between 1881 and 1900; that some of the first penny lilacs, by far the rarest, had fourteen dots, sometimes called 'pearls', in each corner, while some had sixteen; that the London issue was in 'pale lilac' and the country issue in 'deep lilac'; and that there were to be many errors in its production, usually fascinating to philatelists, including printing on the gummed side. Even the word 'lilac' was and has since been questioned. 'Shades of purple' has sometimes been preferred.

There were to be many shades of imperial purple at the two royal Jubilees of 1887 and 1897, but before the first it had been decided to withdraw the De La Rue unified series on the grounds that there was too much confusion of colours and designs between the different denominations – particularly the 3d and the 5d. Nor did the Post Office or philatelists much like them. For these reasons a Departmental Stamp Committee, which included two members of the De La Rue family, was set up in 1884 under the chairmanship of Thomas Jeffrey, the Controller of the London Postal Service, who had himself submitted colour essays in 1881.

The Committee met for eleven days, calling Judge Philbrick as one of its witnesses, and doubtless paid attention to a comment in the *Pall Mall Gazette* that each of its readers should 'borrow from some schoolboy of his acquaintance a collection of foreign postage stamps.' 'Might we not try to come a little nearer,' the *Gazette* asked, 'to the excellent taste displayed in this matter by France and Switzerland?' For *Truth* also, there was need to look abroad: 'Our postage stamps were a satire on all our fuss about art education.'

The Committee – and its successor – recommended bi-coloured stamps or stamps printed in distinct colours – pink, blue and yellow – and after many colour trials this recommendation was followed in the design of the so-called 'Jubilee issue' of 1887, an issue which had nothing to do with the Jubilee itself. For the origins of Empire commemorative stamps, we have to turn to New South Wales, which led the way with centennial stamps issued in 1888 showing a map of Australia, a portrait of Captain Arthur Phillip, the First Governor, and (inset) Lord Carrington, the then Governor. In 1897 Barbados was to follow with Diamond Jubilee stamps showing Victoria in a chariot drawn across the ocean by six horses.

In design terms the British 1887 issue is interesting in that it reveals clear-cut changes in taste. Indeed, it expressed the lavish and often vulgar styles of the 1880s far more obviously than the design of the penny black had reflected the battles of styles during the 1830s. There was certainly little imagination except that the profile of the Queen's head was smaller in size than it had been in earlier stamps. For real imagination we have to turn again to the Empire – to Barbados and to the Sudan, where in 1898 one of Kitchener's field officers, Colonel Stanton, produced stamps, also printed by De La Rue, showing a camel postman carrying bags of mail marked 'Berber' and 'Khartoum', the latter still to be captured. Stanton got his idea from an advertisement of a carpet firm in the *Illustrated London News*, which depicted a camel carrying rugs up Ludgate Hill. These stamps, themselves not objects of great beauty, were long to outlast the British 'Jubilee' series. Indeed, they were to remain in use until 1948.

One stamp in the first De La Rue British issue of 1880 deserves special attention – the halfpenny green. There had, however, been two earlier halfpennies of a very different kind. Ten years before, following a Parliamentary vote against the Government, the Government of Gladstone and of Lowe, the postage rate on inland newspapers and on inland printed matter and samples had been reduced to a halfpenny, and in consequence new wrappers bearing an upright rectangular halfpenny stamp with rounded corners had been issued. There had also been a small half-size halfpenny stamp, in Rigo de Righi's words 'compact like a miniature rose': it was printed from twenty plates of 480 stamps. They were 'comb perforated' which meant that one side was usually imperforate.

This, too, was a landmark, as was the appearance of the first $1\frac{1}{2}$d stamp issued in the same year, showing the Queen's head within a curious three-sided frame. Although there was no immediate use for such a stamp plates had been prepared in 1860: indeed, it has often been claimed that this was the reason why the stamp was issued in 1870. Four years later, trials of farthing stamps were prepared, but the stamps were never issued. It may well have been that the Post Office was contemplating using them for payment for the delivery of circulars on a regular basis. There are six farthing essays, made by Perkins, Bacon and Company, in the R. M. Phillips collection in the National Postal Museum. There are also De La Rue essays of the same date.

During the 1880s Post Office officials feared that there might be an even bigger landmark than the introduction of the $\frac{1}{2}$d stamp – a halfpenny post, for which there seemed to be mounting pressure. In a period of falling prices, it seemed to many that the price of stamps should fall also. Yet the Post Office, afraid of an alarming deficit, resisted the pressure. It had had a quite different reason for considering halfpenny rates in 1870, however, before the price level began to fall – the introduction of the first postcard, somewhat bleak in character, with a halfpenny stamp printed on it within a 'Greek pattern rectangular frame', to the left of which was the Royal Arms. And printed very firmly beneath were the warning words in capital letters 'The

Address Only To Be Written on this Side'. In the light of later history, these were the most inflexible of all postcards. De La Rue manufactured them, and at first they were sold at their face value until retailers protested and the price was soon slightly raised, to be further raised in 1875.

Few observers would have guessed at their first inception that here was the beginning not only of a huge new development in postal communication but of yet another collecting hobby which claimed in time, particularly when the postcards became pictorial, to be an art. The famous diarist, the Rev Francis Kilvert, received a postcard on the first day of their issue, 'very bright and cheery', and sent his own first cards two days later. 'They are capital things', he wrote, 'simple, useful and handy, a happy invention.'

By the late 1890s, postcard collectors had so established their position that the author of a well-researched handbook on philately writing of the postcard stated that while compared with the postcard 'the adhesive stamp possesses quite a venerable culture', 'a work on Philately would be incomplete if Mr Gladstone's favourite medium of political utterance was not treated with something more than incidental mention.' To have Gladstone as well as Kilvert as a sponsor was no mean achievement.

# VII

Although thought of today as an 'invention of yesterday' – and suitable, therefore, for inclusion in Chapter 10 of this book on 'new things', like the telephone – the postcard has been given a far longer pedigree by historians of 'popular culture'. They have traced its history back, indeed, long before it was called a postcard, searching for origins in the story of prints and broadsheets, Mulready and other envelopes, postal stationery, *cartes de visite* and advertisements. Few of the specialist historians, however, have looked at the relationship between the postcard and the stamp. They have seemed more anxious at times to argue with each other incessantly about who first thought of the postcard or – a question more difficult to answer – who produced the first pictorial card.

It is sensible to begin where contemporaries began. An interesting article in *Chambers's Journal*, published in September 1870, the month before the new British postcard – and the halfpenny stamp – appeared, had as its either/or title 'Postcards v. Envelopes'. 'The envelope', the author claimed, 'is not likely to be knocked off its perch of vanity by any mere card.' The author knew well, of course, how little envelopes had been used before penny postage – if only because the receiver of a letter in an envelope would have had to pay extra for the weight – but he added new 'information' about a Brighton bookseller and stationer, S. K. Brewer, who was making envelopes cut from metal plates at about the same time as John Walker was making matches in Stockton (see page 128.) Dobbs and Company of London took up the idea, which again was by no means entirely new, although Charles Lamb gave the word a graceful twist when he described writing a 'naked note' to a great man at the court 'such as Whitechapel people interchange with no sweet degrees of *envelope*.' 'I never enclosed one bit of paper in another,' he added, 'or understood the rationale of it.'

Would he have understood the rationale of a postcard which could not be folded and had to be left 'unscreened by any cover or wrapper'? Certainly many people had difficulty in doing so in 1870, for quite different reasons. Even twenty years later, a manual of 'mistakes and improprieties' called *Don't* warned its readers not 'to conduct correspondence on postal cards. It is questionable whether a note on a postal card is entitled to the courtesy of a response.'

More seriously postcards seemed for some people to threaten privacy. What could be more absurd than 'writing private information on an open piece of cardboard that might be read by half a dozen persons before it reached its destination?' The author in *Chambers's Journal* even thought that the messages might have to be written in cipher to prevent 'inquisitive eyes' from seeing them. He did not take up, however, what soon became another popular debate – whether or not writing postcards would reduce the desire to write letters. This was a sequel to the 1840s debate about the effects of penny postage on working-class letter writing. And it is interesting to note that by the end of the century postcards were already being introduced which did almost everything for you without writing too much. You could fix the time of an appointment by marking the hour on the provided outline of a clock or you could be given printed phrases to follow up at your own whim.

Makers of postcards were most ingenious in contemplating such uses, with Messrs Raphael Tuck prominent amongst them once the plain card had given way to the picture card. In their well-known 'Write Away' series, the title of the picture, printed in imitation handwriting, said to be that of Adolph Tuck himself, 'the King of Postcards', gave the writer of the card the necessary inspiration to go on. 'It struck me very terribly' was one such opening gambit: the picture showed a footballer receiving the ball from a powerful kick to his stomach. Less contrived scenes, like a view of a mountain top or of a beach, might speak for themselves with scarcely any addition. 'A little card', wrote Margaret Meadows in the *Girls' Realm* in 1900, 'will suggest what we cannot put into words. The picture postcard meets alike the needs of those slow of expression or too hurried to write.'

The picture postcard came to Britain years after the kinds of cards produced by the British Post Office in 1870; and the fact that the latter had gladdened the heart of Gladstone – even, he said, lengthened his life – was based on a very different kind of rationale for their existence than illiteracy. No one could ever have said that Gladstone was short on words, and in 1875 he managed to order from the Post Office specially made 'stout' cards, costing a penny a dozen more than the 'thin' ones, to give greater permanence to what he wrote on them.* It was not in Britain, however, but in continental Europe that the plain postcard had first appeared, taking off significantly, perhaps, in that great mid-Victorian boom, which made all new ventures look possible and which offered Governments tempting possibilities of new revenue. It is said, too, that half-a-million people passed through St Martin's Le Grand on the first day of issue of Post Office postcards, and that 70 million postcards were sold in the first year. By the end of the decade, over 150 million postcards had already been posted – with picture postcards still to come.

The idea of a Post Office postcard may well have been put forward for the first time by an influential German Post Office official, Dr Heinrich von Stephan, who was to play a major part in the setting up of the General Postal Union (later to be called the Universal Postal Union) in 1874. While attending an Austro-German Postal Conference in Karlsruhe in 1865, one of many such conferences at this time, he made a ponderous speech in which after looking back at letter writing across the ages, he looked forward in the future to the wide circulation of an *offenes Postblatt*, 'an open post sheet', made of stiff paper and sold, like stamps, in Post Offices. This, he said, was a medium of communication which would offer simplicity and brevity. There should be a fixed place for the address, he suggested, and postal rates should be kept deliberately low.

The idea was taken up by an Austrian, a Professor at Vienna's Military Academy. Dr Emmanuel Hermann is important in the story because in 1869 he actually persuaded the Austrian Post Office to introduce such a *Correspondenz Karte* – it was buff-coloured – and because he was given honours in his own country and outside – if not in the North German Confederation – when nearly three million such cards were sold in the Austrian Empire during the first three months. The North German Confederation followed with postcards in July 1870, and Britain on October 1st 1870, the day of the issue of the first halfpenny stamp. And postcards, though not for long in buff or violet, were to outlast the halfpenny stamp which was taken out of general use in 1965 and quietly withdrawn in 1969.

The first newspaper in Britain to advocate the introduction of the postcard had been *The Scotsman*, and the first person to raise a petition to persuade the Government to act had been Lyon Playfair, who spoke of a 'card post'. Interestingly, however, the Society of Arts, which earlier in the century had pioneered many initially controversial schemes, including the great Exhibition itself, this time was hostile. It suggested instead light-weight letter

---

* What would he have thought of a postcard exhibited at a Düsseldorf Exhibition around 1890 on which was written the first three books of the *Odyssey*? One American postcard was used by Rita Kittredge, aged 77, of Belfast, Missouri, to hand down to posterity the 15,000 words of President Cleveland's message to Congress.

sheets tucked inside envelopes – for it, these were now *de rigueur* – and it even produced specimens which might have appealed to Cole. A different and superficially tenable objection which it expressed to postcards was that they were produced by a Government monopoly. In fact, from the start some enterprising firms added printed and decorated messages to the official looking new object: they included on the very first day an advertisement from the Royal Polytechnic Institution of Regent Street welcoming 'the Introduction of the Half-Penny Postage' and advertising a programme of entertainment. Soon afterwards Christmas greetings were incorporated on the card, sometimes lithographed in colour.

The Christmas card, of course, had a longer history than the postcard, as did the birthday card, the Valentine card and the New Year card, all of which were older still and the second of which, unlike the first and third, could be cruel, even vicious, rather than sentimental. The Christmas card was first invented in Britain in 1843 – by Henry Cole, who chose a design by J. C. Horsley, which was, if more modest, slightly worse than that of Mulready: it showed a family Christmas dinner with three generations present, although there was no tree, another Victorian innovation, in this case imported from Germany.

The mid-Victorians (and their progeny) were prepared to accept far worse designs for Christmas cards than those of either Horsley or Mulready, although they also bought and sold cards which still have character and charm. Late-Victorian artists included Kate Greenaway and Walter Crane. De La Rues produced such cards, as did several other firms, but the company which received the Royal Appointment in 1893, by which time the postcard for all seasons was well and truly established, was Raphael Tuck and Sons, who were to make the very most of the new postcard medium and to encourage the freeing of its production.

If postcards were first advocated because of the brevity and simplicity of the messages they would deliver, and if there were fears that they would become libellous, most of the earlier greetings cards which preceded the postcards, like many of the *cartes de visite* (see page 132) were impregnated with sentiment, expressing it with or without flowers:

> May you long each other love
> With benediction from above,
> And your faithful hearts when olden
> Celebrate the wedding golden.

There were doubtless some links with older popular culture here, although the style was unmistakeably Victorian.

Most of the first British postcards were circulated, like the older greetings cards, within the country, but in 1875, following the setting up of the General Postal Union, a new postcard for overseas was issued at half the letter rate. It bore the words 'FOREIGN POSTCARD. For Countries included in the Postal Union'. The cards also bore the apparently innocuous words in French – 'UNION POSTALE UNIVERSELLE, Grande Bretagne', thus stating a national location which it had been deemed unnecessary to state on adhesive postage stamps. And inevitably this was a distinctively British complication. For the Victorian Irish there was no such single country in the world as Great Britain, and the words 'Great Britain and Ireland' had to be substituted later in the year.

The Post Office faced a more time-consuming challenge during the 1870s as attempts were made by business firms to undercut its postcard prices. From 1872 it was possible for private firms to print their own cards, including pictures, subject to qualifications. They had to look like and to be as nearly as possible the same in size as official cards, they were not allowed to show the Royal Arms, the cardboard used had to be whiter than that used by De La Rues, nothing but the address could be written on the address side, and, most important of all, after being printed they had to be sent to the Inland Revenue Department to have a halfpenny stamp printed or engraved upon them and, this done, they never thereafter had to be altered.

These were serious restraints, but within the limits they imposed a few enterprising firms undercut the Post Office and sold their own postcards at 2s 6d per hundred. This was possible because they included advertisements: one, with a churchy appeal, advertised – along with photos of the Lambeth Conference – 'vino sacro, the unique Church Wine, A Boon to the Clergy', the Burial, Funeral and Mourning Reform Association, and the monthly magazine Mission Field. In New Zealand advertising had already been tried on the gummed side of postage stamps themselves – for Beecham's Pills and Sunlight Soap. Pears Soap, however, had failed to persuade the British Post Office to adopt a similar scheme five years earlier.

Less adventurous, but perhaps politically more articulate, business (and other) interests were soon pressing with the enthusiastic prompting of Henniker Heaton, who had found another new cause: for an even bigger, though basically very simple, change – the end of the Post Office monopoly and the opportunity for all firms to produce postcards on which members of the public would simply attach adhesive postage stamps as they did on letters. Clearly De La Rues as manufacturers of the 'official' postcards by Government contract were open to pressure also, and Henniker Heaton, who himself had interests in stamp delivery machines, did not spare them in his demand for the end of the Post Office monopoly.

It was not until 1894, however, that the Government capitulated, and agreed that adhesive stamps could be used on postcards, and even after 1894 it continued to exercise control in a manner that was characteristic of the Post Office (and doubtless of the Treasury). Henceforth postcards could be privately printed and sold, but they had to be of a specified size, and this was a different size from that used across the Channel. There were no fewer than fifteen scheduled provisions in the relevant Treasury Warrant published in the *London Gazette*, and any pictures associated with the cards still had to be printed on the message side, leaving the other side open for the address.

There was a further widening of choice in 1895 when a second size of card was permitted – 'court' size ($4\frac{1}{2}$ inches by $3\frac{1}{2}$) – but these postcards, said to appeal to Queen Victoria, still remained smaller than the controlled size (they had something in common with playing cards) and they were even less suitable for pictorial display than the standard cards. The first series of British views are said to have been produced by George Stewart and Company in Edinburgh – with London and Leicester close behind – but British firms were slow to take advantage of their new opportunities after 1894, and foreign producers were eagerly eyeing the lucrative British market.

France had already played a key role in the development of picture postcards, as had Germany and Switzerland. Indeed, what has often been hailed as the very first pictorial card, a *Souvenir de la Guerre de 1870*, was produced by a stationer near to Le Mans, Léon Bésdarneau. Soldiers welcomed such cards, and they could be carried economically by balloon when Paris was under siege. Other European countries were also producing picture postcards, including views of towns and countryside, during the early 1870s; and in Britain itself, Gustave Doré's drawing of St Paul's was printed on the address side of an official postcard by Grant and Company in 1872, with official permission, to advertise Doré's serialized *London*.

Paris again seemed to be at the centre of Europe at the time of the 1889 exhibition, and *Le Figaro* successfully projected a postcard which could be posted from the Eiffel Tower. It long survived the exhibition itself, and after it had been shown in 1900 at a Jubilee Postal exhibition in Leeds, the British Post Office flattered it by imitation, printing its own postcard version of the top of the Eddystone Lighthouse. The Americans, too, produced their first picture postcards for the Chicago Exhibition of 1893.

There was another burst of postcard writing at the Paris Exhibition of 1900, but you no longer needed to be present at a great event in a great city to rush for a postcard. Scenery would do. G. R. Sims in a copy of *The Referee* during the same year described how at the top of a mountain in Switzerland 'directly we arrived at the summit, everybody made a rush for the hotel and fought for the postcards. Five minutes afterwards, everybody was writing for dear life. I believe that the entire party had come up, not for the sake of the experience, or the scenery, but to write postcards and to write them on the summit.'

In the previous year Adolph Tuck had won a campaign on behalf of somewhat unenthusiastic British manufacturers – one observer in 1899 called them 'apathetic' – for them to be permitted to produce postcards in the same size as continental countries, and he had been given six months' notice to produce his own cards in the shops on the appointed day. Yet it was the Boer War rather than foreign tourism that made the appointed day propitious for British postcard producers. Soldiers in khaki could now appear on postcards of the right size, and if the cards revealed as little about the actual nature of that war as prints and photographs had done of the Crimean War (see page 162), they were none the less popular for that.

After the picture of the Queen, the most popular Tuck cards were said to be those commemorating the relief of Mafeking and Ladysmith. Khaki was the right colour too – it had come in through mid-Victorian India – but this did not inhibit the sales of a glamorous series of cards showing Grenadier Guards or Gordon Highlanders in full uniform. A Wrench series was called 'Links of the Empire' and a Blum and Degen series 'the Army through the Ages'. Other Tuck series in 1901, which recalled earlier Victorian series in other media, included Harold Copping's Shakespeare set and a popular 'Rough Seas' set printed by collotype in blue, green and sepia. *The Times* thought that they were 'almost too good to send through the post.'

Whatever the pedigree of the postcard – and there was a fine art pedigree in this last case – many of the producers of the new postcards, including Tuck's, had fascinating personal pedigrees. Gale and Polden of Aldershot, who made military cards, had made other militaria before. Harry Payne, who drew many of the Tuck Boer War cards, had specialized earlier in illustrating books of military history. Tom Browne, who made his name with comic seaside cards produced by Valentine's, had worked with *Punch*. George Stewart and Co of Edinburgh, who had claimed to be the first firm in Britain to publish postcards with views, had already published views on notepaper. James Bamforth of Holmfirth in Yorkshire, who was to make his name with 'Song and Hymn Cards', incorporating 'Real Life Photos', and with comic cards, had established his reputation by 1900 as 'King of the Lantern Slides', dealing both in magic lanterns and the production of lantern shows. (See page 137.) Lewis Wain, who along with German postcard makers was to produce anthropomorphic animal postcards, had written his *Madam Tabby's Establishment* in 1886 when he was twenty-six years old.

'Pretty postal missives', wrote E. W. Richardson, the editor of the recently founded sixteen-page *The Picture Postcard Magazine of Travel, Philately and Art* (July 1907), 'may in their small way subserve large issues', and he was thinking, as Cole had done early in Victoria's reign, of propaganda for good causes. Yet the early collectors of postcards were not usually driven, as he was, by social – or artistic – purpose. 'Young ladies who have escaped the philatelic intention or wearied of collecting Christmas cards', we are told in the *Standard* in 1899, 'have been known to fill albums with missives of this kind received from friends abroad; but now the cards are being sold in this country, and it will be like the letting out of waters.' By then, there was talk even in *The Times* of a postcard collecting 'mania', although, it was added, it had not yet reached 'such a pitch as it has in some foreign countries'.

The American journal *The Postcard* had been launched as early as 1889, and the first international postcard exhibitions took place in Leipzig in 1898 and in Venice in 1899. Ten years later, the first number of *La Carte Postale Illustrée* appeared. Yet there were twists in the story. Serious philatelists were uneasy about picture postcards, actually preferring the officially issued Post Office message cards, 'splendid specimens of the engraver's art,' and for them there seemed to be something meretricious about the pictures. Artists, too, seem to have ignored the possibilities of offering pictures of their own for postcards; and in the bureaucratic Austro-Hungarian Empire, despite the fact that it had been the first country to produce plain postcards, the sale of postcards of Titian and Rubens paintings in the Imperial Gallery in Vienna was forbidden in 1901.

Whatever the early inhibitions, the desire to collect picture postcards – nobody yet spoke of 'deltiology' – very quickly overcame them, and in 1900 itself Messrs Tuck organized a competition with £1000 in prizes for collectors of Tuck postcards. They had to have been posted, and the prizewinner, a lady in Norwich, submitted over 20,000 of them. Finally, the last Post Office obstacle was overcome when in 1901 the authorities agreed to allow postcards to include both a message and an address on the same side of the postcard – 'or even an advertisement' – 'so long as such matter' did not 'interfere in any way with the legibility of the address'. There seems to have been no new formal regulation or de-regulation, but a notice to this effect appeared in the *Picture Postcard Magazine* in January 1902.

By then, of course, Queen Victoria was dead, and the golden age of the postcard was about to begin. The editor of the *Picture Postcard Magazine* had two things to say about that. First, 'not known as a great collector of postcards ... had she lived it is possible the Queen might have developed into one'. Second, 'Many portrait postcards of Queen Victoria appeared during her life. None was so good as those published after her death.' One was called 'the Mother of her People'.

# 10
# New Things – and Old

Novelty, give us novelty, seems to be the cry.
Heaven and earth and the wide sea cannot obtain the forms and fancies that are here displayed ... like the whimsies of madness.

HENRY COLE, *Journal of Design*, 1849

'It's one of those horrid telegraph things, mum', she said, handling it as if she were afraid it would explode and do some damage.

LOUISA MAY ALCOTT, *Little Women*, 1868

AD 10,000. An old man, more than six hundred years of age, was walking with a boy through a great museum. The people who were moving around them had beautiful forms, and faces which were indescribably refined and spiritual. 'Father', said the boy, 'you promised to tell me today about the Dark Ages. I like to hear how men lived and thought long ago.' 'It is no easy task to make you understand the past', was the reply.

W. HARBERN, *In the Year Ten Thousand*, 1892

We were making the future and hardly any of us troubled to think what future we were making.

H. G. WELLS, *When the Sleeper Awakes*, 1899

# I

It was easy to confuse novelty and innovation in Victorian Britain, particularly in the decade before Queen Victoria died. There was an element of play, also of entertainment, both in fashion and in invention; and in the discussion of scientific inventions there could be an active element of fantasy. There were many 'eccentric ideas'. Indeed, as early in the reign as 1845, the *Westminster Review* had written of the 'sanctuary of science' being 'invaded by clamorous cries of the half-educated masses.' It was referring then to scientific or pseudo-scientific theory, however, particularly to theories of evolution, and so too was J. A. Froude a generation later when he complained of science 'stepping beyond its province, like the young Titans trying to take heaven by storm.' By the end of the century, it was the impact of science on the world of things rather than on the world of ideas which was catching the popular imagination, and by then a cluster of new things had been brought into existence with the promise of far more to come.

The limits of the possible were being pushed further and further back. As the *Popular Science Monthly* put it in 1898, 'As the nineteenth century draws to its close, there is no slackening in that onward march of scientific discovery and invention which has been its chief characteristic. At the beginning of the century the telegraph was as yet undreamed of, and the telephone and the dynamo utterly unimaginable developments. Had anyone dared to conceive that signals could be made to pass in a second of time between Europe and America he would have been considered a fit candidate for Bedlam ... Today these things are considered commonplaces.' Nonetheless, a writer in the *Strand Magazine* in 1896, an *annus mirabilis* in the social history of the application of invention, was right to point out that the idea of a new thing was not in itself an invention. 'Every practical inventor knows that *ideas* are common to nearly everybody who will exercise their minds a little ... Some apparently impossible suggestions are realized by men such as Edison. But there are many ideas which even the wizard Edison could not lick into shape.'

The writer did not add that the *Strand Magazine* specialized in such 'impossible' ideas, while other periodicals specialized in warnings about the likely effect on people of ideas successfully realized as things. 'It is quite evident that many useful inventions ... while they may quicken the pace of life do not prompt either to physical or to intellectual exertion', the *Popular Science Monthly* insisted, 'and that the vast provision made today for the entertainment and amusement of the multitude has little educative value and may even tend to the injury of the reflective powers ... It sometimes seems almost possible that the modern world might be choked by its own riches.'

The *Electrical World* combined wonder and warning. Discussing in September 1890 'music on tap' by telephone, an 'idea ... most luxurious and

**GIVING THEM WARNING.**

*Electricity (to Submarine Cable and Land Telegraph).* "I DON'T LIKE TO GET RID OF OLD AND VALUABLE SERVANTS, BUT I'M AFRAID I SHALL NOT BE ABLE TO KEEP EITHER OF YOU MUCH LONGER."

*Electricity proclaims her future,* Punch, *1899*

371

attractive, fit ornament of a symbolic age', it foresaw 'a vista of dreadful possibilities' – 'the horrors of having one's disposition wrecked by a "popular programme"' of 'appetite-destroying tunes . . . turned loose at feeding time'. It even forecast the BBC when it demanded that any company providing 'music on tap' should be given an 'exclusive charter, for the probability of cut-rate competition and an orchestration in every boarding-house is really too horrible for contemplation.'

Such journalistic, intellectual or plain middle-class, middlebrow, notes of concern or contempt should be distinguished from militant resistance to invention on practical grounds on the part of workers who were suspicious of new machines, or defensive resistance on the part of vested interests which were rooted in the technological *status quo*. The complaint, also advanced in the *Popular Science Monthly* in 1898, that as a result of new inventions 'literature is more and more taking on the forms suited not so much to busy as to idle people', and the view of *The Electrician* that 'we are getting perilously near the ideal of the modern Utopia where life is to consist of sitting in armchairs and pressing a button' were very different from the efforts of telegraph companies to hold back the power of the telephone.

There is a wealth of evidence, however, to suggest that, whatever the reason, invention was seldom universally acclaimed in Victorian Britain. For some people the invasion of new things carried with it an element of threat. For more people there was a sense that new things upset old ways. There was a countervailing curiosity, of course, and in the event enough adaptability to ensure relatively rapid acceptance of change. Yet even among industrial employers there might well be little trust in science so long as profits were maintained.

In the alkali industry, for example, the crude but profitable Leblanc system survived long after the ammonia-soda process had established itself overseas. 'A manager can be too much of a chemist' was one of the depressing British opinions quoted by C. T. Kingzett in a book of 1877 on the 'alkali trade'. A second British opinion was that while the British invented things, they did not know how to exploit them; and a third opinion, that expressed in 1881 by Professor Sir Henry Roscoe, the President of the Society of Chemical Industry, was that 'whilst it is true that the most general and most important discoveries in the alkali trade have been made by Englishmen, it still remains the fact that many improvements and suggestions due to foreign skill and enterprise are not taken up in Britain as they deserve to be'.

Change in the chemical industry has figured less prominently in the twentieth-century literature of inventiveness than those changes in communications and in the sources of power which transformed attitudes to time and space. If the clock rather than the steam engine was 'the key machine of the modern industrial age', as Lewis Mumford called it, 'the foremost machine in modern technics', Britain lost its competitiveness in the clock industry in the very century when time was being measured and synchronized more generally – and more effectively – than ever before, even if it was standardized in 1884 with Greenwich as the reference point. It was the Swiss – and the Americans – who through their enterprise benefited most economically from enhanced time-consciousness: late-Victorian Britain, which had a highly prestigious, high quality business in clocks, watches and chronometers in London, was importing large numbers of Swiss watches and American clocks: indeed, as early as 1854, a Liverpool importer claimed that 'American clocks are imported from the United States by almost every vessel in small boxes containing dozens or half-dozens'.

When the Lancashire Watch Company was set up in 1889, significantly not in London or in Coventry, but at Preston – belatedly entering a field of mass production in which it soon became a successful competitive enterprise – even there workers resisted the adoption of new technologies. The experienced artisans whom the firm had decided to employ were, according to one observer, 'very much against any alteration to old things'. 'Now the Swiss, when they introduced the cheap watch', he went on, 'didn't take the men who had been used to the good quality work ... they trained up another lot which hadn't got the tradition, you see, so there was no prejudice behind them using those sorts of [new] things.'

The economic lesson, clear by 1901, was that if resistance to technology succeeded in Britain, there were always other places, particularly Germany and the United States, willing to take up the technology. And British customers, more enterprising than manufacturers, were not reluctant to import things from overseas which with more enterprise might have been manufactured in Britain. In such circumstances, late-Victorian industrial protectionism in Britain was neither an attractive nor a healthy industrial response. At best, it was an attempt to hold time back. At worst, it actually limited rather than encouraged the play of inventiveness, never a uniquely British product, in Britain itself.

Curiously, Britain's last Victorian Prime Minister, Lord Salisbury, a true conservative in politics and a true aristocrat, loved all new things which had an element of science in them. He dabbled in chemistry, installed electricity in his great house at Hatfield to the horror of many of his own guests, and in an address to the very first dinner of the Institution of Electrical Engineers in 1889 he extolled the social power of electricity far above the power of the steam engine. Nineteenth-century scientific discoveries, he argued, in words that might have been used by H. G. Wells, had had a bigger impact 'not only upon the large collective destinies, but upon the daily life and experience of multitudes of human beings, than even the careers of the greatest conquerors or the services of the greatest statesmen'. According to *The Electrician*, which reported his speech in full, this sentence, which was placed in the middle of his speech, was received with 'cheers'.

Salisbury certainly appreciated the global significance of invention, the fact that both the origins and implications were international; and H. G.

Wells was to claim that 'obsolescent particularisms' would disappear as communications technology advanced. Yet even this line of thought was not completely new. Before either of them had turned to the subject of the shrinking of distance, Gladstone had once remarked piously that 'each train that passes a frontier weaves the web of the human federation'.

It was in Canada, where there were huge distances without frontiers, that some of the most enthusiastic prophets of communication were to be found, as they were to be found still more in the twentieth century. The use of the telegraph, wrote Sanford Fleming, a Canadian engineer whose vision encompassed space and time, 'subjects the whole surface of the globe to the observation of civilized communities and leaves no interval of time between widely separated places proportionate to their distances apart.' In Australia, the Melbourne *Argus* in June 1853 considered the telegraph 'the most perfect of modern inventions ... Anything more perfect than this is scarcely conceivable, and we really begin to wonder what will be left for the next generation upon which to expend the restless enterprise of the human mind.'

## II

In his 1889 speech a generation later, Lord Salisbury insisted that there was much that was left, and looked forward to a not too distant future when 'you can turn on electric power in the house of the artisan as now you can turn on gas'. This, he claimed, would reinforce the most conservative force in society, 'the integrity of the family'. When Salisbury looked back, however, towards a not very distant past, it was still the electric telegraph, a 'strange and fascinating discovery', which moved him most: it too had had a direct influence upon 'the moral and intellectual nature and action of mankind'. 'The electric telegraph', he claimed, 'has achieved this great and paradoxical result: it has, as it were, assembled all mankind upon one great plane, where they can see [*sic*] everything that is done, and hear everything that is said, and judge of every policy that is pursued at the very moment when these events take place.'

When Salisbury made remarks of this kind, he was talking, perhaps, more of the potential of things than of their actual impact and he was obviously leaving out much, perhaps most, that was relevant to a proper assessment of 'the moral and intellectual nature and action of mankind'. Yet scientists and engineers themselves made very similar remarks. For Sir Gabriel Stokes, responding to Salisbury at the dinner, 'nowadays the whole earth resembles, in a measure, one of our own bodies. The electric wires represent the nerves, and messages are conveyed from the most distant regions to the central place of government, just as in our bodies, where sensations are conveyed to the sensorium.'

The metaphor, significantly different from the older metaphor of the circulation of the blood, was to have a long life ahead of it, but that was not the servant's reaction to telegraphy in Louisa M. Alcott's's *Little Women*. At the family level, after telling her mistress that the 'penny postman' had not yet arrived on 'our day for a letter', there was a knock at the door and 'one of them horrid telegraph things' was brought in. Her mistress's reaction was similar. 'At the word "telegraph" Mrs March read the two lines it contained, and dropped back into her chair as white as if the little paper had sent a bullet to her heart.'

Obviously there were messages and messages, just as there were homes and homes – of every variety – as well as 'central places of government'. The telegraph, a new Victorian experience, carried both personal and public information: it figured in letters, diaries and novels, therefore, even more than in blue books, and most of all in newspapers. In announcing to the London public the birth of Queen Victoria's second son, Alfred Ernest, at Windsor in 1844, *The Times* had declared itself 'indebted to the extraordinary power of the Electro-Magnetic Telegraph' for being able to be the first with the news. 'By telegraph' soon became newspaper blurb. 'Telegrams are for facts,' Moberley Bell, the managing editor of *The Times* told correspondents. 'Background and comment must come by post.'

W. F. Cooke and Charles Wheatstone's telegraph patent, taken out in the year Queen Victoria came to the throne, was based on deflection by magnetic needles, with signals causing the needles to point to the letters of the alphabet. Yet long before Victoria an 'expeditious method of conveying intelligence' had been sought; and in the early-nineteenth century Francis Ronalds, who has claims to be 'the father of English telegraphy', had been in touch with an uninterested Admiralty. 'Why,' he asked, 'should not the Government govern at Portsmouth as promptly as in Downing Street?' Official rebuffs turned Ronalds from telegraphy to meteorology – and from Portsmouth to Kew – but he received a knighthood for his services to electric telegraphy in the year before he died, 1870. The word 'electric' mattered increasingly by that time. Indeed, the editor of *The Electrician* refused to publish articles on the subject of signalling unless they omitted all the 'non-electric parts', including flags, semaphore and hydraulic telegraphs.

Before its multiple uses became apparent, the telegraph is quickly said to have saved lives in accidents – this was always a bonus for any new invention, as it was to be for wireless – and the first Electric Telegraph Company was set up in 1846.

One man who had to be bought off in the final business deal was Alexander Bain, who held patents both for a telegraph and an electric clock. There was nothing unique about this. Almost all Victorian patents were to be the subject of arbitration, litigation and buying off. Money was at stake, not just techniques or ideas. Both the idea and the technique of Cooke and Wheatstone's telegraph had, in fact, been anticipated by the German Baron Paul Schilling, who had displayed his telegraph at a meeting of German naturalists in Bonn in 1835.

The story of the telegraph in the United States has similar features to that in Britain, although paths were to diverge and there, Samuel Morse, a remarkable man of multiple talents, who had been the first President of the American Academy of Design, gave a private demonstration of telegraphy in 1837. 'If I can succeed in working a magnet ten miles I can go round the globe', he is reported as having said a year earlier, but it was not until 1844 that he built the first telegraph line from Baltimore to Washington. Morse's telegraph system carried a code of letters tapped out on a keyboard – this was the task of an operator – and recorded at a distance by a register and a moving stylus on a strip of paper. His dot-dash 'alphabet' drew on the work of his collaborator Alfred Vail, with whom he entered into partnership in 1837, and immediately became known as the 'Morse code'. Already developed by 1838, it passed into international use, constituting both 'a system of signs by which letters and consequently words and sentences are signified' and 'a set of type, adapted to regulate and communicate the signs'.

The word 'telegraph' means 'writing at a distance', and Morse was as interested in the alphabet as in the electricity. Indeed, he actually counted the number of letters he found in each box of printer's type case and examined them carefully, an example of direct transference from an old technology to a new one. Morse messages were written on paper, and the first of them, transmitted in 1844, ran, grandiloquently – 'What Hath God Wrought!'

It might be argued that the Western Union Telegraph Company, set up twenty years later, wrought still more than God had done following a consolidation of soundless telegraph businesses. By 1866 it operated through 2,250 offices and had 100,000 miles of telegraph line; and in 1872 its operations were made far more efficient than ever before with the perfection of the duplex system by Joseph Stearns of Boston. This invention doubled telegraphic capacity through the simultaneous wire transmission of messages, and by 1877 Western Union had over 90,000 miles of telegraph line and 7,500 offices. Out of duplex came quadruplex, sextuplex, and multiples.

Other American companies besides Western Union introduced new devices of their own both to speed up messages and to record them: there was even facsimile telegraphy, albeit at high cost. Yet in the United States it was Morse who was always thought of as the founder of it all rather than his American predecessor Professor Joseph Henry, or foreign scientists, particularly the Dane, Hans Oersted, who had discovered in 1819 that an electric current causes the deflection of a compass needle, not the least important of all the many needles (see page 208). For a writer in *Scribner's Magazine* in 1889 'the world has lost nothing, nor is it less to his [Morse's] credit, if parts of the invention which he esteemed most have, like the false works of an arch, been removed. When they became an encumbrance, their absence was doubtless as important as had been their presence, to give the structure its original shape and strength.'

In the history of the telegraph in Britain there was always a distinctive touch of imperialist rhetoric, particularly after the submarine Atlantic cable, 'a thread across the sea', had been successfully laid in 1866, two years after India was connected to Britain. In 1851 T. R. Crompton had announced the laying of the London – Paris cable in the Crystal Palace when Queen Victoria was leaving the platform after declaring the great Exhibition closed; and in 1858 Charles Bright, a 26-year old engineer, received a knighthood – he was the youngest man people could remember to do so – for completing the first Atlantic cable. His cable was not to last, but *The Times* called it 'the greatest discovery since that of Columbus', a 'vast enlargement ... given to the sphere of human activity'.

Nonetheless, there was argument as well as rhetoric in Britain concerning the telegraph before the Telegraph Act of 1863 first regulated aspects of the business, for between 1846 and 1870, the year when Ronald received his belated knighthood, the development of telegraphy in Victorian Britain, as in the United States, was in the hands of profit-making private enterprise. The Act regulated certain operations of the companies and restricted the sale of any of them without the consent of the Board of Trade. Yet complaints persisted of high charges and slow deliveries, and in 1868 Disraeli's Conservative Government introduced a Telegraph Bill 'to enable the Postmaster-General to acquire, maintain and work the Electric Telegraph in the United Kingdom'. Private enterprise was thought to be inefficient, even though by then there was a national system of telegraphy which had grown remarkably, if unevenly and patchily, since 1846, just as there was a national railway system.

The year 1851 had been a very special year, and between then and 1855 the number of messages transmitted had increased more than seven times, from 99,216 to 745,880. Two years later, the Electric Telegraph Company, the major group in the system, had merged with its rival, the English and Irish Magnetic Telegraphic Company, to form a new 'Magnetic' with (from 1859) imposing head offices in Threadneedle Street, close to Bagehot's Lombard Street, and with links throughout the whole world. Also in 1859 a London District Telegraph Company was formed – with links with the Magnetic. As it set about wiring London, Dickens, sensitive to the earlier impact of railways on the metropolis, wrote in *All the Year Round* how 'the sturdiest Englishman is ready to give up the roof of his castle in the interests of science and the public good when he finds that hundreds of his neighbours have already led the way'. Dickens believed that 'in an age of express trains, painless operations, crystal palace ... and a hundred curiosities such as our grandfathers and grandmothers never dreamt about' the telegraph was 'of all our modern wonders the most wonderful'.

Despite the wonder and the progress, the years from 1836 to 1867 were not the only years when the issue of public ownership was raised – indeed, it had been raised in relation to railways still earlier – and there was always scope for comparison since both France and Germany had developed public railway and telegraphic systems. 'Is not telegraphic communication as much a function of government as the conveyance of letters?' the *Quarterly Review* asked in 1854. As was to be the case in all subsequent development in communications technology, including radio, and in the making of electricity supply systems, the same technology was to be employed in different societies according to traditions and attitudes which had little to do with the inherent characteristics of the technologies themselves.

Among the cluster of issues which affected judgements on the issue of public versus private ownership were the powers of the companies *vis à vis* the owners of private property, the structure of tariffs charged to different categories of users, the role of the railways as the most powerful of communications interests, the extent of geographical coverage and, above all, attitudes towards monopoly *versus* competition and the effects of each on the quality of service and on the level of investment.

One user was more influential than the rest. The Press, influenced in its content and even in its language by the telegraph, was interested as a major customer both in what information it could collect and transmit by telegraph and what it would cost. As early as 1854, more than 120 provincial newspapers, the most favoured of the beneficiaries, received columns of Parliamentary news by telegraph; and in 1859 Reuters, then a young news agency, secured exclusive rights to supply foreign telegrams to all towns in the kingdom. A year later, 'the Electric' erected an office at Newmarket to provide racing news which had previously been carried by 'hard riding'. In 1854 it had introduced a 'pneumatic despatch' between its central office and the Stock Exchange.

It was a blow, therefore, to considerable sections of the Press, as it was to many business interests and to private interests, when in July 1865 the British telegraph companies, acting in unison, withdrew the uniform low rate of 1s for 20 words, addresses free, that had been in force since 1861 between certain large cities. Some of the protests came from exactly the same cities, among them Edinburgh, which had pressed for uniform postage rates during the 1830s. The acquisition by the state of the telegraph companies was, they maintained, 'essential to the progress of the mercantile and manufacturing interests of the country.'

However surprising it might seem in the 1980s, it was not surprising at the time that it was a Conservative Government which introduced telegraph legislation in 1868 that was designed to shift ownership from private companies to the state. After all, the *Quarterly Review*, which had asked the key question in 1854, was an established Tory periodical. It is more surprising, perhaps, that one of the most forceful advocates of 'the transfer of telegraphs to a public department' was the free-trader Member of Parliament for Stoke-on-Trent, John Lewis Ricardo, nephew of the political economist David Ricardo, particularly since he had been founder-director and chairman of the Electric Telegraph Company until 1858.

A more likely advocate, although to begin with he was fully preoccupied with another exercise in national enterprise, the Post Office Savings Bank, was Frank Scudamore, 'small, bright-eyed, eager and alert' public servant, who had joined the Post Office in 1841 and who had been appointed Assistant Secretary in 1863 after a spell as Accountant General: the half-penny postcard had been his responsibility (see page 348). Scudamore found international comparisons useful. The percentage of telegrams to letters was no higher in Britain in 1865 than it had been in Switzerland in 1853. In Belgium the state-controlled institution, set up in 1850, had reduced charges during the 1860s with the result that the use of telegrams increased by 400 per cent while the use of letter post increased by only 45 per cent.

Scudamore's manipulation of detailed statistics recalled that of Rowland Hill. So, too, did his estimates of future revenue, which impressed the Postmaster-General, and among others W. S. Jevons and Edwin Chadwick. The Conservative bill of 1868, designed 'to enable the Postmaster-General to acquire, maintain and work the Electric Telegraph of the United Kingdom', survived Disraeli's Parliamentary defeat in the general election of April 1868 and became law in July 1868. Indeed, the principle of nationalization also survived the replacement of Disraeli by Gladstone. An amendment that the new government monopoly should be limited to seven years was defeated.

The terms of the take-over as set out in 1868 were criticized more than any other aspect of the measure, and Robert Lowe, the Chancellor of the Exchequer, washed his hands of them, but there seem to have been few people who followed *The Railway Times* in objecting to what it called 'the stagnation and dreary routine inseparable from official regulations' or who pressed for complete free trade, allowing the right of any association to erect public telegraph poles along any public way. Seventy-seven petitions in favour of Disraeli's bill had been received from local Chambers of Commerce and other bodies and 177 from the Press, which supported the proposal vigorously in editorials. Moreover, of the petitions against the bill ten came from companies, 319 from their shareholders, and only one from a person who was not a shareholder.

The fact that the well-organized opposition campaign was supported by large sections of the 'railway interest' which straddled the House of Commons did not, in fact, sway the outcome. On this memorable occasion, at least, vested interest did not prevail. Part of the reason was the appeal of a uniform rate, promised in the bill, as attractive as the idea of a uniform postal rate (see page 328). A stronger reason still was the fact that the Press, particularly the provincial Press, favoured the change. J. E. Walker, the Editor of the *Manchester Guardian*, had been in the forefront of an agitation for change since 1858, and was infuriated by the unwillingness of the companies to deal with the Press Association, formed in 1868. As *The Economist* wrote 'the Press when united, is stronger than any other interest, and has suffered for years under the shortcomings of the private [telegraph] companies'.

The effect of nationalization was an expansion of services, but the price was financial crisis. On the eve of the legislation which gave the Post Office a public monopoly, more than three million inland messages had been sent in 1868 from over 3,000 stations, a third of which were located in railway stations, while nearly 3,700,000 messages had been international. By 1872/3 there were over 5,000 telegraph offices, 1,900 of them added in 1870 itself, and over fifteen million messages were being transmitted. The policy of ensuring that 'a cheap telegram in order to be successful should go everywhere' meant substantial extra expenditure on lines as remote areas began to fall within the aegis of the system. By comparison the development of a postal system had been cheap. To cover the cost of expansion – and a far greater purchase price than he had originally estimated, Scudamore did not hesitate to divert resources, including a large sum from Post Office Savings Bank funds, which would have otherwise gone to the Exchequer, fully knowing that what he was spending in total was in excess of his Parliamentary vote. But when he was attacked, he was unrepentant. 'You might as well expect a canary to hatch a sitting of ostrich eggs', he told Gladstone, 'as to expect the Treasury to dry-nurse the telegraph system.'

It was the Treasury that won, and in 1875 Scudamore had to go, still unrepentant; and in 1875 he left London far behind him for the very different task of organizing the posts and telegraphs of the Ottoman Empire. He did not leave, however, without honour. Trollope, Dickens, Gladstone and, not least, *Punch* had been amongst his friends. Scudamore always insisted that his actions were fully justified in terms of the increase of traffic. In particular, the number of telegraphic messages transmitted by the Press had increased three times between 1870 and 1875. 'The transmission of news to the Press throughout the kingdom – should be regarded as a matter of national importance', he maintained, and charges for such transmission should include 'no greater margin of profit than would suffice to make the service fairly self-supporting'. The *Edinburgh Review* went further: 'some loss may be wisely undergone rather than a most important means of communication be curtailed'.

There were others, therefore, more subject to criticism, who wished to go further in reducing charges for the service as a whole than Scudamore had done, and in 1883 Dr Charles Cameron, a Glasgow MP, forced a reduction of telegraph charges against the wishes of Gladstone's Chancellor of the Exchequer, which inevitably involved government subsidy. From October 1885 onwards the rate for a twelve-word inland telegram was reduced to 6d. – the twelve words now had to include the address – and at the expense of increasing Post Office deficits the number of messages transmitted rose still further to over 50 million in 1886/7, 66 million in 1890/1, and over 90 million at the end of the century. This was the highest total for any country in the world. Given these figures, it seemed to matter little to most people that Post Office deficits increased and that in the words of a Select Committee of 1888 on the Revenue Departments' Estimates 'a great commercial department like the Post Office' was disregarding 'commercial principles'.

There were many further technical developments in late-Victorian England, and the Society of Telegraph Engineers, founded in 1871 with Charles W. Siemens as President, took a professional interest in all of them before and after it changed its name to the Institution of Electrical Engineers in 1889. One of the last of them was the 'telautograph' of 1901 which claimed not for the first time to transmit the actual handwriting or drawing of the person sending the message. There were no further public enquiries into the telegraph system, however, despite the fact that there were well-informed British critics who felt that the Post Office monopoly did not help necessary scientific research and that America was now ahead. More seriously, by 1900 the appeal of the telegraph had been challenged in ways that would have seemed impossible in 1868 and 1869, but had become apparent since 1876, the year after Scudamore left the Post Office.

## III

It was in March of that year that Alexandra Graham Bell patented the telephone and demonstrated it at the Philadelphia Exhibition (see Chapter 2). Sir William Thomson, later Lord Kelvin, who saw it and heard it there, described it as 'the most wonderful thing he had seen in America'. He brought back across the Atlantic a pair of Bell telephones wrapped in newspaper, which he himself and W. F. (later Sir William) Preece, the Assistant Engineer-in-Chief of the Post Office and a founder member of the Society of Telegraph Engineers, displayed to members of the British Association at Plymouth in 1877. 'Hey, diddle-diddle, the cat and the fiddle', recited Thompson on one telephone. 'Please follow that up', and the reply came back – to his and his audience's delight – on the second telephone, 'There he goes – he says – "the cow jumped over the moon"'.

There was something even more appropriate in the content of this exchange than the first words Bell had succesfully transmitted to his lively and highly inventive partner Thomas Watson in March 1876 – 'Mr Watson [please?] come here, I want you'. The direct personal quality of that request from a man in trouble – Bell had spilt battery acid over his clothes – could not then be answered on the telephone by Watson with the comforting words, 'I'm coming', since Bell's telephone could transmit sound in one direction only. Yet in the future, when the telephone had become an instrument not of information but of communication, the message was to be compared favourably with telegraphy's rhetorical exclamation 'What Hath God Wrought'.

Nursery rhymes belonged naturally both to the prehistory and to the history of the 'harmonic telephone', but so, also, did Shakespeare: it was 'to be or not to be' that the Philadelphia audience had heard at the Centennial Exposition. There was, in fact, both a theatrical and a therapeutic pedigree. Bell, born in Edinburgh in 1847, had a grandfather who had moved from cobbling to the stage as a 'comedian' and from jokes to Shakespeare: he was the author of two books, *The Practical Elocutionist* and *Stammering and other Impediments to Speech*. Bell's father became a 'professor of Elocution', and as a pioneer of 'visible speech' to assist the deaf it was he who introduced Alexander to the problems of speech which were to point him in novel fashion towards the telephone. As Watson put it, having made deaf mutes talk, he wanted to make mute metal talk also. Yet the telegraph was always in his mind. In Bell's own words of 1875, 'if I can make a current of electricity vary in intensity as the air varies in density during the production of a sound, I should be able to transmit speech telegraphically'.

The serious and the trivial were juxtaposed as Bell and Watson demonstrated the uses of the one-way telephone to Americans and Canadians with dramatic soliloquies and poems, trombone solos and songs like *Yankee Doodle*, *Pull for the Shore*, *Do not trust him, gentle lady* and *Home Sweet Home*. Watson himself is said to have had 'a steam organ voice' developed by 'months of shouting in the laboratory', and Bell once said that his dream was that 'all the people of the United States will sing "The Star Spangled Banner" in unison by means of the telephone'.

In London, Bell had chosen a talented American woman journalist and publicist, Kate Field, to present a brilliantly conceived *Matinée-Téléphonique* to coincide with the opening of Parliament in 1877, and later Gilbert and Sullivan in HMS *Pinafore* were to include the telephone in the lyrics of a quartet led by Dick Deadeye:

He'll hear no tone,
Of the maiden he loves so well.
No Telephone
Communicates with his cell.

By then, however, the telephone was associated with conversation as well as with transmission so that *Punch*, an invaluable, if sceptical, guide to Victorian invention, could develop the idea of lovers' telephone chat with suggestions that kissing by telephone might be an early refinement. A whole generation earlier, it had talked mischievously but precociously of songs and pieces of music being sent by telegraph: 'It must be delightful for a party at Boston to be able to call upon a gentleman in New York for a song'. And it added that the telegraph was 'too good a thing to be confined to public use' and should be introduced into 'the domestic circle'.

There had been less play with the telegraph than there was with the telephone, a word invented in 1863 by Joshua Coppersmith, who was arrested for trying to extort funds from 'ignorant and superstitious people' by exhibiting a device which he claimed would carry the human voice any distance over wires. The play continued, moreover, after 1876. In August 1877, the *Daily News* reported a demonstration by Cromwell F. Varley at the Queen's Theatre, Long Acre, of a 'musical telegraph by which sounds of variable pitch can be conveyed from one place to another by electricity'. The demonstration began with 'Where, and oh where, is my Highland laddie gone?' and it was received with loud cheers. As the *Musical Times* put it, 'the sounds reproduced were certainly not of the sweetest kind, but the interesting and important fact was that they were there'.

Given such responses to inventiveness, it is not surprising that many members of the public treated the first one-way Bell telephones as 'electrical toys'. Yet the sense of a telephone being a toy paradoxically had its own serious side. At a time when there was an increasing demand for entertainment, which twenty years later could become a cause of concern, what in retrospect has been called 'a radio concept of telephony' – the use of the telephone as an instrument not of conversation, but of transmission of music, drama and news – was logical enough. Even the highly serious periodical *Nature* could contemplate 'dancing parties' where there would be no requirement for a musician, while G. Vidal's supremely serious French study *Le Téléphone* (1886) talked of the sound of music 'turned on by a switch "just as we get water when we turn on a faucet"'.

In the universe of invention, the telephone belonged, therefore, not only to the sphere of the telegraph, but to that of the phonograph, another invention of the late 1870s, first described in the *Scientific American*, and first actually tested by its inventor Thomas Edison with the words of 'Mary had a little lamb'. Edison himself developed his tin-foil cylinder phonograph while working with Bell's telephone receiver, and when it was introduced to the editor of the *Scientific American*, it 'spoke for itself' with a record enquiring after his health, asking him whether he liked the machine and wishing him goodnight.

Not surprisingly, the phonograph shared the headlines with the telephone as a major 'topic of the day'. 'There is no reason', wrote one Canadian newspaper, *The Daily Expositor*, in March 1878, 'why we should not have all the great men of the age, as well as all the brilliant singers and actresses, taken possession of and driven off their course by the phonograph ... We shall all waste a portion of our substance on these little instruments.' *Leslie's Weekly* went further. The phonograph would 'turn all the old grooves of the world topsy-turvy and establish an order of things never dreamed of even in the vivid imaginings of the Queen Scheherazade in the 1001 Night's Entertainments'.

For various reasons, mainly technical, it was the telephone which continued to hit the headlines until Edison took up the phonograph again later in the 1880s, telling the *Scientific American* proudly in 1887 that he could now read the whole of *Nicholas Nickleby* on four cylinders. Two years later the (bewitched) conductor von Bülow was recording *inter alia* Beethoven's *Eroica* and the prelude to Wagner's *Die Meistersinger* and Gladstone was addressing 'a band of excursionists at Hawarden'. A year after that an applicant for a post in an opera company offered to send 'a cylinder from which you can judge near enough to place me in the chorus'.

Meanwhile, at the Paris exhibition of 1881 long queues had gathered to listen to music transmitted by telephone from a mile away, and long after the exhibition was over 'theatrephones' in the boulevards were linked with Paris theatres. The most highly organized and efficient 'radio telephone' service was popularized not in Paris, however, but in Budapest, when regular programmes were broadcast by telephone each day from 1893 onwards. The main features of the Hungarian scheme were highly publicized in Britain by writers like Arthur Mee, future editor of the *Children's Encyclopaedia*, for whom 'the pleasure telephone' opened out 'vistas of infinite charm'. 'Who dares to say that in twenty years the electric miracle will not bring all the corners of the earth to our fireside?'

London lagged well behind Budapest in its recognition both of the possibilities and of the practical problems, but in London also an Electrophone Company was founded in 1894 – it was not thought to be a new idea – following previous experiments in both London and in the provinces. It had a capital of £20,000, and its object was 'the hiring out of an instrument designed to enable subscribers to hear at their own homes or at certain central offices the performances at theatres, halls, concert halls, etc.' 'A regular supply of the most up-to-date music, the most recent plays, the latest *cause célèbre* or the best passages of a sermon by one of the most eminent divines' would be 'laid on' in the home, it promised, along with 'the water, the gas and the usual accessories'.

It was thanks to this London company that Queen Victoria was 'amused' by a demonstration in May 1899, although more than twenty years earlier still she had invited Bell to Osborne, had listened to him explaining his techniques, had heard Kate Field singing and had heard Preece humming the National Anthem which she thought 'very badly played'. In 1889 she listened at Windsor Castle to boys from naval and military schools rendering their version of 'God Save the Queen' at Her Majesty's Theatre in London. Four years earlier, the farewell address of Dean Farrar at St Margaret's, Westminster had been heard by 'hosts of admirers in other districts of London' and in city hospitals. Other churches using the electrophone were said to be St Anne's, Soho, St Michael's, Chester Square and St Martin-in-the-Fields, a church which was to play an interesting part in the early history of broadcasting. Pulpit and stage, religion and entertainment, were now drawing closer together.

The management of *Telephon Hirmondo*, founded by Theodore Puskas in Budapest, learnt from experience about most of the difficulties that broadcasting organizations would face in the twentieth century – 'balancing programmes'; 'giving the people what they wanted'; dislike by the Press of a rival news service; performing rights; and, not least, self-censorship and 'how much advertising?' By comparison, the experience of London's Electrophone Company was severely restricted. Yet one lesson seemed clear. As *The Electrician* stated in 1882, it was 'problematical' whether any government department would ever wish directly to 'enter upon this kind of business'. Offering a service involving what we would now call 'programming' was not, like telegraphy, a matter for the Post Office.

It says much for Bell that while he was interested in such leisure uses of the telephone – he wished he had taken ivory telephones with him when he visited the Queen – almost from the start he had emphasized with remarkable prescience, like *The Electrician*, that its uses in business and in government were far more important. When he gave his early lectures on the new instrument, this was his main theme, and he made the most of it *before* all the necessary technology was available to realize what he wanted to do. Unlike America's foremost electrician, Elisha Gray, who had himself developed invention in this field and who, it has been suggested, suffered from all the limitations of the expert, Bell did not just compare the telephone with the telegraph. He saw the potential of long-distance verbal telephonic dialogue through a network.

Another American in a privileged position who did not see the potential was William Orton, President of Western Union, the big American Telegraph Company, founded in 1856 and by then the biggest corporation in the United States, who turned down an offer from Bell in 1876/7 to acquire all his patent rights for $100,000. Orton posed a would-be decisive question – 'What use would this company make of an electrical toy'? – and the answer seemed to him obvious. Telegraphy was so well established and by then supplied so many specialized services, some of them on 'ticker tape', that it was unassailable. In 1876 there were 214,000 miles of telegraph wire in the United States, delivering over 30 million messages.

In Britain, too, the Post Office had a similar vested interest, but Disraeli's Conservative Postmaster-General, Lord John Manners, was relatively enthusiastic about the telephone, and there were early demonstrations of it at Aldershot, the military centre, as well as at Osborne. Preece might question its immediate usefulness in a country where there was no shortage of domestic servants, errand boys and 'things of that kind', and John Tilley, a more important Post Office official, was even more sceptical, but the Post Office took it seriously and *The Times*, while noting many 'extravagant and erroneous statements' about the future of the invention, described it as 'a most startling one – too remarkable, indeed, to be discredited by any amount of exaggeration'.

The British were impressed also by Thomas Edison's improved telephone transmitter, which included a carbon lampblack button, patented in 1877, and the Post Office was soon involved both with the new Edison Telephone Company of Great Britain and with Bell's company. 'In England we had fun', Edison wrote later. 'Neither the Bell people nor we could work satisfactorily without injuring each other.' To prove the merits of his own devices he had arranged for his nephew to recite Shakespeare, Tennyson and Emerson before an audience in Piccadilly Square, and for Gladstone and Mrs Gladstone to have a private audience. He was somewhat disturbed when Mrs Gladstone had to ask whether it was a man or a woman at the other end of the line.

George Bernard Shaw was one of Edison's paid publicists – he was called 'a wayleave manager' – but it is doubtful whether he was any more impressed than Mrs Gladstone: later he was to suggest that the chalk drum telephone was 'a much too ingenious invention ... of such stentorian efficiency that it bellowed your most private communications all over the house instead of whispering them with some sort of discretion'. More pertinently, with resistance to invention, not invention, in mind, he noted how contemptuous Edison's American workmen had been of 'the artfully slow British workman who did as little for his wages as he possibly could' and 'never hurried himself'.

It was to the Napoleon of inventors, Edison, born within days of Bell, but very different in personality, outlook and behaviour, and, indeed, in power to prophesy, that Western Union turned when it realized very quickly that its President had made a serious mistake in rejecting Bell, even though Orton had once told Preece that Edison had 'a vacuum where his conscience ought to be'. By then, however, Western Union was in the midst of fierce financial manoeuvring between Jay Gould and William H. Vanderbilt, and a new National Bell Telephone Company, set up in 1878 – without Bell – was able to establish itself quickly under the leadership of Theodore N. Vail, son of Morse's collaborator, Alfred Vail.

There was litigation about patents, of course, then and later, much of it protracted, some bitter, like a Tennessee suit filed in 1885 which reached the Supreme Court, but when in 1879 Western Union sold its telephone interests to the National Bell Telephone Company the way was clear for the full exploitation of Bell's patents which would last until 1893/4. In 1880/1 there were 132,692 Bell telephones in use compared with 6 in the summer of 1877, 3,000 in November 1877, and 61,000 a year in 1879/80, and there were only nine cities with a population of 100,000 or more that did not have a telephone exchange. By 1890, when long-distance services had been developed in America, Bell's net earnings were five times as large as they had been a decade earlier.

It is possible to trace back to this time the beginning not only of a telephone network in the United States, but of a telephone culture. Mark Twain's short story 'A Telephone Conversation' with a woman at each end of the line, was written as early as 1880, one year after he had had a telephone installed in his house: the conversation covered everything from beauty care to religion and ended with protracted goodbyes. Six years later, Benjamin Franklin Taylor, a poet with just the right Christian names, described how

> Your little song the telephone can float
> As free of fetters as a bluebird's note

and referred to 'the Lightning' as 'God's electric clerk'. As in the case of the telegraph, accidents played a part in the creation of the culture. The first news of a terrible railway accident in Connecticut was telephoned to a Western Union office in 1878. It created a stir and it quickly brought in doctors as subscribers. Advertisers made as much use of the affair as reporters.

The technical developments of the 1880s were mainly associated with the great cities – the first underground cable, a quarter of a mile in length; the opening of the first switchboards; the introduction of the first telephone number system (recommended by a doctor in Lowell, Massachusetts during a measles epidemic in 1880); the first successful automatic switches, devised by a Kansas City undertaker in 1891; the first dials in Milwaukee in 1896. As Colin Cherry has written – and as Vail himself, like Bell, fully appreciated – 'it was the introduction of the telephone *exchange* system and the growth in the *network* that finally converted Graham Bell's invention from a toy into a social instrument of immense organizational and economic power'. By the time that Bell's patents expired, there were over a quarter of a million telephones in use; and by then the main areas of growth were beginning to be not urban but rural, with the telephone becoming a major instrument of social transformation.

Not all Victorian things were so handled. Nor did all modes of handling, including those of American Bell and of the American Telephone and Telegraph Company, originally American Bell's New York City licensee, win the approval of the Press. Yet for the *Electrical Engineer* of New York in 1895 there was 'no escape from the self-evident fact that the telephone has been managed with energy and enterprise, while the telegraph has been gradually confined to the old conservative grooves, blind to the march of events, and deaf to the demands of development.'

In Britain, the story was significantly different, although the first telephone exchange was opened in London in 1879 – in Coleman Street – and by the time the first list of subscribers was printed in 1880 there were seven London exchanges or 'stations' as they were then called. There was almost as much excitement when London was linked with Birmingham in 1890 and with Paris in 1891 as there was in the United States when Boston was linked with Providence in a line dismissed at first as 'Vail's folly'. If in the United States Vail insisted that he was the one who took responsibility, in Britain the parallel insistence came from the Post Office with contrasting results. Using the Telegraph Act of 1869, itself harking back to railway legislation, the Post Office imposed in 1880 licensing regulations and controls on the United Telephone Company, created in May 1880 to link Bell and Edison interests that otherwise would have conflicted; and soon it opened public lines and public telephone exchanges of its own. The subsequent policies and operations of the Post Office were inconsistent, and while there were varieties of advice from behind the scenes there were also shifts in public opinion, culminating in a widely held, if erroneous, view expressed in the *Quarterly Review* five years after the death of Queen Victoria that 'by common consent we have the worst telephone service in the civilized world'.

From the beginning there had been an argument in Britain between the supporters of monopoly and supporters of competition which had been far sharper than the earlier argument about telegraphy. From the beginning also there had been pressure from business interests to lower and standardize telephone charges just as there had been in the case of the telegraph. 'It seems axiomatic to us that telephony must necessarily be a monopoly', wrote *The Electrician* in 1881, when the ratio of telephones in London was 1 for every 3000 people as against 1 for every 200 in Chicago. Yet it did not seem axiomatic to the political economist Henry Fawcett, Postmaster-General in Gladstone's government of 1880 to 1885, nor to *The Spectator* which stated in 1884 that 'had it not been for the hateful effects of state monopoly we should have been the most wire-speaking country in the world'.

The numbers of British businessmen prepared to use the telephone increased, but the Bank of England had no telephone until after 1900, and any 'telephone culture' that existed was negative. Robert Louis Stevenson was not alone in worrying about the telephone 'bleating like a deserted infant' as it penetrated 'our bed and board, our business and bosoms'. Even *The Electrician* claimed in 1895 that 'if a round robin could be got from all quarters we suspect that a majority could be obtained for voting the telephone an unmitigated nuisance which everybody would wish to see abated and perhaps even abolished altogether'.

Those people who possessed a telephone in Britain – there were only 45,000 of them in 1890, 0.12 per cent of the population, and 210,000 of them in 1900, 0.51 per cent – had many complaints about the service provided both by the Post Office and by the companies, while *The Economist* complained further in 1892 of telephone company 'profits swollen by abuse of their monopolies'. In the same year, the Treasury accepted the then Post Office view that the Post Office should acquire and operate the trunk lines itself, but the Postmaster-General stated frankly that the main reason for the Treasury minute to this effect was the desire 'to see that whatever revenue arises from the telephone, a portion should go to the public'. The idea of large numbers of the public becoming telephone users did not cross his mind.

The transfer of the trunk lines to the Post Office was finally settled in 1896 and completed by February 1897. When in 1899, following a Select Committee Report, the local systems were opened up to the municipalities as well as to the private companies, only 13 (among them Glasgow, Brighton and Hull) applied for a licence and only 6 of them established services, none in operation before 1901. The system had not worked well, nor were there any reasons for thinking it would in the future. Why should the Post Office take a ten per cent royalty on gross company receipts? Why should the Treasury seek to hold back efficient Post Office development on the dubious grounds that they were unwilling to see the Post Office employ a 'large army of staff'? Why should a late-Victorian Liberal Postmaster-General, Arnold Morley, claim that while 'gas and water were necessities for every inhabitant of the country, telephones were not and never would be'?

Morley did not quite dismiss them as 'luxuries', but was convinced that it would be of no use 'to try to persuade ourselves' that 'the use of the telephone' could ever be 'enjoyed by the large masses of the people in their daily life'. Salisbury significantly made no reference to the telephone in his speech to the Institution of Electrical Engineers, although, like Bismarck, he had already installed a telephone in his house – at Hatfield. One obvious reason for such attitudes was 'the fear' as *The Times* put it, that 'any great increase in the use of the telephone would be at the expense of the telegraph', not an entrenched interest, but it was not the only reason. Nor did everyone blame the Post Office, where opinions were divided. 'The government alone is able to undertake this system and develop and work it properly', the Duke of Marlborough told the House of Lords in 1889. 'It was on such a principle that the Post Office acted with regard to the Parcels Post, and most successful and admirable that arrangement has been.'

One place which did welcome the thought of the telephone with 'unashamed delight' was Brighton, the town which also welcomed – and pioneered – the cinema. A newspaper there called it 'a wonderfully versatile appliance', and when a connection was made with London in 1884 it was promised that 'you will be able to bask in the sunshine of the Marine Parade and chat to your managing clerk in the fog of the city'. Meanwhile, in industrial Sheffield there was bitter competition between telephone companies; and in Oxford, where the first telephone was installed as early as 1877 – between the Central Fire Station and 'Engineer Neill's residence' – the University's *Oxford Magazine* (1880), with purely local horizons in view, observed that 'the dream of the sluggard – to take his first lecture in bed – is now brought within the sphere of practical politics, and rumour already whispers of an anti-proctorial telephonic association, by which the members can gain precise information of the position and movements of the Proctors [the guardians of university discipline] at any given time'. There were, in fact, 96 subscribers and 2 call offices in Oxford in 1895, and among the subscribers were the Eye Hospital, the Warneford Asylum, several doctors, surgeons, chemists and a dentist. Clearly the telephone was operating mainly as an emergency service, with the City Police Station sharing the same number as the Fire Brigade.

Oxford, criticized for lagging behind, was ahead of some other places. 'Telephonic communication is not desired by the rural mind', Salisbury's Chancellor of the Exchequer, Michael Hicks Beach, a free trader, could generalize freely, if unimaginatively, in 1901. No more imagination was evident, however, in a comment in *The Times* in 1902 that 'when all is said and done the telephone is not an affair of the millions. It is a convenience for the well-to-do and a trade appliance for persons who can well afford to pay for it.'

The inhibitions and controls of English social life were never more evident than they were at the end of Queen Victoria's reign when it was almost as cheap to pay for a domestic servant as it was to pay for a telephone; nor was there much optimism even when the statistics occasionally looked encouraging. Thus, when the total number of telephone subscribers doubled between 1890 and 1895 and doubled again between 1895 and 1900, *The Times* paid no attention to such encouraging figures, still claiming that an overwhelming majority of the population was most unlikely ever to use the telephone at all.

The number was to double again between 1900 and 1905, yet the optimism even of a historian blessed with hindsight must be limited too after reading the advice given in 1898 by a man who ought to have been optimistic, I. A. H. Hastie of the Association for Protection of Telephone Subscribers – 'The telephone should be primarily answered by a servant and there should be further internal connection ... with other rooms'. The traditional social system was immeasurably stronger than the embryonic telephone system. For Hastie the telephone was a superior speaking tube.

It is fair to add that in New York the first subscribers to the telephone were business offices, not homes. The charge for a direct line business line telephone, $240, was two-thirds of the average annual wage of a factory worker. Moreover, in a very different American community which has been studied in detail, Pawtucket, Rhode Island, only 16 out of 161 telephones in service in 1897 were residential. Nonetheless, there was a confidence on the other side of the Atlantic which was missing in Britain, that this state of affairs would not always persist. Chicago, where as early as 1896 almost 30 per cent of the entries in the *National Telephone Directory* were residential, pointed the way to the future in this as in so many other respects. (See *Victorian Cities*, Chapter I.)

Doubtless it will be the study of an emerging system and the limits to its use that will be of most interest to the historian of the telephone as a new Victorian thing and he will be able to compare it with the evolution of the system of electrical generation and transmission. Yet the telephone as a thing itself has proved of interest both to cultural historians and to collectors on both sides of the Atlantic as early telephones have become vintage pieces like gramophones or like sewing machines in a way that telegraphic equipment never has done. Moreover, they sometimes figure, if less prominently than 'wireless sets', in histories of design.

In Britain, the Post Office telephones were appropriately all in black, like top hats. The National Telephone Company telephones by contrast were sometimes nickel-plated. 'Skeleton types' are now particularly highly prized. By the late 1890s some desk sets were fashion objects, although even in America no President was to have a desk telephone until President Hoover: the first White House telephone had been installed under President Rutherford B. Hayes and President Eisenhower was to be presented with the fifty millionth telephone. Already by 1901, however, there were 81,000 'nickel-in-the-slot' pay telephones, for most people necessities. It is interesting that at a time when there was much speculation about the future 'evolution' of clothes (see page 274) and of houses, there was little speculation about the future aesthetic form of the telephone. It was still very much of a Victorian thing.

## IV

The phonograph was another of the new things which was beginning to come into its own during the 1890s, with Berliner introducing a lateral cut form of recording on flat discs, not cylinders, along with a new name, 'the gramophone' in 1887. Seven-inch gramophone records (or 'plates' as they were first called), among them *The Old Folks at Home*, appeared on the market at fifty cents each in 1894. The lowest-price gramophone then cost $12, and the term 'record' was now in regular use. Edison had employed vertical-cut 'hill and dale' cylinders, and although his trade in them began to prosper during the 1890s, he remained unsure about the future of his own $40 phonograph even in 1896 when he formed a new National Phonograph Company. Was the bias of recording to be towards entertainment? Four years earlier the coin-in-the-slot nickelodion had been invented. Was that not a more lucrative line of development than classical music or recording the voices of the great?

As early as 1878, Edison, who disliked tinfoil, had arranged for the publication of an article in the *North American Review* in which ten possible uses of the phonograph were listed. It was not just to be 'a talking machine', although the third use, with an eye on Bell, was to be 'the teaching of elocution'. The second use was 'phonographic books which will speak to blind people without any effort on their part', and the eighth 'the preservation of language by reproduction of our Washingtons, our Lincolns, our Gladstones'. The fourth use, however, was music ('the phonograph will undoubtedly be liberally devoted to music'); and the sixth use – and perhaps it seemed most to the point at the time –was the offer of a child's doll, 'which may speak, sing, cry or laugh'.

There is no evidence that such a doll ever appeared, and by 1887 among other new possible uses listed were recording of sermons and of the voices of animals. 'The invention may even be pressed into the detective service', Edison then told the editor of the *Scientific American* (compare the camera, page 134) and used as an 'unimpeachable witness'. 'It will have but one story to tell, and cross examination [a technique familiar to Edison] cannot confuse it'. In fact, music was to be the main long-term beneficiary of the phonograph, although many musicians were as suspicious of it as boiler-makers were of electric power.

The fact that you could repeat the listening experience, a point made by historians of the gramophone and by Daniel Boorstin in his wide ranging study The *Democratic Experience* (1973), received less attention at first than the fact that you could record sound. There was no emphasis, therefore, on musical appreciation or musical education. Nor was there much emphasis on mass circulation. Nonetheless, an 1899 catalogue of the phonograph, which included forty illustrations of its uses, picked out dancers 'gliding over the polished floor, the orchestral music being supplied by the phonograph', a pair of lovers resting in a shady grove with background phonograph music from Gounod's *Romeo and Juliet*, 'a little street arab, the *gamin* of Paris, who has dropped two sous into a public phonograph and is enjoying the song of the Toreador from *Carmen*', and a young lady at a piano practising a concerto with the orchestra 'on the phonograph'. To get the balance right, however, there was a reference to a phonograph record of a sermon slotted into a country service and a picture of an old man of seventy listening wistfully to the sound of his own voice when he was 4, 14 and 24.

*The Electric World* in 1890 envisaged a further 'historical' use of the phonograph – as a phonographic newspaper: 'Fancy an interview with Gladstone or Bismarck reproduced not only in their own words, but with the very intonations of the great statesmen'. Two years earlier, *The Spectator*, which had dared to suggest that the telegraph 'produced more misery than it relieves', had expressed horror at Edison's initial eighth use and at the idea of 'phonographic libraries', a suggestion put forward by Edward Bellamy, author of *Looking Backward* (1888). Moreover, it had added a visual dimension to the horror, *The Spectator* added, linking phonograph records and statues or portraits. 'Imagine a man in the next century whose great-grandfather was a Gladstonian, whose grandfather was intrusted with a command in the war with Ireland to which home rule had led, and whose father had sided with the Irish in resisting the oppressions of the restored government'. Surely if he looked at the portraits of his ancestors and heard their voices, he would 'carry into life a consciousness even more hesitating and divided than even that which gives birth to our 19th-century vacillations?'

It was a fanciful if tortuous question, but unlike many such questions it not only carries that nineteenth-century note of concern which accompanied invention but has retained part of its point in the real 'next century'. 'We have a very strong belief', *The Spectator* explained, 'that the scientific ingenuity of our day, acting under the imperious guidance of sensibilities which are as narrow as they are tender, will continue to fill the world we leave behind us much too full of us for the free growth of our posterity.'

In the twentieth century, but not for many decades, radio and television rather than the phonograph were to provide both 'phonographic news-papers' and historical records of the great and the small; and although Valdemar Poulsen, a Danish scientist who invented magnetic tape in 1898 – his 'telegraphone' was displayed at the Paris Exhibition of 1900, where it won a Grand Prix – decades were to pass before there were tape recorders. Long before then, the words 'phonograph' and 'gramophone' had disap-peared from the American, though not from the English, language. Neither word was ever used by the Victor Talking Machine Company, incorporated in October 1901.

## V

What was true of tape recorders was for rather less long equally true of wireless. Guglielmo Marconi certainly had no long-term purposes in mind when he arrived in London in mid-February 1896, with two large bags containing 'a number of brass knobs, a large sparking coil, and a small glass tube from each end of which extruded a rod joined to a disc fitted in the tube and . . . metal filings'. Marconi had transmitted his first wireless messages in an improvised Italian country house laboratory which had previously been used for storing trays of silk worms, and Preece quickly arranged a demonstration in London and for the army on Salisbury Plain. Whatever the long-term purposes the Post Office had in mind, they had nothing to do with broadcasting. It had long been interested – and it was not alone in this – in the possibility of using 'Hertzian waves' to carry telegraphic messages. As a maritime nation Britain's interest was a very special one.

The only object was to substitute wireless telegraphy for telegraphy by cable, and the broadcast element in wireless was thought of as a handicap rather than an advantage: people would pick up confidential person-to-person messages for whom the messages were not intended. The *Electrician* in 1899 had a further worry: 'Messages scattered broadcast only waste energy by travelling with futile persistence towards celestial space', doing mischief on the way 'by interrupting the everyday business of stations in the vicinity'. 'If only the Marconi waves would confine themselves strictly to business', it concluded, 'the prospects of wireless telegraphy would be enormously better than they now are.'

Nonetheless, even before Marconi arrived, the *Electrical Engineer* had suggested in 1895 that since telephones were becoming 'more and more useful', in the future 'we may hope to have communications by telephone without wires', and it had even gone on to ask 'Shall we also see by electricity without wires?' Indeed, on the eve of Marconi's visit to London, which could not have been better timed, the air was charged both with electricity and with prophecy. Nor was London the only place of action. In St Petersburg, A.S. Popov, a physics instructor at the Russian Navy's torpedo school, gave a lecture in May 1895 which he later claimed anticipated Marconi.

In public Marconi preferred to talk in London to the 'lay Press' before he talked to scientists, and by the end of 1897, when his wares had been demonstrated to the Admiralty as well as to the Army, in London's East End at Toynbee Hall, at Osborne, and to the Royal Institution, the popular periodical *Science Siftings* described wireless as 'a fitting tribute to the enterprise of this *fin de siècle* age. The invention will, in truth, add a fresh lustre to the year of the Jubilee.'

'To Marconi is due', it was stated at the time in the *Electrical World*, 'the great credit of devising a practical apparatus which, if not yet commercial in form gives much promise of becoming so.' It was a balanced verdict, for it was recognized that if the future was unknown – and there were to be many twists and turns in it – there was a well charted scientific past in the history of wireless. It led back in time beyond Heinrich Hertz's experimental demonstration in 1887 of 'radiation' – hence radio, the generation of electromagnetic waves which could travel at the speed of light – to James Clark Maxwell's claim in 1863 that this was theoretically possible. Edison himself had played with 'sparks' in 1875 before he played with the phonograph, and the *New York Herald* had predicted that the application of his 'etheric force' would render redundant 'cumbersome appliances' like 'telegraph poles', 'insulating knobs' and 'cable-sheathings'.

In England in 1892, Sir William Crookes in a more quoted article had offered 'the bewildering possibility of telegraphy without wires, posts, cables or any of our present costly appliances granted a few reasonable postulates', and in 1897 Sir Oliver Lodge, who felt that his own claims to be an inventor as well as a theorist had been slighted by Marconi, applied for no fewer than four patents. Preece, too, was a persistent experimenter as well as an eloquent talker, yet just as he had had little faith in the immediate promises of Bell in 1877, so he had little faith in the immediate promises of Marconi twenty years later: 'A single cable to France could transmit 2500 words a minute without any difficulty, whereas a single Marconi circuit could not transmit more than twenty words a minute.' And five years later, when Marconi had exchanged wireless telegraphic messages between Britain and France, Preece was still telling the Society of Arts that 'wireless telegraphy in its present form and limited speed cannot be named in the same category as the old system'. *Chambers's Journal*, reporting his speech, placed it alongside an item called 'Her Majesty's Pigeon Messengers'.

There were many knowledgeable British observers who preferred Preece's cautious prediction to the promises of the Wireless Telegraph and Signal Company which Marconi set up in 1897 to exploit his inventions. For them wireless was 'immature', and it was safer to depend on the Post Office than on the Wireless Telegraphy Company. 'The fact is, it is about the worst thing possible for an invention of this sort to get into the hands of a company. We have only to look at the telephone to be convinced of this, and yet it was urged against the nationalization of the telegraph thirty years ago that it would tend to stifle invention.'

One point was clear – that whether or not the Post Office would stifle invention, it would certainly seek to regulate it. If there was a direct line in Edison's career as an inventor from telegraphy through telephony to the phonograph and the cinema, there was to be another direct line in Britain between railway legislation, telegraph legislation and wireless legislation; and it was under the auspices of the Post Office that the BBC, at first the British Broadcasting Company, was to be brought into existence in 1922. 'It looks as if it might soon be thought necessary to nationalize the ether', wrote the *Electrician* in 1899, although it added as a parenthesis 'or municipalize it'. 'Otherwise it might resemble the Pool of Bethesda in being of use only to the individual who first avails himself of it.'

For those in 1900 who were less interested in organization than in invention itself there was still time to contemplate what the great journalist W. T. Stead, who doubtless would have fared well in an age of broadcasting and television, called 'spirit mysteries'. 'The great triumph of the 19th century', he claimed, as the old century came to a close, 'has been the subjection of time and space by the mind of man.' As a result, the 'materialism' of the century had been pushed into the background, its citadels destroyed. Things were now less inspiring than waves. The telephone following in the wake of the telegraph had 'mounted sound upon the wire' and had annihilated distance, just as the phonograph had annihilated time. 'Countless generations mourning the dead have cried with vain longings to hear the sound of the voice that is still. But in dreams alone or in those rare visions vouchsafed to finer souls was the prayer ever granted. [Now] the very sound and accent of the living words of the dead whose bodies are in the dust have become the common inheritance of mankind.'

Wireless meant that 'it was perfectly possible for mind to communicate with mind' through the 'ether', and there were certainly 'spirit mysteries' there. As the *Popular Science Monthly* put it, 'wireless telegraphy is the nearest approach to telepathy that has been vouched to our intelligence, and it serves to stimulate our imagination and to make us think that things greatly hoped for can always be reached, although not exactly in the way expected.' 'The possibility of seeing through things, which our forefathers used to believe was only possessed by supernatural beings', Stead went on, 'is now in possession of everyone who is capable of using the Röntgen rays' – X-rays, discovered in 1896 – through which 'you can now see through the human body itself'. For the public, though not for the spiritualist Sir Oliver Lodge, the mystery of Röntgen rays (Kelvin refused to believe in them) exceeded that of Marconi's wireless waves. The almost incredible 'new photography', producing pictures of what could be seen by X-ray, was demonstrably more different from the old photography than Marconi's wireless was from the old telegraphy. After all, wireless did not mean that you did without wires.

Stead, like other journalists, added 'seeing at a distance' to the range of 'spirit mysteries'. 'We are told of a new marvellous invention', he wrote, 'by which visitors to the Paris Exhibition will be able to see by the aid of the telelectroscope scenes that are occurring at a distance of hundreds of miles. The precise nature of this invention has not been made public; but from the inscriptions which have appeared it is evident that it is to do for the eye what the telephone does for the ear.' 'If the telephone has removed the barriers which render it impossible for human beings to be audible to each other, the telectroscope makes this planet transparent as a crystal.'

# VI

No contemporary discussion of 'spirit mysteries' in mid-Victorian or in late-Victorian Britain would have been complete without a lengthy part of it being devoted to electricity. For every theory concerning electricity there was a myth, for every inventor a charlatan, and for every practical invention in its history – and Edison was responsible for many of them – there was an 'object of fraud and superstition'. On one side of the account was the electric light bulb, on the other the Harness Electropathic Belt, the eidoloscope, 'capable of recording and reproducing luminous pulsations', and the 'gigantic heliograph' capable of sending messages to the moon. There could be doubt even among experts, about the side on which certain things should be placed. Thus, the American dynamo-maker Edward Weston described Edison's 1879 high-speed 'Faradic machine' for converting mechanical energy, steam power, into electrical energy as 'more or less like a perpetual motion machine'.

Given such uncertainty both about the practicality of certain uses of electricity and about the physical character of electricity – 'High authorities', wrote Crookes in 1892, 'cannot yet even agree whether we have one electricity or two opposite electricities' – it was far more difficult, therefore, for laymen to understand the genuine mysteries of electricity than it had been to understand the simple operations of the steam engine. The two technologies provoked very different responses. There were many metaphors of steam, but for most people the very conception of electricity itself was metaphor, and scientists themselves resorted to metaphor when they tried to explain 'how it worked'.

Communication did not necessarily seem to help. 'An almost inevitable result of the rapid developments of the last three decades especially', the Chairman of the American Association for the Advancement of Science claimed, 'is that much of what goes by the name of science is quite unscientific. The elementary teaching and the popular exposition of science have fallen, unluckily, into the keeping largely of a purely literary view of phenomena. Many of the bare facts of science are so far stranger than fiction that ... untrained minds fall an easy prey to the tricks of the magazine romancer or the perpetual motion promoter.'

At least one new electric thing seemed to be a triumph of fact – the electric light bulb – although even that could be called 'the Light of the World'. Edison, who himself was quite capable of romancing, and romancing happily, was extremely matter-of-fact, when he contemplated replacing gas by electricity. 'The electric light', he wrote after the event, 'has caused me the greatest amount of study and has required the most elaborate experiments.' But he was quite clear what he wanted to do before the event, clear in a way he was not clear either with the phonograph or the kinetoscope. As he stated in an almost terse note:

> Object: E. to effect exact imitation of all done by gas, to replace lighting by gas by lighting by electricity. To improve the illumination to such an extent as to meet all requirements of natural, artificial, and commercial conditions. Previous inventions failed – necessity for commercial success and accomplishment by Edison. Edison's great effort – not to make a large light or a blinding light but a small light having the mildness of gas.

The explicit references to gas are striking. So, too is the emphasis on 'a small light' requiring little current: elsewhere Edison called it a candle. He was not thinking of an arc lamp, therefore, or of lighting in theatres, where electricity was already beginning to replace gas, but of lighting in the home; and there was no doubt that the demand for superior lighting in the home was already there. An average household in Philadelphia, for example, is said to have increased its use of illumination twenty times between 1855 and 1895.

The 'literary' approach to electrical lighting had concentrated not on the home but on 'grand effects', beginning in time in 1808 with Sir Humphry Davy's demonstration by galvanic battery of an arch of 'dazzling lights' between separated pieces of carbon, and continuing through the story of what had been achieved or was being achieved, often in spectacular, if expensive, fashion in 'searchlights' in lighthouses on both sides of the Atlantic. The story usually skipped from headline to headline ending at Hall Gate in New York's East River in 1884. The 'effect' there of nine lights supported at a height of 250 feet by a light iron tower was said to be 'magnificent'. Yet this particular story, at least, did not have a happy ending. After several years of use, it was decided by the Lighthouse Department that the costly lighting 'did not afford the expected aid to navigation' and the nine lights were duly removed in 1888. Nonetheless, after the closure, a writer on electricity and its uses in *Scribner's Magazine* as late as 1891 still chose this as one of his big examples before turning almost apologetically to 'the numerous lights of moderate intensity employed for general domestic illumination'.

Edison was not alone in defining his apparently far more modest object so specifically. In Britain, Joseph Swan, a chemist born twenty-three years before him, had been working on electric lighting for decades. Indeed, it was before Edison's birth that he began to experiment with materials to be used in the fine filament of an electric lamp, beginning, as Edison was to begin, with strips of carbonized paper. Swan claimed that he had first become interested in electric lighting when he heard a lecture on electricity at the Sunderland Athenaeum, while Edison, who played with wet cell electric batteries when he was a child, regarded the day when he bought a second-hand copy of Michael Faraday's *Experimental Researches in Electricity* as a landmark day in his life. It was Swan's chemistry, however, that came to his assistance after years of unrewarding trials, at times abandoned, of a wide range of fragile materials for a filament and of different kinds of vacuum pump. It was not until 1878 that he found a solution, finally using for his filament threads of cellulose, which he had carbonized by immersion in sulphuric acid and careful washing with water.

Meanwhile, Edison was testing and went on to test natural products of all kinds, for example bamboo, brought to his Menlo Park laboratory from distant parts of the world, coconut shells, grass fibres, horsehair and even human hair provided by one of his helpers on the spot. As in the case of the gutta-percha used in telegraph cables, nature was being called to the assistance of human invention. Edison was willing when necessary to pore over botany books, and when for a time he had to fall back on platinum as a filament he sent out so many prospectors to find the metal that a friend warned him against 'the indiscriminate examination of rocks', an activity offensive not only to all Victorian geologists but to all Victorian businessmen.

Edison was working in a climate far more favourable to invention – and to publicity – than Swan was, for when in December 1878 the latter demonstrated to the Newcastle Chemical Society a carbon filament lamp, a tubular bulb with conical ends carrying a straight thin carbon conductor of a diameter of one twenty-fifth of an inch, there was relatively little public excitement. The fact that his lamp burnt out after several minutes through excessive current might have seemed more important than that it gave out light at all, although Swan rectified this fault in later lecture demonstrations, culminating in an impressive address to the Institution of Electrical Engineers in 1881. By that time his lamps had been installed in Kelvin's house and at the Cragside home of Sir William Armstrong, the armaments manufacturer.

There might well have been another ruthless patent war between Swan and Edison – although the former did not take out a patent until after the latter had done so – but instead the Edison Electric Light Company, founded in 1881 with British capital, and Swan's company decided on a merger in 1881, and the Edison and Swan United Electrical Light Company was formed. For the most part Edison himself disliked litigation – 'A law suit', he wrote in his diary in 1885, 'is a suicide of time'. Yet even after the merger, litigation was forced on the new company. Ironically it pivoted on how close Swan had been in 1860 to anticipating Edison in 1875. Was his first carbon conductor, which he had described openly, really a filament? It was decided in 1888 that it was not. To the benefit of the United Company, therefore, the Edison patent stood.

Long before this outcome, which made possible the rapid expansion of the United Electrical Light Company, Edison had proved that he was capable of illuminating the contours of the future so brilliantly that he could attract, sometimes it seemed to the British almost without difficulty, both financial and scientific support. His American Edison Electric Light Company, formed as early as November 1878, had connections both at Western Union, through Vanderbilt, and with J. Pierpont Morgan. His experiments, for which there were now substantial available funds, were assisted by a team of scientists, including a brilliant mathematician-physicist, Francis R. Upton, who was said to have juggled with integral and differential equations like an Oxford wrangler. Later, when he turned to the problems of the dynamo, Edison was assisted by the brilliant English physicist and engineer, Dr John Hopkinson, who made a unique contribution to electrical engineering.

Outside Edison's laboratories, there were some distinguished mathematician-physicists in England, including Preece, who thought at first that an incandescent electric light bulb was an *ignis fatuus*: it would contravene Ohm's law. (This was not to stop Preece at a later stage from ordering lights from the Edison Electric Light Company for the Post Office building in 1882.) It was fortunate at the critical stage, therefore, that Edison and his helpers, however much they might exaggerate what they immediately had to offer, persisted in the face of outside criticism in their efforts to 'subdivide electrical light'. Moreover, because they had raised substantial funds, they were able to draw not only on outstanding scientific know-how but to secure the most modern equipment and the most skilled labour from Europe.

The two points Edison always insisted upon in experimenting with his bulb were high resistance and minute filament diameter. This meant that his lamps used less current. And the importance of this feature was recognized when his lamps won a prize, which carried with it more than prestige, at the Paris Electrical Exposition of 1881; there they were placed one class above Swan's low resistance lamps and the high resistance lamps of another Englishman, St George Lane-Fox. A year later, when Edison's lamps were demonstrated in the Crystal Palace, a journalist in the New York *Herald* picked out and italicized a more obvious feature which would surely have interested Voltaire had he been able to return to the Crystal Palace yet again in 1887. 'The light without flame' could now be 'ignited *without a match*.'

Edison had long been a favourite of journalists, as had been shown in October 1879 when he held his first big demonstration in New York: one of his lamps then burnt continuously for forty-five hours. There had been a second and far bigger demonstration on the last day of the year, well publicized in the New York *Herald* a few days before it happened. The fact that there was more than a touch of wizardry about all this made it excellent copy. Edison clearly recognized, however, that neither wizardry nor publicity was enough. Electric lamps would not be saleable in large quantities, he perceived, unless electric power was laid on in people's homes. As in the case of the telephone, there had to be a system, and it would require dynamos of a new and improved type, underground mains, short circuits, safety fuses, insulating materials, sockets and, not least, switches.

There was no such electrical system in existence in 1880, but there was an 'analogous system', as Edison called it, in relation to gas, a system which was shaken but by no means dislodged when rumours of new electrical invention led to a slump in gas shares on both sides of the Atlantic in 1879. Edison had never liked gas – it was dirty and it smelt – but it had always figured in his thinking and he learned everything about its organization, including its costing. He also doubtless learned about the systemic problems of gas pipes and gas explosions, while fully appreciating that they frightened ignorant people less than the use of electric wires and switches and the often terrifying 'electric accidents', usually starting with 'leaks', which characterized the early years of the exploitation of electricity. Gas was the model, although Edison had also had early experience of the telephone system, which required far less capital and equipment.

At this point new financial problems inevitably arose. The successful provision of electricity required heavy 'public utility' investment as well as individual outlay on electrical installation; and, if only for this reason, the capitalism of electricity, which pointed to the planned capitalism of the twentieth century, was different in form from carboniferous capitalism (see page 289). Edison had been able to attract funds from Wall Street to invent his electric light bulb, but the financiers from whom he attracted them were in general more interested in obtaining royalties from his patents than in producing new things. Nor did most of them think in terms of creating a public utility: they wanted the initial risks of developing a system to be borne by others. 'Practicability, economy and profitableness' had to be established, as the directors of the Edison Electric Light Company put it in 1883.

The ultimate pattern was to be twofold – a public utility system and an electrical manufacturing industry, each backed by research and development organization and each dependent on aggressive salesmanship – and a new General Electric Company was to be created as an amalgamation of manufacturing interests in 1892 (with Westinghouse interests, incorporated in 1885, outside it). Public utility corporations were to follow. Yet during the risk stage, before this pattern took shape, Edison's early financial backers left him personally to take all the risks. 'Machine-rich and cash poor' though he was, he had to organize many different things at the same time – to build a power station in New York's Pearl Street, 'the biggest and most responsible thing I had undertaken'; to create a new manufacturing industry, which involved first making efficient electric dynamos, an extraordinarily difficult task, as well as electric light bulbs; and to run a headquarters and showroom (at 65 Fifth Avenue) as well as factories. Moreover, he not only had to carry out every conceivable kind of research and development task – in 1882 he applied for no fewer than 141 patents – but to provide skilled electrical maintenance at a time when the number of people able to guarantee it was small.

Edison's real instinct was 'looking for things'. Now he not only had to work by something other than instinct, but he had to restrain his instinct: when Pearl Street came into operation, there were so many risks that he had to prevent publicity. In the process he not only had to sell his own shares in the patent-controlling company which had been brought into existence in his name in order to acquire funds to develop new manufacturing enterprises, but he had to be told by that company not to move fast. There were conflicts of interest – and many rows. The result was that although the price of electric light bulbs fell sharply from over $1 a lamp to 22 cents during the late 1880s, 'light was not used on anything like the scale' Edison had 'reasonably' expected.

# VII

Gas interests remained particularly strong in Britain because of the dominion of British coal, although by the end of the century it was estimated that $2\frac{1}{2}$ million electric lamps were in use in London alone. What is fascinating is that 'natural gas' had itself been spoken of at first as a 'spirit' and was 'more or less of a mystery'. It is also remembered as adding a touch of mystery to Victorian London – 'Fanny by gaslight'. In fact, a really effective incandescent gas mantle, the counterpart of the electric light bulb, was not perfected until 1885.

The effort to produce one had been more protracted than the effort to produce an electric light bulb, and there had been many technical obstacles. As early as 1848, a Frenchman, using the same material as was used in the early electric light bulb, platinum, had devised a small gas mantle made of platinum which became incandescent through a flame of burning water gas, but the metal quickly deteriorated because of the action of carbon monoxide. All other later devices involved deterioration. Edison himself had joined the

contest in 1878, and another inventor was appropriately named Franken-
stein. There was a British version by Professor Lewis in 1881, and a French
version, displayed a year later at the Crystal Palace, which was praised for
the 'purity, penetration, steadiness and brilliant whiteness of its light'.

The successful patentee – in 1885 – was an Austro-Hungarian aristocrat,
Carl Auer von Welsbach, a pupil of Professor Robert von Bunsen, who
realized – and it was a dubious moral principle in Victorian England – that
chemical mixtures were more effective than 'pure substances' in the making
of the fabric of the mantle. He impregnated the cotton thread fabric of his
new mantle, therefore, with a patented chemical mixture which offered a
shell of incandescent material that would achieve what was and what has
been hailed since as a romantic Victorian yellow glow. Professor Lewis, who
was present when the mantle was demonstrated, noted, however, that it had
other symbolic Victorian characteristics also. 'It was such a delicate thing
that every door and window had to be carefully closed in order that a
draught shall not blow it to pieces.'

In many places it was difficult for the new mantle to compete with
kerosene or paraffin lamps which had been available in large quantities since
the 1850s and which had supplanted the oil lamps and paraffin wax candles
which had themselves largely supplanted beeswax and tallow candles. The
candle, too, had had its period of innovation during the thirty years between
1820 and 1850.

The Incandescent Gas Light Company set up in 1887 in London – within
Westminster – nine years after the Edison Electric Light Company, proved
almost as delicate a thing as the new gas mantle itself. If it was difficult to
make the fragile mantles, it was even more difficult to distribute them safely.
Indeed, the problem of breakage was not overcome until the introduction of
'collodionizing' (soaking the mantle in collodion) in 1897. The mantles cost
five shillings each at first, as much as Edison's electric light bulb first cost,
with the burners costing one guinea in addition. The company found,
however, that there were considerable defects in production and in 1890 it
was forced to withdraw its mantles when a change in the impregnating fuel
rendered the mantles useless.

The company would have faced further difficulties in a later age, for
another product used in the sewing of the fabric tops was asbestos thread.
Reconstructing the company preceded the reconstruction of the mantle
itself. Three years later, there was a row with another company which, it was
claimed, had infringed the Welsbach patent, although in the 'Battle of the
Mantles', as it was called, the reconstructed Incandescent Light Company
won.

As it was, during this late-Victorian age the number of gas burners sold
rose from 20,000 in 1893 to 105,000 in 1894 and 300,000 in 1895, and the
company was given a further boost in the last of these years when it secured a
large order to supply a new type of anti-vibration burner to the London

municipal authorities. They were still lighting their own streets with gas, not with electricity, so that when Charles Booth wrote the first volume of his *Life and Labour of the People in London* in 1892 he made much of 'the flaring lights' and in the same year *The Strand Magazine* had a long article describing the Beckton works of the Gas Light and Coke Company capable of turning out $56\frac{1}{4}$ million cubic feet of gas per day. There was no cross reference to electricity. Welsbach himself was keeping up more with the times. Indeed, in 1900 he was to contribute his skills to a new phase in the evolution of the electric light bulb after himself switching from gas to electricity.

The reign of the incandescent gas mantle, a very late-Victorian thing, seems in retrospect, at least, as short as the life of the individual mantle. Yet the mantle survived the end of the reign of Queen Victoria, and had it not been for the development of electricity, it would doubtless have been hailed in retrospect as a great triumph of invention and related to another line of Victorian invention – artificial silk, the first man-made threat to natural fibres. Indeed, the fabric material of the incandescent gas mantle was known as the stocking. Given how familiar a thing the gas mantle was to become, the language of Welsbach's patent was as abstruse as Rowland Hill's when he described his postage stamp (see page 328): it was to be 'an illuminant appliance in the form of a cap to be rendered incandescent by gas or other burners so as to enhance their illuminating power.'

There was a late-Victorian twist to the design of the incandescent gas mantle and of the burner. The first 'illuminant appliance' gas mantles had

*Gas in the palace: patented gas apparatus for Blenheim, 1862*

all been upright, and this meant that light moved upwards and produced odd reflections from the ceilings and the walls. In the year of Queen Victoria's Diamond Jubilee, however, a new burner was designed which made possible the inversion of the gas mantle. The 'gas fixings' in the comfortable late-Victorian home were beginning to look very different, therefore, from those in the mid-Victorian home. And since there was far more willingness to cook by gas than there had been, electricity had a hard fight ahead of it in Britain.

As in the case of the telegraph and the telephone, and as was to be the case with the radio, Britain and the United States were facing up to continuing technical challenge in different ways, responses which have recently been studied systematically by Thomas P. Hughes in his important analysis of systems, *Networks of Power, Electrification in Western Society* (1983). In Britain, where the first electric 'power station' was built at Holborn Viaduct *before* Edison's Pearl Street station in New York came into precarious operation, an Electric Lighting Act of 1882, amended six years later, empowered municipalities to buy up street and residential and business lighting systems after a period of twenty years at market values. This undoubtedly diminished the opportunities for private enterprise, although it speeded up procedures. Hitherto, private bills had been necessary for each proposal, and they had all been referred to a Select Committee under the chairmanship of Lyon Playfair. New general conditions were laid down.

It was Joseph Chamberlain as President of the Board of Trade who introduced the 1882 legislation. It attracted few takers, however, until it was amended in 1888, and in retrospect it seems to have held back progress. Nevertheless, there were several signs of enterprise. Thus, the energetic and enterprising Colonel R. E. Crompton, who owned an electrical engineering factory in Chelmsford, founded the Kensington Court Electric Light Company in 1886: his own house in Porchester Gardens, it has been claimed, was the first private house in London to be supplied effectively with electric lighting. After 1888 the Kensington Court Company was taken over by a bigger Knightsbridge Electric Lighting Company, one of a number of London companies which built power stations. Brighton, too, was a pioneering centre, with the (Robert) Hammond Electric Light Company supplying customers for a charge of 12s per lamp per week as early as 1881. These were exceptional ventures, however, and the demand for electricity increased more rapidly in the United States than in Britain. 'Isolated' business firms were among Edison's first enthusiastic customers – but Edison himself, who was uninterested in book-keeping, was inevitably 'squeezed out'.

It did not help Edison that, having seen the necessity for 'a system', he failed to see the obvious advantages of a system based on alternating current. Indeed, he regarded alternating current as dangerous. Nonetheless, the die was already cast before he made this serious mistake. Nor was he alone in making it. 'Electric lights are too old for me', he is reported to have said jocularly just at the time that they were still young and exciting, past the inventive stage and into the stage of mass production. When the new General Electric Company was founded in 1892 not only was there no Edison name in the title, but Edison received news of its foundation not directly but through a New York newspaper office.

By then, there were many American publicists of electricity, the most remarkable of them Nikola Tesla, born in Croatia in 1856; and while many of them dealt in ideas, not in things, others talked enthusiastically of 'new uses' of electricity in the universe of things. In particular, they concerned themselves with the generation of electrical power for other purposes besides lighting. Tesla, in particular, thought that these purposes were almost limitless. He had been a protégé of Puskas, the owner of the Budapest telephone system, and when he arrived in the United States in 1884 he had had a letter of introduction to Edison. Yet there was a distinctive visionary note of his own in what he had to say, not least about alternating current, that made his critics accuse him of extravagant exaggeration. When newspaper headlines described him as 'Our Foremost Electrician', which they did in 1893, or 'Greater Even than Edison', they provoked jealousy as well as criticism.

As early as 1878, Edison had talked eloquently of electricity being used not just for lighting but as a source of power for heating, cooking, sewing, and running an elevator and a train. Then in 1887 the American, Park Benjamin, had published his book *The Age of Electricity* and described one by one the multiple uses of electricity, 'simply legion', most of them 'automatic in their action'.

For Benjamin, electricity was 'a vigilant and sleepless sentinel' which guarded the signals which 'protect the swift-rushing express' and warned of 'the inroad of thieves or the outbreak of fire'. On the other hand, it was 'a most treacherous foe', driving and exploding 'the deadly torpedo' and firing 'the hidden mine'. 'From its inert, harmless-seeming wires the most casual touch' might bring forth 'instant death, swift as the greater lightning.' In the hands of the physician, 'the curative effects of the electric current' made it 'a potent ally for the relief of human suffering'. Yet its 'destructive certainty' would 'in time render it the instrument of execution of the last penalty of the law'.

It 'annihilated time and space in the telegraph', yet it could govern time simultaneously in hundreds of clocks, ringing chimes in bells and in kitchens, and measuring space as it was 'traversed by the railway train or the steamship'. It could impel the locomotive; and equally it could 'control the brake which stops its motion'. It could 'light up the inner cavities of the living body, so that the eye of the surgeon may explore them; or illuminate the eternal darkness of the depths of the great sea, so that the retina of the camera may see and record their mysteries. It will indicate for us the heat of the steel furnace, or that of the far distant stars. In one form it will tear asunder the atoms of water: in another, cause them to re-unite. It will set, type and drive the printing press; operate the intricate pattern-mechanism and move the loom.'

It was already in use to control 'the warmth of the hatching egg': and it had been proposed to use the current to cremate the bodies of the dead. It could protect a freezing-chamber from too high a temperature, or a vineyard from the effects of frost. It could make engravings and etchings, and aid in dyeing and in bleaching. In time it would 'reveal the approach of the earthquake or the rumblings of the volcano, or the almost imperceptible sounds of the human heart ... It will record the votes which change the destiny of a great nation, or set down the music of the last popular melody. It will talk in our voices, hundreds of miles away.' 'Where in the history of all magic', the author concluded, 'are there wonders greater than these?' Had not 'a "genie of gigantic size"', whom we have named Electricity, come to us – if not at the rubbing of a lamp, certainly at the rubbing of a bit of amber? And what did Aladdin's genie do half as wonderful as ours has done?'

There was little that was 'homely' in Park Benjamin's message, although almost a decade earlier one group of judges at the Philadelphia Exhibition had claimed that amongst the 'varied' applications of electricity, its application to 'social economy' was especially important; and by 1896 a writer in *Scribner's* could make the most not only of electricity in the hospital, in the city, on the seas and on the battlefield but of 'electricity in the household'. 'It would be strange, indeed,' he began, 'if so readily controlled an agent as electricity, an Ariel before whom time and space seem to vanish, did not cross the threshold of our homes and enter into our household life. We find, in fact, that the adoption of electrical appliances is daily becoming more widespread, here adding a utility, and there an ornament, until in the near future we may anticipate a period when its presence in the household will be indispensable.'

It is disappointing that after this stirring lead in to his subject the author could give no more exciting a first example than the electric bell, but it was a sign of the novelty even of this modest invention that like others before him in describing new things, he had to resort to circumlocution – 'the pressure of the finger on the button brings two strips of metal into contact and completes a circuit, forming as it were an electrical endless chain for the battery, through the wires, bell and annunciator'.

The author followed up this example with the thermostat, the fan, the clock, the lamp again, the telephone and the telegraph, the fire alarm, and – with no touch of irony – the hand-gas igniter. There was only the most cursory reference to heating, although he made the point that electric lighting was 'primarily and essentially electric heating'; and when he turned to the heating of things he did not choose to mention an oven, but rather a coffee pot. 'The advantage to a man whose duties call him out during the night, of being able, from his bedroom, to set an electric coffee-heater to work in his dining room, so that by the time that he is ready to leave the house he finds hot coffee awaiting him ... far outweighs the three or four cents for electrical power that the beverage has probably cost him.'

There was no reference to the woman in this statement. Yet it was she who was to benefit most from the new universe of electrical appliances. And once again asbestos obtruded alarmingly into the picture. One convenient electrical coffee heater would be 'a kettle in an asbestos lining round which circulate coils of wire, the passage of the electric current through these coils generating the heat'.

The limits then set to the use of electricity in the home were as obvious even in the United States as its potentialities for the future. What would be the source of electrical supply? Batteries were troublesome to maintain and very expensive to use. 'Dynamo-machines driven by steam engines' might well involve far more difficulties with the employment of the steam engines than with the generators. Edison's Jumbo dynamo was as huge and cumbersome as his light bulb was small and economical.

Long before Henry Adams compared the cult of the Virgin and the cult of the Dynamo there were religious parallels: the spaces in Edison's plant were called in 1880 'cathedral shops' because of their lofty ceilings. Adams could only have written as he did, however, because of major advances in the theory and construction of dynamos between 1880 and 1890. It was then, in the words of J. A. Fleming, that 'the dynamo was ... perfected so that from being a machine very liable to breakdown and failure, especially in electric insulation, and at low efficiency, it was capable of sustaining non-stop runs'. Hopkinson was one of the pioneers: his construction of Edison's Jumbo was similar in size and weight, but greatly increased available power. Already in 1879 he had stressed the need for establishing standards for judging dynamos.

It was the power of the dynamo which impressed Henry Adams, and it was another Adams, Edward Dean Adams, who described the most fascinating example of its power in his story of 'the harnessing of Niagara' for electrical purposes in a book which was privately printed for the Niagara Falls Power Company in 1895. It justified Henry Adams's enthusiasm. The impressively named Cataract Construction Company, set up in 1889, took the bold decision to employ alternating current, although no less a person than the future Lord Kelvin described it as a 'gigantic mistake'. West-inghouse, committed to it – and to Tesla – had already pointed the way in 1893 when it exhibited a complete alternating current system at the Chicago World Fair. Yet it was Professor George Forbes, a Fellow of the Royal Society and former President of the British Electric Light Company, who designed the remarkable generator which made it possible to harness Niagara and to distribute electrical power over a distance of twenty miles between the Niagara Falls and Buffalo.

Forbes himself was as clear about his purpose as Edison had been when he set about producing the electric light bulb. 'The officers of the company and myself ... looking at the purposes for which our machinery is being set up, therefore felt sure that the proportion of electricity which would be used for lighting purposes would not be large, and that we must look upon our whole plant as a *power* producing and distributing plant, and that our object must be to distribute *power* in the most efficient and economical manner.'

When the Cataract Construction Company was voluntarily liquidated in 1899, there were eight 5,000 horse power units in operation and one industry, not mentioned in the original proposals, the electrochemical industry, was using more power than lighting and electric motors together. There were to be other surprises of that kind. Meanwhile, Salisbury envisaged the 'distributive power' of electricity leading, unlike steam, to 'centrifugalism': electricity could be distributed 'over the whole land, while 'steam railways can only be great arteries'. The city would 'drift towards the country and the country into the city, so that fifty years hence the city would be very closely assimilated to the country' and people would look back on 'the present city' (see *Victorian Cities*, Chapter 2) as 'a half civilization'.

Some writers believed that electricity would be used just as much in agriculture as in industry. 'The use of electricity as a motor will haul long lines of farm waggons loaded with produce quickly to market ... It will dispense with the cost of most of our hired men and expense of feeding horses'. And if 'electric gardens' could be successfully established, the produce of both gardens and farms might well be doubled in quantity.

These were dreams, just as anticipations of the uses of electricity in warfare were nightmares. Yet for some observers there was another nightmare too – that electricity would throw 'a crude white glare into every crack and cranny of life'. Tesla thought he saw further. For him, at least, there would be great advantages if electricity could turn war into a mere spectacle or play to be seen on a screen, however great the crude, white glare. With 'the number of individuals [necessary to wage war] continuously diminishing, merely machines will meet in a contest without bloodshed, the nations being simply interested, ambitious spectators'. Through a new science of 'telautomatics' it would be possible to 'control the movements and operations of distant automatons'.

# VIII

Not all the new things of the late-Victorian years were electrical. Nor were all of them associated with such a bold vision. One of the main centres of change was neither the home nor the plant but the office with the typewriter as the newest thing inside it. 'In its way', one writer said of the typewriter, 'it is as great an invention as the telegraph or the telephone.'

The word 'typewriter' was frequently employed at the end of the century not to describe the thing itself, a generic term, but its user, not an automaton, but a clerk. More often than in the past the clerk was a woman, who in using her new machine speedily transformed into neat typescript, not copperplate script, the shorthand which itself had been one of the first Victorian things. The elliptical curves favoured in mid-Victorian handwriting gave way to standard type, although the type came in different varieties and was delivered by machine in a variety of different ways.

It was possible, however, even in the case of the typewriter to relate it to the electrical complex. Thus, a writer in the *Electrical World* predicted in 1890 that stenographers would disappear as 'phonographs' (i.e. recording machines) came into use. Mechanical stenographers, genuine automatons, would take their place, never making mistakes, never arriving at the office two hours late, never 'stopping one in the middle of a well-turned period to request repetition', and never asking for an increase of wages. Paradoxically the same word 'phonograph' that Edison used had been applied earlier by Isaac Pitman to his shorthand system devised in 1837. Curiously, too, in late nineteenth-century America the Gramophone Company changed its name for a time to the Gramophone and Typewriter Company and produced talking machines, which were successful, and typewriters, which were not.

One late-twentieth century device, which has transformed the modern office even more than the typewriter did, was not developed because it rested on mechanics rather than on what came to be called electronics – the computer, much to the chagrin of at least one eminent Victorian, Charles Babbage, who died in 1871. As early as 1823 Babbage had persuaded the British government to finance an 'analytical engine' that would undertake all kinds of calculations. It was mechanical, not electrical, of course, and used a punch-card system which was to be taken up later in the century within a different context by Herman Hollerith in the United States. Babbage got his own idea from cards from the Jacquard loom, another example of a transfer from one technology to another.

Derided by many enemies, but also supported by many friends, including Wellington, Darwin, Dickens, Tennyson, Browning and Longfellow, Babbage, who was a sensitive but irascible man, persisted after 1848 with his work on what he called 'Difference Engine No. 2'. He had the rare distinctions of quarrelling both with Peel and with Disraeli and, despite the interest of Prince Albert and of Playfair, of having his 'Difference Engine No. 1' excluded from the Great Exhibition of 1851. Nonetheless, part of it was shown at the Exhibition of 1862, if only in what Babbage called 'a small hole', where no more than six 'anxious and curious observers' could see it at a time and if they were lucky listen to Babbage explaining it.

Babbage died with his work unfinished. He saw the significance of the computer, however, both for government and for industry in both of which he was interested. In 1832 he had written a little treatise *On the*

*Economy of Machinery and Manufactures* which revealed how fascinated he was by industrial processes and their costs and by the political economy of invention. Indeed in 1851 Playfair would like to have had him made Chief Industrial Commissioner.

It did not help Babbage's dealings a year later with Disraeli, then Chancellor of the Exchequer, when he claimed that his new difference engine could not only 'calculate the millions the ex-Chancellor squandered', but could deal with the smallest quantities: 'nay it feels even for zeroes'. The Victorians had to continue with their traditional modes of calculation. Moreover, Peel, who did so much to lay the foundations of Victorian Britain – and had distinguished himself as an undergraduate reading mathematics at Oxford – had been too much caught up in his own society to see any further than Disraeli. 'I should like a little previous consideration,' he had told J. W. Croker, 'before I move in a thin House of country gentlemen [the House of Commons] a large vote for the creation of a wooden man to calculate tables for the formula $x^2 + x + 41$.'

Words proved easier to manipulate than figures during the nineteenth century – and it was the handling of words which was to change most in both government and business offices. Already when Peel dismissed Babbage, Isaac Pitman's shorthand had begun to establish itself. It had first been set out in a booklet *Stenographic Soundhand* which appeared in the year Queen Victoria came to the throne: Pitman was so busy writing it that he had no time to celebrate her coronation.

Neither shorthand nor typing appeared out of the blue. In the year 1837 itself, at least thirty new 'shorthands' had been advertised in England, only a few of them looking back to the tradition of 'secret writing', the original motivation of Tudor shorthand; and Pitman shorthand itself, the favourite brand in Britain, was to go through ten versions between 1837 and Issac Pitman's death sixty years later. By that time, however, there were far more versions of the typewriter, a machine without a standardized design, than there were of shorthand. The typewriter, too, had pre-Victorian forerunners, including the 'Family Letter Press' of William Austin Burt, made in Detroit in 1829, 'a pretty and exceedingly ingenious piece of mechanism', and a French manual 'keyboard' machine of 1833.

In 1850 J. B. Fairbank was granted a patent for 'the first typewriter with a continuous paper feed'; 'typographs' were on prominent display at the 1851 and 1862 Exhibitions, with G. A. Hughes the prize-winner; and in 1855 the Italian Giuseppe Revizzo produced a typewriter which was to be honoured dubiously in centennial celebrations in 1955 as the machine which provided 'the answer' to 'all technical problems'. In fact, the search for answers to such problems was and remained continuous, and while Italy deserves a special place in the story of the typewriter as in many other branches of modern 'technics', other countries figured prominently also. In one year alone, 1891, no fewer than 149 typewriter patents were taken out in the United States.

Many of the very mixed band of inventors, including Edison, who devised an electric typewriter – he also devised an electric pen – looked backwards to more primitive 'writing machines' for inspiration. Nor did they always have businessmen in mind when they were thinking about who would use their products. Pitman's first publisher, who told him to insist on the 'novelty' of his invention, dealt not in ledgers but in Bibles, and Pitman himself was a dedicated Swedenborgian. Before he became a businessman – and a highly successful one – he set out to propagate shorthand not through a business operation but through a 'movement' on the same lines as the Anti-Corn Law League or Hill's Mercantile Committee, and John Bright was one of his enthusiastic backers. 'Shorthands', Bright observed, 'are of little use if known only to the select few.'

In the case of the typewriter, many inventors concentrated most on the value of their products to novelists, poets and scholars and still, above all, to the blind. 'Grand old Milton', a speaker told the Society of Arts in London in 1888, 'would have been independent of his "flippant daughters" had he possessed this "scimitar of power". At last modern invention has espoused the cause of the penman, and in the typewriter has given to the world of letters an instrument that banishes at a sweep cramp in the hand and illegibility, and doubles, nay trebles, the speed of writing.'

Members of the Society of Arts had listened to an earlier talk on the typewriter – accompanied by a demonstration – as long ago as 1867, but while inventors of typewriters were never absent in Britain or in other European countries and remarkable 'tailor made' individual typewriters were produced, like one for the Czarina of Russia incorporating enamel and mother of pearl and one for Queen Victoria herself with ivory gold-plated keys, it was in the United States that progress in salesmanship was most rapid, if often most controversial. In that same year, 1867, Christopher Latham Sholes, Samuel Soule, and Charles Gliddon were at work in Milwaukee on a machine for numbering the pages of a blank book, and between then and 1873 Sholes turned out no fewer than twenty-five working machines. In the words of a late-Victorian writer on the evolution of the typewriter in *The Strand Magazine*, Sholes was fully aware from the start of the 'vast possibilities that lay hidden in the tangled collections of cams and cogs and levers'.

It was the Remington Company, previously associated mainly with the rifle and now diversifying its activities after the Civil War, that took up the Sholes machine in 1873, introducing the Sholes and Gliddon Typewriter which was displayed, without attracting much notice, at the Centennial Exhibtion of 1876. And this typewriter became the Improved Model I of 1878, which served as the prototype for all Remington typewriters (and many other typewriters) until 1908: by then there had been ten Remington models. The 'Caligraph' was a related machine, which beat the Remington in a much publicized speed test in 1888. By contrast, the 'Columbia' and the

*Early typewriters: 1877 and 1887*

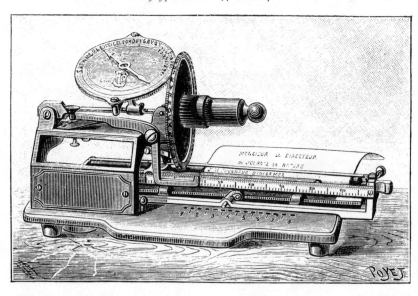

*'Typewriters' at work*

'World' had no type-bars and the 'Hammond' and the 'Writing Ball' were quite different products.

Remington was never without critics or competitors, but it did not have to face up to effective British competition. As late as 1897, when *The Strand Magazine* writer surveyed the field, only one well-known typewriter, 'The North', was being made in England. The writer had no explanation to offer, although he pointed out, as the speaker to the Society of Arts, John Robinson, had done in 1888, that the British were creatures of habit and that long-hand writers were suspicious of machines. His only suggestion was that there should be protection. 'If the Government were to decide tomorrow to clap a 25 per cent *ad valorem* duty on all foreign-made typewriters, there is not the slightest doubt that factories for manufacturing machines on English soil would be quickly established.' The suggestion was made no more convincing when the writer added that Americans had one advantage over the British in that they had trained operatives in their plant, whereas 'anyone establishing a typewriter factory in England would be obliged to find his own workmen'.

While Britain was demonstrating its business backwardness both in using

413

typewriters and in manufacturing them, the situation in the United States itself revealed a different version of protectionism. In 1893 a Union Typewriter Company, a trust promoted and joined by several hitherto competing firms, was formed, not only to fix the price of standard typewriters of various makes, including the Caligraph, at $100, but to ward off competition from makers of those rival typewriters which offered the great advantage that what was being typed was 'visible' to the typist. By comparison other typewriters seemed 'blind'. 'Testimonials' from their grateful users were used for advertising, and fifteen years later the Union Typewriter Company itself went 'visible'. Not all of Remington's competitors had offered its salesmen a free piano if they sold ten Emersons in three months.

Sales statistics of typewriters are patchy, although it has been estimated that 304 Remington Model IIs, introduced in 1878, were sold in 1880, 27,000 in 1887, and 65,000 in 1890, and that 17,000 'Worlds' were sold in its first year, 1886. All in all, it has been claimed, 150,000 typewriters were in use in the United States in 1896. A writer in *The Strand Magazine*, a year later, recorded that in Britain there were still 'scores and hundreds of old-fashioned firms where a writing-machine was absolutely tabooed. Only recently, a distinguished barrister, well-known on the home circuit, had declined to receive a typewritten brief.' Such 'blind unreasoning prejudice' the writer concluded, would soon be overcome, however, as the advantages of the typewriter became as apparent in Britain as across the Atlantic. There its operators had quickly become 'devotees'. In Britain itself, after all, 'the refusal in the early forties of certain old-fashioned people to make use of trains' had not stopped the 'introduction into England of railways'.

It is interesting to note that as late as the 1890s the railway parallel was still considered as the natural one to select in discussing the resistances of 'a naturally conservative people'. Indeed, in the story of Pitman shorthand the 'progressive' role of the railway was chosen as a parallel at many points in the story. 'Stenographic soundhand', Isaac Pitman wrote in 1837, 'must roll upon its own wheel', and Pitman's first biographer, looking back over fifty years of progress, compared the first 1837 system with the first locomotives, the Rocket and the Puffing Billy.

## IX

By the time that these comparisons were made, the railway, source of wealth, of power, of ideas and of images, was itself under the threat of competition on both sides of the Atlantic, although there were few who realized it. Changes in the pattern of physical communication had been at the centre of the pre-Victorian and early-Victorian experience of invention; and they were to be associated at the end of the century with what perhaps in retrospect were the most innovatory of all late-Victorian things – automobiles. Unlike the railway, the automobile was a thing for the individual – and the rich individual at that. Yet it was preceded by the tram, a thing for 'the people', and the bicycle, a thing for people, including people who were poor, and women as well as men. The cluster of new inventions had the bicycle at the centre. You might go to a bicycle shop to buy your phonograph cylinders and your records, and the same firm might also produce bicycles, typewriters – and sewing-machines, still the most intricate objects of the three. Of course, you might also go to a blacksmith for your petrol.

The new chapter in the story of physical communication was to change the role of the horse, 'the most noble of animals', as much as it was to change the ways of life of the human being. Victorian society had been so heavily dependent on horses – and on all the Victorian things connected with horses – that Michael Thompson has described it as 'the horse-drawn society'. And it remained so in the 1880s. Before new powered things, therefore, came berlins and britzschas, things with imported names, and broughams and Victorias, very British, not to speak of 'sociables' and 'sulkys'. To leave them out completely from a book on 'Victorian things' – or all the other 'horsey things from bit to bridle' – would be like leaving out all pre-electrical signalling in a history of the communication of messages. There was even one Victorian, reported in the *Manchester Sporting Times* in 1888 who, thinking that his horse was short-sighted, had his eyes examined by an oculist, who certified that the horse had a 'Number 7 Eye' and required concave glasses.

The Victorian air smelt of horses and of horse-manure. The Victorian aristocracy were connoisseurs of the stable. Victorian city streets were often jammed by horse traffic, Victorian horse racing was *the* racing of Victorians and thousands gambled on horses who had never been to a racecourse, while mechanical power, the greatest pride of the Victorians, and every other form of power, including the harnessed power of Niagara, was measured in terms of horse power. Not surprisingly, therefore, the motor car figured first as a 'horseless carriage' – the title of a new American periodical of 1895 – and its salesmen were at pains to explain how much cheaper it was to maintain a motor car in a garage than it was to maintain a horse in mews. As the Chairman of the new Daimler Company optimistically told the first annual meeting of his shareholders in London in 1897, 'There are no saddles to be rented, no feed, no trouble about the horse being out of order or sick. Looking after a motor car is child's play compared to attending to a horse'. The same points, he went on, had been made to the owners and drivers of London's horse omnibuses, each of which, according to *Household Words* in 1866, required ten horses to operate it, each of which consumed twenty-one pounds of oats and hay each day.

A lecturer speaking in the Camera Club in the same year as the Chairman of the Daimler Company – the location was appropriate – was reported by *Autocar*, a new magazine founded in 1895, as saying 'he hoped as soon as possible to see the horse abolished and found only in the hunting field and parks (laughter)'. He might have stilled the laughter by pointing out how many steps had already been taken to abolish the horse, if not the name. The first effective pre-Victorian bicycle, invented in 1817 by a German, Baron Karl von Drais, as instinctive an inventor as Edison, had been nicknamed 'the hobby horse' or 'dandy horse', and, of course, the railway locomotive itself had been known from its infancy as the 'iron horse'. Old images, as always, were used to familiarize new things.

The first motor car in Britain was an imported product from Germany that cost £80 – a three-horse power Benz two-seater, bought in 1894 by Henry Hewetson, who was to go on to sell no fewer than 1300 early Benz cars. Both Karl Benz and Gottlieb Daimler – they never met – had taken out patents for petrol-driven four-wheel cars with internal combustion engines eight years ealier, and Benz had sold his first four cars in 1887–8. Hewetson collected his model at the docks, and as he drove it proudly to Charing Cross Station he was stopped by the police for the offence, prescribed under the Red Flag Act of 1865, of not being preceded by a man on foot, and was told not to commit it again.

It was the offence, however, not the car, which soon disappeared. For the most part, fines imposed on offenders seem to have been largely nominal before 1894, and in 1878 the red flag itself had ceased to be obligatory. Now in 1896 the man went too. The Act of 1865, with steam carriages in mind, had restricted speeds to four miles an hour in the country and two miles an hour in the towns, but now in 1896 maximum speed limits were raised to fourteen miles an hour, still far lower of course than the speed that the new motor cars of the 1890s were capable of reaching: speeds of up to fifty miles an hour were themselves exceeded at speed competitions, which attracted journalists as well as car enthusiasts.

However enthusiastic pioneers like Hewetson might be about the new automobile, a note of alarm was often struck. There was also hesitation on the part of people able to afford the new vehicles. 'It seems to be part of the sturdy Briton's character', *Chambers's Journal* wrote in 1899, echoing a familiar theme, 'that he should be conservative in his suspicion of new-fangled inventions; anyhow, he is slow to adopt inventions and discoveries which other nations are willing at once to assimilate.' 'The habit', the writer went on, 'has its drawbacks; but it has the pretty constant advantage that we leave the great expense and trouble of experiment to others, and profit much in the end by their labours. It has been especially so with the motor car.'

The proposition was doubtful. Britain had been backward even in the development of the steam carriage, with the French proving themselves capable of producing steam carriages that even during the 1890s could outpace the new automobiles; so that it was not correct to attribute the greater interest in internal combustion engines in France and Germany to the fact that Britain had cheap coal and steam and France, in particular, had not. Another argument advanced was that France, in particular, had far better roads. It had, but this scarcely seems an adequate explanation.

Whatever the reason, France certainly produced the first commercially successful gas engine in 1869, and even after Germany forged ahead during the 1870s, 1880s and 1890s, with Rudolf Diesel producing *his* first model – with the help of Krupps in 1893 – the French were quicker to take out Daimler licences than the British, as *La France Automobile* proudly proclaimed. Moreover, of 150 vehicles France produced in 1898, over 120 were exported across the Channel – bad roads or not. When Harry J. Lawson, flamboyant son of a Non-conformist minister, eventually acquired the Daimler manufacturing rights in Britain in 1895, his British Motor Syndicate seemed most interested in exploiting a monopoly that would serve his own interests rather than those of the infant car industry.

Frederick Henry Royce, who had started life as a telegraph messenger, was still making lamp holders and electric light bulbs in Manchester, and his first two cylinder car did not take to the roads until 1904. By then, however, Frederick Lanchester, scientist as well as engineer, had secured capital for his Lanchester Engine Company; Montague Napier and Selwyn Francis Edge were producing quality cars; the Automobile Club of Great Britain was seven years old; and 8,500 cars had been licensed. It had greatly helped too that the Prince of Wales had become both an enthusiast and a customer, buying three Daimler cars in 1900. When as King Edward he granted a Royal Warrant to the Company in 1902, he was ensuring that early motor cars are now thought of less as Victorian than as characteristically Edwardian things. They went well with the 'plutocracy' that many influential Victorians, particularly Gladstone, saw as a threat to the future of the country.

Lawson had provided the late-Victorian rhetoric of the motor vehicle prospectus: during the Edwardian years, never short of rhetoric, there was genuine achievement in production also – along with continuing controversy. Another car enthusiast, Rudyard Kipling, was to dwell not on the thrills but on the more chastening experiences of motoring – the 'agonies, shames, delays, chills ... burns and starvations'. 'Any fool can invent anything', he went on, 'as any fool can wait to buy the invention when it is thoroughly perfected; but the men to reverence, to admire, to write odes about and erect statues to are those Prometheuses and Ixions ... who change the inchoate idea to fixity up and down the Queen's Highway.' Kipling did not care whether they were plutocrats or not.

In the United States the automobile was to be associated with a mythology, yet during these early years both the first and the second parts of the *Chambers's Journal* proposition were to hold. While there was relatively little early interest in the internal combustion engine – steam carriages and electric cars were far more popular – once the switch had been made, it was the internal combustion engine that attracted outstanding entrepreneurial talent, adequate capital and the promise of a popular and expanding market. There, too, for a time Lawson had intervened as a dubious promoter, joining forces with get-rich-quick Edward Joel Penington, who purported to have manufactured the appropriately named 'Hot Air Engine'. Yet across the Atlantic the slick prospectus very soon gave way to the still slicker assembly line. Ransom E. Olds produced 600 'Merry Oldsmobiles' in 1901, and Henry Ford, once Chief Engineer of the Edison Illuminating Company, had made his first 'quadricycle' in Detroit in 1896, where the first car dealer appeared two years later.

While it was the German Mercedes-Simplex motor car of 1901 which first set the shape and style of the twentieth-century automobile, it was Ford's universal Model-T which set the pace: it was to take to the roads in 1909, based on the principle, unpopular with many fashion designers, that the way to make automobiles is to make one automobile like another automobile, a principle which both the British and the French, for different reasons, would have found it difficult to enunciate, let alone accept.

It is impossible to tell the story of the motor car independently from that of the bicycle, and it is equally impossible to tell the story of physical communications and leave out the tram. Karl Benz's first motor car was in its essentials an internal combustion engine set on wheels within a 'sociable' light tricycle framework, and in Britain the first home-produced petrol driven engine was the petro-cycle of Edward Butler, son of a farmer, designed in 1885. Lawson, too, rose on the cycle boom before turning to motor cars.

As had been the case with the different features of the railway, each feature of the bicycle, like the motor car later, had its own pre-history before the 'combination' began to work. In the case of the railways it had been locomotives and track signals; and in the case of the motor car it was to be internal combustion engines, power transmission, sprung suspension, steering gear, headlights and horn. In the case of the bicycle it was steering (1817), pedals (1839), front-wheel cranks (1861), pneumatic tyres (1890), and geared front drive (1889–1896). It was by continuing combination as much as invention, therefore, that quadricycles and tricycles gave way to 'boneshakers' and boneshakers became 'safety bicycles'. France played a prominent part in this process too. Already by 1868 Ernest and Pierre Michaux, coachmakers in Paris, were making twelve 'boneshakers' or velocipedes a day.

The social history of the bicycle also went through phases. The 'hobby horse' had been a toy for the gentry. The velocipede and later the 'ordinary bicycle' – note the adjective – introduced in 1870 – appealed to a bigger public. Indeed, from 1868 to 1870 – at the height of the great Victorian boom – London, like Paris and later New York, was struck by 'velocipedomania', and at least fifty English manufacturers, some of them traditional craftsmen, followed the Michaux brothers in manufacturing iron-tyred bicycles. The bicycle was to give a new lease of life to Coventry, an old city hit by the collapse of the silk ribbon trade (in face of French competition), particularly when importing French bicycles became difficult during and after the Franco-German war of 1870. Its population, which had been declining or stagnant for twenty years grew rapidly thereafter, more than doubling (from 45,000) in the next thirty years, and going on to attract the automobile industry after the great bicycle boom collapsed.

The speed of the velocipede had been its main selling point – it was four times faster than walking – but it was difficult to mount, and since it was dangerous to ride on steep hills there were critics of it who claimed that while a mad dog could be avoided because it ran straight, 'a madman on a velocipede' ran anything but straight. Part of its appeal, however, and part of the appeal of the improved bicycle, lay in the fact that it was very much a thing in itself, a kind of 'leviathan', as Keith Falconer, 'the best cyclist of his day', called it. It was a piece of personal property, as the motor car was to be, but cheaper and less dependent on a network of services, and like all such pieces of property it was to become a collectors' piece. Charles Wade, who started to collect bicycles in 1920 when few people showed much interest in them, assembled a remarkable museum of them at Snowshill in an old granary re-named 'Hundred Wheels'. From a different angle, of course, the bicycle, as one French writer put it, was an 'extension of man'. There was a sense that the man on the bicycle was not just a man and a machine, he became 'a faster man', rather than 'two different things like man and horse.'

Given such a 'philosophy' the imagination of bicycle enthusiasts turned inevitably to flying: 'We have wings'. Real flying was to come later, although 'new flying machines', 'much heavier than the air', had been already invented, some power-driven, some 'gliding'. One active experimenter in 1898 was Alexander Graham Bell, who began building kites to study lift and drag. There was a feeling, as the inventor, Professor S. P. Langley, secretary of the Smithsonian Institution, put it in 1897, that 'the great universal highway overhead is now soon to be opened'.

Wells introduced flying machines into his stories. Meanwhile, however, he was cycling on Britain's rough national highways – and local tracks. In such a setting the experience of cycling, which could be as thrilling and chastening as that of motoring was to be for Kipling, changed as the pattern of the bicycle evolved. Between the velocipede and the safety bicycle came the 'penny farthing' or 'the ordinary', often wooden wheeled, and James Stanley's model patented in 1870 was called significantly 'the Ariel'. It was shrewdly developed between 1870 and 1878, when many other patents were taken out, most of them described in *The Bicyclist*. The tubular steel frame became commonplace and the weight of the bicycle was reduced. The whole design was challenged, however, in 1885 after J. K. Starkey, James's nephew, and Sutton introduced at a bicycle club their new safety Rover machine with a driving chain to the rear wheel. This 'set the fashion to the world', including the United States, and it opened up 'the delights of cycling' to a new and greatly extended public.

In longer term perspective it prepared the way for 'motoring, not least by drawing attention to the state of British roads, as enthusiasts with enough money, like the journalist Alfred Harmsworth, later Lord Northcliffe, recognized at the time. So, too, did the American pioneer of the automobile, Hiram Percy Maxim, son of the inventor of the Maxim gun, who wrote with conscious hindsight in his lively autobiography *Horseless Carriage Days* that 'the bicycle could not satisfy the demand which it had created. A mechanically-propelled vehicle was wanted instead of a foot-propelled one, and we now know that the automobile was the answer.'

Price was the major element in choice. New bicycles, which cost between $100 and $150 in 1893, cost $15 or less by 1901: the cheapest automobiles still cost ten times more. In England bicycles cost between £12 and £25 during the 1870s. By 1894 they could already be bought for £4.50 and were regarded as 'the Working Man's Friend': there was also a flourishing trade in second-hand bicycles. During the 1890s, with safety bicycles now equipped with pneumatic tyres, many working men were riding by bicycle to work more cheaply than they would have done had they taken any other mode of transport.

Bicycles were considered by then 'the most democratic of all vehicles' on both sides of the Atlantic, unless tandems were even more popular: the popular song 'Daisy Bell' goes back to 1892:

> I will stand by you in 'wheel' or woe, Daisy, Daisy!
> You'll be the bell(e) which I'll ring, you know! Sweet Daisy Bell!
> You'll take the 'lead' in each 'trip' we take, then if I don't do well;
> I will permit you to use the brake, my beautiful Daisy Bell.

Three-wheelers were popular, too, and Queen Victoria had several of them. Moreover, sport figured in the literature as well as romance: crowds of over 20,000 were gathering at Wolverhampton during the 1880s for championship races. Far outside royal circles, many cycling clubs hailed democracy as enthusiastically as their own bicycles. The Bicycle Touring Club was founded by Stanley Cotterell in 1878, the National Cyclist's Union in 1883, and Robert Blatchford's Clarion Clubs soon afterwards. The first of these had 22,000 members in 1886, and towards the end of the century reached its peak in 1899 with 60,000 members. Bicycles, pianos – and perambulators – were the most expensive pieces of property most families owned.

There were still some people who could not cope with two wheels and asked for four, so that the *Illustrated London News* hailed the horseless carriage as 'a great institution for ladies with plenty of pluck to go about alone who can steer themselves, but with not enough vital force to propel a bicycle.' Most people who could cope with neither two wheels nor four or who could not afford to discover whether or not they could, still had to travel by train – or in the cities by omnibus or by tram.

Significantly, perhaps, Britain's first electric tramway was opened not in London but in the popular holiday resort of Blackpool in 1885: already a 'mass' resort, the three-mile ride along the length of the Promenade was an attraction in itself, as was the Victoria Pier opened in 1893, complete with a photographic booth – and a phrenologist. Other places in Lancashire quickly followed, so that by 1901 61 local authorities owned electric tramways – Manchester was one of the largest – and 89 tramway undertakings were managed by private enterprise. In Leeds which pioneered electrification there were no longer any horse-drawn trams in 1901.

London had developed its underground system since the 1860s – 'as aerial navigation is not yet an accomplished fact', wrote the *London Magazine*, 'the only alternative left to us is to burrow under the earth like rabbits'. The advent of electric trams had been fiercely resisted: two years after Queen Victoria's death 500 million passengers a year were still being carried by London's 4,000 horse omnibuses and only 165 million on the tramways.

The pattern of electrification of rail transport had been set in the United States following the opening in 1888 of Frank Julian Sprague's Electric Union Passenger Railway, although there were many earlier experiments. Edison had invented a not very efficient electric train in 1880, which he thought of as a possible streetcar or as a substitute for a steam train on a track, and a year earlier Werner Siemens, Germany's foremost electrical inventor, had exhibited a full-size electric train in Berlin. The American breakthrough came during the 1890s. Between 1893 and 1895 the mileage of electric tramways rose from 7,466 to 12,583, while the 'horse mileage' fell from 3,497 to 1,232. General Electric and Westinghouse, keenly competitive, sold between them over 50,000 trams between 1890 and 1898. This was the beginning of what Charles Klapper has called 'the golden age of tramways', and one popular General Electric Model, the GE 800, deserves to be remembered along with Ford's later Model T automobile.

While in London some horse omnibuses seemed 'only fit for firewood', a complaint of 1893, and moved so ponderously that in the reminiscences of Gwen Raverat 'a running child could beat them easily', in late-Victorian Britain well-bred and well-trained horses were still attracting bigger crowds on the race-courses – and more betting off them – than bicycles or cars. The jockey Fred Archer, who committed suicide in 1886, had long ago joined the gallery of fame, and his image was as well known outside as inside racing and betting circles. The Prince of Wales, who had a place in the gallery for different reasons, won fame of a new kind when his horse won the Derby ten years later in 1896. The Liberal Prime Minister, the fifth Earl of Rosebery, had been a Derby winner in 1894.

# X

The often repeated story, apparently untrue, was that Rosebery had had three ambitions – to become Prime Minister, to win the Derby, and to marry a Rothschild. He had certainly achieved the third of these ambitions relatively early in 1878, when he married Hannah Rothschild, the richest heiress in the country, who four years earlier had inherited among other possessions Mentmore, the house her father had built and furnished a quarter of a century earlier. Not far from another Rothschild house, Waddesdon, it had been built by Paxton and stood imposingly in the middle of a 700-acre estate in the Vale of Aylesbury. 'I do not believe that the Medici were ever so lodged at the height of their glory', wrote Lady Eastlake. The house was, in fact, Jacobean, as different from the Crystal Palace as possible except that its courtyard was entirely covered in with a forty-foot high roof of glass.

It is fitting that the last chapter of a book on Victorian things should include sections both on Menlo Park, the laboratory which Edison created for himself in New Jersey and on Mentmore. Menlo Park, 'a wonderful place', as *Harpers' Weekly* called it in 1879, was full of new things, even if some of them were 'fragments of old machines': Mentmore, wonderful in a very different sense, was full of old things, even if some of them had been repaired and polished to the point of newness. Both were cluttered – or 'crowded' as *Harpers* preferred to describe Menlo Park. Both had a library: Edison called his a 'thought laboratory'. There was a stuffed eagle in it from the 1889 Paris Exhibition, but its eyes were made to shine by a miniature bulb in its head. Most of the names of the Mentmore objects had already figured in collectors' lists and in sales catalogues. Some of them were very old, like the Gobelin tapestries: few, however, were medieval. Few, too, were British, and even fewer purely functional. The guest bedrooms were fitted with Louis XV or Louis XVI commodes, the marble tops of which had been pierced and fitted with basins and taps.

Mentmore was not Puginesque. Nor would Rothschild – or Paxton – have had much sympathy with a Pugin disciple's assessment of a Victorian hansom cab in 1858 – as 'so truthful, so-so-so medieval.' What happened *after* the middle ages counted. It was left to William Burges to produce a sketch of a 'Gothic paddle steamer'. This was one of many examples of the Victorians crossing the centuries. In 1851 at the Great Exhibition Alexander Bain had displayed his electrically powered clock in a richly scrolled rococo French-styled case which would certainly have appealed to Lord Rothschild.

'Our age is retrospective' Emerson had complained in the 1840s. Why, he asked ponderously, should it not proclaim 'an original relation to the universe?', a question not very different from the favourite Victorian question posed by architects, why should they not have 'an architecture of our period, a distinct, individual, palpable style of the nineteenth century?' The burdens of history could be as real as its excitements. For the architect Gilbert Scott, 'the peculiar characteristic of the present day, as compared with all former periods, is this – that we are acquainted with the history of art.'

Because such questions were asked and many different, even contradictory, answers given, it is as difficult to generalize about the universe of old things in Victorian times and how it was related to the universe of new things as it is to categorize and to interpret Victorian new things. There was parody as well as derivation, escape as well as exploration, individual fantasy as well as imitation. Nor did you need to subscribe to a mid-Victorian philosophy of eclecticism (compromise?) to be eclectic: it might come naturally. The *Contemporary Review* was never short of pieces on the middle ages.

Mentmore is best known now for the great sale which took place there in 1977 and for the five catalogue volumes, almost as impressive as the house, which were produced by Sotheby and which cover furniture and furnishings, works of art, silver, porcelain, paintings, prints and drawings. In early-Victorian England in 1842, there had been an equally remarkable, if far less financially successful, sale – that of the contents, not all of them Gothic, of Horace Walpole's Strawberry Hill, which preceded the full mid-Victorian recognition of 'antiquity' as a saleable asset. *The Times*, reflecting the changes in taste since Walpole and the current attitudes toward 'the old', stated then that 'there was nothing for which a good judge would have travelled a step out of his road', but Gerald Reitlinger in his indispensable study *The Economics of Taste* (1963), which uses relative price changes as indicators, noted 'how Walpole's ghost would have been amazed to see his expensive French furniture and porcelain [the kind of objects which were to appeal to Rothschild] fetch less than his Renaissance furniture and his armour.'

There was more than a touch of *The Old Curiosity Shop*, the title of Dickens's novel, in the Strawberry Hill sale – 'suits of mail standing like ghosts in armour here and there, fantastic carvings bought from monkish cloisters, rusty weapons of various kinds, distorted figures in china and wood and iron and ivory: tapestry and strange furniture that might have been designed in dreams'. These were the residues of 'older times', but at the end of *The Old Curiosity Shop* we reach a place where 'Time itself seemed to have grown dull and old, as if no day were ever to displace the melancholy night.' Dickens was as different from Pugin as Paxton was. As Humphry House has written, 'the church in which Little Nell at last finds rest is a monstrous curio rather than the relic of a great civilization.'

Yet in the middle years of Victorian England – after the Great Exhibition – there were markedly different attitudes not only towards 'antiquity' (what Thackeray in *The Newcomes* called 'the Hantique') and towards the Middle Ages, a favourite refuge for poets, but towards 'expensive French furniture, particularly eighteenth-century furniture, and porcelain'. The Victoria and Albert Museum, offspring of the great Exhibition, bought many old things – often still at extraordinarily cheap prices – like the Eltenburg Reliquary and a Limoges casket by Martin Didier – as well as new things. There was a sense then that the things of the past could and should be captured and placed in a great treasure house, since the new things of the present and the future might be evanescent. The sense was particularly strong in the late-nineteenth century United States. For one visitor to the Chicago World Fair of 1893, 'if we should have another exhibition twenty-five years from now, the probability is that not one of the things which seem so wonderful will then be valued.' That was a different sentiment from that which had been expressed by Samuel Palmer in 1862 – 'The Past for Poets: the Present for Pigs' – but it was part of the same clusters of responses.

They were complex as well as changing responses. For Reitlinger, who was mainly interested in 'high art', the period from 1875 to 1885, which has often been thought of as a period of economic depression and, equally often, as a period when a new cluster of things appeared, saw 'the high-tide mark of the *objets d'art* market'. 'Some of the highest prices which were paid in gold in 1875–85 were never repeated again.' The general price graph was falling, but this particular price graph was not.

Reitlinger was right to insist that 'the value of a work of genius bears no relation at all to the basic cost of living'. Yet most of the *objets d'art* which fetched high prices were not works of genius. Businessmen who realised that falling prices of the 'new things' they made or sold would increase sales, often paid the highest prices for 'old things'. Nor were things always well maintained or displayed. Much of the lumber and clutter of Mentmore could be found elsewhere in less ambitious homes even when it was becoming increasingly fashionable to limit lumber and cut clutter. For one American critic of the late-nineteenth century years, working in the 1920s, you had to be 'philosophical when you discussed 'the public neglect that greeted the telephone at its birth' and recall 'that the eighties were dull and stupid years full of fat pomposities and varnished gimcracks, an era of mansard roofs, iron deer, horsehair furniture, antimacassars, bustles and whiskers'.

Mumford's 'brown decades' saw many curious juxtapositions; as in Tennyson's *The Princess*, you might confront

A Gothic ruin and a Grecian house,
A talk of colleges and of ladies rights,
A feudal knight in silken masquerade
And yonder, shrieks and strange experiments.

It was difficult during the 1880s and 1890s, therefore to know what 'something made to suit the time and place', to use another phrase from *The Princess*, really would be.

Leaving on one side all questions of status, class and 'poverty in the midst of plenty', most of which were raised by the census of 1901, taken in the year of Queen Victoria's death, there was no one single universe of Victorian things for those who possessed them. What was not shared was at least as significant as what was.

*Victorian Cities* ended with a chapter similar in title to this chapter – 'Old Cities and New'. The cities not only co-existed: almost all the new incorporated elements of the old, and almost all the old incorporated elements of the new. As far as things were concerned, they could, of course, be completely new or old. Yet old and new things co-existed too – within the home, within the factory, within the warehouse, within church and chapel, and, not least, within the city; and they continued so to co-exist down to the 1950s when many old Victorian things were rediscovered, at a time when many new things were being introduced. Corner shops, more representative of Victorian villages, towns and even cities than department stores, survived too, as yet unpressed by supermarkets. There were still many 'necessities' which had changed little, although many of the new things of the 1880s and 1890s, including motor cars and trains, were already being thought of as vintage things.

The history behind all this is relevant to the present as well as interesting in itself. There are always surprises, but as the wisest interpreters of things, like W. J. Lethaby, have never hesitated to say, 'would you know the new you must search the old ... To forget the past would be to ignore the future.'

# BIBLIOGRAPHICAL NOTE

This bibliographical note is highly selective. No book is mentioned twice. It is designed primarily for the reader who wishes to pursue further in other books the subjects of the individual chapters in this book. It also includes a number of books which have particularly interested or influenced the author. It leaves out contemporary and later articles, often the only sources for the text, and exhibition catalogues, a major source. However many words are read, there is no substitute for *seeing* collections of things.

## 1. THINGS AS EMISSARIES

The best lead-in is S. Giedion, *Mechanisation Takes Command* (1984), although this pioneering study should be compared with A. Forty, *Objects of Desire: Design and Society, 1750–1980* (1986). The latter concludes with a useful bibliography that includes some of the books and articles studied in parallel by me. See also T. J. Schlereth, *Artifacts and the American Past* (1980) and the much earlier book by J. A. Kouwenhoven, *Made in America* (1942).

Basic studies of Victorian design and taste include J. Steegman, *Victorian Taste, A Study of the Arts and Architecture from 1830 to 1870* (1970), a re-issue of his older book *Consort of Taste* (1950) with a useful foreword by Sir Nikolaus Pevsner putting the book in perspective; Pevsner's own *High Victorian Design* (1951), his essays *Studies in Art, Architecture and Design* (1968), and his *Pioneers of Modern Design* (1960); R. Lynes, *The Tastemakers* (1949); the first two chapters of F. MacCarthy, *A History of Design, 1830–1870* (1979), originally published in 1972 with the tempting title *All Things Bright and Beautiful* (with useful bibliographies); A. Böe, *From Gothic Revival to Functional Form* (1957); B. Denvir, *The Early Nineteenth Century, Art, Design and Society, 1789–1852* (1984), *The Late Victorians, Art, Design and Society, 1852–1910* (1984), two volumes in his useful documentary history of taste in Britain; H. Schaeffer, *The Roots of Modern Design* (1983); and L. Grow and D. von Zweck, *A Style and Source Book; American Victorian* (1984), again with a good select bibliography.

Readers interested in pursuing the subject through Victorian writing should begin with the works of William Morris (there is a Penguin anthology edited by me (1984 edn.); with Sir Henry Cole's *Fifty years of Public Work* (1884); and with T. Wemyss Reid, *Memoirs and Correspondence of Lyon Playfair* (1899). The last of these opens up perspectives not opened in any of the previous books cited in this note. So, too, does J. A. V. Chapple in *Science and Literature in the Nineteenth Century* (1986).

There is no entirely satisfactory social history of Victorian science in twentieth-century perspective, but see for a popular contemporary account R. Routledge, *Discoveries and Inventions of the Nineteenth Century* (1884) and for a late-nineteenth century assessment A. R. Wallace, *The Wonderful Century* (1898). Technology has been covered better. See, for example, L. T. C. Rolt, *Victorian Engineering* (1970) and W. H. G. Armytage, *A Social History of Engineering* (1961) which, like all Professor Armytage's books, is peppered with fascinating references. There is a place for human beings as well as for machines in books like G. Dodd, *Days at the Factories* (1975 reprint). See also J. Kasson, *Civilising the Machine: Technology and Republican Values in America, 1776–1900* (1977).

The differences in approach between strictly economic history and both technical and cultural history are well brought out in parallel study of R. Floud, *The British Machine-Tool Industry, 1850–1914* (1976) and W. Steeds, *A History of Machine Tools, 1700–1910* (1969). There is a similar gap between J. B. Jefferys, *Retail Trading in Britain 1850–1950* and A. Adburgham, *Shops and Shopping, 1800–1914* (1964). An American study of French retailing – M. B. Miller, *The Bon Marché, Bourgeois Culture and the Department Store, 1869–1920* (1981) to some extent bridges the gap. So, too, does D. Landes in his *The Unbound Prometheus* (1969). See also my *From Ironbridge to the Crystal Palace: Images of Industry* (1979) and *The Power of Steam* (1982) and I. C. Bradley, *Enlightened Entrepreneurs* (1987). Miller's book should be compared with R. H. Williams, *Dream Worlds: Mass Consumption in Late-Nineteenth Century France* (1982); I. M. G. Quimby, *Material Culture and The Study of American Life* (1987); D. Boorstin, *The Americans: The Democratic Experience* (1973); A. Trachtenberg, *The Incorporation of America* (1982); and D. F. Noble, *America by Design: Science, Technology and the Rise of Corporate Capitalism* (1979).

S. Kern, *The Culture of Time and Space, 1880–1918* (1983), particularly relevant for the last chapter of this book, is concerned with literature too. For the best approach to Victorian things through literature, see P. Conrad's stimulating book *A Victorian Treasure House* (1973); H. House's *The Dickens World* (1960) remains valuable. See also *inter alia* J. McMaster, *Thackeray, the Major Novels* (1971); J. Bayley, *An Essay on Hardy* (1978); P. Thompson, *The Work of William Morris* (1967); and P. Stansky's *Re-designing the World* (1985).

There is a huge mass of writing on collectors, collections and 'collectables', the last of these the title of J. Mackay's short illustrated dictionary *Collectables* (1979). Compare T. Curtis, *The Lyle Price Guide to Collectibles* (1983) (note the different spelling of the key word) and M. Edwards, *A–Z Guide to Small Collectables* (1985). There are many handbooks like *The Victorian Collectors' Handbook* (1970) by C. P. Woodhouse, which includes an appendix on 'Victoriana on View in Britain'. Far more Victoriana are on view now, however, than then. See also J. Laver, *Victoriana* (1966); E. Swenson,

*Victoriana Americana* (1976); and J. Gabriel, *Victoriana* (1970). Compare C. W. Drepperd, *Victoriana: the Cinderella of Antiques* (1950). For thorough but limited studies of the economics of art and art objects see *Taste*, 2 vols. (1960, 1963). Compare the wide-ranging book by M. Thompson, *Rubbish Theory* (1979). *Exchange and Mart; Selected Issues, 1886–1948*, a David and Charles reprint with an introduction by G. Viewing and J. Mendes (1970) is a valuable complement.

Works of reference on particular categories of art objects include H. Osborne (ed.), *The Oxford Companion to the Decorative Arts* (1975) and S. Jervis, *The Penguin Dictionary of Design and Designers* (1984), a complementary volume to *The Penguin Dictionary of Decorative Arts* (ed. J. Fleming and H. Honour, 1977).

The Victorians themselves liked dictionaries and encylopaedia and some of them have recently been reprinted. See, for example, M. Henderson and E. Wilkinson, *Cassell's Compendium of Victorian Crafts*, republished in 1977 by its original publisher. Compendia included C. Tomlinson, *Encyclopaedia of Useful Arts, Mechanical and Chemical* (1854); G. Bevan Phillips, *British Manufacturing Industries*, the 1854 volume of which dealt with guns, nails, locks, screws, bolts and spikes; and G. Matéaux, *Wonderland of Work* (1883), referred to in my chapter. At the other end of the scale there were many 'mini-books'. For a recent post-Victorian example, see G. Williams, *Collecting Victoriana* (1970).

Among books by writers in different disciplines which raise theoretical issues the following are of direct interest – K. Marx, *Gründrisse* (1973 edn.) and many of his other writings; W. Benjamin, *Illuminations* (American edn.1969), with an introduction by Hannah Arendt); A. Giddens, *A Critique of Historical Materialism* (1981); A. Heller, *Everyday Life* (1984); C. Geertz, *The Interpretation of Cultures* (1973); R. Barthes, *Mythologies* (Paris, 1957); J. Baudrillard, *Le système des objets* (Paris, 1968); A. Moles, *Théorie des objets* (1972); H. Lefèbvre, *Critique de la vie quotidienne*, 2 vols (Paris, 1961, 1968); M. Rheims, *La vie étrange des objets* (Paris 1959); G. Perec, *Les choses* (Paris 1965); L. L. Cavalli-Sforza and M. W. Feldman, *Cultural Transmission and Evolution, A Quantitative Approach* (1981); S. Ewen, *Captains of Consciousness; Advertising and the Social Roots of the Consumer Culture* (1976); R. Marchand, *Advertising the American Dream: Making Way for Modernity* (1985); M. Douglas and B. Isherwood, *The World of Goods: Towards an Anthropology of Consumption* (1978); P. Wright, *Living in an Old Country* (1985); U. Eco, *Travels in Hyperreality* (1986 English edn.); H. T. Odum, *Systems Ecology* (1983); and M. Csikszentmitalyi and E. Rochberg-Halton, *The Meaning of Things, Domestic Symbols and the Self* (1981).

Delight in things and curiosity about them rather than concern for meanings is present in the admirable Shire Album series covering briefly, but with illustrations, a wide range of categories from agricultural hand tools to woollen textiles. Shire Publications has also produced a 'Discovering Series', and Cassell a Collectors' Pieces series. Among the many bigger books on particular categories of Victorian things not listed in references in later chapters, see J. Ayres, *British Folk Art* (1977); T. S. R. Boase, *English Art, 1800–1870* (1959); D. Farr, *English Art, 1870–1940* (1978); K. Gardiner, *An Introduction to Victorian Painting* (1985); R. Culff, *The World of Toys* (1969); T. White, *Antique Toys and their Background* (1971); C. Bartholomew, *Mechanical Toys* (1979); B. Barenholtz and J. McLintock, *American Antique Toys, 1830–1900* (1938); G. White, *Toys, Dolls, Automata, Marks and Labels* (1975); P. Beaver, *Victorian Parlour Games* (1974); B. Morris, *Victorian Table Glass and Ornaments* (1978); G. Wills, *Victorian Glass* (1876); G. W. Beard, *Nineteenth Century Cameo Glass* (1956); P. Hollister, *The Encyclopedia of Glass Paperweights* (1969); A. C. hedges, *Bottles and Bottle Collecting* (1975); C. Gore, *Victorian Jewellery Design* (1972); P. Wardle, *Victorian Silver and Silver Plate* (1963); P. Wardle, *Victorian Lace* (1968), one of a Victorian Collector Series published by Herbert Jenkins; J. E. T. Clark, *Musical Boxes* (1961); J. Bedford, *All Kinds of Small Boxes* (1964); R. F. Jordan, *Victorian Architecture* (1966); and R. Dixon and S. Muthesius, *Victorian Architecture* (1978), which includes a useful biography and a brief dictionary of architects.

I found much of delight myself in G. Buday, *The History of the Christmas Card* (1954); L. Lambton, *Vanishing Victoriana* (1976); J. Morley, *Death, Heaven and the Victorians* (1971); and S. Lasdun, *Making Victorians* (1983).

## 2. THE GREAT VICTORIAN COLLECTION

The Crystal Palace is examined within the context of the year 1851 in my *Victorian People* (1954), later editions of which include a brief bibliographical note on books on the subject that appeared since the date of first publication. Among books on the subject published since 1954 are C. H. Gibbs Smith, *The Great Exhibition of 1851* (1964); P. Beaver, *The Crystal Palace* (1970); G. F. Chadwick, *The Works of Sir Joseph Paxton* (1961); and U. Haltern, *Die Londoner Weltausstellung von 1851* (Münster, 1971). The last of these books has an excellent bibliography. See also S. Koppelkamm, *Glasshouses and Winter Gardens of the Nineteenth Century* (1981); S. Bayley, *The Albert Memorial* (1981) and J. Physick, *The Victoria and Albert Museum: The History of its Building* (1982).

For the nineteenth-century Exhibition sequence, see J. Allwood, *The Great Exhibition* (1977); B. Benedict, *The Anthropology of World Fairs* (1984); J. Maas, *The Glorious Enterprise: The Centennial Exhibition of 1876* (1973); R. C. Post (ed.), *1876, A Centennial Exhibition* (1976); B. Reid, *The Great American Fair: The World's Columbian Exposition* (1979); J. Harriss, *The Tallest Tower – Eiffel and the Belle Époque* (1975); *Chicago, 1893, Memorial Volume* (1893); P. Julian, *The Triumph of Art Nouveau – Paris Exhibition, 1900* (1974) and R. D. Mandell, *Paris 1900 – The World's Great Fair* (1967).

For arguments on taste and design, some still topical, see Q. Bell, *The Schools of Design* (1963); S. Macdonald, *The History and Philosophy of Art Education* (1970); A. Scharf, *Art and Industry* (1971). Contemporary works include G. Semper, *Wissenschaft, Industrie and Kunst* (1852); A. W. N. Pugin, *Designs* (collected studies, 1972); R. N. Wornum, *Analysis of Ornament* (1856: 8th edn. 1893); O. Jones, *Grammar of Ornament* (1856); C. Dresser, *The Art of Decorative Design* (1862), *The Principles of Decorative Design* (1873) and *Japan, Its Architecture, Art and Art Manufacture* (1882); R. Redgrave, *Manual of Design* (1876); W. Crane, *The Bases of Design* (1898); W. R. Lethaby, *Form in Civilisation* (1922); and C. Fry, *Vision and Design* (1920). There is an illuminating discussion of some of the key issues in E. Gombrich, *The Sense of Order* (1977). See also R. Watkinson, *Pre-Raphaelite Art and Design* (1970); G. W. Yapp (ed.), *Art Industry, Furniture, Upholstery and House Decoration* (1878) with 1200 engravings and diagrams; E. Aslin, *The Aesthetic Movement*: (1969); I. Anscombe and C. Gere, *Arts and Crafts in Britain and America* (1978); S. T. Madsen, *Art Nouveau* (1967); I. Anscombe, *A Woman's Touch: Women in Design from 1860 to the Present Day* (1984); A. Crawford, *C. R. Ashbee: Architect, Designer and Romantic Socialist* (1985); J. Brandon-Jones, *C. F. Voysey, Architect and Designer* (1978); P. Selz and M. Constantine (eds.), *Art Nouveau: Art and Design at the Turn of the Century* (1975 edn.); and admirable among mini-books Marabout Flash, *Le Style 1900* (Paris, 1968).

## 3. THE PHILOSOPHY OF THE EYE

Ruskin provides the most important entry into this chapter. For his career and significance see Q. Bell, *Ruskin* (1943) and J. D. Rosenberg, *The Darkening Glass* (1963). For his vision see T. Fellows, *The Failing Distance: the Autobiographical Impulse in John Ruskin* (1975); R. Hewison, *John Ruskin, The Argument of the Eye* (1976); and E. Helsinger, *Ruskin and the Art of the Beholder* (1982). See also M. Hardman, *Ruskin and Bradford: An Experiment in Victorian Cultural History* (1986). The last of these highly original books – and Ruskin encourages original interpretation – has a good brief bibliography.

On the eye and spectacles, see D. Lardner, *The Museum of Science and Art*, Vol. V (1855), 'The Eye'; C. S. Flick, *A Gross of Green Spectacles* (1951); F. W. Law, *The Ophthalmological Society of the United Kingdom, A Hundred Years of History* (n.d.) and *The Worshipful Company of Spectacle Makers – A History* (n.d.).

For the Victorian camera and its changing significance see B. Coe, *Cameras from Daguerrotypes to Instant Pictures* (1978) and M. Aver, *The Illustrated History of the Camera* (1975). The role of photography is discussed, although sometimes unconvincingly, in P. Bourdieu, *Un art moyen* (Paris 1965); S. Sontag, *On Photography* (1978); G. Freund, *Photography and Society* (1980); and A. Rouille, *L'Empire de la photographie, 1839–1870* (Paris, 1982).

There are many books on the history of photography, among them J. M.

Eder, *Geschichte der Photographie* (4th edn. 1932); H. Gernsheim, *The History of Photography* (1969); J. A. Keim, *Histoire de la Photographie* (Paris, 1970); B. Newhall, *The History of Photography* (4th edn. 1964); J. Willsberger, *The History of Photography* (1977); S. Hartmann, *The Valiant Knights of Daguerre* (1978); and J. Hannavy, *Masters of Victorian Photography* (1976). See also N. Lyons (ed.), *Photographers on Photography* (1966).

More detailed studies include H. Gernsheim, *Incanabula of British Photographic Literature, 1839–1875* (1984); R. Lassam, *Fox Talbot, Photographer* (1979); J. M. Cameron, *Victorian Photographs of Famous Men and Fair Women* (1973 edn.); M. Bartram, *The Pre-Raphaelite Camera* (1985); A. Hopkinson, *Julia Margaret Cameron* (1986); and M. F. Harker, *The Linked Ring* (1979).

For examples of the work of photographers see C. Ford and R. Strong, *An Early Victorian Album* (1974); W. Sansom, *Victorian Life in Photographs* (1974); B. Hillier, *Victorian Studio Photographs* (1976); D. Wilson, *Frith's Travels, A Photographic Journey through Britain* (1985); and, above all, C. Ford and B. Harrison, *A Hundred Years Ago; Britain in the 1880s in Words and Photographs* (1983). J. Maas, *The Victorian Art World in Photographs* (1984) is a fascinating and well illustrated study of artists as subjects of photographers and as photographers themselves.

For the moving picture see E. Barnouw, *The Magician and the Camera* (1981); P. Hammond, *Marvellous Meliès* (1974); C. W. Ceram, *Archaeology of the Cinema* (1965); G. Hendricks, *Beginnings of the Biograph* (1964) and *The Kinetoscope* (1966); R. Jeanne, *Cinéma 1900* (Paris 1968); G. Jowett, *Film* (1976); and J. Barnes, *The Beginnings of the Cinema in England* (1980).

For pictorial arts, covered in this and the next chapter see F. Jussim, *Visual Communication and the Graphic Arts* (1974); R. J. Godrey, *Print Making in Britain* (1978); W. M. Ivins, *Prints and Visual Communication* (1969); A. Garrett, *A History of Wood Engraving* (1978); A. M. Hind, *A Short History of Engraving and Etching* (1908); B. Denvir, *Pictures to Print* (1984); R. K. Engen, *Victorian Engravings* (1975) and H. Guise, *Great Victorian Engravings: A Collector's Guide* (1980). For illustrated books see P. H. Muir, *Victorian Illustrated Books* (1971) and G. Wakeman, *Victorian Book Illustration: the Technical Revolution* (1973).

## 4. IMAGES OF FAME

Queen Victoria is at the centre of this chapter. See S. Weintraub, *Victoria* (1987), an 'intimate biography' which has much to do with images, and H. and A. Gernsheim, *Queen Victoria, A Biography in Words and Pictures* (1958).

For Staffordshire figures in their historical context begin with J. and J. May, *Commemorative Pottery, 1780–1900, A Guide for Collectors* (1972). The best account of the economics of Staffordshires is in A. Oliver, *The Victorian Staffordshire Figures* (1971). For the objects themselves and their attraction for collectors see R. G. Hagger, *Staffordshire Chimney Ornaments* (1955); T. Balston, *Staffordshire Portrait Figures of the Nineteenth Century* (1958); P. D.

Gordon Page, *Staffordshire Portrait Figures* (1970); B. Latham, *Victorian Staffordshire Figures* (1953); and J. Hall, *Staffordshire Portrait Figures* (1972). The experience of potters is discussed in the autobiographical sketch *When I was a Child* by 'An Old Potter' (S. Shaw); H. Owen, *The Staffordshire Potter* (1901); and R. G. Hagger, *A Century of Art Education in the Potteries* (privately printed, n.d.). See also B. Hillier, *Master Potters of the Industrial Revolution* (1965).

Good general studies of pottery, commemorative and otherwise, include G. Bemrose, *Nineteenth Century English Pottery and Porcelain* (1952); and G. A. Godden, *Victorian Porcelain* (1961) and *British Pottery and Porcelain, 1780–1850* (1966).

For fairings see W. S. Bristowe, *Victorian China Fairings* (1964) and in a mini-book M. Anderson, *Victorian Fairings* (1982). For Goss see J. D. Magee, *Goss for Collectors* (1973). For pot lids see H. G. Clarke, *The Pot Lid Book* (1931) and C. Williams Wood, *Stafforshire Pot Lids and their Potters* (1972). There is little work on Parian ware, but see Shire Album 142 by D. Barker, *Parian Ware* (1985), the prelude to his *The Parian Phenomenon*, and C. and D. Shinn, *The Illustrated Guide to Victorian Parian China* (1971).

On Victorian statues see B. Read, *Victorian Statues* (1985) and A. Byron, *London's Statues* (1986). For Victorian memorial brasses, see D. Mearn, *Victorian Memorial Brasses* (1983). See also E. V. Gillon, *Victorian Cemetery Art* (1972 edn.) and J. S. Curl, *A Celebration of Death; introduction to some of the building monuments and settings of funerary architecture in Western European tradition* (1980).

For Baxter prints, see C. T. Courtney Lewis, *The Picture Printer of the Nineteenth Century, George Baxter, 1804–1867* (1911); H. G. Clarke, *The Centenary Baxter Book* (1936); and A. Ball and M. Martin, *The Price Guide to Baxter Prints* (1974). There is no book that relates Baxter to his cultural context. See, more generally, for early Victorian England, L. James, *Print and the People, 1819–1851* (1954), and for the United States, H. T. Peters, *Currier and Ives, Printmakers to the American People* (1942).

See also *The Illustrated London News, passim*; J. Hatton, *Journalistic London* (1882); M. Jackson, *The Pictorial Press* (1885); and H. Vizetelly, *Glances Back Through Seventy Years* (1893). Techniques and their transfers are discussed in W. Turner, *Transfer Printing on Enamels, Porcelain and Pottery* (1907); H. G. Clarke, *Colour Printed Pictures of the Nineteenth Century on Staffordshire Pottery* (1924) and *Underglaze Colour Picture Prints* (1949).

For Stevengraphs, see G. Godden, *Stevengraphs and Other Victorian Silk Pictures* (1971) and A. Sprake and M. Darby, *Stevengraphs* (1968). Prices used in *Rubbish Theory* are set out in A. Sprake, *Price Guide to Stevengraphs* (1972).

R. Pearsall's book on *Victorian Sheet Music Covers* (1972) does not cover the ground covered by W. E. Imeson in his *Illustrated Music Titles* (printed for the author, n.d.). For trade union banners and emblems see R. A. Leeson, *United We Stand* (1971).

P. Newman deals with *Discovering Militaria* in a 'Shire Discovering Book'. See also D. E. Johnson, *Collector's Guide to Militaria* (1976), which includes not only a brief bibliography but a guide to museums and collections. There is even a *Collector's Pictorial Book of Bayonets* by F. J. Stephens (1971). Medals are dealt with in M. James, *The Art of the Medal* (1979); L. L. Gordon, *British Battles and Medals* (1971) and more briefly in W. A. Steward, *The ABC of War Medals and Decorations* (1918). Toy soldiers are the subject of J. G. Garratt, *Model Soldiers, A Collector's Guide* (1971). see also I. McKenzie, *Collecting Old Toy Soldiers* (1975) and P. Johnson, *Toy Armies* (1982). See also D. Clammer, *The Victorian Army in Photographs* (1982).

Books on the Crimean War figure in the bibliography of *Victorian People*. See also, however, R. Wilkinson-Latham, *Uniforms and Weapons of the Crimean War* (1977); *R. Fenton, Photographer of the Crimean War*, with an essay by H. and A. Gernsheim (1954); J. Hannavy, *Roger Fenton* (1975); L. James, *The Crimean War in Photographs* (1982); and, a sign of new American scholarship, M. P. Lalumia, *Realism and Politics in the Art of the Crimean War* (1984).

For the Boer War and other wars see F. Villers, *Pictures of Many Wars* (1902). See also J. Lewinski, *The Camera at War* (1978). For early *Punch* see A. and S. Briggs, *Cap and Bell* (1972) and for the whole history, R. G. G. Price, *A History of Punch* (1957).

## 5   THE WONDERS OF COMMON THINGS

Reading for this chapter is scattered and fragmentary. See A. Williams, *How It is Made* (n.d., 1907?) Among the topics which it discusses are money (the first chapter), paper, matches, biscuits, guns, saws, files, pens, pins and needles. It does not include a bibliography. See also E. J. Wiseman, *Victorian Do-It-Yourself: handicrafts and pastimes of the 1880s* (1976), a selection of practical advice and technical drawings from the late-Victorian *Amateur Work*. There is much of importance in local studies like S. Timmins (ed.), *The Resources, Products and Industrial History of Birmingham and the Midland Hardware District* (1866).

For needles see M. T. Morrell, *History and Description of Needlemaking* (1854); E. S. Bartlett, *History of a Needle* (1887); H. Page, *The Sewing Needle* (1896); and J. G. Rollins, *A Short History of Redditch* (1970). See also L. Hayward, *Surgical Needles, Ancient and Modern* (1961) and E. Bordoli, *The Boot and Shoemaker* (4 vols., 1935).

Collectors with a limited interest in Adam Smith – or Timmins – can turn to books like L. Baker, *The Collector's Encyclopaedia of Hatpins and Hatpin Holders* (Kentucky, U.S.A., 1976) and T. Wright, *The Romance of the Shoe* (1922). See also, however, S. Groves, *The History of Needlework Tools and Accessories* (1973) and Gertrude Whiting, *Tools and Toys of Stitchery* (1928). Eleanor Johnson has written Shire Album 96 on *Thimbles* (1962).

For matches see M. Heavisides, *The True History of The Invention of the Lucifer Match* (1909); P. Beaver, *The Matchmakers, The Story of Bryant and May* (1985); W. H. Dixon, *The Match Industry* (1925); M. F. Cross, 'A History of the Match Industry' in the *Journal of Chemical Education* (1941); and R. E. Threlfall, *The Story of a Hundred Years of Phosphorus Making* (1951). Ian Hay's novel *A Safety Match* was published in 1911. There is no good book on the match girls' strike. See, however, A. H. Netherhurst, *The First Five Lives of Annie Besant* (1960).

For pens see J. I. Whalley, *Writing Implements and Accessories from the Roman Stylus to the Typewriter* (1975) and for one of the first steel pen makers, J. T. Bunce, *Life of Sir Josiah Mason* (1882).


## 6.  HEARTH AND HOME

The key books for this chapter are *Mrs Beeton's Book of Household Management* (1st edn., 1861) – it had previously appeared in 24 monthly parts – and C. L. Eastlake, *Hints on Household Taste* (1868). Julia McNair Wright, whose encyclopaedic *The Complete Home* (1879) provides the lead into my chapter, has no fewer than 38 entries in the catalogue of the New York Public Library. She is one of the missing names in the attempt at a general study by W. Rybezynski, *Home* (1986). So, too, is Mrs Beeton, who also produced an equally famous *Dictionary of Everyday Cookery* and through Ward Lock and Company was named in *Beeton's Housewife's Treasury*. For a brief account of her life see H. Montgomery Hyde's readable *Mr and Mrs Beeton* (1951).

Significant Victorian titles – and I have concentrated on these – figure in the text of this chapter rather than in this note, but to those mentioned should be added Lady Barker, *The Bedroom and the Boudoir* (1828) and J. Mayr Smith, *Ornamental Interiors* (1887). Mrs Haweis must be read copiously, particularly her *The Art of Housekeeping, A Bridal Garland* (1889), and various encyclopaedias of different dates should be compared – for example, T. Webster, *An Encyclopedia of Domestic Economy* (1844) and Cassell's *Book of the Household* (1890).

Much later writing on the Victorian home is one-sided or incomplete. See, however, R. Harling, *Home, a Victorian Vignette* (1938); R. Dutton, *The Victorian Home* (1976); H. E. Priestley, *The English Home* (1970); D. Yarwood, *The English Home* (1956) which includes a useful bibliography to that date; and J. H. B. Peel, *An Englishman's Home* (1978). On the United States see as a contemporary text C. E. Beecher and H. Beecher Stowe, *The American Woman's Home* (1869) and for a modern survey D. Handlin, *The American Home, Architecture and Society, 1815–1915* (1917).

For the house itself see H. Muthesius, *The English House* (1904–5: Eng. tr., 1979 by J. Seligman); G. Stamp and A. Goulancourt, *The English House, 1860–1914* (1986); M. Girouard, *The Victorian Country House* (rev. edn., 1979) and *Sweetness and Light: the 'Queen Anne' Movement, 1860–1900* (1977); and J. Franklin, *The Gentleman's Country House and Its Plan, 1835–1914* (1981). Two works by John Gloag are perhaps mainly now of historiographical interest. *Victorian Comfort* (1961), however, is less dated than *Victorian Taste* (1962). See also R. Furneaux Jordan, *A Picture History of the English House* (1959); R. A. M. Stern, *The Pride of Place, Building the American Dream* (1986). S. Nicholson, *A Victorian Household* (1988) is a sensitive account of a Victorian upper middle-class home in Kensington which can now be visited.

For interiors, see M. Praz, *An Illustrated History of Interior Decoration* (1982) which begins with Pompeii and ends with *art nouveau*; P. Thornton, *Authentic Décor, The Domestic Interior, 1620–1920* (1984); and N. Cooper, *The Opulent Eye, Photographs of late-Victorian Domestic Interiors* (1976) which provides a link between this chapter and Chapter 3. So does W. Seale, *The Tasteful Interlude: American Interiors through the Camera's Eye, 1860–1917* (1982).

There are two agreeable books by Lawrence Wright, *Clean and Decent, the History of the Bath and the Loo* (1980) and *Warm and Snug: the History of the Bed* (1962). Contemporary studies of the different rooms of the house are dealt with in the text. For tiles see J. Barnard, *Victorian Ceramic Tiles* (1972); J. B. Austwick, *The Decorated Tile* (1980); and H. Van Lemmen, *Victorian Tiles* (1981).

For furniture, see F. G. Roe, *Victorian Furniture* (1952); R. W. Symonds and E. B. Whineray, *Victorian Furniture* (1962); E. Aslin, *Nineteenth-Century English Furniture* (1962); S. Jervis, *Victorian Furniture* (1968) and E. Mannoni, *Meubles et ensembles; style 1900* (1968). Compare M. Comino, *Gimson and the Barnsleys* (1980) subtitled 'Wonderful furniture of a Commonplace kind', with D. P. Bliss, *Charles Rennie Mackintosh as a Designer of Chairs* (1974). See also G. F. Lenoir, *Guide to Upholstery* (1962).

There is a huge literature about Victorian gardens, but it is most revealing to look back to contemporary books like W. Robinson, *The Wild Garden* and *The English Flower Garden* (1899) or G. Jekyll, *Wood and Garden* (1899). See, however, T. Carter, *The Victorian Garden* (1984). See also N. Scourse, *The Victorians and their Flowers* (1983).

Domestic service has been dealt with by many writers in recent years. Useful books include P. Horn, *The Rise and Fall of the Victorian Servant* (1975); T. M. McBride, *The Domestic Revolution: The Modernisation of Household Service* (1976); and for one example of a big household, Erdigg, M. Waterson, *The Servants' Hall* (1980).


## 7. HATS, CAPS AND BONNETS

Hats have been studied by several writers, the first R. Turner Wilcox, *The Mode in Hats and Head-dress* (1959). F. Clark's *Hats* (1982), published in Batsford's Costume Accessory Series, has a useful brief bibliography. It deals with both women's and men's head-dress and makes good use of contemporary journals. See also G. de Curtois, *Women's Head-dress and Hair styles* (1973) and H. Amphlett, *Hats: a History of Fashion in Headwear* (1973). J. Woodforde, *The Strange Story of False Hair* (1971) is interesting.

Costume history has been a major pursuit inside and outside museums, and the reading is voluminous. C. W. Cunnington's magnificent but exasperating *English Women's Clothing in the Nineteenth Century* (1937) is indispensable. See also J. Laver, *English Costume of the Nineteenth Century* (1929) and *Taste and Fashion* (1945); A. Buck, *Victorian Costume and Costume Accessories* (1961); C. Willet and P. Cunningham, *English Costume in the Nineteenth Century*; C. H. Gibbs Smith, *The Fashionable Lady in the Nineteenth Century* (1960); B. Baines, *Fashion Revivals* (1981); and for the depiction of fashion, an important subject, V. Holland, *Hand Coloured Fashion Plates* (1933); J. Laver, *Fashion and Fashion Plates* (1943); and A. Gernsheim, *Fashion and Reality* (1963). Men's clothes over the centuries are dealt with in P. Byrde, *The Male Image: Men's Fashion in England, 1300–1970* (1979) and D. de Marly, *Fashion for Men* (1985).

The author of the last of these books has also written a biography of Worth, *Worth, Father of Haute Couture* (1980). Another business study with a biographical flavour is F. Whitbourn, *Mr Lock of St. James's Street* (1971). Compare E. Saunders, *The Age of Worth* (1955).

C. Walkley's *The Ghost in the Looking Glass* (1981) is limited in scope and depth. See also I. Pinchbeck, *Women Workers and the Industrial Revolution* (1930). Trade-union history is outlined but by no means fully covered in M. Stuart and L. Hunter, *The Needle is Threaded* (1964). For the crafts see B. Morris, *Victorian Embroidery* (1962); S. M. Lovey, *Discovering Embroidery of the Nineteenth Century* (1971); E. N. Van der Poel, *American Lace and Lace Makers* (1924). See also G. Warren, *A Stitch in Time: Victorian and Edwardian Needlework* (1976).

For the sewing machine see R. Hersberg, *The Sewing Machine* (1864) and G. R. Cooper, *The Sewing Machine: Its Invention and Development* (1976).

A number of local histories deal with hatmaking, among them C. Freeman, *Luton and the Hat Industry* (1976). At the other end of the spectrum see R. Barthes, *Système de la mode* (1967), translated and published in New York as *The Fashion System* (1983). Compare E. Canter-Cremers-van-der-Does, *The Agony of Fashion* (1980) and H. Hill and P. Bucknell, *The Evolution of Fashion* (1967).

For wedding fashions see A. Landsell, *Wedding Fashions* (1983) and for funeral fashions L. Taylor, *Mourning Dress: A Costume and Social History* (1983). P. Cunnington and E. Lucas were still more ambitious in their *Costume for Birth, Marriage and Death* (1972).

## 8. CARBONIFEROUS CAPITALISM

The unforgettable phrase 'carboniferous capitalism' was coined by Lewis Mumford. See his *Technics and Civilisation* (1934) which should be studied alongside his *Culture of Cities* (1938) to which there are many references in my book *Victorian Cities*.

Annie Carey's non-Mumfordian *Autobiography of a Lump of Coal* appeared in 1870 five years after W. S. Jevons, *The Coal Question* (1865). See also *The British Coal Trade* (1915) written by his son: in a David and Charles reprint of 1965 there is a useful introduction by B. F. Duckham. It would have been impossible to write this chapter, however, had not R. D. Collison Black edited with great thoroughness in seven volumes the correspondence of W. S. Jevons. Volume I (1972) includes Jevons's biography and personal journal, Volume VI (1977) his *Lectures on Political Economy*.

More recent studies of coal include A. R. Griffin, *Coalmining* (1971); M. W. Kirby, *The British Coalmining Industry, 1870–1946* (1977); B. R. Mirfield and P. Deane, *Economic Development of the British Coal Industry, 1800–1914* (1984); R. A. Church, *The History of the British Coal Industry*, Vol. III, *1830–1913* (1986), which is sub-titled *Victorian Pre-eminence*; and, most useful for the themes of this chapter, J. Benson, *British Coalminers in the Nineteenth Century – A Social History* (1980). Regional studies of the coal industry include, for Wales, W. E. Minchinton (ed.), *Industrial South Wales, 1750–1914* (1969); F. J. North, *Coal and the Coalfields in Wales* (1931); J. H. Morris and L. J. Williams, *The South Wales Coal Industry, 1841–1873* (1958); and M. J. Daunton, *Coal Metropolis, Cardiff, 1870–1914* (1977).

For iron and steel see W. Fairbairn, *Iron, Its History, Properties and Processes of Manufacture* (1861); Sir Isaac Lowthian Bell, *The Iron Trade of the United Kingdom* (1886); D. W. Burn, *The Economic History of Steel Making* (1940); and J. C. Carr and W. Taplin, *History of the British Steel Industry* (1977).

There is a useful Pitman series on 'common commodities of commerce', started in the early twentieth century, which included coal (by F. H. Wilson), iron and steel (by C. Hood), cotton, oil, rubber, silk, wool and tobacco. For paper, see D. C. Coleman, *The British Paper Industry, 1495–1860* (1958) and A. H. Shorter, *Paper Making in the British Isles* (1971). There were late-Victorian attempts to see the history of paper in perspective by M. L. Evans, 'Paper Making', a lecture given at the Dickinson Institute in 1896, and in the 25th anniversary number of the *Paper Trade Journal*, vol. XXVI (1897). For a modern perspective in an age when there is much paperless information, see D. Saltman, *Paper Basics: Forestry, Manufacture, Selection, Purchasing, Mathematics and Metrics, Recycling* (1978). For papier-mâché see J. Toller, *Papier Mâché in Great Britain and America* (1962).

For the evolution of the Press, see S. Koss, *The Rise and Fall of the Political Press in Britain: The Nineteenth Century* (1981); L. Brown, *Victorian News and Newspapers* (1985); and M. Schudson, *Discovering the News: A Social History of American Newspapers* (1978).

Trade unionism, important in relation to all the trades and industries described in this chapter, is covered in A. E. Musson, *The Typographical Association: Origins and History up to 1890* (1954); R. P. Arnot, *The Miners, Years of Struggle* (1953); and P. S. Bagwell, *The Railway Men*, Vol. I (1963). The most straightforward lead into the whole subject is via A. F. Thompson and H. Clegg, *A History of British Trade Unions since 1889*, Vol. I (1964).

## 9.  STAMPS – USED AND UNUSED

Many books on stamps are solely of interest to philatelists. J. Watson's *The Stanley Gibbons Book of Stamps and Stamp Collecting* (1984) is a marked exception and provides a good introduction to this chapter. So, too, does the file of past numbers of the Post Office's *Philatelic Bulletin*.

There is little about the history of stamps as things in M. J. Daunton's carefully researched *Royal Mail, The Post Office since 1840* (1985), which does not entirely supercede H. Robinson, *Britain's Post Office: A History of Development from the Beginnings to the Present Day* (1935). Victorian studies of the Post Office, brightly written, include W. Lewins, *Her Majesty's Mails* (1864) and 2nd edn., 1885, and J. W. Hyde, *The Royal Mail, Its Curiosities and Romances* (3rd edn., 1889). There is an important essay by R. H. Coase on the postal monopoly in J. K. Eastham (ed.) *Economic Essays* (1955). See also J. Y. Ferrugia, *The Letter Box* (1969). For the United States, see W. E. Fuller, *The American Mail, Enlarger of the Common Life* (1972).

Contemporary reading must include R. Hill, *Post Office Reform* (1837) and R. and G. B. Hill, *The Life of Sir Rowland Hill and the History of Penny Postage*, 2 vols. (1880); E. Edwards, *Sir Rowland Hill* (1879); A. Trollope, *An Autobiography* (1883); and A. Potter, *The Life and Letters of Sir John Henniker Heaton* (1916).

On the history of the Victorian postage stamp, see Robson Lowe's *The British Postage Stamp of the Nineteenth Century* (1968), an admirable guide to the collection R. M. Phillips presented to the nation to found the National Postal Museum. Yet one of the most sensitive of philatelic historians, F. Marcus Arman has managed to say sometimes different things in *The Reginald M. Phillips Collection of 19th Century British Postage Stamps: A Short Account* (1966). Earlier works include E. D. Bacon, *The Line Engraved Postage Stamps of Great Britain* (1954–1965). See also R. A. G. Lee, *The Penny Lilac* (1963); S. Rose, *Royal Mail Stamps, A Study of British Stamp Design* (1980); J. Easton, *The De La Rue History of British and Foreign Postage Stamps* (1958); and L. Houseman, *The House that Thomas Built, The Story of De La Rue* (1968).

There is as yet no adequate history of stamp collecting in book form. For a lead into the subject see S. Phillips, *Stamp Collecting*, characteristically no date. Compare with F. Body, *The Stamp Collectors' Guide* (1862). See also P. J. Anderson and B. T. K. Smith, *Early English Philatelic Literature* (1912).

For postcards (and deltiology) see W. J. Scott, *All About Postcards* (1903); J. R. Brodrick, *Picture Postcards* (1957); R. Carline, *Pictures in the Post* (2nd edn., 1971), with a good bibliography; F. Staff, *The Picture Postcard and its Origins* (1966); C. W. Hill, *Discovering Postcards* (n.d.); W. Duval with V. Monahan, *Collecting Postcards* (1978); T. and V. Holt, *Picture Postcards of the Golden Age* (1971); S. Zeyons, *Les cartes postales* (Paris, 1979).

## 10.  NEW THINGS – AND OLD

For the electric telegraph, see J. L. Kieve, *Electric Telegraph, A Social and Economic History* (1973) and the fullest Victorian account of its beginnings J. J. Fahie, *A History of the Electric Telegraph* (1884). The latter should be compared with Dionysius Lardner, *The Electric Telegraph Popularised* (1855). C. Bright's *Submarine Telegraphy* (1898) is informative. See also C. Briggs and A. Maverick, *The Story of the Telegraph and the Great Atlantic Cable* (1858). R. L. Thompson, *Wiring A Continent: the History of the Telegraph Industry in the United States* (1947) should be compared with A. Moyal, *Clear Across Australia, A History of Telecommunications* (1984), an admirably comprehensive history. See also P. Dunheath, *A History of Electrical Engineering* (1962).

There was an abundance of writing on the history of the telephone around the time of its centenary in 1976. The best collection of well-footnoted essays was edited by I. de Sola Pool, *The Social Impact of the Telephone* (1977). See for Britain F. G. C. Baldwin, *The History of the Telephone in the United Kingdom* (1925). The technology is discussed in S. F. Smith, *Telephony and Telegraphy* (1978) and G. F. Blake, *A History of Radio Telegraphy and Telephony* (1926).

On Edison, the subject of a lively and impressive Edison Papers Project at Rutgers, see, pending its publication, M. Josephson, *Edison, A Biography* (1959). The best history of the electric light – A. A. Bright, *The Electric-Lamp Industry: Technological Change and Economic Development from 1880–1947* (1949) – should be supplemented by H. C. Passar, *The Electrical Manufacturers, 1875–1900* (1953). A recent model study is T. P. Hughes, *Networks of Power: Electrification in Western Society, 1880–1930* (1983), which raises fundamental questions. See for a very different book, stimulating in its attempt at an assessment I. Hunt and W. W. Draper, *Lightning in his Hand: The Life Story of Nikola Tesla* (1977).

For the phonograph, see R. Gelatt, *The Fabulous Phonograph 1877–1977* (1977 edn.); it has no bibliography. See also Joe Batten's book *The Story of Sound Recording* (1956).

For radio see H. G. J. Aitken, *Syntony and Spark: The Origins of Radio* (1974); A. Briggs, *The BBC, The First Fifty Years* (1985), chapter one of which (with bibliography), deals with 'first things'; and S. J. Douglas, *Inventing American Broadcasting* (1987). Marconi has been the subject of many books, including R. N. Vyvyan, *Marconi and Wireless* (1974) and W. P. Jolly, *Marconi* (1974).

There is a useful *History of the Marconi Company* by W. J. Baker (1970). For Sir William Preece and the Post Office, see E. C. Baker, *Sir William Preece* (1974).

On the bicycle see J. Woodford, *The Story of the Bicycle* (1970); H. Adams, *Cycles and Cycling* (1965); and H. O. Duncan, *The World on Wheels* (1927). For transport in general see N. E. Lee, *Travel and Transport through the Ages* (1958) and more fully, P. S. Bagwell, *The Transport Revolution from 1970* (1974).

On inventions in general see L. de Vries, *Victorian Inventions* (1973) and E. de Bono (ed.), *How and When the Greatest Inventions Were Made* (1974); J. Jewkes, D. Sawers, R. Stillerman, *The Sources of Invention* (1958); A. H. Kenwood and A. L. Longheed, *Technological Diffusion and Industrialisation before 1914* (1982). There are links between issues raised in *Victorian Cities* and *Victorian Things* in A. R. Preed, *Urban Growth and the Circulation of Information* (1973).

For other aspects of the social and cultural context of the late-nineteenth century in addition to books mentioned in the reading lists of previous chapters, see L. Mumford, *The Brown Decades* (1931); J. Lears, *No Place of Grace: Anti-Modernism and the Transformation of American Culture, 1880–1920* (1981); J. Mordaunt Crook, *William Burges and the Higher Victorian Dream* (1981); T. Howarth, *Charles Rennie Mackintosh and the Modern Movement* (1977 edn.). A key contemporary book is H. Adams, *The Education of Henry Adams* (1907). See also A. R. N. Roberts (ed.), *W. R. Lethaby* (1957) and G. Rubens, *William Richard Lethaby* (1986).

For history and prediction see I. F. Clarke, *Voices Prophesying War, 1763–1984* (1966) and *The Pattern of Expectation, 1644–2001* (1979).

# INDEX

# INDEX